Sir Elton
THE DEFINITIVE BIOGRAPHY

PHILIP NORMAN has an international reputation as a chronicler of popular music and culture. *Shout!*, his ground-breaking 1981 biography of the Beatles, was a best-seller in both Britain and America and has been translated into many languages. In 1984 came *Symphony for the Devil*, his classic biography of the Rolling Stones, of which Craig Brown said in the *Mail on Sunday* 'I have not read a better book on the real world of rock 'n' roll.' In 1996, he produced an acclaimed definitive biography of Buddy Holly.

Also an award-winning writer of fiction, Philip Norman was named one of the original twenty 'Best of Young British Novelists'. His newspaper and magazine articles have been collected in three books, *The Road Goes On For Ever*, *Tilt the Hourglass and Begin Again*, and *The Age of Parody*. Married, with one daughter, he lives in London.

D1314355

By the same author

Sir Elton
THE DEFINITIVE BIOGRAPHY

PHILIP NORMAN

CARROLL & GRAF PUBLISHERS, INC.
NEW YORK

First published in 1991 as *Elton*
First Carroll & Graf trade paperback edition 2001

Carroll & Graf Publishers, Inc.
A Division of Avalon Publishing Group
19 West 21st Street
New York, NY 10010-6805

Library of Congress Cataloging-in-Publication Data is available.
ISBN: 0-7867-0820-4

Manufactured in the United States of America

TO JESSICA ROSE

Contents

Acknowledgements

Thanks are due to *Rolling Stone* for permission to quote from their interview with Elton John.

PROLOGUE

'Goodbye, England's Rose'

Westminster Abbey, London, 6 September, 1997

THROUGHOUT Elton John's career there have been times when his natural politeness and humility have given way to outbursts of infantile temper known as 'Elton's Little Moments'. But his life is far more notable for Big Moments, when he has risen further and still further above the attitudes and aspirations usually expected of a pop star. We are about to see Elton's Biggest Moment ever.

For six days the nation has been in shock. Diana, Princess of Wales is dead – killed along with her Arab playboy lover Dodi Fayed when their chauffeur-driven car crashed in a Parisian underpass while apparently fleeing from paparazzi. Now, on a Saturday as golden as her hair, as balmy as her smile, she is to be laid to rest. In death, even more than in life, she will present Britain with some of the strangest, most unsettling scenes it has witnessed in this or any century.

Diana made royalty even more of a spectacle than Elton John made rock music. Before she came along in 1981, Britain's Royal Family received almost no media coverage outside the plodding, dowdy routine of state ceremonial and overseas tours. Thirty years ago, who could have imagined royalty transformed into an endlessly mesmerising romance-cum-tragedy-cum-farce that would make the behemoths of pop culture seem dull and predictable by comparison? In 1995, the surviving Beatles announced the reunion for which billions had waited almost a quarter of a century, with Paul McCartney, George Harrison and Ringo Starr overdubbing accompaniment on some 'lost' vocal tracks by John Lennon. Alas, its release happened to coincide with the BBC Panorama interview in which Diana exposed the sham of her 'fairy-tale' marriage and gave her husband, the future king, a flaying of such subtlety as had not been seen since the Spanish Inquisition. In competition with that, even the Beatles' Second Coming was doomed to be an also-ran.

Now she has gone, which means she is more ubiquitous than

ever, filling every TV screen with that 18-carat mop, those sky-blue eyes, that oddly asymmetric nose, those long legs, that halting, childish voice, and all those endlessly contradictory phases of her sixteen years in the spotlight. Here is the creamy-faced bride under a virginal veil . . . the Eighties sloane in frills and Laura Ashley prints . . . the fun mum, plunging down theme park water-chutes and sprinting without her shoes on school sports days . . . the sumptuous fashion-plate dressed by Versace and Lacroix . . . the angel visitant, unafraid to pick up a maimed African child or cuddle an AIDS sufferer . . . the effortless beauty who looked her most sensational after being drenched with rain during Pavarotti's Hyde Park concert . . . the worrier about her own supposed physical defects, who exercised obsessively and forbade photographers to shoot her in profile . . . the exquisitely tailored, lonely figure on a bench in front of the Taj Mahal, palpably wishing for a husband who'd love her a millionth as much . . . the hater of media 'intrusion' who couldn't live without cameras . . . the shopaholic, the hysteric, the bulimic . . . the helpless, the cunning . . . the classy, the vulgar . . . the crassly foolish, the idiotically brave . . . the totem of shrink-speak and victim culture . . . the exploiter even of her own children in pursuit of public affection . . . the campaigner against landmines . . . the unhealthily fascinated observer at surgical operations . . .

For these all too human flaws as well as her near-divine radiance the world came to love Diana as no star, certainly no princess, was ever loved before. Only those who remember the death of King George VI, forty-six years ago, have seen public grief on such a scale in Britain. People cling together and weep in a way familiar among warm-blooded European races but hitherto anathematised by chill, reserved Anglo-Saxons. People of all ages, all classes, all ethnic origins, cling and weep. Some of it is for the benefit of hysteria-hungry television crews, all of it may be the result of watching too much Oprah Winfrey and Jerry Springer, but it is undeniably, overwhelmingly, sincere. At Kensington Palace, Diana's former London home, the floral tributes left at the gate have become a plastic-wrapped ocean that almost fills the surrounding park. Queues stand patiently, day and night, to sign the books of condolence.

In the suicide-rush of her life, she made the House of Windsor wobble. With her death, she rocks it to its very foundations. The Prince of Wales stands condemned long since as a cold, selfish twit whose rejection of his adoring young bride and inexplicable prefer-ence for his weatherbeaten mistress, Camilla Parker Bowles, have cast grave doubts on his fitness to inherit the throne. Throughout various unbecoming imbroglios that have beset the Royal Family over the

years, the Queen herself has always remained immune from criticism.
But no more. There is audible anger that in the days following the
accident she and Prince Philip remained sequestered at Balmoral,
their Scottish estate, offering no word of grief for their former
daughter-in-law or of sympathy toward their stricken subjects. The
new Prime Minister, Tony Blair, is forced to intercede, like Disraeli
with the reclusive Queen Victoria 150 years earlier, persuading his
sovereign to appear on television and pay tribute to Diana, however
grimly, 'from my heart.'

The funeral is an uneasy compromise between the will of the
people and the ill-will of the establishment. Multitudes line a two-
mile processional route from Kensington Palace to Westminster
Abbey; massed television cameras wait to beam the event to a
worldwide audience calculated at 2.5 billion. But the full military
honours of a state funeral are withheld. The cortège consists of a
single antique cannon and horse-drawn limber from the Royal Horse
Artillery's King's Troop whose gold-braided gunners fire ceremonial
salutes on royal birthdays. The gun bears Diana's coffin, an artefact
weighing 40 stone, wrapped in a Union Jack and topped by a spray
of lilies. Her sons, William and Harry, walk behind, Victorian-style,
with their father, grandfather and uncle. There is eerie quiet, broken
only by the rhythmic tolling of a bell, the jingle of horse harness,
shrieks of un-British anguish from the onlookers and, bizarrely,
periodic bursts of clapping.

Inside the abbey, things get even heavier. Diana's brother, the
young Earl Spencer, rails at the monarchic chilliness and insensitivity
he holds responsible for hounding her to her fate, and pledges that
her 'blood family' will be the one to shelter and nurture her boys. It
is as if a gauntlet is being flung down in some Shakespearian tragedy.
The Queen sits, frozen-faced, watching the dynasty she has worked
so long to maintain being pilloried in the very place where, forty-
four years ago, she received her sacred anointing and had the crown
lowered on to her head. At this moment, there is only one Queen of
England and her name is not Elizabeth. Despite the muffling thick-
ness of the abbey's thousand-year-old walls, the crowds outside
somehow sense what is happening. Every new lance thrust by the
hot-headed earl unleashes further distant bursts of applause.

There is perhaps only one person alive who can save the day. He
rises from among the massed VIPs, a familiar stocky figure wrapped
in a plain dark suit of ultimate cost, his puggy features set in a resolute
frown, his eyes masked by tinted glasses that on this occasion are
doubly needful. As he walks towards the grand piano specially placed
in the abbey nave, a moment that was unreal beyond conception

becomes like so many others back through the chaotic decades to his childhood in Pinner, Middlesex. A voice whispers in his ear as irresistibly as when he was a resigned but dutiful eight- or nine-year-old and it was his mother speaking. 'Come on, it's up to you . . . They're waiting . . . You can't let them down . . . Be a good boy.'

At the beginning of the Nineties, Elton John seemed to have enjoyed – or, at least, experienced – every Big Moment conceivable. After meeting Elvis Presley, Mae West, Liberace, Elizabeth Taylor, Katharine Hepburn and Groucho Marx, after duetting on record with John Lennon, after seeing Los Angeles declare an 'Elton John Week' and planting his footprints among those of his greatest idols on Hollywood Boulevard, after bringing his football club, Watford, from obscurity to the Wembley Cup Final, after playing tennis with world champions like Billie-Jean King, Jimmy Connors and Martina Navratilova, going out to bat at Lords, taking tea at the White House and jiving with the Queen at Windsor Castle, what could possibly be left for a fat boy from Pinner to dream?

As a songwriter and performer, he seemed to have reached a similar plateau, albeit one of Everest-like altitude. At the turn of the decade, he made good the one flaw in an otherwise peerless recording career when 'Sacrifice' became his first-ever number one single in Britain (solo single, that's to say, as distinct from 'Don't Go Breaking My Heart', his chart-topping 1976 duet with Kiki Dee). Were he never to have sold another record or concert ticket, his place was secure in pop music's tiny topmost echelon alongside Presley, Dylan, the Beatles and the Stones, that little coterie of world conquerors instantly identifiable by just their Christian names – Elvis, John, Paul, Mick, Keith, Bob, Elton.

Even amid the hyper-inflated numbers of Nineties pop, his achievement still made eyes dilate and jaws sag. No one else, singer or band, had equalled his mid-Seventies run of seven consecutive American number one albums, four of them at number one simultaneously in America and Britain. Of the thirty-odd albums he had released since 1969, twenty-four were certified to have 'gone platinum' with sales of more than one million copies. His total record sales were hazily estimated at around 100 million. One music paper calculated that he accounted for 3 per cent of all singles, albums and tapes sold annually throughout the world.

But here was no mere sacred rock-relic, content to exploit the nostalgia for songs like 'Rocket Man', 'Bennie and the Jets', 'Goodbye Yellow Brick Road' and 'Daniel' with which he personified the glorious shoddy glitter of the Seventies. In advancing middle age he remained as determined to stay at the cutting edge as he had been in his twenties at the high tide of Glitter Rock. Other great figures from his era, like the ex-Beatle George Harrison, might rail at the modern charts like curmudgeons from their chimney corner. But Elton kept up with every style and fad, enjoying the best – and worst – of whatever was around. Newcomers to the business revered him, freely acknowledging his influence on their look and sound. At any premium gig he would probably be backstage, hugging and kissing all the latest golden boys and girls and being hugged back by them as if to do so was like touching some lucky talisman.

When I spoke to him at length in 1991, he seemed to have resolved every part of the troubled inner life that had always existed in ironic counterpoint to his outward triumph. He had netted one million pounds in out-of-court libel damages from *The Sun* over its allegation that he consorted with rent boys, not only forcing the paper to publish an apology as its front page lead ('SORRY ELTON') but putting the fear of God into any other tabloid that ever considered publishing unsubstantiated dirt about a rock star. He had ended the painful charade of his marriage to his former recording engineer, Renate Blauel, and, at long last, had emerged from the camouflage of so-called bisexuality to come out as 100 per cent gay.

He had beaten his ghastly full hand of addictions: drugs; drink; sex; the eating disorder that for years had led him alternately to gorge and starve himself. He had found true love with Hugh Williams, the manager of a Baskin-Robbins ice-cream parlour in Atlanta. Then he had found it again, seemingly for good this time, with a 30-year-old Canadian advertising executive named David Furnish. He had vowed that all his old Elton craziness was behind him: the spectacles fitted with windscreen-wipers or Venetian blinds; the shopping trips through Cartier with a supermarket trolley; the split-second mood swings from wild exuberance to black misery; the imperious demand that someone make the wind outside his hotel suite blow a little more quietly; the suicide attempts, including one in front of his own assembled family.

He had even solved the age-old problem of his hair loss, finally abandoning the expensive but largely fruitless transplant operations with which he had so long tormented his unlucky scalp. Not since the late Seventies had he been seen in public – or, indeed, in performance – without a camouflaging hat. Now the myriad straw boaters and bowlers and trilbies and jewelled Nehru caps were cast off to reveal a thick reddish thatch, like an expensive feather duster, fringed in modish retro-Beatle style. The rejuvenating effect was uncanny: we could almost have been seeing his teenage self back in the mid-Sixties when he was still plain Reggie Dwight, pounding his Vox organ in a no-hope band called Bluesology.

In short, it was a totally new Elton, grown up and toned down, with the ability that had always eluded him to count his extraordinary blessings. Enough of the old Elton remained, however, to keep him in the headlines as consistently as he had always been. Despite his reformed lifestyle and promises of a new asceticism, he continued to show pop's rising generations that no one could flaunt it, spend it and camp it up quite like he could. For his fiftieth birthday in March 1997, he spent £300,000 on hiring the naffest possible venue, the old Hammersmith Palais ballroom in West London, for a fancy dress ball whose guests included Lord Lloyd-Webber as a footballer, Sir David Frost as the Phantom of the Opera and Shirley Bassey as Cleopatra. Elton's own silver brocade Louis XIV costume, three-inch heels and two-foot tall powdered wig were so unwieldy that he had to be delivered to the party in an articulated lorry and lowered from it to the ground on a pneumatic lift.

In 1991, he had said he felt the time had come for him to get off the album-making, concert-giving treadmill and 'take time to smell the roses'. But, of course, it didn't happen. The touring went on unabated, the albums kept coming out. He also realised his long-standing ambition to compose music for films and the theatre. In collaboration with Sir Tim Rice he wrote five songs for Disney's *The Lion King*, which was to be first a blockbuster animated movie and video, then a smash hit on both the Broadway and West End stage. A song from the film, 'Can You Feel the Love Tonight?', won him and Rice an Oscar in 1995. Even more rarified recognition seemed increasingly on the cards as, one by one, pop's other good boys were rewarded with knighthoods – Cliff Richard, Paul McCartney, the Beatles' former producer George Martin. Elton's long history of charity work, stretching back decades before such things were fashionable, made him a natural candidate for the sword touch on the shoulder, although it was to be delayed until the Queen's New Year's Honours list of 1998.

Elton, of course, had been into royalty long before it was the stuff of tabloid headlines and *Hello!* magazine. Princess Margaret and the Queen Mother became devoted fans as far back as the early Seventies. After we learned that the newly created Princess of Wales spent her leisure time roller skating the Buckingham Palace corridors, listening to pop music on a Sony Walkman, it was clearly just a matter of time before she took over the Buckingham Palace branch of the Elton John Appreciation Society. They met at a Windsor Castle ball when Elton arrived early, found the princess there by herself and the two danced the Charleston alone for twenty minutes. Thereafter they met frequently through charity works, especially the AIDS organisations in which both, for different reasons, were deeply interested. It became a genuine friendship from much in common: their shared experience of broken homes, sham marriages, media persecution, eating disorders and depression; their two global followings; their two lost souls.

They overlapped additionally as top trophy clients of the same flashy unisex Italian couturier. Gianni Versace dressed Diana in the most brazenly effective of her gowns and also provided Elton with the mutedly eccentric wraparound suits of his later 'mature' period. (While other celebrity Versace clients expected to be outfitted gratis in exchange for publicising the label, Elton conscientiously paid for everything, spending up to £250,000 at a time.) On one famous occasion the tables were turned, and Elton modelled glitzy Versace frocks for a Richard Avedon fashion spread. It was perhaps his strangest incarnation yet, lounging in décolleté sheaths and strappy shoes, his copious body hair planed away, his skin as unnaturally smooth and shiny pink as glazed pink marzipan.

On 15 July, 1997, Versace was shot dead at the gate of his Miami mansion while walking back with the morning papers, 'BLOWN AWAY IN HIS VERSACE FLIP-FLOPS', as the Daily Mirror put it. Elton and Diana joined the chief mourners at his funeral and during the service were pictured clinging to each other and weeping like children robbed of a parent. Thus it is only natural that, in the numbed aftermath of this infinitely more shocking bereavement a month later, the world should turn to one person above all to mirror and express the universal grief.

Just who first had the idea that Elton should sing at Diana's funeral service will never be absolutely clear. He himself will later say he was personally asked to do so by Diana's elder sister, Lady Sarah McCorquodale. A contradictory account comes from the Virgin tycoon Richard Branson, another of Diana's celebrity friends and a moving spirit in the funeral organisation. Branson will afterwards claim credit for approaching Elton, then securing the consent of the abbey choirmaster, the Dean, the Spencer family and finally – with Tony Blair's help – the Royal Family itself.

The number that Elton first considers playing is 'Your Song', his first-ever hit from way back in 1970, a simple, sweet, poignant ballad but one whose first line ('It's a little bit funny . . .') may not be quite suited to present circumstances. Far better in every way is 'Candle in the Wind', the ode to Marilyn Monroe from his 1973 Goodbye Yellow Brick Road album, a song articulating his passionate empathy with the

woman who until now has been fame's best-known golden-haired
casualty. For years, it has been the farewell encore of every Elton
John concert, moving the audience to strike matches and cigarette
lighters and hold them aloft as in one huge, dark altar of frailly
flickering candle flames.

To become Diana's funeral ode, the original lyrics must be revised
– not because they are inappropriate to her, one suspects, but because
they are rather too appropriate. The story of Marilyn's hectic rise to
stardom and her poignant dying fall offers several analogies likely to
grate on regal nerves. 'They crawled out of the woodwork and they
whispered into your brain/ They set you on a treadmill and they
made you change your name . . . Loneliness is tough/The toughest
role you ever played . . . Even when you died, the press still hounded
you . . .' The Royal Family have indicated that they are especially
uncomfortable with that last line. Elton therefore contacts Bernie
Taupin, the Lincolnshire-born poet, three years his junior, who has
written words for the vast majority of his songs since 1967 and who
now lives permanently in Los Angeles.

As collaborators, the pair have seldom known the pain of tortured
creativity. Words drop from Bernie's pen as obligingly as chord
patterns form under Elton's pudgy fingers. 'Candle in the Wind' was
just one of twenty-three songs whose tunes he dashed off in three
days back in 1973. It has already been a mega-moneyspinner for
twenty-four years; now, with a few swift retouches, it is to ascend
into the stratosphere.

So the good boy takes his seat at the piano, watched by the
Queen, the Prime Minister, the massed dignitaries and celebrities and
much of the planet. He flexes his hands and turns to the teleprompter
he has requested in case emotion should blur even his meticulous
memory. Those familiar tinkly opening chords echo in a vaulted
space accustomed to the blast of huge organ pipes. The voice which
for all its Latino tinge, all its studious Deep South enunciation,
remains ineluctably redolent of English suburbia, floats up into the
firmament of medieval arches and stained glass. Not the 'Goodbye,
Norma Jean' that millions of lips involuntarily shape, but:

> Goodbye England's rose.
> May you ever grow in our hearts.
> You were the grace that placed itself
> Where lives were torn apart.

The voice is brittle with anguish, but it never slips, never cracks,
never falters. There is probably no other performer alive who could

deliver such a rendition under such pressure. One has only to remember his Australian tour of 1986. Convinced that he had throat cancer, unable to sing without coughing up gouts of blood and mucus, he still went onstage. Dressed as Mozart.

> *You called out to our country*
> *And you whispered to those in pain*
> *Now you belong to Heaven*
> *And the stars spell out your name.*

Maybe it is in dubious taste for a funeral service to be turned into live gig, and a Glam-Rock song about a dead film star to be heard in Britain's premier place of worship. Maybe it does show the sad state of the culture which once raised this sublime edifice, that it can now only understand emotions filtered through Hollywood or pop music. Even so, Elton's performance creates a highlight on a day oppressed with lowlights. For the few minutes it lasts, it dispels the weirdness and sense of embarrassed compromise that has tarnished the very sunshine. It seems to blow away the clouds of bitter reproach around the nation's rulers and of dysfunctional grief among its subjects. In some barely explicable way, it restores sanity. And, like it or not, you know how much she herself would have loved it.

> *Your footsteps will always fall here*
> *Along England's greenest hills.*
> *Your candle's burnt out long before*
> *Your legend ever will.*

This afternoon, a single hearse carries Diana's coffin out of London, through blizzards of thrown flowers, to her last resting place on an island at Althorp, the Spencer family estate. Elton, meanwhile, is at Town House Studios in central London, recording the tribute version of 'Candle in the Wind' under the supervision of Sir George Martin. It will then be rush-released as a single whose royalties will be donated to the fund established in Diana's memory. The plan sparks a row between Elton and Richard Branson, still a record-company boss at heart, who thinks the track will benefit the fund more as part of an all-star tribute album. But – as so often in past years – Elton's instinct is triumphantly vindicated. Sales of the single will eventually reach thirty-one million, taking it past Bing Crosby's 'White Christmas' to become the best-selling song of all time. Fifteen months later, it will still be in some countries' top 10 charts.

The Big Moment is still far from over. Tabloids that once revelled

in anti-Elton smears and sneers now hail him as something close to a
saviour of his country. *The Sun*, in particular, prints the new words
of 'Candle in the Wind' in larger type than was ever granted any
conventional Poet Laureate. When he appears at a Watford match,
the 12,000 crowd give him a standing ovation. In a television
interview with Sir David Frost, he praises the British for the way
they have expressed their feelings for Diana. 'So much love . . . and I
am so proud of the way people responded . . . It's up to everybody
now not just to grieve publicly for a week and then forget about it,
but to try to carry on what she was all about . . .' He also vows never
again to perform 'Candle in the Wind' in public, except for Prince
William and Prince Harry if they request it.

The week afterwards, he is in Florida to play in a fund-raising
tennis tournament for his AIDS foundation. At a press conference,
dressed in a multi-striped tracksuit, he finds his role has become that
of national agony aunt. What advice does he have for the millions he
has left still in anguish across the sea? He answers with the rugged
good sense that even drug addiction, alcoholism, suicidal depression
and wearing four-inch platform heels and necklaces of outsize bananas
could never quite chase away. It's time to end the tears, he affirms,
and put one death, however shocking, into the context of a world of
human tragedy. 'Princess Diana would not want this sadness to
continue . . . I've lost two great friends [Diana and Versace]. You
have to grieve and you have to move on.'

'ELTON JOHN TELLS NATION TO STOP GRIEV-
ING', runs one British newspaper headline. 'Only' rock 'n' roll, did
someone say?

I

MR FRANTIC

ONE

The Buttoned-up Boy

'LIVERPOOL!' Dick James the music publisher exclaimed quizzically on a famous occasion. 'So what's from Liverpool?' His power of prophecy would have been still more profoundly paralysed by Pinner.

In 1930s Britain, the future advanced with audible tread. From grubby, cramped Victorian London, the brand-new suburbs ribboned out along brand-new carriageways, lined with brand-new factories making aeroplanes, motor cars, electric stoves and vacuum cleaners, punctuated by new shopping 'parades', recreation grounds, hotels, pubs and quasi-Elizabethan roadhouses. At regular intervals along the blowy way to a brave new world stood the monumental redbrick tower and circular portals of an Underground station.

It was the world named 'Metroland' after its vital artery and chief cultural influence, the Metropolitan Line. These were days when public transport was a public pride, and each Underground line gave a distinct character and voice to the area it served. Especially the Metropolitan Line, whose posters and brochures exhorted migration to the new Middlesex dormitory suburbs in an accent of deep-piled cosiness. If the London office-worker would choose Metroland, what best of all worlds would be his! In the morning, abundant trains could whisk him in no time up to his City desk. At night, equally abundant trains would carry him home to his Olde English Nirvana of leafy woods and quiet avenues, box hedges and box Brownies. Pipe, tobacco and plaid slippers before the Magicoal fire. Hot Horlicks or Bournevita, then up the wooden hill to Bedfordshire. English order and normality at its best!

Pinner lies on the Metropolitan Line's north-westerly branch, where the station-names are like a row of leather-bound volumes in an Art Deco book-case. Before Pinner come Jane Austeny Northwick Park and Surtees-flavoured Harrow-on-the-Hill; after it come

Wild West-sounding Northwood Hills, Enid Blytonish Chorley-wood, the Walter Scott-like heraldic grandeur of Chalfont and Latimer. Three subsequent branch-lines extend into authentic countryside, penetrating Buckinghamshire as far as Chesham and Amersham, and Hertfordshire as far as Watford.

Though the future never did arrive, and the Metropolitan Line is sunken into squalor like all the rest, Metroland lives on a little in Pinner. There is still the broad shopping parade where fortunate Metrolanders foregathered on Saturday mornings for Camp coffee and Fuller's cakes, ordered their *Daily Sketch*, *Woman's Weekly* and *Everybody* magazine, purchased their Bird's Custard, Symington's soups and Bile Beans and entrusted their dry-cleaning to the winged pageboy on the logo of the Achille Serre company. Order and decorum endure in the police station's neo-Gothic flourishes. Beyond lie wide verges and topiary-trim hedges, bordering the mock-Tudor gables and Art Deco apartment 'courts' of prewar Elysium.

Pinner Hill Road, where Elton was born and spent his earliest years, is an ascending way, as long as the avenue where two hooded and gaitered toddlers walked in the old Tube-wall poster for Start-Rite Shoes. On the left stands a tall, dark clock tower, remnant of some local squire's 'folly' back in the pre-commuter dark age. Isolated among the gabled roofs and neat gardens, it seems to feel Pinner's crushing disapproval of anything ostentatious or flamboyant.

A hundred years ago there was no fast train between Chesham and Pinner, nor any but the most limited concept of social mobility. The place you were born was the place where you died. Your station – especially if it was low – bound you eternally to a horizon of a mile or two.

The Dwight family first surfaces up there in Buckinghamshire, in the vast permanence of the late nineteenth century. William Dwight, Elton's great-grandfather was – by a coincidence the future platform-heeled wonder would appreciate – a shoemaker, of Waterside, Chesham. His wife Jane, *née* Palmer, like many a dutiful Victorian wife, was unable to write her own name. An X marks her signature on her marriage lines and the birth certificate of her son, Edwin.

The quickened industrial pace of the early twentieth century was what finally set the Buckinghamshire Dwights in motion, though still not towards leafy Metroland. Elton's grandfather Edwin Dwight, a cable factory worker, moved forty-odd miles due south to join the cable firm of Callander's in Belvedere, Kent. Callander's was an old-fashioned patriarchal employer, solicitous for the recreation as well as sweated labour of its workforce. The firm had a name for music, boasting a brass band that won many a silver cup and rosette in inter-factory competitions. It also offered good facilities for sport, especially football, a passion with all Dwights, past and to come.

Edwin and Ellen Dwight – he, small and inoffensive; she, large and voluble – had six children, five sons and a daughter. Their youngest son, born in 1925, was Elton's father, Stanley.

The household at 6 Stapley Road was further increased by family tragedy. Edwin and Ellen's son Ted lost his young wife after the birth of their daughter, Susan; then Ted himself fell mortally ill with tuberculosis. He and his two small sons, Roy and Dave, came to live at Edwin's tiny house, where the only place to nurse an invalid was a couch in the walk-in living room. When Ted died, aged only thirty-four, his sons stayed on with their grandparents.

For Roy and Dave, growing up with old people, themselves not in the best of health, could occasionally be dull and stifling. The consolation was their uncle Stan, still living at home and young enough to seem more like an elder brother and ally than a censorious adult.

Stanley Dwight was a stockily-built young man with bushy eyebrows, a strong chin and a modest, reserved manner which – like his son's in later eras – concealed a romantic and an extrovert. His father, Edwin, played soprano cornet in the Callander's company band, and had taught Stanley to play trumpet. He performed with several local amateur swing bands and grew proficient enough to be asked to sit with classy professional outfits like the Lou Praeger Orchestra. His nephew Roy remembers often hearing him 'have a blow' in his bedroom, the notes mingling with the sound of a circular saw in the neighbouring woodyard.

Stan was as keen on football as all the family, and shared their intrigued realisation that young Roy seemed a better than ordinary player. Money being too short to buy him proper equipment, he would turn out with books pushed down his socks as shin-pads. His grandfather Edwin – who repaired all the family's shoes – fitted some leather strips under his boots to make up for the absent metal studs.

In those days, Stanley Dwight seemed an archetypal young man of his class. After leaving Dartford Grammar School, he had gone to work for a boatbuilding firm named Walkers in Rickmansworth, Hertfordshire, proving so neat and efficient that he became personal assistant to Mr Walker, the company's owner. The Second World War was then at its height and in 1942, when he was 17, Stanley volunteered for the Royal Air Force Naval Reserve. He was accepted for aircrew training to fly on bombing missions but, again, was quick to show superior qualities. Within only months of joining up, he was selected for officer-training. Despite being a model recruit, trumpet-playing remained his passion, and he formed his own band in the service under the name 'Stan Wight'. One of his early postings was near Lord's cricket-ground in north London. He would later recall how he persuaded friendly sentries to let him sneak back on base in the small hours of the morning after gigs at local night-spots.

One night in 1942, not long after joining up, 17-year-old Stanley was sitting in with the Eric Beaumont band at an hotel unalluringly called the Headstone in North Harrow. Among the audience was a 16-year-old-girl named Sheila Harris whose petiteness belied the strenuous wartime job that had fallen to her. With so many men away in the forces, young women everywhere were having to fill occupations never before considered possible for a female. Sheila Harris was delivering milk for the United Dairies company.

Sheila came of south London stock. Her father, Fred Harris, served with the Welsh Guards in World War I, afterwards becoming groundsman at Hatch End Tennis Club, Middlesex. For the sake of the job, Fred's guardsmanlike figure cycled forty miles each day, from home in Peckham to Hatch End and back again. Eventually, with his wife Ivy and three children, he migrated to Middlesex, living first at Kenton, then Hatch End and finally Pinner Green.

The Harris family home was 55 Pinner Hill Road, a semi-detached council house in the row just south of that Victorian clock tower which looks over Metroland. In the style of late-Thirties municipal housing, number 55 was solid, even spacious, with a back garden that Fred lovingly tended, along with two vegetable allotments. Beyond the hedge lay the green turf and metal scoreboard of Pinner Cricket Club.

Stanley Dwight's courtship of Sheila was a slow and characteristically decorous affair, lasting almost three years. He had his RAF duties and Sheila had joined the ATS, working as a clerk at Coastal Command's complex at Northwood in Middlesex. They were married at Pinner Parish Church in January, 1945, and moved in with Sheila's parents at 55 Pinner Hill Road. Finding a place of their own was a problem for any young couple in the immediate postwar years. Besides, Stanley's service duties frequently took him away from home. Sheila needed the company of her parents, her younger sister, Win, and her brother, Reg.

Stanley Dwight's RAF commission was not merely a temporary thing, as with so many other young men in wartime. At the war's end, he stayed on in the service, a sign of indispensability confirmed by rapid promotion. By 1947, when his son was born, he had become a flight lieutenant. Sheila, now pregnant, did not like his frequent absences from home, and for a time Stanley thought seriously of leaving the RAF and returning to his former job at Walker's boatyard. His elder brother Percy, however, told him he'd be a 'bloody fool' to give up the RAF with its allowances and security, and take a job at much lower pay. For the sake of the baby, Sheila agreed it was best that he remain in uniform.

They had only one child, Reginald Kenneth Dwight, the future Elton Hercules John, born at his grandparents' council house, 55 Pinner Hill Road, on March 25, 1947.

The profound bitterness which Elton would afterwards cherish against his father can be traced right back to what he believed a slight on his very birth. The story – still capable of making the millionaire superstar boil over in resentment thirty years later – was that, when Sheila went into labour, Stanley was absent overseas on RAF service. 'I was two years old when he came home. Mother said "Do you want to see him?" He said "No, I'll wait till morning." He'd been in Aden or somewhere, and he came home after two years, after not seeing me born or anything.'

In fact, Stanley Dwight was then on a home posting, with the RAF's Number 4 maintenance unit at nearby Ruislip. He was in the house when Reggie was born, and registered his son's birth on the following day. For almost the first year and a half of Reggie's life Stanley was stationed at Ruislip but living off-base: he would return home to his wife and baby each evening just like any normal Metroland commuter.

It was well-known in the family that Sheila had really been hoping for a girl. Baby Reggie very nearly granted her wish. Early photographs show an infant of radiant beauty, with massed golden curls that Shirley Temple might have envied. Sheila was a devoted and also fastidious mother. The baby possessed innumerable changes of outfit.

In 1949, Stanley Dwight received a two-year posting to Basra in Iraq. His family doubtless could have accompanied him, but Sheila elected to remain with 15-month-old Reggie at her parents' house in Pinner Hill Road. Though certainly a dedicated career officer, Stanley seems to have been heartbroken by the long separation from his toddler son. For their first Christmas apart, he arranged with Hamley's, the West End toyshop, for an expensive pedal car – the first of many future flash motors – to be delivered to Reggie.

The world Reggie first saw about him was anything but a colourful one. Though the war had been over for two years, Britain remained in the grip of food-shortages and rationing, a chill, grey place under officially prescribed 'austerity' where any self-indulgence or surfeit was accounted downright sinful. In ordinary households, the only respite was 'the wireless', from which the BBC Light Programme poured out an unrestricted supply of morale-boosting variety shows, like *Stand Easy* and *Workers' Playtime*, and the turbaned housewife's mid-morning portion of *Music While You Work*.

Among the future superstar's earliest memories was to be his parents' collection of big, breakable 78 rpm records, and the American stars of that pre-pop era: Guy Mitchell, breathy and good-humoured, on 'Red Feathers' or 'Truly Fair', Kay Starr, lovelorn and lingering on 'Wheel of Fortune', Les Paul and Mary Ford, a girl whispering in harmony with what few people then could identify as an electric guitar. Almost before Reggie learned to read, he could recognise all the different record labels. He also possessed the aesthetic sense that many children have at a young age, but can find no words to express. He still remembers vaguely resenting the dull, muddy liveries most of the labels wore and his pleasure in the one great exception, MGM's bright yellow and black.

With his father away in Iraq, Reggie lived in an almost wholly feminine atmosphere until he was four, cosseted equally by his mother and adored 'Nan', Ivy. A neighbour in Pinner Hill Road, Jacky Reppington, remembers him as an overprotected toddler, not allowed to run riot with other children on the field behind the council houses. He would usually be in the garden by himself, playing with his many toys, carefully and decorously.

Like many ordinary households in that pre-television era, the Dwights had an upright piano. As the future superstar would one day recall before a Hollywood audience, it was his grandmother, Ivy, who first encouraged him to play, picking him up and depositing him on the piano stool with cheery words of encouragement when he was no more than three. He took to it instantly, and would bang away at the keys while his mother did the housework. One day – the family legend goes – he astonished her by suddenly starting to pick out the melody of 'The Skaters' Waltz'.

The family talent that had drawn his grandfather to the soprano cornet and his father to the swing trumpet was manifest in a perfect musical ear. Even as a toddler, Reggie Dwight could hear a piece of music just once, then sit at the piano and replicate it note for note.

At the age of four he started at the local state primary school, Pinner Wood Junior and Mixed Infants. After only a year he was taken away and sent to Reddiford School, a small private academy of about a hundred pupils run, in their back garden, by an elderly man named Mr White and his spinster sister. By the age of six, he was also having piano lessons from a Pinner woman named Jones, whose husband was an accomplished classical musician. A Reddiford class-mate, David Lewis, remembers walking home with Reggie one day and asking him what he wanted to be when he grew up. 'A concert pianist' was the firm reply.

The life of a small boy who plays the piano is, to a large degree, pre-ordained. At school he is a celebrity, older than his years as he arrives with his adult briefcase full of music, grave in his demeanour as he settles down to perform. His skill is frequently co-opted by authority, to show the school off at concerts and open days, perhaps even play the hymn for morning assembly when the music teacher is indisposed. Preoccupied with his staves and rests, he has little time or opportunity to be other than utterly conformist and conventional. The small boy who plays the piano tends to be a very good boy indeed.

To his family he is a live-in entertainer, called upon whenever grown-up conversation falters. The first of many times this happened to Reggie was when he was seven, at the wedding of his grown-up cousin Roy Dwight. 'Stan was my best man,' Roy remembers, 'and Reggie was a page boy. After the wedding breakfast we'd got a band booked, but they were a bit late in turning up. So Reggie was put on the piano in his little white tail suit and bow tie. He kept things going until the real band arrived.'

An early snapshot − destined to be many times reproduced − sums up everything that could possibly be said about his early childhood. A plump small boy with a round pug face sits at an upright piano, hands poised on white notes, looking over his left shoulder. Even at seven or eight his chubby-cheeked smile has the resigned quality of the pro who must perform whether he feels like it or not. There is an implicit air of celebrity but, even more, of virtue. Hair neatly slicked down and parted where other boys' would be tousled. Plump knees peeping from traditional flannel shorts where other boys would demand blue jeans. Neat white shirts and starched handkerchieves. Socks correctly pulled up and polished shoes. Framed certificates and silver cups. His name in the local paper every now and then. A very, very good boy.

In 1953, at the young age of 28, Stanley was promoted to Squadron-leader and posted as service supply officer to Lynam in Wiltshire. Sheila and Reggie moved down to join him in a 'prestige' four-bedroom house provided by the RAF. Reggie seemed to settle in well enough, so Stanley believed, but life as a service wife did not suit Sheila. He later said she had objected to the 'snobbery' of an RAF officer's life, even though he had already been an officer when they first met. Within a short time, she had taken Reggie back to her mother's in Pinner, and Stanley had moved into the officers' mess.

The future superstar would portray his father as a cold, unloving disciplinarian who continued to behave like an officer in his own family circle and treated his son as little more than a despised parade-ground malingerer. He would describe the strict code of behaviour and table manners that Squadron-leader Dwight imposed, the petty rules and regulations about not making noise or kicking his football around the garden in case it damaged the rose bushes. Most rancorously would he describe his own dread of his father's homecomings from abroad, and the overpowering gaucheness and clumsiness that always affected him under Stanley's gaze. The abiding, awful image is of Reggie being afraid even to bite into a stick of celery in case his father objected to the crunch.

The portrait was to mystify Stanley in later life as much as it hurt him. He was certainly a strict, old-fashioned parent, requiring the same order and discipline in his home as he did as a senior supply officer. On his visits home, he also felt a need to counteract the otherwise wholly feminine influence on Reggie, and his resultant tendency to be a bit of a pampered mummy's boy (a vice he would freely admit on television almost half a century later).

No outsider can possibly know the truth or plumb the complexities of a father–son relationship. Only Elton can be the judge of how he felt as a child. But Stanley seems to have been very far from cold. On his postings abroad, he kept a picture of Sheila and Reggie beside his bed, and wrote home almost every day. A photograph exists of his solitary service bedroom in some desert waste or other; it is as meticulously neat and well-ordered as his son's mansions would be one day. To assuage his loneliness, he would organise sports and swimming lessons for the children of his service colleagues. Towards the sad end of his life, he would recall how, on those visits home to Pinner, he would try to make it up to Reggie for the months they had been apart. He remembered them on pre-Christmas walks, seeing who could count the greater number of Christmas trees in neighbours' windows. A photograph of them both on a beach, taken when Reggie was about nine, could not show a more idyllic-looking Fifties 'Dad and his lad'.

Indeed, as Stanley would eventually confess, he was often the one to feel rejected. In 1956, he received a further posting to Iraq, where he became caught up in the chaos following the assassination of King Faisai, and then moved on to Aden and another high-level administrative job. In 1957, he was accidentally electrocuted, suffering a paralysis that required many months in hospital. In February 1958, he was flown home to Britain for a three-month recuperation period. During all that time, Stanley would later say, he was not visited once by Sheila and Reggie.

On his recovery, he was appointed to the Headquarters Signals Group at RAF Medmenham in Marlow, Buckinghamshire. This long-term home posting meant he could at long last settle down in one place with his wife and son, although Sheila still would not move too far away from her mother. The answer was a small detached house in Potter Street, Northwood, just a couple of miles from Pinner. So uncomfortable were to be the associations of this modest villa that later, when Reggie's past life became of interest to journalists, he would always omit it from the chronology. Stanley and Sheila had by now both recognised that there was an irreconcilable gulf between them, but agreed to stay together 'for the sake of the child'. One has to have lived in such a house to know what a chill wind always blows.

The consolation for Reggie was a large and loving family circle. His mother's side of the family all lived around Pinner – his Nan in Pinner Hill Road, his namesake Uncle Reg and two cousins, John and Cath. The circle increased when Sheila's younger sister, Win Robinson, returned from overseas, bringing her baby son, Paul. They were the kind of family that always got together at Christmas and even took their summer holiday together. One such perfect Fifties box Brownie scene was a camping expedition to Ilfracombe, Uncle Reg in charge, Sheila and Win hooting with laughter together, baby Paul bedded down each night on the back seat of the car.

Reggie was just as attached to Stanley's side of the family, especially his grandparents, still living in Belvedere, Kent. He loved to sit on this grandfather's knee and play with the watch-chain on which hung two medals that Edwin had won for cornet-playing. The musical Dwights were especially delighted by his prowess on the piano. He would entertain them by singing and playing a current pop hit with a certain prophetic quality – 'I'm a Lonely Little Petunia in an Onion Patch'. He had inherited the Dwight love of football and, like his father, became a passionate supporter of Pinner's local team, Watford. Some of the happiest moments Stanley would remember were on the terraces at Watford's Vicarage Road-ground, with Reggie curled up inside his father's service great-coat.

The family's interest was further sharpened by what had happened to Roy, the orphan nephew whom Stanley had befriended in prewar days down in Kent. At the age of fourteen, while playing in a kickaround on Dartford Heath, Roy had been spotted by a talent scout for Fulham, the celebrated Second Division club. After a probationary period on Fulham's ground staff, he had turned professional (signing on the same day as future England manager Bobby Robson). In his debut season, he had been picked to replace Bedford Jezzard in the star centre-forward spot. He had scored in each of his first eight games, culminating with a four-goal tally against Sheffield United.

In mid-Fifties Britain, professional footballers were national pin-ups – none more so than Roy's Fulham colleague Johnny Haynes, who combed back his hair with a smug smile in advertisements for Brylcreem. Reggie's greatest excitement as a small boy was to be taken to see Haynes and Co. play in their brilliantine and baggy shorts at Fulham's Craven Cottage ground. Sometimes as a special treat Roy would arrange for him to watch the match sitting on the touchline.

Break-time games in Reddiford School's garden had shown that Reggie himself, though keen and energetic, possessed no comparable spark. He was more useful at tennis, for which many openings existed in leafy Metroland. But, most of all, he was a boy who practised long hours alone, whose briefcase bulged with grown-up names like Chopin and Brahms, and whose puggy, patient face was turned towards the next, more arduous grade examination set by the Royal Academy of Music in London.

Whether or not under his father's influence, Reggie had become a boy of almost painful self-restraint – careful, neat, methodical and anxiously polite. His nature was considerate and thoughtful, punctilious about writing Christmas and birthday thank-you letters and buying gifts for his mother and family. His only fault was a tendency to temper tantrums, usually arising from the stress and fatigue of piano practice. These would blow up in a moment, and usually disappear as quickly as they had come.

Radio – and now television – presented his chosen instrument in very different guise. It was the great age of star piano entertainers: Semprini with his Viennese charm, Joe 'Mr Piano' Henderson with his oleaginous charm, Russ Conway with his dour charm. Most of all, beamed from America, Liberace with the oozing charm no one yet recognised as high camp; his lace ruffs, duck-egg-sized diamond rings, piano-top candelabra and violin-playing 'brother George'.

The performer of later life would owe a manifest stylistic debt to

Liberace. But more influential still was Winifred Atwell, an amiable black entertainer who, in the middle and late Fifties, enjoyed a string of massive piano hits like 'Coronation Rag' and 'The Poor People of Paris'. All Reggie liked that was both extrovert and good-natured seemed to be in that glossy, overflowing figure – on Jack Payne's TV show, or Billy Cotton's – switching from Bechstein grand to her honky-tonkish 'other piano', smiling and roguishly winking as her jewel-studded fingers dashed to and fro.

The one instance of outrageous live performance his childhood witnessed was at a Saturday night variety show at the London Palladium, starring the 'Red Feathers' man Guy Mitchell. 'At the end of his set, he took off his sock and whirled it round his head. I thought, "What a funny guy!" And, do you know, I always remembered that.'

When rock-'n'-roll music first hit Britain in 1955, Reggie Dwight was not yet nine years old. He was far too young – and, in any case, Metroland saw little of those first surreal moments when close-cropped and tweed-jacketed English youths suddenly grew sideburns like Mississippi cardsharps, put on cylindrical coats with velvet collars, thick-soled 'brothel-creepers' and bootlace ties, and mumbled their knee-trembling worship of an unfathomable American song entitled 'Houn' Dog'. Nor, as a pianist, was he swept up by the related skiffle phenomenon, when English boys – who hitherto would sooner have disembowelled themselves than be caught singing in public – rushed to form groups with cheap guitars, tea-chest basses and kitchen washboards, and discordantly chorus hobo and work songs written by impoverished black men half a century earlier in the obscurity of America's Deep South.

Like most other British adults – and all with any claim to professional musicianship – Stanley Dwight at first found the new music bafflingly raucous and shapeless. The future superstar would sardonically recall that on his ninth birthday, in the year of Bill Haley's 'Rock Around the Clock' and Lonnie Donegan's 'Rock Island Line', his father gave him an LP record by the jazz pianist George Shearing. But, to be fair, Shearing's silky modern jazz style was youthful and hip in 1955. And Shearing standards like 'Roses of Picardie' and 'September in the Rain' would nurture the superstar's musical imagination as much as rock ever did.

It was Sheila Dwight – then only just turned thirty – who became the household's prototype rock-'n'-roll fan. The first Reggie knew of it was when his mother brought home two new 78s – 'Houn' Dog' by Elvis Presley and 'ABC Boogie' by Bill Haley and his Comets. The boy with the doggedly virtuous face and the head full of theory listened in amazement to these wildly pulsing and pounding intimations of how different a piano-player's life could be.

In September 1958, he joined the brown-blazered throng at Pinner County Grammar School. A boy named Peter Emery sat next to him in the first music lesson when the teacher, Mr Stoupe, asked each pupil in turn about his musical interests and attainments. 'A few of us said we played the piano,' Peter Emery remembers. 'One or two said they'd done Junior Royal Academy to Grade 5. When Mr Stoupe got to Reggie, he said he was Grade 8. Stoupe didn't realise what he'd said at first – he carried on for a moment, then did a huge double-take.'

Pinner County Grammar was another perfect manifestation of Metroland. Built in 1937, its streamlined frontage and square central tower epitomised Art Deco futurism and environmental progress for all. Save that boys and girls occupied segregated quarters, its air was more that of an American high school. No more cinder playgrounds, pothooks and squeaky slates but a veritable campus amid the trees and bulbous Morris Minor cars of Beaulieu Drive.

Behind the Norman Rockwell façade lay an ethos more like that of some exclusive fee-paying school: a heraldic badge of a stag rampant with the motto 'Honour Before Honours'; a house and prefectorial system; a sixth-form club, The Stag, owing something to the Pop fraternity at Eton; even pointless but rigid 'traditions', like that forbidding all but sixth formers to cross the frontage from girls' side to boys'. The headmaster, Jack Westgate Smith, was a teacher of the best old-fashioned sort, a stern but just disciplinarian with the gift of maintaining order through affection rather than fear. Pinner County Grammar could boast a record of scholastic and sporting achievement second to none among Middlesex state schools. It was also a tolerant place, free from bullying and with no hidebound view that all children ought to be the same. Under Jack Westgate Smith, the singular or eccentric pupil received equal interest and encouragement.

Music was one of the school's greater strengths. Mr Westgate Smith was himself a classical pianist, a frequent performer as soloist or in duet with the music teacher, W. G. Stoupe. The history master, Bill ('Scruff') Johnson was a blues enthusiast, a friend of the music historian Paul Oliver. The school's concerts and recitals were famous throughout the district. Among its proudest possessions was the Steinway grand piano in its assembly hall.

R. K. Dwight of Downfield House initially seemed set fair to add further lustre to Pinner County's musical prestige. At the age of eleven, he had been interviewed at the Royal Academy of Music in London for possible enrolment on its Junior Exhibitioners – i.e. part-time scholarship – scheme. Not only did he win the scholarship but the course director, Margaret Donington, recommended him to Sub-professor Helen Piena as a piano student of special interest.

Helen Piena taught him at the Royal Academy of Music for the next four years. The classes were every Saturday morning at the Academy's Gothic building in Marylebone Road: schoolroom tuition in theory and composition, choir practice and a forty-five-minute individual lesson.

The first thing Helen Piena noticed – and set out firmly to thwart – was his astounding natural ear. 'I remember once playing him a prelude by Handel, four pages long. As soon as I'd finished, he played it straight back to me just like a gramophone.'

That annoying facility aside, she remembers him as a model pupil, hard-working, punctilious and polite. 'I always called him by his full name, Reginald. But he was very affectionate, too. He'd send me letters with kisses on the bottom. Once he sent me an embroidered skullcap from Switzerland, where he'd gone on holiday with his school.'

At Pinner County Grammar, he was making no such mark. Fifteen years later, when his flashing reincarnation bestrode the world, the same astonished question would be asked by almost everyone who had known him at school. 'That can't be Reg Dwight, can it?'

Then he was a boy of such averageness and conventionality as to be almost invisible. Though imaginative and quick-witted, with an excellent memory and wonderously neat handwriting, he did not shine in class. Even with his best subjects, like English and languages, he followed a line of least resistance, doing only just enough to satisfy his teachers and get by in examinations. 'Satisfactory', 'Of average achievement', 'Not particularly distinguished' were common judgements in his end-of-term reports.

His fondness for sport was hampered by the school's pretensions. At Pinner County Grammar they did not play football, but the more upper-class game of rugby. Where Reggie longed to dribble the ball like his famous cousin Roy, his small stature and bullet head made him a natural for hooker in the thick of the set scrum. There, at least, his dogged determination earned some notice. 'He'd come out, looking like a chewed-up monster,' Peter Emery says. 'But he'd always go back in again for more.'

Even his musical talent and status as a Royal Academy exhibitioner did not win him unstinted praise. Mr Stoupe the music teacher – a New Zealander afflicted with an unfortunately appropriate stoop – seemed almost resentful of this extracurricular distinction. When Reggie produced composition homework better than anyone else's, and instantly hummable, he would risk censure for having done it too easily; the schoolmaster's crime of being 'casual'.

Musically, too, he preferred to be just one of the crowd. In a typical school concert, R. Dwight's rendering of 'Les Petites Litanies de Dieu' by Groylez was buried in a full programme that also included Patricia Corry's violin performance of Bach's 'Gavotte in D'; M. Wheeler's cello rendering of Mozart's 'Ave Verum'; T. White's trumpet solo, Allegro from Haydn's 'Concerto in E flat'; and Messrs Stoupe and Westgate Smith's piano duet in Arthur Benjamin's 'Jamaican Rumba' and the Polka from Weinberger's 'Schwanda the Bagpiper'.

In appearance he was equally unexceptional, a neat, orderly boy whose school uniform bore no trace of the Teddy-boy flourishes that even Metroland youth was starting to sport. It was to be another bitter charge laid at the door of his father that he was allowed none of the trendy flourishes that could be added even to school clothes, like tapered trousers, a leather waistcoat or socks in any colour but regulation kitbag-grey. The 'in' footwear for British youths in the late Fifties were suede shoes called Hush Puppies, whose trademark was a doleful-looking basset hound. The future superstar would one day recall – with an expression every bit as doleful – how even Hush Puppies were denied him under Squadron-leader Dwight's strict dress code.

A school group photograph, taken when he was about thirteen, shows a boy no longer just chubby or plump, but unequivocally fat, his hair mousy dark, his round pug face resignedly studious in half-frame glasses. He wore glasses not because he needed them but in homage to Buddy Holly, rock music's first four-eyes, who died in a plane crash in 1959. Alas, in Reggie's case the resemblance would often seem closer to Billy Bunter, the Owl of the Remove in Frank Richards's stories of Greyfriars school. But he persisted in imagining himself Buddy, not Billy, and in the process managed to make himself genuinely myopic.

By now, like virtually every other blazered and cricket-capped British schoolboy, he was possessed and besotted by rock 'n' roll. One has to have been there to fully appreciate its brilliant presence amid the boredoms of adolescence in late-Fifties Britain. On the one hand, Mr Macmillan and Mr Gaitskell; on the other, Elvis Presley's 'King Creole'. On the one hand Purchase Tax and the Motor Show;

on the other, Danny and the Juniors' 'At the Hop'. On the one hand, Prince Philip inaugurating International Geophysical Year; on the other, Marvin Rainwater's 'Whole Lotta Woman'. On the one hand, black-and-white TV, red phone boxes, brown GPO vans and beige Austin saloon cars. On the other, Johnny Otis and his Three Tons of Joy. Disapproving adults used to condemn rock 'n' roll as sexually suggestive, but actually it was utterly childish; the ultimate form of play, with its silly names, silly voices, silly words like 'bop-shoowop' and 'rama-lama-ding-dong'. Reggie Dwight, in Pinner, was one of the generation it would spare from ever having to grow up.

The taste in Britain now was for softer pop, like the hiccupping Buddy Holly parodies of Adam Faith. But Reggie remained true to the prototypes his mother had first brought home. Reggie – not entirely fashionably – was a true rock-'n'-roll fan.

His idols were the two wildest, freakiest stars of the genre, both brilliant piano players as well as inimitable vocalists. He had all Little Richard's records: 'Tutti Frutti', 'Long Tall Sally', 'Lucille' and 'Good Golly Miss Molly' – stentorian shrieks of joyous gibberish accompanied by manic pounding on innocent keys. As well as the madness, he loved the theatricality of the tiny dervish figure with its lounge-lizard moustache and wobbling drape suit. He managed to see it 'live' just once, in a package show at Harrow's Granada cinema. As Little Richard jumped over his piano, the virtuous fat boy had a spellbinding thought: 'I wish that was me.'

Even his switched-on mother drew the line at Jerry Lee Lewis, whose 1958 British tour was cut short when it emerged that he had married his thirteen-year-old cousin. The 'Killer' was rock-'n'-roll outrage personified with his permed hair, his cherry-red suit, his habit of concluding a session at the piano by dousing it in petrol and setting it alight. Reggie was entranced by Jerry Lee Lewis, and struggled to stretch his own small hands into the same wicked rippling runs that tore up piano keyboards like rotten linoleum.

Other teenagers could socialise over music at youth clubs and coffee bars. But Reggie was cut off from most friends and after-school activities by his parallel career at the Royal Academy of Music. With school and piano practice every day, the Academy on Saturdays and homework on Sundays for the next Monday morning, he scarcely had an hour to himself in the whole week.

Almost all his spare time was spent in his bedroom at 111 Potter Street. He would be hours up there alone, tending his record collection, already considerable. Each single, LP and EP had its own protective brown-paper cover and was meticulously catalogued. As much as the music, he loved records as physical things: their labels and covers, back as well as front; the madly hip language of their meagre liner-notes, even the addresses of the pressing plants, like EMI, Hayes, Middlesex. The shine of the velvety blackness as it turned, the playing-arm's little click as it moved across, were almost living things, keeping him company. As the future stupendous hoarder of possessions would admit, 'I grew up with inanimate objects as my friends.'

Loneliness combined with obsessiveness made him a born fan, able to derive almost complete happiness and fulfilment from follow-ing and extolling the achievements of others. As well as a rock-'n'-roll fan he was a sports fan, mad about cricket and tennis, and a football fanatic like all males on the Dwight side of his family. After music, he gave greatest fervour to supporting his local team, Watford, attending as many home games as possible at the modest Vicarage Road ground, using their triumphs and disasters, their ups and downs in the Football League, as a surrogate for his own uneventful, unexpectant life.

The only small fame he seemed destined ever to enjoy was as cousin to a famous footballer. For Roy Dwight was still going from strength to strength. Having helped take Fulham to the FA Cup semi-final in 1957–8, Roy had been signed by First Division Not-tingham Forest for the then hefty transfer fee of £15,500. Among the trophies of his growing fame was a wallet autographed by Hollywood's blonde bombshell, Jayne Mansfield. 'I was judging a beauty contest in Mansfield, Notts., and they somehow got Jayne Mansfield to judge it as well.'

The 1958–9 season began as a magic one for Roy Dwight. Not only did he score four hat-tricks in as many matches, but at the end came the climax of which every player dreams. Nottingham Forest made it through to the FA Cup Final, playing Luton at Wembley Stadium, watched by the Queen and the Duke of Edinburgh.

Roy, at outside-right, scored in the ninth minute, confirming his reputation as an audacious goal-snatcher. Then in the thirty-third minute, he was heavily blocked by Luton's full back, Brendan McNally, and rolled on the Wembley turf clutching his right leg. When his team trainer attempted to manipulate the leg, Roy gave a yell of agony. His tibia, the shin bone, had sustained a compound fracture.

Rushed to a local hospital, Roy showed his own measure of Dwight doggedness by refusing to be X-rayed until he had seen the remainder of the match. Still in his player's gear, he was put in a wheelchair and pushed into a ward to join a circle of astonished old men round a TV set which, only minutes before, had shown him being carried from the Wembley turf.

One Saturday, during Reggie's piano tutorial with Helen Piena, he told her he might have to give up his scholarship at the Royal Academy. Naturally perturbed, Helen asked him why. Reggie answered that his parents were about to get divorced.

Stanley and Sheila Dwight had, in truth, been divorced for years in everything but name and strained outward appearance. The void at the centre of Reggie's life was as familiar to him as sleeping or waking. Low-burning chronic unhappiness is, however, infinitely preferable to unhappiness dragged out under a spotlight and minutely examined. A home in any state is better than one finally and irrevocably broken.

The unhappy family ménage at 11 Potter Street, Northwood, where Reggie felt afraid to bite into celery or kick his football, had been of mercifully short duration. In 1960, Stanley was posted by the RAF to Harrogate in Yorkshire, this time with no question that his wife and 13-year-old son might accompany him. Reggie could settle back into the indulgent care of his mother and grandmother with no male disciplinarian to upset matters – although, by Stanley's later account, he enjoyed travelling up to visit his father during school holidays.

A few months into his posting, Stanley later said, he was rung up by Sheila and told that she'd met someone else and wanted a divorce. The 'someone else' was a local builder and decorator named Fred Farebrother whom she had first met during the war. The decree was granted in 1962, on the grounds of Sheila's adultery with Farebrother.

In a passionate outburst almost a quarter of a century later, the superstar would accuse his father of making Sheila pay the costs of the divorce and taking almost all their combined assets, even though he, too, had been having an affair at the same time. To set the seal on young Reggie's feeling of rejection, Stanley quickly married his new love and had four sons with her in rapid succession. What further proof could there have been that he'd never really wanted Reggie in the first place and was delighted to be rid of him now?

From Stanley's side, however, came a rather different story. He said he paid all the costs of the divorce and gave Sheila half the proceeds from the sale of 111 Potter Street, plus their car and all the furniture and contents except for two silver-framed photographs of Reggie – which he was to keep beside his bedside until the day he died. He continued to support both Sheila and Reggie until the divorce, and went on supporting Reggie until he left school. Stanley's version also sheds interesting light on his supposed strict refusal to let Reggie wear trendy clothes. He said he opened an account at a West End Branch of Horne Brothers, the outfitters, where Reggie was free to go and choose whatever clothes he wanted. He even arranged for a kindly member of the Horne's staff to take his son to football matches now that he himself would no longer be able to do so.

In Harrogate, Stanley had, indeed, met someone else in his turn, a 33-year-old lab technician named Edna Clough, who was there recovering from the recent death of her elderly mother. But he did not begin seeing Edna until 1962, when his divorce from Sheila was about to be made absolute.

The first response of almost any child in such circumstances tends to be naked self-interest. How will it affect me? Can I still play football next Tuesday? Or in Reggie Dwight's case, would he have to give up his scholarship at the Royal Academy of Music? To his teacher, Helen Piena, he confided another, related anxiety. His parents had always said that, if he really buckled down to his studies, they would get him a new piano to replace the rather battered upright he had been using. But, with all their money going on lawyers, presumably he could forget about that now.

As a musician himself, Stanley had been immensely proud of Reggie's Royal Academy scholarship and (as even the future superstar would not deny) had always encouraged him to work hard and acquire the most thorough possible musical grounding. Stanley was quick to reassure Reggie, and also his teacher, that there was no question of his leaving the Royal Academy and that he could still have his piano. A receipt from Hodges & Johnson's music store of Romford, Essex, proves he was as good as his word – £68 paid on 26 February 1963, for a 'secondhand upright pianoforte by Collingwood, walnut finish'.

Far from swanning off into the blue with his new wife and family as legend has it, Stanley seems to have taken pains not to make his son feel rejected and to maintain a relationship with him. Reggie had been given the choice of living with him or Sheila but, unsurprisingly, chose Sheila. Stanley then gave in his notice to the RAF in order to move back down south to be near his son. His northern-born second wife, Edna, agreed to the migration, realising how important it was to him. Stanley served out his RAF time at the Air Ministry in London, with occasional liaison duties in Yorkshire. Then he and Edna took a small toy and stationery shop in Chadwell Heath, Essex, far enough away to forget his unhappy former home but near enough to stay in regular contact with Reggie.

Stanley's letters to Edna reveal a man who was anything but cold, who worried about his son's feelings over the divorce and was hugely relieved when Reggie seemed to harbour no resentment about his remarriage. Witness this, dated 2 December 1962: 'In the afternoon I met Reggie and told him about us, pet, and he was very pleased. Indeed, he was really delighted. He took the news exactly as I said he would, dear, and said that all he wanted was for me to be really happy and now he is really looking forward to meeting you – especially as you play the piano. He saw your photographs, pet, and said "Yum! Yum!" Cheeky imp! Ha! ha!'

And on 17 December: 'This weekend Reggie came over [to Stanley's sister Ivy's house in Kent] and brought us a nice magazine and newspaper holder for our wedding present, dear. I took him to the cinema last evening to see Constantine the Great, which was quite good. Yesterday, Ivy, Henry [Stanley's brother-in-law], Reggie and I went to see Dartford play Wisbech and beat them 5–2.'

After Stanley and Edna's wedding, Reggie wrote his father a four-page letter in his neat handwriting, thanking Stanley for a gift of 10s (50p) and reiterating his feelings about the event. 'I am glad you had a nice honeymoon but you didn't mention anything about your new wife. I was rather hurt, because you know that I do not mind you getting married again . . .'

The letter also mentions hintingly that Reggie's white mackintosh is 'in a disgusting condition' and that he is 'desperately in need of a new one' as well as of new tennis shoes. He has just taken his mock GCEs and come top in English language with 73 per cent, but is afraid he has done 'terribly' in geometry. 'I also know what I want to do when I leave school,' he adds. 'Actually I have known for a long time but I have never said so before because I thought everyone would laugh at me. I want to entertain – that is, to sing and play the piano. I know that it is not easy to become an entertainer and I appreciate that it takes a lot of hard work and of course luck, but I know I would really enjoy doing it. I hope you don't think I'm foolish but I thought I'd tell you anyway.'

Reggie, Sheila and the Collingwood upright grand had now set up home with Fred Farebrother, the builder and decorator, who was himself leaving another family behind. Fortunately for Reggie, there was to be no awkwardness about sharing his mother or fitting in with her new partner. Fred was a simple, homely character who took pains to be a friend and ally to Sheila's boy at a time when he was plainly upset and disoriented. He was, indeed, more like an elder brother, enthusiastic about pop music, liberal with pocket money and lifts in his ex-Post Office van, unfailingly amused when Reggie addressed him as his name spelt backwards, 'Derf'. Very quickly Reggie took to describing Fred as 'my dad', even though he and Sheila would not marry for 10 years yet.

Their home was in Frome Court, one of the colonies of maisonettes on the long, leafy road between Pinner and its adjacent suburb, Northwood Hills. Although technically an apartment block, Frome Court was like a double-winged Metroland villa with stained-glass heraldic devices set into its windows and front doors of mock-Tudor design. Derf, Sheila and Reggie lived in flat number 30a, on the ground floor to the left.

Moving to a new home and new neighbourhood increased Reggie's solitariness. His world was still mainly his bedroom – an even smaller one now in the tiny Frome Court maisonette. His best friends remained his records in their brown-paper covers, his books on sport and the movable counters of his Football League chart.

He was fond of his Auntie Win's son Paul, a cheerful little boy who used to bring Sheila her newspapers every Sunday. Paul would be allowed into his room to look at his League table and hear about a wonderful new group called the Beatles. 'He said they were the greatest thing there'd ever been,' Paul remembers. 'We'd sit there with an album-cover and he'd tell me which one was John, Paul, George and Ringo.'

He was galvanised by the Beatles, their energy and humour and also the extraordinary possibilities they opened up to all such bedroom-bound British youth. The songs with which they turned the charts upside-down were not cover versions of American hits, but had been written by two of them, Lennon and McCartney. It was a transfixing thought to a boy with a musical ear that had always made tunes spontaneously dance in his head. With everything else, the Beatles were themselves record fans, acknowledging a debt to backwaters of American blues and soul known only to serious aficionados like Reggie Dwight. In particular he watched the Beatle named John Lennon, whose shadow of a cynical smile first hinted to him that rock-'n'-roll performance need not be entirely in earnest.

'He took me to a Beatles concert once,' his cousin, Paul Robinson, remembers. 'We'd gone up to London to see a schoolboys' exhibition. That was boring, so Reg said, "Do you fancy seeing The Beatles?" They were doing one of their Christmas shows at Hammersmith Odeon.' Another great eye-opener was to see John, Paul, George and Ringo prancing around the stage in pantomime fancy dress, even coming on in drag. No one had thought of putting pop together with slapstick fun before.

He was unusual in liking female pop singers, a tiny faction then. His particular favourite was Dusty Springfield, who left a folk trio to find solo success in 1963. Not since Winifred Atwell had a female performer so interested Reggie. Along with a smoky gospel-edged voice went over-the-top Barbie Doll glamour: spun-up bouffant hair, bow-tied balloon-skirt dresses and enormous black-smeared eyes. Despite apparently singing straightforward love songs to straight-forward men, she also projected a curious sense of uninvolvement and aloneness. Reggie had pictures of Dusty Springfield, cut from *Reveille* magazine, pinned all round his bedroom wall.

The usual pains and tensions of puberty seemed to trouble him remarkably little. He had the advantage of attending a co-educational school, where girls were a daily fact rather than, as for so many English boys, distant figures of fantasy and speculation. Despite his podgy build and puggy, four-eyed face, he had a good rating on Pinner County Grammar girls' grapevine. He was funny and interest-ing; he possessed the unusual attributes of good manners and polite-ness, and the still more unusual one of knowing how to be friends with girls. Going on a date with Reg Dwight was totally free of the usual physical unease. He was happy to see a film or a pop show, walk his partner home, then say goodnight. Girls were relieved to know someone with whom they could spend an evening, free from the ultimate dread of a spotty lunge and a knee driven among their layered petticoats.

Julie Westaway, the daughter of his English teacher in the fifth year, was one of several such regular female 'mates'. Another was Janet Ritchie, who had known him since they both started at Pinner County. Reggie was a regular visitor at both their houses, approved of for his punctilious good manners. Even in 1963 it was becoming rare to find a boy like this, who got up when a lady entered the room, and addressed all older men as 'sir'.

Janet became a particular mate because her uncle was secretary of Chelsea Football Club and she a comparable football enthusiast. Reggie and she would go together to Chelsea matches and to pop shows at the Harrow Granada. She also was one of the few school-friends, of either sex, he ever liked and trusted enough to invite home to Frome Court. He even took her into his room to show her his precious brown-paper-covered record collection and the meticu-lous cataloguing system that went with it. But he'd never lend a record, even to Janet, for fear it might come back scratched.

At school, she was one of a clique who went in for Goonish humour and conversed in a private vocabulary largely invented by Reggie. A favourite trick was to drop initial letters, so that the class

lookout would signal a teacher's approach by a hiss of 'She's 'oming'.
Anything good was termed 'dos muchos', 'diode' or 'small'. The
height of understated enthusiasm was to look momentarily shame-
faced, as Reggie did so well, and apologetically murmur 'small
hyperbole there'.

He also was a gifted mimic, able to bend his light, accentless
voice to almost any timbre, male or female. He could recite whole
segments of TV and radio comedy shows back through his childhood:
*The Goon Show, Hancock's Half-hour, Round The Horne, Take It From
Here.* Most of all he loved *Steptoe and Son*, Galton and Simpson's
classic sitcom about a genteel rag-and-bone dealer, his disreputable
old father and their patient horse, Hercules.

He seemed to have got over the trauma of his parents' divorce,
and to be just as comfortable with his father's new partner as with his
mother's. His stepmother, Edna, remembers him coming to stay with
them in the flat above their Chadwell Heath shop, and being always
affectionate to Stanley and friendly and immaculately well-mannered
toward her. Stanley continued to write to him, take an interest in his
musical studies and answer his desperate SOS messages for new
clothes. When a 'classic' raincoat bought for him by his father was
not acceptable, Stanley and Edna took him to Horne Brothers in
London and let him choose one in the new shortie style. Whatever
reservations Stanley may have had against trendy clothes seemed to
have vanished by this point. One colour snap taken of Reggie on a
visit to Chadwell Heath shows him in a shirt with thick vertical
yellow and black stripes. Another shows him playing miniature golf
in a Robin Hood trilby and what look suspiciously like Hush
Puppies.

'Reggie enjoyed himself when he came to stay with us,' Edna
remembers. 'We were both busy a lot of the time in the shop, but
he seemed quite happy upstairs, playing my piano or picking out
letters on a portable typewriter we had. One day I saw that he'd
typed over and over again, "Stan Dwight is my father, Sheila Dwight
is my mother." I felt a great sense of sadness that at such an
impressionable age a boy should be separated from one of his parents,
and wondered if this had been preying on his mind as he sat there
typing.'

Thanks to his more stable home circumstances, Reggie became
noticeably more relaxed and happy during his last two years at Pinner
County Grammar. In his fourth year, one of the Downfield House
sixth-formers was a girl named Gay Search, later to become a
successful journalist and broadcaster. 'Yes, Dwight – I can see him
now with his blazer buttoned across his chest and his bum sticking

out. He had a walk that I won't put an adult gloss on and call "mincing", but it was an odd little walk, special to him. I remember him as being totally different from the general rabble of younger boys. He had an air of being far more grown-up, more civilised. He wasn't a sycophant, he didn't creep, but as a fourth-former he was someone a prefect or sixth-former could talk to on equal terms.'

Pinner County Grammar now knew R. K. Dwight for something other than 'Les Petites Litanies de Dieu'. That beautiful Steinway piano in the assembly hall felt a very different pressure on its immaculate keys. To the amazement of his peers, the earnest Royal Academy student also could play like Jerry Lee Lewis, or nearly, rippling with a manic index finger to and fro, kicking away the piano stool to stand there and hammer, his duck-like rear thrust out under his blazer hem. To still greater general astonishment, the buttoned-up fat boy revealed he could sing, and even sing while playing just like the crazy drape-suited figures up on the cinema screen in *High School Confidential* and *Disc Jockey Jamboree*. It was the last kind of voice anyone had expected from that shy dumpling face – keening rock-'n'-roll gibberish in a flamenco-high tenor, bursting every tight stitch of his former self-consciousness and reserve.

He would perform at end-of-term socials and at odd moments in term-time when the sacred Steinway was unsupervised. In these dull interludes of school, any entertainer is highly prized. And Reggie did not just entertain. He astonished. He excited. He drew crowds. It was an authentic marvel, how dumpy R. K. Dwight had somehow emerged from his bedroom, spinning off 'Great Balls of Fire'.

A star among his classmates, he now found himself against the grain of authority for the first time in his life. Mr Stoupe the music master had a loudly-vented hatred of all pop music, and bitterly upbraided him for so wasting his abilities. Bill Johnson the history master, and blues buff, was more sympathetic. 'I remember at one end-of-term party he wanted to rig up a microphone at the piano. I found him a bit of wood that he could nail it to.' The first in a multitude of increasingly long-suffering roadies.

As rock 'n' roll took stronger and stronger hold, his interest in his classical studies dwindled to vanishing point. In his Royal Academy class with Helen Piena, the once model pupil grew casual and slapdash. Some Saturday mornings he would leave home with his briefcase, but never arrive at the Academy. As the superstar would admit in later life, 'I'd come up to Baker Street, get on the Circle Line and stay there for three hours, then go home again.'

In his fourth year, a school group including Janet Westaway, Peter Emery and Reggie went on a trip to Annecy in France. During the week of educational visits, their itinerary somehow became combined with that of some girls from a French lycée. 'These lycée girls literally used to clamour to be on the same coach as Reg,' Peter Emery remembers. 'I can see him now, sitting at the back, with French schoolgirls all round him, beating out rhythm on the seat-back and singing Elvis Presley songs.'

George Hill was among the most go-ahead landlords in the chain of pubs operated by Benskins brewery. He and his wife, Ann, had made such a success of the Hare, at Harrow Weald, that Benskins offered them a place more than twice as large, though not as immediately attractive. In 1961, therefore, with many misgivings, George and Ann Hill accepted tenancy of the Northwood Hills Hotel, just outside Pinner.

The Northwood Hills bore little resemblance to their previous idyllically pretty country inn. Situated immediately opposite North-wood Hills tube station, it was a large detached building, in size and gloomy aspect more like some abandoned Rural District Council offices. It had, indeed, been built as a hotel in the years of Metro-land expansion, but all the room-and-board side had long ago vanished.

Within were three enormous bars lined in dark Olde English oak panelling, with heavy, knobby furniture and drab brown industrial linoleum. Six sad cheese rolls under a plastic dome represented the only catering. When the new tenants arrived, trade was so slight that one person could easily tend all three bars at once.

George and Ann Hill set out to change all that. They reopened the defunct dining-room, putting on special lunches for employees of the nearby headquarters of Vehicle and General Insurance. For the evenings, George saw he must appeal to the growing teenage element. He therefore decided to have live music in the saloon bar on Friday and Saturday nights.

Among the benefits of the Hills' previous pub had been two highly popular saloon-bar pianists. 'One was an old lady who used to play the honky-tonk style,' George Hill remembers. 'Then we had Bob. He was an albino who just turned up one day with his white walking-stick. But he was a marvellous pianist – and a real showman. He used to jump up and down, get really carried away. The customers loved him.'

Bob followed the Hills to their new pub, played there a couple of weekends, but said he'd have to stop as the travelling was too much for him. George still had not found a satisfactory replacement when a man he had not seen before came into the saloon bar and asked for a word with him. 'It was Reggie's father. He asked me if I needed a pianist, because his boy wanted to have a go. I said, "All right. I don't mind having a look at him."'

Reggie's 'father' was, in fact, Sheila's man-friend Fred Farebrother, who not only got Reggie his try-out at the Northwood Hills but also delivered him there, along with a rudimentary microphone system to augment the saloon bar's decrepit upright piano.

The initial impression was hardly that of a Saturday-night showstopper. 'He was only about fifteen, still at school,' George's wife, Ann, remembers. 'His hair was cut very short. He wore a collar and tie, and grey flannel trousers. And this Harris tweed sports jacket that was a kind of gingery colour. He was very shy. But he did tell us he'd written a song that was called "Come Back, Baby".'

Picture the scene, that inaugural night in the Northwood Hills saloon bar. The sprawling old bar, still more full of echoes than people, with its dingy panelled walls and faded lampshades, its brown lino worn by generations of feet and supine dogs. The brightly lit bar counter with a go-ahead new husband-and-wife team, pulling Benskins pints or turning for push-ups at the spirit optics. A few incurious eyes turn to the piano, where a bespectacled boy in a ginger tweed sports jacket is setting up some kind of microphone and loudspeaker, helped by a man and a petite, vociferous woman, plainly his mother. Man and woman retire to a side table, leaving boy alone. Dogged bespectacled face nerves itself as for plunge into cold swimming-bath. A sudden passionate salvo from the yellow piano-keys. A voice from the loudspeaker fabric, keening the lovelorn words of Ray Charles's Country and Western classic:

> *Take these chains from my heart and set me free.*
> *You've grown cold and no longer care for me . . .*

To begin with, the customers didn't appreciate it. 'They gave him terrible stick,' George Hill remembers. 'They'd shout "Get off!" or "Turn it down!" He'd have empty crisp packets and ashtrays thrown at him – we only had tin ones, so they didn't hurt. Or somebody would sneak up and unplug the leads of his PA system. I think he had quite a few pints emptied into that piano as well.'

But, with the ringside support of his mother and Fred Farebrother, Reggie stuck it out. And after a few nights, the hail of scrunched-up crisp packets and tin ashtrays was somewhat moderated. The leads from the mike were left alone, and the piano innards spared their baptism of Benskins best bitter. Here and there, under a knobby oak table, a foot began to tap on the old brown lino. Hands even loosened their grip on pints and gin glasses to clap along in time.

Enormously in the boy's favour was that he did not only do 'modern stuff'. Like his early exemplar Winifred Atwell, he would play anything his listeners showed the smallest signs of liking. If he could not reach them with Ray Charles or Jim Reeves, then he would try with English bar-room evergreens like 'Roll Out the Barrel' or 'Bye Bye Blackbird'. Some nights, he would be joined in performance by the amateur vocalists every English pub can produce. 'There was one old girl from the East End, called Mary Whitmarsh,' George Hill remembers. 'She used to like to get up and do all the traditional Cockney things, like "The Old Bull and Bush". And there was a bloke named Toby Barry, who really fancied his voice. He'd play the spoons on his knee as well, or beat time on a tray.'

After a few weeks, George was forced to admit he had found an attraction at least the equal of albino Bob. 'But I still don't think Reggie was as good a piano-player,' he insists to this day. 'As far as I'm concerned, Bob was the one who ought to have become a star.'

George Hill's object of drawing 'the young crowd' worked, if anything rather too well. 'It was quite a hard pub, actually. We used to get this crowd in from South Ruislip who had a scrap every Friday night. I remember a punch-up starting one night while Reg was playing. There was a window near the piano, and he just went out through that like a flash.'

Reggie was the Northwood Hills' weekend pianist for almost two years. His pay was thirty old shillings (£1.50) a night, plus the collection which Mary Whitmarsh, the old Cockney lady, would make for him on a glass-ringed tin tray. In all that time, he did not ask for a rise, or for his name to be displayed outside the Northwood Hills Hotel, as indeed it never was.

While the boy in the Harris tweed jacket pounded the yellowed piano-keys, Britain was in the grip of Beatlemania and its vast cultural backwash. If Liverpool could have an internationally popular and commercial sound, then why not any other hitherto remote, unfashionable British city or town? Consequently, there was soon a Manchester Sound, spearheaded by the amiable, sub-Beatle-ish Hollies. There was a Birmingham Sound, represented by the Apple-jacks, with their amazing novelty of a girl bass-player. There was even a Tottenham Sound, briefly incarnate in the white-trousered Dave Clark Five. There were potentially Scottish, Irish, Welsh and West Country Sounds. But never in the keenest entrepreneurial eye the smallest glimmer of a Middlesex and, especially not, a Pinner Sound.

To date, Reggie Dwight's home area had produced only one pop musical attraction, of somewhat special appeal. This was Screaming Lord Sutch, a Medusa-haired rock maniac whose stage properties included Viking horns, a coffin and a Jack-the-Ripper-style Gladstone bag, and whose family home was in Northolt Road, Harrow-on-the-Hill.

It was in these decorous London suburbs, however, that the next great musical generation was taking shape. Across in Ealing, in a packed club room under the ABC teashop, Alexis Korner's Blues Incorporated presented a roster of unknown young vocalists including Rod Stewart and Long John Baldry. In front of the grandstand at Richmond's Old Deer Park, corduroy-clad boys and girls jazz-stomped to an unregenerate rhythm-and-blues band called the Rolling Stones. Southward, at the Wooden Bridge Hotel, Guildford, you could hear Rhode Island Red and the Roosters, featuring Eric Clapton. At the Railway Hotel, Harrow and Wealdstone, just down the road from Pinner, one would soon be able to catch the Mann-Hugg Blues Brothers, later Manfred Mann, and a wild West London Mod group called the Detours, soon to be transmogrified into the High Numbers and finally the Who.

In his fourth year at Pinner County Grammar, Reggie had gained admittance to a local amateur group named the Corvettes. Its founders were two Northwood Secondary School boys, Stuart Brown and Geoff Dyson, on guitar and bass respectively. The drummer's father ran a pub, The Gate, near Mount Vernon Hospital. Their name was inspired by the Chevy Corvette sports car driven by two young freebooting heroes in an American TV series, *Route 66*.

The Corvettes played a mixture of blues and rock 'n' roll. Stuart Brown, who had a huskily soulful voice, did the blues numbers. Reggie Dwight, at the piano, did the Jerry Lee Lewis 'shouters'. Their celebrity was not great. The most Geoff Dyson ever remembers them being paid was £2 a night at the youth club in St Edmund's Roman Catholic Hall, Pinner Road. 'Reggie had to play whatever piano was there, which nearly always would be horribly out of tune. Stuart and I used to try to tune our guitars to the piano. The other thing I remember was how dapper and conventional-looking he always was. While the rest of us would be in jeans, he'd be in grey flannels.'

The Corvettes disbanded after a few unspectacular months, and Geoff Dyson took his bass guitar to another local group, the

Mockingbirds, good enough to 'open' for big-time R & B bands like the Yardbirds. Then he met up with Stuart Brown and Reggie Dwight again. They told him they were starting afresh, with a new name and new serious intent. They were now Bluesology, in homage to a number by the gipsy jazz guitarist Django Reinhardt.

Geoff Dyson agreed to rejoin them on bass guitar, though there was another role in which he could be still more useful. While with the Mockingbirds, he had played at glamorous Soho music venues like the Marquee Club. With his contacts there, he could act informally as Bluesology's booking manager.

Not that Bluesology would show much sign of promise, for quite a long time yet. Most of its personnel were more interested in chasing girls and fooling around. 'But we always knew Reg was going to make it,' Geoff Dyson says. 'He'd look at the rest of us sometimes, and say "Oooh, you lot! But I'm going places."'

TWO

A Bit of Outrage

H E had reached that stage of school life when a Careers Advisory Officer arrived in the late afternoon period to conduct individual interviews amid piles of helpful literature about opportunities in banking, insurance or the Forestry Commission. For male Grammar School leavers in those monochrome early Sixties, official advice was virtually always the same. A good all-round GCE, followed by college or, at least, technical college. Your place thus assured on the morning platform for the Metropolitan Line train up to town. Work, a cheese roll lunch, and more work. Home at five to your pipe, slippers and Ovaltine in Metroland.

Among the new generations of prospective commuters there were always a few renegades, inquiring about offbeat jobs for which the Careers Advisory Officer possessed no official literature. One such at Pinner County Grammar School was a portly fifth-former named R. K. Dwight, who had announced that he wanted to go into the 'music business'.

Viewed from rural Middlesex in 1964, the 'music business' was a mystery as remote and impenetrable as the diplomatic service or the BBC. Music was not, as it is today, a visible, pullulating industry. Pop was a barely emancipated part of a tiny professional enclave, ruled by dynasties and nepotism and centred on a couple of streets in London's West End. As with the film business, you got in by grabbing any opening, wherever it occurred. Being in that old-fashioned music business for Reggie Dwight could have meant managing the Royal Philharmonic Orchestra or selling pianos in a department store. It could have meant cutting records in a factory, etching sheet music or filing and cataloguing in the BBC Gramophone Library.

He had turned several other possible careers over in his mind, including the possibility of following his father into the RAF. There, doubtless, his neatness and efficiency would quickly have gained him a commissioned rank like Stanley's on the bureaucratic side. Stanley, of course, knew of his half-shamefaced wish to become 'an entertainer' and, as a former semi-pro trumpeter, understood better than most what an unstable basis that was for a career. One of his post-divorce letters to Sheila – destined to be chuckled over many years later – urged that Reggie be talked out of this implausible wish to become 'a star'. Even so, Reggie thought enough of his father's wisdom to suggest Stanley should sit in on his forthcoming interview with the Careers Officer.

He had sat his GCE Ordinary Level exam at sixteen, passing in only four subjects: English Language, English Literature, French and Music. It was the typical result of the clever but torpid pupil who had done next to no work, merely getting by in those subjects where he possessed innate ability. Even in Music, he had reached only the lowest pass grade. He was now in the sixth form, the only one in his year to be studying music at A-Level. But his teacher, Mr Stoupe, complained that he wasted his ability – and unconscionable amounts of study-time – in messing around with a pop group. Clearly, not a boy destined to set the world alight. A boy who might possibly get his wish and find a minor niche in some office, shop or outlet connected with music. But where?

Of all unlikely people, it was Reggie's footballer cousin Roy who found that elusive opening. Roy's 1959 Cup Final accident had put paid to his stardom, though he played on for a while, first with Fulham, then under Jimmy Hill's management at Coventry. From playing he would move into coaching, and tireless work with young people in several departments of sport which continues to this day.

Roy had stayed on friendly terms with Sheila Dwight after her divorce from Stanley, and had good-naturedly promised to help Reggie if possible via his many contacts in the sporting and showbiz world. It happened that a football friend of Roy's knew Pat Sherlock, who worked for the West End song publishers Mills Music. Roy arranged for Sherlock to interview Reggie, and himself conscientiously accompanied the lad up to town for the occasion.

'I can see him now, sitting in my office,' Pat Sherlock remembers. 'I remember thinking what small hands he had for a piano-player. He had this nervous mannerism of pushing his glasses back up his nose. And a funny little pouting look.' Reggie was, of course, an excellent interviewee with his shy and studious air and his habit of addressing older men as 'sir'. A further interview with Mills' managing director, Cyril Gee, confirmed the favourable impression. He was offered a job as Mills Music's office boy at a starting salary of £5 per week.

His decision to leave school in early 1965, a term before his A-Level exams, caused universal protest. As well as being the school's only A-Level Music pupil, he had also been due to take English, a subject in which he could be brilliant when he chose. With two A-Levels added to his four O-Level passes, he could have competed for admittance at several redbrick universities, if not the Royal Academy of Music. His Academy tutor Helen Piena was particularly dismayed at what seemed a perverse squandering of promise, academic as well as musical. 'I remember sitting with him for about three-quarters of an hour, trying to talk him into going to university. All he said was that he wouldn't because no one in his family ever had before.'

Stanley Dwight, predictably, was most unhappy about the decision, and bitterly reproached his nephew, Roy, for setting up the Mills Music interview without consulting him. It was in fact to be a watershed in his relations with his son, although Stanley did not realise it at the time. He still prided himself on maintaining a good relationship with Reggie and kept him supplied with clothes and pocket money, even though frequently short of cash himself. Reggie seemed fond of his stepmother, whom he called 'Aunt Edna', and had been delighted when she bore the first of his four half-brothers, Stanley, in April 1964. 'How is the new baby and how is Aunt Edna?' he asked his father excitedly on the phone while Edna was still in hospital. 'Send her my love and tell her I'm really looking forward to seeing my baby brother.'

But Stanley, as was made clear to him, had no say whatever in his son's career choice. His widow now remembers it as a culmination of many signs that Reggie no longer felt the same respect and affection for him and that his place – even as a provider of clothes and pocket money – had been usurped by the easygoing rough diamond, Fred Farebrother. So rejected and disillusioned did Stanley feel, Edna now says, that he gave up trying to compete with Sheila and Farebrother for Reggie's affection. Not long afterwards, he sold his stationer's shop in Chadley Heath and he and Edna moved back to her part of the world, the Cheshire Wirral.

A far more serious stumbling block to Reggie's plan was Pinner County's stern head, Jack Westgate Smith. Reggie broke the news to him in trepidation, well aware that Mr Westgate Smith had the power to jinx the plan if he chose. 'He asked me if it was really what I wanted to do,' the star would remember later. 'I said "Yes", and he said "All right. You have my blessing." I was flabbergasted.'

R. K. Dwight's last recorded attendance at Pinner County Grammar School was on 5 March, 1965. Bill Johnson, his history master, delivered a philosophical farewell. 'I told him if he really wanted to be in the music business, this was probably the most sensible way. "When you're forty," I told him, "you'll either be some sort of glorified office-boy or you'll be a millionaire."'

Denmark Street, London's version of Tin Pan Alley, is a brief thoroughfare between Charing Cross Road and the sour, windy wastes under the Centre Point skyscraper. When Reggie Dwight arrived there in 1965, the days were long gone when songwriters in poky offices would try out a tune on any old 'tin pan' or rush into the street to see if some passing tramp could instantly whistle it back (hence 'the old grey whistle test'). But Denmark Street remained the hub of what was still not quite the British music industry.

Here, as half a century before, any composer must come to have his work published, in sheet-music form, the words even of wildest rock-'n'-roll numbers written below the notes with archaic hyphens and accents. Here, before the age of private recording studios, aspiring groups must come to make their 'demos' in eggbox-lined confessionals at £5 per hour. Here, among shades of Music Hall and Variety and smells of jangly upright pianos and violin-dust, the next week's teenage Top 10 was still put together by men in their late forties and early fifties, chain-smoking Player's or chewing on wet Wills Whiff cigars.

In barely a hundred yards could be found all one needed to get on in pop music. Publishing houses like Southern, Pickwick, Grosvenor, Mills and KPM. Recording studios like Regent Sound, where the first ever Rolling Stones sides were cut. Promotion men like Brian Sommerville, who had first taken the Beatles to America. Film and variety agents like Lipton and Andy Lothian. Not to mention L. Lennox, the music-engravers; the Tin Pan Alley Club; and Musical Exchange with its window full of Fender and Gretsch guitars, black Vox amps, organs and zebra-skin-covered bongo drums.

Though thrustful new Tin Pan Alleyites were to be seen everywhere in their Carnaby Street clothes, the monarchs were still figures embodying continuity and tradition. Of these none was greater than Dick James, once a small-time danceband crooner, now the Beatles' music-publisher. It had been in Tin Pan Alley, or not many yards away, that Brian Epstein had been stood up by another publisher, then walked into Dick James's hole-in-the-wall office to find James fortuitously at his desk. Since then, of course, Dick James had risen

to far more sumptuous offices, in nearby New Oxford Street. But his
regal promenades through Denmark Street and his regular court at
the Gioconda coffee bar remained a symbol and affirmation of just
how lucky a man in this business could get.

Mills Music was an American firm, born in New York's original
Tin Pan Alley, whose catalogue included such illustrious names as
Fats Waller, Duke Ellington and Leroy Anderson. Its UK catalogue,
though more modest, covered the spectrum of British pop, from
Cliff Richard's 'Move it' to 'Side Saddle', 'Snow Coach' and other
piano hits by the dour Russ Conway. Not that Reggie Dwight put
so much as a toe on the ladder to such things. His job was in the
warehouse at the rear of Mills' premises, in Denmark Place, filling
casual orders for sheet-music, brewing tea, packing parcels and
wheeling them on an old-fashioned hand-barrow to the Post Office
depot in Kingsway. His closest brush with celebrity would be when
he was sent with a piece of music or a message to the Regent Street
office of the veteran bandleader Joe Loss.

On his Tin Pan Alley bosses he seems to have made scarcely
more impact than on his schoolteachers. Cyril Gee, the managing
director, was aware only of 'this podgy kid' who persisted in calling
him 'sir'. 'I remember him coming to me one day and asking if he
could play one of the arrangers' pianos in the lunch hour.' Even his
original mentor, Pat Sherlock, knew little about him, save that he
played piano at every moment he was not packing parcels or hunting
for something or other among the dusty catalogue shelves. 'That
Christmas, we had a party in the office, with a lot of Chelsea football
players. We kept Reggie back after work, playing a lot of Cockney
things like "The Old Bull and Bush".' Cousin Roy's wedding all
over again.

As well as being poorly paid, menial, boring and submerged, the
job entailed frequent leg-pulling from the far more sassy and streetwise boys who constituted Tin Pan Alley's messenger class. One such
was Caleb Quaye, office boy for Paxton's wholesale music-delivery
firm in Old Compton Street, who used to call at Mills every day on
his rounds. The son of prewar bandleader Cab Quaye, himself flashily
proficient on guitar, piano and drums, Caleb at this stage spotted no
fellow spirit in Reggie Dwight. 'I just used to laugh at him because
he looked so much like Billy Bunter.'

But Reggie was starting to change. His girl 'mate' Janet Ritchie
received another privileged invitation into his bedroom at Frome
Court to try on some new things he had bought in the trendy
boutiques and second-hand clothes shops around Carnaby Street. 'I
remember, he'd got a fur coat. One of the short ladies' ones all the

boys were starting to wear. And a Mickey Mouse T-shirt. I'd never seen such way-out stuff before. "I like a bit of outrage," he said.'

Meanwhile, his new group, Bluesology, struggled in continuing birth pangs. Their style was meant to be cool, sophisticated and worldly, something like the hugely popular Georgie Fame and the Blue Flames. Putting aside simple rock and even simple blues, they experimented with the more complex, less cheerful repertoire of Mose Allison and Jimmy Witherspoon. As the star himself would later admit, this was usually far over the heads of teenage audiences at dances in the Pinner area. 'We were always playing the wrong stuff, trying to appeal to minority tastes. Bluesology were either two months too late or three years too early.'

Despite being largely held in church halls and British Legion clubs, their gigs were not immune from excitement or physical danger. One night at South Harrow British Legion, a squad of black-clad rockers rode their motorbikes into the club and demanded that Bluesology call a halt to Jimmy Witherspoon and do some old-fashioned rock-'n'-roll. On that terrifying occasion, the least terrified was Reggie Dwight. He did not mind at all going back to being Jerry Lee Lewis. And he secretly loved the 'bit of outrage' that turned the flag-hung war veterans' hall into a scene Marlon Brando might have played in *The Wild One*.

Bluesology now numbered five. With Reggie on piano and Stuart A. Brown on guitar and vocals, there was Mick Inkpen on drums and Rex Bishop, replacing Geoff Dyson, on bass. Emulating the Blue Flames, they also acquired a tenor-sax player named Mike, somewhat older than the others, as brass sidemen then tended to be. In nearly every teenage R & B outfit there would be one member who looked like the others' big brother, if not father.

With the elder Mike among them, blowing lustily if erratically, Bluesology now felt ready to move up another notch. They began to enter for the amateur talent contests that, in the beat-group craze of 1965, were frequently put on by dance halls and clubs. Though large entertainment chains like Mecca did offer alluring prizes – even recording contracts – most were simply a wheeze to get five or six hopeful bands to perform free of charge. Bluesology entered one contest at the Wimbledon Palais, another at Rory Blackwell's club in Islington. In both they were beaten by more practised groups with material more accessible than Jimmy Witherspoon.

On Sunday afternoons they would meet to practise in the big back bar of the Northwood Hills Hotel. Though ready enough to grant that favour George Hill remained deaf to any hints that he might allow Bluesology to augment Reggie's weekend piano spot, or possibly put up money for new equipment. 'I never knew what went on when Reggie brought them all in,' Hill remembers now. 'I just knew there was always a hell of a noise.'

Georgie Fame's number one hit 'Yeh Yeh' had made the electric piano massively popular. Geoff Dyson remembers that at the Wimbledon Palais talent contest, one of the groups who trounced Bluesology already possessed this treasure. 'Reggie was allowed to have a go on it. He thought it was wonderful.' Shortly afterwards he approached George Hill at the Northwood Hills and asked for the loan of £200 to buy an electric piano for Bluesology. 'I had to say "No",' Hill remembers. 'I hadn't got two hundred pounds to lend him.'

A more serious patron was acquired through their drummer Mick Inkpen, who worked as an apprentice to a jewellery manufacturer in Bond Street. Inkpen persuaded his employer, Arnold Tendler, to come and see Bluesology at one of their Pinner church-hall gigs. 'After having had my arm twisted to go and see them, I was really bowled over,' Tendler remembers. 'At the piano there was this little roly-poly boy in clothes even I called square. But when he played, he was marvellous. Even then he used to kick away the piano-stool and play sitting on the floor.'

Arnold Tendler became Bluesology's first real manager, putting up money for new instruments, stage uniforms and a Ford Thames van. At the same time, using every penny of his savings and pub earnings, Reggie managed to raise the price of a Hohner 'Planet' electric piano and amplifier.

Between Bluesology's good-looking vocalist and its owlish tweed-jacketed one, there was no contest as far as Arnold was concerned. 'No matter what he looked like, Reg was the one who made that group. Stu Brown had a good voice, but it could be flat. And it always took him a bit of time to get going. Whereas Reg just had to open his mouth, and there it was.'

Despite being well into his thirties – an almost prehistoric age to sixteen- and seventeen-year-olds – Arnold Tendler entered into the spirit of Bluesology, accompanying them on most of their outings to disappointing talent competitions. 'And I used to go down and watch Reggie play at that pub in Northwood Hills, even though there'd be a fracas most weekends. At the time, I remember, he had a girl friend with red hair, called Gipsy.'

The jeweller's money also financed the making of a two-side demo record at a studio in Rickmansworth operated by the son of bandleader Jack Jackson. On one side Bluesology did Reggie's song

'Come Back, Baby', with the composer himself on vocal. The other side featured Stuart Brown's soulful voice in Jimmy Witherspoon's 'Times Getting Tougher Than Tough'. Armed with this, Arnold Tendler made the rounds of the London record companies. He struck gold – or, at least, rolled gold – at Philips, whose head of Artist and Repertoire, Jack Baverstock, was sufficiently impressed to offer a recording contract with Philips' associated label, Fontana.

Tendler had not pulled off such a marvellous coup. In that post-Beatlemania spring of 1965, record companies would sign up virtually anything, so long as it featured long hair, hipster trousers and guitars. Bluesology were just one of hundreds of amateur bands from all over the United Kingdom, contracted on royalty rates of fractions of a penny and run quickly through the system, like baggage through an X-ray machine, to see if they might be a Fab Four, Five or Six.

But for the band concerned, it was still a thrilling moment. Most thrilling was it for Reggie Dwight, who would feature on the A-side of the debut single, singing his own song, 'Come Back, Baby'. To complete his triumph, 'Come Back, Baby' was also accepted for publication by his daytime employers, Mills Music.

Actually, it was a measure of Fontana's perfunctoriness merely to let Bluesology re-record the two sides they had cut as demos in Rickmansworth. The recording took place at Philips' London studios, under Jack Baverstock's supervision, on 3 June, 1965. It speaks volumes for Reggie's self-effacing manner in those days that Baverstock does not remember noticing him during the three-hour session.

The future Elton's debut on record is a half-pint ballad, full of the sidelong chords and macho wistfulness of the Merseybeat era. Its lyric is lifted complete from the songwriter's phrasebook: 'Come back, I'll treat you right. Come back, I'll hold you tight.' The voice is recognisably Elton's, clearer and higher than almost any dared be in those days, holding together the cheap blur of sound and Mike's lone, off-key saxophone. The piano chords give the good value one would expect from a Royal Academy junior exhibitioner. Key changes are heralded by emotional pounding, as in the very best of Bobby Vee. The B-side version of 'Times Getting Tougher Than Tough' might have been thought marginally more commercial in those rhythm-and-blues-crazy days. Stuart Brown's husky café-au-lait voice has more than a touch of Georgie Fame. Reggie is represented by piano boogie infillings and a long middle solo in the groove of a Northwood Hills Saturday night.

The single came out in July, in company with the cream of the British and American beat boom. Also released, that twangling Op-Art midsummer, were the Rolling Stones' 'Satisfaction', the Hollies'

'I'm Alive', the Animals' 'We Gotta Get Out Of This Place', the Byrds' 'Mr Tambourine Man', the Kinks' 'Set Me Free', the Yardbirds' 'Heart Full of Soul' and the Who's 'Anyway, Anyhow, Anywhere'.

The star still remembers the thrill of hearing his voice crackling on a car-radio, when 'Come Back, Baby' got its first play on Radio Luxembourg. After that, it rapidly sank under the thousand-watt tank-tracks of the Yardbirds and the Stones. There was not even the faintest seismic hint of an appearance in the charts.

Nevertheless, a watershed had been reached. Bluesology were no longer an amateur group, playing for school hops and Catholic socials. As 'Fontana recording artists', they could aspire to serious London R & B venues like the Last Chance and the 100 Club. When they played, it was in the uniform of dark blue pants, red polo shirts and blue-and-white blazers bought for them by Arnold Tendler at Irvine Sellars's Carnaby Street boutique.

On 22 July, they received their first national publicity – a story in the trade paper *Record Retailer and Music Industry News*:

Bluesology, a group of five talented young musicians, take their name from the title of a record by the famous French jazz guitarist Django Reinhardt. Their first Fontana record release was 'Come Back, Baby', composed by the group's singer–pianist, Reg Dwight. 'We play blues music mainly after the style of Jimmy Witherspoon, Memphis Slim and Muddy Waters with, dare I say it, a slight jazz flavour,' says spokesman drummer Mick Inkpen (17).

Above was a minuscule picture of the talented young musicians – four of them slim, hollow-cheeked and fashionably handsome, the fifth bespectacled, his face set in the glower of a Bunter who has just learned that the Greyfriars tuck shop is out of cream buns.

Arnold Tendler was successful in getting them bookings, though of a somewhat variable and unpredictable kind. One was at the Phoenix Theatre, in Charing Cross Road, supporting Eric Burdon and the Animals. 'The audience threw so much stuff at the stage that Eric had to go out, sheltering behind a dustbin lid, and threaten no one would play if it didn't stop. Another time, I got them in at the restaurant on top of the Hilton Hotel in Park Lane. When we arrived, the lady in charge said "We like it very quiet." So the lads played just one number, "The Girl From Ipanema", making it last about twenty minutes.'

Towards the end of 1965 Pat Higgs, an experienced dance band trumpeter, read in a music press ad that an up-and-coming blues band sought recruits for its newly inaugurated horn section. The only slightly disconcerting thing was that auditions were to take place in Pinner, Middlesex.

Pat Higgs made it out to Pinner, and found Bluesology. They told him they had to get a proper brass section before they could make their next record. Though several years older than any of the personnel, Higgs thought he might as well join up. The same auditions produced tenor saxophonist Dave Murphy, another noticeably older recruit whose previous experience had been mainly in theatre orchestra-pits.

The expanded Bluesology's first major foray was to a talent contest-cum-audition for bands, run by a contact of Arnold's named Trevor Witchelo. The venue was the State, a huge circuit cinema modelled on New York's Empire State Building in the heart of Irish Kilburn. After their three numbers, they were approached by a representative of the Roy Tempest Agency, which at that time handled a large number of touring pop package shows. The Tempest man asked if they would be interested in backing American R & B solo performers on tour in Britain. If they were to accept, it was obvious that Reggie Dwight could not continue in a daytime clerical job, as he had previously managed to do. He therefore turned fully professional, handing in his notice at Mills Music and exchanging a regular £5 pay packet for the excitement and uncertainty of life on the road. Little did he guess where that road would lead – or that he was destined never to get off it again.

The first American R & B artist to whom Bluesology were offered as sidemen was Wilson Pickett, born in Pratville, Alabama, singer of 'Mustang Sally', 'In The Midnight Hour' and 'Land of 1,000 Dances', most aggressive of the new funky generation on the Memphis Stax label, and a difficult companion in almost any circumstances.

Alas, Bluesology were not to experience life on the road with 'the Wicked Pickett'. At the audition, his guitarist took against them and ordered Roy Tempest to find Pickett another backing band. 'All those American acts used to be very organised,' Pat Higgs remembers. 'They'd have their song-arrangements all written out, and expect the backing band to be the same. Bluesology had never used arrangements. Before we went up for the next audition, I had to try to scribble a few out.'

Their first successful audition was with Major Lance, a high-register soul man, named in the grand tradition of the Duke of Earl, whose best-remembered song bears the title 'Um Um Um Um Um

Um'. Pat Higgs having got the horn arrangement down on paper, Bluesology were booked for their first fully pro tour in December 1965.

For Reggie Dwight, who naturally knew every word of 'Um Um Um Um Um Um', the next two weeks were unforgettable. Merely to shake hands with Major Lance was a thrill almost beyond expression by the shy, pug face. Never mind to travel and socialise with him and, each night, gamely try to reproduce his original arrangements on the stage of some noisy little club. The ultimate music fan had found a way of being closer to his idols than the very best seat in the front row. Twenty-five years later that same, undiminished music fan would still maintain, 'Backing Major Lance was probably the biggest thing that ever happened to me.'

More idols followed, from the mainstream and also the back-waters of Reggie's record-collection. During early 1966, Bluesology toured as backing band for the Drifters, the Ink Spots, Billy Stewart, Doris Troy and Patti LaBelle and the Bluebells – or 'Blue Bellies', as one provincial club poster announced them.

Working for the Roy Tempest Organisation was no rest cure. As well as importing genuine veteran US groups like the Drifters and Ink Spots, Tempest also put on groups of the same name who, at the most charitable estimate, were no closer than fourth or fifth cousins to the originals. Most of the groups stayed in a flat owned by Roy Tempest, for which they were charged a hefty rent. 'Tempest used to con us, really,' Pat Higgs says. 'We'd be shown a two-week tour sheet with just a few dates, and proper rest days. Then when we started, all the spaces would have been filled in. We'd find ourselves doing two, sometimes three gigs in a day.'

The future star's memory would also be of virtual slave labour. 'There was one day with Billy Stewart we did four gigs – in London and Birmingham. We started off in the afternoon, playing an American servicemen's club in Lancaster Gate, finished that at four, raced up to Birmingham and played the Ritz and Plaza there, then came back to London and played the Cue Club in Praed Street the same night. And we never had road managers in those days. At the time we didn't think anything of it, humping our equipment up and down all the stairs.'

Arnold Tendler, the Bond Street jeweller, continued as their manager, patiently bailing them out when equipment was lost or stolen, even forking out for a new van when the other was wrecked on a trip to Norway. 'I think Arnold was having a bit of financial trouble at the time,' Pat Higgs remembers. 'Still, he always paid us all right. Sometimes he'd open his car boot and it'd be full of watches. He'd dole out one to each of us, so that we could go off and sell that.'

Not all the American stars Bluesology backed had the cult status of Major Lance. The Ink Spots were the original late Forties vocal group, combining pre-doowop harmonies with an archaic comedy routine. 'I remember we went with them to this really hip black club around Liverpool Street,' Pat Higgs says. 'Suddenly in the middle of the number, one of these Ink Spots starts taking his clarinet to pieces. The audience nearly pulled us off the stage.'

The star's own fondest recollection would be of Patti LaBelle, who both mothered him with home cooking and took a small fortune from him at suitcase-top cards. And of Billy Stewart, another hero of Reggie's for his gymnastic scat versions of 'Summertime' and 'Sitting in the Park'. 'He died very shortly after he left us – was shot to death back in America. An enormous man. I mean, I remember stopping alongside the motorway on the M1, waiting for him to relieve himself, and it was like waiting for a train.'

In between, Bluesology would do gigs on their own at London clubs like the Cromwellian in South Kensington, or the highly fashionable Scotch of St James's. At the latter, Reggie had a traumatic experience with his new acquisition, a Vox AC 30 electric organ, painted a lurid shade of orange. 'In the very first number, one of the notes got stuck. I was so embarrassed. But later on, Eric Burdon of the Animals came up and said "Never mind, lad. That happened to us once, too."'

The Vox became hallowed on a later night at the Cromwellian, when Stevie Wonder, the Motown prodigy – then only just metamorphosed from 'Little Stevie Wonder' – borrowed it for an entire set. Reggie was still a starstruck fan above all, thrilled that music could smuggle him in to places like the Scotch, where the faint profile of a Beatle or, at least, a Gene Pitney, might glimmer through the high-priced darkness.

Bluesology's second single for Fontana, recorded the previous November, was released in February 1966. The A-side, 'Mr Frantic', was another Reggie Dwight composition, a soul number rather oddly slow and tentative, befitting this nearest-ever approach to self-portraiture. The B-side was a traditional R & B boogie, 'Every Day I Have the Blues', sung by Stuart Brown. Despite the vastly fatter, more confident sound of the new horn section, airplay was minimal and chart-action nil.

At this point, something strange happened to Reggie Dwight. From being undisputed front man in the group he had co-founded, he was relegated – or relegated himself – further and further into

Bluesology's background. A mixture of chagrin and guilt at having failed to sing a hit seemed to undermine his confidence, his extrovert showmanship and determination to 'go places'. The lead singer became merely the Vox organist, loyally backing up this or that American star, on solo gigs giving up his limelight to the handsome, husky Stuart A. Brown. That he still passionately wanted to sing could be divined by an anguished flash in his glasses whenever Stu Brown started giving it hot. But, in some obscure self-destructive mood, he felt he couldn't, or shouldn't.

It was enough for him to be in a busy band, with regular money and a full engagement book. In the new van financed by the long-suffering Arnold Tendler, Bluesology voyaged to Britain's furthermost music venues, like the Whisky-à-Go-Go, Newcastle-upon-Tyne. With Doris Troy they even played the Cavern Club in Liverpool, dank subterranean birthplace of the Beatles. Reggie's Pinner friend Janet Ritchie, who was doing teacher training in Liverpool, hitched a ride in the van and helped carry their equipment down the eighteen famous steps from Mathew Street.

In the six-strong line-up, fat Reggie was odd man out – quiet, neat and self-contained, inhabiting his own little patch of order amid the travelling chaos. Most indulgences of a blues musician's life seemed to pass him by. He barely drank and didn't smoke, either cigarettes or marijuana. He showed no interest in the girls who clustered at Bluesology's feet as they played and followed them backstage or to the pub afterwards if they liked. Reggie's only interest in girls seemed to be for conversation. 'If nothing was happening, he'd just go to sleep,' Pat Higgs remembers. 'He had a special little pillow that he used to carry round with him.'

Within the group he was the comedian and clown, the one most likely to raise a laugh from their punishing itinerant life. On long road journeys he would entertain the others with streams of punning wordplay, or his wide repertoire of funny voices from radio and TV shows: Eric Morecambe, 'Professor' Stanley Unwin, Bloodnock and Bluebottle from the Goons. 'And when we broke down – which was a lot – we'd say "Come on, Reg. Do us your little dance",' Pat Higgs remembers. 'He'd get out and do this special little dance for us on the hard shoulder of the motorway.'

There was also the other Reggie, troubled, bashful and unconfident, buttoned up inside a mod jacket as tightly as he once had been in his brown school blazer. His hair had already become a problem, receding from the temples and thinning at the crown, so that his regulation Beatle busby required more and more elaborate maintenance with shampoo, hair-dryer and comb. In 1966 the idea of going

bald was a pop musician's ultimate nightmare. Ghastly to end up like
the Hollies' drummer, who was forced to hide his terrible affliction
under a wide-brimmed cowboy hat.

The other torment was his chronic weight problem. He had
chosen the very worst life to keep slim, eating as he most often did
in pull-up musicians' cafés like the Blue Boar, whose walls were like
action paintings, zigzagged with the tomato and egg stains of late-
night food fights. Not that he was gluttonous like the real Billy
Bunter; as he often remarked bitterly, he had only to look at a
doughnut for the pounds to pile on. In desperation, he started to
take amphetamine slimming pills, the kind that promote weight loss
by speeding up the metabolism. 'He said he'd pinched them from his
mum,' Pat Higgs remembers. 'He handed them out to the rest of us,
too, to help us stay awake.'

Following the Beatles' path, five years too late, Bluesology even
did a stint on the Hamburg Reeperbahn, playing at the self same
club, the Top Ten, where Beatlemania had first taken root. 'Though
Reg usually didn't drink much, he did have a bit of a go in
Hamburg,' Pat Higgs says. 'I remember him dancing among the
traffic out on the Reeperbahn.'

It was the summer of 1966. The Beatles were far away from
grubby Hamburg with their chastely black-and-white-jacketed album
Revolver. *Time* magazine had dubbed London 'The Style Capital of
Europe'. England won the World Cup, snatching two goals from
West Germany in the last seconds of extra time. Girls' bumblebee-
striped dresses climbed four inches above the knee. England was
drunk with sunshine, football and sounds. Bluesology still couldn't
get a hit.

In a single day they did three London gigs, then drove straight
down to the South of France to play for a month at the St Tropez
Papagayo Club. When they arrived, the accommodation to which
they were shown was a completely bare room. The club owner
explained that his previous resident band had destroyed all the beds
and furniture. 'I remember the Papagayo because Reg electrocuted
himself on his gear one night,' Pat Higgs says. 'He was out for quite
a few minutes. We had to call a doctor to give him an injection in
his bum. The rest of us stood round the bed and watched.'

Among British blues singers of this era, none was so distinctive as
Long John Baldry. A London policeman's son, six foot seven and a
half inches tall, blond of hair and pink of face, he combined a voice
oozing Southern molasses and hominy grits with a manner which, in
either sense, could accurately be termed high camp.

Camp was not a thing much encountered in blues circles then, and Long John's appearance made it the more striking. As well as being immensely tall, he was a notable dandy, fond of flipping open his jacket to display the LJB monogram patterned over its silk lining. The Deep Southern voice that growled macho blues ballads each night was by day exercised in all the parodied gambits of a screaming old queen. Whereas other musicians called each other 'man' or 'cat', Long John preferred the appellation 'dear' or 'she', as in 'She's bold today!' A saxophone player who travelled with him remembers once passing a full troop of Boy Scouts, trudging along replete with Baden-Powell hats, khaki shorts, woggles and toggles. A satirical cry from Long John Baldry rang out in tones to curdle the blood of any scoutmaster. 'Ooh look, dear! Trade!'

Onstage he was equally unlikely, his immaculate figure towering through the cigarette smoke, a Savile Row suit straight out of some Mississippi bayou. To his teenage audiences his manner was at best caustic, at worst downright testy. On one famous night, he actually tapped an inattentive girl spectator on the head with his microphone. When feminine chatter interrupted his emotional rendering of 'Black Is The Colour of My True Love's Hair', Long John broke off to shout that they were 'just a lot of Woolworth's shop girls'.

Like Mick Jagger, Long John got his big break as a singer with Alexis Korner's Blues Incorporated under the ABC teashop in Ealing. He had subsequently joined another great British blues eccentric, the harmonica-playing Cyril Davies. When Davies died in early 1964, Long John took over his backing band, renaming them the Hoochie Coochie Men and bringing in a sandpaper-voiced youth named Rod Stewart as second vocalist.

Unlike most blues purists, Long John Baldry had his eye firmly fixed on commercial success. His next venture was Steampacket, an early supergroup combining Rod Stewart with Julie Driscoll and Brian Auger, the duo who would later produce a classic Sixties single, 'This Wheel's on Fire'. There were, indeed, too many potential stars in Steam Packet for it to last, and by late 1966 Long John was looking for another backup band.

Dropping in at the Cromwellian Club, South Kensington, one night, he happened to catch Bluesology playing in the basement. 'They were a good tight band,' Long John remembers now, 'though they didn't have a guitarist. And the Vox Continental their organist was playing looked rather hideous.' There and then Long John Baldry offered them the job of backing group to himself, paying them a flat weekly wage via his managers. Though Bluesology were already under contract to the jeweller Arnold Tendler, they instantly accepted.

Long John's managers at the time were John and Rik Gunnell, sharp-operating brothers who had started the famous Flamingo Club in Soho and now had a virtual monopoly of white blues and soul acts, from Georgie Fame and Alan Price to Chris Farlowe and P. J. Proby. As well as the Flamingo, they ran the Bag o' Nails in Kingly Street, currently the in-club for London's rock-music aristocracy. Their reputation as tough guys was considerable. Arnold Tendler did not try to resist the poaching of his boys.

As Long John Baldry's sidemen, Bluesology were re-outfitted in yellow shirts with frilly fronts and cuffs, and green John Stephen suits whose double-breasted jackets buttoned from left shoulder to right hip. There was also an influx of bigger-time musicians, all but obliterating the original Pinner line-up. Mick Inkpen and Rex Bishop were replaced on drums and bass respectively by Pete Gavin and Freddy Gandy. A talented lead guitarist named Neil Hubbard took over from Stuart Brown. A clean sweep of the horn section brought in Marc Charig on trumpet and a tenor sax-player with an unusual Christian name, deriving from ancestors in Nottinghamshire. His name – half of it destined for immortality – was Elton Dean.

The new style was that Long John took the spotlight in his monogrammed silk suit, with husky-voiced Stuart Brown demoted to backup vocalist, and Reggie Dwight to backup backup vocalist. After a few weeks, Long John brought in another singer, Alan Walker, to harmonise with Stu Brown. Now Reggie wasn't even needed to do 'Oohs' and 'Aahs'.

A photograph of him in this period shows a figure anything but fulfilled, happy or comfortable. His hair is wedged into a Beatle fringe, as rigid and unnatural as the strip of handkerchief in his breast pocket. His pug face, with its unfashionable half-frame spectacles, is set in a resigned glower. His high-lapel jacket visibly strains at all three of its buttons. His discontent and frustration are almost ectoplasmic.

He kept in constant touch with Sheila and Derf at home in Pinner and, like a good boy, sent picture postcards of the more exotic locales to his relations and friends. Although his father now lived far out of his ken, they still corresponded regularly, and Stanley Dwight always sent him a present on his birthday and at Christmas. Having sold his shop, moved to Cheshire and started a large second family, Stanley Dwight was now in some financial difficulty. At his time of life, the only work he could find were poorly-paid office jobs for which, as a former senior RAF officer, he was absurdly overqualified. He worked for Littlewoods home-shopping catalogues and Cammell Laird's shipyard before finding a better niche at Unilever, the chemicals conglomerate, where he would remain until his retirement.

To add to the pressures on Stanley, his baby son Robert, his third child with Edna, fell seriously ill with gastroenteritis just before Christmas, 1966. All seasonal cheer was forgotten amid the anxieties of nursing the baby through the life-theatening crisis. Shortly afterwards, Stanley received a hurt note from 19-year-old Reggie, wondering why he had received no Christmas gift as he usually did from his father.

When Bluesology played a gig at Liverpool University, he managed an afternoon to visit Stanley and Edna over on the Wirral. Remembering how he used to enjoy his food, Edna prepared a lavish buffet lunch. Both she and Stanley were shocked to see how thin and pinched-looking the once-ample boy had become. He explained that if he wanted to be a pop star he had to stay on a strict diet, and hardly ate anything. 'What do you live on?' Stanley asked him. 'Mostly crispbreads,' he replied.

Long John Baldry says now he was not aware that Reggie Dwight ever nurtured ambitions as a vocalist. 'As far as I was concerned when I took on the group, Stuart Brown was the leader and the one with the voice. Later on, I even produced Stuart on a couple of demos of songs that Reggie had written.'

Bluesology's new sax-player Elton Dean first noticed Reggie as a dispirited, silent figure out on the margin, not playing conspicuously well. Despite the modish prestige of the Vox organ, he never felt comfortable on it, or properly mastered its fingering. 'He didn't make mistakes. He didn't inspire you particularly, either,' Dean remembers. 'He was just Reggie – or Bunter, I used to call him, 'cos he was a little bit portly and always used to wear striped blazers.'

To newcomers like Elton Dean he seemed more like the band's archivist, the one who would find out-of-the-way blues numbers on forgotten labels to bolster their repertoire. 'He'd write songs and bring them to rehearsals, but none ever got done onstage. I never even knew he sang until I heard him do a number one day at a sound-check. Then I thought he sounded great. Just like José Feliciano.'

His frustrations became harder to restrain, especially under the influence of the amphetamine pills he was still taking in an effort to control his weight. The sudden squalls of his childhood reappeared, in what Long John satirically described as 'screaming fits'. Elton Dean remembers how, in a moment, the band's cheery fall-guy and one-man Goon Show could change to a glowering dressing-room recluse. Another couple of minutes and he'd be himself again. His fellow musicians used to call them Reggie's Little Moments.

THREE

'I feel lost'

E VERY so often Britain's TV audience is treated to selected re-runs
of the Sixties pop programme, *Ready Steady Go!* Modern music
fans can look back, with amusement or nostalgia, to a quintessential
expression of Swinging London. They can see the stuffy old Rediffu-
sion Television studio at the Aldwych end of Kingsway, which, each
Friday just after tea, became as 'in' as the trendiest West End club.
They can see the format, so daring for those primitive black-and-
white days, that put musicians and audience together in open plan
with the unconcealed hardware and freneticism of the studio floor.
Everyone from polo-necked Beatles and barefoot Sandie Shaw to
Martha and the Vandellas and James Brown's Famous Flames, surrounded by Mod crowds of their near-equals dancing along industrial
catwalks or draped around iron fire escapes. A poignant monochrome
memento of the last days when pop didn't have a care in the world.

The audience is of equal fascination, fresh-trawled from Carnaby
Street or King's Road, in its hipsters and Mary Quant bobs, shaking,
frugging, ponying, monkeying or hullygullying among the sound-
booms and trundling cameras. Especially those young men one
glimpses alone in the crowd, running combs through their Ringo
mops and staring round them with eyes as bright and unblinking as
baby piranha fish. The next generation of hustlers, entrepreneurs and
tycoons is watching and waiting to get a fingernail or squared-off
boot-toe into the business, anywhere.

Ray Williams first went to *RSG* as a fifteen-year-old fan from the
Heathrow, Middlesex, area, following his local soul band, Cliff
Bennett and the Rebel Rousers. When the band did well enough to
be asked back, so was their loyal entourage. As Cliff and the boys
belted out their first chart success, 'One Way Love', Ray appeared
on camera, dancing in a gallery.

The thing about Ray Williams was his almost ludicrous prettiness. His hair was thick gold, his skin liqueur honey brown, his Delft china-blue eyes as wide open and ingenuous as Christopher Robin's. It was inevitable that, after a couple of weeks frugging with the extras on *Ready Steady Go!*, he should come to the notice of the show's presenter, Cathy McGowan. She made him her unofficial assistant, helping audition other girls and boys who hoped to feature as dancers. When he arrived at the TV studios on Friday nights, screaming girls would mob him as if he, too, were a pop star.

It was the high summer of Mod style, striped box jackets, peg-top trousers, button-down shirts and fringed faces composed into becoming scowls. Ray Williams grew famous as the ultimate speci-men, regularly featured in *Mods Monthly* magazine. When any foreign camera team came to London to report on 'the scene', they usually ended up interviewing and photographing Ray.

At *Ready Steady Go!* he met a great many useful people, notably Brian Epstein, the Beatles' famous manager, and Brian Sommerville, their original public-relations man. The golden good looks were again decisive. He became Brian Sommerville's assistant, working out of a Tin Pan Alley office only yards from where Reggie Dwight was making tea and packing parcels. Not that anyone suggested that so gildedly handsome and right-looking a youth as Ray Williams should ever dampen his Mod blazer on an electric kettle or soil his mitred shirt cuffs with anything so mundane as brown paper and string.

At barely sixteen he was doing PR work for the Kinks, Sonny and Cher and Tommy Roe, a Buddy Holly clone who spirited him off to work in America. Thence, with a single Cuban-heeled leap, into publishing, running Lowry Music for Tommy Roe's manager. Thence into corporate life with his own organisation, Mayfair Public Relations, working with two young partners, Simon Hayes and Allan McDougall, from a house in Bruton Mews, off Berkeley Square. He was not yet quite eighteen. So things went in the summer of 1966.

Mayfair Public Relations represented Sonny and Cher, Buffalo Springfield, the Hollies and Cream. Simon Hayes also did some PR work for Brian Epstein, at that time becoming estranged from the Beatles and attempting to console himself with management of a West End theatre, the Saville.

The defection of Simon Hayes, in 1966, brought an end to Mayfair Public Relations. With the company went most of Ray Williams's resources, including the briefcase Tommy Roe had given him and the camera that had been a present from Sonny and Cher. But he retained his matchlessly good contacts, most crucially with Allan Clarke, Graham Nash and Tony Hicks of the Hollies.

In 1967, the American Liberty record label, previously licensed through British EMI, decided to set up its own self-contained European operation. By thought processes utterly logical to that youth-obsessed time, eighteen-year-old Ray Williams was appointed Liberty's European head of Artist and Repertoire, and installed behind an executive desk in Albemarle Street, Mayfair.

Two slight snags lay in this. The first was that Williams had no experience whatever in A & R, a job combining talent scout and record producer. The second was that Liberty – famed as the label of transatlantic legends like Bobby Vee and the Chipmunks – had virtually no artists under contract outside America.

The blond teenage tycoon was entirely undaunted. On his executive desk he drafted an advertisement, inviting would-be recording talent to come and audition for him at Liberty. The ad ran as a quarter-page in the *New Musical Express*, on 17 June, 1967. The aureoled face of New York's Statue of Liberty and her upheld torch drew attention to the enticing words:

LIBERTY

WANTS TALENT

ARTISTES / COMPOSERS / SINGERS / MUSICIANS

TO FORM NEW GROUP

Call or write Ray Williams for appointment or mail audition tape or disc to 11 Albemarle Street, London W1. Tel. Mayfair 7362.

Among the flood of applicants was one whom Ray Williams would have special cause to remember. 'This little dumpy guy came into my office,' Williams recalls. 'He was a bit fat, a bit forlorn-looking, dressed in blue denim, with all his stuff in a carrier bag, like Tiny Tim.' It was Reggie Dwight, of Pinner, Middlesex.

Reggie had seen the advertisement while gigging with Bluesology in Newcastle-on-Tyne. To an unhappy organ-player, somewhere to the rear of Long John Baldry's coat tails, it had seemed too good to be true. Liberty Records – another name of magic from his lonely bedroom hops – were not full to capacity with talent like Bobby Vee and the Chipmunks. In some humble or invisible capacity, there might be room for him, too.

Ray Williams's lordly title and letterhead had led him to expect some senior, intimidating management figure. Instead, he beheld the goldenly handsome young man of his own age, beautifully dressed, impressively secretaried but otherwise friendly, pleasant and sympathetic. 'We got on well from the start,' Williams remembers. 'We started talking like mates, really. He told me he was in a band, backing John Baldry, that he really wanted to sing, but Baldry wouldn't let him. "I feel lost" he said. What struck me most was how unloved he seemed. Plus coming out with a thing like that, which you'd hardly say even to a very close friend. I just felt so sorry for him.'

The Liberty advertisement, indeed, had come at a moment of terminal despair for Reggie. With no chance to sing in Bluesology, and no alternative prospects, he was thinking of quitting stage-performance altogether. He had even secretly gone to Philips Records and asked for a job as a record plugger, back in the painless faint glamour of Tin Pan Alley. Time and again through these early years, a kindly Providence would thwart his instinct to do exactly the wrong thing. Philips turned his application down. His mother bolstered his confidence and resolve yet again, helping him draft a reply to the *NME* ad in his neat music-student's writing.

Here he was, as a result, seated at Ray Williams's office piano, twitching his spectacles back up his nose and spreading his diminutive hands. At this crucial opportunity to display his talents, all memory of upbeat Bluesology material fled from Reggie's mind. Instead, he chose a slow country-and-western number, Jim Reeves's 'He'll Have To Go', charging its mournful, fatalistic words with all his own feelings of frustration and hopelessness.

The keening voice was like none in pop, save perhaps the young Latin-American José Feliciano. The song, in that time of Monkees and flower power, was practically an antique. That he was clearly an excellent pianist did not help at all. Under the long-running dominance of four-man guitar groups, the piano had been relegated to an old-fashioned parlour joke. A solo singer-pianist was as archaic a notion as Russ Conway or Winifred Atwell. Ray Williams could barely count the ways in which he was totally unhip.

A string of similar numbers followed in the same lachrymose vein from the Jim Reeves and Ray Charles song books, each as far as it could possibly be from current pop fashion. The climax was a plaintively whiteface version of Al Jolson's 'Mammy'. Williams still remembers how the forlorn figure changed completely as the music took hold. 'He didn't look sad and lost any more, but totally in command and relaxed.'

Despite the unsuitable songs and passionately non-commercial performance, Ray Williams was impressed. He suggested that, as Reggie had brought no audition tape, he should make a demo record. This Williams promised to play at the first opportunity to his

American boss, Bob Reisdorf. For, despite the grandeur of his title, he himself had no power to sign talent on his own authority.

The demo was made at Regent Sound in Denmark Street, the studio where Andrew Loog Oldham had first recorded the Rolling Stones. 'Reggie just did the same numbers he'd already played in my office,' Williams remembers. 'At Regent, studio time still only cost five pounds an hour. I think we did it all inside one hour, with another hour for the mixing.'

In the course of that afternoon, Reggie admitted a further handicap. Though he could write tunes almost instantly and ad lib, he said he was 'no good' at lyrics. This even though song-lyrics by him had already been recorded, and even published as sheet-music.

Then Ray Williams remembered a letter from the huge shoal he had received after his *NME* advertisement. It was from another would-be songwriter with a handicap as large as Reggie's, in that he could not write music, only words. With the letter had come a sheaf of lyrics, typed on an ancient faint-ribboned machine. Quirkily interesting as Williams found them, he had seen no immediate practical use for them. Now his entrepreneurial instinct went to work, putting two and two – or, rather, one and one – together. He found the letter, handed it over with the lyrics that were enclosed, and suggested that Reggie have a crack at putting them to music. If there were any justice in the world the making of this one connection would have given Ray Williams riches for life. But, we can be assured, there is no justice in the world.

The letter had come from Lincolnshire, that slightly mysterious eastern county of flat farmland, mists, gypsies, medieval stone gargoyles and village names outlandish even by the standard of the English gazetteer. The address at the top of the page was 'Maltkiln Farm, Owmby-by-Spital'. The signature also was exotic: Bernard Taupin.

The name familiarly pronounced 'Torpin' by a generation of pop fans is, in fact, French, deriving from *taupe*, a mole, or *taupinière*, a molehill. It is a suitable trick of etymology for French stock that became transplanted to the deepest English countryside. Not bad, either, in its later espionage connotation, for someone destined to be the supreme underground worker of popular music. Working silently as he has behind a blazing frontal talent, pursuing his own private, subterranean paths, shunning the light and limelight, Bernie Taupin could very well be classified as a 'mole'.

The Taupin family originated in Burgundy. Bernie's paternal grandfather was a wine shipper who set up business in London but still preferred to raise his four sons and one daughter in wholly French style. Robert Taupin, Bernie's father, was born in London but sent to boarding school in Dijon. He intended to be a lawyer, but poor health interrupted his studies at the London School of Economics. Instead, the lycée-educated Frenchman decided to become an English farmer.

The literature and learning that were to influence Bernie's life came largely from his mother's people, the Corts, originally a family of Anglican clergymen in north-west England. His maternal great-great-grandfather and great-grandfather both served as vicar of the parish of St Anne's, in Sale, Cheshire. His grandfather, John Leonard Patchett Cort, was a schoolmaster, a Cambridge MA who taught on the naval training ship HMS *Conway* and later co-owned a private prep school in Reigate, Surrey.

His mother, Daphne, was academically gifted, although circumstances ruled out the university degree she might otherwise have taken. Just before World War II, the Corts moved to Switzerland, hoping to find a cure for Daphne's mother's acute asthma. There Daphne became fluent in French and studied French literature and Russian. On her mother's death, her father returned to England, but Daphne stayed in Switzerland throughout the war. There she became involved with the relief organisations bringing both Swiss and French children over the frontier for brief respite from the privations of Nazi-occupied France. Daphne herself would cross to the German side, risking internment as an enemy alien.

She met Robert Taupin in London just after the war, while working as children's nanny for his brother Henry. They married in 1947, and immediately set forth on Robert's farming career. Their first son, Tony, was born in 1948. Their second, Bernard, arrived in 1950. A third, Kit, was to follow eleven years later.

Bernie's memory of his early upbringing has the roseate glow of Laurie Lee's famous country autobiography *Cider with Rosie*. Robert Taupin worked as a stockman for a large farm estate near Sleaford. The family lived in feudally tied accommodation, first a farm then a rambling old house named Rowston Manor, full of nooks and passageways that were paradise to an imaginative small boy.

The great influence on Bernie and his elder brother, Tony, was their grandfather Cort, the classics master, now both widowed and retired. 'Poppy', as the boys called him, fostered their interest in nature, teaching them to recognise plants, birds and butterflies. He also read them the great poems of English literature: Tennyson's 'Charge of the Light Brigade', Coleridge's 'Rime of the Ancient Mariner', Lord Macaulay's 'Lays of Ancient Rome'. While other village boys played simple cowboys and Indians, Bernie's infant games were all based on schoolroom classics, Scott's Lochinvar and Macaulay's epic tale of Horatius. 'Whenever I charged down a field, I was always Lochinvar. I'd take my friends down to the little stream we called the beck, which had a tiny bridge over it. I'd make them be the Tuscan hordes while I was Horatius, keeping them at bay while I recited the poem. I knew every stanza, word-perfect.'

His other initiation was into *Winnie-the-Pooh*. He loved A. A. Milne's archly *faux-naif* tales of the Bear of Very Little Brain, Piglet, Rabbit and Eeyore. His great treat with Poppy was to play 'Poohsticks' – throwing twigs into the stream off one side of the bridge, and seeing which twig would come out first on the opposite side. Little did Bernie Taupin then dream his future destiny as Pigletish accomplice to a Pooh colourful beyond any illustration by E. H. Shepard.

The move to Owmby-by-Spital marked Robert Taupin's first independent farming venture as a smallholder and battery-chicken farmer. Maltkiln Farm comprised two dilapidated houses in the dead centre of the tiny hamlet, keeping company with its marshy field, a single barn and the chicken battery-house. In the beginning, there was neither running water nor mains sewerage. Baths had to be taken in a tin tub before the fire. The only lavatory was a chemical closet in the cellar.

Yet in this austere English setting, the habits of Robert's French upbringing prevailed, with evening dinner instead of high tea, oil-and-vinegar dressing instead of salad cream and wine served on occasions when Lincolnshire neighbours would have had bitter beer or sticky sweet sherry. Where other families went to church or 'chapel', Robert and the boys attended the Catholic church in nearby Market Rasen, where Bernie served as an altar-boy.

Encouraged both by his grandfather and his mother, he absorbed books through every pore: *Winnie-the-Pooh*, *The Wind in the Willows*, the Narnia stories of C. S. Lewis. He became fascinated by the American West, going beyond the pasteboard Hollywood version to read the true-life, often squalid adventures of Jesse James, Billy the Kid and Wyatt Earp. His parents had by now moved from their draughty, inconvenient farmhouse to a new bungalow a few yards away. Bernie used a room in the old house to create a museum of the fall of the Alamo, with a broken breadknife doubling as Jim Bowie's eponymous blade, an old fur coat as Davy Crockett's coonskin cap, copper pennies as Colonel Travis's uniform buttons and bits of boundary-railing as Mexican lance-heads.

Almost as soon as he could read he had begun to write, stories and poetry. At the age of ten he decided to write a book on the American West, filling half a dozen pages of a school jotter and sending it boldly off to a publisher in London. 'I got a very sweet letter back, saying "There's nothing we can do with this at the present time",' Bernie remembers. 'I was as thrilled by that as if they'd said they'd publish it.'

Like many another super-imaginative Fifties child, he was considered academically dull. While his brother Tony attained the glory of De Aston Grammar School, Bernie was relegated to Market Rasen Secondary Modern, a Treblinka-like establishment largely attended by half-witted farm boys whose hobnailed boots struck sparks off the concrete paths. Much of his first term was spent in hiding, to avoid the ritual initiation of having his head dunked in a toilet bowl.

Music was added to his excitements long before the onset of adolescence. On a visit to his father's brother Henry, in Putney, he discovered a stack of dusty 78 records by Woody Guthrie, 'Leadbelly' and their English interpreter Lonnie Donegan. For Bernie, it was a perfect extension of his fascination with Americana. In particular he loved Donegan's 'Rock Island Line', its story in droll recitative, building up to a triumphant comic pay-off. 'It was American history, the kind I could never get enough of from books. I loved the grittiness and reality of it.'

As a teenager he was still small and slight, with looks that seemed to come less from his French ancestors than from the gypsies that haunt Lincolnshire's roads and fens. His face, habitually shy and downcast, could break into a grin that was wolfish, even faintly dangerous. With the dreamy, romantic eyes went a libido that was active – even hyperactive – though his virginity was to remain intact until well after he had left Lincolnshire behind.

Living in Owmby-by-Spital meant being roughly two years to the rear of current teenage fashion. For a long time, Bernie's only contact with developing pop culture was a battered transistor radio his father used around the farm in the daytime. On this, after dark, he would listen to Radio Luxembourg or AFN, the American Forces Network, broadcast to the many US bases throughout East Anglia. Much as he loved rock 'n' roll, his preference was always for songs with a cowboyish, narrative feel: Johnny Cash's 'Ring of Fire', Johnny Horton's 'North to Alaska', especially Marty Robbins's doomy Mexican-flavoured ballads, 'El Paso' and 'Devil Woman'.

With pop to help him, the Catholic altar-boy grew up rough, racy and rash. He abandoned literature, birds and butterflies for the more dubious charms of Market Rasen, hanging out at a clothes boutique named Banger Hall's which kept its catalogue for winklepicker shoes chained to the counter. His appearance changed constantly, varying from Mod high collars to the blue jeans and patches of a Woody Guthrie hobo. He went with a gang that indulged in petty burglary of mobile shops and fish-and-chip vans, and was himself not above vandalising contraceptive machines, even filching the occasional five-pound note from his hard-working father's wallet. In pursuit of girls, he frequented all the toughest Saturday night dances, relying on luck or fast-talking chutzpah to avoid trouble with Lincolnshire's archaic but no less frightening Teddy boys. 'If you said you liked the same music they did, that always helped. In a tight spot, you could try mentioning Little Richard or Jerry Lee Lewis. It was like Androclese taking the thorn out of the lion's paw.'

His interest in writing flared up and lapsed erratically until one memorable night under the covers with his father's transistor radio. On crackly Radio Luxembourg, he heard Bob Dylan's 'The Times They Are a-Changin''. 'I'd only seen Bob Dylan's name written down before. I didn't even know how to pronounce it. Suddenly through the static comes this plaintive guitar and this amazing voice. To me, folk music had always meant tunes you heard on BBC *Children's Favourites* – Burl Ives or "An English Country Garden". This voice was like broken glass, like spitting. The words were like arrows, being shot straight into the heart of the Establishment. That was what made me realise what the words of a song could do.'

Not that the lesson seemed of any practical use. Leaving school at fifteen, he tried to get a job as a reporter on a local paper, the *Lincolnshire Standard*, but instead found himself apprenticed in the printroom. It was a steady job, such as was then prized, with ancillary night-school courses leading to a diploma five years hence. To alleviate the boredom and hatred of setting up wedding invitations and raffle-tickets on an antiquated Heidelberg press, he took to drinking heavily. One night he was discovered in a field near his home, trying to feed crème de menthe to cows to discover if it would produce green milk.

From here on, as in some eighteenth-century poem heard at his grandfather's knee, Bernie started to go to the bad. Tempted by a job as a fruit-machine mechanic, he threw up his printer's apprenticeship, badmouthing the foreman and tossing a valedictory ink trowel into the Heidelberg press. When the slot machine life did not materialise, he frowsted at home, living off his parents, contemplating no career beyond vague notions of life as a professional housebreaker.

It was early 1967. In the world always tantalisingly two years ahead of Owmby-by-Spital, pop songs now teemed with words and

images such as had always filled Bernie Taupin's head. He himself
was working as a labourer on a chicken farm, carting hundreds of
corpses to be incinerated during an outbreak of fowl pest. 'I've got a
photograph of myself bundled up against the wind, surrounded by all
these dead bodies, looking like some scene from *The Killing Fields*.'

At night in his bedroom he would scribble endless, yearning
parodies of the Beatles' 'Strawberry Fields Forever', Bob Dylan's 'Mr
Tambourine Man', Procol Harum's 'A Whiter Shade of Pale'. That
June, when he chanced on Ray Williams's advertisement in the *New
Musical Express*, he had been fired from the chicken farm and was
'literally at a dead end'. In common with another pessimistic youth a
hundred miles away, he could not imagine that 'talent wanted' meant
what it said. 'I was so far from the centre of everything. I had no
idea how record companies or songwriters worked. I just thought
that maybe something I'd written might be of some use to someone,
somewhere down the line.'

On an ancient portable typewriter he picked out a letter to Ray
Williams and enclosed a sheaf of his newest poems. He then put it
on the living-room mantelpiece and, by his own account, 'forgot all
about it'. Fortunately, his mother noticed it there and posted it for
him.

The result was a scene Bernie had read so many times, with
envious longing, in Enid Blyton books for older children. The village
postman coming up the path, bearing an ivory-white envelope with
a London postmark. A crested letter, thanking him for his poems and
suggesting he should call in and see Ray Williams at Liberty Records,
next time he happened to be in Albemarle Street, Mayfair.

To Reggie, the visit to Albemarle Street at first seemed just another
dead end. Friendly and sympathetic as Ray Williams had been, he
could offer no quick way out of the situation with Bluesology. In
the immediate term, all he could offer was a sheaf of lyrics with
mystifying titles like 'Sad-Eyed Queen of Laughing Lake', and 'Year
of the Teddy Bear'. And a promise to put the lyricist, Bernie Taupin,
and Reggie together as soon as possible.

The truth was that Williams's *NME* advertisement had produced
other applicants of far more obvious potential than Reggie Dwight.
The most obvious find was a group of modish eccentrics called the
Bonzo Dog Doo-Dah Band, soon to enjoy a hit with the quasi-
comic 'Urban Spaceman'. Two other young men originally signed
by Ray Williams to Liberty would go on to massive money-spinning
chart success in the early Seventies. One was Jeff Lynne, later of the

Move and Electric Light Orchestra. The other was Mike Batt, musical director to the Wombles.

Despite all these more colourful attractions and distractions, Ray Williams went out on a limb for Reggie Dwight as far as he could. He still felt certain there was 'something' in the voice and the stubbornly unfashionable piano style. He also felt strangely obligated to the forlorn figure who had confessed so readily to feeling lost and desperate, yet was also funny, unpretentious and engaging. Like many afterwards, Ray Williams took Reggie's part, most of all, because he liked him.

He played Reggie's audition tape to Liberty's European head, Bob Reisdorf, and the head of promotion, Andrew Lauder. Neither could see anything in the mournful mix of Jim Reeves and José Feliciano that would warrant putting it under contract. Williams's secondary hope was that Liberty's publishing company, Metric Music, might sign up Reggie on the basis of his songwriting alone. But Metric's boss, Alan Keane, also declined the opportunity.

It so happened this was not the first time Williams's instincts had been thwarted by his Liberty bosses. A few weeks earlier, he had unsuccessfully tried to interest Metric Music in a pair of young Midlands songwriters named Nicky James and Kirk Duncan. Rather than let them go, Williams had taken them on independently, quartering them in his Bruton Mews house, renting a piano for them and, in airy teenage tycoon style, promising to form a company to divide the proceeds of their songs when these should eventually materialise. The company name – an amalgam of Nicky, Ray and Kirk – was to be Niraki Music.

From there, thanks to his past life as a PR man, Ray Williams had been able to wheel a further deal. He was still on friendly terms with Graham Nash, Allan Clarke and Tony Hicks of the Hollies. Graham, Allan and Tony had their own acronymic publishing company, Gralto, which in turn was managed by Britain's most successful song publisher, Dick James. It was easy for Ray Williams to strike an agreement whereby Niraki's output would be published by Gralto, under the umbrella of its parent organisation, Dick James Music.

Hence Ray Williams's power to offer at least a crumb of compensation to Reggie Dwight for failing the Liberty audition. He introduced Reggie to Nicky James and Kirk Duncan, both of whom were adept at writing the lyrics Reggie could or would not. He also brought Reggie, at however distant an initial remove, into the orbit of Dick James.

★

Dick James's legendary luck did not show itself for the first three decades of his life. Born in 1919 of Polish parentage in London's East End, he began life as a dance-band crooner, changing his name from Isaac Vapnick to cut a more romantic figure at the microphone. Throughout the Forties and Fifties he earned a decent living with British bandleaders like Geraldo and Cyril Stapleton, but was never up in the big league like Dickie Valentine or Ronnie Hilton. Unluckily losing his hair, he was obliged to perform romantic numbers like 'Tenderly' in a 'rug'. His biggest moment on record came in 1955, with the launch of commercial television in Britain. An early children's series, *The Adventures of Robin Hood*, took him into the Top 20 with its memorably tacky theme song.

Fortune did not smile on Dick James until November 1962, after he had quit the dance bandstand and set up as a music publisher in a poky office in London's Tin Pan Alley. He was not doing well – was, in fact, doing very badly – when his friend George Martin, head of Parlophone Records, rang up to try to interest him in the work of an unknown pop group from Liverpool. The publisher gave a cuddly laugh into which was gathered twenty years of know-how and experience. 'Liverpool!' he echoed. 'So what's from Liverpool?'

Dick James's first stroke of luck was getting a second chance. George Martin kept badgering him until he agreed to see the new group's manager, Brian Epstein, and hear a just-pressed copy of their record, 'Please Please Me'.

It was on the day of his meeting with Brian Epstein, however, that James's luck grew gorgeous and glorious. Epstein had meant to see another publisher first but on arriving for this appointment was told the other man hadn't turned up. Instead, it was suggested he should play his group's new record to the office-boy. Stalking out in crimson-faced fury, he arrived at Dick James's half an hour early. By a last semiquaver of Heaven-sent fortune, James was already there, and amenable to seeing his flustered visitor without delay. That is how he became publisher of John Lennon and Paul McCartney, the most stupendously successful and profitable songwriting partnership ever.

Luck, of course, is nothing unless tempered with energy and vision. The vision of Dick James was not to absorb Lennon and McCartney into his own existing organisation on the traditional meagre 10 per cent royalty. Rather, he created a separate company, Northern Songs, to be managed by him on their behalf, the proceeds split 50–50. It was a genuine example of fair-mindedness prompted by James's own days as a vocalist, when he would be paid only a flat £15 studio fee even for recording an international hit. Hence the ancillary miracle of the Beatles, managed by Brian Epstein, recorded by George Martin and published by James. The biggest show-business phenomenon of all time was directed by three honest men.

Of these, Dick James was always the most universally liked. A sunny-natured man, older than his forty-odd years, he was the archetype of the avuncular impresario, bald, pear-shaped and bespectacled, with a voice that retained its woofly calm, whether ringing round his matchless business contacts or calming the neuroses of his youthful protégés. Happily married, with a lovely home, a lovely car and lovely friends, he lived each day in a state of visible pleasure and gratitude to Providence, often exuberantly breaking out into one or other of his old hits, 'Tenderly' or the theme from *Robin Hood*.

The brainwave he had for Northern Songs was ironically to spell the end of James's own Tin Pan Alley milieu. Writing and publishing their own work, it was not long before the Beatles also began supervising their own sessions in the recording studio. In the rush to emulate them, Denmark Street's cosy hierarchy of chain-smoking professional songwriters, arrangers, pluggers and A & R men had been all but swept away. Only Dick James, the ultimate Tin Pan Alleyite, could be said, with his astounding luck, to have stayed ahead of the game.

In the hugely transformed music business of 1967, his name was still a synonym for heaven's most profligate bounty. Northern Songs had become a public company, reaping vast dividends for its managing director in exact proportion to its unstoppable creative partnership. His own organisation, Dick James Music – which published no Beatles material after 'Please Please Me' – had waxed powerful in its own right, with numerous other catalogue acquisitions that seemed to confirm an unfailing Midas touch.

The new, improved headquarters of Dick James Music at 71–75 New Oxford Street, situated symbolically above the Midland Bank, could lay some claim to being the powerhouse of British pop. In administering Northern Songs, it was the most visible adjunct of the Beatles' empire – not yet formalised into Apple Corps – a calling-place for individual Beatles with their retinues, and for all seeking to cover Beatle songs, from Peter and Gordon to the London Symphony Orchestra. James's partnership with Brian Epstein, a company called Jaep, published the million-selling Merseybeat hits of Cilla Black and Billy J. Kramer and the Dakotas, and brought further large helpings of glamour in through the doors of 71–75 New Oxford Street.

In the four years since his Northern Songs coup every young songwriter who dreamed of becoming a Lennon or a McCartney had beaten a path straight to Dick James's door. No successful pobp act who copied John and Paul and formed a publishing company felt it was quite complete without his name on its masthead. Dick James Music was a warren of such companies, run by James on the same triumphantly equitable split. He owned 50 per cent of the Hollies' Gralto company, of Gerry Marsden's Pacermusic and the Spencer Davis Group's Spencer Davis Music. He was a partner in Cookaway Music, formed by Roger Greenaway and Roger Cook (a duo later globally successful with songs like 'Home Lovin' Man' and the Coca-Cola theme, 'I'd Like to Teach the World to Sing'). He was the publishing side of impresario Larry Page's Page One organisation, so enjoying a share in contemporary chart smashes like the Troggs' 'Wild Thing'. To the young writers, performers and session musicians who daily thronged his premises he seemed like some great, bluff broody hen that, ever and again, would shift its grey worsted wings to reveal yet another golden egg or gold disc.

Large as the DJM operation had become, it still functioned in the comfortable way of old-fashioned family business. The only share-holders were Dick James and his old friend and accountant Charles Silver. The executive staff were mostly men of James's own age who had known him since the days of sheet music and Geraldo's orchestra. His only son Stephen, now aged twenty, had worked in the business since leaving school at sixteen, and was very obviously the apple of his father's eye. A former employee remembers the morning execu-tive meeting in Dick James's office as a running dialogue with Mrs James on the telephone and Stephen at his right hand. 'Your mother says, "Is the new shirt all right?" He says, "The new shirt's fine." '

Though as inclined to arrogance as any boss's son of twenty, Stephen James had shown genuine flair for music publishing and management. He was a successful plugger of DJM songs, having matched 'I Can't Let Go' to the Hollies, 'Needles and Pins' to the Searchers and 'Wild Thing' to Larry Page's Troggs. As the Beatles and Northern Songs claimed more and more of Dick James's atten-tion, he gave Stephen increased executive power, eventually entrust-ing him with the whole organisation's day-to-day running.

By 1966, Stephen James was growing impatient with the tra-ditional empire his father ruled at 71–75 New Oxford Street. To him, the job of hawking songs around until they reached the right performer seemed a time-consuming, labour-intensive way of earning not very much. With the Beatles and so many other hit artists writing their own songs, it was becoming harder and harder to persuade anyone to record a number written by someone else. Just as ulti-mately unrewarding was DJM's 'umbrella' method of handling sub-publishing for American record labels like CBS and Liberty, whereby one sedulously built up a catalogue's value only to lose it at the end of a two- or three-year agreement.

The ascendancy of the singer-songwriter – like the American Bob Dylan and his English counterpart, Donovan – offered far more attractive economics. With such an artist under contract, DJM could bypass the whole time-consuming, low-profit rigmarole of matching material to performer. They could also look forward to publishing all ten tracks on an album, instead of just one or two. All this Stephen James successfully argued with his father – and also the immediate requirement for implementing it. The company had always had taping facilities for writers to put down basic outlines of voice and piano or guitar. Stephen urged that, to nurture singer-songwriter talent, Dick James Music must have its own in-house recording studio.

To carping onlookers this, of course, looked very much like adoring impresario father giving son a recording studio for his birthday. None could have dreamed it would bring Dick James his second piece of once-in-a-lifetime luck.

The studio was established in an empty space at the rear of DJM's first-floor executive suite. As in all DJM interior décor, thrift was the watchword. 'I bought a Studer four-track system secondhand from EMI, Abbey Road,' Stephen James remembers. 'A guy I knew, who went on to build Neve mixing desks, put a little mixing outfit together for me in his garage.' The original plan had been to produce only demos – rough demonstration versions of new songs. But the guy in his garage built a mixing desk sophisticated enough to produce masters, or finished versions, ready for manufacture.

Along with the new studio, Stephen set up a production company to handle the in-house talent that might eventually evolve, named with a more than faint tinge of boss's-son arrogance. 'I called it This Record Co., because "this" is an anagram of "hits" and "shit".'

At that stage it was not a sufficiently grown-up studio to necessitate hiring a grown-up manager and technical staff. Instead, the job was given to a teenager whose father Dick James had known in the dance-band days and who'd just joined DJM from Paxton's sheet music wholesalers. It was Caleb Quaye, the same who used to tease Mills Music's office boy for looking so very much like Billy Bunter.

The studio was available to all the songwriters and musicians of whose companies DJM owned a part: Roger Greenaway and Roger Cook of Cookaway Music, Spencer Davis, Eddie Hardin and Peter

York of Spencer Davis Music, Graham Nash, Allan Clarke and
Tony Hicks of the Hollies' Gralto. With the Hollies came the two
young songwriters whom Ray Williams had recommended to them:
Nicky James and Kirk Duncan. Tagging along with Nicky and Kirk
came Williams's other protégé, the forlorn piano player Reggie
Dwight.

Nicky and Kirk had begun to do extremely well. Not only did
the Hollies like their work; so did the man who owned 50 per cent
of the Hollies' Gralto publishing company, and towered over the
whole pop industry. Dick James himself had put them each under a
£10 weekly retainer in expectation of songs they would write, if not
for the Hollies then for other performers serviced by Dick James
Music. They also had virtual *carte blanche* at the in-house studio to
produce demo versions of their work.

This facility they generously extended to their new collaborator,
Reggie Dwight. Throughout the hot summer of 1967, all Reggie's
time off from touring with Bluesology was spent with Nicky James
and Kirk Duncan at the Dick James studio. A scratch band evolved,
with him on piano, Dave Hinds on drums and Tony Murray – later
of the Troggs – on bass.

They were producing only demos of the songs written by Reggie
with either Nicky or Kirk, which the Niraki company could then
offer the Hollies' Gralto company for possible use by them or some
other established pop artist. Reggie Dwight's vocals were no more
than blueprints for how the song might eventually be worked out.
Kirk Duncan remembers how little confidence he seemed to have in
his singing voice. 'He was very quiet, very humble,' Duncan says.
'Whenever I mentioned he might be good enough as a vocalist in
his own right, he just didn't want to know.'

It had not helped Reggie's confidence to realise the studio
engineer was Caleb Quaye, his fellow messenger, and leg-puller,
back in Mills Music days. The Bunter tag first attached to him by
Caleb had dogged him ever since. The last thing he thought was that
anyone would ever want to hear a song sung by the Fat Owl of the
Remove.

If Caleb's first instinct had been to start teasing Reggie again, it
changed on seeing the professional musician he had become. Even
on this humble demo work, his approach was brisk and businesslike,
sitting straight down, spreading his stubby fingers and getting on with
it. When Caleb himself left the control room to sit in with the band
on guitar, his attitude to Reggie changed from respect to downright
admiration. 'It was so obvious he'd got something special,' Caleb says
now. 'Every day, a little bit more of it would come out.'

Quiet and businesslike as he usually was, there were moments when he could become exuberant, extrovert, even slightly demented. 'I remember once, we'd been working non-stop,' Kirk Duncan says. 'Reg was leaning on the desk, and he started shouting like some mad Hollywood agent. "I'm going to make you a star, my boy! A star!" He ran outside, down the passage, through the cutting-room, back through the studio and out again, screaming at the top of his voice. And he'd sometimes do the same thing in the street.'

In the first-floor studio he met all the big names from the current Top 10 and his own Pinner record collection. Often, to his amazement, they were not the standoffish demigods he had imagined, but just friendly young men a little older than himself, interested in his work, unselfishly willing to offer help and advice from their own practical experience. Graham Nash of the Hollies – who were to publish Niraki's eventual output – became such an adviser and friend. Another was Roger Greenaway, who had formerly been a pop star with Roger Cook (David and Jonathan) and was now a successful songwriter and pioneer of ad hoc studio-only bands like White Plains.

Kirk Duncan gives a poignant picture of how unknown back-room boys like Reggie Dwight and himself were swept up into the entourages of heedlessly wealthy pop stars. 'We hardly ate, we hardly slept, we were paupers. And all night we'd be around with people like Graham Nash and Allan Clarke of the Hollies. We'd go to the Bag O'Nails. There'd be a bottle of Scotch, a bottle of brandy and a dozen Cokes on the table – and no food! We were in these swish places, literally starving, and down at heel. Graham Nash had to buy me a pair of shoes once.'

It was only a week or so after Reggie's unsuccessful audition at Liberty that Bernie Taupin, mustering every resource at his command, managed to 'happen to be' in Albemarle Street, Mayfair. To the innocent Lincolnshire farm boy, Ray Williams's airy suggestion that he should call in and 'have a word' about his lyrics seemed like the summons of Destiny. So he successfully portrayed it to his long-suffering parents, ex-colleagues at jobs he'd failed to hold down and cronies around the chained-up shoe-catalogue at Banger Hall's boutique. Like Dick Whittington, Pip in *Great Expectations* and every other worthwhile hero in his hundred favourite books, Bernie was off to London to seek his fortune.

It was arranged that, pending the making of this fortune, he should lodge with his father's brother, Uncle Henry, in Putney. His spinster aunt Tati, who lodged in the house and to whom he was very close, promised his mother to keep an eye on him. His departure brought a moment of closeness with his father, the taciturn farmer to whom he had latterly been such a trial. As Bernie's early morning train to Kings Cross left St Mark's station, something made him lean forward and kiss Robert Taupin hard on the cheek.

His first meeting with Ray Williams at Liberty Records was enough to convince Bernie that he'd jumped straight into the big time. 'As I went in, I saw Graham Nash of the Hollies on the stairs. Graham Nash of the Hollies! My mouth just fell open.'

Like other respondents to Williams's *NME* ad, Bernie was amazed by the youth and blond beauty of Liberty's A & R chief. An agreeable conversation ensued, in which Ray Williams broke it to him that his lyrics were of no immediate use to Liberty Records. However, there was a piano player, working indirectly for Williams, who needed someone who could write words. The unpromising name of that piano player was Reggie Dwight.

Ray Williams set up a meeting between Bernie and Reggie Dwight the next day, at Dick James Music. Bernie travelled up from Putney to New Oxford Street in the nearest his small, battered suitcase could muster to a 'trendy' outfit. 'I only had the one jacket – a hideous moth-eaten blue double-breasted thing that was much too small for me.' To hide his extreme nervousness, he sported thick sunglasses.

When he arrived at DJM, Reggie was busy in the in-house studio doing a piano overdub. Bernie sat and waited meekly in the control room. At one point, the engineer, Caleb Quaye, turned round and inquired 'Are you supposed to be here?' The sunglasses he had worn in an effort to be cool produced another disconcerting moment. 'Somebody said "Nice shades, man." And I had no idea what they were talking about.'

After a while, Reggie came out, noticed him there and said 'Hi, are you the lyricist?' Bernie admitted that he was. The two of them went for a cup of coffee at the Lancaster Grill in Tottenham Court Road.

The initial bond was between two pop music fans of equal fanaticism and encyclopaedic knowledge. Despite the three-year difference in their ages, they discovered they felt the same about everything that mattered: Tamla Motown, the Beatles, the words of Bob Dylan's 'Subterranean Homesick Blues', the Spanish guitar solo on Marty Robbins's 'Devil Woman'. Their mutual shyness vanished as they exchanged the lore and trivia they had soaked up for years from tinny record players in bedrooms a hundred miles apart. Reggie warmed at once to the slight, shabby boy whose extreme diffidence was tempered with flashes of gypsyish mischief. Bernie instantly liked the podgy piano player who, twitching his specs up on his nose, confessed to being not nearly the big shot he had initially seemed. 'Even though he was there on the scene, plugged right into the circuit,' Bernie remembers now, 'I got the feeling he was rather isolated from it all.'

The more they talked, the more their disparities drew them together. Their childhoods, blissful and miserable. Their fathers, loving and remote. Their homes, a suburban maisonette and a farm. Their most recent work experience, playing in a blues club and carting chicken corpses to the incinerator.

'We were complete opposites – town mouse and country mouse,' Bernie Taupin says. 'But the one thing we had in common was being mad about pop music. And both being desperate to write songs.' Over two cups of coffee in the Lancaster Grill, they decided to give it a try.

Bluesology's third and final attempt to be a hit band in their own right was recorded in August 1967. They had switched labels from Fontana to Polydor and put themselves in the hands of Kenny Lynch, a pop star turned producer (afterwards to become a well-known TV compère and comic). As well as producing them, Lynch co-wrote the A-side, 'Since I Found You, Baby', and the B-side, 'Just a Little Bit'. If Reggie Dwight had felt smothered before, he now felt wholly disinvented. Not only did Stuart A. Brown sing lead vocal on both sides, but the billing on the record was amended to 'Stu Brown and Bluesology'. The finished product was so lacklustre that Polydor sat on it for two months, finally releasing it in October, to deafening public apathy. Like Jack Baverstock at Fontana, Kenny Lynch cannot now remember anything about working with the future Elton in the studio.

In the travelling band that supported Long John Baldry, his life was more frustrating than ever. The hubristic Long John had now added a third singer to the backup line that kept Reggie in keyboard-pounding obscurity. The newcomer was an ebullient black girl named Marsha Hunt, later to achieve fame as the star of *Hair* and the mother of Mick Jagger's first daughter. Though visually stunning, she possessed but a marginal singing voice. 'She only knew one number – "Love Is a Many-Splendored Thing",' the future star would recall. 'She didn't know what key she wanted, so she had to do it unaccompanied. And she was really terrible. But looked amazing. So Baldry said "All right dear, you're in."'

In London Reggie had by now introduced his new collaborator

to his two associates in Niraki Music. Nicky James and Kirk Duncan both leafed through Bernie Taupin's lyrics and agreed there could well be 'something' there. They did not at all object to Reggie's starting an additional songwriting partnership with the seventeen-year-old boy in absurdly cool 'shades' who made himself as small as possible in corners of the DJM control room.

The new team's first song came from a Bernie poem, redolent of his Lincolnshire farm background, called 'Scarecrow'. Reggie then made a demo version of it in Nicky and Kirk's studio time at Dick James Music. It never became a finished track either on a single or album, and has long since disappeared into the vaults of its composers' past. Bernie Taupin still remembers the thrill of taking the first rough acetate back to Putney to show his Uncle Henry and Aunt Tati.

The idea had been that Reggie should write with Bernie in alternation with Nicky James and Kirk Duncan. 'But as soon as they got together, it was obvious that magic was starting to happen,' Kirk Duncan remembers. The song list that has survived shows what a dichotomy was instantly at work. With Kirk Duncan Reggie would write something called 'Who's Gonna Love You?'. With Nicky James he would write something called 'Where It's At'. With Bernie Taupin he would write something called 'A Dandelion Dies in the Wind'.

Neither Nicky nor Kirk objected to this either. They were happy to see Reggie and Bernie evolve as a separate partnership that would be a further asset to Niraki Music. The deal with Dick James was that when Niraki accumulated £10,000-worth of song copyrights, it would become a full company within the Hollies' Gralto company, within Dick James Music. It would then be able to put Reggie and Bernie under contract and take a share of their earnings. Nicky James and Kirk Duncan accordingly gave Reggie and Bernie every encouragement.

Having nerved themselves to begin, they found they could work at phenomenal speed. Within a week or so, they had produced more than a dozen songs to add to Niraki Music's embryonic catalogue. In this initial phase, they worked together only intermittently. There were frequent breaks when Reggie was hauled reluctantly back on tour with Bluesology, and Bernie wrote on in isolation at his Uncle Henry's, or back home in Owmby-by-Spital. As each new set of lyrics poured from him, he would post them to Reggie out on the road.

The postal method was to continue in much the same way even after they had come within permanent earshot of one another. Shyness and embarrassment on both sides dictated the *modus operandi*.

Bernie would arrive at the Dick James studio with a sheaf of words, which, at some point, Reggie would take off to a piano in another room. In ten minutes or so, the song would be delivered back to Bernie, parcelled up tight in robust, professional chords.

As each new song was written, Reggie would demo it in the Dick James studio. Caleb Quaye, the engineer, allowed virtually unlimited time for each to be worked on, less and less as a rough sketch for some future performer than as a refinement of Reggie Dwight's own, gradually more confident and distinctive version. With Caleb's indulgence, the sessions went on late into each night, using Dick James's electricity and amenities long after most lights had dimmed along that rather isolated stretch of New Oxford Street.

For a break, they would go to the nearby Gioconda coffee bar, a place now empty of its daytime Tin Pan Alley clientèle and more likely to be occupied by drunks and derelicts. Or to the Lancaster Grill, that businessmen's venue in Tottenham Court Road, where Reggie and Bernie first sealed their partnership. Or to a cheapo Indian restaurant, L'Orient, which football-mad, pun-mad Reggie renamed Leyton Orient.

It surprised the country mouse at first that the town mouse was willing to sing everything he wrote, without the slightest quibble or demur. He did not realise how glad Reggie was to be saved from any part of lyric-writing, that old, inexplicable blind spot. No lyric was too literary, fanciful or obscure for this process of instant ventriloquism. Reggie's part in the words was purely sub-editorial, switching a verse here, reprising one there, occasionally cutting one altogether. Nor did Bernie try to influence the tune beyond tentative suggestions that this might be a slow ballad, that an uptempo rocker. Not infrequently the slow ballad he had imagined would come back to him as an uptempo rocker, and vice versa. For almost all his life as a lyric-writer, he was never to be quite certain what the postman would bring.

FOUR

Hits and Shit

ALL through that fabled 1967 Summer of Love, Reggie Dwight and Bernie Taupin were outsiders, looking on wistfully with noses pressed against the glass. They saw the coming of hippies, of kaftans, sandals, tinkly bells and smoking joss-sticks. They heard the siren-soft voice of Scott McKenzie, bidding them go to San Francisco, see the 'gentle people' and wear flowers in their hair, even though at the time they were hard put to raise a double bus-fare across London or the price of a toasted sandwich at the Gioconda. Like half Britain's young men, Reggie became a quasi-hippy, draping his cardboard Carnaby clothes with hopefully mystical necklaces, pendants, thongs and amulets. Bookish Bernie became swept up in the hippy craze for J.R.R. Tolkien's medieval fantasies, *The Hobbit* and *The Lord of the Rings*. Lyrics handed or posted to Reggie suddenly teemed with echoes of Bilbo Baggins, Frodo, Gollum and the Dark Lord of Mordor.

With the new 'underground' counterculture came billow after billow of new pop sound, transfixing to the two record fans, inspirational to the two incorrigible copycats. The nasal sneer of 'electric' Dylan, the brassy strut of Memphis soul, the acid blues of Cream, the shivery pyrotechnics of the Jimi Hendrix Experience, the accents, licks and riffs of Jefferson Airplane, Canned Heat, Pink Floyd, the Foundations, the Warm Sound, the Flowerpot Men, the Honeybus, all worked their way, somewhere or other into the late night sessions in Dick James's demo-studio.

Above all, the Beatles continued to be a seven-league leap ahead of all competition. That June, they had released *Sgt. Pepper's Lonely Hearts Club Band*, their album masterpiece, combining high-fashion psychedelia and mysticism with the whimsical mateyness of a Liverpool variety show. *Sgt. Pepper* instantly set a new style for pop LPs with its narrative form, its elaborately in-joking cover, its cargo of giveaway novelties, paper sergeant's chevrons and false moustaches. It was no sooner in the shops than the Beatles embraced hippydom, chanting their simplistic anthem 'All You Need Is Love' in a TV broadcast by satellite that reached an estimated world audience of 400 million.

That summer was the time of greatest-ever Beatles songs, 'She's Leaving Home', 'Lucy In The Sky With Diamonds', 'A Day In the Life'. All were handled by the world's luckiest publisher, Dick James, in blissful unawareness that, on his own premises after dark, two unknown songwriters were producing a parallel Beatle-cum-Tolkien repertoire: 'Regimental Sergeant Zippo', 'Year of the Teddy Bear', 'Mr Lightning Strikerman', 'The Tide Will Turn For Rebecca'.

Few now remember what a dark underside the Summer of Love often revealed or how, along with the feathers and bells, its recurring motifs were pitiless warfare, official vindictiveness, mob fury and profligate death. In America, as the hippies sunned themselves in Haight-Ashbury, northern cities erupted into racial violence. In Vietnam, the helicopter gunships spread their healing flame over thatched villages. In Egypt, Jordan and Syria, the tanks incinerated their trapped consignments of young men.

While half Britain was intoxicated by pop music, the other half railed against it with the ferocity of seventeenth-century witchfinders. Composite villain and martyr of the hour was Mick Jagger of the Rolling Stones, the band most condemned for turning young people to rebellion, immorality and drugs. In reality a negligible drug-user, Jagger had been 'exposed' as a boasting dope-fiend by the gutter-press *News of the World*. His attempt to sue for libel only turned the paper loose on a vigorous campaign to dig up some genuine dirt that could be passed on to an overtly receptive police force. The result was the famous drug bust at Keith Richard's house, where Jagger was caught in possession of four innocuous amphetamine pills, subjected to a vicious show trial and clapped into jail amid audible public rejoicing.

Though Jagger was quickly freed – largely thanks to a courageous editorial in *The Times* – his mistake would stand as a lesson to all pop stars over the next twenty years. However gross the lies written about you in sensationalist newspapers, there was no point in trying to sue. The papers were too powerful, with their huge resources, their batteries of lawyers and teams of muck-raking spies and sneaks. Anyone who took them on could only get in deeper and deeper.

On the August Bank Holiday weekend of 1967, the Beatles left London by excursion train, accompanying their new-found Indian spiritual teacher, Maharishi Mahesh Yogi, for a course of transcendental meditation in Bangor, North Wales. That same week-end their manager Brian Epstein walked out of a dinner-party in Kingsley Hill, Sussex, to return alone to his Belgravia house. Next morning, he was found dead of what a coroner would later describe as 'incautious drink and drug overdoses'.

Epstein's death increased the high public profile of the Dick James Organisation. Helpless without their all-protecting manager, the Beatles instinctively turned to those whom Brian had made part of the original, impermeable shield, their record-producer and their publisher. Had James wished, there is little doubt he could have assumed their management; temporarily perhaps, but for long enough to avert the huge financial and emotional chaos of their efforts to run their own affairs.

Dick James knew that, whatever short-term healing might take place, the deepening rift between John Lennon and Paul McCartney must inevitably finish the Beatles. His most urgent worry was as managing director of Northern Songs, the company he had created as a joint venture with Lennon and McCartney to publish their prodigious output. Northern had gone public in 1965 and now had 3,000 shareholders, to whom James owed as much duty as to his own large residual stockholding. The nervous souls of the Stock Exchange could not be expected to understand that, whatever happened, Lennon and McCartney's song catalogue would continue earning fortunes for ever. Any rumour of a Beatles breakup would be sure to send Northern's share price plummeting. With these and other Fab Four preoccupations filling his mind, Dick James had little attention to spare for goings-on at his own offices.

The goings-on might never have come to light but for DJM's position above the New Oxford Street branch of the Midland Bank. Though relaxed enough about daytime traffic up and downstairs, the Midland was understandably sensitive about activity near its strong-rooms after dark. Anyone working late at DJM had to give due warning to the bank's security staff.

Late one night, DJM's office manager, a former dance-band drummer named Ronnie Brohn, chanced to be driving past 71–75 New Oxford Street. To his alarm, he saw a light in the first-floor executive corridor. Going up to investigate, he came upon Caleb Quaye, Reggie Dwight and the others at their usual after-hours work in the demo studio. An angry scene ensued in which Brohn accused Caleb of using office resources without authority, and said that the matter would be reported first thing the following morning.

Since Stephen James had charge of day-to-day office business, it was to him that Ronnie Brohn angrily complained. 'He came into my office fuming,' Stephen James remembers, 'saying Caleb had been letting all kinds of people come in and use the studio. "He'll have to go," Ronnie kept saying. "He'll have to go."'

Twenty-year-old Stephen – himself on less than good terms with Ronnie Brohn – was inclined to take a milder view of the matter. Summoning Caleb Quaye, he learned that a Reg Dwight had been making demo records on the basis of vague arrangements with Nicky James, Kirk Duncan and the Hollies' Gralto company. If this Reg Dwight did not exactly fit Brohn's outraged description of rag, tag and bobtail off the street, misusing DJM's electricity, sofa fabric, instant coffee and lavatory paper, he was hardly a bona fide studio musician either.

'My attitude was, I didn't mind people using our studio as long as we had the chance to hear what they produced,' Stephen James says now. 'I asked Caleb what the material was like. He said, "There are half a dozen songs, and they're not very good."' The upshot was that Stephen asked to listen to the demos himself. 'I thought there was something interesting there,' he remembers. 'When my father came in, I took the material and played it to him. He thought there was something interesting there as well.'

A relieved Caleb Quaye was not sacked but asked to relay a message to Reg Dwight and his partner, Bernie Taupin, that Dick James himself desired their presence. 'I remember them both sitting outside Dick's office,' says Caleb, 'dead scared because they thought they were going to be hauled over the coals.' Instead to their astonishment, they were greeted with the utmost affability by James, motioned to chairs next to the great man's large executive desk and cross-questioned by him at length about their backgrounds, their musical ambitions and their immediate plans. Glancing with incredulity at the gold discs and sacred Beatle photographs around the walls, they realised they were not being reprimanded, but courted.

Dick James, for his part, was pleasantly surprised to find that Reg and Bernie were not the uppish young street urchins he had expected, but a pair of shy middle-class boys whose extreme politeness was tinged with palpable hero worship. Especially did he warm to the plump, bespectacled one who, despite diffidence and confusion, was quick, sharp and funny in a way no young pop hopeful had been since the first days of John, Paul, George and Ringo. 'We always believed in Reg, and thought he had talent,' Stephen James says now. 'But the main thing was, we just liked him.'

To Dick James, the matter was trifling enough. He merely followed the instinct of a man with proven colossal luck, that

anything new in the music business was worth taking 50 per cent of.
Finding there were two young songwriters of promise rolling about
loose inside his organisation, he merely shifted his weight on the
nesting-box to envelop them, along with Gralto, Pacer, Cookaway
and the rest. His offer was to put Reggie and Bernie under contract
as songwriters with Dick James Music.

For the two awestruck figures in facing chairs, it was a moment
that made the world suddenly tilt askew. Reggie, in one bound, saw
his escape from the months of frustration with Long John Baldry and
Bluesology. To silent Bernie it was simply beyond his wildest story-
book fantasies. 'To actually be given money for writing songs! I
couldn't believe they were really serious.'

In the general euphoria, a small point was overlooked. This was
that Reggie and Bernie had been supposed to sign with Nicky James
and Kirk Duncan's Niraki Music, when Niraki accumulated enough
song copyrights to warrant its becoming a proper company.

To Nicky and Kirk, the signing of Reggie and Bernie direct to
DJM was presented as a *fait accompli*. An angry Nicky James complained to Graham Nash of the Hollies, whose Gralto company was
to have published Niraki's output. Nash and Ron Richards, the
Hollies' producer, went in to see Dick James, leaving Nicky waiting
outside the office door.

James was, as ever, a reasonable man. A deal was struck with
Nash and Richards wherein the songs that Reggie had written with
Gralto's writers, or that Reggie and Bernie had written under Gralto's
sponsorship, should be copyrighted to the Hollies' company, along
with ten more still to come, a total of some two dozen songs in all.
Since Dick James part-owned Gralto, he would, in any case, share
those royalties.

'When Graham Nash came out of Dick's office, I was still sitting
there waiting,' Nicky James remembers. 'He told me, "It's all right,
everything's fixed."'

Everything was fixed, save for the partners in Niraki Music, on
whom it rapidly dawned that they featured in these satisfactory
arrangements not at all.

For Ray Williams – who had put not only Niraki but also Reggie
and Bernie together – it was no great tragedy. In his job as A & R
head at Liberty Records, he was now on to numerous other projects
(among them recording Rolling Stone Brian Jones in a drugged-out
band named Hapshash and the Coloured Coat). Little dreaming how
history was destined to repeat itself, Ray Williams shrugged and
accepted being cut out of the Reggie Dwight deal.

But for Nicky James and Kirk Duncan, poor and struggling as

they were, the event proved terminal. Despite all the promises of their pop star friends, Niraki Music never did become a fully fledged company. Shortly afterwards, for reasons they never understood, Nicky and Kirk even lost the weekly retainer they had been paid by Dick James Music via Gralto.

Both still maintain that Dick James ditched their whole future by spiriting Reggie and Bernie away from Niraki Music. 'We'd brought them on, given them our studio time, fixed up cover versions for them,' Kirk Duncan says now. 'If we couldn't have managed them, we were connected with people who could. Spencer Davis, I know, was talking about signing them and taking them off to work in America.'

After leaving DJM, Nicky and Kirk struggled on for a while, but met with so little success that both decided to quit the music business. Today they have only vivid memories, and an abiding bitter taste. Such tales are commonplace in the rising of a star.

Keenly as he had sought a singer-songwriter for DJM to nurture, Stephen James at first did not recognise such an apparition in Reggie Dwight. The dumpiness, glasses and carrier bag were like nothing from even the weirdest echelons of the new counterculture. And Reggie himself expressed no ambition to be anything but the backroom boy he was at present.

All Stephen initially thought that DJM had acquired was a songwriting team with a strong line in melody and a fancy twist in words, whose songs might best suit one or other of the female singers who had at last broken through in the British charts. Reggie and Bernie accordingly were instructed to study the latest successful recordings of Sandie Shaw, Dusty Springfield and Lulu, and see if they couldn't come up with something similar.

On 7 November, 1967, they formally signed their contract with Dick James Music. As they both were still under twenty-one, the signature of each had to be witnessed by a parent: in Reggie's case his mother and in Bernie's, his father. Under the publishing agreement, they assigned DJM world copyright of their songs, which were to comprise at least eighteen titles, over an initial, renewable three-year period. For this they would receive a £100 advance against royalties calculated at 10 per cent of the marked selling price of each copy (after the first 250 copies) and 50 per cent of proceeds from recording, live performance, radio and TV broadcasting and sub-licensing abroad. In addition to their £100 joint advance, Reggie and Bernie would each receive a weekly cash retainer of £10, to be set against future royalties. Since, on reflection, Reggie's job as singer and pianist as well as writer seemed somewhat the more onerous, his weekly payment was upped to £15.

On Stephen James's next round of the record company A & R men, he took with him a selection of the demos Reggie had made in the DJM studio. The product he had to sell was the songs themselves, the vocal only a rough sketch of what a real singer might do. An early call was on Johnny Franz at Philips, who recorded Reggie's boyhood pin-up, Dusty Springfield. While regretting the song was not quite Dusty, Franz expressed interest in the voice on the demo. The same interest was shown by Tony Hatch, writer of many hits, like Petula Clark's 'Downtown'. 'He said the songs were too original to be covered by other people,' Stephen remembers. 'But the demo singer might be good enough to record them on his own account. "The voice isn't terrible," Tony said. "It might need working on a bit." It was only then that I mentioned to Reg that he might do his own record. He told me he'd always wanted to, but he didn't think anyone would be interested.'

The murmurs of vague interest, on top of his own, prompted Stephen James to offer Reggie a recording deal with DJM's This Record Co. It would not be a very big deal, since TRC was but a small production company, licensed through Philips, the label on which Bluesology had already made two unsuccessful singles.

Still, if he were to record, he would also have to make live concert appearances. If he hadn't already got a manager, Dick James advised him, then he'd better get one fast. At which – so Stephen James recalls – Reggie gave Dick a look that was both despondent and appealing, and said 'Can't you do it?'

This slight surge of encouragement over his voice prompted Reggie to one last attempt to break the jinx inside Bluesology. To prepare for it, he starved himself and took Sheila Dwight's slimming pills until he had lost more than two stone. His face lost its Bunter roundness, growing gaunt and long, down to the cleft in a single chin. In place of owlish Buddy Holly frames, he bought rimless granny glasses like John Lennon's in the Beatles and Roger McGuinn's in the Byrds. His stripe-blazered torso was now as girlishly lean and flat as anyone's in the line-up. Only the legs and arms remained chunky, and the fingers that stretched over the organ keys.

Reggie and Bernie's partnership was interrupted again when Bluesology left on a short tour of Sweden. Reggie took his new figure with him, euphoric at having proved he could do anything he set his mind to. On his return, he resolved to tackle Long John Baldry yet again about singing with the band.

He might have managed it, but for a wholly unforeseen event. For some time, Long John had been anxious to exchange the impecunious blues world for the far more lucrative one of mainstream pop. In the winter of 1967, encouraged by his manager John Gunnell, he recorded a schmaltzy slow ballad entitled 'Let the Heartaches Begin'. To everyone's amazement – not least the vocalist's – it zipped into the Top 20, reaching number one on November 22. Long John Baldry was suddenly a teen heart-throb.

With this radical change of style came an equally radical change of audience. As a blues singer, playing the studentish pub-'n'-club circuit, Long John had been lucky to clear £100 a night. But with a number one hit, the hard-nosed Gunnell could book him into the cabaret and gambling clubs which now dotted the industrial north. As Gunnell's other protégés Georgie Fame and Alan Price already knew, a successful artist in the northern clubs could earn up to £20,000 a week.

Bluesology changed form yet again, dropping Marsha Hunt from the backup vocal line and acquiring an extra guitarist in Caleb Quaye, DJM's studio engineer. Its bookers were the Marquee and Klooks Kleek no longer, but Batley Variety Club or the Bailey Organisation, whose bird-of-paradise venues sparkled amongst the pit-heap fogs of County Durham and Teesside.

To the management of Club La Bamba, Darlington, or the Flamingo, Billingham, all that mattered about Bluesology's set was that it should be short, allowing the punters to get back as quickly as possible to spending money on blackjack and roulette. 'I remember one club, in Southport,' Long John Baldry says. 'The owner told us to play for twenty minutes, no more. When I overran a couple of minutes, the curtains closed in front of us. Just as if someone had got a nasty shock and snatched their front-room curtains together.'

There was now no question of Long John's sharing the limelight, vocally – or even instrumentally if he could help it. 'Let the Heartaches Begin' had been recorded solo voice, with Mantovani-ish violin accompaniment. When Long John performed it in the clubs, his R & B sidemen were silenced in favour of a pre-recorded instrumental tape. Bluesology's horn section and organist would just stand there in their green Brummel drag, trying to look appropriately lovelorn.

For Reggie, the northern cabaret club circuit was the last straw. His mind was now firmly made up to quit Bluesology, return to London and take whatever chances there might be with Dick James. But there were still endless nights in the smoky Las Vegas dark of Stockton or Darlington, playing against a buzz of conversation or a clash of cutlery as people ate their basket meals of scampi and chips. His private rebellion began with ritual maltreatment of that symbol of frustration and imprisonment, his orange Vox Continental organ. 'It was all falling to bits. It used to fart and make terrible noises. I finally destroyed the amplifier, my Vox 80, by kicking it in during a Bingo session.'

He also nearly took another wrong turn, secretly auditioning for the Mike Cotton Sound, a former trad-jazz band now briefly cashing in on pop. Again, the hand of Providence intervened. When the Mike Cotton Sound faded into oblivion a few months later, Reggie Dwight was not among their number.

On 10 January he signed a five-year agreement with This Record Co. wherein he undertook to record 'at least four sides of seven-inch records in each year', the content to be specified by TRC. For this he would receive a royalty 'equal to 20 per cent of all net monies received by the company in respect of the master recordings, after the cost of musicians, singers, musical directors, orchestrations, copy-ing, cartage of musical instruments, studio-rentals, technicians, tape-costs, editing, dubbing and re-dubbing and all like production expenses incurred by the company in respect of any of the master recordings shall first have been recouped by the company.' This did not, as might be thought, mean 20 per cent of what each record earned in the shops. It meant 20 per cent of This Record Co.'s income from its manufacturing licensee, Philips – that is, 20 per cent of 10 per cent, equivalent to only about 2 per cent of each record's retail selling price.

With the contract went what a future High Court judge would describe as an 'imposing' addendum, signed by Reggie's mother (though she herself would later admit she had barely understood a word of what she was ratifying). 'I, Sheila Eileen Dwight, being the parent/guardian of Reginald Kenneth Dwight (who is a minor) have carefully considered the provisions of the above agreement and have advised my child/ward thereon. I am satisfied that the agreement is for the benefit of my child/ward, who has entered into the agreement with my approval. In consideration of the company entering at my request into the agreement with my child/ward, I hereby guarantee the performance of my child/ward's obligations under the agree-ment.'

Her child/ward's farewell appearance with Bluesology was in December 1967, in Edinburgh. On the shuttle flight back to London, he canvassed the others for a professional name, in place of the clearly unsuitable Reg Dwight, to be signed on the pending management agreement with Dick James Music. Bluesology's tenor-sax player

Elton Dean remembers Reggie coming along the aisle to see him
shortly before the plane began its descent to Heathrow airport. 'He
said "I'm leaving the band. To become a pop star. Is it all right if I
call myself Elton Dean?" I said "That's a bit strong, Reg." So he
went away. Then he came back and said "OK, is it all right if I call
myself Elton John?"' 'John' had been a flash of inspiration, looking
over the seat-backs to Long John Baldry's towering blond head.

Neither Dean nor Baldry objecting to this shotgun marriage of
their Christian names, it was Elton John who stood on the concourse
at Heathrow, waiting for his holdall on the baggage carousel.

During that crossover Christmas season, when every radio played
Long John Baldry's misty-eyed hetero love lament, another wholly
unexpected thing had happened. The newly named, newly slimline
Elton had amazed his road companions by finally pulling a 'bird'.

It happened in Sheffield, where Bluesology were appearing at a
Bailey circuit cabaret-club, the Fiesta. Between sets, Long John
Baldry got talking to a midget named the Mighty Atom who worked
as a disc jockey at the city's Locarno ballroom. With him that night,
the Mighty Atom had a girl almost six foot tall, blonde, skinny and
vaguely upper class in manner. Her name was Linda Ann Woodrow.

During the evening, the Mighty Atom's companion and Bluesology's usually shy and unamorous organ player fell into conversation.
In Long John Baldry's sardonic words 'young love blossomed'.

Linda, then aged twenty-four, came from a colourful background.
Her father, Alexander Dane Woodrow, had been a drummer in the
Cameron Highlanders, a standup comic on the variety halls, a
promoter of all-in wrestling and a conjurer skilled enough for
admittance to the Magic Circle. As Al Woodrow, he now owned
and ran a Soho drinking club, the New Cottage, in Litchfield Street,
a favourite watering-hole for traditional jazz musicians like Acker
Bilk and Mick Mulligan. There 'Cottage Al' cut an impressive figure,
whether demonstrating magic at the bar or robustly warning Soho
hoods like Big Maltese Frank that if they didn't behave properly,
they'd be thrown out on their necks.

The Woodrow family owned Epicure, an old-fashioned manufacturer of pickles and preserves. As a pickled-onion heiress, Linda had
been educated at a select girls' academy in Reigate, then at finishing-
school in Eastbourne. Provided with a generous trust fund, she lived
a life of peripatetic leisure, tinged by 'Cottage Al's' show-business
proclivities. In 1968, she was staying with her remarried mother in
Sheffield and working as a disc jockey at a club above the Mecca
skating-rink.

Until this point there seems to have been no doubt in Elton's mind – or anyone else's – that he belonged utterly to the sexual mainstream. His lack of overt interest in girls, save as friends, was easily explicable by his shyness and vulnerability. The one sure way never to be rejected is never to advance even one step. None the less, like nearly all young men of 1967, he supposed he would meet 'someone' sooner or later and, like everyone normal, in the pop business as well as outside it, be married by his early twenties. What there was to learn about sex and love would keep until that notional wedding night. To be a male virgin at twenty, while nothing to shout about, was nothing abnormal either.

Why did his usual buttoned-up reserve disappear so spectacularly when he met Linda Woodrow? The answer seems not to have been sexual so much as social. The elaborately dressed and coiffured girl – who towered over him scarcely less than over the Mighty Atom – spoke in a middle-class accent much like Elton's own. With her finishing-school manner she was, indeed, somewhat superior to Middlesex and Metroland. But their accents were alike enough for understanding to gel. After years as a social outsider around working-class pubs and clubs, he had finally found someone to talk to.

Elton himself was later to give a lurid account of his meeting with Linda, claiming she had been the Mighty Atom's girl-friend and that he – Elton – had spirited her away from frequent ill-treatment at the midget DJ's hands. One can understand the need to blot out with comedy what was to prove a confusedly traumatic period in his life.

The story as Linda now tells it is much more circumspect. She was never the Mighty Atom's girl-friend, only his companion that evening. Elton asked her to show him round Sheffield next day, then suggested she should follow Bluesology on to their gigs in the north-east. He was a 'perfect gentleman', reserving her her own separate room at the band's hotel. In Newcastle, they did nothing more scandalous than go roller-skating together.

They began to go steady, seeing each other in between Elton's final spells on the road with Bluesology. Linda would come and stay with Sheila and Derf in Pinner at the Frome Court maisonette – always decorously occupying her own room. When Elton quit Bluesology and returned to London for his new career with DJM, they decided to set up house together.

They found a basement flat in Furlong Road, Islington. Bernie Taupin also moved there with them, an arrangement Linda would later have cause to rue. In addition there were her two pet dogs – small, yapping specimens which deposited ordure freely along the entrance-hall. 'I used to go to my room singing the tune of "Old

Macdonald",' Bernie remembers. '"Here a turd, there a turd, every-where a turd-turd."'

Bernie was not the only one of Elton's London circle to wonder why he had chosen such a girl-friend, three years older than himself as well as inches taller, coiffed and dressed with a formality that seemed almost middle-aged. 'Everything about her seemed to be artificial – her hair, her eyelashes, her nails. When she went to bed at night, she used to totally disassemble.'

The explanation now looks fairly simple. Ashamed of his own long indifference to girls, Elton was ready and willing – if not determined – to fall for the first one who came along. He seems to have begun the affair with Linda in the spirit of a non-swimmer, plunging headlong with eyes shut and fingers pinching nose, hoping that, if he went straight in at the deep end, everything would somehow sort itself out.

Alas, the opposite was the case. Their first attempt to make love was a disaster, setting the tragi-comic tone of subsequent events. Linda remembers that, for some reason, Elton had taken her to stay at one of the ornate old Victorian hotels on the border of New Oxford Street and Bloomsbury. 'When we rolled into bed, he was clumsy and, frankly, didn't have a clue.' Linda, at the time, detected no malaise other than inexperience, shyness and nerves. 'He was a gentle person by nature, and he was that way in bed. I was so keen on him that I didn't really mind.'

In all sorts of other ways, domestic life in Furlong Road proved trying and traumatic. The only person Elton had lived with before was his mother, that doting, protective figure who cooked, washed, ironed and did everything for him. Linda vehemently refused to be a party to any such mollycoddling. Elton was forced to take his turn at cleaning and cooking and visiting the local launderette. The habit remained of consulting Sheila about everything and instinctively turning to her whenever he felt under stress. Linda's abiding memory of this time is how often he would be on the telephone home to Pinner.

For a time, on the outside at least, it seemed a thoroughly conventional romance. Linda took Elton to meet her father, 'Cottage Al' Woodrow, the club owner and magician. 'I remember her bringing him up to my flat in Ridgemount Gardens,' Cottage Al says. 'This apparition walked in, wearing a tatty old fur coat. Linda said to me "He writes wonderful songs, he's going to be an enormous star." "Oh yes," I said. "Pull the other one."'

Elton introduced Linda to trusted Pinner mates like his old school friend Janet Ritchie. Both attended Janet's wedding, Elton in his now rather worn Bluesology Beau Brummel suit. After the reception, Janet and her new husband made a foursome with Linda and him, travelling back by train to London for a long night round the Soho music clubs.

In the second-hand Hillman Imp car which Elton's mother had lent him £25 to buy, they travelled to Newcastle, for Linda's brother Neil's twenty-first birthday, and to Lincolnshire to visit Bernie Taupin's parents. On the way they were involved in a seven-car pile-up which totally wrecked Elton's Hillman. He himself escaped unhurt, but Linda sustained an arm injury. 'I thought at first that I'd broken it. But it was cured by putting it on an air-cushion.'

Bernie was an amiable sub-tenant, tolerant of Linda's little dogs, content to live on the household's diet of sausages, instant puddings and Indian or Chinese takeaways. He, too, had by now lost his virginity, to a girl named Tottie whom he had met up in Lincolnshire. To Bernie the main attraction of Furlong Road was a room of his own in which to continue these delightful experiments.

He admits he was 'shit-scared' of Linda, who, since she met most day-to-day expenses from her pickled-onion trust fund, ruled the basement ménage somewhat like a school matron. When Bernie wanted to put up a Simon and Garfunkel poster on his bedroom wall, Linda told him he mustn't.

Since Linda had a day job as a secretary, Elton and he spent long hours together, if not at Dick James Music, then watching their socks and underwear rotate at the local Washeteria. 'I remember once putting a new cashmere sweater into the machine, then bringing it out shrunk down to the size of a postage stamp,' Bernie says. 'Elton was laughing so much, he literally rolled on the floor.'

One thing they could not do at Furlong Road was work at their embryonic partnership. The basement did not have a piano. And besides, Linda had her own ideas of the way Elton's career ought to shape. She wanted him to model himself on Buddy Greco, the American cabaret star.

From time to time she would come with Elton to the Dick James Studio, raising incredulous eyebrows among all collected there. Caleb Quaye could not subdue his old propensity for tactless mirth. 'I remember one night we'd all been out to dinner and were on our way back to the studio. Elton was trotting along beside Linda in his fur coat, with one of her little dogs on its leash. He looked so ridiculous with her towering over him, I just rolled on the pavement, laughing.'

To Dick James, Elton John was the smallest, most insignificant part of his daily concerns. Now and again, amid vastly bigger deals, he would remember the £25 he paid out every week and ask his son Stephen how that little side project was going along. Even the name of the little side project sometimes eluded him, and he would absent-mindedly call Elton 'Elvis'.

To Elton, James was a figure of absolute awe, the man who had helped discover the Beatles, intermediary of every glorious hit from 'A Hard Day's Night' to 'I Am the Walrus'. Elton's greatest pop idols and exemplars hung like a golden halo around Dick James's bald head. Merely to associate with the publisher of Lennon and McCartney was privilege and achievement enough. Never mind if no song he himself wrote for James ever made it onto vinyl.

Yet, long before Dick James brought any advancement to Elton, or Elton represented anything like profit to James, a bond of genuine warmth grew up between them. The former dance-band crooner and the former pub pianist were not so very different, notwithstanding the vast gap in their ages, prestige and background. Dick James's former world of swing, boiled shirts and scalloped music-stands was one that Elton had known and loved vicariously through valve wireless sets in Metroland. As James's dulcet voice discoursed, Elton loved to remember those same tones issuing from a cabinet TV, amid the twang of synthetic longbows, on mid-Fifties Sunday afternoons. It was a source of wholly unironic pleasure to him that his publisher had sung the *Robin Hood* theme.

In all kinds of ways, Dick James was destined to fill the greatest emotional void of Elton's childhood and adolescence. From the very start, he reposed total faith and trust in James, turning to him for advice on every problem, absorbing his pronouncements in reverential silence and following them to the letter. As time passed, their relationship would become less that of entrepreneur and artist than of increasingly indulgent father and increasingly dependent, and demanding, son.

The first Elton John single was released by This Record Co. via Philips in March 1968, the month of his twenty-first birthday. Disregarding the pile of exotic works that already existed on demo, Stephen James opted for safety and convention. 'I've Been Loving You' was a routine Elton ballad whose routine lyrics also happened to be his, though Bernie Taupin still received credit as joint composer. It had been recorded before Christmas in the DJM studio, with Caleb Quaye producing, and the usual modest in-house backup band. Elton himself disliked the result, which seemed to him all too much like the soupy effusions of Engelbert Humperdinck. But that was the one Dick James liked, and who knew better the constituents of a hit?

Even for whimsical 1968, the Christian name of Philips' new recording artist struck an incongruous note. Most who heard it then instantly thought of Elton Hayes, a genteel folk performer whose Olde English ditties were still ineradicably engraved on Fifties childhood's inner ear:

> Oh I'll sing a song, a rollicky song, as I roll along my way.
> With a hey derry-dow and a herry di-doo
> And a riddle-de-diddle-de -day-de-day
> And a riddle-de-diddle-de-day.

'John' was not much better, seeming merely a weak imitation of earlier pop stars who'd used Christian names for surnames, like Cliff Richard and Keith Richard. There was also the point that in America 'John' meant toilet.

The bearer of this unluckily twice-evocative name possessed few obvious attributes of a pop heart-throb. Even the sympathetic lens of Philips' publicity photographer could make him no more than marginally good-looking, with his newly gaunt face and granny specs, his expression its usual mixture of self-conscious shyness and faint dread. With his hair now cropped short and combed down over his forehead, he looked more like some troubled young Roman tribune than the requisite arrogant Carnaby Mod. There being neither time nor budget for grander settings, he was shown, in his tab collar and creased little box jacket, posing against a corrugated iron fence.

Philips' publicity department did their stuff none the less, billing 'I've Been Loving You' in the trade press as 'the greatest performance on a first disc' by '1968's great new talent . . . You have been warned.' The warning was to no avail. 'I've Been Loving You' sailed out into a sea of silence just like Bluesology's two attempts on the same label. The sensation of 1968 was not to be Elton John. It was a group from Birmingham named the Move, whose outrageous publicity stunts had even got them into legal trouble with Prime Minister Harold Wilson. Elton remembers going to see a concert by the Move around this time and feeling his spirits lurch downhill again. 'I thought, "I'm still not getting anywhere."'

As 'I've Been Loving You' stayed firmly out of the charts, Elton and Bernie resumed their duties as in-house songwriters at DJM. And once again Dick James in his wisdom – and on the strength of the £25 he paid them each week – instructed them to forget the airy-fairy stuff they had been writing before, and produce some solid commercial tunes that other artistes could cover.

A cross-section of their efforts survives on a cassette-tape made from some of the studio demos by Elton's footballer cousin, Roy Dwight. The background is Sheila Dwight's tiny lounge at Frome Court, with Roy's small son, Stephen, occasionally chirruping in the background. 'This is the first of Reggie's recordings,' Roy's voice announces with stolid pride. 'He now goes under the name of Elton John . . .'

The main item is entitled 'I Can't Go on Living Without You', sung by Elton in Latin style, punctuated by cod cries of 'Yariba! Yariba!' 'A group named the Plastic Penny has just recorded this one,' DJ Roy continues earnestly. 'It's called "Turn to Me" . . . This one is called "Sorry to See Me Go".' 'If only you knew what I'd been through,' runs the tenaciously unimaginative refrain, 'you'd be sorry to see me go!' A solitary lyric in true Taupin style, 'Smokestack Children' – with one line about 'the tapestry of children's faces' – has been slipped in like a packet of dope in a suitcase of woollen underwear.

The DJM organisation was not totally hostile to these surreptitious 'non-commercial' efforts. Lionel Conway, the young head of DJM's publishing division, was an enthusiastic fan of Elton and Bernie's work, though, alas, possessing insufficient clout to change so firmly made-up a mind as Dick James's. With Conway's support, a number of their more poetic efforts were covered by other artists within the large DJM network. 'Turn to Me' was recorded by the Plastic Penny, a group belonging to Larry Page's affiliated Page One Music. 'Thank You for Your Loving' (a song credited to Elton John and Caleb Quaye) became the B-side of a single by a group called the Dukes Noblemen. 'When the First Tear Shows' was recorded as the A-side of a November release by a DJM solo protégé, Brian Keith. 'Taking the Sun from My Eyes' was the B-side of a single by a children's TV 'story lady' named Ayshea. A song from their very earliest batch, 'The Tide Will Turn for Rebecca' ended up as a curio single for another DJM acquisition, the actor Edward Woodward.

Most successful was 'Skyline Pigeon', the wistful song of a captive bird turned loose by a prisoner. Elton's demo version came to the notice of Roger Greenaway and Roger Cook, the prolific writing team whose Cookaway Music also was run by DJM. So enthusiastic were they about the song that they arranged with Dick James for Cookaway to publish it, plus two further John–Taupin titles. Roger Cook, a singer in his own right – soon to front a string of hits by Blue Mink – released 'Skyline Pigeon' as an A-side in August 1968. A second A-side cover appeared that same month by a singer named Guy Darrell.

For every glimmer of success in tiny print on a revolving record label, there were a dozen disappointments when big-name cover versions they had pinned their hopes on failed to materialise. 'I used to get more down about it than Elton did,' Bernie Taupin says now. 'Usually he'd be the one keeping both our spirits up. What used to bring him down was when I'd go off back to Lincolnshire for a time. I know he once wrote in his diary: "Bernie away. Very depressed."'

While grinding out songs to Dick James's specifications, they continued surreptitiously writing their own uncommercial material. Elton's studio demos of these forbidden tracks, like 'A Dandelion Dies in the Wind', now amounted to a full album's worth. But, under all the rules of pop, they knew it was hopeless. No one ever recorded an album without the prior achievement of at least one Top 10 single.

The one faint hope of changing their luck was that some influential music journalist might be persuaded to listen to their songs, and write a story about them eulogistic enough to change Dick James's mind. But the national music papers, *Melody Maker*, *New Musical Express* and *Disc and Music Echo*, though right on Tin Pan Alley's doorstep, all seemed remote and unapproachable as the music mandarins at the BBC. To date, they had met only one journalist, a girl named Nina Myskow who worked as a fashion-writer for *Jackie* magazine, published by the penny-pinching D. C. Thomson group from Dundee, Scotland. Fleeing down to London for stories as often as she could, Nina soon made contact with the varicoloured pop musical life around Dick James Music. Elton John, at that stage, was nowhere near big enough to rate a mention in *Jackie* magazine. But something about him compelled Nina Myskow's attention. 'For a start, he was so funny and entertaining to be with, even though he often seemed depressed about the way his career was going. Once he told me he didn't think the partnership with Bernie was working out, and asked if I'd ever thought of writing words to songs. Silly bitch that I was, I never took him up on it. Later on, he told me he'd written a song called "Nina".'

To supplement his weekly £15 retainer from DJM, he also began doing freelance session work, both as a pianist and backup singer. He became one of the network of hardy musical pros, sent in to studios like kamikazes to beef up the sound of this or that ephemeral Top 20 act. During 1968 he played anonymously on hits by two comedy groups, the Barron Knights and Scaffold. He was also an indistinguishable voice in the chorus behind Tom Jones's melodramatic number two smash 'Delilah'. For a time he had a second career as pianist in a pubbish group named the Bread and Beer Band with other DJM musicians: Caleb Quaye on guitar, Roger Pope on drums and Bernie Calvert on bass. They even released a single on Decca, 'Breakdown Blues', and cut an album that reached test-pressing stage before being mysteriously cancelled.

Even when not working at DJM, Elton and Bernie would hang around the office, soaking up all possible propinquity with the men who knew the Beatles. At the time, Dick James had just hired Geoffrey Ellis, boyhood friend of Brian Epstein and one of the last to see him before his lonely death. A solicitor, impeccably dressed and inscrutably respectable, Ellis now looked after contracts and artist relations at DJM. He first noticed Elton as a down-at-heel figure, sitting with Bernie outside Dick James's office, for all the world like two schoolboys waiting to see the headmaster.

Paul McCartney would sometimes drop in to use the DJM studio with his new Welsh protégée, Mary Hopkin. On one memorable occasion, Elton and Bernie saw him at EMI's Abbey Road studios, where the Beatles had lately recorded the White Album. 'We were there talking to the Barron Knights,' Bernie Taupin remembers. 'Suddenly Paul came in, sat down at the piano and asked us if we'd like to hear this new thing he'd written. It was "Hey Jude". God, we thought that was just so cool.'

Neither Elton nor Bernie could ever bear to be far from pop music and records. Their constant port of call was the Musicland record shop in Berwick Street, London's best place for American import discs. They would spend hours there, riffling through the boxes or squashed into an audio booth, soaking up ideas like hippy magpies for half a dozen new songs that Dick James would prefer them not to write. Elton became so well-known to Musicland's two assistants, Ian and John, that he was allowed behind the counter and even took turns at serving customers. Little in Elton's afterlife was ever to match the excitement of queuing up, amid Berwick Market's banana boxes and squashed cabbage-stalks, for the newest albums by Leonard Cohen or Soft Machine. The high spot of each week was Friday, when Musicland's new import stock came in. Bernie Taupin still remembers the ecstasy with which they first listened to *Music from Big Pink*, by Bob Dylan's former backing group, the Band.

Bernie's weekly £10 was mostly going on rent, and buying successive volumes of Tolkien's *Lord of the Rings*. Often he couldn't afford to buy the record he wanted. 'So Elton always used to say "Never mind. I'll buy it and we'll share it."'

The early relationship between Elton and Bernie Taupin has often been speculated on. It was a bond of pure brotherly love. Throughout his solitary childhood, Elton had often wished he had a brother. In gregarious country mouse, with his warm family background and two brothers, town mouse found – or seemed to find – everything that was missing. 'I loved Bernie,' he would admit. 'Not in any physical way. It was just fantastic to know that someone else knew how I felt.'

For Bernie also, the relationship was utterly natural. His country upbringing had made him quite accustomed to living at close quarters with brothers and school mates. Elton and he worked, travelled, drank, ate and roomed together as uncomplicatedly as if they were going through school, college or military service.

Innocent and platonic as their relationship was, it brought Elton face to face with his true nature for the first time. For, whatever he still did not know about himself, one thing he knew beyond any shadow of doubt. He could not face marrying and settling down with Linda Woodrow.

In the basement flat in Furlong Road, Islington, the old psychologist's axiom had come true, that whenever three people are together, two will invariably turn against the third. On one side were Elton and Bernie, their hopes and disappointments, their similar musical tastes and shared LPs. On the other was Linda with her hairpiece, her false eyelashes, her two little dogs and her hope that her fiancé would cultivate the suave piano and vocal style of Buddy Greco.

Bernie Taupin remembers how they would gang up on Elton's supposed loved one behind her back like a pair of naughty schoolboys. 'One night, I remember, the two of us made a treacle sponge pudding. When we brought it out of the oven, we accidentally dropped about half of it into the sink and it got mixed up with gunge and Ajax powder. As we scraped it up, Elton said, "We'll give her this bit."'

Elton was afterwards to give semi-farcical accounts of the relationship, claiming that Linda so dominated and intimidated him, he dared not even try to end things with her. To one magazine, half a dozen years later, he described Linda habitually beating him up; a too perfect comic reversal of her own earlier alleged ill-treatment by the midget Mighty Atom. Bernie's more ordinary recollection is of rows in which the much taller female party would frequently lash out, and make contact. Linda herself denies even that. 'I never hit him, or any other fellow I went out with. If I had, I know I'd remember it.'

The truth is that Linda did not coerce him nearly so much as he coerced himself, further and further down the path where it was impossible for him to go. Like H. G. Wells's Mr Polly, he longed for escape, yet was powerless to stop the social forces he had set in motion.

He got engaged to Linda on his 21st birthday, in March 1968, presenting her with a ring she had bought for herself at a jeweller's in the Holloway Road. On 4 April, he wrote a thank-you letter to his father and stepmother for the briefcase that had been their present to him. 'I became engaged on my birthday to my girlfriend Linda,' he told them. 'We do not intend to get married yet, or at any rate not until my career takes shape. She is a very understanding girl and realises that at the moment my work comes first . . .' He invited his father to the wedding, but Edna Dwight remembers Stanley prophesying that it would never happen.

'As you know, I have just had a record released,' the letter continued, 'but I don't think that it will be a hit because none of the disc jockeys like it very much. So I will just have to wait until I can find something they do like!! I am enclosing the sheet-music so that Aunt Edna can get in practice again!!!'

Despite this outward light-heartedness, he was also in a trough of depression about the failure of 'I've Been Loving You' and the endless false hopes and disappointments of trying to sell his songs to other performers. Bernie Taupin remembers how his initial buoyancy changed to dull resignation, as no chart action registered, and yet another big-time cover version failed to materialise. 'He got really down about it. I remember him often saying "Why doesn't anything ever work out for us?"'

It tormented him that, in almost nine months of living with Linda, he had found it difficult to establish any successful physical relationship with her. Linda's own relative tolerance and forbearance on this front could not remove the cloud that lay over their happiest domestic moments, the inward question, asked by so many young men in that same bewildered darkness: 'What's wrong with me?'

Nobody realised the extent of his gloom and desperation until one afternoon at the Furlong Road flat. 'The three of us were supposed to be taking a nap,' Linda remembers. 'I came out of my room and Bernie came out of his, both thinking we'd heard a noise. We went into the kitchen, and there was Elton lying with his head in the gas oven.'

A few telltale clues suggested that his decision to end it all was somewhat less than wholehearted. 'He'd only turned the gas on to "low", and left the kitchen window open,' Bernie Taupin says. 'And he'd thought to take a cushion to rest his head on.'

Bernie pulled him clear of the unfatal jets – a succour that would one day be celebrated in a song. Linda took a more sceptical view, merely remarking on the waste of good gas.

Everyone around Elton strove to dissuade him from rushing into marriage with Linda. His mother, Sheila, in particular, said that if he went through with it, she'd never speak to him again. Fervently as he might agree with them all, the arrangements still went forward with deadly inexorability. A local registry office had been booked for a civil ceremony. Linda and he had already been out choosing furniture, and looking for a new flat in the middle-aged suburb of Mill Hill. A wedding cake was on order. Long John Baldry was to be best man.

The wedding date was only three weeks away when Elton and Bernie went out drinking with Long John at a Soho club called the Shazz. Linda had also been invited but, providentially, said she preferred to stay home that night.

At the Shazz, and later at the Bag O'Nails, Elton's friends rejoined battle to save him from his impending nuptials. 'Baldry kept on at him all evening,' Bernie Taupin remembers. 'It's absurd, you don't really love her, you're just being a damned fool . . .' Other music figures joined the discussion like supernumerary agony aunts, among them P. J. Proby and Cindy Birdsong of the Supremes, who had once gone out with Bluesology's lucky vocalist, Stuart Brown.

By the time the Bag closed in the early hours, Elton's resolve to end it with Linda had been stiffened. 'We were both pretty drunk,' Bernie says. 'We walked back up Furlong Road arm in arm, to give ourselves courage. On the way, I fell against a car and set its burglar alarm ringing.

'When we got to the flat, Elton said "I'm going to tell her." I said, "I'm going into the bathroom to throw up." Then I bolted straight into my room and shut the door, with all hell breaking loose on the other side. A little while later, there was a knock, and Elton's voice said "I'm coming in there with you." I think he spent the rest of the night on the floor.'

The next morning, in contemporary parlance, was 'heavy'. Linda announced she was pregnant, and threatened dire consequences if Elton called the wedding off. 'She locked herself in the bathroom and shouted out she was going to commit suicide by injecting an air bubble into her vein,' Bernie Taupin says. 'I remember the two of us outside, saying, "She can't, can she? She hasn't got a syringe."'

For Elton, there was now only one possible way out. He got straight on the telephone with an SOS to his mother.

Shortly before noon, a van drew up outside. In it was faithful Derf Farebrother, a one-man Dunkirk fleet for the evacuation of

Elton, his household effects, his record collection and his songwriting partner. In little more than an hour, the wrathful Linda and her two little dogs were left behind. Elton and Bernie sat in the safety of Derf's van, heading home to 30a Frome Court, Northwood Hills.

The idea had been to seek sanctuary with Sheila and Derf just for a week or two, until the Linda furore had died down and they could find another flat in London. Little did Bernie Taupin realise they were destined to remain out in leafy Metroland for something like the next year and a half. Until well past the point when Elton John had taken the pop world by storm, he would still be living at home with his mum.

The only vacant space in the 1930s maisonette was the bedroom where Reggie Dwight had spent so many solitary hours. With Sheila's indulgence, this was now converted into a self-contained bedsitter for Elton and Bernie, with its own oil heater and television set. Their two fun-fur coats hung behind the door, where Reggie's solitary school cap and blazer used to be. The room was too small even for two single beds, so they had to go out and buy themselves metal-framed bunk beds, the kind that small boys sometimes have to share at seaside holiday hotels.

Both town and country mouse, fortunately, were neat and methodical and able to coexist quite happily in the tiny space. On one side were their records, scrupulously marked with an 'E' or a 'B', and the stereo system they were buying together on the instalment-plan. On the other was a cabinet with doors, housing the leather-bound volumes from the book club to which Elton subscribed.

The weeks of monastic seclusion at Frome Court brought one great benefit to Elton and Bernie. Their songwriting – in virtual abeyance during Elton's domestic traumas – now hit full stride, in the form it was to retain henceforth. Bernie would sit on the lower bunk bed, scribbling lyrics on a pad on his knee. He would then take them along the minuscule hallway and into the living room, where Elton sat at the piano. Back in the bedroom, a few moments later, he would hear chords begin to vibrate through the wall.

Sheila Dwight would come home from her job with the Ministry of Defence, cook Elton and Bernie an evening meal and listen to the day's compositions. Frequently, the audience would be swelled by Sheila's sister, Win, and her next-door neighbour, Mavis.

True, it was not the most convenient address from which to pursue a career as Tin Pan Alley tunesmiths. Each morning, wearing their mousy furs, they had to walk up Pinner Road, turn left at the

traffic roundabout and go along the parade of shops to Northwood
Hills tube station, opposite the gloomy hotel-pub where Elton's
performing career had begun. Thence on the Metropolitan Line,
winding through Pinner, Harrow-on-the-Hill, Northwick Park and
Wembley, with its distant view of the stadium's towers, and finally
Baker Street, with a change to the Bakerloo Line, then another to
the Central Line for Tottenham Court Road, Tin Pan Alley and
DJM. The last train home left Baker Street before midnight just as
things were hotting up in their favourite Soho haunts, the Shazz and
the Bag O'Nails.

Surprisingly enough, it was this tedious journey on the Metropolitan Line, rather than hanging around DJM, that gave Elton and
Bernie's career its next nudge forward. Returning home alone one
day, Elton spotted a familiar face in the commuter crowd. It was
'Muff' Winwood, elder brother of Stevie, the teenage vocal star of
the Spencer Davis Group, with whom Bluesology had often shared
gigs. Muff had now left the group to become a producer with the
new progressive Island record label and, with his wife Zena, lived
only a mile or so from Northwood Hills.

Elton began playing tennis, in his fiercely competitive way, with
Muff Winwood. He also played him some of the demos of 'non-
commercial' songs he had made illicitly at DJM. Like Lionel Conway,
Muff thought them brilliant. He couldn't understand why Dick and
Stephen James kept such songwriters on a treadmill of easy-listening
and Europop, nor why Elton wasn't being more adventurously
launched as a solo performer. Muff Winwood's suggestion was that
he should approach Island's whiz-kid young boss, Chris Blackwell,
to see if Blackwell would take over Elton's contract from DJM.

Meantime, Elton and Bernie had a friend and adviser, living only
minutes by car from Frome Court. 'We used to go over and see
Muff regularly every week,' Bernie Taupin remembers. 'We always
took his wife, Zena, a box of Black Magic chocolates and a bottle of
Mateus Rosé, and spent the evening playing table football. Muff used
to give us this really great advice about what to do when we finally
did make it and became famous. "Remember," he'd say, "a concert
promoter will give you anything you ask for, but you'll always end
up paying for it in the end."'

The meticulous day-by-day diary that Elton kept – and still keeps
– records this era in capital letters, often with the flavour of a
prototype Adrian Mole:

January 7, 1969. STAYED AT HOME. WROTE EMPTY SKY,
FLOWERS WILL NEVER DIE.

January 12. WENT TO LJB'S [Long John Baldry] BIRTHDAY PARTY, HAD ROW WITH BERNIE.

April 10. RECORDING AT OLYMPIC – IT'S ME THAT YOU NEED. SESSION WAS GREAT. HELPED IN MUSICLAND TODAY.

April 12. CAUGHT THE 9-30 TRAIN AND WENT IN TO MUSIC-LAND. GOT 'DUFFED UP' ON WAY HOME. WENT STRAIGHT TO BED.

May 28. PINNER FAIR. WENT UP TO GET PAID. WENT TO THE FAIR WITH MICK AND PAT. I WON A COCONUT AND TWO GOLDFISH – JOHN AND YOKO!!

May 29. MY GOLDFISH DIED TONIGHT. VERY UPSET!!

May 30. WENT TO GET SOME MORE GOLDFISH – GOT A TANK AND FOUR FISH. PLAYED TENNIS WITH TONY'S FRIEND, MARK. WON 6-2, 6-4, 2-6, 4-6, 6-0.

August 14. DIDN'T WAKE UP UNTIL 3-0. BERNIE WENT TO THE DENTIST . . . GOT DRUNK ON MERRYDOWN. BERNIE VERY ILL.

August 30. GOING TO THE I.O.W. TO SEE BOB DYLAN. TOO MUCH!!

To Bernie as well as to her natural son, Sheila Dwight was endlessly good-natured, cheerful and encouraging. He still does a fond impersonation of her, chain-smoking and nodding vigorous approbation for a 'nice ballad'. Her one domestic stricture was in throwing out his fun-fur coat, which, especially in wet weather, used to smell like an unhygienic woolly dog.

For Elton – especially after what had gone before – it was a happy, if not carefree time. Bernie and he were like nothing so much as study chums in some safe, cosy tale of Greyfriars school. Sharing prep and talking after lights-out, the darkness friendly and familiar – what more could anyone need in a relationship?

Bernie remembers moments of high farce, like the time Elton's glasses exploded on one morning train journey to Baker Street. 'It was his first pair of John Lennon glasses. He'd bought them at a shop in Charing Cross Road. As I watched him, they just spontaneously flew apart on his nose.

'There was another time when Sheila had gone away and we had to cook dinner for ourselves. We tried to cook sausages, chips, peas and make Instant Whip. Everything got spoiled, excepting the peas.

While I'm burning the sausages, Elton's mixing up the Instant Whip
with one of these gun-type mixers. When he tries to look at what
I'm doing, he takes the gun out of the bowl and starts spraying
Instant Whip all over the ceiling. "Look what you're doing!" he's
shouting, and I'm shouting "No! Look what you're doing!" '

On quiet evenings in, Bernie would read *The Lord of the Rings*
and Elton would sit watching football on television. The last thing
country mouse would see before going to sleep each night was the
rail of the bunk bed, with town mouse's hippy chains and amulets
draped over it.

In September 1968 Dick James had persuaded a moustachioed young
song-plugger named Steve Brown to leave EMI and join the expand-
ing operation at DJM. The son of a Salvation Army officer, Brown
had started out as a musician, playing baritone sax in Emile Ford's
group, the Checkmates. Naturally ambitious, he saw the DJM job
as a means of advancement from plugging to full-blown record-
producing. His true niche in pop music, however, was to be as one
of its very few genuine altruists.

Among the first assignments given to Steve Brown was the
motivation of DJM's two in-house songwriters. He accompanied
Elton John and Bernie Taupin into the studio and listened to all their
material, both the 'commercial' songs they had been forced to write,
and the non-commercial ones they had gone on mutinously producing for the album no one would sanction. Then he delivered a
verdict which lifted both their hearts. The uncommercial stuff was
far superior to the commercial, Steve Brown told them. They should
waste no more time in trying to ape other styles and voices. From
now on, they must write only what they felt from the heart. 'It was
a very brave thing for Steve to do,' the star would afterwards
acknowledge. 'He was only an employee. He was telling us "Don't
take any notice of the boss." '

Among the elderly Tin Pan Alleyites at DJM, Steve Brown came
as a bright ray of salvation. Though only slightly older than Elton
and Bernie, he seemed an omniscient figure, combining the know-
how of big-time commercial pop with hippyish sensibility and
sympathy. His encouragement of them to be themselves had instantly
positive results, rousing both to the challenge of being commercial
without necessarily selling out.

It began, as usual, with Bernie, who came up with a lyric entitled
'Lady Samantha', combining his favourite image of a medieval damsel
with a highly fashionable Sixties name. This Elton wrapped in piano
chords and a vocal performance which began in the sad cypress

bleakness Bernie had meant it to, but then dissolved into a gutsy chorus, as if the Lady of Shalott were suddenly revealed in black net stockings and a red garter. On Steve Brown's strong recommendation, Dick James accepted 'Lady Samantha' as Elton's long-delayed follow-up to 'I've Been Loving You'. It was also agreed a suitable opportunity for Brown to make his first essay as producer. 'Lady Samantha' and a B-side, 'All Across the Havens', were recorded in the DJM studio on 18 October, 1968.

The session got off to an uncomfortable start. Elton's hired Wurlitzer piano had a key out of tune, which prevented his playing a crucial note in the 'Lady Samantha' arrangement. Though Steve Brown and everyone else pronounced the finished track excellent, he still worried and fretted about that missing note. Attempts at reassurance did nothing but bring on one of Reggie's Little Moments. He said he hated 'Lady Samantha', and didn't want it released. Brown's diplomatic suggestion was that he should go away for a few days, then listen to it again to see if he still felt the same. After two or three days, Elton listened again, and gave in. ' "Okay", I said. "Release it. You know, it can't do me any harm." '

'Lady Samantha' was released by Philips on 10 January, 1969. It did not reach the Top 20, or even the Top 50. But it received good notices everywhere that mattered. The *New Musical Express* called it 'professional and musicianly'. *Disc and Music Echo* thought the lyrics 'sensible and worthwhile' and the singer 'a promising talent'. The all-important *Melody Maker*, which gave ratings rather like a musical *Michelin*, commended a 'sturdy voice' and 'an interesting, guitar-ridden sound that could create waves of interest. Very good, and a gold star.'

More importantly, the song-plugging team of Stephen James and Steve Brown secured reasonable airplay on the BBC's new pop network, Radio One. To harassed BBC producers, fending off the druggy and the free-loving on every side, a quasi-Arthurian ballad, wherein no one spoke of 'turning on' or 'getting high', came as a welcome relief. Every major disc jockey, like Tony Blackburn and Johnny Walker, made room at least once among the Move, the Herd and Vanity Fair for 'Lady Samantha'. The cerebral John Peel gave it a special mention on his late night show, which in those days ran as late as almost midnight.

Though sales amounted to barely 4,000 copies, Elton was on the map as a performer at last. The BBC called him in for audition by its production panel, to determine if he was good enough to perform live on Radio One. He played 'Lady Samantha', 'Skyline Pigeon' and 'All Across the Havens' in a trial session which its producer,

Aidan Day, called 'highly original and inventive', even though Elton had previously warned he was suffering from a migraine. Not all the six-man BBC tribunal were so impressed. 'Male vocal in the 1969 feeling,' ran one report. 'Thin, piercing voice with no emotional appeal. Don't think this singer doing his own weird material is right for radio at present.' 'Writes dreary songs and sounds like a one-key singer,' another said. 'I suppose he must be available for anyone who wants his four-minute numbers, but I do not . . .'

With three votes for him and three against, Elton received the benefit of the doubt. He performed the same three numbers on a Radio One Saturday-morning session and afterwards was briefly quizzed by Britain's senior disc jockey, Brian Matthew. 'Any plans for personal appearances?' Matthew asked, in evident surprise there had as yet been none. 'I'm getting a band together at the moment,' Elton answered, in a voice both strained and shy. 'I've got a partner, who writes the lyrics to my songs. I've been very lucky. Well, I haven't had a hit yet, but I've still been lucky.'

One 'turntable hit' under their belt, Elton and Bernie now enjoyed further mild success via one of the numbers they had churned out to appease Dick James. It was a song called 'I Can't Go on Living Without You', composed with an ear half-cocked to the sub-Bacharach style of the barefoot chanteuse Sandie Shaw. Thanks to vigorous lobbying by Dick James, musical unoriginality and banality reaped the highest possible reward. 'I Can't Go on Living Without You' was chosen as a British candidate for the Eurovision Song Contest.

The annual satellite-linked event in which Europe's nations compete to produce execrable pop music was not quite so vomit-inducing three decades ago. In those days, established performers rather than gawky newcomers sang Britain's entry. Established song-writers did not practise the boycott that afterwards arose. Elton and Bernie were in highly respectable musical company.

'I Can't Go on Living Without You' was one of six potential British entries sung by the Scots star Lulu in successive editions of her weekly BBC TV variety show throughout January and February of 1969. She then reprised all six in a special *Song for Europe* programme on 1 March. A viewers' vote selected the one to go to the Eurovision final in Madrid on 29 March.

Despite a spirited performance by Lulu, the viewers did not choose 'I Can't Go on Living Without You'. Nor did they choose 'Come September', co-written by the prestigious lyricist Don Black. Their overwhelming choice was Peter Warne and Alan Moorhouse's 'Boom-Bang-a-Bang', a song destined, weirdly, to tie with three others for first place in the Eurovision final, and usher in a tradition of Esperanto-ish nonsense titles that continues to this day.

For Elton and Bernie, the only consolation was a brief TV walk-on appearance as writers on the *Song for Europe* programme. When their big moment came, Michael Aspel, the compère, announced them as 'Elton John and Bernie Poppin'. Bernie's local paper up in Lincolnshire subsequently carried the headline LINCS BOY WRITES A SONG FOR LULU.

During late 1968 and early 1969, the affairs of the Beatles loomed over Dick James Music like a mop-topped mushroom cloud. Elton's career, in both short and long term, was to be crucially affected by Fab Four fallout.

Over the past three years, James's relationship with the Beatles had dramatically deteriorated. The syndrome is a familiar one in show business, experienced by almost all those fortunate enough to sign up phenomenal talent on the ground floor. Financial arrangements that seem fair and equitable on the ground floor tend to look somewhat different after the talent has shot through the roof.

So had it become with the 50–50 deal Dick James had made with John Lennon and Paul McCartney for publication of their music through a jointly owned company, Northern Songs. To two unknown boys in 1963 it had seemed almost unbelievably generous. But to history's most successful songwriters in 1969 it seemed a wholly unwarranted and excessive portion of themselves. The 23 per cent of Northern which James had kept after public flotation loomed large in their growing sense of being exploited and trammelled by what John Lennon bitterly called 'the men in suits'.

Nor was Dick James any longer the impressive figure he had seemed to John and Paul in their naïve early days. Instead, he represented a brake on creativity with his grey suit and bald head, his pleas, as the White Album took its avant-garde course, to send Northern Songs more nice, tuneful numbers like 'Michelle' and 'Yesterday'.

To James must be ascribed a certain lack of intuition and tact. Sure of his own integrity – as he had always been and would be – he could not see how 'the boys' could have any cause to resent him. Nor could his amiable nature comprehend the pressures within them as they fought to find a saviour from the chaos of their business venture, Apple Corps, and reach some basic consensus on musical policy. That January of 1969 found the Beatles on a freezing sound stage at Twickenham film studios, near-paralysed with anger and misery over what would become their final album, *Let It Be*. Matters were not helped by Dick James's cheery visits and his Christmas gifts of plastic playing-cards bearing the DJM monogram.

The great worry to James was his responsibility as managing director of Northern Songs, and the adverse effect on 3,000 shareholders (among whom he was himself a major one) in this season of virtually nonstop anti-Beatle press coverage. Worse even than the Apple business fiasco had been John Lennon's public affair with Yoko Ono, their conviction for drug-possession and the series of headline-grabbing performance-art stunts on which they were now embarked. Each time John and Yoko crawled under a giant paper bag, planted symbolic acorns for peace, or issued pictures of themselves as full-frontal nudes, Dick James would give another gulp and turn to Northern's share quotation in the *Financial Times*.

With the appointment of Allen Klein, a tough New York accountant, to sort out the chaos at Apple, Dick James decided his nerves could stand no more. Early in 1969 – taking advantage of a moment when both Lennon and McCartney were abroad – he sold out his 23 per cent of Northern Songs to Lew Grade's ATV organisation for something over one million pounds. ATV then set about acquiring the other stock (beginning a chain of ownership that would end, three decades later, with the Sony corporation).

Though DJM continued to administer Northern Songs, and would do so for the next three years, a great personal incubus was lifted from Dick James. His immediate thought – so his son Stephen remembers – was that, in building up and running Northern, he had not paid enough attention to his own company. He was thus prepared to put unusual effort into developing DJM's one and only home-grown talent.

With only nominal protest, therefore, Dick James yielded to the pleas of his young assistant Steve Brown that Elton John and Bernie Taupin should be given their creative heads. The turntable success of 'Lady Samantha' proved that their non-Eurovision music might not be so uncommercial after all. They could go ahead and make the album they had been dying to for almost a year.

From a music mogul as traditionally minded as Dick James, the concession was enormous. Record albums in the late Sixties were nothing like the gargantuan self-contained business they are today. Performers who sold albums still tended to be those with a large residual singles following, like the Beatles, Bob Dylan and the Beach Boys. 'Album only' artists, like Leonard Cohen and Leon Russell, were still almost wholly a transatlantic oddity. To advance an unknown singer into this rarefied company showed an extraordinary degree of faith and indulgence.

Not that Elton's first album mobilised anything like the spend-thrift resources of a *Sgt. Pepper* or *Pet Sounds*. The venue was the DJM studio, with its second-hand Studer four-track. The band was the usual rake-up of session mercenaries, led by Caleb Quaye on guitar. Steve Brown was producer, still very much feeling his way. By using in-house facilities, and cutting every corner possible, the final cost was barely £2,000.

All but one of the tracks had been written by Bernie, sitting on the lower bunk at Frome Court, then carried, postman-like, along the tiny hallway to Elton at the piano in the lounge. Sheila Dwight, her sister Win and her next-door neighbour Mavis had received sneak previews of most, while the composers' dinner simmered on the kitchenette stove.

The two daydreaming fans and inveterate mental hoarders poured forth a motley magpie cache. From Bernie came two- and three-minute storylines drawn from the literature and mass culture he had devoured since childhood, echoes of Walter Scott, Macaulay and Alfred, Lord Tennyson, of Kenneth Grahame, C. S. Lewis and J. R. R. Tolkien, of *Buffalo Bill's Annual* and *Eagle* comic books, of BBC Monday-night radio plays and Technicolor cinema screens on Saturday afternoons. From Elton came melodies just as instantly assembled from the years of playing he already had behind him, chords and progressions formed in each long epoch from the Royal Academy of Music to the Twisted Wheel Club, thrown into an instant stew of all his keyboard heroes from Russ Conway to Stevie Wonder, from J. S. Bach to Winifred Atwell.

The titles were a highly self-conscious mixture of poesy, sub-Kerouac parody and laboured *Goon Show* pun. 'Empty Sky' returned to one of Bernie Taupin's favourite themes, a prisoner bemoaning lost liberty. 'Val-Hala' rang with echoes of torch-lit Viking movies starring Kirk Douglas. 'Western Ford Gateway' celebrated the American frontier landscape Bernie Taupin had yet to see. 'Hymn 2000' was a Joe Ortonesque fable of maternal incest, church and chocolate. 'Lady, What's Tomorrow?' was a lament for vanishing rural beauty in the voice of a child evacuee. 'Sails' was an unconscious reworking of John Masefield's poem, 'Cargoes'. 'The Scaffold' had a feel of Spanish conquistadors, invoking both Eldorado and the Minotaur. 'Skyline Pigeon' – Elton's belated version of a song already twice covered – returned to yearnings from the prison cell. 'Gulliver' was about one of the dogs on Bernie's father's Lincolnshire farm. All these far-sighted visions of country mouse, myopic town mouse wreathed about him in the light, clear, angst-ridden voice that still reminded its listeners most of José Feliciano.

The album took the title of its opening song, 'Empty Sky'. In contrast with the tortuously self-indulgent studio epics of Beatles or Beach Boys, it was completed in a few days during February 1969, at the astoundingly low cost of £150 per track. When the sessions ran late and the composers missed their last train back to Pinner, Steve Brown took them to sleep on the floor of his father's flat above the Salvation Army centre in Oxford Street.

The finished master was then handed to Dick James's son, Stephen, for release through This Record Company's distribution label, Philips. Much as Stephen liked what he heard, he could see the problems ahead. Since *Sgt. Pepper*, British record companies were just about reconciled to the theme or concept album. *Empty Sky* had no detectable theme, save perhaps the amount that could be borrowed from every department of a record shop like Musicland. From conventional acid rock, it swung to Olde English roundelay; from country and western to Afro-Caribbean; from Procol Harum to Jimi Hendrix; from the Rolling Stones to the Band. Poetically introspective, it still contrived to end on a note of saloon-bar cheeriness. The play-out track, 'Hay Chewed', a tortuous pun on 'Hey Jude', featured Elton and saxophonist Don Fay in an extended jazz-boogie duet.

Stephen James's misgivings proved well founded. Johnny Franz, the Philips A & R head, would not consider releasing so 'strange' an album by someone who had not yet made a proper hit single. Stephen's nettled response was to invite him to tear up This Record Co.'s contract with Philips, which Franz obligingly did. In a bravura show of youthful confidence, Stephen announced he would put out *Empty Sky* on a wholly independent DJM record label. Rather than merely employing the resources of its distribution label, DJM took on the whole creative and marketing process excepting actual manufacture (a job passed from Philips to Pye). As well as its studio, 71–75 New Oxford Street now also needed an expanded publicity and promotions office and an art department to design record-sleeves. Large corporate steps, all on behalf of little Elton and Bernie.

To design *Empty Sky*, Steve Brown brought in a young graphic designer friend of his named David Larkham, who worked freelance for various magazines and newspapers like the London *Evening Standard*. Larkham produced the simple dark blue sleeve on which Elton John confronted his listeners for the very first time. An unrecognisable figure, sidewhiskered like a Victorian paterfamilias, leaned back from its keyboard against a vista of psychedelic cloud. Stubby fingers rested on the keys, just as in every such pose back to the age of six. His herringbone tweed jacket was only one step on from the hairy ginger job of the Northwood Hills Hotel. On unseen pedals below, one could almost visualise the Hush Puppies.

Overleaf on the sleeve was a facsimile note in Elton's neat music-student hand, thanking the various helpers and 'Auntie' BBC, one of whose disc jockeys, David Symonds, provided some modish gobble-degook by way of testimonial:

> Elton John plays and pleases on this album but . . . he does not confine himself to the brighter side of life. The runcible has since changed to the smouldering crucible of a million injustices. It's a sign of the times. I too want to hear the pealing bells of distant churches sing. When it does happen, it will be a sign of tomorrow. And Elton will have a song about that as well.

Elton's first publicity launch also owed a debt to Beatle fallout. The new DJM label's promotions man was Alistair Taylor, who had worked in Brian Epstein's Liverpool record shop, subsequently becoming personal factotum to Paul McCartney. With Allen Klein's appointment as the Beatles' manager, Taylor found himself summarily and brutally fired. Hearing of his predicament, Dick James had good-naturedly offered him a job.

Alistair Taylor hyped *Empty Sky* almost as if it were a Beatles album, booking advertisement space on what are called the 'back earpieces' of 100 red London double-decker buses. For some days in June 1969 puzzled Londoners beheld pairs of receding posters on which a bespectacled face was outlined in silver dots against a background psychedelically purple. In true enigmatic Sixties style, no copy appeared but the name 'Elton John'.

Despite this bold gesture, Empty Sky ended up by selling fewer than 4,000 copies. Its best review, in the London *Evening Standard*, said it was 'nicely recorded but unadventurous . . . While the music is sweet, the lyrics seem to be a bit self-consciously cultured and "poetic" in a highly fanciful style. To be fair, though,' the *Standard*'s critic patronisingly continued, 'he has talent. When he gets less fanciful and less pretentious he will, I'm sure, have a worthwhile contribution to make.'

FIVE

'If you'll distribute him, I'll give him to you'

No decade ever ended as slowly and reluctantly as the 1960s. As a rule when each ten-year span draws to a close, there is a rush of excitement, a quickening interest and curiosity as to what the unfamiliar numeral will bring. So it had been when the Sixties approached with their illusory promise of realism and sleek modernity. By their utterly transformed end, to their millions of youthful beneficiaries, they had grown as mellowly comfortable as some old over-laundered, patched and darned denim jacket. Everything that was happy and easy had come to be identified with the number six. And suddenly, with a feeling of cold queasiness, people were having to think about sevens.

No other last year of a decade can have contained so many of its quintessential events. Nineteen-sixty-nine was the apogee of hippydom, with the Blind Faith and Rolling Stones' free concerts in Hyde Park, the festival which brought Bob Dylan to the Isle of Wight, and the half-million strong blue-denim bivouac at Woodstock. Other things happened, too, including the opening shots of terrorism and inflation, and man's first footstep on the moon. The abiding picture, however, is of millions of young people lying all over the earth, as if their blessed sunlit season truly could be spun out to eternity.

With winter came a growing dread, symbolised by that dread which emanated from a white Georgian house in Savile Row, Mayfair. The Beatles were breaking up, so how could the Sixties not follow? All the sadness of a fading golden age seemed gathered into Paul McCartney's great cow eyes as he sang the valedictory hymns of the *Let It Be* album.

The first bleary, hung-over day of 1970 was a stricken one for multitudes, all over the world, whose every impulse for joy and celebration since 1964 had been dictated by the Beatles. Suddenly they looked, and there was nothing.

And what of the person destined to soak up almost all that empty sea of fan-worship? As his *annus mirabilis* begins, we find him in yet another low-rent studio, trying to forget he is Elton John or ever possessed style or material of his own. Shutting his eyes like a heretic under torture, he swallows his natural voice and pulls down the shutter in his throat. From his grimacing lips there emerges a thin, reedy note, filled with the tremulous angst of a pullet about to have its neck wrung. All present agree it to be horrendously like Robin Gibb of the Bee Gees.

Times being tougher than tough, Elton could not afford to turn down any kind of freelance session-work. He would appear even on the cut-price LPs, sold mainly by Woolworth's stores, whereon anonymous artists produced wobbly counterfeit versions of current smash hits. During late 1969 and much of 1970, his talent for mimicry earned him at least as much as did his true persona.

Copying Robin Gibb on a pseudo-Bee Gees 'Saved By The Bell' was the most punishing of these vocal masquerades. For bargain-basement labels like Avenue or Ace of Clubs, he also impersonated Stevie Wonder singing 'Signed, Sealed, Delivered'; Mungo Jerry singing 'In the Summertime'; and Andy Fairweather-Low singing 'Natural Sinner'. He was there, singing or playing backup, on 'Woolies' 'versions of the Beach Boys' 'Cottonfields', Christie's 'Yellow River' and Creedence Clearwater Revival's 'Up Around the Bend'. He even recorded with the treacly Mike Sammes Singers and participated in a cover version of 'Back Home' as originally sung by the England World Cup football squad.

As a Motown child prodigy, a crewcut surfer, a Mississippi swamp rocker, even an English footballer with the vocal range of a tired moose, he was utterly convincing. The only characterisation that continued obstinately not to gel was that of Elton John.

After *Empty Sky*, his first single on DJM, 'It's Me That You Need', had belly-flopped. His only sniff of the Top 10 had been as session man on two '69 winter hits, the Hollies' 'He Ain't Heavy (He's My Brother)' and the Scaffold's remake of a Wolf Cub camp-fire song, 'Gin Gan Goolie'.

Out of the studio, he bore only the most superficial resemblance to a would-be pop star. He and Bernie Taupin were still living at his mother's flat in Pinner, sleeping in little-boy bunk beds, hammering out songs in two-minute bursts on the living-room's upright piano. Every free day was still spent hanging round the reception area at

Dick James Music, scrounging cups of tea or coffee and watching glumly as not only a new year but a new decade rolled off the blocks without him.

Nineteen-year-old Sue Ayton became the junior of Dick James's two secretaries late in 1969. Her first sight of Elton was when he and Bernie came in with a greetings card for her departing predecessor. As the plump, good boy in Metroland had been, so did the fiercely slimmed-down pop musician remain punctilious about remembering birthdays, writing thank-you notes and buying flowers.

'One day I was walking through Reception with a tray of dirty teacups,' Sue remembers. 'He was sitting there with Bernie, as always. As I went by, he put his foot out and tripped me up. Not viciously; just to get a laugh from everyone else. I was furious, and hit him. He hit me back, just in a jokey way. I told him what I thought of him, and stormed off to the tea-making room. He followed me in there, looking really worried. "Don't be cross with me," he said.'

Sue Ayton's duties included the issuing of Elton and Bernie's weekly retainer cheques, and receiving their formal receipts, for £15 and £10 respectively. She also looked after the cupboard where file copies of records by the Beatles and other DJM-affiliated artists were kept. 'I used to let them go through everything that came in and take what they wanted – until I found out I wasn't supposed to.'

To Sue and the other office staff, Elton was still a figure utterly without conceit or arrogance, courteous, considerate, almost painfully grateful for anything they did for him. At the end of the day, a whole group of them, singer, lyricist, producer, musicians and secretaries, used to adjourn to a pub round the corner. 'Elton always used to wear the same old tweed jacket and cords. A black trilby hat. A herringbone maxicoat with big lapels if it was cold. Another thing he lived and died in was a rainbow-coloured waistcoat his mother had knitted him. But he always looked businesslike. He always carried a briefcase.'

Bernie she remembers as an almost invisible figure, tagging on Elton's maxicoat-tails, more often than not moonstruck with love for some girl he had just met or daydreaming of new comic-book epics to compress into a song-lyric. 'We were all going along once, and Bernie walked straight into a lamp post. It was quite a nasty cut. I remember his Lincolnshire accent saying "It 'urts". Next day when he came into the office, he told everyone he'd been in a fight.'

At the same time, DJM's launch of Elton John the live performer was under way, despite some dogged resistance from the performer. The frustrations and discouragements of the past four years had flattened the confidence of the one-time keyboard showman and extrovert. He had developed a psychological block against going out on stage, in case someone told him to shut up and pushed him out to the sidelines again.

Better the life of a backup singer, where he need not be noticed even in the most public situation. Paradoxically, in this period of greatest reluctance to show himself, Elton made two separate appearances on BBC TV's *Top of the Pops* show. With Roger Cook and a female session trio, the Ladybirds, he was an indistinguishable part of the studio decor behind Brotherhood of Man singing 'United We Stand'. Another night, he was a face in the backup vocal crowd for a group named Pickettywitch.

When money was really short he would reluctantly return to his old frustrating role of backup musician. His journalist friend Nina Myskow never expected to run into him on her beat for *Jackie* magazine around Dundee, Scotland. But she got a surprise when she went to see a fading one-hit group called Simon Dupree and the Big Sound perform at a club in the remote Scots fishing port of Arbroath. 'There on the stage behind Simon Dupree was Elton, playing piano. When I talked to him afterwards, he said, "Is there any way I can get a game of tennis up here?" I had to take a day off work to play tennis with him.'

Stephen James remembers feeling deep dismay on first seeing Elton face an audience on his own. 'He seemed to have terrible problems communicating. He'd just sit at the piano, play six to eight songs, then say "There it is. That's it." For a long time, I don't remember him saying more than two words at a time during his set. My father and I had to go on and on at him about loosening up and projecting.'

Even the James organisation's entrepreneurial muscle could not secure him more than a sparse handful of bookings at obscure clubs, mostly in the London area. He would appear with all or some of the *Empty* Sky session musicians, Caleb Quaye on guitar, Roger Pope on drums, Dave Glover on bass. A contingent from the office would always be there – Bernie Taupin, Steve Brown, and Sue Ayton – fervently clapping, cheering, whooping and whistling. 'He went on stage to play in the same old tweed jacket and cords he always wore,' Sue Ayton says. 'I remember one night he'd bought a pair of jeans to wear, but when he tried to put them on, he just couldn't get into them. So he went out and played in his old cords again.'

Within the safety of the group, Elton began to take an interest in nineteen-year-old Sue, who was both his enthusiastic fan and a robustly down-to-earth character. The Linda Woodrow disaster had by no means ended his hopes of finding conventional happiness. Sue

Ayton and he would go out on dates together, as well as with the office group. 'He was a very warm, loving person. We'd hold hands or have a bit of a kiss and cuddle. But it was all very innocent. Anyway, I was still living with my mum, and he was living with his.'

The truth is that both sides in the Elton John project were rapidly running out of hope. DJM had spent more than two years in trying to launch him, an effort not devoted to the Beatles, the Rolling Stones or any other pop newcomer. He had been pushed with maximum force down every possible music avenue, from Europop composer to progressive singer-songwriter. Yet still the breakthrough refused to happen.

Elton, for his part, had passed through the phase of dumb wonder and gratitude at that patience and indulgence, and was now at the more querulous stage of asking why the man who had harnessed the Beatles seemed able to do so little for him. In his deepening gloom, as one false dawn followed another, he had even started to wonder how much better he might do under management less celebrated but more go-getting. As far back as January 1969, when 'Lady Samantha' failed to chart, he had gone to his old Mills Music boss Cyril Gee and asked for help in getting out of his DJM contracts. Though Gee, as a friend of Dick James, preferred not to be involved, he gave Elton the name of a solicitor who might act for him. But Elton – in the new exhilaration of recording *Empty Sky* – decided to let the matter drop.

His feelings of discontent were exacerbated by the fact that another record company was by now actively trying to poach him from DJM. His friend Muff Winwood, the young producer for Island Records, had kept his promise to play Elton's demos to Island's boss, Chris Blackwell. Blackwell loved them and immediately offered a £10,000 advance, provided the existing agreements with DJM could be legally circumvented. On reading through these, he told Elton that, in his opinion, there were holes in them, and that Elton could easily get out of all or part of them. 'Most of my contracts void,' Elton jotted in his diary.

In the crusade to prise Elton away from DJM, Muff Winwood had joined forces with Lionel Conway, who had now left his job with DJM publishing to pursue impresarial ambitions of his own. During 1969, on four separate occasions, Muff Winwood and Lionel Conway approached Dick James with schemes for Island to take over Elton's recording contract. James firmly resisted these overtures, though he said he would be willing to sell Elton's management contract. A new agreement between Muff, Conway and Elton was drawn up – and signed by Elton – one night at the Speakeasy Club.

But then Muff Winwood baulked at a manager's role, saying he would rather 'stay friends'.

That July of 1969, after *Empty Sky* had come out and flopped, Elton's spirits nosedived again. He told Stephen James he was fed up with failure after failure, and definitely wanted to leave DJM. A meeting with Dick James hurriedly took place, at which James was able to mollify, reassure and reinvigorate him.

Much as the Jameses liked Elton, they could not ignore the large sums of money already uselessly spent on his advertising, promotion and, most of all, enough studio time to produce almost a hundred finished masters as well as innumerable demos. Altogether, Stephen James calculates, Elton's development cost DJM about £70,000, a sum reckonable as close to half a million today. 'We were getting to the point where we knew we had to say "That's it."'

It was Steve Brown's urgent contention that Elton must make another album, to build on the undoubted creative development of *Empty Sky*. Dick James agreed to this further investment late in 1969, though with an emphasis which none present could fail to notice. Elton's second album was to be, in other words, his last chance.

Steve Brown, that singular altruist, laboured to ensure that, if this were indeed the final throw of the dice, then it would be a good one. For the album sessions he persuaded Dick James to let him quit the severely limited DJM recording facility and, instead, book time at a modern, well-equipped West End studio, Trident. In a further burst of selflessness, he declared that he himself was not an experienced enough producer to bring Elton to full potential. Instead, a top-flight man should be brought in from outside.

Brown's first choice was George Martin, the Beatles' producer, now running his own studio, AIR-London. Martin was amenable, but insisted on arranging as well as producing, and Steve Brown preferred that the two jobs remain separate. His nominee as arranger was Paul Buckmaster, who had dreamed up the eerie orchestration for David Bowie's 1969 hit, 'Space Oddity', the first (but not last) pop song about a disenchanted astronaut. Buckmaster agreed to participate after hearing two piano and vocal demos by Elton intended for the new album, a historical minidrama called 'The King Must Die', and a ballad called 'Your Song'. Buckmaster, in turn, introduced Brown to Gus Dudgeon, who had produced 'Space Oddity' as well as albums for the Bonzo Dog Doo-Dah Band. As an established and highly fashionable producer, Dudgeon at first was not keen to take on a virtual unknown like Elton John. What swayed him was the undoubted promise on the two demos, plus a handsome royalty cut and Steve Brown's promise of *carte blanche* at the sessions.

Elton himself was intimidated by the resources mustered for his final attempt to make good. In addition to the usual backing band, Paul Buckmaster's arrangements called for a full symphony orchestra, complete with harp. As the star later recalled, it was like suddenly being projected backwards to the era of Royal Academy concerts and frowning teachers named Stoupe. 'All the notes were written down, even the rhythm notes. I had to play live with everything. I mean, they had all these brilliant musicians standing there, and if I made a mistake, they all went.'

The main part of the album was recorded in January 1970, in conditions as different as they could possibly be from the late-night indulgence of Beatles or Stones. The musicians kept office-hours, breaking for coffee, tea and the occasional Chinese lunch in nearby Wardour Street. Elton himself set the prevailing tone of good humour and dogged professionalism. Nevertheless, it quickly became clear to Gus Dudgeon that Dick James's budget of £6,000 would not nearly finance all the further instrumental flourishes Paul Buckmaster had in mind. Midway through the recording, Dudgeon had to go and beg a £1,500 extension. When this, too, was rapidly spent, he went to Dick James again, taking some of the half-completed tracks. After listening to what was there, James nodded and said 'Finish it.'

Even to those who saw it develop layer upon layer, the completed album was a revelation. The raw material was essentially the same as on *Empty Sky*, a motley of images from Bernie Taupin's favourite stories, poems and films, welded together with chords from pudgy, capable hands. Again, the song-titles mixed elaborate literariness with throwaway pun: 'No Shoe Strings on Louise', 'First Episode at Hienton', 'Sixty Years On', 'Take Me to the Pilot'. Again, the only sexual tone was blushing chivalry, in 'I Need You to Turn To', and 'Your Song'. Again, the style was utterly eclectic, glancing off Shakespeare and Mary Renault in 'The King Must Die', colliding with Dixie gospel in 'Border Song', punching up every and any musical influence, from Chopin études learned ten years previously to the latest Friday night stop-press import at Musicland.

The difference was all in the recording: the depth and perspective lent by Paul Buckmaster's chamber music arrangements, the masterly blending by Gus Dudgeon of poetic introspection with acid-edged rock, the constant, artful switch of moods from the manic to the sensitive, from regicidal rabble-rousing to bashfully tongue-tied charm. The difference, above all, was in the voice, performing with a new energy and confidence down all the pinball zigzag of its emotion. By the time the last switch was thrown, Elton had delivered his first virtuoso performance.

Though Dudgeon and Steve Brown knew they had something very special, the great fear was that Dick James – faced with a bill now nearer £10,000 – would simply shake his bald head in bafflement. But James also was instantly captivated. Sue Ayton remembers the day the full album was first played, from one DJM executive suite to the other. 'Everyone said how brilliant it was. No one could talk about anything else.'

For Elton, it meant an immediate change of role. No longer was he just the kid who had monopolised the demo studio and camped out in reception. Every door was open to him, every executive sofa his to command as the inspired mosaic was reviewed again and again. From Dick James came a new tone of respect as he declared the album was 'out of the area of experimentation', and 'quite outstanding'. Not only that, he told Elton it 'deserved the distinction of a worthwhile recording agreement'. In March 1970 the 1967 recording agreement was cancelled and a new one took its place, binding Elton to DJM for five years, with an undertaking to make six, instead of the previous four, album sides each year. Instead of 20 per cent of This Record Co.'s receipts from Philips, he would get 40 per cent – that is, 40 per cent of 10 per cent, a sum equivalent to roughly 4 per cent of the record's retail selling-price. In two years, this would be increased to 60 per cent – or 6 per cent of the retail selling-price.

Great time and expense were devoted to a sleeve that would do justice to the album within. David Larkham's front-cover design showed half Elton's face and one outsize spectacle lens emerging from the black of some latter-day Rembrandt. In the same mood of definitive talent classily understated, it bore no title but the small, white-lettered name 'Elton John'. Overleaf, the principal players stood in line – Paul Buckmaster, Bernie Taupin, Gus Dudgeon, Caleb Quaye, Steve Brown, some in wide-brimmed hats, like Wild West outlaws on identity parade. Elton here was just one of the band, slimmer and more bushy-haired than he would ever look again, in cherry-red trousers and rainbow-striped waistcoat.

Pleasant arguments raged back and forth about which of so many different strong and varicoloured tracks should be released as a single in advance of the album. No one at that stage even considered the modest little ballad that began side one with a note of diffident infatuation: 'It's a little bit funny, this feeling inside . . .' The vote was for 'Border Song', a quasi-spiritual, more than somewhat reminiscent of the Edwin Hawkins Singers' 'Oh, Happy Day'.

'Border Song' was released on 20 March. Though it did not reach the charts, enough impact was made to get Elton a booking on BBC TV's *Top of the Pops*. Brotherhood of Man's backup singer made it to his own podium at last, set about by jigging girls in maxiskirts, razor-cut pageboy hair and sateen lace-up boots. Backstage at Television Centre, he finally met Dusty Springfield, his teenage pin-up bouffant and pink taffeta dream. Dusty's enthusiasm for 'Border Song', the star would afterwards say, 'made my year'.

Top of the Pops was recorded a day in advance of its Thursday transmission. 'We all watched it at the office, on Dick's colour television,' Sue Ayton remembers. 'I could see Elton sweating as he saw himself on the screen.'

Dick James was now in a free-spending mood. To promote the album, he engaged DJM's first full-time press and publicity officer, a girl named Helen Walters, who had just quit her job as a schoolteacher in Croydon. With no previous music industry experience, she found herself responsible for organising a lavish press launch on 26 March, at London's most fashionable club, the Revolution. Its climax was James's presentation to Elton of a tape deck for his twenty-third birthday, the day before. A photographer afterwards snapped smiling mogul and side-whiskered protégé in one of the Revolution's Louis XIV-style banquettes, enjoying a cup of tea together.

The *Elton John* album was far more successful than its maker ever realised. In later years, he would remember it as a critical triumph but a chart disappointment that barely scraped into BBC Radio's Top 50 albums. In fact, it reached number 11 in the newly instituted nationwide chart compiled by the British Market Research Bureau. It stayed in the chart for fourteen weeks, through May and June 1970, competing with giants like the Beatles' *Let It Be*, Simon and Garfunkel's *Bridge Over Troubled Water*, Bob Dylan's *Self Portrait*, Paul McCartney's eponymous first solo album, and *Led Zeppelin II*.

The reviews were as good as they could possibly be. The *New Musical Express* called Elton 'a big talent . . . who sounds as if he has lived in Nashville all his life.' On *Melody Maker*'s page of album notices, he received billing above Grand Funk, Blodwyn Pig, Toe Fat and Nirvana, only losing the lead slot to Lord Sutch's Heavy Metal Friends. The reviewer's initials RW belonged to Richard Williams, one of the earliest to recognise Elton's potential. Williams called *Elton John* 'a truly great record', citing 'brilliant production' and 'superbly crafted songs'. He followed this up with a full-page feature interview, detailing Elton's tortuous history from Mills Music to Bluesology, giving thanks for his 'Border Song' appearance as a breath of fresh air on *Top of the Pops*, and quoting his hero-worshipping but articulate enthusiasm for other artists like Van Morrison, Neil Young, the Band, especially 'people like Jagger and [Frank] Zappa, who don't give a—'. The piece was headed IS THIS THE YEAR OF ELTON JOHN?

The album's sale of 10,000 copies was excellent in that market at that time. More important, everyone throughout the tight-knit British music business had now heard of Elton John as a singer, the John–Taupin songwriting partnership, the DJM record label and a new phase in the career of pop's luckiest man.

What was still lacking, however, was the breakthrough to the mass singles market in which Dick James had invested so heavily. A third Elton single on DJM, 'Rock and Roll Madonna', was released in June to capitalise on the first flush of the album's success. Like every other Elton single for the past four years, it vanished without trace. So did an American single, 'From Denver to LA', used – unrecognisably – on the soundtrack of a Michael Winner movie, *The Games*. Cult success though Elton John might be on fashionable stereos, his face was still virtually unknown. In this period he made a further television appearance, playing piano for the American singer Lou Christie on BBC2's *Disco Two* programme. Throughout the number only his back was visible in an embroidered coat, pounding the keys like the manic ghost of some eighteenth-century highwayman.

Dick James's diagnosis was simple. Elton could not expect to work like Bob Dylan or Leonard Cohen, releasing albums every now and then and otherwise remaining shrouded in poetic mystery. He must go on the road and work all-out at acquiring a following that would look for his records in the shops. It was the last thing that Elton, with his caved-in confidence, wanted to do, and he has admitted he fought against it 'tooth and nail. But I suddenly decided it was the only way if the records were going to sell.'

As a live performer, his most pressing short-term need was for a full-time manager. Dick James was doing the job only with reluctance, leaving his day-to-day supervision to Steve Brown, the selfless A & R man. Brown, with his hippy wisdom and subtle powers of persuasion, would have suited Elton to perfection. But he was married, with a baby daughter, and did not want to be constantly off on the road.

Elton himself racked his brains for a candidate among his contacts in the music industry. One person he approached was Don Black, the songwriter who had just won an Oscar for his movie theme, 'Born Free'. Black also was published by Dick James and, in addition, managed the ballad singer Matt Monro. Though a fan of Elton's work, Don Black was too busy with his own songwriting to take on another client. However, he referred Elton to his long-time business partner, Vic Lewis, who – in the industry's endless game of musical chairs – had recently taken charge of Brian Epstein's old agency, NEMS.

Though NEMS and Dick James Music had long ceased their old intimate relationship – and now, indeed, ran competing record labels – Vic Lewis and Dick James remained very old friends. Rather than poach Dick's boy, Vic Lewis agreed that NEMS should take on his agency work, though with one major proviso. If Elton were to go on the road, he could not do it as a soulful solo pianist. He must have his own full-time band.

Dick James agreed to this further investment, although with a sharp eye to thrift and making do. 'Band' is, in fact, far too grand a term. Elton was launched on the road as a trio, backed by drums and bass, doing the instrumental donkey work himself as well as singing. Both his new sidemen were from the pool of musicians awaiting fame or oblivion at 71–75 New Oxford Street. Dee Murray, the bass player, had been in Mirage, on Larry Page's Page One label. Nigel Olsson, the drummer, had been in Plastic Penny, for whom Elton and Bernie had once been hopeful songwriters.

Against their reluctant piano-leader, the two long-haired new-comers provided strong visual counterpoint. Nigel Olsson was elfin and dark, like some clever foreign girl in an Enid Blyton school story. Dee Murray was large, fair and cheery-looking, like the same school's hockey or lacrosse captain. But, makeshift though they might be as a unit, their playing gelled right from the start. 'As soon as we got together, everything felt right,' Dee Murray remembered. 'It was just like magic. Elton was great to play with because he gave you complete freedom. Other people might not like you to improvise – they'd cut you out as soon as you stopped playing right on the beat. Elton would always discuss what you were doing, and might suggest you did it a different way. But he'd never ever try to cramp you.'

It was arranged they should split the concert proceeds, 60 per cent to Elton, 20 per cent each to Nigel and Dee. Dick James also provided a van and a single roadie, Bob Stacey, who had formerly been with the Spencer Davis Group.

The tie-up with Vic Lewis proved fortuitous in another way. NEMS, at the time, had just bought up the business of a rock band agent named Bryan Morrison. As part of the deal, Morrison joined the parent company, bringing with him a young associate with Nordic blond hair, china-blue eyes and almost ludicrous good looks.

It was Ray Williams, whose want ad for Liberty records, two years before, had first brought Elton and Bernie Taupin together.

The thwarting of his plan to sign Elton to his Niraki company had scarcely checked Williams's easy ascent through the London music scene. After a successful term as head of A & R at Liberty, he had gone on to manage Jeff Lynne's band, the Idle Race, precursors of Lynne's subsequent creation, the Electric Light Orchestra.

Ray Williams met up with Dick James and Elton again just at the moment he was on the lookout for an act to manage that would strengthen his rather tenuous standing at NEMS. With his sharp ears and blue eyes he quickly recognised his opportunity. Neither James nor Vic Lewis, in their middle-aged eminence, wanted the bother of being a full-time manager. Elton himself, moreover, still felt grateful to the personable young man who had shown him a first way out of feeling 'lost' with Long John Baldry and Bluesology. As Williams remembers it, Elton came to him with a straightforward entreaty – 'Manage me.'

The initial plan was that Bryan Morrison and Ray Williams should buy out Elton's management contract from DJM. But the price that Dick James set was more than Vic Lewis felt NEMS should pay. 'Vic said "For that money, his gigs would have to average £75,000 a year",' Williams remembers. 'When I said they could do that, everyone else just laughed.'

When no deal could be made through NEMS, Dick James came up with an alternative plan. This was that Williams should manage Elton on behalf of DJM, working in-house for a 50 per cent share of the management commission. The arrangement was incorporated into a new three-year management agreement, dated 11 May, 1970, assigning DJM 20 per cent of Elton's earnings in the entertainment field, excluding songwriting. Ray Williams's share was to be 50 per cent of 90 per cent of that (10 per cent being deducted for the office facilities he would receive). He would draw a salary of £40 per week on account, with £5 per week in advance expenses.

Williams's arrival coincided with Elton's launch, or relaunch, as a reluctant stage performer. The opening gigs were for £50 a night at provincial universities or day jobs at the fag-end of the free festival era. The band travelled round in a single van, much like early Bluesology: Williams, Elton, Nigel, Dee and Bob Stacey the roadie, humping the rather basic equipment that had been financed by Dick James. 'Dick bought them about £1,000-worth of stuff, which I think he got wholesale,' Ray Williams says. 'I had the most terrible job getting him to pay to insure it.'

Only Dee and Nigel had their own equipment. Elton played

whatever piano was available, however beaten-up or hideously out of tune. At one early northern gig, the piano he was supposed to use had both its foot pedals missing.

In performance, the trio's star quality was anything but apparent. Concert audiences by then had grown used to band ensembles numbering anything up to seven or eight. Huge spaces seemed to yawn between Elton at the piano and two sidemen who barely redressed the sense of physical oddity. Elfin Nigel Olsson all but disappeared behind an outsize kit that would eventually expand to thirteen amplified drums. Dee Murray was an amiable but scarcely charismatic figure, picking at his bass with a leisurely index finger and smiling his lacrosse captain's smile.

And, indeed, their first big chance on an international stage ended in total disaster. Vic Lewis at NEMS had booked them as warm-up act on a European tour by Sergio Mendez and his Latin-American orchestra. On opening night in Paris, an all-too-typical French audience booed them off stage. Bernie Taupin – watching in the wings with a bottle of Courvoisier brandy – also remembers bits of hot dog being thrown.

Almost as traumatising in a different way was an appearance in Belgium, at something called the Knokke Festival. This was not, as they had supposed, a pop-music event but a competitive television festival. Elton – whose Belgian following none had suspected – found himself performing in an elaborate set, surrounded by a troupe of dancing girls. To the amazement of its subject, 'Portrait van Elton John' was judged the festival's winning entry.

During these up-and-down weeks between Paris and Halifax, Ray Williams saw Elton's huddled shyness at the keyboard gradually break down, to be replaced by a revived energy and relish for taking on an audience. He also began to show the personal flamboyance that had been virtually buried since Janet Ritchie visited his bedroom at Pinner to try on his new fun fur.

A decisive sartorial moment occurred on a further short European foray when – with the sublime bad taste of old-fashioned pop – Elton and his band posed for publicity pictures against a background of the Berlin Wall. They also visited Sweden, to play at Stockholm University, and a local club. 'Afterwards, the club owner took Elton and me into this boutique,' Williams remembers. 'Elton was just in the denim jacket and jeans he always wore. They showed him an enormous jockey cap, three or four times normal size, blue with white polka dots. When he said he liked it, the club-owner bought it for him. He also liked the look of some men's handbags they had in the shop. Suddenly, there he was, camping it up in his jockey cap, swinging a handbag over his shoulder.

'I was the last one to get on the plane back to London. As I walked out across the tarmac, I could see Elton in one of the plane windows, wearing this stupid great jockey cap. When I went into the cabin, he was sitting there, grinning at me, and everyone else obviously thinking we were a couple of you-know-whats.'

That summer's most prestigious booking was at the Roundhouse, an old north London tram shed, then enjoying its brief season as hippydom's Albert Hall. Elton's trio appeared in one of the regular Roundhouse 'Pop Proms', warming up for the stars of the evening, Tyrannosaurus Rex. Performing for 2,000 promenading longhairs under the soot-black industrial rafters brought another victory over Elton's performing block. 'While he was playing, he accidentally kicked his piano-stool over,' Ray Williams remembers. 'It got a terrific reaction from the audience. So, at the next gig, he kicked it over on purpose.'

As Britain was brought round to Elton John by sweated labour and infinitesimal degrees, America remained steadfast in not wanting to know him.

Of no help at all was the fact that DJM Records had an American licensee, the Bell label in New York. Despite the close bonds implied, American licensee labels were historically reluctant to pick up on talent submitted by their British counterparts. Dick James himself could all too well remember how EMI's American outlet, Capitol, had blithely turned down the first three British hit singles by the Beatles.

Bell, likewise, turned down Elton John's 'Lady Samantha' in January 1969, oblivious of its status as a British 'turntable hit'. Several other New York labels having passed on it, the only course was to put it out on an American DJM label, thereafter it vanished without trace. When *Empty Sky* was released that June, Dick James sent it over to Bell's Larry Uttal, with a personal plea to recognise a unique new talent. But – like Johnny Franz at British Philips – Uttal could see no future in releasing an album by someone who had yet to make a hit single.

The year 1969 was, in any case, a bad time to be sending British music to America. The phenomenal mid-Sixties 'British Invasion' of Beatles, Stones, Herman's Hermits et al., had long since sputtered out. American bands, like Buffalo Springfield, the Flying Burrito Brothers and Creedence Clearwater Revival, now laid decisive claim on the native idioms which British boys had temporarily borrowed. America's most successful British musician was Graham Nash, formerly of the Hollies, now manifestly the junior partner in an amalgam of American group talent, Crosby, Stills, Nash and Young. No less propitious moment could be imagined for a British solo performer, playing so unhip a thing as a piano. *Empty Sky* went the rounds of other East Coast labels, and received a unanimous thumbs-down.

The West Coast record companies were bound to be even more xenophobically fixated on bands of West Coast flavour. None the less DJM's New York representative, Lennie Hodes, thought he had better try. Leaving on a short business trip to Los Angeles that summer, Hodes packed a copy of *Empty Sky* and one of 'Lady Samantha'.

It happened that Roger Greenaway, Elton's fellow DJM songwriter and long-time supporter, was also in New York, preparing to go on to Los Angeles. He and Lennie Hodes travelled on the same flight and checked into the same hotel, the Continental-Hyatt on Sunset Boulevard.

The Hyatt was a rendezvous for music people from home and abroad. Breakfasting together in its coffee shop, Hodes and Greenaway spotted two familiar faces. One was the songwriter Don Black, currently enjoying a US number one with his theme song for the movie *To Sir With Love*. The other was Russ Regan, lately appointed head of Uni Records, a small offshoot of the giant MCA corporation.

'Lennie Hodes told me he'd got this terrific guy that no one in New York wanted to sign,' Russ Regan remembers. 'I said "How much do you want for him?" Lennie said, "Nothing. If you'll distribute him, I'll give him to you." '

Regan agreed to listen to the album and single that everyone on the East Coast had turned down. As Hodes went to fetch them, Don Black added his own warm recommendation of Elton. 'If Don Black likes him,' Regan said, 'that's good enough for me.'

When Lennie Hodes went to Uni Records for Regan's verdict, Roger Greenaway accompanied him. 'Russ Regan played about four tracks of *Empty Sky* as we sat there,' Greenaway remembers. 'Then he said, "I don't think this is for us. It's too introverted." He asked me what I thought of Elton. I said, "Well, I'm biased because I've seen him play live" – which I hadn't actually. I told Russ "This is someone who's going to be really huge and if you don't grab him, you'll be a very unhappy A & R man." '

Regan, it turned out, was far more interested in another DJM act, a new band called Argosy. Lennie Hodes's offer – relayed from

Stephen James in London – was that if Uni Records would take on Elton, they also could have Argosy. For Argosy, a band destined to sink without trace, Russ Regan paid DJM an advance of $10,000. For Elton John, under the quid pro quo arrangement, he paid nothing.

Uni at first would do no more than rerelease 'Lady Samantha' – coupled with Elton's earlier flop, 'It's Me That You Need' – on its Congress label in January 1970. 'Border Song' followed the same cautious route in June, and made similarly little impact save, for some reason, in Memphis, Tennessee.

By then, however, much had changed in America's musical climate. The Beatles' slow motion smash-up had refocused attention on Britain, albeit via bizarre rumours that Paul McCartney was now dead. The Rolling Stones had made their first American tour for four years, its mounting mayhem climaxed by the murder of a spectator at the ghastly Altamont festival. It was clear that no American band could yet claim to surpass either of these phenomena from the country of Dickens and Shakespeare.

In the California brain of Russ Regan, similar mystical changes had taken place. When Regan received *Elton John* – an album better produced, but essentially no different in tone or style from the 'too introverted' *Empty Sky* – his ecstasy rivalled Pilgrim's at the gates of Paradise. 'I just flipped! I couldn't believe my good fortune. I kept saying to myself "How lucky can I get, to be given such a great piece of product!" I called the whole staff of Uni into my office, about thirty people. We put all the phones on hold and I played them the album through. Everybody fell in love with it.'

Regan's overjoyed message of acceptance to Dick James was accompanied by an urgent *cri de coeur*. When Uni released *Elton John*, late that summer, it was imperative that the artist himself be in America to help with promotion. Dick James's largesse, however, did not run to paying Elton's transatlantic air fare merely for the odd press or TV interview. If he were to go – and, indeed, attract the notice required – it must be on the basis of a proper concert tour.

Vic Lewis at NEMS then contacted his American associate, the agent Jerry Perenchio – and the familiar story began again. Perenchio could make no worthwhile concert bookings for an unknown English singer-pianist. Lewis, in exasperation, decided to bypass Perenchio and see what he could do off his own bat. He had previously sent a group named Pentangle to a successful appearance at Los Angeles' famous folk club the Troubadour. Contacting the Troubadour's owner, Doug Weston, he talked Weston into giving

Elton's trio a week-long engagement, opening on 25 August. The clincher was Lewis's promise that, if Doug Weston gave this chance to a British unknown, he would be sure of 'a club full of stars'.

Money was of minor importance against the Troubadour's reputation as a showcase for quality rock talent and a listening-post for the West Coast music industry. Far more important was that Elton's trio would headline over David Ackles, a folk singer who, it happened, was among his and Bernie's chief American influences. For the whole week's engagement, Doug Weston offered only $500. Built into the contract was a booking at Weston's other Troubadour club, in San Francisco, plus an obligation to play return dates at the LA Troubadour over the next two years.

The exciting news filled Elton with something like horror. He had only just ventured back on the road, with a wholly untried band; now they were trying to shoot him off to America. He protested to Dick James that it was 'too early': he should not attempt America until better established in Britain, say in a year or so. Nor could he see how one week at a small folk club could possibly break his album as DJM's American people suggested.

He agreed to go simply because it would be a nice trip, both for him and his indispensable lyricist, to the very seat of the culture both had worshipped since early boyhood. If the performer baulked, the pop fan and inveterate record-buyer was eager. 'We thought we might as well go over,' Bernie Taupin says, 'just to check out the record shops.'

Elton's doubts and forebodings persisted, however, to such a degree that the Elton John Trio almost did not keep its appointment with destiny at the Troubadour. And he himself was only prevented in the nick of time from consigning himself to the same outer darkness as Reggie Dwight in Bluesology.

Playing the Speakeasy club with Dee and Nigel one night, he was approached by Jeff Beck, formerly of the Yardbirds, now Britain's most famous guitarist after Eric Clapton. Beck was so impressed with the trio, he asked to sit in at one of the rehearsals they were currently holding at Hampstead Town Hall. After a session miraculously enhanced by Jeff Beck wizardry, he offered to join up with them permanently.

For a heady time, it seemed that the Elton John Trio had struck paydirt. Beck had a large following in America as well as in Britain, and would ensure them far better things over there than gigs at West Hollywood folk clubs for rates below the Musicians' Union minimum. Indeed, Beck's first advice was that they should immediately cancel the Troubadour engagement. He also wanted to bring in a 'name' drummer, Cozy Powell, to replace the elfin Nigel Olsson.

Elton was all for the plan, even though Beck clearly saw himself as both lead instrumentalist and vocalist. Dick James's efforts to talk him out of it only brought on one of Reggie's Little Moments. 'I heard them having a terrible row about it,' Sue Ayton remembers. Elton was shouting, "I want to do this. I've worked my arse off and got nowhere . . ."'

His enthusiasm waned when Jeff Beck's agent came on the phone and said that Beck would expect 90 per cent of the new group's earnings. The argument was that even Elton's one-third share of 10 per cent would amount to far more than he currently made. If they toured in America, Jeff Beck's name out front might pull in as much as $25,000 per night. Dick James then made a pronouncement that seemed grandiose. 'In six months' time, Elton John will be earning $25,000 a night on his own.'

Another problem now confronted Elton, one that can blight the most hopeful journey (which this one was not). When he opened at the Troubadour on 25 August, what was he to wear? Obviously, his old cords, his home-knitted rainbow waistcoat and badge-bespattered denim Levi suit would not do for Los Angeles. Yet, apart from an outsize jockey cap, blue with white polka dots, he possessed almost nothing else. Right back to the ginger tweed jacket he had worn while singing Ray Charles to Northwood Hills drinkers, clothes had never really been the point.

The only London clothes boutique that attracted him was Mr Freedom's shop at the bottom of Kensington Church Street. Mr Freedom in real life was an ebullient Cockney named Tommy Roberts whose clothes designs reflected both his irrepressible swagger and his own rotund shape. He was outrageous in designing for leisure only, and with blithe disregard for his customers' height, age or silhouette. After the pinched, winklepicker Sixties look, boys and girls alike plunged with relief into Mr Freedom's outsize T-shirts, emblazoned with appliqué Old Masters, his bright red or yellow boiler-suits and his range of roomy though wacky boots and shoes, some embellished with little Mercury wings.

Mr Freedom well remembers Elton's first tentative visit to the Kensington Church Street shop. 'He didn't wear anything way-out then. Just a donkey duffel and a college scarf. I used to have a room where special customers could change, and have a drink if they wanted one. Everyone used to go in there and whip the clothes on and off without worrying. But Elton didn't like taking his trousers down in public. I remember seeing him over in a corner, fumbling.

'He came in one day and said he wanted a few things to take with him to America. I remember I made him a yellow boiler-suit with a grand piano appliquéd on the back. And some white boots with green wings. Just normal-size heels, those first ones had.' Elsewhere he acquired a floppy tweed cap, a hipster belt with two outsize metal Texan stars and a T-shirt inscribed ROCK 'N' ROLL

At the DJM office, much banter went on about the forthcoming trip. Looking at Elton as he helped with mail-outs or photocopying, or put on the kettle in the tea-making cubicle, no one could see a transatlantic conqueror to follow the Beatles, the Stones or Herman's Hermits. Much leg-pulling went on about the fact that he'd started to grow a rock star-ish beard. Sue Ayton told him jokily to watch out for the Plaster Casters, two American groupies so named for their unique method of memorialising rock stars' penises.

Ray Williams, as Elton's personal manager, was put in charge of the trip. Eight in all flew to Los Angeles on TWA, economy class: Elton, Bernie Taupin, Williams, Steve Brown, the musicians Nigel and Dee, the designer David Larkham and the roadie Bob Stacey.

Behind them Elton and Bernie left the tiny room with bunk-beds which they had continued sharing at Sheila Dwight's maisonette in Northwood Hills. Sue Ayton subsequently received a note from Sheila:

'Have only just got in. Was at work when they went. Reg has left the whole place full of flowers.'

Uni Records' publicity consultant, a frenetic man called Norm Winter, had been assigned to bring Elton John to the attention of Los Angeles. Winter is the kind of hyper who will tell you he loathes hype – unless, of course, the product to be hyped really and truly merits it. Elton's album fell as such a precious rarity into Norm Winter's life, causing him to forget all normal instincts towards understatement and decorum. 'I knew it was special as soon as Russ Regan played me some of the tracks. I knew this was something you took your pecker out for, and put it on the table.'

The first taste of Winter's PR style was shown to Elton and his seven companions when they emerged from the arrivals hall at Los Angeles International Airport. Tired and rumpled after the eight-hour economy flight, they had looked forward to sinking into some restful air-conditioned record-company limousines. Instead, Norm Winter proudly showed them to the mode of transport he felt most eye-catchingly suitable for new young music stars from Swinging London. This was a red double-decker bus, filled with rollicksome

Uni staff and hung with banners in the same typeface as the album, saying ELTON JOHN HAS ARRIVED.

The arrival photograph speaks eloquent volumes about Norm Winter's coup. Every English face ranged against it shows what a world-shattering thrill was the concept of being greeted by a London bus. By symbolic accident, Ray Williams seems the centre of the group with his gold hair and sideburns and his air of creativity, arrested in flight. Elton, on the extreme left, in dungarees and glasses, his arms resignedly folded, might be just another supernumerary roadie.

Grinding down the freeway to the City of Angels on hard bench seats, surrounded by reminders of a life Elton and Bernie thought they had left behind – '6 Passengers Standing', 'Used Tickets', 'Press Bell Once to Stop' – could not be called a promising start. And, indeed, things were to get a lot worse before becoming even faintly better.

The bus stopped first at the Troubadour Club, at 9079 Santa Monica Boulevard, and Elton was shown the unspectacular-looking 300-seat space where he would open in two nights' time. Thence to their hotel, the Hyatt, on an unglamorous uphill stretch of Sunset Boulevard. To be well in time for the Troubadour's Tuesday opening night, they had arrived on a weekend. Once Norm Winter's enthusiastic patter had faded and the London bus engaged its noisy gears and pulled away, there was nothing scheduled for approximately the next thirty-six hours.

As team leader, Ray Williams volunteered to get on the phone to see what entertainment he could find. It happened that none of the party had remembered to bring a hair-dryer, essential for the shampooing of apostle-length hippy hair. Williams called an old girlfriend of his named Joanne, to see if she had a hair-dryer. Joanne had gone abroad, but her sister Janice was at home. Janice had a hair-dryer, and volunteered to bring it right over. With her she also brought a girl friend named Maxine Feibelman, at the sight of whom Bernie Taupin's dark eyes immediately kindled.

With Janice and Maxine, Ray Williams hatched a plan for the following, free day. They would all take a trip down to Palm Springs in Janice's car. Six out of seven in the party accepted the idea eagerly. Only one – Elton – said he didn't want to go. 'At the time, I didn't think I was dealing with a star,' Ray Williams says now. 'To me, we were just a group of mates away on a trip together. So I told Elton, "The majority want to go to Palm Springs – see you when we get back". The six of us went off for the whole day in this girl Janice's car. I was getting on very well with Janice, and Bernie was getting on very well with Maxine. We spent the day in Palm Springs, and all got quite pissed.'

When he met up with Elton again that night, Ray Williams saw at once that something was seriously amiss. 'Elton was very very weird. I realised that being left alone all day had put him in some kind of bad mental state. He was sulking – and petrified. I heard later that he'd been on the phone to Dick James in London, and Dick had had to calm him down. The next morning at breakfast he was even worse. He said he wasn't going to play the Troubadour date, and was getting on the first plane home. I basically had a fight with him. I said, "You've got to do it, you can't spend all this money for nothing." He said "I don't give a fuck, I'm going."'

It was one of Reggie's Little Moments in excelsis. It was, indeed, the first of Elton's Little Moments. All Ray Williams's efforts on the spot and Dick James's over the transatlantic phone were needed to mollify the attack of mingled peevishness and terror, and stop him calling a cab for the airport.

Meanwhile Norm Winter, Uni Records' PR man, had been working at fever-pitch. All the main LA record stores displayed posters of Elton and piles of his funereally black-covered album. Every important disc jockey had been primed with free copies and press kits. When the cost outran what Uni were prepared to spend on an unknown British act, Winter approached Elektra Records, whose artist, David Ackles, was second on the bill to Elton. Elektra agreed to pay for half the hype, even though none of it was destined to benefit Ackles.

This latter gambit had to be carefully kept from Elton, himself a long-time fan of David Ackles via Musicland's imports box. While Winter laboured deviously to throw Ackles into the shade, Elton worried because his name appeared in bigger letters than Ackles's on the Troubadour's marquee. He and Bernie Taupin both thought it 'terrible' that idiosyncratic folk talents like Ackles, Tim Buckley and Tom Paxton enjoyed so little status and respect in their own country.

For the Tuesday first night, Norm Winter and Vic Lewis between them had succeeded in giving Doug Weston his 'club full of stars'. Winter had enticed in a galaxy of rock celebrities: singer-songwriters Gordon Lightfoot, Mike Love of the Beach Boys, David Gates of Bread. Supporters from England included the two songwriters who had done so much to promote Elton, Roger Greenaway and Don Black. Working on Vic Lewis's behalf, Black brought along the arranger Quincy Jones, the composer Elmer Bernstein and the conductor Henry Mancini. The greatest coup of all had been to persuade Neil Diamond, then the hottest American pop troubadour – and, by happy chance, also a Uni artist – to introduce Elton onstage. Many of the industry people, press and radio disc jockeys arrived under the mistaken impression that they were to witness a performance by Neil Diamond.

Waiting in the tiny backstage area, Elton was almost incoherent with nerves. As well as the audience of his musical heroes out front, there were reviewers from every important West Coast publication, from underground papers like *Rolling Stone* and the *Los Angeles Free Press* to the stodgy but all-powerful *Los Angeles Times*. Robert Hilburn, the *Times*'s rock writer, had meant to go to the Coconut Grove that night, but Norm Winter had persuaded him instead to give an ear to this obscure import from London.

The moment of walking out before this glittering assembly was awesome. Yet it also was strangely familiar. It had happened nine years before, when the crop-headed schoolboy played his first Friday night at the Northwood Hills Hotel. Then he had looked out at olde oak walls, brown lino and tin ash-trays. Now, it was darkness lit by glass-cupped candle flames. Then he had worn a ginger Harris tweed sports jacket. Now he wore dark glasses, a grimy growth of beard and a T-shirt inscribed ROCK 'N' ROLL. But, just as at George Hill's cavernous pub, there was a yawning pit in front of him. And once again, to the boy nurtured on timidity and caution, the only possible way out was to take the plunge.

Robert Hilburn was not initially impressed when Elton struck up on a nod to his two sidemen. 'He started going through his songs in a somewhat distant, businesslike manner. He looked scared, keeping his eyes on the piano and microphone in front of him.

'I don't remember now what the first song he did that night was. I think it was from the *Elton John* album. But I do remember it had the kind of distinctiveness and personal vision you look for in a new pop act. The really impressive thing was that the strengths of the songs were all different. The songs, for instance, that hit me hardest that night were "Your Song", a gentle tale of romantic affection, "Sixty Years On", a touching look at the loneliness of old age, "Country Comfort", a country-flavoured sentimental song about going home, and "Burn Down the Mission", a raucous, straight-ahead rocker.'

Not everyone was as attentive as Robert Hilburn. This was, after all, a totally unknown British act, and the conventions of West Coast 'cool', besides, forbade overt enthusiasm about anything. The Troubadour audience therefore carried on their usual habit of lingering at the bar, greeting their friends and talking noisily among themselves.

To Elton, it wasn't much better than playing with Bluesology in a Tyneside cabaret club while people marked their bingo cards and ate their chicken-in-the-basket.

Around the third or fourth number, his temper snapped. 'He got really furious,' Don Black remembers. 'He stood up, kicked away his piano-stool and shouted "Right! If you won't listen, perhaps you'll bloody well listen to this." Then he started pounding the piano like Jerry Lee Lewis.'

The Troubadour crowd was taken utterly by surprise. On the evidence of the album-sleeve's shadowy face, they had supposed they were in for a rather serious set from some sombre, introspective British folkie. What they got was totally American – Greenwich Village coffee-house poems of Bob Dylan in the chicano wail of José Feliciano, pounded out in the torn-up keyboard riffs of the 'Killer' at his most recklessly manic. Of all the people Elton surprised that night, none was more astonished than himself. In his temper, he had come upon stores of passion and pazzazz not seen since breaktimes at Pinner County Grammar and nights at Northwood British Legion Hall.

The frosty cool of the Troubadour vanished like mist from a Martini glass. Instead of the usual polite applause, there were cheers, whistles and whoops of welcome back to the glorious disreputable old ghosts of rock 'n' roll. During 'Take Me to the Pilot', the huge silhouette of the soul singer Odetta became visible at the back, frugging for all she was worth. By the finale of Bernie Taupin's new Western epic, 'Burn Down the Mission', Elton was playing down on his knees, just Reggie Dwight, at the very start with the Corvettes.

Britishness broke through only when he had finished his selection from *Empty Sky*, *Elton John* and his imminent new album, *Tumbleweed Connection*, and started a run of Little Richard and Jerry Lee oldies much as he might once have settled down to 'The Old Bull and Bush' or 'Bye Bye Blackbird'. Then the bearded owl gave his audience a smile that was pure Winnie Atwell, and told them they were welcome to join in the choruses if they liked.

Afterwards, so many people wanted to meet him that Norm Winter had to set up an almost royal receiving line. The piano-kicking showman became a fan once more, shaking his heroes' hands with dumb reverence, uncomfortable amid their accolades, wanting far more to talk about great things they had done. Arranger Quincy Jones (the future mentor of Michael Jackson) brought his whole family backstage. 'He seemed to have about 900 children,' the star was to remember. 'I just kept on shaking hands coming through the door.' A rash Uni PR man introduced him to Quincy Jones as 'a genius'. Elton was thrown into an anguish of embarrassment and stormed at the PR man, 'Never do that to me again.'

The next morning brought a flood of congratulatory phone-calls from those who had witnessed Elton's triumph, and those who wished they had. Among the latter was Bill Graham, America's foremost rock promoter, begging to put Elton on at his Fillmore East in New York. Graham offered $5,000, the largest sum that a first-time performer at the Fillmore East would ever have received.

The second night at the Troubadour brought a further influx of stars, not attracted by PR hype this time, but by excited word of mouth. Among them was Leon Russell, rock's prototype singer-pianist, an eerie-looking silver-haired man, as sour and cynical in appearance as his voice sounded on record. 'I didn't see him until the last number,' Elton remembers. 'Thank God I didn't, because at that time I slept and drank Leon Russell. When I saw him, I just stopped. He said "Keep on."

'I lost my voice during the next day, and he invited me up to his house. I thought he was going to tie me to a chair and say, "Listen, motherfucker, this is how you play piano." But he was so nice. He gave me a gargling potion that I continue to use to this day.'

Bernie Taupin went along, too, a star-struck back-seat passenger. 'It was the first time I'd ever seen a rock star's house. It was a huge place, completely empty but for some beds, instruments and stereo. For some reason, all rock stars' houses were exactly the same.'

He and Elton were given a grand tour of LA rock society by Danny Hutton from Three Dog Night, a band that had covered 'Lady Samantha' and 'Your Song' in America. Hutton took them to call on Brian Wilson, their ultimate pop idol, founding genius of the Beach Boys. The man who had hymned the carefree, crew-cut joys of sun and surf was by then a neurotic recluse. 'I'll never forget arriving at Brian Wilson's house,' Bernie Taupin says. 'Danny Hutton rang at this big security gate and said, "I've got Elton John and Bernie Taupin here." Suddenly a voice on the intercom started singing, "I hope you don't mind . . . I hope you don't mind . . ." It was Brian Wilson, singing "Your Song".

'When we got inside, he insisted we had to see his kids, even though it was the early hours of the morning. He took us into a nursery, picked up each of these sleeping children and waved them under our noses. Then he started playing us marvellous tapes he'd made, that had never been released. But as soon as he started playing one, he'd take it off and start playing another. Both of us wanted to scream, "Let's hear all of it!"'

Elton was now, understandably, on top of the world, thrilled to have met Brian Wilson and Leon Russell, additionally excited to hear that, during his appearance at the San Francisco Troubadour, the tenth anniversary convention of the Tamla–Motown label would also be going on up there.

His one discontent, paradoxically, was on behalf of David Ackles, the pensive folk-poet he was nightly blasting off the Troubadour's stage. As a fortune now came within his own grasp, Elton was scandalised to hear that Ackles's whole year's income could be as little as $5,000. He watched Ackles play each night, an enraptured fan, furious with the audience for talking and fidgeting through the set. Ackles himself was philosophical, buying Elton half a bottle of whisky and saying it had been a pleasure working with him. 'Do you know,' the superstar would say, 'that meant most of all to me.'

He had apparently got over his anger with Ray Williams, pushing Williams into the Hyatt swimming pool to symbolise – as Williams thought – a return to friendly relations. 'I bought him a kimono,' Williams remembers. 'As far as I was concerned, everything was back to normal between us.'

In his punctilious way, Elton sent postcards to everyone at home, including the DJM office staff. '. . . Have not encountered any Plaster Casters yet . . .' he wrote to Sue Ayton. 'Having a great time . . . seem to be going down really well so far . . . Love, Reg.'

To lift his spirits further there was the discovery of Tower Records, a store many times larger than London's largest, the HMV shop in Oxford Street. More exciting even than his Troubadour début was that first journey with a supermarket trolley through aisle after aisle of albums that would not be at Musicland for weeks yet. A friend in London remembers an excited phone call, totally unconnected with having become the toast of LA. 'Hey,' Elton's voice said, in almost hushed reverence, 'I've just got Neil Young's new one, *After the Goldrush.*'

There was also a trip to Disneyland, arranged by Uni Records, a fleet of limos mercifully replacing the London bus. 'We were VIPs by this time,' Ray Williams says. 'They virtually gave us the key to Disneyland. We were loaded with souvenirs, ushered to the front of every line.'

That moment, posing in paper Mickey Mouse ears under the perma-pressed spires of Snow White's Castle, Reggie Dwight was finally laid to rest and Elton John was born. Marvellous, the feel and scent of this land without horizons or nosy neighbours, where good taste did not exist, jumbo and outsize were normal scale and a bit of outrage was everyone's God-given right. He wore the ears onstage that night, together with a pair of baggy shorts, and went down even better. He had broken Squadron Leader Dwight's dress-code for good and all.

On Thursday 27 August – by the grace of Norm Winter's persuasive tongue and a fortuitously less enticing attraction at the Coconut Grove – Robert Hilburn's rock column in the *Los Angeles Times* was devoted to Elton's Troubadour opening. The headline was ELTON JOHN NEW ROCK TALENT. The opening sentence was a single word: 'Rejoice.'

Rock music, which has been going through a rather uneventful period recently, has a new star. He's Elton John, a 23-year-old Englishman, whose debut Tuesday night at the Troubadour was, in almost every way, magnificent.

. . . His music is so staggeringly original that it is obvious he is not merely operating within a given field (such as country or blues or rock) but, like Randy Newman and Laura Nyro among others, creating his own field . . . He has, to be sure, borrowed from country, rock, blues, folk and other influences, but he has mixed them in his own way. The resulting songs are so varied in texture that his work defies classification . . .

While his voice most often resembles José Feliciano, there are at times touches of Leon Russell and Mick Jagger . . .

John's songs are co-written by lyricist Bernie Taupin, whose lyrics often capture the same timeless, objective spirit of the Band's Robbie Robertson . . .

Beyond his vocals, melodies and arrangements there is a certain sense of the absurd . . . that is reminiscent of the American rock stars of the mid-1950s . . .

By the end of the evening, there was no question about John's talent and potential. Tuesday night at The Troubadour was just the beginning. He's going to be one of rock's biggest and most important stars.

There were similar eulogies in the *LA Free Press* ('a marvelous and very resourceful songwriter-performer'), the *Chicago Sun-Times* ('a major star before the end of his first set'), the *San Francisco Chronicle* ('interesting, offbeat and sympathetic to life'), and the *Hollywood Reporter* ('spectacularly exciting'). A local FM radio station, KPPC, took out a full-page press advertisement, thanking Elton for coming to America. But Robert Hilburn's piece eclipsed all. For its message was one irresistible to that tawdry town throughout fifty years of movie-making, the same message even now that the Sunset

Boulevard billboards showed Janet Gaynor and Judy Garland no longer, but Diana Ross and the Jackson Five. The one idea guaranteed to wake up Hollywood from its romantic heart to its greedy head – a star is born.

Elton was 'broken' on the West Coast – and much more. By the strange magic that transmits any novelty coast-to-coast at a thousand miles an hour, all America seemed to know that the Seventies had a new rock star. Within only two weeks of his Troubadour opening, the *Elton John* album had sold 30,000 copies. In Philadelphia in a single day – to quote Russ Regan's ecstatic argot – 'six thousand units were popped loose'.

What had begun as a low-budget flying visit had become a fully fledged tour, going on from the San Francisco Troubadour to additional concert dates in Boston, the Electric Factory in Philadelphia, and a press reception in New York at the Playboy Club. Dick James was contacted in London, and agreed to put up more travelling money.

In Los Angeles, every FM rock station up and down the Strip now played tag with *Empty Sky* and *Elton John*. It is Roger Greenaway's memory of driving to the airport to catch his London plane: the sun, the smog, the scabby palms; a disc jockey's awe-struck voice, saying 'The New Messiah is here.'

II

LORD CHOC ICE

SIX

'Dylan digs Elton'

A FEW weeks after the New Messiah's return to London, he was to be seen in concert at the Royal Albert Hall. The recent headliner in San Francisco and Boston now appeared merely as warm-up act for a folk-rock band named Fotheringay. On opening night Sue Ayton arrived by taxi, bringing Sheila Dwight and Derf Farebrother. They found the New Messiah waiting for them at the Albert Hall's main entrance, unnoticed by anyone in the crowd.

Such was the anticlimactic bump with which Elton returned to his native land in September 1970. In America, he was the biggest thing with a British accent since the Beatles had conquered the continent in 1964. But back in Britain, he reverted to being just another semi-famous pop name among many. When the Beatles had returned home in 1964, they had been greeted by cheering crowds, orgies of celebration in the media and, ultimately, an MBE each for enhancing national prestige and aiding the export drive. Six years later, Britain exported long-haired musicians with as little emotion as safety pins or soap. The pop industry's routine hyperbole had all but exhausted belief in genuine success or achievement. None but a tiny handful of people around the British music scene realised just what Elton had pulled off.

The few scanty press reports of his American triumph were confined to music papers. ELTON STORMS THE STATES, *Melody Maker* announced, though deeming Richard Williams's story of sufficient interest only for an inside page. To Williams, Elton gave a typically modest, humble and grateful account of the LA expedition, paying tribute to Dick James for the finance, and confessing to near paralytic stage fright at the Troubadour, especially when Leon Russell appeared in the audience.

The effect was of a level head, totally unturned by all the West Coast hype and adulation. 'Of course, some of the reviews have been ridiculous. But I know how good I am and what I'm capable of. You simply can't sit back and believe everything people say about you, or you'd get terrible ego problems. I do believe that we write good songs, but I get very embarrassed when people say so.' He added that among his American souvenirs was a gold lamé tail coat, which he planned to wear onstage at the Albert Hall. 'It's from a Thirties Busby Berkeley musical,' he told Richard Williams, adding cryptically, 'I may sew some sausages on it.'

In fact, as he admitted to another journalist, coming back down to earth in Britain, after that wild three-week American roller-coaster ride, had left him feeling 'depressed and shattered'. He also worried that the rave reviews had often overlooked Bernie Taupin's contribution to the music. Bernie, however, was more than happy with the trip. He had fallen in love with Maxine Feibelman, the girl with whom he'd spent an idyllic hot afternoon in Palm Springs. Elton too, as it happened, had 'met someone'. But this could not be admitted for a long time yet.

So, for the present, life resumed a humdrum course, barely enlivened by the release of *Tumbleweed Connection*, his third album, completed the previous August. For this he had still been drawing on the cache of material written at Frome Court, though, fortuitously, the feel was quite different from the *Elton John* album's torchlit paganism. As its title suggests, *Tumbleweed Connection* celebrated Bernie Taupin's childhood love of the American West. Almost all the tracks had a cowboy or Mexican border feel: 'Country Comfort', 'Ballad of a Well-Known Gun', 'My Father's Gun', 'Burn Down the Mission'. The lyrics teemed with references to trains, riverboats, hellfire preachers and rocking chairs, mixed with memories from Bernie's own far frontier in Lincolnshire – the cow sheds, cornfields, squirrels and nightjars; the Angel Tree where he would sit and daydream; even his farmer father, 'the herdsman with his torch'. The mood throughout was folksy and down-home, punctuated with yodels and rebel yells, culminating in Elton's bravura honky-tonk finale to 'Burn Down the Mission' which had already knocked them dead at the LA Troubadour.

Only two tracks were not narratives cribbed straight out of *Buffalo Bill's Annual*. 'Amoreena' was an idyll touched with the spirit of a Renoir cornfield. 'Love Song' – a cover version of Lesley Duncan's ballad – charmed with its gentle persuasiveness, and words that might seem to have been prophetic:

Love is the opening door.
Love is what we came here for.

David Larkham's sepia album sleeve showed what an unreal world America had still been to both composers when the songs were recorded. Elton, in Lenin cap, floral shirt and cowboy boots, sat with his back to the wall on a Victorian station platform covered with enamel signs for Sunlight soap and Mazawattee tea. The shot continued overleaf, Bernie Taupin lounging near a sign for Swan Vesta matches, like some anonymous foot soldier photographed after Gettysburg. Inside was a twelve-page booklet with the lyrics expensively printed amid mock-Victorian woodcuts and cameos. There was also a dedication: 'With love to David' [Ackles].

Tumbleweed Connection was released on 30 October. Despite excellent reviews and steady sales, it made no immediate showing in the UK album charts. Elton was reluctant to put out any of the tracks as a single, and Dick and Stephen James agreed with him that none was 'commercial' enough. Workaholic as ever, he plunged into a fresh project, recording a soundtrack album for a movie, *Friends*, directed by Lewis Gilbert.

In lifestyle Elton remained as unassuming as before conquering America. New Messiah or not, he continued living at home with his mum in Northwood Hills, sharing the tiny bedsit with Bernie Taupin, hanging his hippy chains neatly over the rail of their little-boy bunk beds last thing every night. The only difference was that now Sheila Dwight's telephone rang at crazy early-morning hours with calls from Maxine Feibelman, Bernie's new Californian love.

To the public at large, Elton John still represented upmarket, even esoteric pop, the kind heard late at night on BBC Radio One, announced in the dour Liverpudlian voice of John Peel. 'Now here's another incredibly wonderful track from *Tumbleweed Connection* . . .' Gratifying though it might be to have the track played all through without interruption, it was not the way to mass sales. The way to mass sales was to be on Tony Blackburn's early-morning show, competing with cheeky boy puns and the electronic woof-woofs of Arnold, the dog.

Only a small band of initiates yet could confirm Richard Williams's assertion that 'despite the sombre quality in his recorded work, Elton is nothing if not a raver onstage.' They included the audiences who went to see Fotheringay at the Royal Albert Hall, ready for an evening of whimsical folk-rock songs about dragons, fairies and witches' spells. The opening act, in his gold Busby Berkeley tail coat,

stole the show every night. 'He was determined about that,' Sue
Ayton remembers. 'He was going to blow Fotheringay off the stage.'

In America, meanwhile, waves of excitement and interest continued to swirl around in his wake. The combined effect of four
minuscule dates and Robert Hilburn's review was to propel the *Elton
John* album to fourth position in *Billboard* magazine's chart. When
Tumbleweed Connection was released, it too went into the *Billboard*
chart, eventually reaching number five. Everyone in the music
business, East and West Coast, was talking about this bespectacled
Great White Hope for the Seventies who had come, briefly shone
his light, then departed again, still on TWA economy class.

Clearly, it was imperative for Vic Lewis, his British agent, to send
him back on a full-scale tour as quickly as possible. The complication
was Doug Weston of the Troubadour, who, in return for Elton's
matchless exposure at his club, had obliged Ray Williams to sign a
contract stipulating two further appearances, at the same knockdown
fee. 'In the end, we had to give Weston $100,000 to buy the contract
out,' Vic Lewis says. 'Dick James and I paid it between us.'

This left Lewis and his US counterpart, Jerry Perenchio, free to
set up a coast-to-coast itinerary for Elton, from mid-November to
early December. For the major dates, he would open for his great
idol, Leon Russell. The climax was the two-night booking in New
York at Bill Graham's Fillmore East. Graham, typically, had no doubt
where the future lay. At the Fillmore, Elton's and Russell's names
were to be displayed with equal prominence.

The moment was well caught in a *New Musical Express* headline,
ELTON JOHN, SHY EXTROVERT. The writer, Gillian Saitch, happened
to be with Elton when the Fillmore East news came in, and so
witnessed his mixture of excitement and anguish even to be mentioned in the same breath as Leon Russell. To Gill Saitch, he came
over as sensible, courteous, straightforward, in every way a blessed
relief from the mumbling poseurs who were a pop interviewer's usual
material. 'I get embarrassed by all the publicity,' he admitted. 'It's
very flattering, but it can do more harm than good, because the kids
who listen to music these days want to form their own opinion and
not be hyped into liking something.'

As usual he talked of other people as much as of himself: Leon
Russell, Quincy Jones, Graham Nash, and his latest pop fan enthusi-
asms, Joni Mitchell and James Taylor. Remembering what had
happened in America, he took special pains to emphasise Bernie
Taupin's vital role in the composition process. 'Without Bernie,
there'd be no songs. I get very annoyed when people ignore him.'

'Interviewing Elton John must be one of the most relaxing

occupations around,' wrote Gillian Saitch. 'Although quiet and retiring in some ways, once he starts talking he makes you feel how dedicated he is to his music, and he has very definite ideas about how things should be done.'

The same serious, low-key feel came from his first major performance on British television. This was a thirty-minute *In Concert* programme on BBC2, recorded the previous May but not transmitted until the end of October, just after Elton had left for the States again.

Apart from *Top of the Pops*, BBC TV in those days allowed pop music only if it could be given the guise of a serious, subclassical form. Elton's *In Concert* therefore was subtitled 'The Songs of Elton John and Bernie Taupin', as if part of some ongoing musico-anthropological study. Compounding the sense of upmarket exotica, it went out at the almost inconceivably late hour of 10.30 pm.

Seen now, the programme is a little classic of 1970 earnestness. The title appears in fairground carousel letters of psychedelic red, to the opening chords of 'Your Song'. The letters enlarge and simultaneously grow transparent, revealing Elton at a grand piano with a full string orchestra conducted by Paul Buckmaster. Watching in the round are sixty-odd teenagers handpicked for their fashionable but sensible and mature BBC2 look: girls with madonna-length hair and microskirts, and Indian-smocked, side-whiskered boys. Here and there, over the hirsute young heads and the balding ones of the middle-aged orchestra, hang long Oriental-looking mobiles of tinkly white.

Four months as this was before his Troubadour triumph, Elton gives off few signals of either showman or star. His knitted rainbow waistcoat, salmon-pink T-shirt and pale blue jeans are getting perilously close to shabbiness. Near-blond hair is combed down close as a helmet around squared granny specs. Only the stubby hands have changed, being now covered with chunky silver rings.

With the confident, impassioned singing comes a bare minimum of talk. His main concern seems to get through everything in the time allotted: 'Border Song', 'Sixty Years On', 'Take Me to the Pilot', 'The Greatest Discovery', 'I Need You to Turn To'. To the sedate applause his response is a brief 'Thank you', a gap-toothed grin and 'This next one's called . . .' In frequent arty cutaways we see Paul Buckmaster, like an elegant dervish, playing cello; the sheet music of the violinists; the hands of a lady harpist; the tuba-player's bulb-inflated cheeks; the solemn young audience listening with no movement but occasional flicks of hair from their faces; the ivory-white mobiles winking and shimmering overhead.

The longest pause between songs is for Elton to introduce Bernie

Taupin, sitting in the audience; a shy Cherokee face and a fawn T-shirt. 'He's my partner ... Actually he's more important than me because he writes the words. This next one, I think, is the finest lyric he's ever written ...'

On the clapperboard where a recorded TV show's production details are chalked, 'The Songs of Elton John and Bernie Taupin' was classified for BBC archives as 'Folk'.

The Los Angeles trip had done permanent damage between Elton and Ray Williams, his personal manager. It was all the fault of that unfortunate initial free day, when Williams had taken Bernie and the band for a trip to Palm Springs with two girls, leaving Elton alone at the hotel.

Like many good-looking people, Ray Williams was somewhat lacking in imagination. He assumed Elton would treat the episode as just one of those things that happen when you're abroad with a group of mates. He did not realise that, in Elton's new but fast-developing concept of affairs, he was now no longer a mate, but a functionary. Still less did he realise that, to Elton, that day alone on Sunset Boulevard was rejection and abandonment akin to being tied with a label and put on a cattle train across Siberia.

Back in London, the Palm Springs episode continued to reverberate. Dick James made no secret of his view that, by going AWOL and stirring up Elton at that crucial moment, Williams could easily have ruined the whole American trip. In the political circles that now existed around Elton himself, opinion began to run against the blond-haired Adonis. It began to be whispered that in other management matters, too, he had been less than brilliant, lackadaisical in the organisation of Elton's gigs, and too reliant on the power of his looks and easy-going charm.

On the other hand, his vast importance to Elton and Bernie couldn't be denied. Not only had he found them both, with his want ad at Liberty Records, and put them together as songwriters, he also had brought them to Dick James Music, via his publishing company, Niraki.

At first the problem seemed amiably resolved. After their return from Los Angeles in September, Elton told Williams over lunch that he thought the management arrangement 'wasn't working'. 'I totally agreed with him,' Williams says. 'I could see the kind of manager he needed, and it wasn't someone like me. What he needed was the person who eventually did wind up managing him. Another thing was that, with his success, he was starting to get away with murder. He was very quick, very witty, very funny, and people just let him do anything he liked. I'd been standing up to him and that hadn't been going down well. It was also the time he was starting to find himself sexually. I found that another pressure on our relationship.'

According to Ray Williams, Elton and he agreed informally to sever their association at the end of Williams's current one-year contract with DJM, in May 1971. The share of the management commission Dick James was contracted to pay him – 50 per cent of 90 per cent – would be substantial recompense. 'There was the tour coming up, and another one in spring-summer of '71. There were going to be albums, live concerts ... I was looking at a lot of money.'

In mid-November, Elton and the band left for America again. Shortly afterwards, Ray Williams was summoned to Dick James's office. 'Dick just said "I'm tearing up your agreement. You can sue me. Or you can accept £500 settlement." I was totally amazed. I said "I've got an arrangement with Elton, which, after all, has only got about six months more to run." Dick said, "I don't care. I'm tearing it up."'

Williams's first reaction was to try to contact Elton on the road in America. 'As far as I was concerned, we were still friends. He was godfather to my daughter, Amoreena. But now when I called him up, I could never get through to him. Each time, Steve Brown or some other member of the organisation answered the phone and said Elton wasn't available. To this day, I don't know if he ever knew what was going on.'

There was very little else that Ray Williams could do. Despite the grandeur of his 'personal manager' title, he was no more than a salaried employee at DJM, not even privy to the various contracts between Elton and Dick James. His finances entirely dependent on the commission to come, he was living from hand to mouth with a wife and five-month-old baby. He approached a couple of lawyers, hoping one might take his case on the American system of a share in the proceeds, but none would. Meanwhile, his weekly retainer from DJM was stopped. He fell behind with the rent on his Islington house, and was even running out of money to buy food. 'It may sound dramatic now, but that's the way things were.'

In a series of meetings with Dick James the compensation offer was laboriously winched up from £500 to £750, and finally to £1,500. 'Dick was quite vicious about it,' Williams says. 'All the time he was saying, "You can sue if you want", knowing full well that I couldn't.'

Williams saw he had no alternative but to accept £1,500. For that, the contract he had in no way breached was torn up and his unspecified thousands in commission melted away. He also had to agree to the deduction of what he had already received in weekly salary. This meant his payoff finally boiled down to around £1,100. 'At least it was enough to pay my back rent and put some food in the fridge. I wasn't even allowed to take my files out of DJM.'

True to past form, Ray Williams landed on his feet. Shortly afterwards, he formed a partnership with the Kinks' manager, Robert Wace. They discovered a Scots band named Stealer's Wheel, destined to enjoy major chart success in the mid-Seventies and to spin off a solo singer-songwriter talent in Gerry Rafferty.

Today, his blond good looks intact, Williams has a successful company handling soundtrack music for major films like *The Last Emperor*. He does not brood too much over business manoeuvres twenty years ago which bumped him out of a multimillion-pound property, not once but twice. It is only now and again – when Dick James is described in his hearing as the straightest man who ever walked Tin Pan Alley – that a sardonic grin appears on Ray Williams's handsome face.

The new Elton, for the present, was just a wild rumour, wafted home from 5,000 miles away. 'I remember when these pictures started to arrive of him on tour in the States,' Sue Ayton says. 'Everyone back in the office said "What on earth's going on?" But Steve Brown said, "No, it's great. This is the way it's going to be."'

There was, for instance, the picture of Elton clad in striped drawers and ankle socks, to set off his winged Mr Freedom boots, caught in an onstage paroxysm with mouth agape, fists clenched against his sides, sturdy knees turned in, for all the world like some fractious small boy howling because it's bed- or bath-time. The shot was by a young *Rolling Stone* photographer named Annie Leibovitz, who would afterwards build a great career from persuading rock stars to adopt unlikely or unflattering poses. With this one, she had no trouble from the start.

The Elton that burst forth on this second American tour began as a purely defensive measure. He knew that, in all outward manifestations of a 1970 rock star, he was totally deficient. He had no girlish physique, no spindly legs and tiny behind, no long, pale face or long, lank hair to toss to and fro in multi-spotlit ecstasy. He knew he was short and square and squat and all too solid. In Britain, the best way of diverting attention from this was to retreat into shyness and Rembrandt semi-dark. In America – so an infallible instinct prompted – his best disguise was to go all out and over the top, acknowledging and satirising his own shortcomings before anyone else got the chance.

Becoming outrageous was a conscious decision by someone who had been a pro since the age of six. America demanded spectacle; therefore he'd be spectacular in America. Britain preferred seriousness, therefore he'd be serious in Britain. Each time he passed through US Customs and Immigration, Dr Jekyll would turn into Mr Hyde.

This second American visit also began on the West Coast, though in surroundings very different from 300-seat folk clubs in West Hollywood. On 15 November, after a short holiday, Elton opened as top of the bill at the 6,000-seat Santa Monica Civic Auditorium. So great was the ticket demand that four more major concerts had to be scheduled in the Los Angeles area, at San Bernardino, Riverside, Anaheim and UCLA.

It was Santa Monica that saw the new Elton in full flight for the first time. Third on stage after Ry Cooder and Odetta, he appeared in a brown leather top hat, a blue velvet cloak over a jump suit, and high silver boots decorated with stars. His face, now shorn of stubbly beard, sported outsize Afrika Korps-style sunglasses. Pinned to his chest was a Donald Duck badge. At the top of the gusset where his fly should have been was a smiling ceramic face in a miniature bowler hat.

The run of elegiac songs from *Elton John* and *Tumbleweed* was accompanied by slapstick striptease. First the blue velvet cloak went, then the top hat, then the jump suit to reveal a second jump suit beneath. This, too, was soon cast off, Elton popping from its sheath dressed only in a Fillmore West souvenir T-shirt, silver boots and what *Rolling Stone*'s critic incredulously described as 'purple pantyhose'. (They were, indeed, women's tights, worn as a dare from Bernie Taupin's girlfriend Maxine.) In the Jerry Lee Lewis finale, having kicked away his piano-stool, he played standing up, crouching, performing Tiller Girl kicks, even prone under the keyboard, somehow reaching to pound on it with one hand straining crabwise.

Rolling Stone's critic noted the range of grimaces and facial contortions that accompanied all this. 'Sometimes he would stick out his lower lip like Stan Freberg used to do, or grit his teeth or pucker up his face like Alvin Lee. Sometimes he would recoil from the keyboard, his mouth falling open in horror as if his ass had been shot full of lightning.'

At the backstage party, *Rolling Stone*'s reporter, David Felton, noticed the great contrast between Elton onstage and off. 'Compared to the Little Richard–Jerry Lee Lewis acrobatics he went through during "Burn Down the Mission", his demeanour . . . seemed oddly subdued. He was extremely friendly, but seemed shy, almost fragile, rarely even looking at the person he's addressing . . . While scores of writers and industry people consumed tons of champagne and catered goodies, Elton stood off to the side, alone, costumed and silent.'

Despite all the plaudits, he still resolutely refused to consider himself a star. In his own eyes he was just a member of a trio that had miraculously found top form, and somehow kept on hitting it, night after night. 'In all the time Elton, Nigel and I were on our own, I never remember us ever doing a bad concert,' Dee Murray remembered. 'Sure we used to have fun, but there was never that rock thing of being out of your head onstage. The music was always the number one priority.'

Elton made no demand for special accommodation in their hotels or backstage, and was perfectly happy to rough it, if need arose, just as in old touring days with Bluesology. 'I remember, there was a bit of the tour we had to do by road,' Dee Murray said. 'Bob Stacey drove the van with the equipment and I drove the station wagon with Elton and Nigel in it. Once, we had to drive all through the night. But it was still all good fun, a laugh. I think there was only one small row on the whole tour.'

In rest periods, Elton's main interest was adding to his record collection, faithfully detailed in Rolling Stone as '5,000 albums, 2,500 forty-fives, 100 EPs, 60 seventy-eights, 500 eight-track cartridges and 300 cassettes'. His musical knowledge amazed his American interviewers, covering as it did the whole spectrum of pop, country, soul, blues and jazz, even extending back to the barely mentionable eras of Doris Day and Pat Boone. In one typical buying spree in San Francisco, he picked up albums by Albert King, Leon Russell, Gordon Lightfoot and the Flamin' Groovies, plus cassettes by Spirit, John and Beverly Martyn, the Velvet Underground, Santana, Harry Nilsson, Marvin Gaye, David Crosby, the Voices of East Harlem and Seatrain.

On the road, his constant companion was the diary in which in his neat handwriting he recorded each day's events meticulously, the venue he had played, the probable size of the audience and the box-office gross. Driving away from a stadium, bathed in sweat and festooned in towels, he would at once reach for the diary and begin scribbling.

All the time, the plaudits of celebrated music figures continued to rain down. Al Kooper, Bob Dylan's organist and the founder of Blood, Sweat and Tears, described *Elton John* to the *Melody Maker* as 'the perfect record'. When Elton reached Boston, Kooper made a special trip to see him there, and afterward hired a limousine to give Bernie and him a day's sightseeing in Massachusetts.

Still greater accolades waited in New York, where Elton was to play two nights with Leon Russell at the Fillmore East and also do a concert session over WABC radio. Goodwill messages included one from the group of musicians most influential of all to Elton and Bernie in their odyssey through the imports rack at Musicland. It was the Canadian group whose brilliant history, first with Ronnie Hawkins, then with Bob Dylan, glowed through a name of absurd simplicity: the Band. The Band were also in New York, that week, and sent word that they'd like Elton and Bernie to come over to their hotel.

The thought of actually meeting his ultimate heroes, from *Music from Big Pink* and 'Rag Mama Rag', made Bernie Taupin's knees almost buckle with awe. In person, however, the Band were full of the same easy unpretentiousness that made their music the first fully grown-up rock. Especially agreeable was lead guitarist Robbie Robertson, who had taken to the road as a boy even more innocent than Bernie, after his first employer promised, 'You won't make much money, kid. But you'll get more pussy than Frank Sinatra.'

'Robbie was really sweet,' Bernie remembers now. 'He invited us up to his room, and we sat there talking the whole night. He gave us lots of advice in that very sage way he has. He paid me the most tremendous compliment as well. He said he couldn't believe the songs on *Tumbleweed* had been written by someone who'd never been to America or travelled through America.'

The new friends parted in opposite directions, Elton to play the Electric Factory in Philadelphia, the Band to do a concert in upstate New York. But when Elton came off stage in Philadelphia that night, the Band were in his dressing room. To catch his performance, they had put their own show forward a couple of hours and travelled down by charter plane. They asked Elton and Bernie to write a song for their next album, and Elton to record with them at their studio in Woodstock.

On the first night at the Fillmore East, Bernie Taupin felt his knees turn to blancmange again. 'Elton came up to me and said "Taupin, there's someone I want you to meet." I followed him to this booth where Leon Russell was sitting, and Leon said "Bernie Taupin – Bob Dylan".'

It was, indeed, the great poet and recluse of rock, hawk-beaked, bearded and savage-looking as some master of the Spanish Inquisition.

'I can't remember now what I said to him, or what he said to me,' Bernie admits. 'Something about liking one of the songs. I was too overwhelmed. I just couldn't take it in.'

Back in Britain, the music press set up a hearty patriotic cheer. DYLAN DIGS ELTON! screamed *Melody Maker*, in whose purist eyes conquering America was of less significance than impressing the man who wrote 'Subterranean Homesick Blues'. Almost the entire front page was occupied by a picture of Elton, albeit in his last summer's beard and T-shirt, banging a tambourine at the Troubadour. 'Elton, his lyricist Bernie Taupin, bassist Dee Murray and drummer Nigel Olsson are blowing the States apart,' a column in bold type reported. 'His success is such that his manager estimates he will be a dollar millionaire within a year.'

Below were details of his first major British tour, from January to March 1971, playing thirty-eight dates from the south of England to the north of Scotland. Also of a third American tour in April and May, and a fourth – covering fifty-five cities and so guaranteeing his dollar millionaire status – from September through November.

Inside was a telephone interview with Elton, bubbling over with his excitement at meeting the Band and Al Kooper and jamming with Leon Russell at the Fillmore. 'We did a great gig in Philly . . . San Francisco audiences are a little cool at first, like those in London, because they've seen everything, and one night it was like pushing over a brick wall very slowly, but they went in the end. Los Angeles is like home to us, and Philly and Boston are great, too. Every audience is good if you get at them the right way . . .'

Not since the earliest Fab Four days had life on the road sounded so exciting, so wholesome or so much fun.

It wasn't until nearly Christmas that the conqueror returned, and Mr Hyde reverted once more to Dr Jekyll. But a Dr Jekyll whose taste for the loud and flamboyant there was now money enough to gratify. A few months earlier, Elton's idea of a luxurious present to himself had been a leather-upholstered Roberts portable radio. Now – thanks to a cash advance from Dick James – it was an Aston Martin sports car, sprayed pale mauve. He had bidden farewell for ever to the Metropolitan Line.

The DJM office staff, who had cheered him across America, at first found him little changed. He was as thoughtful as ever about bringing home little gifts; as punctiliously grateful as ever to people for doing things for him while he was away. Especially Sue Ayton, who had kept in touch with his mother and carried out other small personal commissions like sending a birthday greetings telegram to 'a bloke named John Reid'.

'We only really understood what had happened to him when it came to the office Christmas party,' Sue Ayton says. 'The previous year, he and Bernie had been the first to arrive. But this year he came late and made a big entrance in a long coat with a fur collar, looking like Greta Garbo.'

Dollar millionaire as he soon would be, Elton's lifestyle clearly had to change. And with that material change – though none realised it yet – came the profoundest of emotional ones. The brotherly love affair between Bernie Taupin and him had reached a natural, amicable end. Bernie was head-over-heels in love with Maxine Feibelman, the California girl he'd met during the Troubadour trip (another debt owed to the luckless Ray Williams). Maxine had joined him on the second tour and afterwards followed him back to London. Bernie had no further use for the lower bunk in that tidy little bedsit at 30a Frome Court. There was not – and never would be – any diminution in their mutual affection and regard. But town mouse and country mouse were now embarked on very different voyages of discovery.

The task of finding Elton a flat in central London devolved on Sue Ayton. She came up with 384 The Water Garden, a brand-new apartment block just off Edgware Road, with a central court full of tropical palms. The property belonged to the Church Commissioners, who required that prospective residents be interviewed by their estate agent, Chestertons.

A dubious Elton went for the interview, accompanied by Geoffrey Ellis, the immaculate lawyer from DJM. 'We were seen by a very snotty young estate agent, who clearly couldn't believe Elton had the money to buy the place,' Ellis remembers. 'Poor Elton went away very much with his tail between his legs. But then Dick James contacted his solicitor, who knew someone at Chestertons, and the deal went through that way.'

An early visitor to the new flat was *New Musical Express*'s reporter, Gillian Saitch. Elton talked to her euphorically of his imminent British and European tour, the 'tightness and funkiness' of his band, the show they had played on WABC radio in New York. 'We had an audience of about a hundred and we got such a buzz, we played for an hour and a half. They stopped the news, commercials, everything . . .'

Gill Saitch also mentioned the brand new pale mauve Aston Martin that stood in the Water Garden's precincts, adding the enigmatic observation that Elton had given his previous car 'to his flatmate'.

Paradoxically, the chief interest of the British record press in Elton was how stupendously well he was doing across the Atlantic. For a British act to break in America before Britain was almost unprecedented, not only in pop music but in any sphere of entertainment. Apart from Charlie Chaplin, there had been the child singer Laurie London with one freak single in 1958. Only a trivia hound like Elton himself now even remembered its name.

The down-at-heel London session musician of January 1970 was, by December 1970, the toast of New York radio, with two American top five albums and an impending gold disc, acknowledging $1 million sales of the *Elton John* album. Any American promoter who wanted to book him had now to be thinking ahead to 1972. In Britain, by contrast, he was merely another prominent new attraction, along with Dave Edmunds, Mungo Jerry, Pickettywitch, Hawkwind and Ashton, Gardner and Dyke. For all the BBC2-ish critical success of his albums, only one had left the faintest mark on the charts. Nor had he yet made the hit single by which, in Britain, pop success was still ultimately judged.

The disparity between abroad and home was underlined by the American and British record press end-of-year popularity polls. In American *Record World* magazine's poll, Elton was named Top Male Vocalist. On the basis of several important US cover versions – notably Aretha Franklin's of 'Border Song' – Elton and Bernie were named Best Composers of 1970 by the New York-based Circle of International Music Critics. Yet in the annual *New Musical Express* popularity poll, Elton was rated only number 14 in the categories for World Male Singer and World Musical Personality, behind obvious giants like Elvis Presley, Cliff Richard, Tom Jones and Paul McCartney, and less obvious ones like Andy Williams and Glen Campbell. Even in the British Vocal Personality section, he was rated only ninth. His solitary win was in the New Disc Singer category, pipping Dave Edmunds, Cat Stevens, Gilbert O'Sullivan and Led Zeppelin's Robert Plant.

What had eluded him in Britain for almost three years happened in America, almost while nobody was looking. As part of the run-up to his second tour, Uni Records unilaterally put out another track from the *Elton John* album. It was 'Your Song', the pensive ballad whose lyric Bernie Taupin had written in fifteen minutes around the breakfast table at 30a Frome Court. Though an integral part of Elton's stage show, and charming to all who heard it, no one at DJM had ever considered it remotely chart material.

'Your Song' was released in America in October 1970 and at first attracted little notice. The impact of Elton's second tour, however, pushed it into the Top 40 in time to be a farewell present on his return to London in mid-December. By January 1971, it was number eight.

Though Elton badly needed to put out a British single – not having done so since the disastrous 'Rock and Roll Madonna' six months earlier – Stephen James still balked at 'Your Song'. For it seemed almost perversely ill-attuned to current taste with its quiet mood, its downcast eyes and tone of tongue-tied bashfulness. Elton has always claimed it was about a rather serious girl with glasses whom Bernie briefly worshipped from afar in Lincolnshire. Bernie himself insists he had no one specific in mind. 'It was just an idea that came to me one morning at Elton's mum's place. I remember writing it in the kitchen, after a plate of bacon and eggs, with Elton in the bath in the next room. The original lyrics have got an egg-stain on them.'

The song had been among a batch of album tracks sent out by Stephen James to the various BBC radio disc jockeys. There was an instant and surprising response from Tony Blackburn, host of Radio One's hugely influential breakfast show. Blackburn said that, if DJM put out 'Your Song' as a single, he would make it his Record of the Week.

The uphill work was in convincing Elton who, with such a stack of failed British singles behind him, still did not believe this could be the one. Dick James prevailed, and 'Your Song' was released in Britain on 8 January. Tony Blackburn kept his word and made it Record of the Week. On 23 January – a year and a day after its recording – it entered the British Top 50. By early February, it was number seven.

The modest little track would turn out to be Elton and Bernie's longest-lived success, their equivalent to the Beatles' 'Yesterday', and one notable exception to a later unwritten rule that other performers did not cover Elton John material. Over the next two decades it would generate some forty-five cover versions by, among others, Andy Williams, the New Seekers, Cilla Black, Lena Horne, Jack Jones, Sacha Distel, Roger Whitaker and even (as if to appease the departed Linda) Buddy Greco.

Few songs have so perfectly suited their moment. After the long era of psychedelic pretentiousness, Bernie Taupin's simple lyric was a breath of fresh air that seemed almost revolutionary. So, indeed, the greatest of all pop revolutionaries considered it. John Lennon later remembered hearing 'Your Song' in New York, where he had

sought refuge from the Beatles' terminal lawsuits and Britain's persecution of Yoko Ono. Lennon was typically open and generous to
the new performer who, in future years, would prove a staunch
friend. 'There was something about his vocals that was an improvement on all the English vocals till then. When I heard it, I thought
"Great! That's the first new thing that's happened since we [the
Beatles] happened."'

Many other people shared this sense that a new musical era was
taking shape at last. No longer clanging guitars, but a quiet piano.
No longer clichés in chorus, but individual, intelligible thoughts. No
longer outsize paper butterflies and Lenin posters on bathroom doors,
but potted palms, Laura Ashley prints and lamps that could be pulled
up and down over kitchen tables of stripped pine.

Albeit by pure coincidence, 'Your Song' ushered in a new pop
musical genre. From then on, the sound of piano keys, a quiet voice
in an empty room, became a recurring feature of both British and
American charts. By the end of 1971, John Lennon had released his
own piano soliloquy, 'Imagine'. The songwriter Carole King had
emerged from Brill Building anonymity with her solo album *Tapestry*.
An Irish Dead End Kid, burdened with the name Gilbert O'Sullivan,
was tinkling a lugubrious ballad called 'Nothing Rhymed'. The age
of Semprini and Winifred Atwell had begun anew.

Another consequence of 'Your Song' was to give Bernie Taupin his
first serious public recognition. It intrigued the music press to discover
that the hits did not spring direct from the head of their vocalist, but
from a separate lyricist with a name almost as unhip as Reg Dwight.
Up until now, the do-it-yourself geniuses of pop had always written
words and music. Not since the days of Lorenz Hart and Ira Gershwin
had there been someone famous for writing lyrics only. And neither
Hart nor Gershwin had ever been taken round by the performers
they supplied, and proudly shown off as '50 per cent of the music'.

Bernie's circumstances had become as different as they possibly
could from study-chum days with Elton at 30a Frome Court. He
was now engaged to Maxine Feibelman, and making plans for their
wedding with all the heady haste of his twenty years.

Maxine was, indeed, a catch: blonde and willowy, with the
warm-voiced cool of the classic 'Valley girl'. Her father was an
inventor, responsible for such scientific breakthroughs as a microphone that worked by 'ear-tones'. Like many a California girl then,
she had a barefoot, earth-mother folksiness that was bound to appeal
to Bernie's romantic nature. An accomplished needlewoman, she was
always on hand to do running repairs on badly stitched rock-'n'-roll

clothes, and conform to the general chauvinistic idea of a 'chick', even though her tongue could occasionally be sharp. Some, indeed, who knew the sensitive Bernie felt vague forebodings on his behalf. 'I remember one day they were looking at some wedding presents together,' an ex-DJM employee says. 'Bernie made some comment and Maxine said "No, dummy!" I thought it was a funny expression to use to someone you were going to marry.'

Thanks to Dick James's largesse, Bernie also now owned a car, though somewhat more modest than a pale-mauve Aston Martin. 'It was a silver Mini, which I loved. The trouble was, I hadn't yet passed my driving test. Maxine used to have to drive me around.'

The interest in Bernie's writing, allied to his Lincolnshire burr and gypsy good looks, had given Dick James a further bright idea. Why not dress him in a dinner jacket and get him onstage reading his poems as an opener to Elton? Though Bernie was too shy – and possessed too much innate taste – for that, he had no objection to trying his hand at recording on his own. Moreover, he had a cache of lyrics which, for one reason or another, had proved unsuitable to become Elton songs. It was agreed he should make an album for DJM, reading his poems with an instrumental accompaniment in the tradition of W. H. Auden, Dylan Thomas and John Betjeman.

No such lofty pretensions are evident in the figure interviewed by *NME*'s Roy Carr in February 1971. The accompanying picture shows Bernie in Levi jacket and sweatshirt, looking less like latter-day Auden than some student thumbing a lift beside the M1. For most of the piece he talks to a not wholly comprehending interviewer about the many books and authors that have inspired him. It could be the first-ever mention in *NME*'s columns of C. S. Lewis, J. R. R. Tolkien and what a printing error unfortunately renders as 'Winnie-the-Poo'.

As Elton has ceaselessly pushed him, so Bernie now springs to Elton's defence against American critics who have taken to condemning the bizarre stage outfits as an unnecessary gimmick. 'What particularly annoys me is that the so-called in-crowd who were continually predicting great things for Elton are knocking him since he became big . . . People say why does he have to do rock 'n' roll and wear all those funny clothes? But that's Reg. He's an eccentric in the nicest possible way.'

Despite the impending poetry album, Bernie tells Roy Carr he has no desire for fame or limelight. He says he lives 'in a fantasy world. I'm not very realistic. I never read papers or listen to the news. To be honest, I can't take politics and violence.'

Bernie and Maxine were married early in 1971, back on his

home territory of Market Rasen, Lincolnshire. Elton was best man, and a large party travelled up from Dick James Music by coach. For their honeymoon, they joined Elton on tour in Hawaii.

Even crossing and recrossing the continent in Elton's baggage train had not exhausted Bernie's infatuation with America. Accompanied by Maxine, he made his own long pilgrimage through the Far West, visiting famous Wild West sites like Dodge City and Tombstone, and Civil War battlefields in the South.

After that, his ambitions were simple. All he wanted to do was take his Californian bride back to live in the Lincolnshire countryside he had so loved as a child, and spend the rest of his life there, reading, writing and imagining.

In those days, Elton's dealings with journalists were all of the very happiest. To a record-company publicist, he was a dream client. Helen Walters, still feeling her way in the job at DJM, never had a moment's difficulty with him. Whatever interview he was asked to do he did, cheerfully and generously. Female writers, like *Disc*'s Penny Valentine and *NME*'s Gillian Saitch, seemed to find him specially *sympathique*. En route to concerts, he would often call for Gill Saitch in his mauve Aston Martin, creating the natural, widespread assumption that they were dating.

The music press now recognised a prize interviewee, articulate and funny as no pop star had been since John Lennon. His air of normality, of health and wholesomeness, was something quite new in a world where the prevailing fashion had always been tubercular skinniness, sickly pallor, sunken cheeks, smoker's coughs and hair hanging in greasy rat's tails. Here was a musician of day rather than night, who didn't mumble cosmic gobbledegook, didn't smoke dope or screw six groupies a night, who got up and went to bed at normal hours, who had wind enough left to turn out on cricket pitches and tennis courts, and whose great passion, after music, was his local football club, Watford.

Throughout early 1971, Elton performed as tirelessly in print as on stages throughout Britain and mainland Europe. *Melody Maker* launched a four-part 'Elton John Story', featuring him in detailed question-and-answer with Richard Williams, tracing his career back to Long John Baldry and Bluesology. *New Musical Express* soon afterwards began its own three-part 'Chat-in With Elton John'.

The music papers took to using him as a commentator on any and every aspect of pop, from new American bands like Bread to Phil Spector's controversial production of the Beatles' farewell album, *Let It Be*. Elton possessed the gift of plain speech without sour grapes, neither mincing his words nor being gratuitously offensive. His background knowledge of the business was frequently more illuminating than any professional reporter's. 'I think [Phil Spector] did a bloody good job for the Beatles, because he made an album out of nothing. If you'd heard the original tapes, you'd know what Spector did for them. The only thing I can really get against him is "The Long and Winding Road", which was beautiful without strings and all the other rubbish.' A typical *NME* foot-of-page trailer reads: NEXT WEEK ELTON TALKS ABOUT ROCK 'N' ROLL, CRITICISM, COPYING, PRESS RECEPTIONS, HYPES, MICK JAGGER.

In *Melody Maker*'s Face-to-Face session Richard Williams asked how he reacted to the critical backlash which now condemned the *Elton John* album as precious and overproduced. Elton replied that a bit of knocking would probably do him good. 'Own up – people are getting sick of reading about Elton John, the Wonder Human Being. I'm a bit cheesed off with it myself . . . Yeah, I've had a ball, but if it all ended tomorrow I could go out and get a job.'

At the same time, there were inklings that the cheery, voluble new star had a less robust, more troubled and vulnerable side. On 23 January, *Melody Maker*'s lead story reported that Elton had 'narrowly missed a nervous breakdown' through starting his British tour too soon after returning from America. With two more American tours in prospect, his doctor had faced him with the stark choice of slowing down or burning himself out. As a result, three British concerts had had to be cancelled, at Southampton, Loughborough and Hull.

It happened at the moment Elton was due to fly to Cannes, to appear in the prestigious MIDEM international music convention. *Melody Maker* reported that he arrived there 'on a diet of vitamin pills'. To make things worse, MIDEM proved a total disaster. Elton, representing Britain, was scheduled to play after Eric Burdon, ex-vocalist with the Animals, representing America with his new band, War. However, Burdon refused to leave the stage after his allotted fourteen minutes, and continued blasting with War for almost an hour and a quarter. Elton was reported to have stormed out of the theatre.

That week's *Melody Maker* loyally took Elton's part, reproaching Eric Burdon for a 'staggering display of selfishness'. Elton himself was ruefully apologetic, as always after one of his Little Moments. 'I've been feeling so rough, and I can only think it's been the strain of all the work . . . We've been travelling too much for any sort of comfort, and last week I felt really rotten. I was exhausted. It's funny, but I never even wanted to go on the road. All I ever wanted to do was make records and maybe produce. Now look at me.'

Dick James's bland communiqué – that Elton had merely been over-excited about receiving his second gold disc, for *Tumbleweed* – underlined the continuing chronic deficiency in his life. He had a music publisher who was the best in Britain, an inspirational song-writing partner and an agent of infinite experience. He had a top-flight record producer, a distinguished arranger, an excellent band. He also now had an accountant and a solicitor. What he did not yet have, and needed more desperately each day, was a manager.

The overpowering sense one gets from these first frenetically famous months is a lack of any firm voice or steady hand on the tiller. Elton is being worked into the ground, flung back and forth around Britain and Europe as a prelude to two more, almost consecutive American tours. His public image became oddly unfo-cused and contradictory as plans were made and bookings accepted with a fine disregard for overall strategy. In March alone, he could be seen at totally opposite ends of the pop-music spectrum. Here he was, one night, back in élitist BBC2 mode, playing the Royal Festival Hall with Paul Buckmaster, a full symphony orchestra and chorus. Here he was another night on BBC1, joining a Las Vegas-style finale with Ray Charles on the *Andy Williams Show*. Here he was, on yet another night, sweating it out in a basement blues club in West Hampstead. Everyone on every side was saying 'Yes' for him. Somebody should have been there, but wasn't, saying 'No' for him.

His career on record was in a similarly overwrought state. By May 1971, two more albums had joined *Tumbleweed* and *Elton John* in the British and American shops. One was the movie soundtrack album *Friends*, whose arrangement had been among Ray Williams's last managerial acts. At the time, Paramount Pictures had turned down the offer of a full Elton album, taking only five John–Taupin compositions to be interspersed with theme music from Lewis Gilbert's unmemorable tale of teenage romance.

Finding *Tumbleweed Connection* in the US chart, however, Para-mount rush-released *Friends* ahead of the movie, in a drab pink sleeve showing boy kissing girl, like the cover of a cheap contact magazine. *Friends* reached only number 36 in the US chart and did not register at all in Britain. The title track did little better as a single, charting only in America at number 34. Paradoxically, the album was to earn Elton another American gold disc, having reached $1 million worth of sales to record outlets. No account was taken of the sale-or-return system, whereby an album that went out gold might come back cardboard. Such an inveterate visitor of record stores as Elton was all too painfully aware how quickly it was remaindered. 'I mean,' he commented wryly afterwards, 'you can go into any record store in the States now and find *Friends* for $1.98 with a hole punched through it.'

Also out was the live album he had made in New York, titled after its performance date, 17 November, 1970. A beady-eyed manager might have talked Elton out of the workaholic insecurity which turned a one-shot session on WABC radio into the follow-up to *Tumbleweed Connection*. The result was another odd mishmash, mixing a new John–Taupin song, 'Can I Put You On', with the Beatles' 'Get Back', the Stones' 'Honky Tonk Women' and Arthur 'Big Boy' Crudup's 'My Baby Left Me'. It made 11 in the *Billboard* chart but, like *Friends*, sank without trace in Britain.

Elton himself realised the absurdity of having four albums simultaneously on sale. 'I was getting more and more unhappy about it,' he recalled later. 'I thought "We've worked so bloody hard to get this far, and now we're blowing it."'

His management agreement was still the three-year one signed in June 1970 when Ray Williams had been drafted in to look after him. On Williams's departure that September, a rider had been added to the agreement, reallocating managerial duties to Dick James, his son Stephen and Steve Brown, the A & R man. But it was an arrangement that could never work satisfactorily. Dick James was far too grand to get involved in the daily minutiae of management work and Stephen was too busy, running This Record Co. Steve Brown was primarily a DJM employee, powerless to make major decisions on his own, and, besides, did not want to leave his wife and daughter too much to accompany Elton on tour.

In addition there were still managerial nibbles of interest from Island Records, via Muff Winwood and Lionel Conway, resulting in yet another pressure on Elton's time and a further odd refraction of his image. Under Conway's aegis, he went into the studio to record a non–Bernie Taupin song called 'Honey Man', in duet with Island's biggest artist, Cat Stevens. But, Island and DJM being unable to agree on a royalty split, the track was never released.

By early 1971, the need was growing desperate for someone to be with Elton around the clock, seven days a week; someone strong enough to protect him from outside pressures and also, on occasion, from himself. Stephen James remembers how, in that disorganised spring, Elton himself came up with yet another candidate. 'He said it was a friend of his named John Reid, who was label manager at Tamla-Motown.

'I went and asked Steve Brown if he knew this John Reid. "Oh yeah," Steve said. "Elton's a big Tamla-Motown fan. He goes over to John's office to hang out, and gets records out of the cupboard."

'"Elton wants him to be his manager," I said. "Do you know anything about it?"

'"Oh yeah," Steve said. "They're living together. John has moved in with Elton at the Water Garden."'

SEVEN

'At least he'll have someone to get him up in the morning'

Before colour entered British men's clothes, their only touch of colour – only touch of class – came from Paisley. For business-men or father at Christmas there was the Paisley tie in muted red or blue silk, printed with that inexplicably traditional pattern of large or small amoebas under a microscope. For sports car types, in gauntlets and Kangol caps, there was the yellow and red Paisley scarf. For men-about-town or would-be Noël Cowards, there was the green and red Paisley dressing-gown.

Few products have so little resembled their place of manufacture. Paisley lies a few miles to the west of Glasgow, in the industrial conurbation that straggles down the Scottish Central Lowlands next to the River Clyde. There is not much fine silk about the drab town with its looming Victorian mills and threadbare streets. Not many clothes-conscious dandies can be found, there or in the council estates that spread outward to merge into the colourless suburban weave of Dumbarton, Renfrew, Rutherglen, Motherwell and East Kilbride.

Aside from its contribution to the male wardrobe, Paisley can point to nothing remarkable. It suffers an identity problem common to all medium-sized towns in the hinterland of a great and notorious city. What Birkenhead, Wallasey and New Brighton are to Liverpool, so Paisley, Renfrew and Motherwell are to Glasgow, now a modish 'City of Culture' but in the mid-Sixties still the most luridly notorious city in the United Kingdom. Glasgow of the great rail terminus and Sauchiehall Street. Glasgow of shipyard cranes along the Clyde, and fiery union demagogues. Glasgow of the Gorbals, where razor gangs reconstituted the clans, under chieftains with names like Red Rory of the Eagles. Glasgow, epitomising all that most worries the lowland Briton about the Scot's impulse to aggressiveness and uncontrollable violence.

★

John Reid became an entrepreneur at the age of eleven. He had the idea of collecting up the old newspapers which neighbours put out for the dustman, and selling them to a local greengrocer as wrappers for vegetables. The scheme turned such a quick profit that he soon could subcontract other children to collect the newspapers for him, paying them a percentage of what the greengrocer paid him. Thus did he simultaneously increase his dividend and remove the need to get his hands dirty.

The story is one of very few Reid would tell about himself in later years, when he ran a business empire worth £40 million and controlled the world's number one rock star. Generally, he has no need to be his own biographer. There are people enough to tell John Reid stories from all over the world, in tones varying from warm affection to bitter hatred, and from amusement to outright terror.

Little of his remarkable future could be prophesied for the boy born in Barshaw Hospital, Paisley, on 9 September, 1949. His father, John senior, was a thread-reeler in one of the mills that gave the town its purpose and the very thoroughfares their names. John and Elizabeth Reid lived at number 1 Thread Street. Betty Reid, née King, whom John had married two years earlier, was a vigorous woman with a temper he had learned to respect. She bore him two sons, Bobby and John, a year younger. John was easily the brighter and better-looking of the two, slight and dark with large liquid eyes and a face whose pointed alertness seemed more Latin than Celt. Take away the acrid Clydeside accent and he could easily have been some little French boy named Georges or Armand.

His modest upbringing contained one exotic interlude. John senior had abandoned mill work to become a welder with Crittle Ltd, a local engineering firm. In 1959, when John junior was ten, Crittle shut down their workshops in Paisley and transferred the whole of their workforce to Auckland, New Zealand. The Reids emigrated under the old neocolonial system, paying a nominal £10 each for a lengthy sea voyage out via the Panama Canal. John and Bobby found themselves in an easy-going land of sunshine and lushness at the furthest possible extreme from Scottish rain and fog.

Then, as now, New Zealand was famous for its Maoris, to be seen most spectacularly performing ceremonial war dances on state visits by the Queen. Who could have guessed that, one far distant day, Maoris would mass to dance in honour of John Reid, or that he would round off the occasion by spending a month in jail?

Despite the charms of New Zealand, Betty Reid became home-sick for Scotland. In 1961 the family returned to Paisley, settling in a

small house in Gallowhill, on the main road between Renfrew and
the Firth of Clyde. John senior became a welder at the Chrysler car
plant in nearby Linwood. Bobby and John junior were enrolled at St
Mirin's Academy, the Catholic grammar school that lay just a couple
of hundred yards from their house.

At St Mirin's John Reid proved a model pupil. Though a year
younger than the other boys of his class, he came consistently near
the top in every academic subject. His demeanour was bright and
co-operative, his blazer of blue and gold always immaculate. Outgo-
ing and personable, he took a leading part in the school's social life,
music, amateur dramatics, 'anything that was going', according to his
former chemistry teacher, John Clews. After school he would return
to his home a little way along Renfrew Road and, shortly afterwards,
be seen out walking the family's large Alsatian dog.

In the fifth form he became a school monitor, responsible for
supervising younger boys in the playground at break. This he did
with a conscientiousness which, to the supervised ones, naturally
seemed more like bossiness and oppressiveness. Among the boys
under his jurisdiction was one named John Harvey. 'He used to
come and try and catch me and my pals when we were in the
smokers' corner,' Harvey remembers. 'He was always nosing after us.
We used to call him Wee Alsatian-Face.'

Though nowhere near the scale of Glasgow, Paisley had its tough
quarters and its gangs. Ferguslie Park (later mentioned in a Gerry
Rafferty song) was one place where the prudent did not venture at
night. Wars went on intermittently between local triads with names
like the Young Disciples and the Gallowhill Team.

John Reid had little − although not nothing − to do with such
things. His adolescence was utterly typical for a working-class Scottish
boy in that Beatle and beat-boom era. With his friends he went to
dances at St Peter's youth club and pop shows at Paisley ice rink. His
main social stamping ground was a coffee bar called the Sherwood
Café. He was popular with the opposite sex and had several girlfriends, though not one particular steady one. As an old schoolfriend,
Charles Palmer, remembers, 'He went through them all.'

In his mid-teens he got a Saturday and holiday job working at a
menswear shop called Stylecraft in Moss Street, Paisley. Stylecraft
specialised in fashionable knitwear and the − for Scotland − slightly
outré Ben Sherman style of button-down poplin shirt. The sharp-
faced, dapper grammar-school boy quickly proved a natural salesman.
John Palmer, the shop's proprietor, remembers him enthusiastically
as 'brilliant'.

Like almost everyone his age, he got involved in amateur pop music, joining various unsuccessful folk groups with his elder brother, Bobby. An entrepreneurial streak revealed itself when he offered to manage two other St Mirin's pupils, a pair of singing brothers named McBride. The relationship brought painful consequences, however, after the McBrides had managed to offend some or other element in Paisley's teenage gangland. One school lunchtime, as John Harvey remembers, a gang member appeared in St Mirin's playground, and began systematically beating up both McBride brothers. When John Reid tried to go to their aid, he too was badly beaten.

'I knew that scene so well from the movies,' Harvey says now. 'The fight in the school playground with everyone ganging round, shouting and cheering. But the chilling thing, when the McBrides and John got beaten up by this heavy, was that it all happened in total silence.'

Reid left St Mirin's in 1966, at the age of sixteen, with an exemplary tally of eight passes in the Scottish General Certificate of Education. His original ambition – fostered by the long sea voyages to and from New Zealand – was to become a marine engineer, and he began a diploma course at Stow Hill engineering college in Glasgow. Show business, however, was starting to claim more and more of his attention. He joined the amateur dramatic company centred on the Glasgow Pantheon Club and appeared in several musicals, once attaining the third lead in *Kiss Me, Kate*. He also spent a brief period as a vocalist with the house band at the Glasgow Locarno ballroom, singing cover versions of current hits like 'There's a Kind of Hush'.

The decisive influence on his career was a Scots friend named David Bell, later to become head of light entertainment at London Weekend Television. In Bell's view, the job in which John Reid could best combine his passion for music with entrepreneurial push would be as song plugger for one of the London music publishers. He therefore abandoned his Glasgow engineering course, moved down to London and 'knocked on a lot of doors', but could find no openings. To tide him over, he got a job in the shirt department of Austin Reed, the Knightsbridge menswear shop. From his department there was a back view across to the pale cream luxury of Montpelier Square, Belgravia. A particular large, elegant town house in the square always caught John Reid's eye, and he vowed to himself that one day he'd own it or one like it . . .

After a few weeks at Austin Reed, his big break came. He was offered a job with Ardmore and Beechwood, a small publishing company owned by the giant EMI record company, based above their HMV record store in Oxford Street. It was with Ardmore and Beechwood that Brian Epstein's luck had finally changed after having the Beatles turned down by every major London label. And for seventeen-year-old John Reid, four years later, they brought a similar transformation of fortune. One week, he was selling shirts in Knightsbridge; the next he was responsible for plugging the catalogue of a new American singer-songwriter called Neil Diamond.

His new employer, EMI, was in those days Britain's largest and most prestigious record company. On its namesake label, or equally famous subsidiaries like Parlophone, it mustered the élite of British recording talent from Cliff Richard to the Beatles. Through an agglomeration of licensing deals with American companies like Capitol, Bell and Motown, it imported such transatlantic moneyspinners as Frank Sinatra, the Four Tops, Stevie Wonder and the Supremes.

Despite its huge success, EMI was an organisation of archaic stuffiness, run on bureaucratic lines close to those of the BBC. At its headquarters in Manchester Square, young producers and promo men were still not allowed to come to work in jeans or have stereo equipment in their offices. Secretaries were forbidden to wear trousers. Employees who arrived after 9 am had their names entered in a penitential 'late book'.

In these surroundings, John Reid rapidly prospered. His short hair, smart suits and Austin Reed salesman's manner gave him an affinity with EMI's middle-aged command structure. At the same time, he worked with ferocious zeal to acquire all possible knowledge and expertise about music publishing, selling, accounting and contracting. It was not long before he came to the attention of Ken East, EMI's managing director. East and his wife Dolly took up the pleasing young man socially.

In 1969, a vacancy occurred for label manager of EMI's hottest American franchise, Tamla-Motown. Berry Gordy's Detroit-based company at the time was on its great winning streak, pumping out hits by Marvin Gaye, the Miracles, the Supremes and the Temptations with the consistency of an auto-factory conveyor-belt. To be Motown's man in London was a plum job for any would-be record executive.

Among the applicants were John Reid and a young man named David Croker, then manager of a progressive London record store, One Stop. Neither Reid nor Croker was given the coveted job. But about a year later it fell vacant again, and this time John Reid got it. He was still only nineteen.

David Croker had then just joined EMI as label manager for the American Bell label. Among the contacts he brought with him from

One Stop was a producer named Gus Dudgeon, an A & R man named Steve Brown and a struggling singer-pianist, still called Reggie Dwight, whose passion for records surpassed even Croker's own.

He recalled Reid's arrival to take over Tamla-Motown, amid some dissension from people who felt that a more experienced person should have got the job. 'I remember a sort of a groan – "Oh, oh, John Reid's coming." A feeling that he'd only got it because of who he knew in the company.'

Managing an American label within EMI was generally a one-person operation. The label manager decided which tracks should be released in Britain, supervised publicity and promotion, and looked after his American artists when they visited London. The comparatively low salary was offset by abundant perks: free records, entertaining expenses, constant parties and receptions, the chance to mingle with the famous and, in that idyllic late Sixties time, virtual freedom from stress, insecurity or fear.

John Reid's job was particularly congenial thanks to Tamla-Motown's current run of enormous British chart hits. Under EMI's bureaucratic paternalism, label managers received points for each successful release, accruing to a cash bonus. An early glimpse of Reid's celebrated ferocity came when it was suggested that he might share his bonus points with his colleagues.

David Croker remembered him as a figure apart from the other label managers, short-haired and dapperly suited, tidy and meticulous, with an air of sophistication unusual for a 19-year-old, especially in that sub-hippy milieu. Whatever rough corners he had brought down from Paisley were now entirely rubbed away. He was socially graceful, knowledgeable about literature and art, a lover of good food and expensive restaurants. Where other young EMI executives did their entertaining at the local pub or trattoria, Reid preferred ultra-smart places like Inigo Jones in Covent Garden.

He possessed a talent for knowing bizarre as well as important people. One of them was Barbara Windsor, the blonde, busty ingénue star of the *Carry On* films. Reid met her while he was still a record-plugger, and impressed her with his 'dark, very French' looks, and the number of times he had attended her stage show, *Come Spy with Me*. 'He kept coming to the theatre to see me,' she recalls in her memoirs. 'Even though young, he had a good head on him. There was nothing he didn't know about show business. I found this young man very exciting.'

He became an escort to Barbara Windsor, in between her highly publicised involvements with tough characters from the East End. They must have made an arresting couple: the sleek Scots teenager and the pneumatic peroxide Cockney sparrow, some two decades his senior. Windsor remembers how he always said he wanted to be a millionaire and drive a Rolls-Royce by the time he was twenty-one.

She was aware at the time of an uncharitable construction which some people put on Reid's interest in her. 'John himself once said to me, "I hope you don't think I'm using you as a stepping-ladder." But that was not the case at all. I never introduced him to anyone or gave him a step up. I just loved him. But there again, John was so loved by his pals that they didn't want him going out with me. There were always little spokes being put into our relationship.'

Throughout this period, Reid knew Elton only vaguely as someone often seen around the EMI corridors or in David Croker's adjacent office. Some of Elton's early compositions with Bernie Taupin had been covered by EMI bands, like the repellently named Toe Fat. He had got to know David Croker via Gus Dudgeon and One Stop records, and Croker had watched some of the sessions for the *Elton John* album. Everyone at EMI knew him, both as an old pro session man and a hopeless record-collecting freak who would come in to cadge new American products from the various label managers. John Reid's first sight of him, so Reid himself would later say, was 'a dumpy little guy in a funny jumpsuit who put his head round the door and asked to borrow some records.' Croker subsequently gave him a white label pressing of *Elton John* but Reid put it aside without even playing it.

In August 1970, a few days before his twenty-first birthday, John Reid was in San Francisco, attending the tenth anniversary celebrations of Motown Records. Elton had just scored his triumph at the Los Angeles Troubadour club, and arrived in San Francisco to play the newly opened second Troubadour there. 'He rang me up,' Reid later recalled. 'He was bubbling over with what the critics had said, and dying to tell someone about it. I was the nearest Englishman – or nearest thing to an Englishman.' It was a day or so later that Sue Ayton in London got a request from Elton to send a birthday telegram to 'a bloke named John Reid'.

To most people, the situation presented nothing out of the ordinary. Thus far in Britain the sexual revolution had been an almost entirely heterosexual one. There was as yet no general notion of a 'closet' and consequent need or pressure to come out of it. London in 1971 was full of paired young men, unexceptionally living in flats together.

For quite a long time, therefore, close friends of both Elton and John Reid – and even friends they began to make in common –

suspected no more than that. Two young bachelors of like mind, if wildly unalike appearance, happened to be sharing a modern apartment near Marble Arch after a metropolitan tradition familiar from Dickens down through Muriel Spark. As well as flatmates they were close companions who increasingly seemed to prefer one another's company to the girlfriends each was presumed to have. In literal-minded 1971, that could still be the beginning and end of it.

Besides which, these particular two bachelors possessed several additional layers of camouflage. John Reid wore a short haircut, a smart suit, a collar and a tie, all in those days definitive emblems of utter normality. And, to add still more concealing foliage and mottled paint, Elton was a pop star. The medium which, more than anything else, had unloosed Britain's heterosexual revolution was also mainly responsible for its general blindness to any alternative. Pop music had seldom been about anything other than boys chasing girls. The essence of the vicarious excitement in any pop star's rise to fame was how many dozens of girls he would now find at his disposal. Even a pop star who looked like Elton John must surely now be enjoying those same conventional delights.

In character the new flatmates were the total opposites that seldom fail to attract. Elton, in his purple and silver rock-'n'-roll drag. John Reid, in his low-key clerical grey. Elton chunky and wispily pale. Reid small and sleekly dark. Elton the soft-hearted and self-effacing. Reid the hard-headed and self-aggrandising. Elton the seasoned veteran. Reid the newcomer and junior who, for all that, possessed immeasurably greater stores of knowledge, cultivation and *savoir-faire*. Someone, in other words, who could be both kid brother and father.

John Reid entered Elton's complex social circle shyly and diplomatically. He was especially chary of Bernie Taupin, the most visible long-standing attachment in Elton's life. Elton, too, was worried lest Bernie should feel any way superseded or slighted, even though their relationship was plainly quite different and separate. 'I think Elton was more concerned than I was about us not being as close as before,' Bernie says now. 'When John would come and meet him, I'd usually get up and disappear, just to leave them alone. And Elton would always say "Oh, you don't have to leave", which I think made John feel that I didn't like him.'

In fact Bernie says he found Reid 'very personable' and did not feel in the least offended by the new arrangement. 'Elton and I had solidified our relationship early on. We knew we were very different in certain areas and that it was impossible to have continued in such close proximity. It was healthier that way, too. Otherwise we'd just have got sick and tired of each other. My basic attitude towards the whole thing was "Good luck."'

For the present, all most people could see was the instant and enormous change in Elton's lifestyle. With John Reid's advent, he seemed to step up an entire social class.

Their flat in the Water Garden was a world away from bedsitter life at 30a Frome Court. With a total redecoration job by Elton's stepfather, Fred Farebrother, and several hundred pounds' worth of contemporary furniture, the place was a model of a modern bachelor pad. Every surface quickly became covered by the ornaments, toys, souvenirs and keepsakes that Elton acquired everywhere he went. On the shagpile living-room rug stood his precious record collection, with his two framed gold discs in pride of place above. From the spotless bathroom came the expensive reek of his favourite after-shave lotion, Aramis.

Gone, too, was his Pinner diet of chips, peas and Instant Whip. Reid was an accomplished and ambitious cook. 'I remember going there for dinner, and John serving poussins,' David Croker said. 'There were six of us, and he brought out three poussins. I was thinking to myself "How on earth am I going to get through half of one of these?" Then he brought out three more. We were expected to eat a whole poussin each. The other thing I remember was that John was one of those people who start doing the washing up before the guests have left.'

Reid established an instant rapport with Elton's family, getting on especially well with the down-to-earth Sheila. She and Fred (alias 'Derf') were frequent visitors to the Water Garden flat, as were Elton's aunt, Win Robinson, and his young cousin, Paul. 'I remember there being gold discs on the wall,' Paul Robinson says now. 'And getting terribly drunk, for the first time in my life, on vodka and lime.'

All the Pinner relations took to this personable new friend of Elton's who seemed to be organising his life in such a satisfactory manner. Sheila and Derf would frequently go there to visit Reid while Elton was on the road. Indeed, in the first hectic months of 1971, it was Sheila Dwight who first floated the idea that Reid might become his manager.

At Dick James Music it had finally percolated through that Elton and John Reid were 'together'. It caused dumbfounded surprise, not least to the several girls there who had looked at the former Reg Dwight, in his shabby maxicoat, and wondered if they mightn't one day take him in hand. Sue Ayton, the only one he'd actually dated, was, paradoxically, the least surprised by the revelation. 'I think I may have had an inkling, because our relationship was so very innocent,' she says now. 'Anyway it made no difference at all to how I felt about him.'

With Sue, as with Bernie Taupin, Elton seemed anxious to show that the huge change did not alter long-standing attachments. 'I went to a party they gave at the Water Garden flat, and Elton was still just the same Reg. When I had to go, he called me a taxi, terribly apologetic because he couldn't drive me home himself. "I should do, Sue," he said, "but I can't leave the other guests." He was almost getting upset about it.'

So the news eventually reached Dick James that Elton and the young label manager of Tamla-Motown Records were living together, and that Elton wanted his new friend to become his manager.

James was hardly new to such things, having known Brian Epstein, Larry Parnes and the host of other major music industry figures whose proclivities the teenage record-buying public never suspected. His response was a tolerant shrug which he – and, even more, his son Stephen – would have cause to regret.

'Oh well,' Dick James said. 'If he's living with his manager, at least he'll have someone to get him up in the morning.'

John Reid was at first not at all sure he wanted to be Elton's manager as well as closest friend. 'I was quite happy doing what I was doing,' he recalled later. 'And it was generally accepted at EMI that I would be moving onwards and upwards there, so I wouldn't have gone to Dick James on that basis, except that I was being kind of nudged by Elton and his mother. I wasn't the only person who was approached. There were a lot of American managers who were being very pushy.

'I went to America with Elton for a holiday, because he wanted me to go with him to meet all these managers. When we came back, he said "I don't see why I should go with any of them. Why don't you come and do it?" So I gave my notice in at EMI, and [they] went bananas, saying "How can you do this, we were getting you ready for great things?" so I withdrew my notice again. Then, after a month, I thought "Oh shit! I really should do it." I was pretty scared because I'd no management experience, no legal experience, no financial experience.'

The plan could not come to fruition for several more months, since Reid had to work out his notice with EMI. In the meantime, Elton's business affairs continued to be divided among many hands, sometimes making anything but light work.

In late 1970, when it became clear that he stood to earn large sums of money, Dick James had advised him to appoint a solicitor in addition to his accountant, Barry Lyons. James's associate Geoffrey Ellis had recommended his own solicitor, Michael Oliver of Berger, Oliver and Co. Michael Oliver played a large part in the subsequent complex refinements to Elton's agreements with the James organisation that John Reid was to spend so many subsequent years challenging and attacking.

On 21 September, 1970, DJM had exercised its option to extend the publishing agreement, made with Elton and Bernie in 1967, for a further three years. Dick James proposed three alternative new arrangements. (1) Elton and Bernie could extend the period of the agreement by two years, with a rise in composers' royalties from 50 to 70 per cent. (2) They could keep to the present three years, with a royalty rise only to 60 per cent. (3) They could form a company in partnership with James (his well-tried formula) in the ratio 1–1-3, to which they would be bound for a further ten years.

Michael Oliver's discussions with Dick James raised a subject which would have repercussions fourteen years hence. Elton was now becoming a star, not only in Britain and America, but throughout the world. What could he and Bernie Taupin expect to earn from the many other countries where their songs were heard?

The practice as it stood was as old-fashioned and comfortable as Tin Pan Alley cigar smoke. The British music publisher licensed sub-publishers in North America, in major European capitals and elsewhere over the globe where his works found a public. In each country, the appointed sub-publisher collected royalties on the works, and then himself deducted a royalty. From the percentage of the income paid over by the sub-publisher, the main publisher then paid the performer his percentage.

Dick James Music operated a cat's cradle of such foreign arrangements and affiliations. In America it had a wholly owned subsidiary, DJM USA, with a separate staff and office in New York. It also had wholly owned subsidiaries in Australasia and in France, covering territories from Luxembourg to Morocco, Algeria and Tunisia. These, however, were not DJM offices, but local publishers, managing for a fee. In addition, there were copyright-policing and royalty-collecting agreements with independent (or third-party) publishers in West Germany, the Netherlands, Italy and Scandinavia.

The system was explained to Elton and Bernie in terms of relative benefit to themselves. The foreign wholly-owned subsidiaries of DJM paid a royalty of 50 per cent to British DJM. The foreign third-party publishers paid 50 per cent on recordings made within their territories, but on recordings made outside their territories, 75 per cent (or 85 per cent in the case of Beatles product). Thus Elton and Bernie earned 50 per cent of 50 per cent from their song publishing in the USA, Australasia and France, with the compensating advantage of direct control from DJM London. But under the third party arrangements in West Germany, the Netherlands, Italy and Scandinavia, they would earn 50 per cent of 75 per cent.

Oliver's advice to Elton and Bernie was to accept the second of Dick James's three new proposals on publishing: that they should keep to the prescribed three-year term, with a royalty increase from 50 to 60 per cent. Elton was said to have 'gratefully accepted' the increase, which demanded no quid pro quo from the composers, but was an expression of Dick James's goodwill.

At this point, the topic was first raised that would cause even greater repercussions in the future. Under the publishing agreement, Dick James held the copyright in Elton and Bernie's work for the full copyright term, that is, for the rest of their lives and until fifty years after their deaths. Through Michael Oliver he was asked if he would allow the copyrights to revert to them.

The question touched on one of the few regrets in James's life at that point. Although he was John Lennon and Paul McCartney's music publisher, he owned the copyrights of only two early, insignificant songs by them.* True, the company he had set up for John, Paul and himself had reaped him large rewards. But how much larger still if he himself had kept title to such evergreens as 'Michelle', 'Penny Lane' and 'Yesterday'? So Dick James would not consider letting Elton and Bernie have their song copyrights back. To do so, he said, would make him 'just an agent'.

Elton's agreements with This Record Co. – through which he recorded on the DJM label – had undergone similar refinement and elaboration. In March 1970 he had signed a new five-year agreement with TRC – the 'worthwhile' agreement which Dick James said was merited by the still-unreleased *Elton John* album. In June 1971, with his music booming all over America, DJM made a new deal for him with his US record company, MCA. This, too, ran for five years, for a basic royalty of 15 per cent (of each record's retail price). This Record Co. undertook to supply MCA with seven Elton John albums at specified intervals. A $1-million advance would be paid, with a further $1 million to follow in May 1972.

As a result of the MCA deal, This Record Co. made a further improvement to Elton's recording agreement. In respect of all net proceeds received from MCA after January 1971, his share would

* 'Please Please Me' and 'Ask Me Why'

rise from 40 to 50 per cent, as it would in respect of the album currently in production, *Madman Across the Water*. For all future master recordings supplied to America, Elton's share would be 60 per cent. TRC also undertook to pay him 60 per cent of MCA's $1-million advance. Fourteen years later, these figures would be produced in support of the argument that, if his British record royalties were on the meagre side, his American ones more than compensated for them.

A further elaboration was necessitated by British income tax, then reaching a maximum rate of 83 per cent. Another lesson was well learned from the Beatles, who had ended their career amid horrendous tax problems, both collective and individual.

To mitigate Elton's tax liabilities a scheme was drawn up separating his overseas earnings from his domestic ones and routing each through a company with which he himself had an 'employment contract'. Overseas earnings were to be received by a company named Sackville, of which Elton's solicitor, Michael Oliver, was a director. Domestic earnings were to be received by a company called Rencey, whose name was subsequently changed to William A. Bong Ltd.* A corresponding scheme was drawn up for Bernie Taupin, whose overseas earnings would now be paid through Sackville and his domestic ones through his own company Vanwall.

The simplest agreement was the management one which Elton had re-signed in May 1970, extending for a further three years. Under this, DJM initially received 30 per cent of his earnings in every field except composing. By the rider agreed after Ray Williams's departure, DJM's commission was reduced from 30 to 20 per cent, and Elton's recording activities were also excluded from the agreement.

It might be asked why Dick James, that tireless accumulator of musical property, so readily gave up 20 per cent of Elton John to the totally unknown and inexperienced twenty-two-year-old John Reid. The answer is that he felt he controlled quite enough of Elton already, and didn't want the 'aggravation' of being his manager also. For the first time in many years, Dick James had made a decision that would not reap bountiful good luck.

The plan was for Reid to come on board initially as an employee of DJM, acting as a liaison man between Elton and the company, much as Ray Williams had formerly been supposed to do. But unlike Williams he was to be paid the, for then, handsome salary of £4,000 a year. And it was clearly understood that, in March 1973, when

* a tortuous pun on billabong, or Australian water hole

DJM's management agreement with Elton ran out, John Reid was to manage him exclusively.

In retrospect, the arrangement seems incredibly benevolent. A bloodier-minded man than Dick James might well have kept Reid waiting in the wings for the next two years, then contentedly sat back to see how he might botch the job through inexperience, lack of contacts or any of the other entrepreneurial handicaps he then possessed. As it was, he was being given the chance to learn the ropes at salaried leisure within DJM before spiriting away the company's greatest prize.

While John Reid worked out his final weeks at EMI, Elton was dispatched on another American tour, his fourth in eight months. This time he took his own warm-up act, Hookfoot, a band containing familiar faces from DJM demo days. Among them was Caleb Quaye, the ex-studio engineer, but for whose generosity with Dick James's tape none of this might be happening.

It was the ten-week, fifty-five-city tour that took Elton to dollar millionaire status and, among other things, put him for the first time on the cover of *Rolling Stone*. There he is in the issue of 10 June, 1971, filling the magazine's original tabloid front, from which broadsheet pages used to unfold like a road map. Annie Leibovitz's portrait shows him sitting on the ground, wearing one of the stage outfits that still suggest some wacky Disneyland tourist: shorts, a long-sleeved T-shirt inscribed 'Bernie Taupin' and silver boots with stars over white woolly athletics socks. His hair is mod-crop short. His glasses are normal size and serious. The issue's two main inside stories are billed together: 'Kent State One Year After. Elton John One Year On'. The early Seventies counterculture saw nothing incongruous in juxtaposing the massacre of Kent State University students by National Guardsmen with the rise of a pop star.

His fifty-five-city itinerary took Elton to New York, Boston, Philadelphia, Detroit, Baltimore and San Francisco. It took him for the first time into the American South: to Houston, San Antonio, Dallas, Fort Worth, New Orleans, Memphis and Atlanta. It took him to Oklahoma City and Omaha in the Midwest, Denver and Boulder in the far west, Seattle in the north-west, and over the Canadian border to Vancouver. It took him out across the Pacific to Honolulu; to Miami, Tampa and Jacksonville, Florida; to Sacramento, Fresno and Anaheim, California. It took him to Ashbury Park, New Jersey, where Bruce Springsteen was still a grimy loiterer on the boardwalk. It took him to Cincinnati, Cleveland and – twice – to Providence, Rhode Island.

As if on some evangelical crusade, the frantic little tourist, who sometimes also resembled a dumpy wing-booted Mercury and an astrological Wolf Cub, spread tidings of joy. There truly was life after the Beatles. Boys and girls would climb on to the stage to try to hug him as he played. Now and again he would stop and make an announcement, as politely as of yore in Pinner British Legion Hall. 'Look – you'd really better get off the stage, or the police will beat your heads in.'

His growing success with the crowd brought an inevitable highbrow backlash. Even more than on the previous tour, serious rock critics tut-tutted at the yellow jumpsuit, Mr Freedom boots and top hat. Where was the earnest troubadour of 'Sixty Years On' and 'First Episode at Hienton'? His climactic rock-'n'-roll medley was discussed with the gravity of some liturgical outrage at a church synod. Elton himself was becoming so used to this kind of thing, he even made an announcement before his rock-'n'-roll finale. 'This is for those of you who don't mind theatrical things. For those critics who don't like it, you can leave now. We're just here to have a good time.'

On 8 May *Melody Maker* struck a more seriously negative note in a report by its Los Angeles correspondent Jacoba Atlas. 'Elton John seems to be having a problem with the middle part of the USA,' Atlas wrote. 'His concerts have not been selling out, and, in the words of one observer, "He's dead in New York. And everyone knows New York is the centre of popular opinion."'

Rebuttal came swiftly, from no less an authority than Bill Graham, owner of the New York Fillmore East. 'The report that Elton John was dead in the USA is not true,' Graham wrote to *Melody Maker*. 'Elton John was alive and well at the Fillmore East. He played to five packed houses in April, which were sold out five weeks in advance, and we returned 6,000 mail-order envelopes. I consider Elton one of the truly great entertainers working today.' He had, indeed, upstaged all competition at the Fillmore East, including the British band Wishbone Ash, one of whose members was seen to goggle incredulously from the wings as Elton launched into his piano handstands. 'He can't do that,' the Wishbone Ash man protested. 'He's too fat.'

Rolling Stone's cover story minutely examined the individual whose failure to meet all normal rock-star specifications was endearingly ludicrous, rather as if Britain had sent over another Charlie Chaplin, rather than another Fab Four.

He had just come from Maui and a week in the sun, and his forehead was peeling and blotchy, giving his face a prisoner-of-war quality. His knees were bruised and dirty from scampering round the stage that night.

Elton's still single. He almost got married once, but it turned out the girl wasn't pregnant. So I asked him the usual smutty questions about groupies.

'I don't have any trouble with groupies. I couldn't stand that sort of thing. Nigel has a groupie in every town, but there's no sort of plague. Anyway, they seem to be more sophisticated now. They've become – how should I put it? – they've become less sluttish.

'Bernie and I do seem to attract weirdos. I don't know why, because we're not really weird ourselves. People give me pineapples. And some girl gave me her knickers. Yeah, in Scotland some girl took off her knickers and threw them onstage. Along with a bowler hat. Can you get that one together?

'What upsets me are people who are really spaced out. Like last night there was this guy as we were driving out, he was clinging onto the car, shouting, "I must go home with you! Let me be a person!" What can you do, you know. You can't be rude to people. I couldn't say anything to him because he would have completely . . . we left him sobbing on the ground.'

Elton began rubbing his forehead where it was peeling. He looked tired and dazed.

'I've got no time for love affairs. You wake up in the morning – even if you have a day off – and the phone will ring. Your solicitor will phone you up, or your accountant or your manager or your publicist. Then you have the day-to-day things to worry about, like your car will go wrong, or the stove will blow up. It's amazing how many things go wrong in life.

'I've got about eight close friends and that's it. I haven't got any hangers-on. I couldn't bear that. I don't go to clubs. I sit at home and listen to records mostly. I hate parties.'

In future, Elton himself would say of such tours, 'They just kill you. They physically kill you.' It was not only the endless travel, the monotonous Holiday Inns and arid coffee shops, the bad diet, lack of sleep, and perpetual motion, varied by the boredom of an occasional rest day in somewhere like Omaha, Nebraska. The grimaces that were becoming his trademark arose from real physical pain. His knees were perpetually bruised and scraped from his Little Richard kneelings and pratfalls. Banging the piano as he did for over an hour, night after night, broke fingernails, at times made his hands actually bleed.

By half-way through each tour, he would have developed the calluses of a trapeze flier.

In New York he played Carnegie Hall, making the pictures of Brahms and Beethoven jog on the vestibule wall, just as John, Paul and Co. had in 1964. He also became the first rock star in history, so far as is known, to be joined on tour by his mother.

The arrangements to bring Sheila Dwight and Derf over were made by Elton's New York promoter, Ron Delsener. They were there to see him play Carnegie Hall, appear on the Dick Cavett TV show and receive his third gold disc, for the *Friends* soundtrack album, backstage at the Fillmore East. They were also with him at the gates of Disneyland, to witness a small sartorial contretemps. 'Elton John was the latest in a series of freaks to be refused admittance to Disneyland,' *Rolling Stone* reported aggrievedly. 'Despite his short hair and the company of his mum and dad, Elton was turned out because of numerous patches on his jeans. But John convinced the guards that the Disneyland concessions sold patches, and was let back in.'

Sheila wrote to Sue Ayton at DJM on her return, saying how great the trip had been and how happy Reg was to have her there. Among other news in her note from the Frome Court kitchenette was that he had just bought Derf and her a 'gorgeous' three-bedroom house ('Isn't he just too much!') and that John Reid would be starting as his manager in August.

'Have just got in from work,' Sheila ended, 'and am just trying to boil up some of Reg's washing to try to whiten it up a bit. Have just let it boil over (silly moo!). Must close now and get mopped up.'

From British rock critics that summer, the feeling was not of backlash so much as ceremonial flogging around the fleet.

ELTON BORES 'EM AT THE PALACE announced *Melody Maker*'s 'Caught in the Act' column on 7 August. The venue was not a Royal Command Performance − yet − but Crystal Palace, former south London site of the cast iron and glass edifice which once housed Queen Victoria's Great Exhibition. Here, in 1971, hippydom tried to reassure itself that nothing had changed with a series of rock 'garden parties'. The freaks stripped off to their sallow torsos to hang out in the variable sun or wallow in an artificial moat filled with flaccid rubber fish. Beyond the moat was a stage, where Elton featured in rotation with Hookfoot, Fairport Convention, Rory Gallagher and Yes.

At Crystal Palace, Elton faced a backlash of a completely different kind. What the beery British freaks wanted wasn't complex tracks like 'Levon' and 'Rotten Peaches' from his imminent new album. What they wanted – and threw beer cans if they didn't get – was plain old rock-'n'-roll. By the time Nigel and Dee had joined the red jumpsuited figure on stage, and 'Whole Lotta Shakin'' was belatedly underway, hundreds could be seen drifting out of the ground. 'It was all somewhat sad,' wrote *Melody Maker*'s Roy Hollingworth, 'this man and living myth, darling of America, the ultimate of local boys making good, struggling like a pygmy centre-half with just several thousand of his own people.'

Elton was paying the pop industry's customary price for going too far too fast. A single bad gig – not that it was so very bad – instantly wiped away the memory of a hundred good ones. It was a classic case of performer overkill. There were too many albums on release, too many tours on the go, too many rapturous noises from across the Atlantic. The British music press, quite simply, was growing bored. Critics who had so recently hailed Elton John as the hope of a new decade now began to write him off as just a nine-day wonder, a publicist's invention, without real consistency or staying power.

Elton was now by no means the only new thing to be found in British pop. After the 1970 hiatus, 1971 had seen a whole crop of rival contenders to define the new decade. Two great names from the Sixties were born again and flourishing under the alien numeral. The Rolling Stones had re-launched themselves with their own eponymous record label and a new, spare, stripped-down sound, to match the stripped pine. George Harrison had emerged from his underdog role with the Beatles to release a hugely successful solo album, *All Things Must Pass*, in which Radha Krishna temple chant met Laura Ashley print. With his new-found confidence, Harrison had gone on to organise the spectacular New York concert when he, Bob Dylan, Leon Russell and assorted fellow superstars performed in aid of the starving millions in Bangladesh, so giving pop music its first faint breath of altruism and dignity.

As Elton's first success had prophesied, the time had come for singers without bands. There was Cat Stevens with his Florentine beard and songs of Mabel Lucie Attwell mildness (little hinting at the Muslim who would one day condone the *fatwah* against Salman Rushdie). At a rival piano, there was Gilbert O'Sullivan, in his orphan boy's cloth cap and hobnailed boots a more bizarre-looking figure than Elton would be for quite a long time yet.

There was also a youth with a long anteater face, combining Cockney and Scots ancestry, whose sandpaper scrub of a voice had been heard in semi-famous bands right back to Long John Baldry's Steampacket. After years of obscurity on the blues club circuit, Rod Stewart had joined with the rump of a Sixties teenybop band, the Faces, to score the biggest hit for a British vocalist in America since Elton's in 1970. Stewart's 'Maggie May', a morning-after lament to some backstage hag, foreshadowed every theme in early Seventies pop. Pleasure to the point of boredom. Glamour to the point of squalor. Sex to the point of needing vitamin-A pills.

In the music papers where all these new phenomena were noted, Elton John now tended to draw only adverse criticism, if he was not ignored altogether. The general view was that his first great flush of fame would probably turn out to be his last. As 1971 drew to a close, one columnist acidly remarked that the best song for him to release next might be 'Death of a Clown'.

It was hardly the best moment for Elton's hitherto shy and private lyricist to step boldly forth into the limelight. Bernie Taupin's words had also begun to attract criticism for what was now seen as deliberate obscurity and pretentiousness. And when his solo poetry album, *Taupin*, was released on DJM Records in September, it shared in the same harvest of disenchantment.

Bernie's chief concern about the album was that it should not in any way exploit his association with Elton. He would not let Elton play on any of the sessions, and only one track, 'The Greatest Discovery', had previously been released as an Elton song. When *Taupin* was picked up by Elektra Records in America, Bernie stipulated that Elton's name must not be mentioned in any of the publicity.

The reviews were at best condescending, at worst downright horrid. Even critics who acknowledged Bernie to be a fresh and original voice among pop lyricists declared that he had absurdly overreached himself. Allan Richards, writing in *Crawdaddy* magazine, put it most brutally. 'Taupin is hardly a great poet, more a better-than-average storyteller, and his interpretations are tediously monot-onous. His chosen musical accompaniment also drags like a horse with a lame hoof . . . I walk away from this recording a better man for never having to hear it again.'

The experience seemed to have cured Bernie of any further desire for individual celebrity. With advances against royalties from DJM, he had bought a tiny stone cottage in Tealby, a picturesque village near Market Rasen, Lincolnshire. There, he told everyone, he would be content to spend the rest of his life with Maxine and his collection of Wild West memorabilia, writing songs and poetry among the shades of his literary influences, Tolkien, Kenneth

Grahame and A. A. Milne. In honour of Milne, and of Winnie-the-Pooh's equally famous, faithful sidekick, Bernie named the cottage 'Piglet-in-the-Wilds'.

John Reid's arrival within the Dick James Organisation initially made no great waves. The 21-year-old possessed all the canniness of his native land. He knew he was just a learner, and that unlimited scope to learn was being handed him on a plate. He therefore kept a low profile, with eyes and ears avidly open.

To begin with he seemed little more than Ray Williams and Steve Brown had been before him, a liaison man between Dick James and Elton on the management side, and between Stephen James and Elton on the recording one. This function he performed with the same quiet diligence previously seen at St Mirin's Academy and the Knightsbridge branch of Austin Reed. His position was somewhat like that of an articled clerk in legal chambers, studying the vast case law of contracts and percentages, songs that had sold a million and acts that had stormed the world.

His zeal to learn found a ready response in Dick James, who had always been more than willing to share the fruits of thirty years' experience with anyone who'd listen. 'John used to spend a lot of time in my father's office,' Stephen James says now. 'I believe my father taught him a very great deal.'

Reid's arrival, in August, coincided with the wave of critical backlash against Elton, but no let-up in his treadmill work schedule. In September he was to make his sixth tour of America, going on from there to Japan and Australia. He was also still recording tracks for his sixth album, *Madman Across the Water*, due to be released in November. It was therefore a great relief for Elton's puppet masters to know there was someone with him all the time, both selflessly devoted to his welfare and with enough influence over him to ensure he always did what he was supposed to. As far as Dick James was concerned at that point, John Reid came as a boon and a blessing.

Yet Reid's advent did bring immediate change, most obviously in the relationship between Elton and James himself. Though still cordial on both sides, it now lacked a vital central element. For Elton now had no need of a father figure.

Stephen James is emphatic about the degree to which his father filled that seeming void in Elton's life. 'They used to have long, long talks behind closed doors, not just about music but about personal subjects, too. I think my father was one of the very few people in whom Elton confided about his private life and the difficulties he'd been having with girls. I know that if I was there, my father would

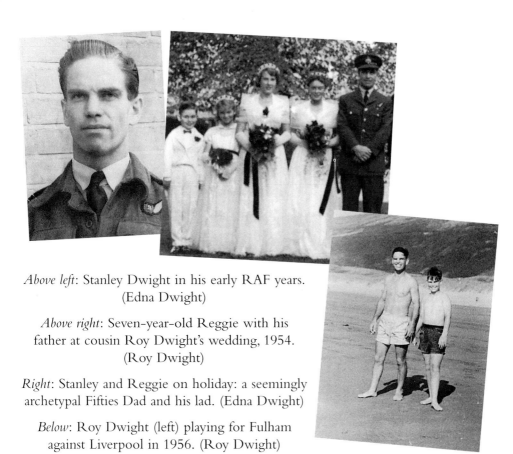

Above left: Stanley Dwight in his early RAF years.
(Edna Dwight)

Above right: Seven-year-old Reggie with his
father at cousin Roy Dwight's wedding, 1954.
(Roy Dwight)

Right: Stanley and Reggie on holiday: a seemingly
archetypal Fifties Dad and his lad. (Edna Dwight)

Below: Roy Dwight (left) playing for Fulham
against Liverpool in 1956. (Roy Dwight)

Above: Reggie aged 13 on a visit to his father. (Edna Dwight)

Left: Where the road began: Elton (second from left) aged 13 at a birthday party in Metroland. (Janet Edroff)

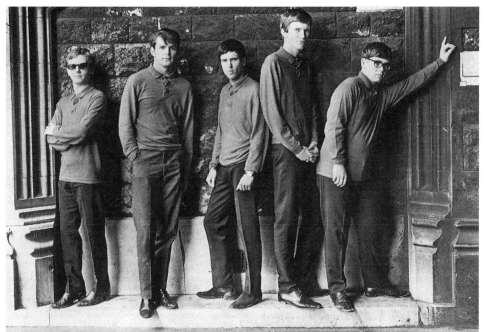

Above: Reggie (extreme right) with Bluesology at the time of their signing to Fontana. (Arnold Tendler)

Right: Co-lead singer in Bluesology. 'Stu Brown always took a bit of time to get going. But Reg just had to open his mouth and there it was.' (Geoff Dyson)

Below: The newly named Elton with new partner, Bernie Taupin. 'We were total opposites. Town mouse and country mouse.'

Left: Dick James (left), 'the luckiest man in pop music', with Elton and Vic Lewis, 1970. (Philip Gotlop, Photographs Ltd)

Main photograph: Elton with John Lennon onstage at Madison Square Garden, Thanksgiving, 1973. (Rex Features)

Right: The Elton John Band: Clockwise l to r Dee Murray, Davey Johnstone, Elton, Nigel Olsson. (Bryan Forbes)

Below right: Elton and Bryan Forbes's daughters, Sarah and Emma. (Bryan Forbes)

Above: Dodger Stadium, 1975. (Terry O'Neill, Camera Press)

Below left: Elton and Bernie take a break between composing sessions. 'To me, songs are like postage stamps. You lick them, put them on a letter and never see them again.' (Rex Features)

Below right: Elton and John Reid: 'the opposites that seldom fail to attract.' (Richard Young, Rex Features)

Above: The most inventive piano showman since Liberace. (Alan Davidson, Camera Press)

Right: Woodside, his mansion in Old Windsor. (Rex Features)

Above: Elton in his study: a place for everything and everything in its place.
(Terry O'Neill, Camera Press)

Below: Air on a piano: aboard the customised tour jet.
(Terry O'Neill, Camera Press)

sometimes ask me to go out of the room so that they could talk in complete privacy.'

Even after Elton became a big enough star to argue with James, their association had still been basically that of omniscient parent and wilful but fundamentally dutiful and grateful son. 'There'd be rows between them,' Stephen James says. 'Elton might get into a paddy and storm out of my father's office. But it never lasted long. A few minutes later he'd put his head round the door and say "Can I have a cup of tea?" '

Now that personal dimension greatly diminished. Elton's wishes were conveyed to Dick James by John Reid. And, in his own obvious power to influence those wishes, Reid also became a power to be reckoned with.

Between Stephen James and him there was almost instantaneous mutual antipathy. Stephen, too, had been used to dealing with Elton on a one-to-one basis on recording matters, and did not care for the new complexity of communication that John Reid introduced. 'Elton and This Record Company had always worked together very simply, as a team,' Stephen says. 'Now, suddenly, it was a matter of us and them. John was supposed to be our employee, but it quickly became obvious, his loyalty was only to Elton – and to himself. I think my father was very tolerant. If it had been up to me, I would have thrown him straight out.'

Elton's backing musicians, Nigel Olsson and Dee Murray, also quickly felt the difference John Reid made, travelling on that sixth tour, to America, Australia and Japan. 'We'd always been equals, like brothers,' Dee Murray said. 'Now, for the first time, Elton started seeming like a big star. You couldn't go straight to him any more. There was somebody else in the way. And it was pretty obvious that John didn't rate Nigel and me that much. At press conferences, it was all Elton. Nigel and I would just sit and not say a word. I said to John once, "Do we really need to be here at all?" He just said, "Aah, don't be so pedantic." '

On the road, Nigel and Dee had been used to only minimal 'management'. 'Steve Brown just used to let us get on with it,' Dee Murray remembered. 'Russ Regan, from Uni Records, used to come to concerts, but all he ever did was hug us and shout, "This is a marriage." With John Reid around, suddenly there was a whole lot more going on. John would comment on the position of the microphones, or say the piano had to be moved.'

Both Dee and Nigel also became aware of a marked change in Elton himself. With John Reid, he seemed to grow moodier, more prone to sulks or his occasional, tempestuous Little Moments. To them – and to many others – it would even appear that, as well as calming Elton's Little Moments, Reid could also bring them on and greatly aggravate them.

The tour itself was a further mixture of critical wincing and huge popular sell-out. When Elton played the Greek Theater, Los Angeles, in September, even his press archangel Robert Hilburn commented adversely on his over-marketing (it was his fourth LA appearance inside a year) and sensed the desperation of a career on the decline. More flak flew at his 'costume gimmicks', even though these still embraced only such items as sleeveless T-shirts, dungarees with braces, badges pinned to his thigh or embroidered on his knee, and winged Mr Freedom boots.

From Los Angeles the party flew to Tokyo, a city bound to fascinate Elton with its phantasmagoric gadgetry and neon-crazed kitsch. The Japanese promoter presented them with kimonos and outsize paper umbrellas, and introduced them to the pre-cholesterol delights of Kobe beef.

Elton's concert in Osaka brought the nearest to a riot he had yet caused. 'In the hall, the kids were behind this long barrier,' Dee Murray remembered. 'They went so wild at one point, we thought the barrier was going to go. Some of them jumped on to the stage, after souvenirs. We finished the performance with about 150 of them up there with us. But it was still all perfectly friendly and polite.'

Thence to Australia, where Elton was to spend some of his very best and very worst times. Back in 1971, it gave little sign of becoming his future second home. 'When he arrived, Elton had dyed his hair orange, with little green bits behind the ears,' Dee Murray said. 'As we were queuing up for Customs, I heard a woman shout "What's this? A bloody travelling circus?"'

It is pure coincidence, but a poignant one, that the first tour that John Reid accompanied also happened to be the first with any faint whiff of offstage controversy. 'We were invited to a reception by the Dean of Perth,' Elton later remembered. 'We were so tired after the flight, we rang him and asked if we could make it the next day. That night on TV there's a big story: "Elton John snubs the Dean of Perth. He says he's in a mood."'

Australia, he announced on returning, had been 'a nightmare'. 'We played at one football stadium, two racetracks and a speedway track – and it was in the middle of winter! The stage blew away on one gig, and we literally played in overcoats. It was raining on the piano . . . New Zealand is nice, though. It's lovely and green, and the people are great. But Australia . . . The band had five days off in Adelaide, and they went mad with boredom. If Mary Hopkin can run into trouble there, well, it gives you some idea . . . But we'll go back again. Why not?'

The year ended on a confused note which one comes to recognise as peculiar to Elton: of euphoria pulled down by anxiety, and disappointment lightened by resolute optimism.

In Britain, his big moment seemed to have come and almost gone. The popularity poll run by *Melody Maker* in September suggested that Elton John was already growing passé. In the British Male Singer category he came fourth, after Rod Stewart, Robert Plant and Robert Chapman. In the Top British Single category – won by George Harrison's 'My Sweet Lord' – 'Your Song' managed only sixth place. In the International Pianist/Organist section, he was third, after Keith Emerson and Leon Russell. In the International Composer section, he was sixth. In the International Male Vocalist section, he did not even make the top ten.

To redress the balance, DJM took out a display advertisement pointing to American achievements that might otherwise have gone unnoticed. In *Billboard*'s year-end analysis of album sales, both by individuals and groups, Elton ranked an amazing sixth, beaten only by domestic monsters like Grand Funk Railroad, Chicago and the Partridge Family. In the solo singer category, he came joint first with James Taylor.

With his sixth album, *Madman Across the Water*, Elton hoped to silence for all time the critical chorus which dismissed him variously as a publicist's hype, a late-night BBC2 fad and a hula-hoopish American flavour of the month. Indeed, while working on it, he had described it to more than one person as 'make or break time'. Nothing would do but that he should come up with something his highbrow critics would pronounce every bit as fresh and exciting as the original *Elton John* album.

Madman, therefore, returned to the style of lushly dramatic orchestral settings, arranged by Paul Buckmaster. But now the songs had an edge which the two untravelled music fans of 1970 could never have given them. When Bernie Taupin wrote about America, it was no longer mere yearning over the pages of a cowboy comic. When Elton played country or cajun piano, it was no longer just guessing how it might be done in the deep South. Their music had ceased to be mere Technicolor dream, and become first-hand Technicolor experience. 'What that album still reminds me of most is simply being in America,' Bernie Taupin says now. 'Driving down the freeways in LA, listening to the car radio.'

The lyrics were suffused with American tour life, mostly as

experienced by Bernie from the wings of arenas or the back seats of cars. 'Tiny Dancer' was a love-song for his wife Maxine, 'Blue jean jean baby, LA lady', who'd 'married a music man'. 'Holiday Inn' was a country-and-western satire on endless domestic flights, with hot towels before landing, and the cheerless motel rooms into which they were decanted each night. Most of the songs were written in the first person, obliging Elton to assume a bewildering array of voices and characters. In the hillbilly-style 'Rotten Peaches' he was a fugitive from a Southern chain gang, who'd 'had my fill of cocaine and pills.' In the melodramatic 'Indian Sunset' he was a full-blooded brave who'd 'read the writings of the smoke . . . learned to hurl the tomahawk and ride the painted pony'. In the mournful 'Razor Face', he was a young wino looking out for a broken-down old one. In 'All the Nasties', he swiped back at the 'sacred cow' music critics who'd been harrying him all year.

Today, *Madman* seems a *tour de force* of shivery English violins and elegant American steel guitars, shot through with a dark cynicism and apocalyptic pessimism for which Leon Russell clearly must take much credit. Two tracks stand out for their utter, wonderful uncommerciality in any age. One is 'Levon', Bernie Taupin's own 'A Day in the Life', about a man born 'on the day the *New York Times* said "God is dead".' The other is 'Madman Across the Water' itself, soliloquy of a lunatic on visiting-day, played by an orchestra schizophrenically uncertain whether it is funeral dirge or slow-motion funk.

The sleeve design was again entrusted to David Larkham, and immediately became involved in acrimonious complications. Larkham's idea this time was to have no pictures on the sleeve, merely the title, hand-embroidered on blue denim. The work was done by his American wife, Janice, on a panel torn from one of his own Levi jackets. Packaged with the album was another expensive booklet with the lyrics in full, the running time of each track, portraits of Elton and Bernie and Victorian photographs with cod captions.

Stephen James considered the process unnecessarily complex and time-consuming. 'I asked the people in our art department, and they told me that exactly the same blue denim effect could be got photographically,' Stephen remembers. 'But no, Elton's people had to have it laboriously done by hand. And on specially expensive matt paper. I was all for good, original design, but what I was most concerned about was making our release date and getting the records into the shops.'

Alas, *Madman* barely measured up to all the effort, hope and stitchery invested in it. True, it reached number eight in the American album chart. But the place where Elton most wanted to prove and justify himself was Britain. *Music Week*'s album chart showed it no higher than number 41. The old problem of penetrating the singles market seemed as insoluble as ever. All the tracks were thought too long to be singles, and Elton would not hear of cutting them. In America, 'Levon' and 'Tiny Dancer' were released uncut, but neither made it into the *Billboard* Top 20. In Britain, nothing was thought worth even trying. Disappointed, and dazed from a year of overproduction and continual motion, Elton experienced yet another of those momentary compulsions to do utterly the wrong thing. 'I thought of quitting. I really thought I'd gone as far as I was going to.'

Instead, he managed to rally and give interviews, looking forward with a good show of brightness to 1972. There was to be another British tour, with American stars England Dan and John Ford Coley. He planned to make a new album in the Rolling Stones' mobile studio at their tax haven on the French Riviera. He also planned to augment his stage line-up with a guitarist whose name he could not yet divulge. The impression was of keeping his chin up and bravely smiling through.

On 8 December, he recorded a BBC TV *Sounds for Saturday* concert, apparently restored to seriousness and decorum, dressed in a conventional high-collared floral shirt, and remaining seated at the piano throughout. Only the occasional grimace of staring eyes and puffed-out cheeks hinted at the past year's wild transatlantic excursions. Between tracks from *Madman*, he did little more than smile shyly, twitch his square sunglasses up his nose, and sip from a BBC paper cup. It truly seemed as though, in the inner war of his two stage personae, Dr Jekyll finally had prevailed.

That very same day, as if to prove to himself there was no going back, he changed his name by deed poll. For a middle name, he looked both to the strong man of classical mythology, and to the broken-winded cart horse in his favourite TV comedy, *Steptoe and Son*. Now Reginald Kenneth Dwight was Elton Hercules John, legally and for ever.

EIGHT

'Can you help me?
How do I acquire taste?'

TURNING up copies of the *Melody Maker* or *New Musical Express*
for early 1972, one is struck by how little everything seems to
have changed in twenty-four months under the alien numeral. The
big names in stories are still Dylan, Stones, Who and Beatles (albeit
as individual performers), plus psychedelic giants like Pink Floyd and
Led Zeppelin. New albums and singles are still reviewed at earnest
length, in minuscule black type. Forthcoming tours are still
announced in screaming full-page ads like the *New York Daily News*'s
front page after Hiroshima. Everywhere one looks, one finds the
Sixties generation still firmly in charge. The idea that there might be
such a thing as a Seventies generation has barely yet risen above a
whisper.

The Seventies generation were nothing like a generation
younger. They were, in truth, only the young brothers and sisters of
the Sixties generation, children in that magical time, and so excluded
from the joys, excitements and indulgences. They were the ones
who had been just too young to choose between Beatles and Stones.
They had been just too young for hipster trousers, Cardin jackets,
Courrèges boots and Op-Art PVC raincoats. They had been just too
young to go to the Marquee, the Ad Lib, the Speakeasy or the UFO,
or to strip naked and frolic in mud or foam at open-air festivals.
They had been just too young for kaftans, gurus, teach-ins, love-ins,
sit-ins, bed-ins, the *I Ching*, the *International Times* or *Hair*.

They were finally old enough, possessed of economic power and
ready for the spree now established as youth's birthright. But the
Sixties generation, their elder brothers and sisters, continued to
obstruct them. The Sixties generation still held all vital installations:
Melody Maker, *New Musical Express*, the Royal Albert Hall, the
Roundhouse, Radio One, BBC2's *Old Grey Whistle Test*. Advancing
into their twenties, with husbands, wives, babies and mortgages, they

still could not imagine any manifestation of youth more vital and colourful – more definitive of the state of being young – than themselves.

The Seventies generation were first manifest in fashion rather than music. As might well be expected, it was a fashion rejecting all the Sixties style for which they had once longed, but been just too young. Out went long hair, washed at home and ironed on ironing-boards. In came shorter hair, professionally styled, razored, curled and permed, dyed scarlet, blonde or ash. Out went long, loose clothes in Oriental prints. In came short, tight clothes in chain-store versions of heavy English tweed or Fair Isle knit. Out went round-necked Indian shirts and collarless jackets. In came collars and lapels as high, broad and floppy as had been sported by 'bucks' in the early nineteenth century. Out went pointed shoes with Cuban heels. In came squared-off shoes with wedge-shaped heels. Out went mysticism and wisdom. In came kid brother and sister cheek and *faux naïveté*. Out went designs of pentangles and Aquarius. In came designs of Bugs Bunny, Superman and Rupert Bear.

Out, in short, went the whole Sixties look of earthiness and naturalness, of lisping love and peace under a smiling sun. In – almost by way of revenge – came a new look of night-time artificiality and decadence; of whitish powder, brownish rouge and wine-dark lip-stick; of slashes, flares, raised seams and gaping pleats; of shoulders extended, lapels sculpted and swaggered, sleeves puffed out and waists nipped in; of embellishments plundered from grandmother's needle-work basket, trimmings of jet, diamanté, spangles and sequins.

The Seventies generation had been told by their elder brothers and sisters that pop's golden age could never come again. They therefore applied their economic power to making it do just that. Pop in the early Seventies thus suddenly ceased going forward, and began to replay itself. The songs and styles of the Fifties and early Sixties underwent wholesale revival. Rock 'n' roll, as once performed by Bill Haley and the Comets, Jerry Lee Lewis and Little Richard. A cappella and 'Doo-Wop', as once performed by Frankie Lymon and the Teenagers, the Platters, the Penguins and the Zirkons. Surfer songs, as once performed by the Beach Boys, Jan and Dean and the Surfaris. Ballads of puppy love, as once performed by Fabian, Bobby Vee, Bobby Vinton and Bobby Rydell. Not only the music of teenagers ten years before, but also their fashions – upswept, greased hair, sideburns and DAs; drape jackets, string ties and brothel-creeper shoes; circular skirts, hula-hoop earrings and ponytails. In the Sixties, every American kid had tried to look like a British one. In the Seventies, every British kid would try to look like an American one.

All these things had once been signs of youth's rebellion. Now they were signs of youth's emancipation, confidence, huge affluence, and the growing tendency among all age groups, as the modern world grew ever uglier, to wallow in nostalgia for the more and more recent past. Where Sixties pop had been almost wholly innovative, Seventies pop would be almost wholly derivative. The dominant mood of hit recordings became one of pastiche and parody. No longer did young people's music reflect, or have the slightest bearing on, social issues, war, famine, politics. The Seventies generation wished only for escapism. Their greatest idols would be those most adept in turning music into froth, fantasy, glitter and pantomime.

Looked at now, those early Seventies phenomena seem a bizarrely ill-assorted bunch. Today, who can fathom the mass hysteria engendered by a family of singing Mormons, as emptily wide-eyed and inanimately dimpled as Cabbage Patch Dolls? Or by the boy star of an American children's TV series, *The Partridge Family*? Or by an ageing warm-up singer for *Ready Steady Go!*, perennially unsuccessful under his former pseudonym, Paul Raven? Or by a group of pre-punk Scots in tartan trews, singing surf ballads with a power and attack that made Pinky and Perky, by contrast, seem Wagnerian? Yet the Osmonds, David Cassidy, Gary Glitter and the Bay City Rollers all would enjoy their stupendous hour in the Seventies generation's revenge.

Among the three runners-up to the ultimate crown, there was little of the conventional teenage heart-throb. David Bowie, white-faced and ambiguous of gender, his voice only marginally trendier than Anthony Newley's . . . Rod Stewart, long of beak and sly of smile, rumpling his slept-in thatch and kicking soccer balls around the stage . . . Marc Bolan, lowered on a cradle before his pre-pubescent fans, with his Clara Bow eyes and Theda Bara scowl, singing words so unintelligible that they might just as well have been Serbo-Croat or Esperanto . . .

And as to the crown itself, who ever would have guessed? The teen sensation of the new age, a former pub pianist from Pinner, of stocky build and thinning scalp, already famous beyond his wildest dreams, and more than half convinced this must be the limit of it.

Elton was as keen as anyone to know what the next pop wave would bring. The incorrigible record buff scanned each week's crop of releases for new directions and trends, sublimely unconscious that the new trend and departure to beat all would, very shortly, be himself.

'I wish the scene would change, and people would get young idols,' he told *Melody Maker* in another of his pop pundit interviews, late in 1971. 'I mean . . . it's crazy. Rod Stewart's in his mid-twenties, Dylan and Lennon are thirtyish. Elvis is an old man – and even I'm twenty-four! Where *are* they? Where are the new Beatles and Stones who are going to come along and shake us all out of our complacency? It's all become so static, so solemn. I don't want another Archies to come up, but things are just terrible as we stand. I can see Lennon still a teenage idol at forty!'

Certainly, the first idols of the Seventies generation all had a distinctly second-hand feel. Marc Bolan, the biggest thing in the British singles charts of 1971 and 1972, had been around since the mid-Sixties, as a male model, flower-power poet and leader of the hippy cult band Tyrannosaurus Rex. It was the first notable pop retread when Bolan collapsed the skeleton of Tyrannosaurus Rex and came back as T-Rex, producing records with names like 'Get It On' and 'Hot Love', aimed specifically at the new 'teenybopper' market.

Elton had opened for the old Tyrannosaurus Rex at the Round-house, and had often told interviewers how much he hated the hippy pretentiousness of their former style. Then one day he met Marc Bolan by chance in a record shop, and immediately took to him. Despite his look of kohl-eyed decadence, Bolan, too, was essentially normal, married and living in suburban Barnes. 'Marc and his wife, June, came to my wedding,' Bernie Taupin remembers. 'He was an incredible egomaniac, but so sweet that you couldn't help liking him. Anyway, that was what made him a star. The little that he had, he flaunted to the ultimate. For someone who was a limited guitarist, and maybe a limited songwriter, *Electric Warrior* is one of the great albums of that time.'

A more erratic relationship grew up with Rod Stewart, the other chart sensation of the hour, who had been around even longer than Elton before finally breaking through. Elton, indeed, could remember seeing him while still at school in Pinner, when Stewart appeared with Long John Baldry's Steampacket at a local Conservative club. 'Afterwards, I went to the pub, and went up to him and said "Excuse me, Mr Stewart, can I have your autograph?" Wild! He used to come on stage with a scarf around his neck, and sing "Good Morning Little School Girl" . . . I thought he was great.'

The two former Long John Baldry apprentices could hardly have been more different. While Elton shunned the excesses of pop-star life, Stewart embraced them all with avidity. He was, indeed, soon to become an early subject of tabloid newspaper headlines for taking snapshots of groupie orgies with his Polaroid camera.

What Elton and he had powerfully in common was their passion for football – in those days, still a fairly novel thing for pop stars to like. Stewart's concerts with the Faces already were more like games at Wembley or Ibrox Park, with fans turning up in colours of Celtic FC, balls intermittently kicked or headed from the stage, and appreciation signalled by thousands of tartan scarves waving between upstretched arms as in a darkened grandstand.

Elton and Rod Stewart also became friends, though their liking for each other was masked by heavily affected rivalry and bitchery. 'Good piano player,' Stewart would concede whenever Elton's name came up. 'Pity his barnet's* falling out.'

What they also had in common was concern over their old mentor, Long John Baldry. Since breaking into the mainstream with 'Let the Heartaches Begin' – and sending Elton off to Liberty Records in despair – Baldry's career had gone into steep decline. He was now managed by Rod Stewart's manager, Billy Gaff, who phoned Elton in New York, asking for help in giving Long John a leg-up. Elton, typically, forgot his unhappy eclipse in Bluesology, preferring to remember how Baldry's acid tongue had helped stop him marrying Linda Woodrow. It was agreed that Elton and Rod Stewart should co-produce an album for Baldry, taking responsibility for one side each.

Baldry's album, *It Ain't Easy*, came as a welcome gear change for Elton in the frenetic summer of 1971. After so long in the spotlight, it was enjoyable to become a session man again, using his vast magpie store of styles and ideas unselfishly for Long John's benefit, and playing piano anonymously in a studio ensemble with guitarist Caleb Quaye and backup singers Roger Cook and Lesley Duncan. It was also a hilarious return to old times at the Marquee and Klooks Kleek, with Baldry as caustically camp as he had always been. The sessions created Baldryesque nicknames that would stick for ever, Elton becoming Sharon, Baldry himself Ada and John Reid Beryl, after the actress Beryl Reid.

Alas, neither this album nor a second Elton–Rod co-production, *Everything Stops for Tea*, early in 1972, was sufficient to restore Long John's British fortunes. Touring with Stewart and the Faces subsequently, he found those 'Woolworth's shopgirls' more disinclined to listen than ever. After sundry other relaunches through the Seventies, he decided to emigrate to Canada. At the time of writing, he was enjoying a new career in TV voice-overs, and had just finished playing Captain Hook in a touring production of *Peter Pan*.

As for Elton, his disappointment and chagrin over *Madman Across the Water* soon evaporated. The workaholic album-maker itched to get busy on his own account in a studio again – though which studio

* Barnet fair – hair

it would be was somewhat problematic. Trident, which had served him so well since the *Elton John* album, was now to be written out of the picture. His accountants advised that, for tax reasons, it would be better if future albums were made outside Britain.

Though modern recording studios existed throughout Europe, almost no British performers had ever thought to make use of them. European pop in the early Seventies was generally thought a joke, exemplified by the annual travesties of the Eurovision Song Contest. Greatest joke of all was France, with its garbled rock-'n'-roll parodies, endless Piaf impersonators and ubiquitous piano-accordions.

France had acquired some chic, however, after the Rolling Stones fled to tax exile on the Riviera, taking with them a fully equipped mobile studio. Elton had been supposed to use it first thing in 1972, but at the very last moment – in true Stones style – word came through that it wasn't available. Hasty inquiries then had to be made by Gus Dudgeon about other possible studios in France or just across its frontiers.

The most promising idea Dudgeon came up with was a studio named Strawberry, established in the seventeenth-century Château d'Hierouville in the countryside 40 kilometres north of Paris. It was a place already known among top American bands, and had recently been used by Jerry Garcia and the Grateful Dead. Elton went over to look at the château, and instantly fell in love with it. 'It had an atmosphere all its own,' he recalled later. 'It was in the middle of nowhere, with a swimming pool, tennis court. You could record in a room with a thirteenth-century chandelier, overlooking nothing but fields.'

With the booking of Strawberry, he could finally name the guitarist he had found to augment his two-man backup band. The newcomer was Davey Johnstone, a blond, lanky Scot who at the time played in an acoustic band named Magna Carta, as well as writing fiddly-diddley folk songs with titles like 'Sponge'. Elton's producer Gus Dudgeon also produced Magna Carta, and had brought Johnstone in on Bernie Taupin's album, playing sitar, banjo, mandolin and lute. Elton was 'knocked out' by his playing, and saw at once what a dimension might be added by translating his flowery acoustic technique to electric rock-'n'-roll lead. 'It's a good time to extend the band,' Elton told *Melody Maker*'s Ray Coleman. 'You get an inner feeling that this is the moment to do something. For the past year, too much has been focused on me – I've been lead instrument, rhythm instrument and voice. I'd gone as far as I could with three men. It was either change completely, or split.'

This came as something of a surprise to Elton's two existing sidemen, Dee Murray and Nigel Olsson. The first Dee knew of it was when Davey joined them en route to record for the first time in France. 'Don't get me wrong – we both got on great with Davey from the start. He was a terrific player, and great for the band. It's just that we had no idea he was coming in.'

To Dee Murray, the affair was another example of how life with Elton changed after John Reid's arrival. 'Before John was around, I'm sure Elton would have discussed the whole thing with us. Now it was as if we just weren't worth consulting – and didn't really matter at all. Before Davey came in, Nigel and I were getting 40 per cent of the concert money between us, and Elton got 60. With Davey in, we just divided it three ways, thirteen and a third per cent each. I was usually the spokesman, so I went to John and asked him if we could get a bit of a raise on that. His answer was no, "and if you don't like it, you know what you can do".'

Recording at Strawberry studio proved an ideal arrangement. The setting of the half-ruined château was breathtakingly beautiful, and wonderfully free of all usual distractions. The musicians occupied basic but comfortable rooms, meeting for meals in a communal dining-area with a piano at one end of it. In the morning, they could get straight up from their breakfast coffee and *biscottes* and start rehearsing. From there it was a walk of only a few yards across a courtyard to the excellently equipped recording complex. 'It was literally like a music factory,' Bernie Taupin remembers. 'I'd be upstairs in my bedroom, writing at top speed. I'd give each set of lyrics straight to Elton at the piano.' With the chords that flowed naturally from the stubby hands, a song could be written in twenty minutes, rehearsed by the band in an hour and recorded that same afternoon.

Creature comforts, however, were not neglected. The château provided first-class cuisine and owned its own vineyard. The studio was run by a young Frenchwoman named Catherine Philippe-Gérard who, like many powerful, authoritative females, became devoted to Elton. He took to her just as strongly, making her part of the inner circle with John Reid, Bernie and Gus Dudgeon, even announcing that the finished album would be dedicated to her.

Such was the energy and euphoria of the Strawberry sessions that in barely three weeks, all ten tracks were finished and ready for mixing in London. The fun atmosphere even extended to Elton's asking his unofficial stepfather, Derf Farebrother, to contribute to one track by playing the spoons on his knee. When Derf could not make it, Elton called over 'Legs' Larry Smith of the Bonzo Dog Doo-Dah Band to simulate the noise of tap-dancing. (It was a poignant twist of fate, since the Bonzos had passed that same long-ago Liberty Records audition which Reggie Dwight had so hopelessly failed.)

There was also a song whose first line had occurred to Bernie Taupin complete, while driving alone in Lincolnshire. 'The words just came into my head: "She packed my bags last night, pre-flight. Zero hour is nine am." I remember jumping out of the car and running into my parents' house, shouting "Please don't anyone talk to me until I've written this down."'

The song was 'Rocket Man' and, like so much of the best of Taupin and John, was anything but original. David Bowie's 'Space Oddity', in 1969, had explored precisely that same theme of a lonely, disenchanted astronaut. As burrowers through Musicland's import box, Elton and Bernie were aware of an even earlier prototype. In 1967, the American cult band Pearls Before Swine had recorded a song actually called 'Rocket Man', written by their leader Tom Rapp.

None of this was to matter in April 1972, when Elton John's 'Rocket Man' came out as a single in Britain and America. Elton had not wanted to release it, thinking it too slow, but the instinct of his producer Gus Dudgeon, fortunately, prevailed. By further happy chance, space happened to be in the headlines with the launch of America's latest three-man moon probe, Apollo 16. In Dudgeon's masterly production, it was as if Elton's voice also echoed down vast black freeways of hyper-space. The very last spot in the universe you would have imagined him to be was a château 40 kilometres from Paris.

It was the instant hit single Elton had longed and sweated for since 1967. More significantly still, it went to number two in Britain while reaching only six in America. From the space capsule whose interior still so much resembled a bedsitting-room in Pinner, Rocket Man might have observed the continents shifting into alignment at last.

One day early in 1972, a young man pushed open the door of a small bookshop in Virginia Water, Surrey. The proprietor who glanced up had a foxy face familiar to anyone raised on British black-and-white war movies of the mid 1950s. He was Bryan Forbes, actor-turned-director and, until lately, head of Britain's last major film studio, EMI. Keeping a bookshop was but one thread in a multistrand life that also encompassed screen- and novel-writing, magazine publishing and frequent appearances in showbiz, society and even royal circles, accompanied by his actress wife, Nanette Newman.

Of the young man browsing in his shop that day, Forbes noted only that he wore spectacles and 'a fur coat which looked as if it had just died. I'd heard that the Bee Gees were supposed to be living in the neighbourhood. My first thought was that he might be one of the Bee Gees. The funny thing was that, though I knew almost nothing about pop music, I happened to be going to a pop concert that very night. I was on the Council of the National Youth Theatre, and we were doing a fund-raising concert at the Shaw Theatre, where they'd got Elton John to appear. I'd heard of Elton John, of course, though I had no idea what he looked like at that stage.

'So to this young man, who I thought was a Bee Gee, I said, "I'm going to a pop concert tonight." "That's funny," he said. "So am I." And that was how I first met Elton.'

They met again that night, and afterwards had dinner together. Elton revealed that he'd just moved to Virginia Water and was living in a bungalow not far from Forbes's house, Seven Pines. Though the star of the night, he was far more absorbed in talking to the man responsible for such British movie classics as *I'm All Right, Jack* and *The League of Gentlemen*. Still more fascinated was he to hear of Forbes's vast circle of movie friends, especially his own idol, the arch Goon Peter Sellers.

A few days later, he paid the first of many neighbourly visits to Bryan Forbes and Nanette Newman at Seven Pines. Having bought the house as a shell in the Fifties, they had made it an opulent showplace, filled with desirable books and excellent art. Elton was deeply impressed. 'He took in every detail of the house,' Bryan Forbes remembers. 'He said "You've got a complete home here, haven't you?"'

He talked in a desultory way about his own new home, the bungalow down the road, and how he was thinking of decorating and furnishing it. Then he turned to Bryan Forbes with a beseeching look – one that Ray Williams, of Liberty Records, would have found all too familiar.

'Can you help me?' he said. 'How do I acquire taste?'

The choice of Surrey's stockbroker belt as a place to live was a familiar one among newly rich British pop stars. Since John, George and Ringo had shown the way, it was almost a *sine qua non* of making one's first million to buy a mock-Tudor mansion or Bel Air-style bungalow out in Weybridge, Esher, Roehampton or Sheen. Pop people even more than stockbrokers appreciated the combination of nearness to London with rural peace and tranquillity, and a lifestyle that was the nearest southern England could offer to the Hamptons or Beverly Hills.

The inhabitants of Weybridge, Esher, Roehampton and Sheen tended to be somewhat less than welcoming. This was because wherever pop people went, so as a rule did thunderous hi-fi, slamming car-doors, revving motorbikes, parties that went on seventy-two hours at a stretch, regular guitar and drum-practice, audible wife- and girlfriend-battering, neglected children with slatternly nurses, villain-ous-looking servants and hangers-on, public drunkenness and lasciv-iousness, periodic police swoops for drugs, chaos, neglect and a squalor that could carry a quarter of a mile on clear summer air. Stockbrokers and their families learned to tremble when neighbouring properties fell vacant, chauffeur-driven Austin Princesses appeared in the drive, long hair bobbed between the topiary work and laid-back voices grew audible, ominously talking about 'good vibes'.

Even sedate Virginia Water, where Elton concentrated his search, had its own resident Minotaur. Among properties for sale was the house of the Who's drummer Keith Moon, aka Moon the Loon, where the eventual purchaser found interior walls peppered with gunshot blasts, the kitchen awash with baked-bean tins, the glass wall to the living room in fragments and a Rolls-Royce Corniche standing submerged in the swimming pool.

Elton eventually found what he wanted in Abbots Drive, part of the exclusive estate surrounding Wentworth golf course. It was a modern split-level bungalow, with a large rear garden and swimming pool, costing £50,000. He moved there with John Reid early in 1972. Commemorating his new identity, and Steptoe's carthorse, the bungalow ceased to be 14 Abbots Drive and was named Hercules.

To begin with, it was very much a standard pop-star home, with large Tiffany lamps, vermilion leather buttonback couches, coffee tables, ceiling-high gilt mirrors, framed reproduction Victorian post-ers, and the hundred-and-one knick-knacks presented for achieve-ment in the record industry. There was the obligatory games room, with ping-pong table, hand-operated football game, fruit machine, golf balls and putter. Along with the stacks of albums in shiny covers and piles of singles in paper ones, there was also now a Fifties jukebox, filled with Elton's personal selection.

Outside on the short, sloping drive stood a thicket of expensive cars: a Rolls-Royce Corniche hardtop, a Rolls Phantom VI, used for touring, a Ferrari Boxer and a Mini GT. In the boot of one Rolls was a moped, which Elton would occasionally whip out and mount if his limousine had been brought to a standstill in London traffic.

The great difference from other pop-star domiciles was noted by

Melody Maker's Roy Hollingworth. Instead of the usual jumble and squalor, fastidious cleanliness and order prevailed. 'From the neatly folded face-flannel in the bathroom to the suit of armour guarding the stairway, all is a kind of tidy perfection one would expect to see at the Ideal Home Exhibition. In fact, Elton's house makes the Ideal Home Exhibition look like a display of Nissen huts shortly before demolition by squads of sanitary engineers. It seemed almost offensive to flick cigarette-ash into the glittering ashtrays.' Hollingworth went on to describe how the interview came to an embarrassing halt when his photographer, Barrie Wentzell, accidentally slopped some Dom Pérignon champagne on to Elton's brand-new living-room carpet. Reporter and photographer watched, bemused, as Elton knelt between them with a bowl of water and a cloth, feverishly scrubbing at the mark.

An early use of the house was as an address on the marriage certificate of Elton's mother, Sheila. In May 1972, she married Fred Farebrother, whose surname she had adopted by deed poll some years earlier. Two witnesses' signatures appear on the certificate: that of John Reid's mother, Elizabeth, and a boldly-inscribed 'Elton Hercules John'.

Despite all the massive changes and upheavals in Elton's life, Sheila remained as central and vital a figure as ever. Only now, in his twenties, did he fully appreciate the struggle she had had, as a single parent, to raise and educate him, and the unquenchable vigour with which she had jollied him along since that day, in Pinner Hill Road, when he hesitantly pecked out the first notes of 'The Skaters' Waltz'. It was among the earliest satisfactions of his new wealth to persuade Sheila to quit her job as a government clerk, move out of the tiny maisonette where they had rubbed along so many years together, and move into the 'gorgeous three-bedroom house' he bought for her in Ickenham, Middlesex.

Sheila's decision to make Derf his official stepfather at last gave Elton huge pleasure, though in truth it made no real difference to their relationship. The genial painter and decorator – who had first delivered him and his PA system to George Hill's pub, and rescued him and his LPs from Linda Woodrow – had always been and would always be 'My Dad'.

At Hercules, Sheila and Derf were fixtures from the beginning. Derf supervised the redecoration and became responsible for the hanging of Elton's growing collection of pictures. When Elton and John Reid were away on tour, Sheila and Derf would move in as caretakers and to look after Elton's spaniel, Brian, and his Alsatian, Bruce.

Sheila, to be sure, was no liability to have around, still only in her late forties, as petite and darkly attractive as ever. She was even starting to take on a little pop style, with blue jeans, big jewellery and baggy T-shirts bearing details of her son's last US tour. Elton made no secret of his attachment to her, nor of his continuing reliance on her plainspoken good sense. 'She's just straight about everything, and she can smell a rat for a mile. She'll say "Don't bloody well trust him. He'll run off with all your money." She's always been right.'

The mother of Elton John was now newsworthy in her own right. A *Daily Mail* writer, Jane Gaskell, visited Sheila while she and Derf were holding the fort at Hercules during Elton's spring 1972 American tour. Both of them chatted freely about his childhood as Reggie and the way their lives had changed since he'd made it into the big time. Derf admitted undergoing some ragging from fellow builders when he wore the scarlet platform-heel shoes his stepson had recently given him. 'But we both feel younger. I expect I look younger, too.'

Sheila talked of Elton's generosity; the £15,000 'gingerbread house' he had bought her at Ickenham, the white MGB sports car he'd insisted she have instead of her old Mini. 'He loves paying out – and he loathes the feeling of owing anyone any money. The first thing he'll do when he gets home is sit down at that desk and write out a dozen cheques. There's been less contact between us, of course, since he became so busy. But he still rings at times and says "I've got the day to myself, Mum – come on over and spend it with me."'

The first parties to be held at Hercules were strictly family ones. Elton's grandmother, Ivy, his Aunt Win, his Uncle Reg, his cousins Paul, Cath and John, all often gathered there for the kind of jolly knees-ups that had always gone on at Frome Court or in Pinner Hill Road. The thoughtful small boy remained just as thoughtful now that he was a star. Chauffeur-driven cars would be sent to fetch everybody and take them home again. Exquisite food would be served by top-class caterers. When Elton's Aunt Win remarried, he insisted both on being best man and holding the wedding reception at his house. 'He organised everything – the cars, the food,' his cousin, Paul Robinson, remembers. 'We had a marvellous party afterwards, next to the swimming pool.'

He was just as pleased to see his Dwight relations, from Kent. His cousin Roy, the ex-soccer star, remembers dropping by one day with his wife, and getting a huge welcome. 'Elton had just come out of the shower,' Roy remembers. 'He took us into the living room still wearing just his bathrobe. It was just a skimpy little thing and, the way he was sitting, you could see everything. But he didn't mind, and we certainly didn't. He sat there, pleased as punch, talking to my wife eyeball to eyeball.'

Otherwise, the main visitors were pop landed gentry who lived in the vicinity: Keith Moon, Rod Stewart, the hippy poet Donovan. There was also a constant stream of interviewers from music papers, to whom Elton described a social life of Jane Austenish variety. 'Donovan's having a party next week, and he's invited the whole world. Keith Moon says he doesn't want any galactic fairy dust, he wants a good booze-up. Rod says he's not much into mushrooms and toadstools, but he'll go . . . David Bowie was just here. I really liked what Mott the Hoople did with his song ['All The Young Dudes'] so I rang him up and invited him for a meal.'

His major new friend in the business was Marc Bolan of T-Rex, whose singles, 'Get It On', 'Hot Love' and 'Ride A White Swan', now stocked the jukebox in his rumpus room. Towards so massive a rival, jealousy and condescension would have been more than under-standable. But such things simply were not in Elton's nature. He recognised Bolan's songs as perfect pop music, expertly tailored to their market. When Elton played the Fairfield Hall, Croydon, late in 1971, Bolan walked onstage as a surprise guest, and they finished the show together, upstaging and outcamping one another like some spangly latter-day Laurel and Hardy.

Bolan lived in Barnes, only a few miles from Wentworth, and often drove over with his wife, June. To Elton, he was the perfect caricature of a pop idol, with his black-ringed eyes and pre-Raphaelite hair; transparently vain, ambitious and exploitative. Yet under the huge ego lay genuine charm, and a healthy root of self-mockery. A tongue-in-cheek contest developed between Elton and Bolan to see which could display the greater hubris and conceit. On Bolan's birth-day, he received a life-size photographic blow-up of Elton. On Elton's next birthday, a furniture-removal pantechnicon drew up outside Hercules. In it was the silver disc Bolan had received for 'Jeepster', and a blow-up photograph of himself, 27 feet high. It was, indeed, higher than the house, and had to be put outside in the garden.

Elton and Bolan even tried to write something together, though the partnership did not progress much further than an ad libbing of 'Jeepster' around the grand piano at Hercules. Clive Banks, a young newcomer to Dick James Music, remembers the occasion as poign-antly illustrative of Sixties- versus Seventies-style talent. 'Elton had a brilliant natural voice, but Marc's was all put together in the studio.

In real life, it wasn't much more than a little squeak. You'd got Elton playing 'Jeepster' and doing a great vocal, and this squeak going on on top of it.'

Elton still did not have the smallest notion of himself as a competitor to Marc Bolan. In his own eyes, he was an oldie from 1971 whose career was experiencing a wholly unlooked-for second wind. With 'Rocket Man' in the British and American charts, he could afford to be indulgent towards new young teenybopper crazes like David Cassidy, the Osmonds and Slade. His tone was that of elder statesman with heart in right place, insisting that youth must always have its say. As he often said, from the encrusted eminence of his twenty-four years, 'It's a sign of people getting old when they start grousing about the groups.'

Big name though he had indubitably become, he was still first and foremost a besotted fan − of rock-'n'-roll stars, film stars, theatre stars, anything with that thrilling golden aura of legend. As he had once made a pilgrimage to Batley Variety Club to see Dusty Springfield, he now went incognito to the London Palladium to see Marlene Dietrich. 'I was totally bowled over by her,' he recalled. 'As I came out afterwards, a girl saw me and said, "Can I have your autograph?" When I'd signed her book, she said, "Here what's this?" I looked, and I'd signed it "Marlene Dietrich".'

His main worry about his new album, released a month after 'Rocket Man', was whether sufficient time had elapsed since the absurd overproduction of 1971, and the somewhat dull thud of *Madman Across the Water*. After *Madman*'s design indulgences, this was a low-profile affair in a custard-coloured cover showing a plain head shot of Elton with his Troubadour beard. The tracks were those recorded at Strawberry studio, amid the unlikely grandeur of the Château d'Hierouville. The title − mixing street jive talk with snob French − was *Honky Château*.

Other than 'Rocket Man', the feel was country and western, with the accent on country. Bernie Taupin had written the idyll of his new life with new-found love, in a thatched cottage named Piglet-in-the-Wilds. The tone was set by 'Honky Cat', an opening track of Zip-a-de-doo-dah jauntiness, with piano chords such as Winifred Atwell might have played in 'Chinatown, My Chinatown'. The space man was also a farm boy after the Huck Finn style, in plantation hat and rolled-up dungarees.

It was an incarnation which seemed to please his audience more than any so far. By early summer 1972, *Honky Château* stood at number two in every British album chart. In America, it became

Elton's first number one, earning him his fourth US gold disc for one million sales. 'Honky Cat' was afterwards released as a single, making eight in America but, oddly for so evergreen an Elton track, only 31 in Britain.

The blending of Bernie Taupin's thoughts with Elton's voice had produced a curious synthesis. Bernie's words were more important than mere song lyrics, each time inventing a wholly new version of their singer's character and psyche. But in another way, they scarcely seemed to register at all. Pop lyrics in the Sixties and Seventies were subject to rigorous vetting, both by the BBC, their all-important British outlet, and by American radio stations, especially those morally hypersensitive ones throughout the Southern Bible Belt. The list of banned records ranged from Screaming Jay Hawkins's 'Constipation Blues' to the Beatles' 'I am the Walrus'. The Rolling Stones had caused international scandal merely by naming a song 'Let's Spend the Night Together'. John Lennon's 'A Day in the Life', a masterpiece by any reckoning, had been outlawed for one drug-flavoured line, 'I'd love to turn you on'.

Yet 'Rocket Man', with its far more narcotically explicit 'I'm gonna be high as a kite by then', blasted unchecked from the transistor radios of two continents. And on *Honky Château*, several even more blatant naughty bits were to be found. 'Slave' cast Elton in the role of Southern abolitionist, vowing, 'I swear one day I'm gonna burn that whore-house down'. 'Mellow' was a cameo of energetic sex: 'wreckin' the sheets real fine'. The Legs Larry tap-dancing track was a cheerful little thing called 'I Think I'm Going to Kill Myself', on which Elton light-heartedly sang of 'buying a forty-four' and 'causing a little suicide'.

It was not that he did not take on his ever-changing roles with total passion, sincerity and conviction. But something in that Latin-inflected voice – the way words were framed by that wide, narrow-lipped mouth – purged the darkest sentiment whiter than white. He was not androgynous so much as genderless, devoid of sexual charge as no male performer had been since the banjo-strumming George Formby. His songs of killing and arson might just as well have been sung by a Teddy bear with a ribbon round its neck; his songs of lust by a castrato from a medieval cathedral school.

As is usually the case with born fans, Elton was also a born collector. Like the urge to follow and worship heroes, the urge to acquire, to hoard and stroke and cherish inanimate objects can become an almost perfect substitute for true happiness. The solitary boy in his Pinner bedroom had long ago learned to draw from toys and possessions the companionship and warmth that human relationships seemed unable to give.

Such taste as he had at the beginning merely reflected the general one. This was 1971 and 1972, when all fashionable interiors lay under the same thrall of nostalgia and whimsicality. Having exhausted London's stocks of Victoriana, the second-hand dealers were now picking over the domestic remnants of Edwardiana, the Great War, the Twenties and Thirties. The craze was Art Nouveau and, at a cheaper level, Art Déco, that cosy Ovaltiney interwar look whose scalloped furniture, dadoed teacups and plaster flying ducks, still current in Metroland, now filled the smart Portobello stalls and Kensington hypermarkets. It was a time rivalling Queen Victoria herself for domestic clutter, when for every one useful household object, fifty would be on show that were useless but 'fun', when no modish mantelpiece could fail to display a set of W. D. and H. O. Wills's cigarette cards, a golliwog in Boer War khaki, a postcard from a soldier in Flanders, a photograph of Jack Buchanan and a menagerie of W. Britain's lead zoo animals and miniature Dinky cars.

With his new pop star wealth, fulfilling his schoolboy dreams, Elton bought on an epic scale. But he possessed nothing casually or haphazardly. The great example was his record collection, still organised meticulously into categories and subsections, with neatly written index cards, even now when trips through Tower Records with a shopping trolley might increase it by 300 albums at a time. His mind was that of an archivist or librarian, cataloguing and cross-referencing all that he acquired, down to the smallest Pinocchio badge from Disneyland. What he lacked was discrimination, or any sense of the dictum 'less is more', a quality he had in common with Elvis Presley. The same rule applied at Hercules in Virginia Water as at Graceland in Memphis, Tennessee. However small, cheap, insignificant or ephemeral the acquisition, once in Elvis's or Elton's possession it stayed there.

By 1972, the bungalow at Wentworth already housed a dozen different collections in progress. There was one of Art Nouveau lamps, supported by streamlined nymphs in every attitude of flowing-robed endeavour. There was another of reproduction posters for such nineteenth-century happenings as *Exposition Internationale de Madrid, 1893–94* or 'Rudge's Rotary Tandem'. There was another of onyx eggs, graded in every size from ostrich to plover. There was another of Pop Art, including Andy Warhol's signed silk-screen print 'Last Suite of the Electric Chairs'. There was another of stuffed animals, including a bear, a cheetah and (*Melody Maker* assured its readers) a warthog. Plus the vast, unclassifiable collection of hypermarket impulse buys and tailor-made technological novelties, from a Victorian cash register to a neon sign spelling Hercules.

There was also the ever-growing and diversifying collection of Elton's clothes and accessories. The down-at-heel denim pirate of 1969 had become the ultimate shiny Seventies fashion plate. No new look could have been kinder to someone of his short and dumpy build. The new platform shoes, with their clubfoot toes and heels stacked up and variegated as layer-cake, added three or four inches to his height. The new trousers, with their gaucho flares, concealed the bulkiness of his legs. The new rigid, nipped-in jackets broadened his shoulders and gave him the appearance of a waist.

His suits, jackets, coats and cloaks, the finest fruits of Granny Takes a Trip in King's Road and Nudie the Rodeo Tailor, filled closet after closet, with pair upon pair of platforms from the Chelsea Cobbler ranged like flotillas of painted sampans beneath. An entire portmanteau was needed for the pairs of spectacles he brought home from every trip to America. A shop in Hollywood made them up to his specifications, with prescription lenses tinted every conceivable shade, and frames of ever-increasing fancifulness. One pair had orange-tinted lenses and white rims. Another had hexagonal rims of translucent blue. Another had heart-shaped rimless lenses, tinted in lateral stripes of red, white and blue. Another had little hoods that could be pulled down over their lenses like supernumerary eyelids.

In Reggie Dwight's Sixties schooldays, pop stars had been identifiable by their fringes and elastic-sided boots. The great star of the Seventies first became identifiable via outsize glasses, allied to footwear so precarious and cumbersome, he could walk only with the slow, measured tread of the circus stilt artist. En route to America in April 1972, four pairs of his platform boots and one pair of his shoes were impounded by US Customs officials who suspected that their eight-inch heels might conceal smuggled narcotics or jewels.

Elton could not claim to be first in what was now officially styled 'glitter rock'. The trend had been in evidence since 1970, with white British bands like T-Rex, Slade, Sweet, even the Rolling Stones, and black American soul groups like the Jackson Five, the Temptations and the Chi-Lites. If the style had any one progenitor it was David Bowie, another Sixties survivor, who had brilliantly seen how his slight singing voice might be projected through a persona of androgynous high fashion and stage shows utilising every dramatic device from Marcel Marceau mime to schlock Hollywood sci-fi.

The difference between David Bowie and Elton John was that between *haute couture* and the rag trade. What Bowie created on the catwalk, Elton rushed post haste into the high street chain stores.

For him, glitter was no more than blessed camouflage. In the stage outfits it was now possible to wear, his physical shortcomings simply melted away. More crucial was the way Glitter Rock abolished the solemnity he had always so hated in live performance, replacing it with whoops and cheers for excesses of flamboyance and kitsch that would have made the Sixties generation wince. He loved it that the newest British chart sensation was a Fifties Teddy-boy caricature actually named Gary Glitter, whom Elton and his circle could remember as an office boy at the *Ready Steady Go!* programme.

In interviews, he constantly stressed that his stage acts were just 'a bit of fun', not to be taken in any way seriously. One music press reporter who called him 'showbizzy' provoked an eloquent tirade. 'It's glamour, but I refuse to say it's showbizzy. I'm sending show business up. I hate show business. I mean, Rod Stewart is exactly the same; he's very flamboyant and wears pink satin suits and that's showbiz, and yet it's not. You can't say I'm showbizzy. I'm so bloody clumsy, and there's nothing graceful about me with a pair of flying boots on. I just like to get up and have a lark. I do it tongue in cheek – with an 'up yours' sort of attitude. It's like an actor getting into his costume for his part. I don't really feel the part until I'm into what I'm going to wear.

'It's a reaction against everything I wasn't allowed to do as a kid. I wasn't allowed to wear winklepicker shoes in case they hurt my feet. I wasn't even allowed to wear Hush Puppies, can you imagine that? Not having had a real teenage life, I'm living all those thirteen to nineteen years now. Mentally I may be twenty-five, but half of me is still thirteen.'

Almost as nettling was the frequent music press insinuation that he worked in obedience to some Svengali-like manager behind the scenes. 'It's incredible – people have the impression that there's someone behind me with a great big button, saying, "You must wear this and you must wear that." I think it was Roy Carr who said they're pushing the Destruct button. Well, that's me, if anyone, because there's nobody behind me.'

Elton's first British tour of 1972 marked his first major foray into glitter rock. He came on in a silver-striped tail coat, red velvet trousers with knee-high green silk turn-ups, multi coloured Lurex socks and silver platform boots, one with a large red 'E' on its side, the other with a 'J'. His hair had changed hue from orange and green to silver. It was part of a conscious – indeed, conscientious – effort to get on terms with a British public which, with his concentration on American tours, he felt he had never really understood. 'In the States, I have no qualms,' he told *New Musical Express*'s Julie Webb. 'But I really don't know what people think of me in this country. I go out and think "What are they expecting?"'

Previously his stage clothes had been a random assembly of things bought at Mr Freedom, picked up at Disneyland or borrowed at the last minute from Bernie Taupin's wife, Maxine. But in this new competitive field of visual extravagance, the way to maintain his edge was clearly to start having performance outfits custom-made.

It happened that Steve Brown's brother Pete had married a girl named Annie Reavey, a freelance designer of shoes for trendy firms like Moya Bowler and Richard Smith's Chelsea Cobbler. Highly gifted and original in approach, she was herself the acme of early Seventies style, from her topply metallic boots to hair that changed colour, or parti-colour, even more often than did Elton's.

For Elton's twenty-fifth birthday, Steve Brown asked Annie Reavey to design and make him a special party outfit. She made him a fur cloak embroidered with palm trees, and a tall quilted hat from which the EJ monogram dangled on a string. Elton loved the ensemble so much that she was asked to start making him clothes to wear onstage.

Annie Reavey remained his chief wardrobe designer for the next three years. To begin with, her creations were relatively simple siren-suit affairs of pink and green woven Lurex, with ELTON in pink across the chest and HERCULES down the side of the right leg. Elton was especially fond of quilted satin, despite the crippling heat it generated during his performances. Another typical Reavey production was a yellow quilted satin suit, its short-sleeved jacket embroidered across the back with a scene of turquoise sea, violet sky, sand, a palm tree, musical notes, a cherry-red transistor radio and a pair of spectacles.

She quickly learned to camouflage the shortcomings of Elton's figure, broadening his shoulders with pads like an American football quarterback's, pluming his trousers like an Argentinian gaucho's to hide the bulkiness of his legs. She also learned that his measurements were seldom constant. If Elton was passing through a period of stress, his waistline could expand alarmingly between the first fitting and the final one. Though prone to indulgence in food and alcohol, he also possessed an ability, given to very few, to know when enough was enough. 'I've got an iron will,' he frequently observed of himself. 'If I want to lose weight, I can just lose it.' Having tactfully let everything out, Annie Reavey would sometimes have to take it all in again.

She also learned there was nothing she could dream up that was too wild, way-out or lacking in all normal masculine dignity for Elton to wear onstage. 'One outfit I made him for St Valentine's Day, I thought he'd never stand for. It was pink and gold Lurex brocade, trimmed with gold lace; it had a pink and gold heart embroidered on it. And short pants. But he loved it.'

The object was over-the-top ostentation and extravagance – but only up to a point. At an Elton John concert, his audience knew they could expect an entrance of surpassing fancy-dress absurdity and self-mockery. But there the posing and posturing stopped. The performance that followed was the same exuberant, unpretentious rock-'n'-roll sweatshop it had always been. The figure punishing the piano was as little aware of its fantastic plumage as a baby is of the designer label on its romper suit.

Not that his acquisitive eye failed to note the increasing use of stage theatrics in Britain by David Bowie and in America by the first male rock star to use a woman's name, Alice Cooper. Elton had attended an early Alice concert, and been overwhelmed by its *grand guignol* inventiveness. 'It was incredible, with the helicopter, the shower of panties, the fireworks. It was the best-produced show I've ever seen. I was caught up in it myself, scrambling for a pair of panties. You can't do anything like that in Britain. You'd get jobsworths backstage, saying "You can't do that here. Who's going to clean up the mess?"'

His belief in value for money onstage was almost Calvinistic in its fervour. He even lambasted his own supreme teenage idol, Jerry Lee Lewis, for giving short measure to concert audiences. 'They asked me to play on his album, but I said no. He was so disappointing when I saw him at the Palladium, and as far as I'm concerned he was the best rock-'n'-roll pianist ever. I went in my drape jacket, and got jeered at by all the Teds. He could have wiped the audience out, but he just sat there and played country and western numbers as if to say "Fuck you". And calling himself the Killer! I could kill more people with one finger than he did when I saw him.'

It is possibly the only instance of Elton being asked to appear on a record and refusing. The ex-session man remained a session man to the core. Even now, on his impossible treadmill of concerts and recording, he could always somehow find time to help out if a fellow musician was in need. He played piano on the debut album of Lesley Duncan, a backup singer and writer whose talent he had always been keen to promote. Not content with co-producing Long John Baldry's second album, *Everything Stops for Tea*, he volunteered to play piano and sing backup vocals, with Rod Stewart, when Baldry made it, once more, to *Top of the Pops*.

He agreed to be in Marc Bolan's film *Born to Boogie*, though predicting, correctly, that Bolan would monopolise most of the action. For Elton, the thrill of the occasion was meeting Ringo Starr, whom Bolan had also persuaded to play a bit part. They had something to talk about since Ringo still hung on in Surrey, living beside the river Wey in Peter Sellers's former house (where, with Liverpudlian practicality, the sixteenth-century oak doors had cat flaps cut into them).

Thereafter, Elton frequently dropped in to see Ringo at the Apple office in London. He was inside the empire of his ultimate heroes at last, even though that empire was now all but extinct, transferred from its Georgian house in Savile Row to a small administrative office in St James's. The general manager, Tony King, had originally worked for George Martin's AIR organisation out of an office at Dick James Music, and had known Elton since his days as struggling Reg. 'He told me I was to call him Elton officially now, but I just couldn't,' Tony King remembers. 'I didn't call him Reg either. I just called him nothing. For about the next two years, I'd say "Phone for you, er . . ." followed by this awful blank.'

His Aunt Win's son, Paul Robinson, was now sixteen and desperate to follow in Elton's footsteps to the music business. For his young cousin Elton did what his own elder cousin, Roy, had done for him at Mills Music, seven years earlier. He used his influence at Apple to get Paul taken on there as a messenger boy.

'I remember Elton coming in all the time, to see Ringo or Tony King,' Paul Robinson says. 'Ringo had a furniture business then – selling things like glass-topped coffee tables mounted on Rolls-Royce grilles. I was always loading stuff like that into the car for Elton. It was when I first properly realised what a big star he'd become. He told me I oughtn't to be cheeky to him any more.'

He was, indeed, becoming famous on a national scale, rather than just in the closed, parochial world of young people's music. National papers then took little interest in pop musicians unless they figured in the expected scandals arising from drug use, insanitary hair or displays of public disrespect. But awareness was growing of this new, very different pop star: not mumbly and sneery, but clear-spoken and polite; not working-class but middle-class; not against the establishment like others of his kind, but happy, even anxious, to become a part of it.

Early in 1972, Elton and his music were the subject of an article by Michael Wale on the 'op-ed' page of *The Times*, a slot which Lennon and McCartney in their glory never attained. That same month, at the other journalistic extreme, he quite defeated the obvious scepticism of the *Sunday Mirror's* showbusiness editor:

> For star quality in the accepted sense, I wouldn't pick him out of a crowd of two. His appearance doesn't help – receding hair, desperately combed forward, stilt-heeled shoes raising him only to medium height, dark glasses that are not so much groovy, more a necessity.
>
> Yet this is Elton John, multi-million disc seller, just back from a triumphant tour of the US. How does he do it? All I can assume is that his music is as honest as he seems to be as a person. It was Elton himself who drew my attention to his defects.
>
> 'Can't grow my hair long – it's too thin. The dark glasses I started to wear when I was thirteen, trying to copy Buddy Holly. Now my eyes are weak, with or without them. So if the fans are thinking about copying me, I advise them to forget it.'
>
> In his private life, too, Elton is scarcely superstar material. There are no groupies either outside his fifty thousand pound house, clamouring for autographs, or inside, begging for bed.
>
> 'I live on my own, without servants,' he told me. 'I do my own housework, ironing, cooking and the rest of it. I like doing these chores. And that way, I know they've been done to my satisfaction. I can't stand tattiness and dirt.'

In America, the good impression was fortified by effective appearances on general TV chat shows, like Dick Cavett's and David Frost's, and by manifest respect and admiration for the American Way. While playing Houston on his spring 1972 tour, with 'Rocket Man' riding high, Elton asked to be allowed to visit the NASA space centre. It was no mere publicist's photo-opportunity. He and the band spent four hours at NASA, lunching with Al Worden, the Apollo 15 pilot, even trying out a flight simulator.

The National Youth Theatre concerts, through which he met Bryan Forbes, belonged to this same period of social entrenchment. Though not previously a theatre enthusiast, Elton was persuaded by his lawyer, Michael Oliver, to attend the NYT's current production of *Good Lads at Heart*, a hard-hitting play about Borstal boys. The production turned him on to theatre in general and the under-financed plight of youth theatre in particular. He gave three fund-raising concerts for the NYT at the Shaw Theatre, one at £1 a head, one at £5 a head, which Princess Margaret attended, then one which NYT members could attend free. He subsequently did a fourth show, and was invited to become one of the Theatre's vice presidents. After that, he kept up with all NYT productions and would even sometimes look in at rehearsals.

His plea to Bryan Forbes to help him acquire taste has the classic Elton note. Unpretentious, honest, trusting and ever so slightly forlorn. The selfsame note as 'I feel lost' and 'Can't you manage me? Please.'

He became a regular caller at the Forbes's bookshop in Virginia Water, frequently buying every book in its window display. 'He loved books,' Nanette Newman remembers. 'He wanted to have them, like we did, all through the house. But not just for show. When you talked to him, you realised how amazingly well-read he was.'

Hercules was only a short walk from the Forbes's house, Seven Pines. Elton became a frequent caller there, too, to the amazement of their two small girls, Sarah and Emma. 'I can see him standing in the hall, holding a couple of gigantic Easter eggs, which he'd brought over for the girls,' Nanette Newman says. 'One of them was a huge pink thing, like something out of Barbara Cartland, which I've still got. One couldn't get rid of it. An Easter egg like that only comes along once in any lifetime.'

He was fascinated by the Forbes's world of movies and studios, and their vast circle of friends in the film business. Bryan Forbes was, in any case, a gifted raconteur, especially on the subject of his close friend, and Elton's *Goon Show* hero, Peter Sellers. 'Once, when Peter and I were coming back from Paris, we told the press we'd discovered a pop singer named Turk Thrust. It even got into the papers that we were going to manage this non-existent pop star, and we kept the gag going for quite a long time. Elton loved that story. He couldn't get over it.'

Nanette Newman remembers how unassuming and straight-forward he was, despite his obvious pop-star eminence and the platform-wobbly weirdness of his clothes. 'He struck me as someone who was totally without conceit. Of course, he had a proper idea of his own worth. If a record was in the charts, he'd tell you, "Hey, guess what — it's done so-and-so . . ." But underneath it all he was truly modest. And it wasn't the affectation of modesty some people put on. With Elton it was completely genuine.'

The Forbeses coached Elton in aesthetics, as far as they were able. They put him in touch with several reputable West End picture and antique dealers and also introduced him to Bryan Organ the portrait painter who had recently painted Nanette. Elton loved Organ's work, with its Pop Art record album feel, and immediately began to sit for his own portrait.

'Another thing he said he wanted to do was go to Cartier's,' Nanette Newman remembers. 'I said I'd take him, because I knew a couple of the people there – but first of all I had to go to Harrods to buy a new washing machine. So I'm there in Harrods' electrical department, trying to choose a washing machine, with this apparition next to me, in amazing clothes, murmuring "Boring, bor-ing!"'

'When we finally did get to Cartier's, the first thing Elton did was to pick up an enormous ring. "God, this is really vulgar!" he said. "It's awful. It's just like some blue-rinsed old woman in Palm Beach or Miami would wear – I love it." While all these terribly smart and correct Cartier people watched, he went round the whole shop, picking things up and buying them. It was as if he was going round Safeway with a trolley. He spent money like Monopoly money. And everyone else had to have presents as well. He bought Bryan a Cartier watch. I certainly didn't want him to buy me anything, and didn't think he had. But when we got into the car afterwards, he said "That's for you", and there was a piece of jewellery on the seat that I hadn't even seen him buy.'

Elton and John Reid became regulars at the Forbeses' parties over at Seven Pines. Nanette Newman remembers them as an attractive couple, openly affectionate with one another. 'John was much more in the background, of course – the fixer who kept things running and made things happen. But he was tremendous company, too, and could be hysterically funny in his own right. I remember him telling us once that he'd been mixed up with Barbara Windsor, somehow or other, and was having terrible trouble with one of her ex-husbands or boy-friends.'

The Forbeses, in turn, would go over to Hercules for Sunday lunch, cooked by John Reid. 'It was always very traditional,' Nanette Newman says. 'Roast beef with roast potatoes. And the house was immaculate. Elton did the housework himself, and was incredibly houseproud. I remember one day they'd been over to us for lunch, and we were going back to the bungalow for tea. Elton rushed off in the car ahead of us. When we got there, he was frantically Hoovering the living room.'

As they got to know Elton more, they discovered the hectic range of his emotions. More than once, he reminded Bryan Forbes of the star he was most avid to hear about: Peter Sellers. 'They were similar in sometimes being able to get on a roll and be hysterically funny for an incredibly long time at a stretch. I remember once seeing Elton compose a whole impromptu operetta, with lyrics and music, about all the shopkeepers in Virginia Water, especially Mr Batty, the grocer. It went on and on, and was totally brilliant. Sellers would have done exactly the same kind of thing, without the music.

'And their temperaments were very alike, too. Either up at the peak or down in the valley.'

He was down in that valley, though soon to be up again, and scaling still higher, shinier peaks.

In June 1972, due to record a second album in France, Elton once more succumbed to the nervous exhaustion that could drop over him like a sack. He cancelled an Italian tour at the last moment, throwing himself into an even worse state at the thought of having let people down. 'It was the second time we were supposed to go there, but pulled out, cancelling the same promoter!' he recalled later. 'In Italy they were holding a competition. "Is he going to turn up or isn't he?"'

On gathering with band and technicians at Château d'Hierouville, he told his producer, Gus Dudgeon, that he couldn't face the work ahead. Dudgeon philosophically suggested postponing the album until September. Then Elton had another lightning change of mood. 'I thought, "I'm going on holiday in July, and it'd be nice to have it all over with by then. It'd be terrible to have come all the way over and not do it." So we did it, although I was very ill.'

He was in fact suffering from glandular fever, and in the very worst possible physical and mental state to begin composing a dozen new songs from scratch. To add to the pressure, Bernie Taupin had provided him with only one finished lyric. Bernie himself was in America, writing to short order and posting each set of words off as he finished them. Then he suddenly turned up at the château, materialising with a flower-child insouciance that Elton, in his overwrought state, found highly provoking. 'He'd been phoning up every night from Los Angeles, and one morning I walked out on the lawn and there he is, behind a bloody bush! In France! Nearly drove me round the bend!'

Iron willpower prevailed. And, once the stubby fingers were spread on the piano keys, ideas began crowding in with their usual facility. Going from bottom to top form in a blink, Elton wrote twelve new songs in two days, seven on one day, five on the other.

Among the lyrics Bernie had produced was a piece of pure Fifties rock-'n'-roll pastiche called, not 'See You Later, Alligator' but 'Crocodile Rock'. Another popped into his head after reading a story in an American news magazine. 'I forget now if it was *Time* or

Newsweek. It was about this guy who'd been wounded in the Vietnam War and had gone back to his home town, just wanting to forget it all and get on with his life. But the people there wanted him to be a hero, and wouldn't leave him alone. In the end, this guy had become so disillusioned, he'd decided the only way out was to leave America altogether.'

The Vietnam veteran's story prompted one of the swiftest pieces of lyric-writing by Bernie since 'Your Song'. 'I got out of bed one morning at the château and wrote this thing, called "Daniel", in about half an hour, and took it down to Elton. Elton got up from the breakfast table, went over to the piano and finished it in about fifteen or twenty minutes, then said to the band "Hey, guys. Let's cut this." We'd done the track by the end of the day.'

The whole of July had been set aside for Elton's first real holiday since becoming a full-time musician. John Reid, Bernie, Maxine and he were to share a rented house in Malibu with Bryan Forbes and Nanette Newman and their little girls, Sarah and Emma.

When Elton arrived at Los Angeles airport from France, he was in anything but a holiday mood. 'As soon as I got off the plane, people said to me "Hey – you're having a nervous breakdown." I was on the verge of a crack-up. Personality-wise, I was unbearable – moody and shouting at people. I'd had bouts of exhaustion before, but had never been in a nervous state like this.'

By the time the Forbeses flew in from London, everything was different again. The glandular fever had subsided, the black moods and screaming Little Moments melted into the Malibu ozone. Elton was back on a roll.

To welcome Bryan Forbes he staged an elaborate joke, partly based on Forbes's old running pop-star gag with Peter Sellers, and partly on his own first inglorious arrival in Los Angeles. 'Elton met us at the airport,' Forbes remembers. 'While we were walking out through the concourse, I knew there was something going on. Outside he'd got a Greyhound bus with LA WELCOMES TURK THRUST written on the side. And a troupe of drum majorettes all twirling and chanting "Hip-hooray – Turk Thrust is in LA."'

The rented house was a rambling affair with a central courtyard, standing right on the beach. With other visitors, like Elton's friend Tony King, there could be as many as twelve people in residence. 'The whole month was like one of those holidays you remember from childhood,' Bryan Forbes says. 'I don't think any of us ever stopped laughing.'

What made the holiday for Elton were the Forbeses' numerous friends in the Hollywood film colony. Every movie star he had ever ogled in *Photoplay* magazines in the foyers of Middlesex Odeon cinemas seemed to be on first-name terms with Bryan and Nanette and available for visits or to visit. For most of that month, the pug face bore a look of blank bedazzlement.

One of the first Hollywood legends he met was Mae West. 'We were all taken into this room that was totally white,' Bernie Taupin remembers. 'We sat down on this big white couch, on this white shag-pile carpet. At the end of the room there was a sort of butler figure, standing in front of a curtain. "Gentlemen," the butler said, "Miss Mae West." The curtain was drawn back, and there she was. She looked at Elton and me on the couch and said, "Well! Wall-to-wall men."

'She came to my birthday party, too; she sat there all evening at the end of the room, not moving or saying anything. It was just like having a stuffed dummy of Mae West at your party.'

Another night, the Forbeses took them to a friend's house where a Groucho Marx movie was being privately screened. When they got there, they found Groucho himself among the audience. On being introduced, he complained that Elton's name was the wrong way round, and thereafter always called him 'John Elton'.

'On the way back, we decided to stop and have a meal in a diner,' Nanette Newman remembers. 'It was one of those places where everything on the menu was "home-style this" and "corn-fed that". When our orders arrived, somehow we'd managed to get more chips than a whole army could eat in a year. Elton took his glasses off – a sure sign with him that something was about to happen. He picked up a handful of these chips and put them in a napkin. "I don't have to eat in places like this!" he said, "I could have been a famous brain surgeon" – and he jammed all the chips down on top of his own head. There was nearly a riot in this place. Bryan got the bill, gave them a huge tip and got us all out before someone called the police.'

A few nights later, an elaborate outing was arranged. Groucho Marx would come to the house for dinner, then the whole party would go on to a performance of a new rock musical *Jesus Christ Superstar*.

Erroneously warned in advance that his guest was a frail and delicate old man, Elton took the precaution of lighting a roaring fire. Groucho arrived in a long overcoat and beret, both of which he declined to remove. He gave Elton such a general ribbing about his name being back to front that Elton at one point held up both hands in mock surrender and said, 'Don't shoot me, I'm just the piano player', so naming the new album he had just made.

Also among the company were Clive Banks from DJM in London, and Strawberry studio's manageress, Catherine Philippe-Gérard. As often happened with Elton, his former obsessive enthusiasm for Catherine had given way to boredom and covert mockery. 'She had rather large breasts,' Nanette Newman remembers. 'While she was out of the room, Elton used to imitate her by putting two grapefruit under his shirt.'

Unluckily, on the night Groucho Marx came to dinner, Catherine had announced she would prepare a typically French meal. 'But everything in the kitchen started to go wrong,' Clive Banks remembers. 'We're all sitting round the table with Groucho Marx, waiting to eat, and there's this sound of terrible panic going on offstage.'

The subsequent outing with Groucho to see *Jesus Christ Superstar* proved equally memorable, as Bryan Forbes describes it. 'In between leaving the car and getting to our seats, Groucho managed to pick up two teenage girls. So I'm sitting there with Elton in his rock-star gear on one side and Groucho Marx in his beret on the other, about to see *Jesus Christ Superstar*. As the performance began, Groucho's voice suddenly rang out: "Does this have a happy ending?" In the Crucifixion scene, it rang out again: "This is sure to offend the Jews."'

Forbes's birthday happened to fall during the month, prompting Elton's most ambitious stunt of all. 'He asked me what sign I was born under, and I said "Leo". On my birthday, when I woke up and looked out of the window, there was a full-grown lion down in the courtyard. Elton had somehow got in touch with a zoo and arranged for one to be delivered, along with a trainer, who was standing there, pointing a gun at its head.'

Groucho returned to the house several times, evidently fond of his new acquaintance, 'John Elton'. 'He'd sometimes sing to us,' Bernie Taupin remembers. 'He used to call up Marvin Hamlisch, who was hardly known then, to come over and accompany him on the piano.' Another visitor was Don Bachardy, Christopher Isherwood's artist lover, who made sketches of Elton, Bernie and Sarah and Emma Forbes.

They also met David Cassidy, the boy actor from the *Partridge Family* TV show, then enjoying his brief reign as teenybop's number one heart-throb. It was evidently a far from pleasant predicament, and it brought out all Elton's best qualities of elder-brother sympathy and rationality. 'Poor guy – we took him to the Troubadour to see a group, and it was the first time he'd been out for two and a half years. He gets up every morning at six, goes to the TV studio, makes an LP, gives a concert. He's like a robot. He asked Bernie and me to write a song for his next album, and I wouldn't mind that at all.

People like him get written off. Because it's the Osmonds, for example, everyone says "Ooh, terrible!" But records like "Crazy Horses" are really good.'

The constant, recuperative pleasure Elton remembered from that month's house party was shopping, acquiring and collecting:

'We used to get up in the morning and say "Right, here we go, looting." Bryan would go with Bernie to a bookshop, and I'd go to a tablecloth shop. We're such great looters, Bernie, Maxine and I. There were sixty-seven cases, and there must have been thirty-two trunks — you know, those Newberry's trunks with the American flag on them. They needed a Greyhound bus to take us to the airport.'

Thus far in 1972, Elton had done only one short American tour, at the time of 'Rocket Man', playing small college-type dates in far-flung places like Oxford, Ohio, and East Lansing, Missouri. To redress the intercontinental balance, a tour on the old gargantuan scale was scheduled for November and December, returning to big-city venues like Carnegie Hall, New York, and also opening up such new territories as Baton Rouge, Louisiana, College Station, Texas, and — perhaps the ultimate Elton conquest — Normal, Illinois.

Learning the lesson of 1971, his new album, *Don't Shoot Me, I'm Only the Piano Player*, was held back from release until *Honky Château* had run its course in the shops. His only new release in late 1972 would be a single from the new album, to create advance interest and also follow up the global success of 'Rocket Man'. Whatever might later be said about John Reid's influence, Elton's career can be seen here assuming a logical pace and strategic intelligence it had hitherto totally lacked.

The choice of a first single from *Don't Shoot Me* provoked what had by now become an almost traditional wrangle between Elton and his record company. Dick and Stephen James were for 'Crocodile Rock', the Fifties pastiche whose carefree sound was so very far from what its performer had been feeling at the time. Elton wanted to put out Bernie's song about the Vietnam veteran, 'Daniel', but the Jameses insisted it would stand no chance as a single. They said it was too slow, too slight, too quiet.

On this occasion, Elton gave in. 'Crocodile Rock', at least, was totally unlike 'Rocket Man', and the first real proof to his album audience (if they hadn't heard 'Rock and Roll Madonna') that he could play fast and furious as well as mournful and slow. With self-immunising pessimism, he wrote off its chances in advance, not least because on its release date, 27 October, he would still be in Britain. He had developed a superstition that no record could be successful if released in a country where he happened to be at the time.

The Jameses' instinct seemed more than vindicated. 'Crocodile Rock' went to number one in America and five in Britain. Bernie Taupin's lyric perfectly caught the breaking wave of teenage nostalgia. The song was like a tour bus crowded with the shades of all Elton and Bernie's favourite jukebox heroes, Bill Haley, Eddie Cochran, Neil Sedaka, Bobby Vee, the Beach Boys. The chorus was a joke falsetto, which the writers of Pat Boone's 'Speedy Gonzales' afterwards claimed had been plagiarised from them. Likewise, Don McLean spotted strong affinities, to put it no more strongly, with his prototype nostalgia hit, 'American Pie'. Elton himself admitted he had plundered ideas for 'Crocodile Rock' with the same enthusiasm that he threw albums into shopping trolleys at Tower Records. 'I wanted it to be a record about all the things I grew up with. Of course it's a rip-off. It's derivative in every sense of the word.'

The three-month American tour of late 1972 included another major British group, Family. It also included Legs Larry Smith of the Bonzo Dog Band, who had provided tap-dancing effects on *Honky Château*, and in whom Elton discovered a kindred soul.

With the spindly shanks that gave Legs Larry his name went Apache-style hair, a long hatchet face, a military moustache, genteel speech and almost unlimited stores of camp whimsicality. On the American tour, when Elton sang 'I Think I'm Going to Kill Myself', Legs Larry came on and tap-danced in American football player's costume of knickerbockers, shoulderpads and silver helmet, topped by a miniature bride-and-groom ornament from a wedding cake. Later he and Elton donned trench coats and fedoras, put up umbrellas and did 'Singin' in the Rain' while dancing-girls high-kicked behind them and glitter was showered over them by a midget, borrowed from a TV frankfurter commercial. The finale consisted of Elton, Legs Larry and Bernie Taupin, playing toy guitars and flinging handfuls of confetti and sweets into the audience.

Elton and Legs Larry also went out 'looting', though this time the object was further idiotic bric-à-brac to incorporate into their stage routine. In a Montreal Woolworth's, they found a picture of Doris Day which had been on display so long, it was covered in dust. Elton bought it to put on his piano that night. It stayed there as a mascot for the rest of the tour.

Despite ecstatic audiences everywhere, the tour went anything but smoothly. Before one gig, Family's stage equipment got lost, and the girlfriend of one of them, the singer Linda Lewis, had to go on in their place. There were also some nasty moments on aeroplanes.

'Larry and I used to hold hands on every flight,' Elton later recalled. 'He used to wind me up by saying "The engine's on fire." One day I looked out, and the engine *was* on fire!'

To add to the strain, half-way through the thirty-odd date itinerary Elton had to return to England. He had been chosen to appear in the annual Royal Command Variety Performance in the presence of the Queen and the Duke of Edinburgh. The invitation had been issued before the tour, but was only finally confirmed as Elton, Legs Larry and the others were working their way through the American Midwest. Though it would mean cancelling his Phoenix concert, flying back to London overnight, rehearsing and performing virtually without sleep and flying straight out again to pick up the tour in Tulsa, Oklahoma, Elton did not hesitate. As he explained later, 'I've always done everything the Queen asked me.'

He arrived back at Heathrow airport early on a Sunday morning, to be greeted by hundreds of hysterical teenage girls. It transpired they were not waiting for him but for the Jackson Five, who were also in the Royal Command Performance and whose flight arrived a few minutes after his. True to the endless replay of the Beatles' story, radio broadcasts had been saying that 200 free T-shirts would be given away: 'a stupid thing,' Elton commented angrily. 'They should give all the kids T-shirts or none at all. It's such a hype.'

He had been almost forty-eight hours without sleep, and was already far from his bonniest. His mood grew still more frayed during the naturally extensive and anxious rehearsals for the show which was to be held at the London Palladium and go out on television to some 25 million viewers. Elton had been asked to do two numbers. The organisers suggested 'Rocket Man' followed by 'Your Song' as most suitable for royal ears. But Elton insisted on doing 'Crocodile Rock', followed by 'I Think I'm Going to Kill Myself', complete with the Legs Larry camp tap-dance routine. Amazingly enough, this was agreed.

Nor did an impromptu press conference he gave during rehearsals strike a totally loyal note. He announced that breaking off his American tour to obey the royal command had cost him £25,000 – 'or it might be £15,000. It's a lot of money, anyway.' 'Why had he done so?' 'Because 25 million people will be able to listen to my latest record, and this is the only chance I've got to plug it.'

The bill was the usual weird mishmash that Her Majesty customarily endures in the name of charity. Among the other performers were Liberace, the Jackson Five, the crooner Jack Jones and the musical comedy star Carol Channing. There were almost two full days of pernickety TV setups and sound checks over the London

Palladium's notoriously poor microphone system. Elton afterwards described it as 'the most horrendous two-day stretch I've ever had'.

The dressing rooms were as crowded as Bombay tenements. Elton shared one with Jack Jones and Liberace, whose jewel-encrusted costumes made a glitter rocker's simple shiny suit seem as modest as the garb of a minister of the kirk. 'He was great,' Elton remembered afterwards. 'He just kept wheeling trunks of clothes in. I just sat there, watching him. He kept calm through the whole thing. All these people were badgering him all the time for autographs and he always did the most ornate autographs, and drew a grand piano around them. He was really nice. He was the most professional person on that show.'

Those who remembered the Beatles' cheekily deferential Royal Command Performance in 1963 were to receive a vivid demonstration of how both times and pop music had changed. Since the Queen herself makes no comment about the show, it will never be known what she made of the shiny-suited figure, in heels several inches higher than hers, pounding a grand piano covered with a pink satin quilt on the hem of which little coloured Christmas lights winked on and off. Nor whether she grasped the import of the second song in which a tall, moustachioed man in a crash helmet tap-danced to and fro, letting off balloons whose farting noises, fortunately, were inaudible to 25 million viewers at home.

Press reviews of the Royal Command Performance are seldom kind. One highbrow Sunday critic said that Liberace had made Elton John 'look like the musical dwarf he is'. No one could have agreed more fervently than the 'musical dwarf' himself. 'Well, I think he did. I think he was the only decent thing on that show. I don't mind. I don't find that offensive at all.'

Elton could afford to disregard such little jibes. His American concerts were sell-out sensations, coast to coast. His records evaporated from stores: not only those currently in the charts but everything he had produced since his first overhyped advent in August 1970. Previous dissatisfactions and disappointments were swept away as questionable gold discs changed into unchallengeable brilliant white ones. By the end of 1972 *Honky Château, Madman Across the Water, Tumbleweed Connection* and the original *Elton John* album all had gone platinum in the US for sales of more than a million copies each. He was no longer a British rock star famous in America. He was America's most famous rock star.

There could have been many ways of marking this moment. Elton celebrated it by going back to Metroland, Pinner and school.

On 7 December he returned to Pinner County Grammar, whose

streamlined façade he had not seen since 1965, when he left ingloriously to become an office boy at Mills Music. The school's sixth form Stag Society had asked him to play at one of their social gatherings. Elton agreed and, with his usual punctiliousness, kept to the appointed date, even phoning the school while on tour in America to reassure them that the visit was still on.

It is always agreeable to return to one's old school as a wealthy celebrity, especially if one has conspicuously failed to shine there as a pupil. Elton made the most of it, arriving by Ferrari in a purple satin suit and red-tinted spectacles with white frames.

Though Jack Westgate Smith was no longer headmaster, many of the staff remained from Reggie Dwight's time. Among them was Bill Johnson, the history master, who'd said that at forty Reggie would be either an assistant in a record shop or a millionaire. Mr Stoupe, the music master who had so often reproached Reggie for wasting his talents, was also still there. A photograph was taken of the visiting rock star warmly shaking his hand as a guide, mentor and friend.

Elton gave a ninety-minute performance, playing 'Rocket Man' and 'Crocodile Rock' on the same Steinway grand he had once used to practise Bach and Brahms and illicit Jerry Lee Lewis licks. Only Stag Society members and teachers were allowed into the hall, even the new head's own children being excluded. 'Security' was provided by the school caretaker and heftier members of the rugby XV, while a low-key police presence kept watch outside. In between numbers, Elton confessed that he was more nervous playing before his old teachers than he would be performing for 15,000 people in America.

Afterwards he looked round the school, stopping to examine a group photograph from which Reggie Dwight looked out resignedly in buttoned-up blazer and Buddy Holly specs. He then kept up with the Stag Society's after-meeting tradition of adjourning to the local pub. 'There was only room for one other person in his Ferrari,' Bill Johnson recalls. 'So naturally he went off in it with the prettiest girl sixth-former in the school. We thought that was completely natural pop star behaviour.'

A few days later – wholly unannounced this time – Elton returned to Pinner County Grammar again. With him he had a colour TV set for the Stag Society's common room. 'He arrived right in the middle of the Second Year Christmas party,' Bill Johnson remembers. 'Of course, the whole lot of them surrounded Elton, going wild. I and some of the other staff had to form a human chain to protect him.'

The headmaster's summary of that term's events mentioned the visit in due context and characteristic style:

Mr and Mrs Pelzer and Miss Young took a party of 19 senior pupils on a skiing holiday to Macugnaga Staffa, Northern Italy, during the half-term break . . .

The Parks Department has recently removed the rubble from the old air-raid shelter and have finished off the area with a layer of top soil . . .

I have already reported to the appropriate committee through the Director of Education the theft on the night of November 3rd/4th of three transistor radios, a typewriter and 30 pence from the dinner float . . .

Meetings of Stag have included talks on 'Forensic Science in Detection', 'The Soviet Union', 'Local History', 'On Being An Air Pilot' and a never-to-be-forgotten visit of ex-pupil Elton John who delighted the younger membership with his songs and pleased the older members with the very real charm and common sense which lies behind the gimmickry of his profession.

It had taken ten years, and untold thousands of miles, but R. K. Dwight of Downfield House was going home with a good report at last.

NINE

Rocket Men

JOHN Reid had made the most of his time on the inside at Dick James Music. Like a good St Mirin's boy, swotting for his GCE, he had pored over the contracts and schedules that applied to Elton: the recording agreements with This Record Co. and MCA in America; the publishing agreement between Elton, Bernie Taupin and Dick James Music; and the cat's cradle of sub-publishing deals with DJM's overseas subsidiaries and licensees by which royalties on their songs were collected worldwide.

He also obtained detailed statements from Elton's accountants of sums so far received as Elton's share of record sales and in publishing royalties. The High Court, thirteen years later, would hear of his immediate 'concern' at the 'low' publishing royalties being received, especially from American 'mechanicals' (ie radio play). To one of the accountants, Mr Lawrence, he queried whether the James organisation's wholly owned American subsidiary, DJM USA, was making deductions of perhaps as much as 40 per cent before accounting to DJM UK.

His behaviour angered Stephen James, who felt that Reid owed loyalty to DJM for as long as it employed him. An awkward moment – also mentioned in the High Court thirteen years later – occurred when Reid was discovered photocopying Elton's recording and publishing agreements with the apparent intention of taking them out of the office for lengthy examination.

In mid-August 1972, John Reid handed in his notice at DJM. On 20 September, eleven days after his twenty-third birthday, his own company John Reid Enterprises was incorporated. The starting capital was £5,000, which Reid borrowed from Barclays Bank's Brook Street branch, using his management contract with Elton as collateral. There were two directors, Reid and his father, John Reid senior.

Long before Reid had any thought of acting for Elton, he knew

SIR ELTON

what business matter was uppermost in Elton's mind. It was the publishing agreement which Bernie and he had signed as minors in 1967, making over the copyright in their work to Dick James Music. A process with which Dick James was already familiar – what might be called the John and Paul Syndrome – was getting into gear again. To two unknown youths in 1967, it had seemed wonderful that a famous music-publisher should wish to put his name on their songs. In 1972, with those songs turning gold and platinum all over the world, the composers saw no reason why anyone but themselves should own them.

It was fortuitous that, in July 1972, a High Court action, Instone versus A. Schroeder Music Publishing Co. Ltd, had caused reverberations throughout the British music industry. The judge, Mr Justice Plowman, set aside a ten-year exclusive agreement between a songwriter and a music publisher, ruling that its terms were 'so unfair as to be oppressive and contrary to public policy'. He said the contract had implied that the publisher would not 'unfairly, unjustifiably or artificially diminish' the income of the songwriter, but that foreign sub-publishing arrangements breached that undertaking, so in effect negating the entire agreement.

On leaving DJM, one of John Reid's first business meetings was with Elton's solicitor, Michael Oliver of Berger Oliver, and the barrister who had successfully represented the plaintiffs in the Schroeder case. Shown Elton's publishing agreement with DJM, the barrister said it seemed 'entirely unobjectionable', but added that a publisher had a duty not to deplete royalties unfairly. He recommended that an audit be made at both DJM USA and DJM UK, that all sub-publishing agreements and relevant documents be examined, and that for the time being Elton should sign no further new material over to DJM. Among notes taken of the conference by Berger Oliver was one that 'Dick James must somehow justify the situation whereby his companies take 70 per cent of the sale proceeds in the United States, leaving Elton and Bernie with only 15 per cent each. This may be the basis for a settlement rather than litigation.'

On 20 October, John Reid met Dick James as his entrepreneurial equal. He complained that Elton's publishing agreements were unfair, particularly with regard to the USA, and that the DJM group was withholding more than its proper share of royalties. Even the emotionless legal document that records this encounter gives off a whiff of Dick James's chagrin at seeing the John and Paul Syndrome breaking out again.

In his own estimation, he had treated Elton magnificently, and his own estimation was very largely true. He had spent three years and an enormous sum in launching Elton, allowed him unlimited indulgence to make the music he wanted, acted not merely as his publisher but also his manager, even his father confessor, and steered him right on occasions when Elton's own instinct had been to steer himself wrong. For Elton, indeed – such was James's belief in him – standard procedures had been waived all along the line. One can only imagine the tension of that moment when fifty-two-year-old music mogul stared at twenty-three-year-old Scotsman, little suspecting how terminal bad luck would set in from here.

Dick James responded with the injured dignity one would expect. He denied that royalties were being unfairly withheld from Elton, and said that 'no fresh ground' existed for renegotiating the publishing agreement. As to the audit recommended by counsel, his company's books were open for inspection at any time.

The history of the Beatles continued to be an insistent subtext to Elton's career. Late in 1972, John Reid consulted John Eastman, the New York attorney, brother of Paul McCartney's wife Linda. Eastman had been McCartney's nominee to sort out the Beatles' finances: his rejection by the others in favour of Allen Klein can be said, as much as anything, to have brought on their final dissolution.

Having looked over Elton's contracts with DJM, John Eastman said that the only one which, perhaps, might be challenged was the publishing agreement. It was felt expedient however, not to press Dick James further, for the present. His co-operation was needed in negotiations with the US Internal Revenue Service, who were withholding a portion of Elton's earnings pending a decision on his tax status in America. Subsequently, John Eastman wrote to John Reid that in his view there was 'a strong case' for claiming DJM had failed to account to Elton satisfactorily, and that the practice of using wholly owned foreign subsidiaries like DJM USA to reduce royalties payable to him was 'not a proper one'.

On 10 May, 1973, DJM's management agreements with Elton, via the two income-receiving companies William A. Bong and Sackville, officially expired. Two months later, new contracts were signed between Bong and Sackville, on Elton's behalf, and John Reid Enterprises.

It was, as few doubted, the beginning of the end between Elton and the Dick James Organisation. The publishing agreement expired the following November and, clearly, was unlikely to be renewed. There remained only the five-year recording agreement with This Record Co., signed in 1970, which meant that Elton John product would continue to be released by DJM until 1975.

But the spirit of Elton – a benign shade in shabby herringbone, haunting the tea kettle and record cupboard – was gone from Dick James Music. In its place was a small but exceedingly active Scots poltergeist that seemed to delight in its power to turn everything upside down, alter the temperature of rooms and make short hairs rise on the backs of necks.

The Beatles were not the first musicians to try owning their own record company. The practice was established in America in the early Sixties by such artist-owned labels as Frank Sinatra's Reprise and James Brown's JB. It was a well-known desire of those who made it big in music to break away from the companies that had originally nurtured them, and gain total artistic control of their own output. There was a time in almost every major performer's life when he wanted to be an entrepreneur, using his wealth and influence to give new talent the encouragement and financial backing he himself might have lacked. Generally linked to that was an ambition to try producing records rather than merely performing, and a desire to show the industry how a totally different kind of business organisation could be created by someone whose heart was in the right place.

The Beatles' Apple Corps had taken such altruism to its ultimate. John Lennon and Paul McCartney had hoped to institute 'a kind of Western communism' under which Beatle money would subsidise not only new recording talent but also new writers, poets, painters, sculptors, inventors and anyone else who turned up at 3 Savile Row with hand outstretched in the regulation manner. The result had been a freeloaders' free-for-all in which the Beatles had seen £2 million of their money wasted, their offices deluged by unusable material, their food and liquor gorged, their fitments, furniture and secretaries' handbags stolen, and, when all else was consumed, the very lead stripped from their eighteenth-century roof.

Though no one ever again went as far as Apple, artist entrepreneurism still flourished throughout pop music. In America, the Grateful Dead now recorded for their own Grateful Dead company, and Jefferson Starship (formerly Airplane) for their own label, the charmingly named Grunt. The Rolling Stones had their Rolling Stones label, Deep Purple their Purple label, the Moody Blues their Threshold label. Two ex-Beatles even nerved themselves to post-Apple business forays, Ringo Starr with Ring O' Records and George Harrison with his Dark Horse label. The fashion waxed equally strong among impresarios: Andrew Loog Oldham with his Immediate label, Kit Lambert and Chris Stamp with their Track label, Jonathan King with his UK label, Gordon Mills with his MAM label and Mickie Most with his Rak label.

Britain's record industry was altogether in a state of bountiful confidence and expansiveness. The huge fortunes trapped in each major company could be sensed by the most casual visitor. In cork-lined outer foyers, gold discs grew in double and triple rows, and overstuffed black leather sofas creaked under the leather coats of those sprawling on them. In twilit inner suites, music burbled softly from giant speakers, underlining an atmosphere of limitless prerogative and perpetual play. New artists were casually acquired, and launched with uniform extravagance. Every night of the week, there was a party to hype someone or other, at Ronnie Scott's Club, Maunkberry's or Les Ambassadeurs. Journalists and disc jockeys were wooed with every kind of favour and gift: free records, cases of Scotch, first-class air tickets, girl companions or, if need be, boy companions.

A new term had been invented, 'ligger', for those many whose whole lives were sustained by the record industry's undiscriminating largesse. Whatever PR launch was going on, liggers by the hundred would always be there, grabbing up the review copies of new albums, wolfing the costly cold buffets, filling the free flights, coaches and hotel rooms, stealing the shampoos, tooth glasses and bathrobes, drinking the minibars dry. A classic liggerfest was the party given by Jonathan King to mark his tenth year as a performer, record producer and all-purpose hypester. From Westminster Pier a riverboat set off up the Thames, packed with champagne-drinking liggers. Near Richmond they transferred to a second riverboat with an open-air barbecue. As the barbecue was ligged, a third riverboat steamed up, letting off fireworks.

All the time Elton had been rising as a performer, he had felt a reciprocal tug towards entrepreneurial roles for which he was equally well fitted. Long John Baldry's two albums had proved him a born producer, imaginative and meticulous. His catholic taste and openness to acts newer and younger than himself made him a habitual talent-spotter. He was filled with idealistic desire to give others the helping hand he himself had so sorely needed: both new performers and established but under-appreciated ones like Lesley Duncan and David Ackles. At moments of greatest hubris, it occurred to him that even idols whom he had worshipped as a teenager, and who were now fallen from fashion, might not disdain a boost from somebody like him. The A & R man manqué was curious to see what he might accomplish on behalf of someone else. The fan was ready, and anxious, to pay his dues.

Recording giant that he had become, he was still bound to a tiny label whose logo was an unexciting wiggly DJM monogram, and whose power over his artistic output was total. From earliest days, he had chafed intermittently against Dick and Stephen James's decisions about what he should release. Now, for the first time, chafing became open war.

As a single to follow 'Crocodile Rock', Elton wanted to release 'Daniel'. But Dick and Stephen James both said no. They thought it unwise to put out another track from the new album, due to be released in only another couple of weeks. Much as they both admired 'Daniel' (James *père* called it 'beautiful and fantastic') they could not see how a song about a blind war veteran could possibly succeed in the teenage glitter market where 'Crocodile Rock' had sold almost half a million.

The ensuing row was loud enough to spill over into the music press. ELTON SLAMS RECORD COMPANY announced *Melody Maker*. DISPUTE OVER DANIEL said *New Musical Express*. When Elton reached an impasse with Dick James, he began his own crusade in the music press, playing 'Daniel' to friendly interviewers like Roy Hollingworth and railing against 'the business' that was trying to stifle it. Dick James also went on record, saying that Elton's US record company, MCA, and even his 'personal co-ordinator' Steve Brown, agreed that releasing it was 'not a good marketing decision'.

Under intense pressure from Elton, and against MCA's wishes, Dick James agreed to release 'Daniel'. But he refused to pay anything to promote or advertise it. Elton retorted that if necessary he'd take out full-page ads in the trade press himself. James then said, with what was meant to be a restoration of joviality, that if it made the Top 10, he would pay for the advertising. 'Christ, isn't that nice!' Elton commented with scathing irony.

'Daniel' (coupled with that oldest of oldies, 'Skyline Pigeon') was released on 12 January, 1973. Its first major British TV exposure came a few days later, when Elton appeared on Michael Parkinson's BBC1 talk show. The now familiar bespectacled figure, clad in one-piece silver like the table ornament of some regimental mess, clumped down the entrance stairway on stilt-like heels, amid applause that was genuinely welcoming. Having talked to Parkinson in his usual fluent, modest fashion, he stilt-walked across to a tripod-mounted electric piano. From the first gently popping notes (very much like Stevie Wonder's intro to 'You Are The Sunshine of My Life'), it was obvious he had a gigantic hit.

Bernie Taupin had intended a straightforward narrative song, as clear and hetero as 'Devil Woman' or 'El Paso'. Daniel, the war veteran, was fleeing America, seen off by his brother at the airport. Unfortunately, most of the details came in a pay-off last verse which Elton, as was sometimes his wont, had arbitrarily cut out. What remained was just the valediction to Daniel by his brother, watching 'the red tail-lights, heading for Spain'.

Sung by the silver-plated figure, with its owlish face and preposterous heels, 'Daniel' turned into something else. It became a love song of man to man, as platonic and unselfconscious as Elton and Bernie's own love had been. The foil-flashy astronaut sang in phrases as down-to-earth as a chat between stops on the Metropolitan Line.

Elton's instinct about the song was vindicated when it went to number two in America and four in Britain. Nor did it have any noticeable adverse effect on the album, released a fortnight later, on 26 January. *Don't Shoot Me, I'm Only the Piano Player* was hailed as an unqualified triumph, not only for 'Crocodile Rock' and 'Daniel' but also for darker, more complex tracks like 'High-Flying Bird,' 'Have Mercy on the Criminal', and 'I'm Going to Be a Teenage Idol', a satire inspired by Marc Bolan. The album cover was a perfect piece of glitter-rock pastiche showing Elton's name outside a 1950s movie-house with a James Dean boy and ponytailed girl buying tickets at the paybox. Irresistible packaging and two proven hit tracks made reviews irrelevant. *Don't Shoot Me* became the first Elton album to go to number one in both America and Britain.

Annoyed as he was about 'Daniel', Elton still recognised that DJM under Stephen James was 'a damned good little record company', which handled him in a more personal and indulgent way than any large company could hope to do. He could record where he liked, hire what musicians he liked, have what album artwork and interior fripperies he liked. Though Dick James had dug his heels in over paying to advertise 'Daniel', he was not usually stingy in that regard. Elton's albums back to *Tumbleweed Connection* had been advertised on British television, not a usual thing for pop records then, and a further £7,500 was currently being spent on TV spots for *Don't Shoot Me*.

The same could not be said of his American record company, the giant conglomerate MCA. For all his albums until now, Elton had been on MCA's Uni label, a small and relatively personal operation under its ebullient chief, Russ Regan. With *Don't Shoot Me* he was transferred to the main MCA label, a move designed to compliment the music division's biggest profit-earner. Instead, Elton found himself marketed with heavy-handed incomprehension in trade ads and promotions that frequently made him cringe with embarrassment. On the week that *Don't Shoot Me* reached number one in America, MCA ran an ad billing it as the 'Latest Adventures of Elton and Bernie in France'. To add insult to injury, it was not even displayed on its own, but lumped into a composite page with such desperately unhip names as Dobie Gray and the country-and-western queen Loretta Lynn.

Chafing as he was against both his English and American record companies, Elton had every selfish reason for starting a label of his own. Paradoxically, what propelled him to the final decision was a desire to help someone else. Davey Johnstone, his guitarist, wanted to make a solo album, but had been unable to find a company in London willing to back it. Elton, Davey, John Reid and Steve Brown were at Château d'Hierouville late one night, drinking the château's home-produced wine and debating how the problem might be solved. Elton said they should start their own label and bring Davey Johnstone's album out on that. 'We all said "Yeah" and went to bed,' he recalled later. 'Next morning, we all got up and said "Was everybody serious?" We decided that we were.'

Firm intent established, the arrangements quickly fell into place. The new record company would be called Rocket, in honour of 'Rocket Man'. It would be controlled by Elton, John Reid, Bernie Taupin, Steve Brown and Gus Dudgeon. John Reid would oversee it in parallel to his management of Elton through John Reid Enterprises.

The objectives, as outlined by Elton, were familiarly straight-forward, sensible and sound. 'We want to start a company that's for the artist, both creatively and money-wise. I got tired of people who aren't in it for the music – just for the money from album sales. There must be room for a company where people don't feel they're being ripped off – or forgotten because five hundred other new albums are also coming out that week. We want to be a friendly record company. We'll pay a good advance and a decent royalty, and when we sign anybody, we'll work our bollocks off for them. It'll be like a family.'

Rocket would be different, too, from creations like Threshold and Purple which existed mainly for the benefit of their performer-proprietors. Elton took pains to emphasise that he himself would not record on the new label, being contracted to DJM until 1975. 'Me not being on it is what's good about it,' he said. 'It would dampen everyone else. It'd be like "Elton John is on Rocket – and so is Davey Johnstone."' His role would be purely entrepreneurial, foster-ing new talent and producing it, as also would Bernie Taupin.

The spirit of the whole enterprise was summed up in the logo soon designed for it. A toytown goods train puffed over an arc of track, its cheeky-faced engine winking one eye, as if to say 'Right on!'. It was, in fact, a virtual duplicate of Thomas the Tank Engine in the children's stories by the Reverend Wilbert Awdry. Amazingly, for all the millions of books it had sold, the design had never been copyrighted. From here on, Thomas the Tank Engine technically infringed the legal rights of Rocket Records.

Behind the nursery-wall whimsy, hard-headed economics went to work. To the lesson of Apple Corps were added John Reid's native prudence and thrift. One thing Rocket Records would not be, above all, was a faucet that could drain away Elton's own fortune. Of the original launch capital, most was provided by American MCA. With Elton's current contract running out in less than two years, MCA's president, Mike Maitland, suddenly awoke to the need to show vision and imagination. In return, Elton agreed to distribute Rocket product through MCA in America, as it would be distributed by his old friends Island Records in Britain. 'MCA aren't so bad,' he had conceded. 'They just need a good kick up the arse every now and then.'

A six-room suite of offices was leased at 101 Wardour Street in the heart of Soho's film district, just a stone's throw from the Marquee Club, where Elton used to play, and the old Bag O'Nails, where Long John Baldry had saved him from premature matrimony. Annie Reavey, his clothes designer, was called in to the room that would be Steve Brown's office, to paint a mural of trains, fields, trees and cows around the wall.

The new label already boasted two signings. One was Davey Johnstone who could now go ahead and make the solo album he wanted. The other was a teenage band named Longdancer, whose personnel included Nigel Olsson's younger brother Kai and a Scots guitarist named Dave Stewart.

On 3 February, 1973, a full page in *Melody Maker* announced the official formation of the Rocket Record Company, with its jolly, winking train puffing over the track and its directorial roster of John, Taupin, Reid, Dudgeon and Brown. Below was a pledge from Elton to the new label's prospective signings that editorial decency could not render without some dilution. 'What we are offering is undivided love and devotion, a f★★★ing good royalty for the artist and a company that works its b★★★★cks off.'

The new company's personnel were lifted more or less complete from the team which had run Elton at Dick James Music: Steve Brown, the A & R man; Gus Dudgeon, the producer; Clive Franks, the sound engineer; and crucial technical people like the head of the art department. John Reid was even able to woo away Maureen, the personal secretary who had worked for Stephen James for the past seven years. Relations between Stephen and Reid thereafter did not improve.

It was on Elton's first British tour of 1973 that the unlikeliest of all phenomena revealed itself. *Melody Maker*'s front page for 31 March was filled by a huge photograph taken from rear-stage during his concert at the London Sundown theatre. In the foreground, Elton crouched at his keyboard, pummelling with stout, bare washer-woman's arms. Beyond him was what seemed a sheer wall of juvenile faces, clapping hands and open mouths. The accompanying banner headline could scarcely disguise its writer's incredulity: NOW ELTON'S A TEENAGE IDOL!

'Crocodile Rock' had taken him straight to the top of the same teenybopper market as T-Rex, the Osmonds, the Jackson Five and David Cassidy. That he himself bore not the slightest resemblance to these school-age objects of desire was irrelevant. The *raison d'être* of teenyboppers was to scream; and, as was now being proved, they could scream for anything. At Elton's concerts, the first five or six rows would be filled by girls of fourteen or even younger, shrieking on that curious long, whistling note, like ceremonial bosuns' pipes at a naval funeral. With the screaming frequently went its allied occu-pation, fainting. At closely packed venues, like those of the new Sundown chain, the only way to remove those who fainted was to lift them on to the stage, past Elton, and off through the wings.

The screams were detectably different, however, from those which greeted David Cassidy or Donny Osmond. 'Elton's fans don't want to go to bed with him,' *Melody Maker* commented. 'They want to mother him or hug him like a friendly Santa Claus after the show.' For corroboration there were cheerfully self-deprecating comments from the new idol himself. 'It's a bit funny to be screamed at, because I'm not your actual sex idol, am I? The only way I ever thought people would scream for me was in horror.'

It all pointed to a remarkable coup which *Melody Maker* – not dreaming any ironic *déjà vu* – headlined THE SECOND COMING OF ELTON JOHN. 'Those who thought Elton had burned himself out through his gruelling work-rate have been proved mistaken ... In the fluctuating world of pop, he has made a dramatic come-back, to answer the doubters. It has turned him into a teen-idol pin-up as well as a respected musician. Few artists these days can wear both crowns, and wear them with such elegance.'

Teenybop hysteria was not confined to London; on the contrary, it seemed to grow stronger the further north Elton went. In Newcastle, the concert-promoter, Peter Bowman, suffered a broken ankle in attempts to protect him from a keening mob. Elton's glasses were snatched from his nose, and he had to bolt down the street with no idea where he was going. In Glasgow it took him an hour to escape from the theatre. Decoys had to be sent out first, and even then the back of his limousine, as it drove away, bore a latticework of prostrate, tearful girls. 'I'd rather they lined up for two hours and I signed autographs for them,' Elton said. 'But they just don't want to do that. There were times when I thought they were going to rip me apart.'

Throughout every performance, girls would jump up on to the stage and fling their arms round his neck like so many skinny pink feather boas. He was forced to carry spare glasses everywhere to replace the pairs continually ripped from his nose or trampled under lurching platform heels.

He himself was at a loss to explain the hysteria. 'It's all very flattering, and it might be something to do with the clothes. They all seem to want to cuddle and mother me, like they're saying "Ooh, isn't he lovely!" I'd get worried if they were screaming all the way through, but they do seem to listen as well. I don't think they're the David Cassidy types, because they know all the songs. When I do something like "Mona Lisa and Mad Hatters" or "Your Song", I can hear them all singing along.'

As well as in the grown-up *NME* and *Melody Maker*, he now found himself the star of teenybopper fan magazines, vying with conventional heart-throbs like David Cassidy and Donny Osmond. His friend Nina Myskow, the fashion writer on *Jackie*, arranged for him to feature in one of its Life Story romantic cartoon strips. 'Elton loved posing for the drawings,' Nina remembers. 'He couldn't believe *Jackie* actually wanted him as a pin-up in that way.' *Jackie*'s publishers, the D. C. Thomson company, were later persuaded to break a lifetime policy and sell the strip's original drawings to John Reid.

With the astuteness peculiar to their kind, Elton's fans quickly discovered where he lived. His bungalow in Wentworth, at that time, possessed no security as such. Only a grass verge separated the front door of Hercules from the road. On quiet Sunday afternoons in his living room, he would look up and see red, weeping faces pressed to the big picture window.

A typical example was Linda Mallarkey, then aged fifteen and going to school in Downham, near Bromley, Kent. A dark, tomboyish girl of partly Irish parentage, Linda possessed that calm air of purpose which so many pop fans bring to their apparent dementia. She had started liking Elton at the time of 'Rocket Man', and stayed loyal to him despite the more obvious attractions of T-Rex and the Jackson Five. 'I don't really know why I liked him so much,' she admits now. 'I knew he wasn't really good-looking. But he seemed a funny kind of person. I mean, sort of fun. Nice. Natural. Just ordinary.'

With a friend, Marie Thacker from Rotherhithe, Linda became the most familiar among the little knot of girls perennially waiting for Elton outside his London ports of call, like DJM and Capital Radio. 'He'd always stop and talk and have pictures taken, and be really nice to us,' she remembers. 'After a while, he recognised us, and even looked for us. When we knew he was coming back from tour, we'd go out to Heathrow and meet him. We'd just find an electric point in the concourse, plug in our cassette recorders and settle down. We waited two days out there for him once.'

On his birthday, Linda and Marie joined forces with two other girls to get him a cake and deliver it to Wentworth in person. 'We took it down all the way on the train. We got him a Buddy Holly book as well, because we'd read that he liked Buddy Holly. When we got there, we were amazed that you could just walk right up to the front door and knock. His mum answered the door and when we told her who we were she was really nice as well. Elton invited us in and showed us his gold discs, and the pictures of him with the astronauts, and we all had a bit of the birthday cake each.

'Afterwards, we read that he liked Dom Pérignon champagne, so we decided to buy him a bottle of that. We bought it in Shepherd's Bush because you could get it there for £12 a bottle; everywhere else, it cost about £18. We gave it to him when he was at Lord's playing in a charity cricket match.'

The girls' reassuring reports to their parents that Elton lived with his mum, in utter normality and respectability, were very nearly true. Sheila Farebrother was constantly at Hercules, serving tea to interviewers, looking after the two dogs, even posing for pictures with Elton beside the Bel Air-size swimming pool. It is said that a mother can never be truly shocked by anything her child may do. Certainly, Sheila seems to have accepted the situation between Elton and John Reid with perfect equanimity, making Reid a part of the warm Harris family as much as Bernie Taupin had formerly been. Only the closest members of Elton's circle ever detected a faint note of ambivalence in her attitude. 'For Christmas, she always used to give

John an electric carving knife,' a former Rocket employee says. 'I used to wonder if there was any significance in that.'

In 1973, Elton moved Sheila and Derf from their Ickenham house into one of the properties immediately adjoining Hercules. Having his mother literally at the bottom of his garden was practically a return to the closeness of Frome Court days. At night, Sheila's house used to be bathed in anti-burglar floodlight which reminded Bryan Forbes of the prison camps he had often tried to escape from in black-and-white British films.

Derf's picture-hanging duties continued unremittingly. Bryan Organ had completed his portrait of Elton, at an open window in a T-shirt printed with Andy Warhol's Marilyn Monroe. The portrait started Elton on a craze for Bryan Organ, as he would afterwards have crazes for Geoffrey Proud, Robert Young, Paul Wunderlich, Edouard Cortes, L. S. Lowry and Rembrandt. By 1973, he already owned two Rembrandt etchings, bought – surprisingly – at Harrods, one for £5,000, the other for £7,000. 'I never dreamed there were Rembrandts still to buy. I thought they were all in museums.' The same Knightsbridge shopping trip netted him a Dürer engraving of a coat of arms and a skull. The piquant fact also emerged that Harrods allowed its customers to buy even precious works of art on the instalment plan. Though Elton did not require this service, the provident John Reid decided to make use of it. 'John bought a Rembrandt etching two inches by one inch on the HP!' Elton kept telling people in amusement.

To other members of his family, he had been just as munificently generous. For his maternal grandmother, Ivy, he bought a house conveniently close to her daughter, his Aunt Win, in Ruislip, Middlesex. On his cousin Paul Robinson's eighteenth birthday, Elton turned up on the doorstep. 'He said "I've got you a present, but it's a bit too big to carry indoors",' Paul remembers. 'I went outside – and there was this brand-new white Mini.'

Up in Cheshire, Stanley Dwight had watched his son's metamorphosis with amazement and real pride – so his widow, Edna, now insists – although, being Stanley, he told none of his office colleagues at Unilever that he was Elton John's father. When Elton appeared at Liverpool's Empire theatre, Stanley and Edna bought two tickets for the show and sent word to the star that they hoped to be able to see him afterwards. During the interval, Edna remembers, John Reid came and found them, identifying Stanley before he could introduce himself because of his resemblance to Elton. After the show, there was time for only a brief reunion in Elton's dressing-room, but Edna remembers he was 'delighted' to see his father and her. 'The next time I play Liverpool, I'm going to pay for your tickets,' he promised. 'And they'll be for the whole family.'

His Dwight relatives in Kent, while following his career with enormous pride, scrupulously distanced themselves from any semblance of 'cashing in'. Finally, his cousin Roy, the ex-footballer to whom he owed his first-ever job, decided to ask for a loan to start a clothes boutique called Lady Samantha. 'I said, "You can say no, and it'll be forgotten, but here's the proposition." The money was there straight away. "And," Elton said, "I'll even come down and open it for you." '

His father never asked for anything, although Elton stayed regularly in touch, sending Stanley postcards from his tours ('Met Gracie Fields [in Italy] yesterday. She was really nice') and a Christmas card that always included his 'Aunt Edna' and four young half-brothers. For Christmas 1972, he sent Nanette Newman's book of children's sayings, *God Bless Love*. On its flyleaf was written, 'To Dad and Aunt Edna, Robert, Stanley, Geoffrey, Simon. With love for a happy Xmas (yes, this is my card) Love, Elton', followed by a row of kisses. Another Christmas letter – written while he was appearing in Newcastle – brought Stanley a cheque for £250, 'a hundred pounds for you and Aunt Edna and £25 each for the boys.'

Early in 1973, when he returned to the Liverpool Empire, he made good his promise the last time he had seen them, providing front-row seats for Stanley, Edna and their four sons. He saw them in the dressing-room afterwards, presenting Edna with a large box of chocolates and the youngest boy, Simon, with a white Teddy bear. The next afternoon he came to their house for Sunday lunch in his white chauffeur-driven Rolls with John Reid following behind in his Jensen. Edna remembers how he took her aside in the kitchen and enquired rather anxiously if his father had minded him dropping the Dwight surname. She repeated what the former bandleader 'Stan Wight' had said at the time: that he understood the necessity of stage-names.

After a chicken and apple pie lunch, Elton kicked a football around the garden with the boys, then played 'Crocodile Rock' on Edna's piano, encouraging Stanley, the eldest of his half brothers, to join in. During the afternoon, Edna remembers, he and Stanley were looking through some car magazines and Elton asked Stanley – who at the time possessed only a Mini – which car he would have if he could choose any one. Stanley replied that, with so many children to ferry around, he would probably plump for a Peugeot 504.

As Elton was leaving, he thrust a piece of paper into Edna's cardigan pocket, asking her to 'give it to Dad'. It was a cheque for

£2,000, the list price of a Peugeot 504, which he had already unsuccessfully tried to give his father. Edna did not want to take it either, but was persuaded by John Reid that such a sum meant nothing to the star Elton was now. 'John said that for Elton to give us that was like someone else giving us a pound,' she recalls. So, to their lasting regret, they accepted the money and bought the Peugeot 504.

Ironically, it proved too expensive for Stanley to run, and he sold it shortly afterwards.

Elton was deeply involved with setting up Rocket Records and creating a roster of deserving artists for whom to 'work his b★★★★cks off'. After Davey Johnstone and Longdancer more acquisitions quickly followed, reflecting Steve Brown's hippyish taste and Elton's feeling for talent hitherto undervalued or misprojected. So Rocket also signed Stackridge, a band well known on the pub-and-club circuit, and two solo singers, Mike Silver and Maldwyn Pope.

Rocket's crusading ideals were never better expressed than when Kiki Dee became its first female signing. For Kiki was the industry's outstanding example of someone who should have made it. Born Pauline Matthews in Sheffield, she had been around since the mid-Sixties, one of those almost-famous female names like Elkie Brooks and P. P. Arnold. Her voice was spectacular; indeed, she had been the only white female performer ever signed to Berry Gordy's Motown label. But even Motown had been unable to do for her what it had for Mary Wells, Gladys Knight and Diana Ross. For some reason, perhaps connected with her rather solid looks, stardom had always refused to come.

Kiki Dee became Elton's special project and protégée. It was not just that he considered her voice second to none among current British female performers. About the sturdy Sheffield girl there was some of the same mixture of smoky soul and total unsexiness that had once drawn him so powerfully to Dusty Springfield. Whatever else Rocket might do, he was determined Kiki would see her name in the Top 20 at last.

He acquired a further influential friend and supporter through the interview he gave to *Rolling Stone* early in 1973, just before his long-postponed Italian tour. The magazine had recently adopted a detailed question-and-answer format after the style of *Playboy* interviews, and to be chosen as a subject denoted election to rock's premier echelon. Interviewing Elton was the idea of Paul Gambaccini, a young American who freelanced for *Rolling Stone* in England while studying at Oxford University. For his enterprise, Gambaccini was rewarded with what stands among the best of *RS* interviews for its articulateness, forthrightness and humour. He himself became Elton's closest media confidant during a subsequent highly successful career as disc jockey and TV interviewer.

Outside the business, Elton's closest friends continued to be his Wentworth neighbours, Bryan Forbes and Nanette Newman. 'He was always dropping over,' Nanette Newman remembers. 'In this spirit of complete normality that was also utterly mad. So this apparition all in silver, with green hair, would sit in the kitchen and drink eighty-seven cups of tea. You'd say "Goodbye" and see him set off that little distance back to his house. Then you'd hear afterwards that on the way home he'd managed to buy a Ferrari.'

The Forbeses were by now well accustomed to Elton's fondness for extravagantly-staged practical jokes. After Turk Thrust, the drum majorettes and the lion came one inspired by Nanette's decision, just before Christmas, to change her car. 'I'd had a Mercedes, and was changing it for a Ford. Elton was horrified. "You can't have a Ford," he kept telling me. Then he said "I think you're exactly the sort of person who should have a Ford – with a nodding dog on the back shelf."

'That Christmas morning, we heard the most terrible commotion outside. Up the drive came this awful old Ford, with Elton behind the wheel. He'd sprayed "Happy Christmas" in fluorescent paint all over it, and on the rear shelf was a nodding dog. He'd gone to so much trouble . . . and, of course, then we were stuck with the old Ford. We had no idea how to get rid of it.'

He loved the two little girls, Sarah and Emma, and showered them with expensive presents that frequently alarmed their parents. 'When Emma was six, he'd give her a pint of Chanel No. 5,' Bryan Forbes remembers. 'One Christmas, he gave her a diamond and sapphire bracelet from Cartier. We put it away for her, but she managed to get hold of it somehow. One day she came home from school and said "Look what I've got. A fountain pen." She showed us this cheap little fountain pen, which she said she'd swapped at school for something else. "What did you swap it for?" we asked her. "That bracelet Elton gave me," she said. A Cartier diamond and sapphire bracelet for a piddly little fountain pen worth about eighty pence! We never did dare tell Elton.'

'We couldn't compete with presents like that,' Nanette Newman says. 'So I used to get the girls to make him things that were special and personal to him. Sarah made him a cushion with a Rolls Royce on it, and the numberplate EJ 1. It took her a year to do. Whenever we went to see him after that, at the bungalow and the big house in Windsor, that cushion was always there.'

Bryan Forbes's stint as a movie tycoon having ended, and his career as a blockbuster novelist not yet having begun, he was in a quiet period professionally. This he decided to occupy by producing, writing and directing two television documentaries. The first was about the doyenne of British stage actresses, Dame Edith Evans. The second was about Elton. Forbes financed it himself, and spent much of the spring and summer of 1973 with a film crew, watching Elton at work and play. A company named Companion Films was set up by John Reid and Forbes to divide the eventual proceeds from TV syndication.

Elton welcomed the project, tickled beyond words to be filmed by the man who had made all those black-and-white classics of his childhood. Some photographs by Bryan Forbes were even used inside the album-sleeve of *Don't Shoot Me, I'm Only the Piano Player*.

He was as dumbfounded as ever by the big star names whom Bryan and Nanette regarded as old friends. On hearing that Katharine Hepburn was to be their house guest, he begged Nanette to bring her over to Hercules for tea.

Hollywood's earliest and most stylish eccentric had lost none of the habit in beautiful old age. Though wafted everywhere by limousine, her preferred method of transport was the bicycle. 'I don't remember if she brought her own bike in the boot of the car, or borrowed one of ours,' Nanette Newman says. 'I remember she biked all around Virginia Water that week, with people gaping and clutching one another and saying, "That can't be Katharine Hepburn!" So when we went over to Elton's for tea, Bryan and I went in the car and Kate went on her bike.'

She arrived at Hercules to find Elton and a magnificent tea waiting, but a painful crisis in progress. A frog had somehow found its way into the swimming pool. Elton was afraid of frogs, and could not face trying to fish it out.

Katharine Hepburn responded with a decisiveness worthy of every brisk heroine she had ever played, in films from *Pat and Mike* to *The African Queen*. She dived into the swimming pool and retrieved the frog.

'That was fantastic,' Elton gasped. 'How did you manage to do that?'

'Character, dear boy,' Ms Hepburn replied. 'Character'.*

★

---

* Asked for corroboration of the story, Katharine Hepburn replied, 'I'm not afraid of

The Rocket Record Company was launched on 30 April, 1973, in a style appropriate to its Toytown railway emblem and the golden age of ligging. A special train was chartered to introduce the music press to Rocket's directors and a selection of its new signings, bands Longdancer and Stackridge, and solo singers Mike Silver and Kiki Dee. The train ran from Paddington to the quiet and beautiful Cotswold village of Moreton-in-Marsh. There a brass band greeted the 200-odd guests and marched with them in noisy procession to the village hall, a sumptuous buffet and performances by Mike Silver and Longdancer, with Elton, Bernie, John Reid and other Rocket executives getting up on stage, to sing the 'oohs' and 'aahs'. In its mixture of whimsicality and gluttony, the occasion was a liggerfest as notable as any the early Seventies recorded. On the return journey, the train's chief steward reported that his entire stock of champagne, wines, spirits and beer had been drunk. As an extra little memento of the occasion, Elton treated himself to L. S. Lowry's painting *Moreton-in-Marsh*, a work later put up for auction at a reserve price of £15,000.

The office at 101 Wardour Street then settled down to serious business. Steve Brown managed it from his office with a mural of steam trains, fields and cows. To Rocket Records, Brown would be much the same guru-like presence that the talented Derek Taylor was at Apple Corps. His younger brother Pete worked under him, as did a hippyish couple named David and Lindsay, two secretaries and a telephonist. John Reid commuted back and forth from the separate office he had established for John Reid Enterprises in South Audley Street, Mayfair.

One of Reid's earliest coups for Rocket was to persuade a well-known music journalist, Penny Valentine, to join the fledgling company as its first press and public relations officer. Valentine was, in fact, London's best-known female music journalist, a columnist on *Disc*, sometime panellist on *Juke Box Jury* and a personal friend of many leading pop stars, including Elton's first pin-up idol, Dusty Springfield.

Penny Valentine had followed Elton's career from the beginning and, like other women journalists, had seemed to develop a special rapport with him. Before even knowing of Elton's fixation on Dusty Springfield, she had noticed a strong similarity between them. 'As performers both of them had the same quality – I can only call it complete lack of sexuality. And both of them were obsessed with the trivia and minutiae of show business.'

---

frogs, and I've always enjoyed upsetting people, but I have no recollection of this incident.'

The job of Rocket's press and PR officer was hardly an onerous
one. Everyone in the music press wanted to write about the new
company, its new acts and crusading aims. The Rocket office was
also a convenient place for Elton to give the interviews he still poured
out unstintingly. Journalists were entertained regally, lunched, dined,
chauffeured and, if necessary, flown first class to Los Angeles and put
up at the Bel Air Hotel.

Rocket's generosity to outsiders was as nothing compared with
Elton's generosity to Rocket. Like his friends, his employees were
showered with gifts: hampers from Fortnum and Mason, chocolates
from Charbonnel and Walker, jewellery and watches from Cartier.
Those small gold watches, with old-fashioned square faces and
Roman numerals, became almost small change in Elton's circle, so
many each year did he give away. 'At Christmas, he'd arrive with a
cardboard box and go round the office, doling things out,' a Rocket
executive remembers. 'Just an ordinary cardboard carton, full of
Cartier watches and pens. He said it was easier that way.'

Rocket, to Elton, was a family – a further source of camaraderie,
approval and affection to fill up the bottomless wells of his childhood
loneliness. On his birthday, if he was in America, it was not un-
common for the whole Rocket staff to cluster around the transatlantic
phone chorusing 'Happy Birthday to you'. Even cynical Penny
Valentine found herself drawn against her will into the atmosphere
of protective babying. 'I remember shouting at him several times,
"I'm not your mother, you know!" One day, just before a press
interview, the hems of his trousers came unstitched, and he got me
to sew them up for him. I found myself kneeling down on the floor
with a needle and thread. "What's happening to me?" I said. "Why
am I doing this?"'

When Elton was not there, the atmosphere at Rocket could be
less idyllic. John Reid was in charge, and now need show no
menswear-store deference to anyone. London's music community
was soon made aware that the most amiable of all pop stars now had
a manager who could not be described in anything like similar terms.
'I met John Reid with Elton at a poll winners' concert,' the former
editor of a music paper remembers. 'I thought I'd never encountered
anyone so unpleasant in my life.'

Working with Reid was Penny Valentine's first introduction to
his explosive and violent temper. As he quickly demonstrated, he was
capable of outbursts that made Elton's Little Moments by contrast
seem the merest trifles. 'You could always tell when he was going to
explode. He'd suddenly go bright red in the face. He'd got one of
those tempers that, for a moment or two, are totally uncontrollable.

What upset him could be something as small as not getting the number he wanted on the phone. Bang! the whole thing would go flying across the room.

'I'd come in in the morning and find him sitting on the stairs with his head in his hands. "What shall I do?" he'd say. "I've fired the whole staff." "Why?" I'd say. "Oh," he'd say. "None of them was in to work on time. Now all the phones are ringing and there's no one to answer them. What am I going to do?" "Ring them all up and get them all back again," I'd say.'

The benign engine face of the Rocket Record Company little hinted at its wobbly, unpredictable steam valve. 'The whole place was in fear of John,' Penny Valentine says. 'But whatever happened, no one ever blamed Elton. Even if Elton might be behind some of what John did, no one ever thought badly of him. Elton was above it all.'

Bryan Forbes's documentary vividly recalls that '73 summer of idyllic hot weather and still-spiralling fame. As a friend, Forbes was given access to his subject's innermost court, in Britain, America and France. He himself acted as narrator and also appeared on camera in an outfit metamorphosed from British POW officer's duffel-coat to pale blue Rocket T-shirt, hipster trousers and cowboy boots.

An early sequence in the film alternates scenes of Elton onstage with one of him walking out to bat at Lord's cricket ground. From the wild night creature of silver and gold, we cut to a sedate noontide figure, fully and correctly attired in white flannels, pads, gloves and cap. He is playing in a charity match, part of a celebrity eleven, raised by his agent Vic Lewis, that also includes David Frost, Peter Cook, Michael Parkinson and Wes Hall. The only departure from tradition is the knot of long-haired boys and girls who leap towards this particular batsman with open arms and autograph books.

'Elton John plays cricket as he plays the piano,' says Bryan Forbes. 'Dressed to kill, and as if his life depended on it. For in his book the greatest sin is to be boring.'

Forbes then establishes his subject in a quick-cutting medley of images. Here is Elton walking onstage, flashing and caped like the most outrageous heavyweight champion all-in wrestling ever knew. Elton half-naked and showing much body hair, beating his chest at his audience like a myopic King Kong. Elton transferred to the Surrey countryside, jogging with his band, a squat, almost waddling figure against their beanpole flares. Elton, short-haired in one scene and, in the next, with hanks of green-patched orange obscuring his ears as stiffly as stale candy-floss. Elton, alone with his grand piano at Hercules, playing 'Daniel' as a Brahms nocturne, then suddenly

turning it into 'She's a Lassie from Lancashire . . .' Elton demonstrating how he used to play 'The Skaters' Waltz' at the age of four in
Pinner Hill Road, and doing 'The Poor People of Paris' in the style
of Winifred Atwell. Elton, opening the drawer of an old-fashioned
cash register whose compartments are stuffed with jewellery. Elton,
with orange hair, tartan trews and red, white and blue glasses,
drinking Rombouts coffee in a kitchen spotless enough to feature in
a Domestos ad. Elton in his bath, holding up a soggy length of
washcloth and talking like Colonel Bloodnock from *The Goon Show*.
Elton, asked what he'll be like in twenty-five years and guffawing,
'Bald, I expect.' Elton deliberately and slowly squashing a cream
doughnut into his own face.

'At twenty-six, he walks confidently on five-inch heels where
lesser angels fear to tread,' Bryan Forbes continues. 'Sometimes as
bright and unyielding as the diamonds he wears on his fingers:
sometimes plunged into self-critical gloom . . . A child with every
toy in the shop, and not a key to wind them with . . . As much an
enigma to himself as to his friends . . . Now possessing no inhibitions:
now totally inhibited . . . Seeking fame one minute: determined to
reject it the next . . . The life and soul of the party: the party-
destroyer . . . Jealous of his privacy: hating to be private . . . Arrogant,
contrite . . . occasionally practising an infant's tyrannies among other
infants . . . Gifted, lonely . . . the superstar who does his own
Hoovering . . .'

Close-up of the face – in pale blue hexagonal glasses now – with
its cleft upper lip, its pugnacious chin, its voice of utter reason and
modesty. 'I'd like to become a legend,' Elton says. 'I'm hung up with
legends. I'd like to become a Mae West, or someone like that. But I
don't think I will be, because those people are so very, very special.'

We see Bernie Taupin up in Lincolnshire, walking alone over
the hills, a simple, plaid-coated figure like some poetic young journey-
man in a novel by Hardy. The next scene shows Bernie in less pastoral
mode, wearing a white Stetson, accompanied by Maxine in platform
boots with her name written in silver down the sides, walking along
the village street in Tealby and entering the garden gate of Piglet-in-
the-Wilds. 'He and his American wife live, snug as country mice, in a
Beatrix Potter dolls' house,' says Bryan Forbes. 'A gentle, unassuming
figure, he has perfected the art of remaining anonymous in a crowd,
the Cartier-Bresson, as it were, of the pop world.'

As usual, Elton takes pains to stress that Bernie's is the more
toilsome job. 'He just comes down to London and hands me a batch
of lyrics. I potter around, and find a chord sequence I like. Usually it
takes me about half an hour a song. I've just written twenty new

songs, and they're my favourites. I think songs should be disposable.
I can't even remember some of the words or chords of albums we
did two years ago, like *Tumbleweed Connection*. To me songs are like
postage stamps. You lick them, put them on a letter, and never see
them again.'

The people closest to Elton appear in telling vignettes. John Reid,
a blandly doll-faced figure in a batik shirt, recalls their first meeting
and subsequent 'gude friendship'. 'He has a Jekyll and Hyde character,' Reid says, in the quiet voice of one who enjoys total emotional
repose. 'You never know what he's going to do next.' Dick James
smiles through thick sunglasses on a rooftop somewhere, son Stephen
standing uncomfortably by. 'He's a paradox,' James says. 'He's very
sincere. He can be very brash as well. He's bringing back to show
business what show business very badly needs. And this is genuine
showmanship.' This wholly predictable remark is followed by a flash
of genuine old showman's wisdom. 'The artist on his way up lives
with failure, magnificently. I've never yet met one who could live
with success.'

His mother, Sheila, is innocently forthright. 'He's had darker
moods since he made it in the pop world than he ever did before.
He's always been a very quiet boy, never been the sort of boy to
have the gay life. I know when he's in a mood, but I never expect
him to be over the moon any time. He's just not that nature.'

The album destined to surpass all others he had made, or would
make, began in troubled circumstances. Elton had planned to record
it in May, at the place that was now like a lucky talisman, the
Château d'Hierouville. But a legal dispute had broken out concerning
the ownership of the château; as a result, the studio was closed
indefinitely.

Instead, he decided to record in Jamaica, a place highly fashionable since the commercial popularity of reggae music and the
migration there of Chris Blackwell's Island label. Two weeks were
booked at Byron Lee's Dynamic Sounds studio in Kingston where
the Rolling Stones had recently recorded *Goat's Head Soup*. Gus
Dudgeon put in an extensive order for special sound equipment and
band amenities including a tabletop football-game like the one at
Hercules.

Elton's party arrived in Jamaica at the worst possible moment, on
the day after the world heavyweight championship fight between Joe
Frazier and George Foreman. Every hotel was jammed to capacity,
and the streets pulsated with aggression. By an administrative mix-
up, Elton had been booked into the Pink Flamingo in the middle of

Kingston while everyone else was staying across the island in the resort area of Ocho Rios.

Terrified even to set foot outside his hotel, he had nothing to do but work on the new batch of lyrics Bernie Taupin had given him. Closeted in his room with an electric piano, he beat even his *Don't Shoot Me* record, writing the music to twenty-one songs in three days. Fortunately, the hotel's resident entertainer was one of his favourite jazz pianists, Les McCann. 'That was a saving grace,' Elton recalled. 'I just used to go and watch him every night.'

Byron Lee's Dynamic Sounds also proved a severe letdown. The studio was situated in one of the worst parts of Kingston, and fortified like a Belfast police station with barbed-wire fences and heavily armed guards. Almost none of the promised special equipment had arrived, not even a grand piano for Elton. The sessions that usually flew by were painfully slow and unproductive. 'We decided "the vibes just weren't right, man",' Bernie Taupin remembers. 'It's hard to see how they could have been with guards holding machine guns outside the door.'

Elton flew into a grand sulk, not moderated even when news came through that *Don't Shoot Me* had made number one in America. While the band held a celebration dinner at the Pink Flamingo, he remained in his room. Suddenly, the others heard a wild shriek. 'This centipede, about fourteen foot long, had crawled over me,' Elton recalled. 'I rushed down into the dining room with just a sheet covering me.'

It was decided to abort the Dynamic Sounds session, fly to New York and reconsider the situation there. But leaving the West Indies proved almost as traumatic for Elton's party as leaving Manila did for the Beatles in 1966. A dispute arose over payment for hotel accommodation. 'Things got so heavy, they even impounded our cars,' Bernie Taupin says. 'We were never so glad to get out of anywhere in our lives.'

In New York, however, there was better news. The legal dispute over Château d'Hierouville had been settled or, at least, suspended. The studio would be available to Elton after all.

The session that ensued forms the most idyllic part of Bryan Forbes's documentary. We see the château looking good enough to be painted by Monet, with shady cloisters and heat-hazed gardens where clouds of midges whirl and dance. At the wide-open main gate, a knot of French teenagers waits politely, like so many concièrges, one of them holding an old-fashioned milk churn. We see the monastic bedrooms, the YMCA-like communal living room, the high-ceilinged refectory, where long-haired beanpoles in floral shirts sit at breakfast with their *baguettes* and *biscottes*. After the horrors of Kingston, a holiday atmosphere prevails.

Bryan Forbes walks through the grounds towards camera, looking like a British officer in Colditz, even with his thumbs tucked into the patch pockets of hipster flares. 'There's a scent of new-mown grass outside,' he says. 'But not a suspicion of it inside' – an observation which caused some little merriment when the film was finally shown. For grass was in as widespread use here as in all pop music circles of 1973. Only Elton and Bernie Taupin were consistent in refusing it.

With the songs already written and rehearsed in Kingston, all there was to do was plunge straight into the studio and record them. In twelve days in May, Elton completed twenty-one tracks.

The material was as eclectic as always, with veers of mood as sudden and schizophrenic as Elton's could be in real life. One of the first into the can was 'Saturday Night's Alright for Fighting', a rave-up rocker, inspired by Bernie Taupin's disreputable teenage years around tough dance halls in Lincolnshire. 'I'd started to feel I was writing too much about American culture and American things,' Bernie says. '"Saturday Night" was my first attempt to write a rock-'n'-roll song that was totally English.'

By contrast, 'Funeral for a Friend' was an instrumental piece, almost Wagnerian in tone, bringing out all that was strange and melancholic on the other side of that wild Saturday-night bopper. 'Gus Dudgeon had always said I should do an instrumental,' Elton recalled later. 'One day, I was feeling really down, and said to myself "What kind of music would I like to hear at my own funeral?" I'd always liked funeral music anyway. I like very sad music of any kind.'

There were lyrics sexier and seamier than Bernie had ever put into Elton's mouth before: 'Bennie and the Jets', about a sci-fi female rock star in 'electric boots and mohair suits'; 'Dirty Little Girl', about an unhygienic nymphet; 'Sweet Painted Lady', about a seafarers' whore; 'Social Disease', about an alcoholic who humps his landlady; 'Jamaica Jerk-Off', about 'honky-tonkin' in the sea'. Nearest of all to the knuckle was 'All the Girls Love Alice', a ballad about a teenage lesbian with a line about 'two dykes in a go-go' which by rights should have sent it straight to the top of every 'banned' list.

Other tracks were steeped as never before in nostalgic yearning for the Wild West, Hollywood and childhood innocence. 'The Ballad of Danny Bailey' was about a heroic gangster shot down by G-men. 'Roy Rogers' was a homage to the squeaky-clean buckskin hero, galloping his horse Trigger across a fourteen-inch TV screen in some

Metroland living room. 'Goodbye Yellow Brick Road' found Bernie plundering imagery from the first film he, Elton and virtually every other postwar child had ever seen, at the same time giving it a backspin of cynicism and disillusionment. In *The Wizard of Oz*, Judy Garland as Dorothy follows the Yellow Brick Road to her heart's desire. But Bernie has already been there, and found it wanting. His dream is to return from his 'penthouse' and 'vodka-and-tonics' to country simplicity, 'back with the howlin' old owl in the woods . . . huntin' the horny-back toad . . .'

There was also a heartfelt song on a theme which, even then, could hardly be called new. Marilyn Monroe had been an icon of pop culture since the late Sixties, when Andy Warhol turned her into a poster image almost as famous as the Campbell's soup can. Bernie had long been struggling with the problem of writing a song about Marilyn that would express both the tragedy of her death and the fascination she continued to exert. 'I wanted to say that it wasn't just a sex thing. That she was someone everybody could fall in love with, without her being out of reach.'

Even the title he chose was not original. It had earlier been said of the rock star Janis Joplin, also doomed to early death from drugs, that she was 'a candle in the wind'.

The subject had equal appeal to Elton, with his love of glamorous legends and his developing understanding that fame could produce despair. 'When I think of Marilyn, I just think of pain,' he says in Bryan Forbes's film. 'I can't ever imagine her being that happy.'

With seventeen out of twenty-one finished tracks clamouring to be used, the obvious course was to follow current fashion among prolix LP superstars and issue a two-record album. Elton resisted the idea, fearing that a double album would be too expensive for his new teenage fans to afford. In addition, both DJM and MCA in America had said they would treat it only as a single work under his contractual obligation to deliver two albums per year.

What persuaded him was the sheer weight of good things this double album would offer. Naming it after its most evocative track, *Goodbye Yellow Brick Road*, suggested further parallels with his great exemplars, the Beatles. '*Revolver* lifted them on to a higher plane, and *Honky Château* did the same for us. *Sgt. Pepper* was their most popular one, and *Don't Shoot Me* was ours. Then they did the White Album, and now we'll have a double, too.' To coincide with its release on 5 October, an American tour was planned, taking Elton for the first time to the country's two ultimate concert venues: Madison Square Garden in New York, and the Hollywood Bowl.

As a foretaste, 'Saturday Night's Alright for Fighting' was released as a single on 29 June. Proving that Bernie Taupin had succeeded in writing a 'totally English' rock-'n'-roll song, it reached number seven in the UK as against only twelve in America. Elton was cast in his most unlikely incarnation of all, a leather-clad rocker, whose favourite sounds were 'a switchblade and a motorbike'. Once again, the ears of the banning brigade seemed fortuitously blocked with wax. What made the song was its incantatory chorus, 'Saturday, Saturday', and the feeling of frantic stage performance created in that tiny French studio. At long last, Elton had a finale wild enough to hammer even Little Richard into the ground.

In the weeks before *Goodbye Yellow Brick Road* was released, he made his main concern the new artists signed to Rocket, in particular his personal protégée Kiki Dee. She has since recalled the selfless hours Elton spent with her as A & R man, building up her confidence and looking for the right song to break her five-year professional jinx. Rejecting the upbeat Motownish things she had previously done, he settled on a dramatic French torch-song called 'Amoureuse'. This Kiki duly recorded – albeit with some Yorkshire misgivings – in a session co-produced by Elton and his sound engineer, Clive Franks.

Rocket had by now also launched an American office, in Los Angeles. A small building was rented in Holloway Drive, just off Sunset Boulevard, literally over the road from Tower Records, Elton's favourite spot of all for 'looting'.

To help organise Rocket USA – and, in particular, work on the forthcoming Elton tour – John Reid hired a self-possessed girl named Sharon Lawrence. Originally a journalist with UPI, she had gravitated into music PR, somewhat against her will, become a close friend of many rock stars, notably Jimi Hendrix, and ended up working for Elton's frenetic publicist, Norm Winter.

Sharon Lawrence had met Elton through Winter at the beginning of 1973. 'I wasn't such a big fan of his at the beginning,' she remembers. 'But I always liked him very much as a person. He was so fresh, so humorous, so enthusiastic – so totally different from the other types of people you had to meet in that business. I'd go with him to Tower Records on his buying sprees. It always impressed me that he refused to take free records: he always insisted on paying for what he had. He'd buy hundreds of albums, and try to buy hundreds for me, too.'

She developed a special rapport with Elton, and gained the reputation of being able to deal with him during his tempestuous Little Moments. John Reid's advent did not remove the need for this. 'I realised the relationship between Elton and John was chaotic.

You had a manager that one day seemed to control his artist completely and another day didn't seem able to control him at all. John would call me sometimes and say, "He's being hateful. He's supposed to do a radio spot, and now he won't." I'd be brought in to talk him into it.'

She agreed to head Rocket USA, fired by the idealistic zest which Elton had for the whole project. 'He cared about the music so much. He'd studied its history. Even after he became so big, he was still in awe of people he considered the great figures of rock 'n' roll. And he cared about them so much as people. If anyone he admired was going wrong, Elton would always try to help them. I've seen him take people aside and say "Look, I've always admired you . . . don't do this to yourself." '

What would go down in pop history as the Yellow Brick Road Tour reached the first of many climaxes before an audience of 16,000 at Hollywood Bowl on 7 September. The two concerts at the Bowl had sold out weeks earlier, fuelled by carefully placed rumours that for his first US appearance in almost a year, Elton intended to surpass all previous displays of excess showmanship. As a teaser, an enormous billboard on Sunset Boulevard had shown him as a Fred Astaire figure in top hat and white tie, winking suggestively from a vista of top-hatted and net-stockinged chorus girls.

The Bowl's scallop-shell stage was furnished as for one of Busby Berkeley's more ambitious dance routines. First, the audience beheld an enormous backcloth of Elton in his Fred Astaire guise, with top-hatted Elton cut-outs flourishing canes and white gloves in a long row beneath. The raising of the backcloth revealed a mass of potted palms and a precipitous, glittering staircase. At the bottom of the staircase were five grand pianos in pale airbrushed hues, one yellow, one orange, one blue, one grey and one mauve.

The compère for the evening was Linda Lovelace, whose book *Deep Throat* had lately become a sub-pornographic bestseller. 'Ladies and gentlemen,' she began. 'In the tradition of old Hollywood, let me introduce you to . . . the Queen of England.' Down the staircase came a lookalike of the monarch whose hand Elton had recently shaken at the London Palladium. More look-alikes followed of idols and current friends, among them Groucho Marx, Mae West, Batman and Robin, the Frankenstein Monster and four counterfeit Beatles.

Elton himself was introduced by a freight train of superlatives, 'the biggest, most colossal, gigantic, fantastic . . .' and the 20th Century-Fox Cinemascope fanfare. Wearing huge white feathery breeches and a white-feathered toque, a cross between Bat Masterson and Queen Mary, he descended the staircase, nodded regally to the kowtowing effigies of Groucho and Batman, stepped on to the lid of the blue airbrushed piano, then platformed gingerly over the hedge bordering the stage proper. As he did so, the lids of all five pianos were raised, revealing the silver letters E L T O N, and 400 white doves were released into the Hollywood night.

Watching this orgy of ego in Bryan Forbes's documentary, it is interesting to see the moment when the last doves flutter away and Elton doffs his feathery bonnet to reveal a somewhat less feathery thatch, tinted scarlet above the ears. Despite the 20th Century-Fox trumpets and the roar of 16,000 voices, what we see is still no more or less than Reggie Dwight, getting down to business in the saloon bar.

Theatrics continued throughout the two-hour show, which suffered somewhat from the Hollywood Bowl's notorious open-air acoustics. While Elton played 'Crocodile Rock', a cloaked figure with a papier-mâché crocodile head backed him on electric organ. (It was Clive Franks, the sound-engineer.) Halfway through, he disappeared to exchange his white feathers for a purple jumpsuit scored with outsize musical notes, and his white-framed glasses for a pair that lit up on his face like the rings of an electric stove.

Melody Maker's report of the concert was headlined ELTON'S FINEST HOUR. In Bryan Forbes's film, the superstar himself describes the sensation of holding so enormous an audience in his grasp. 'I like to lift them up, drop them down, lift them up again. It's the same as having sex. You try to save the very best bit till last. It's like two hours of . . . I don't know. It's like fucking for two hours and then suddenly finding out there's nothing you can do after that. It's so emotional and so physical, you don't ever want to do anything else.'

Gone was the era of all-night drives between gigs in rattletrap station wagons. For this American tour, MCA Records provided Elton with his own personalised Boeing 707 airliner, allowing him to establish a central base and fly to and from his concerts each day. The Boeing's interior was so large, and Elton's entourage so small, he said he often felt like playing inflight hide-and-seek.

Out of his feather bonnet and space rodeo suit, he remained the simplest, healthiest, most clean-living performer rock had ever known. At 8 am, when most other stars were just closing gummy eyes, Elton would be exposing his sturdy legs out on the hotel tennis court. At night, he was scarcely less wholesome than in the morning. Pop concert audiences then were accustomed to seeing their idols punctuate each number with copious swigs from vodka or bourbon bottles and beercans, arrayed like a squalid bar along amplifier tops. Through all of Elton's dehydrating two-hour shows, his only refreshment came from a small bottle of Perrier.

Other touring stars were famous for misbehaviour in hotels, which could include the destruction of TV sets or telephones – sometimes even the entire room. 'That never went on around Elton,' Penny Valentine remembers. 'He was into property. He wasn't into smashing it up.'

Those not in the know marvelled, too, at his self-control where groupies were concerned. With willing female flesh to be had on every side, his hotel suite appeared as chaste as a Trappist monastery. In fact, Sharon Lawrence remembers, the crowds of attractive women who thronged through Elton's dressing rooms occasionally brought a definite gleam into his eye. 'I always felt that he could easily have married and had children – something he often said he wanted to do. Once or twice, I tried to encourage him in that direction. I told him "Don't get stuck with choices now that you'll regret for the rest of your life."'

She was impressed, like many before her, by the neat, meticulous habits that prevailed even amid the whirl of this biggest-ever tour. Driving away after a concert, his first act was still to reach for his diary and jot down his impressions of the place he had just played, the audience size and possible box-office gross. 'At the centre of all that excess and craziness, he was completely self-contained and self-reliant. I always thought if Elton had to do a gig and all the big star support systems broke down, he'd still get there, even if he had to hitchhike and carry his piano on his back.'

This time there had been no argument over which of the new album's tracks should precede it as a single. 'Goodbye Yellow Brick Road' was released at the tour's outset, in September. Within only days, it was number two in America and six in England. The full two-record collection followed early in October, launched by an elaborate TV link-up to the British press from Elton in Los Angeles. He had never released an album while on tour before, and, with his usual superstition, wondered what this might portend. The answer came before the tour's end: number one on both sides of the Atlantic.

Like the Beatles' *Revolver*, though for utterly different reasons, *Goodbye Yellow Brick Road* was an album exactly suited to its moment. One has only to hear that Wagnerian overture of Moog synthesiser and wind whistling round artificial crags to conjure up late 1973 with gruesome clarity. In London, Edward Heath is at 10 Downing Street, about to precipitate a coal miners strike and plunge the country into power cuts and a three-day working week. At the White House, Richard Nixon sits in the Oval Office, still wishing to make it 'perfectly clear' he knows nothing about Watergate. In the Middle East, Sadat holds desperately on to his 'pre-emptive strike' against Israel, and Saudi oil ministers double and redouble the price per barrel. In Belfast, Northern Ireland, and Beirut, Lebanon, terrorist murder in the name of religion becomes an almost daily commonplace. Groups of three or four psychopaths call themselves Liberation Fronts. Psychopaths who blow up children or milk roundsmen call themselves Popular Liberation Fronts. Psychopaths define innocent bystanders as 'legitimate targets' and, having murdered, issue statements claiming 'responsibility'. The word of the decade is 'security', meaning insecurity. Airport concourses become war zones. Inflation bites. Money shrinks. Rules break. Language lies. Scruples vanish.

The result is a desire for escapism as never before in all branches of mass entertainment, movies, television and pop music. Onscreen fires and explosions more cataclysmic than those of everyday life; onscreen murders more vicious and violent than those enacted daily in the street; cars piling up in smashes more demented than on real roads and freeways; shotguns blasting louder; bones crunching more sickeningly; blood spurting redder from super-jumbo exit wounds. And with the cathartic sadism, cathartic sentimentality; a deep hankering for the imagined stability, safety and kindliness of the past. Nostalgia ceases to be the resort of an affected few and becomes the opiate of all classes and age groups. Nostalgia for the Twenties, the Thirties, the childhood idylls of Beatrix Potter and Mabel Lucie Attwell, the 'great days' of Hollywood, the rock-'n'-roll Fifties.

Goodbye Yellow Brick Road perfectly mirrored this mood with its nostalgia and whimsy and, no less, its total lack of concept or focus. Long had the Seventies generation waited for an album so lushly, complicatedly, portentously and passionately adding up to nothing.

Even what little explicitness was there went over the heads of most of its audience. Scarcely anyone noticed the song about the sailors' whore, the unclean nymphet or the teenage lesbian. All that millions upon millions of pop fans wanted to hear were the vague, glowing echoes of childhood and fan-worship: Lucie Attwell, the *Beano* and Saturday-morning pictures; Fred Astaire, Roy Rogers and Judy Garland; Elton not rejecting the Yellow Brick Road, as Bernie Taupin had meant, but linking hands with the Cowardly Lion and the Tin Man, and dancing in high platforms over the rainbow. The production gave his singing a distorted quality, like a sentimental chorale by massed chipmunks. Through that neutral and neuter double voice, Bernie's words were clipped and flattened almost into an alien dialect:

> *Back with the howlin ol' owlinthewood.*
> *Huntin' the hawny black tauwd . . .*

No other Elton album was to stay in the charts so long (more than a year in the American Top 40) or spin off so many single hits. 'Candle in the Wind' was released in Britain, reaching number eleven ironically in a time of epidemic power cuts. Most extraordinary was what befell 'Bennie and the Jets', Bernie's song about a butch sci-fi rock goddess, to which Gus Dudgeon had added the sound effects of a live performance. As well as making number one in the US pop charts, 'Bennie' became a crossover hit on black soul and R & B radio stations across America. A trifling track named 'Harmony', written and recorded in half a day, achieved cult status among the chain of FM stations operated by RKO. In a 'battle of the hits' contest run by the New York station, listeners voted 'Harmony' the winner twenty-three times in succession.

The Yellow Brick Road tour's closing weeks saw Elton raised to a new, dizzy plateau of fame in America. Sharon Lawrence, who was often with him on the road, remembers how the ovations, the adulation and backstage mobbing seemed to surpass themselves each night. 'In Memphis, Al Green came to the concert, which really thrilled Elton. Afterwards, something went wrong with the security, and about 4,000 people seemed to get backstage. Elton was amazed. "My God," he said. "This is really like the Beatles, isn't it?" He was so proud.'

Back at the Rocket office, Sharon's most important job was to tell him his chart placing as soon as the lists were published each Wednesday. 'I'd call him up and say, "Well, I'm afraid I gotta tell you – you're number one again." It was that way week after week after week. One day when I told him, Elton said, "It's going to be terrible to be number two, isn't it?"'

His buoyant mood could always change, and did so more often and unexpectedly as months of travel and performance started to tell. 'He'd stand at the side of the stage sometimes and say, "Fuck it, I'm not going on",' Dee Murray, his bass-player, remembered. 'But he always would – and usually give a killer of a performance. Onstage, I was the one who had most eye-contact with him. For the first few numbers, he'd refuse to look at me at all. Then, at a certain point, I'd meet his eye, and he'd grin. Whatever had been bugging him was all over.

'The thing was, you never knew when he was going to throw a wobbler. And when he did, everyone got it. We were all having dinner one night, in this really smart place, when Elton suddenly got up, said, "You're all nothing but a load of bastards", and walked out. A minute later, he came back and stood there and had another go at us.'

Sharon Lawrence witnessed still worse outbreaks, the kind that, for some reason, only women were ever allowed to see. The biggest rock star in America, whom all show business wanted to meet and court, would lie face down on the king-size bed in his emperor-size suite, mumbling, 'No one gives a damn about me.'

If his spirits were not to take these fearful dips, they had to be kept at a constant hyperactive high. During his appearance in Atlanta, Sharon discovered that the cult star Iggy Pop was appearing at a local club named Richard's. She suggested to Elton that he join Iggy onstage, unannounced, wearing a hired gorilla costume. 'He loved doing that – even though the suit was so hot, he almost suffocated in it.'

For a short hop in the Boeing between New York and Boston, Sharon arranged an equally elaborate surprise. Elton's great hero among black singers was Stevie Wonder, the ex-Motown child prodigy who had recently suffered a serious car crash and was only now inching back to performance. When Elton boarded the plane, Stevie would be at the portable piano in its rear cabin, singing 'Crocodile Rock'.

'But when Elton came out to get on the plane, he was in a terrible mood,' Sharon remembers. 'He hadn't gotten his chart placings that morning, or something. He didn't even see or hear Stevie. He just went straight into the front cabin and sat there, fuming. Stevie carried on playing and singing, and still Elton had no idea. In the end I had to go to him and say, "For God's sakes, Stevie Wonder's back there."

'He and Stevie played together that night, and were wonderful together. Stevie said afterwards that it was the start of things really getting back to normal for him after the auto crash. Elton was on top of the world again.'

The terrible moment was when the machine suddenly stopped. The forces that had kept you pinned to the whirling wall of the rotor-ride gave up their hold. You plunged down and landed with a sickening bump on earth again.

Sharon Lawrence remembers being rung up by Elton on the first night in more than three months when there was no plane ride to take, no white ostrich feather bonnet to don, no two-hour workout to do on callused fingertips, no piano top to strut, above the plantations of waving arms.

'He sounded totally lost. "It's all over," he said. "Where do I go now?"'

TEN

'This is your song,
Your Majesty'

IN late November 1973, mass interviews were held at London's Inn
on the Park hotel to bring the British press up to date with pop
music's most multi-faceted success. For favoured reporters, like the
NME's Charles Shaar Murray, a special bonus was laid on, owing
something to recent close encounters with Groucho Marx. Arriving
in a luxurious panelled suite above Hyde Park, Murray was puzzled
to find a room lavishly furnished with drinks and snacks but only
Elton's chauffeur in attendance. The chauffeur then pressed a button
on the wall, a panel swung around and a folding bed tipped out. Off
the bed rolled a mirthful Elton in white suit, white boots and red,
white and blue spectacles.

It was a fittingly euphoric end to a year that even the most hype-
hardened journalist could only call stupendous. Elton John was now,
undisputedly, the biggest pop star in the world, which by immutable
reckoning meant as big as, or bigger than, the Beatles. Like the
Beatles in the Sixties, he was pop's uttermost peak; the dictator,
inventor and pioneer to whom millions looked for their next era of
fantasy and joy. After his appearance at Belle Vue, Manchester, the
Melody Maker could put only one possible headline above Roy
Hollingworth's ecstatic review: HAIL ELTON! ROCK SAVIOUR!

American superstar or not, he was still the favourite clown of
Britain's music press with his slapstick stunts in folding beds, his first
class quotes in Goon-accented voices – above all, his good-humoured
tolerance of the tradition that praise for his music and showmanship
be invariably accompanied by jibes about his personal appearance.
He would himself repeat the worst insults with apparent enjoyment:
'indubitably lunkish', 'a head like a coconut with a joke-shop mask
attached', 'Godzilla in drag', 'a bald, bespectacled plumpoid', 'a pasty
little troll'.

The biggest pop star in the world remained defiantly normal and

down-to-earth, even about recognising himself as the biggest pop
star in the world. 'You can't be famous and be totally available to the
public,' he told Charles Shaar Murray. 'I don't mean that in a
snobbish sense at all, but if I walked about London all the time,
people would go, "Hmm, he shouldn't do that." They don't want to
see you in Camden Town, buying your vegetables. They don't
associate you with going to the toilet or buying fruit or having
trouble with your plumbing at home. You wouldn't expect the royal
family to go out and buy budgie seed. "Oh yes, saw her yesterday,
walking the corgis."

'If I'm walking down the road and someone says, "Can I have
your autograph?" – sure, that's fine. There's never been a publicity
machine behind me. I'd hate it. There's no image to go with me. I
don't break thousands of girls' hearts at airports. If there's one
photographer there, I'm lucky. I've not got attractive features. I'm
plain.'

Though most journalists now understood the situation between
John Reid and him, none made even the most oblique reference to
it. Seventies pop might visually flaunt the homosexual, bisexual and
'unisexual' but there were still no words to express such a thing in
NME or *Melody Maker*. For propriety's sake Elton would himself
occasionally provide a token alibi. 'When I have kids, I'm going to
call my little girl Umbrella. Umbrella John is a beautiful name. Poor
little girl, she'll really have the piss taken out of her. "Umbrella –
stand over there."'

To his triumphs as a performer he was restlessly adding fresh
achievements as an entrepreneur, talent scout and Svengali. In
December, Rocket Records had its first Top 20 hit with Kiki Dee's
'Amoureuse', the sexy torch song which Elton had matched to the
stolid Sheffield girl, against all appearances. Though 'Amoureuse'
made only 13, the haunting production Elton had given it ensured
its future as a minor British non-feminist classic. Kiki at long last had
the success and recognition she deserved. Here, as everywhere else,
the Elton touch seemed to be infallible.

A further burst of high spirits took him back into the studio to
record his first-ever purpose-made single, albeit in a corny tradition
hallowed since the era of Bing Crosby. 'Step into Christmas' was
completed in a single day at Trident, London, using all the electronic
flimflam of Phil Spector's 'Wall of Sound'. 'I'd like to thank you
for the year,' sang Elton dutifully as a substitute for a Basildon Bond
notelet to his global audience. Though hardly meant seriously, 'Step
into Christmas' reached number 24 in Britain before settling into

the Yuletide radio repertoire. As a further seasonal bonus, Elton played four concerts in London at the Hammersmith Odeon, inaugurating what would become a Yuletide tradition in Santa Claus costume and beard, pounding and pratfalling amid swirls of polystyrene snow.

The new year took off, powered by the euphoric overdrive of the old. *Goodbye Yellow Brick Road* had only just been displaced as number one in the American album chart. 'Candle in the Wind' was released as a British single in February, making number eleven. At the same time in America, its intended B-side, 'Bennie and the Jets', a hit on soul-music stations from Watts to Detroit, crossed over to become number one in the mainstream pop chart. And Elton became vice-president of Watford football club.

It is the nature of all such football fanatics to support their local team or club with total loyalty, however small or inglorious that local team or club may be. For a boy growing up in Pinner, the local club was Watford, five stops north on the Metropolitan Line. Throughout Reggie Dwight's childhood, Watford the football team had been little more glamorous than Watford the town. Small and penurious, stuck permanently in the middle reaches of the Third Division, the club possessed no great players, attracted no great managers, won no great victories, always seemed an infinity away from the yearly Cup Final at Wembley. Yet Reggie had rooted for 'the Hornets' with all his devout fan's nature. He had plotted Watford's unspectacular gains and losses minutely on his League chart; sported Watford's black and yellow colours; cheered from the stands at every possible home game on the modest ground in Vicarage Road.

The club's malady was nothing that couldn't be cured by cash to purchase star players from bigger clubs and pay a charismatic manager to galvanise the team out of its apparent death wish. The days were ending when British sport seemed to run on invisible and bottomless funds. Elton, even so, might never have become involved but for a girl named Julie Webb, who contributed articles to *New Musical Express* and was also a passionate football fan. In late 1973, while interviewing Elton, she mentioned that Watford was making a concerted effort to arrest its long decline and, to this end, was actively seeking new sources of investment and sponsorship. Maybe he could help out by giving them a benefit concert.

The lifelong fan jumped at this chance to help Watford, with both his money and his name. At the same time, embarrassed misgivings all but overcame him. The club's board of directors, in his eyes, was still an august and imposing body. What if they should be embarrassed to receive approaches from a pop star? What if they should regard it as just some publicity stunt? What if they should think his interest merely temporary and feckless instead of profoundly from the heart? A faint, diffident ghost of Reggie Dwight suddenly saw all manner of reasons not to do what he most wanted to.

Enquiries to Vicarage Road banished such fears. The Watford directors would be delighted to have him as an investor, and also grateful for any publicity accruing from his association with the club. In return for the promised benefit concert, and buying a block of shares, he would receive the honorary title of vice-president.

Purely cosmetic though the title was, Elton took it as seriously as if just appointed vice-president of America. Determined to prove his involvement and dedication, he attended all Watford's matches, home and away, missing only a stray one or two from pressure of performing or recording. Though soon to leave Britain and begin globetrotting again, he promised he would stay in constant touch with how Watford was faring in the League.

Self-effacing as he usually was in interviews, he seldom could resist mentioning this honour, outweighing all his heaped-up gold and platinum discs. 'There's nothing to publicise about me,' he insisted to Charles Shaar Murray, 'except that I'm vice-president of Watford.'

On his last American tour, Elton had heard of a recording studio even more appealingly novel than the Château d'Hierouville. This was Caribou, a studio on a ranch 9,000 feet up in the Colorado mountains. The owner was Jim Guercio, an American rock prodigy of background not unlike Elton's own. Trained in classical composition at Chicago University, Guercio had gone on to play guitar with Frank Zappa's Mothers of Invention, to produce Blood, Sweat and Tears and then create the hugely successful brass-rock band Chicago. He also had close managerial ties with Elton's greatest of all American musical heroes, the Beach Boys.

Elton visited Caribou by helicopter and there and then booked time to make an album at the ranch, first thing in 1974. Talking to Jim Guercio filled his mind with plans for zingy brass effects like Chicago and Blood, Sweat and Tears. He also had expansive ideas for backing vocals and asked a large group of musician friends to participate, among them Bruce Johnston and Carl Wilson of the Beach Boys, Danny Hutton of Three Dog Night, and Dusty Springfield.

The album introduced a fourth, highly idiosyncratic figure into

Elton's permanent backup band. Rather than a predictable new guitarist or keyboard player, he chose to bring in percussionist Ray Cooper, ex-stalwart of the studio band Blue Mink. Tall and thin, with the censorious face of some stern Baptist elder, Cooper was almost as much of an onstage extrovert as Elton himself. To his classical ensemble of cymbals and tympani he added sound effects à la Spike Jones: whistles, rattles and Donald Duck quacks. Elton adored him, perhaps taking some subliminal comfort from the fact that Ray Cooper, too, was noticeably sparse on top.

The *Caribou* album – so it would eventually be titled – was squeezed into the smallest time frame yet. Only ten days could be spared, in mid-February, before Elton and the band started a tour of Japan, Australia and New Zealand. From there, Elton and John Reid were due in Los Angeles for final negotiation of a new recording contract with MCA.

Seven months of perpetual motion since *Goodbye Yellow Brick Road* had left little time for Bernie Taupin and Elton to write new material, let alone anything as strong as 'Candle in the Wind' or 'Bennie and the Jets'. The songs they took with them into the Colorado wilderness were little more than hasty ad libs. There was, for instance, the time just after their last US tour when Bernie had been at Hercules, listening to Elton in a cross mood, badmouthing everyone he could think of. Maxine Taupin had entered the room at that moment, nodded knowingly and said, 'Oh-oh. The bitch is back.' The line sparked off an instant Bernie lyric that the 'bitch' in question indulgently set to a frantic rock-'n'-roll beat.

The session began with Elton on top form, charging round the ranch's snowy slopes on a Snowmobile as frenetically as his fingers found chords for Bernie's words. But unfortunately, no one had taken into account the totally different process of recording an album in America. It took two precious days at Caribou to adjust to the studio's unfamiliar monitor system. Repeated technical hitches threw Elton into a 'moody', lasting a day and a half. The entire album therefore had to be finished in barely a week, before he and the band left for their Far East tour.

The most troublesome track was an emotional ballad called 'Don't Let the Sun Go Down on Me'. 'When Elton sang the vocal track, he was in a filthy mood,' Gus Dudgeon remembers. 'On some takes, he'd scream it, on others he'd mumble it. Or he'd just stand there, staring at the control room. Eventually, he flung off the cans [earphones] and said "Okay, let's hear what we got." When I played it to him, he said "That's a load of fucking crap. You can send it to

Engelbert Humperdinck and, if he doesn't like it, you can give it to Lulu as a demo."'

This tour of Japan, Australia and New Zealand was among the last to be set up for Elton by Vic Lewis at the NEMS agency. Elton's agreement with Brian Epstein's old firm was a subsidiary of his expiring agreements with the Dick James Organisation. John Reid had made it clear that, like Dick James, Vic Lewis belonged to the bad old days, and was to be shaded from the picture as soon as legally possible.

It was cavalier treatment for a man who had played almost as crucial a part as James in Elton's early development. Vic Lewis was the one who had largely coerced him from his songwriter's obscurity, forcing him to raise his original band and go back out on the road. Nor might there have been any miraculous American breakthrough in 1970 but for Lewis's fortunate contacts with the Los Angeles Troubadour Club.

The ex-bandleader, with his little matinée-idol moustache, had hitherto enjoyed the warmest possible relations with Elton. Both were avid sports fans, with kindred passions for tennis, football and cricket. Vic Lewis ran his own celebrity cricket team, and had put on the charity match which allowed Elton to bat at Lord's the previous summer. He also shared Elton's fondness for Goonish high spirits and comical accents. 'I used to do Peter Sellers as an Indian, going "oh dear, goodness gracious me", that Elton always adored.'

Numerous gifts from Elton underlined their special rapport. 'The year he first appeared at the Troubadour, he arranged for a television set to be delivered to my home, so that I'd come home and find it working. I had a gold Parker 51 pen set from him, specially inscribed "To Vic". Another time, he came round and said, "I've got something for you" in an Indian voice. It was a gold ring in the shape of a turban, and the turban part was set with diamonds.'

Traditional married man that he was, Vic Lewis had been pained by the later developments in Elton's private life. He disliked John Reid and considered Reid's influence on Elton wholly deleterious. Nonetheless, he was still Elton's agent and, as such, flew out to join the tour for its concerts in Australia and New Zealand.

The concerts themselves were spectacular sell-out successes. Australia by the mid-Seventies had awoken from its long cultural trance and become a market for pop as demandingly up-to-date as America and Britain. Elton was the continent's number-one pop star, a fact in itself reflecting the huge change in public mores. He, in return, liked Australia for its blissfully predictable climate, its American luxury without American stress, above all the sense of being as far as one possibly could from England's littleness and nosiness. In Australia, he always felt his freest and happiest. Australian audiences, consequently, saw him on a roll that even America seldom did.

Backstage, however, there was tension from the beginning. The opening concert was in Perth, at the ground of the West Australia Cricket Club. John Reid got into a dispute with the promoter, Christopher Cambridge, over the box-office take. As a result, Vic Lewis found himself with Cambridge in a room at Perth Town Hall, having to count out all the ticket stubs and check them against the takings.

Any pop-star manager worth his salt will always keep a sceptical eye on concert promoters, to ensure the maintenance of standards for his client, both onstage and off. But to Vic Lewis, John Reid's behaviour throughout the five days of Australian concerts was counterproductively aggressive and challenging. 'Chris Cambridge was an excellent promoter. I'd booked all my other acts with him, like Cilla Black. All the time, John seemed to be doing his best to be difficult and obnoxious. To show that he controlled Elton, so he called the shots.'

Similarly, problems with Elton – those sudden, unpredictable prima donna tantrums and sulks – were things that, in Vic Lewis's view, only seemed to happen when John Reid was around. In Reid's rare absences, he reverted to the straightforward, well-brought-up young man of old. In Melbourne, Reid went off to visit friends, leaving Vic to take Elton to dinner. They discussed sport throughout the meal, starting with cricket, working round to football. Elton talked of his passionate desire to help Watford and his ambition to be more at the club than just an honorary vice-president. His ultimate dream, he said, was to join the club's board of directors. In the light of subsequent evenings, Vic Lewis was to remember this one with nostalgia as 'wholly pleasant'.

Their rapprochement was cemented by revival of a favourite mutual joke. 'Elton was having guests up to his hotel suite for drinks, so we decided to do my Indian gag. I'd got a terrific tan anyway. I put a red spot on my forehead, wrapped a white sheet round my body and head, and sat cross-legged on Elton's bed. When the guests arrived, they thought he had a real Indian guru praying in his bedroom.'

Elton's single concert in New Zealand was to be his biggest ever in Australasia. On 28 February he was to appear at the 34,000-seat Western Springs Stadium just outside Auckland. The plan then was

for Elton, John Reid, the band and Vic Lewis to go to Tahiti for a
week's holiday before Reid and Elton flew back to negotiate the
new MCA recording contract in Los Angeles.

The party flew out of Australia on 27 February – coincidentally
on the same day that the Queen flew in to perform the state opening
of Parliament in Canberra. Their spirits, already good, lifted still
higher as New Zealand's North Island materialised like a patch of
rural Surrey in the ocean. Elton was especially buoyant, remembering
what a haven New Zealand had been after his bumpy Australian tour
of 1971. Those who did not know already were apprised of the
interesting fact that John Reid had spent three years there as a small
boy.

New Zealand was to welcome back its favourite rock star with
almost royal ceremony. On the afternoon of Elton's arrival – the day
before the concert – his Australasian record company, Festival, had
organised a lavish press reception at an Auckland park, the Parnell
Rose Garden. When the tour party arrived, they were to be greeted
by massed Maoris performing a ceremonial war dance.

Every available Rolls-Royce in the North Island had been hired
to take them from their hotel to the park in open-topped cavalcade.
But, as the Rolls-Royce fleet awaited, a crisis suddenly blew up.
John Reid was found not to be at the hotel. Urgent enquiries by Vic
Lewis could produce only the vague explanation that he'd gone
'yachting'. Elton flatly refused to leave for the reception without
him.

By the time Reid reappeared and the procession reached the
park, the Maori dancers were almost ready to wreak carnage in
earnest. The situation was saved by Elton, who entered wholeheart-
edly into the spirit of things, pretending to recoil in terror as the
chanting natives advanced with levelled spears. Good humour apparently restored, the party then moved indoors to the press reception.

The press's long wait had made heavy depredations on the bar
provided for the occasion. John Reid asked for some whisky, and
was told that supplies had run out. What was later described as a
'heated' argument took place between Reid and the party's organiser,
Kevin Williams, with Reid accusing Williams of incompetence.
Offered a glass of champagne instead, Reid threw the contents of the
glass at Williams, and stormed out of the room.

About ten minutes later – according to subsequent courtroom
testimony – he returned to the bar. Sitting there was a woman friend
of Williams's, a journalist named Judith Baragwanath, who, in
forthright antipodean fashion, rebuked Reid for his earlier behaviour.
Reid then hit her, knocking her to the floor.

Neither Elton nor Vic Lewis witnessed the incident. 'I was right on the other side of the room,' Lewis remembers. 'The first I knew of it was when one of the organisers came up and tugged at my elbow. "Get Elton John and your whole party out of here as quickly as possible," he said. "A woman reporter says Elton's manager has just hit her in the face."' Star and entourage were hurriedly shepherded out to the Rolls-Royce fleet and back to their hotel.

That evening, there was a concert by David Cassidy at Auckland Town Hall. Elton, Reid and Vic Lewis attended the concert and afterwards went on to a party for Cassidy at a local night club. Among the journalists present was one David Wheeler, a friend of Judith Baragwanath's. During the party, Wheeler spoke to one of Elton's entourage about that afternoon's episode at Parnell Rose Garden. He was alleged to have said that, because of what had happened to Baragwanath, Elton and his party were 'all marked men'.

The supposed threat was communicated to Elton, who reacted with unwonted truculence, marching up to David Wheeler, grabbing him by the shirt front and asking him whom he thought he was threatening. John Reid then intervened, knocking Wheeler down and kicking him as he lay on the floor.

To hit one person in the course of a day may be considered unfortunate. To hit two – especially in a foreign country, under a foreign legal system – exceeds even Lady Bracknell's definition of carelessness.

The immediate effect was to put Elton's whole party – bar Vic Lewis, who had left early – in imminent fear of retaliatory beatings-up. 'We left the club post-haste,' Elton later remembered, 'and were all physically threatened that anyone to do with the Elton John tour had better watch it. Then when we got back to the hotel we got a phone call [from David Cassidy's security manager] saying, "There's a carload of people on the lookout for you, so just stay inside your hotel."'

Next day – the day of Elton's giant concert at Western Springs – a posse of police arrived at the tour hotel. An agitated John Reid had been concealed in an outlying bungalow, leaving Vic Lewis with Elton. 'The police said they were looking for Elton John's manager,' Lewis remembers. 'At first they thought it was me they were looking for. I had to work quite hard to explain the difference between a manager and agent, and convince them I hadn't thrown champagne or hit anyone. But they finally realised I couldn't possibly fit the description they'd got.'

A strenuous effort was made to smooth matters over. John Reid apologised to Judith Baragwanath and offered to pay out-of-court damages to both her and David Wheeler. But the Auckland police were not to be mollified. Reid was arrested and charged with assaulting Baragwanath at the Maori reception and Wheeler at the night club. Elton, too, though he had merely grabbed the reporter's shirt front, was arrested and charged with assaulting Wheeler.

Later that same day, John Reid was arraigned before Auckland magistrates. After a short preliminary hearing, the case was adjourned until the following day. Reid's application for bail was denied and he was remanded overnight to Mount Eden prison.

Thursday 28 March, 1974 was a day of the highest drama Australasia had known for some years. In Canberra, Australia, while the Queen performed the state opening of Parliament, an armed aboriginal demonstrator held four people hostage in the nearby Department of Aboriginal Affairs as a protest against alleged racial discrimination in its policies. That evening in Auckland, New Zealand, 34,000 Elton John fans converged on Western Springs Stadium, blissfully unaware that both their idol and his manager were facing trial for assault, and that the concert itself was within an inch of being cancelled.

Elton had been released from police custody, but was distraught at Reid's imprisonment and would not contemplate going on stage without him. The only hope was to go to New Zealand's Supreme Court and appeal the magistrates' refusal to grant bail. Frantic lawyer activity finally located a Supreme Court judge, Mr Justice Mahon, who was willing to sit for the appeal. The hearing took place at the judge's house, just ninety minutes before the concert's scheduled starting time. Mr Justice Mahon accepted that Reid was indispensable to the concert and granted bail on condition he surrendered his passport. The feathered space cowboy took to the boards that night as advertised.

Next day, when they should have been en route to Gauguin's island paradise, superstar and manager stood in the dock at Auckland magistrates court.

Elton's trial for assaulting David Wheeler was but a token official slap on the wrist. To such a lifelong good boy, it was none the less awful for that. Wearing a beige bolero suit with laterally-striped lapels, an open-neck striped shirt and yellow glasses, he said nothing in court, other than admitting the charge. His counsel, I. W. Brown, QC, submitted that the offence had been a minor one. Elton had only grabbed Wheeler by the shirt front, and had taken no further part in the assault. He was, his counsel said, 'non-aggressive, sensitive, sensible and concerned for other people, especially the young'. His conduct had been 'totally uncharacteristic of a person who is essentially a gentle individual'. As evidence of his character and public standing, a letter was produced from Princess Margaret, thanking him for work on behalf of her charity, the Invalid Aid Association. Thanks in part to this royal testimonial (which he evidently valued highly enough to carry around the world with him) Elton was discharged without conviction, and ordered to pay $50 NZ in costs.

To John Reid, no such leniency and latitude would be given. Photographs of Judith Baragwanath were produced, showing 'an injury above one of her eyes'. The attack on David Wheeler was said to have caused 'a cracked tooth, a chipped tooth, a black eye and bruises'.

His counsel, R. I. Maclaren, said that Reid admitted the two assaults, but that both had been the result of provocation. He had just experienced the pressure of supervising Elton's tour of Australia, and had arrived in New Zealand in a state of exhaustion. At the Maori park reception, Judith Baragwanath had used 'foul and derogatory language' to him. Baragwanath herself admitted she had called Reid 'a rotten little bastard' for throwing champagne at her friend Kevin Williams. But, under cross-examination, she denied that her remarks had included the word 'poof'.

David Wheeler said that, at the David Cassidy party, he had expressed 'a little bit of concern' over that afternoon's incident with Baragwanath, who was a friend of his. But he denied he had said, as Elton's side claimed, 'We have planned to get Elton John tonight. If not tonight, tomorrow night.' A few minutes later, he had been 'completely baffled' to be confronted by Elton, Reid and two other people, and accused of having threatened Reid.

In the witness box, Reid said he had struck Judith Baragwanath 'as a reflex action' when she confronted and abused him. In retrospect he thought it 'a despicable thing' to hit a woman, and now felt 'very bad' about it. He had attacked David Wheeler at the night club, thinking a fight was about to start. Menaced, as he believed, by several people, his instinct had been to protect Elton. As Wheeler had fallen, Reid was turning to go and had kicked him once, he thought, on the shoulder.

Reid's counsel said that the assaults were 'completely out of character', and that Reid had already been considerably punished by the publicity the case had received. But the Auckland stipendiary magistrate, H. Y. Gilland, was unmoved. He said he was prepared to accept that Reid was 'apparently not a violent man'. But the two assaults in one day must be considered more than an aberration brought on by strain or misunderstanding. Reid had shown 'an ill-mannered, arrogant indifference to people in the way he dealt with them', which could not be punished simply by a fine. He was sentenced to a month's imprisonment for assaulting Wheeler and a further seven days for assaulting Baragwanath, the sentences to be concurrent.

Reid's application for bail pending an appeal was refused by the magistrate but later allowed by a Supreme Court judge in chambers. The appeal was set down for hearing in the Supreme Court the following Tuesday, 3 March. Meanwhile, the *New Zealand Herald* reported, Elton and Reid had checked out of their hotel and gone into hiding.

Urgent overseas phone calls to high-powered lawyers – including Paul McCartney's brother-in-law John Eastman – produced little comfort. New Zealand law would have to take its course. Vic Lewis and the band dispersed for their holiday in Tahiti, leaving Elton behind in Auckland with Reid. In pop-music lore, it is usually stars who get into trouble on tours, and have to be protected by their managers. Here, the manager had caused the trouble with conduct that the most unruly star would have found it hard to equal.

Reid's appeal to the New Zealand Supreme Court, four days later, was dismissed outright. The judge, Mr Justice McMullin, ruled that the two assaults could 'only be branded as cowardly'. He was unimpressed by Reid's payment of $2,500 to Judith Baragwanath and $3,000 to David Wheeler, as well as a sum into court to cover a possible fine. Nor was he moved by pleas that Reid had to be in Los Angeles in five days' time to conclude a new worldwide recording deal for Elton with MCA. He agreed with the prosecutor's submission – ironic in the light of Reid family history – that the appellant should not be treated as a celebrity, but 'just like any other New Zealand citizen'. The sentence was upheld.

Back in Britain, the case received only minimal publicity. Elton's light-hearted account, quoted in *New Musical Express*, said that things 'just got out of hand' at a badly run reception. Later, one of the roadies had been threatened with a beating-up. 'We asked who was doing the threatening . . . I went up to him, seized him by the collar and muttered, "You no-good son of an Irish leprechaun, what do you think you're doing?" and was just about to clock him round the face – me of all people! – when my manager stepped in and hit him for me.' He added that the trial had been 'a farce'. 'The magistrates just didn't believe any of us had been provoked. It was all over in twenty minutes without any of us having witnesses. It was a joke.'

At the Rocket Records office in London, where Steve Brown had held the fort, John Reid's restoration to liberty was awaited with deep trepidation. Penny Valentine felt she, at least, could look him squarely in the eye, having made heroic efforts to keep details of the affair at a minimum in the British papers.

'John amazed me, as always,' Valentine remembers. 'The first thing he said when he walked back into the office was, "Where are my press cuttings?" '

The Cartier-Bresson of pop, meanwhile, preferred not to be excluded any longer from the photograph. Bernie Taupin had realised that twenty-three was perhaps too young an age to settle down for good in the Lincolnshire countryside. 'I had this romantic view of myself as still being a country boy whose heart was in the land,' he says now. 'But it was only a romantic view, because of the great childhood I'd had. I was trying to go back and recreate a chapter that was past.'

Having an American wife meant that, while living his country idyll in Tealby, Bernie also made constant trips out to California, staying in a succession of rented or borrowed houses and apartments. While the A. A. Milne side of him loved Lincolnshire, the besotted Western fan longed to put down permanent roots in America. In 1972 he bought a second home in Los Angeles, paying $170,000 for a house on North Doheny Drive, next door to the film director George Cukor.

Soon afterwards, he sold Piglet-in-the-Wilds, and moved down with Maxine to join Elton in the Surrey stockbroker belt. 'I went from the sublime to the ridiculous. We'd been living in a tiny four-room cottage. Now we'd got a house in LA and this other enormous place called Bourne Lodge right on the Wentworth Golf Course – a Tudor hunting lodge with, I think, a bit of Georgian thrown in – just down the road from Elton at Hercules. Far grander than his place. I mean, he was just living in a bungalow. I was living in a hunting lodge. I think he was a bit put out by that.'

Bernie and Maxine were quickly absorbed into the social circle that revolved round Bryan Forbes and Nanette Newman at Seven Pines. 'They came to all our parties,' Nanette remembers. 'And, of course, Bernie was an even better customer at the bookshop than Elton. What I noticed about him and Maxine was how incredibly neat and meticulous they both were. And their house was as neat and perfect as a doll's house.'

Living at a distance from Elton, meeting only in the studio and on tour, Bernie had not realised the vast change in his old roommate's acquaintanceships. His first inkling was the charity concert Elton gave at the Royal Festival Hall for Princess Margaret's Invalid Aid Association. Afterwards, Elton, Bernie and the band were invited to dinner with Princess Margaret and Lord Snowdon at Kensington Palace.

The Queen's younger sister had had a penchant for unconventionality since marrying a society photographer, the former Anthony Armstrong-Jones, at the start of the Sixties. She was still the most glamorous 'royal', a faintly raffish, as well as faintly tragic, figure, known to be atypically interested in the arts, fond of music and musicians – especially pianists – at times seeming less like a princess of the blood than a performer manquée. Still, it was stretching even Princess Margaret's bohemian lifestyle to invite a bunch of pop people back for a meal after a show.

'The whole night was very odd,' Bernie Taupin remembers. 'The thing that amazed me was that there didn't seem to be any kind of security at Kensington Palace, other than a policeman at the gate. You just rolled up, knocked at the door and were let in. The other thing I remember is that, getting out of the car, I split my trousers at the crotch. I had to borrow one of Lord Snowdon's dressing gowns while a lady-in-waiting sewed them up for me.'

The occasion was anything but formal. Two photographer earls were present, Snowdon and the Queen's cousin Lord Lichfield, both – Bernie Taupin remembers – 'getting plastered in a back room'. Nigel Olsson's girl friend, Josie, who collected celebrity telephone numbers, took the opportunity of copying down the palace's. Princess Margaret herself richly lived up to her reputation for earthy eccentricity. As the pop people stood in line to meet her, they noticed the evidently essential accoutrements of gin and tonic and wreathing smoke. At one point, mislaying her pack of American cigarettes, Her Royal Highness turned to a footman and demanded, 'Where are my fucking Winstons?'

Bernie Taupin's position in the mid-Seventies seemed an enviable one, perhaps even more so than Elton's. For Bernie could enjoy the fruits of their phenomenal success while experiencing almost none of its pressures. The tours that racked and crucified Elton were for him just free rides on a switchback of parties, receptions and room service. The album sessions, when Elton would scourge musicians and studio staff like Simon Legree, were for Bernie just pleasant interludes in France or the Colorado mountains. The closest he came to stress was those four weeks in every year when thirty-odd new lyrics must emerge. For the other forty-eight weeks, he need do nothing but sit and watch the figures change in his bank balance.

He had undertaken a few extracurricular projects; recording his solo poetry album; producing an album, *American Gothic*, for David Ackles; toying with various literary schemes including a children's book. Motivation was not strong when ten minutes' work could earn him a sum greater than most poets saw in their whole lifetime.

Bernie, too, was now seriously rich, though with none of Elton's zeal to acquire sophistication and aesthetic sense. 'I had no notion of taste in those days,' he admits now. 'What I had in the cottage at Tealby was just like any other pop *nouveau riche* – black walls, lava lamps and sand candles. Heavy Victorian furniture everywhere. Orange couches, covered with Liberty prints. No co-ordination whatever. The things I wore were just as bad – denim jackets, covered in patches, fringed buckskin jackets, Navajo jewellery. I'd go to shops like Take Six and buy those awful three-piece suits with the big, wide lapels. Only, being me, I'd buy twelve of them at a time.

'In my most flash period, I had a magenta Rolls-Royce, and a friend working for me as a driver and personal assistant. I even had a phone put in the Rolls – one of the very earliest type, when you still had to ask an operator for the number. I never called anyone on it because of all that hassle of going through the operator. One night, we were sitting in the car outside the BBC, and we suddenly heard a beep but had no idea what it was. Then I realised. "My God! It's the car phone! Ringing for the very first time!" I rushed to answer it, but before I could pick it up, it stopped. I never discovered who the call was from. And it never rang again.'

While Elton rose steadily up the social register, Bernie preferred to stay among the street urchins of Britain's rock biz. He became a habitué of Tramp, the celebrity discothèque in St James's. As in boyhood, he took to running round with a gang. 'There was me, Rod Stewart, Ringo, Gary Glitter. Others came and went, but Rod, Gary and I were the nucleus. You'd see our picture in *Melody Maker* with a caption saying, "Yes, it's the same old crew again."'

With Rod Stewart, he developed somewhat the same love-hate relationship as had Elton. 'Rod lived at Ascot, only a couple of miles from Wentworth, so if I'd fallen out with Maxine, I'd go back and sleep on his floor. He was always fighting with his girl, Dee, so another night he'd come back to my place. We used to have a thing about copying one another's clothes. If I got a tuxedo from Yves St Laurent, Rod had to go and have one made exactly the same. Then I'd try to get shirts made the same as his.'

Gary Glitter – then at the height of his transmogrification from obscure warm-up man to camp teenybop heart-throb – was the gang's clown and occasional fall guy. 'He used to wear that terrible

fur coat and that awful toupee,' Bernie remembers. 'Part of it was a
toupee, anyway. I remember we pulled it off his head one night and
threw it out of the car in the Cromwell Road.

'It was just like still being schoolboys, really. You did the same
thing every night – went to some club and got legless while your car
waited outside. Then drove around, pulling people's shoes off in the
car and throwing them out. We took some poor guy's trousers off
one night outside Tramp, threw them over a pawnbroker's sign and
left him there – drove off and when we came back half an hour later,
he was in a doorway without them, shivering. Silly, cruel things like
that.

'I'd end up so wasted, I wouldn't even know which of the cars
outside the club was mine. I put Harry Nilsson into what I thought
was my car one night, and told the driver to take him back to his
hotel. Next day, I found it hadn't been my car at all, but some Arab
sheikh's. He comes out of the same club later with two hookers –
and it's gone!'

In spring 1974 Elton became a director of Watford Football Club.
Vic Lewis had arranged it for him as a memento of that pleasant
dinner in Melbourne, before the Auckland nightmare set in. On
returning to London, Lewis contacted Watford's chairman, Jim
Bonser, and told him of Elton's passionate desire to graduate from
mere honorary vice-president. With the club still problematically
short of cash and good publicity, Bonser was only too glad to
commend the idea to his fellow directors. As a gesture of appreciation, and to be company for Elton at matches and meetings, Vic
Lewis also was invited to join the Watford board.

Probably no other moment in Elton's career, past or to come,
gave him quite such elation as this. 'The day I took him along to
finalise the details, he was over the moon,' Vic Lewis says. 'With a
grin which spread from ear to ear and back again, he told me, "This
has to be the happiest day of my life."'

His new appointment, for the moment, drove all other thoughts
from Elton's mind. The music papers were suddenly full of football-
oriented Elton John interviews, carrying headlines like THE STACK-
HEELED STRIKER. Julie Webb in *New Musical Express* described him
on the way to a game, waving a yellow and black Watford scarf in
determinedly proletarian manner from the buzzed-down automatic
rear window of his Rolls-Royce Corniche. His tone had the exhilaration of one thankfully regaining touch with roots: 'I've got such
pleasure, mixing with ordinary people again. You do lose the value
of things when you're racing around all the time on tour. Your

lifestyle changes, your standard of living changes. And your appreciation of things lessens to a degree. You forget how much joy you can give by giving an autograph to a person who is actually knocked out at getting it – or a record, and you think "Christ, it's only a bloody record!"'

Mixing with ordinary people, as opposed to adoring fans, did have one slightly disagreeable consequence. As a resplendent Elton took his seat in the Watford directors' box, he realised that not all humanity was involved in the conspicuous camp of glitter rock. Amid the cheers and whistles from adjacent terraces, a lone voice made itself heard like the soothsayer in some classical tragedy. 'You great poof!' it shouted.

On 5 May, Elton gave Watford their promised benefit concert, performing at the Vicarage Road ground where he had, for so many years, been a faithfully star-struck spectator. A crowd of 40,000 – more than Watford had drawn in living memory – saw him all in yellow and black, like some astral traffic warden, hammering out his stadium repertoire with one extra item, the Beatles' 'Lucy in the Sky with Diamonds'. There was also a surprise guest artist, Rod Stewart, swathed in a rival tartan supporter's scarf. After Stewart's four numbers, a violent rainstorm began. Elton came back and led the dampened 40,000 in a chorus of 'Singin' in the Rain'.

The Watford benefit concert and Elton's fund-raiser for Princess Margaret were all his British fans were destined to see of him until the end of 1974. A British and European tour, meant to take him through the summer and reach its climax at Wembley Arena, was cancelled two weeks after being announced. A communiqué from Vic Lewis's office said that Elton and the band were suffering from 'severe strain', and could take on no further commitments outside London. The disappointed fans were mollified by Elton's assurance that there was no serious trouble within that democratic family group. 'I'm very close to them, and they more or less said, "We can't do it any more" and, "Can we relax a bit?" and I think we all deserve a break. But we're not going to become hermits – it's just so that everyone can sit down and plan things a bit better.'

'Serious strain' also flavoured *Caribou*, the album which Elton had virtually abandoned in Colorado the previous January. The rushed sessions with hastily written, inferior songs had caused a serious upset with his perfectionist producer, Gus Dudgeon. 'Until *Caribou*, I thought Elton had never sunk below a certain level,' Dudgeon says now. 'Generally speaking, whatever pressure he was under, the standard stayed incredibly high. But on this one, for me, he suddenly went. It was the first time I ever had a serious quarrel with him.'

The album was largely created in post-production, Dudgeon adding extra vocal tracks by the Beach Boys' Carl Wilson and Bruce Johnston, and brass arrangements by the black soul band Tower of Power. The most inspired reworking had been on a slow ballad, 'Don't Let the Sun Go Down on Me', which Elton, before disappearing to Japan, had said was 'fuckin' crap', worthy only of Engelbert Humperdinck or Lulu. To this Dudgeon had added coolly soaring vocal tracks by Carl Wilson, Bruce Johnston and Toni Tennille, soon to find fame as half of Captain and Tennille. The result had an almost religious air, as if Elton were pleading for his happiness to some higher authority in the clouds.

'There was one bit of Elton's vocal I really wanted to bury,' Gus Dudgeon says. 'When he sang the line "Don't discard me", he put on this really ridiculous American accent, so it came out "Don't discord me". But Toni Tennille said, "No, leave it. It sounds good."' 'Don't discord me', indeed, was the hook that made the hit: number two in America, though only 16 in Britain.

Despite its advance hit single, however, everyone around Elton knew *Caribou* to be a mediocre product, especially as a follow-up to *Goodbye Yellow Brick Road*. The air of haste, indifference and compromise extended even to David Larkham's cover. No over-the-rainbow artwork this time; just a rather banal colour snap of Elton, in marcasite-framed red glasses and tiger-skin bolero, posing with husky swagger against a studio backcloth of mountains and lake. On the reverse, he and Bernie Taupin were shown perched on two stools, stiff and unsmiling, as if almost apologetic for the listing of forgettable doodles like 'Grimsby', 'I've Seen the Saucers', 'Stinker', 'You're So Static', and the unfathomable 'Solar Prestige à Gammon'.

The rock critics generally agreed the whole thing was makeshift and substandard. But who any longer gave a damn what rock critics said? Within a fortnight of release, *Caribou* was in the American top five. By mid-June, it had followed *Don't Shoot Me* and *Goodbye Yellow Brick Road* to number one simultaneously in America and Britain. The only faint hint of censure was the comparatively brief time it spent there: four weeks in America, two in Britain. Gus Dudgeon was later nominated for an award as producer of the year's best album.

With John Reid's release from prison in New Zealand, negotiation of Elton's new American recording contract could belatedly recommence. No trace of that hot-headed Auckland brawler could be seen in the immaculate young man who sat across the table from MCA's president, Mike Maitland, a model of composure and diplomatic level-headedness. With Reid at various times during the negotiations were Rocket's UK press officer, Penny Valentine, and Sharon Lawrence, from the LA office. Though scarcely admiring Reid for his 'chaos' in other directions, Sharon Lawrence could not help but be impressed here. 'He was very proper, very considered, very much in command all through. He never let the other guys rile him, but also never let them take an inch more than they should.'

On 22 June, *Billboard* reported that Elton had arrived in New York to sign what Mike Maitland, with that wonderful vagueness that can come over corporate men, preferred to describe merely as 'the best deal anyone ever got'. Full-page advertisements in both the *New York Times* and *Los Angeles Times* subsequently announced his re-signing to MCA for the US and Canada. The terms were not disclosed, but were widely reported to be $8 million for five albums – the largest sum ever paid to a recording artist. According to John Reid later, trade gossip erred on the side of caution, and the MCA deal was worth 'appreciably more' to Elton than $8 million. With the advance went a hefty increase in his US royalty-rate: from 15 to 17.5 per cent on records already released, and 20 per cent on all product released in future.

With the handshakes and champagne went a proviso, albeit soaked in the honey of American executive-speak. Delighted as MCA were to have yet another number one album, the adverse comments about *Caribou*'s quality could not be ignored. Mike Maitland told Elton that two albums per year were too many and that he should slow down his frantic production rate. Elton's not specially mature reaction was to defend the album by slagging off the critics. 'I'm the big cheese at the moment, so everyone feels bound to have a go at me. I read a good piece by John Tobler in *Zig-Zag* which said the reviews of *Caribou* were probably written before it even came out.' It is revealing that, even with a number-one UK album, he thought he was once again 'cold sick in Britain'.

What he did concede was that *Caribou*, the Australasian tour and its aftermath had left him 'a physical wreck'. His weight had shot up alarmingly again, helped by heavy drinking that now ran at 'about a pint of whisky a day'. His solution was, as usual, to pull down all the shutters, give up spirits and go on a crash diet. He also – for an interlude at least – gave up John Reid, booking himself in singly at a tennis ranch in Arizona. 'It was the first time I'd been on my own for four and a half years. I spent a month doing nothing but hitting a ball around, seven hours a day, and lost twenty-eight pounds.' The tireless competitor could not relax: he won the mixed doubles tournament once and the men's singles twice.

His unexpected holiday from the road was also spent in writing songs for other people: 'Let Me Be Your Car' for Rod Stewart, 'Snookeroo' for Ringo Starr. He spent several months working on a new song for the Beach Boys, agonising about whether they'd even like it when he finally managed to finish it. He got into the falsetto style of new black soul groups like the Stylistics and talked of making a cover version of their hit, 'Rock 'n' Roll Baby'. At the same time, he longed to write material for some traditional, Motown-oriented group like Gladys Knight and the Pips.

Caribou's other spin-off hit was 'The Bitch Is Back', that sardonic tribute of Maxine Taupin's to Elton in waspish mood. Released on 30 August, it reached number four in America, despite some local difficulties. For 'bitch', though a term of mildest chaff in Britain, has an almost Oedipal charge to American ears. Around this innocent rock-'n'-roll shouter swirled a moral furore that all Bernie Taupin's lyrics about murder, arson and lesbianism had not been able to arouse. Many radio stations insisted on bleeping the offensive word. Since it occurs approximately thirty times throughout the song, the result was ludicrous: 'I'm a [bleep!] I'm a [bleep!] Yeah the [bleep!] is back. Stone cold sober as a matter of fact. I can [bleep!] I can [bleep!] I can, better than you. It's the way that I do. The things that I do . . .'

At the behest of his newest fan, one further performance was added to Elton's schedule. Princess Margaret had been greatly taken by his concert for the Invalid Aid Association and, not long afterwards, got in touch with their mutual friends Bryan Forbes and Nanette Newman. 'She said she'd been telling the Queen Mother about Elton,' Nanette Newman remembers. 'The Queen Mother was terribly keen to see him as well.'

This first of many private command appearances took place at the Queen Mother's out-of-town residence, Royal Lodge, Windsor, which happens to be located conveniently only a mile or two down the road from Virginia Water. At dinner beforehand, a nervous Elton picked up what he took to be a silver salt cellar and found himself sprinkling sugar over his hors d'oeuvres. There was further embarrassment when he went into an adjoining room to change from black tie into his cream canvas suit, embroidered with the chinoiserie artwork from the cover of *Goodbye Yellow Brick Road*. He was standing there with his trousers off when the door suddenly opened and Princess Margaret looked in.

The Queen Mother enjoyed the subsequent recital, much as she seems to enjoy everything. 'Elton just did it perfectly,' Nanette Newman remembers. 'In "Your Song", when he got to the line "I'd buy a big house", he changed it to "I'd buy Windsor Castle, Your Majesty".'

The performance over, Her Majesty announced there would now be general dancing. With that, she went to the gramophone, put on her own top pop favourite – a military air called 'Slattery's Mounted Foot' – then seized Elton and vigorously partnered him around the room.

In mid-1974, Steve Brown left his job as general manager of Rocket Records. The ostensible reason was a disagreement with John Reid over the direction the company should take. As another ex-Rocket man remembers, there was a falling-out between them when Reid returned from his enforced stay in New Zealand to find the office, under Brown, not functioning to his satisfaction.

The loss to Elton, in personal terms, was enormous. More than anyone else, Steve Brown had been responsible for putting Bernie Taupin and him on the right creative track. Instead of selfishly commandeering them to further his own career as a producer, he had built them a matchless studio support system that included the indispensable Gus Dudgeon and the brilliant Paul Buckmaster. For more than five years, his enthusiasm, wisdom, judgement and calm had been unshakeable. But in a superstar's life, even the most valued and trusty friend cannot expect to last for ever.

As well as leaving Rocket, Brown left the music business altogether, to pursue a vocation long hinted at by his rustic hippy garb and the mural of fields and cows around his Soho office wall. He became a farmer.

David Croker, his replacement as boss of Rocket, was an almost equally long-standing Elton supporter and friend. Croker had run the Harvest label at EMI when John Reid was running Tamla-Motown and could claim much of the credit for first bringing Elton and Reid together. Indeed, it was always said in their circle that Croker had grown tired of the shabby youth who kept coming to plunder his record cupboard, and had tactfully steered him down the hall to John Reid.

Another new Rocket recruit was Clive Banks, the young pro-motion man whom John Reid had long been trying to woo away from Dick James Music. That meant that almost everyone important to Elton in his DJM days had now transferred allegiance to Rocket.

By the time Croker and Banks arrived, Elton's concept of the perfect record company had come true, up to a point. Rocket, in its first year, had signed eight acts, solo singers and bands, paying nothing like $8 million in advances, but guaranteeing each a generous royalty when success should finally come. The problem was that, try as he might to distance himself from it, Rocket was indivisibly linked with Elton's own stupendous success. Kiki Dee's breakthrough had to a very large extent been due to his personal endorsement and involvement. Having seen that great result, Rocket's other acts expected similar involvement and similar success – a hope, in every case, doomed to bitter disappointment.

They were an oddly mixed bag, reflecting the disparate tastes of the company's talent-spotting directors. Two solo singers, Mike Silver and Tony Bird, had been Steve Brown protégés, and did not long survive Brown's departure. There was a band named Longdancer, containing Nigel Olsson's younger brother and an obscure Scots hippy guitarist named Dave Stewart. There were bands named Stackridge, Casablanca and the Hudson Brothers, the last of whom Bernie Taupin was to produce. There was also a teenage Welsh singer, Maldwyn Pope, who might have suspected his ultimate destiny when, at an early press conference, Elton absent-mindedly referred to him as 'Blodwyn Pig'.

The saddest case was a singer-pianist named Frankie Fish, who joined Rocket as a gofer on a small weekly retainer, very much as Elton and Bernie had originally joined Dick James Music. 'Frankie worshipped Elton – and it was obvious he wanted to be another Elton John,' Clive Banks remembers. 'He'd do his best to dress outrageously – like go around wearing one red sock and one green. He was very sweet, and Elton had a bit of a soft spot for him, kind of like "This is me five years ago". He was given demo time, and mastering time, and more demo time and more mastering time, but nothing really ever came of it. No one knew what to do with him, and no one had the heart to let him go.'

Most of the Rocket signings accepted their failure to ignite with resignation. One who did not was Longdancer's guitarist Dave Stewart, a scruffy, dejected figure, unimaginable as the later charismatic co-star of the Eurythmics. 'I'd go into my office,' David Croker remembers, 'and Dave Stewart would be sitting on my desk with his guitar, waiting to play me his new songs. Sitting on my desk crosslegged! He'd got some kind of job at a record shop in an Underground station, and he'd ring me up from there and stay on the phone for hours.' Stewart himself has since admitted that, thanks to drug-use, the mid-Seventies were a 'blank' period in his life.

Despite Elton's dreams, the sponsorship of new, young talent was not to be Rocket's forte. Aside from Kiki Dee – and Elton himself, in due course – the label's greatest success would come in boosting the careers of two established stars and early Reg Dwight heroes, Neil Sedaka and Cliff Richard. The changeless record fan could thus pay some dues at last for those hours of Dansette joy in his bedroom in Metroland.

Neil Sedaka, in 1974, was suffering the eclipse common to so many early-Sixties jukebox idols. The prototype singer-songwriter, along with Paul Anka, his bubbly dual-tracked hits, like 'Oh, Carol' and 'Happy Birthday, Sweet Sixteen', were regarded as no more than dusty relics in America. His British fans remaining loyal, he had moved with his family to London and was enjoying a revival in the British charts with new songs like 'Standing on the Inside'. Yet he still had no American recording deal, nor any prospect of one.

When Neil Sedaka met Elton that summer, his single 'Laughter in the Rain' had just gone to number 15 in Britain. 'One of the first things Elton said to me was "What's doing with you in America?"' Sedaka remembers. '"Don't ask!" I told him. "Over there, they think I'm a ghost!"'

The two quickly became good friends, finding they had much in common. Sedaka, too, had been classically trained, at New York's Juilliard school, and would still include the odd piece of Bach or Brahms in his stage performances. Happily married for many years, he had two young children, to whom Elton immediately became an unofficial uncle. Hero-worshipped as he was by Elton, Sedaka's friends urged him to seek a contract with Rocket. But he was embarrassed to presume on their friendship.

In August, Sedaka and his wife Leba gave a party at their flat in Mayfair. Elton came along and played 'Daniel' as a duet with Sedaka, apologising that it was 'just an oldie'. During the evening, Sedaka plucked up courage, took Elton and John Reid into another room and offered his British hits to Rocket for release in America. Elton immediately jumped at the idea. '"My God!" he said. "Why didn't I think of this? You're handing us gold bricks."'

Neil Sedaka's 'Laughter in the Rain' was released on American Rocket in October 1974. Twelve weeks later, it was number one, Sedaka's first hit in his native land since 1963 and only the second US number one in his career. It stayed in the American Top 40 for fifteen weeks, also becoming his only single other than 'Breaking Up Is Hard to Do' to sell a million copies.

The result was a Neil Sedaka revival in America, a sold-out appearance at the LA Troubadour and a Rocket album, *Sedaka's Back*, containing his recent British hits, which went gold late in 1975. To complete his triumph, Sedaka subsequently reached number eight with a slow ballad version of 'Breaking Up Is Hard to Do', so becoming the first artist ever to chart with two different interpretations of the same song.

No hungry A & R man ever worked for an artist as Elton worked on the relaunch of Neil Sedaka. 'He even wrote the liner notes for the album cover,' Sedaka remembers. 'He went on radio and promoted it, as EJ the DJ. Here was the most successful recording artist in the world, being the best PR man anyone could have.'

For a time the Sedakas with their children Dara and Marc became another of Elton's surrogate families. Sedaka himself was an intelligent, civilised man, far more satisfying to talk to than most in the superstar's growing entourage. 'He'd call me up from the road sometimes, saying things like he was worried about his voice and whether it would stand up to all the strain,' Sedaka remembers. 'I'd tell him he had to take care of it. Drink tea with honey. Avoid smoky discos.' Leba Sedaka grew fond of him, despite a healthy scepticism about most people in her husband's profession. 'He was extraordinarily sweet and generous. And I don't mean generous in the Elvis Presley way: "You want this ring? Here, take it." For example, he knew that, at that time, I was collecting antique silver picture frames. He went to the trouble of buying me some, finding the right shop, choosing exactly the right pattern.'

The Sedakas also spent time at Caribou ranch during the planning of Neil's American renaissance. Returning with Elton from Denver to Los Angeles produced a scene that Leba Sedaka has never forgotten.

'We were due to fly out of Denver at something like eight o'clock in the morning. The night before, I said to Elton, "We're travelling real early tomorrow, so please don't wear anything outrageous." "I won't," he said. "I've got nothing to wear anyway. I've just been on a diet."

'Next morning, we're waiting for him at the airport. Down the concourse that's full of redneck Colorado types comes Elton dressed all in white – white suit covered in rhinestones, white shoes with rhinestones, a white bowler hat and a cane.

'The next thing is, he has to go up to the airline desk to collect a ticket that's been prepaid for him. The girl at the desk is one of those who hardly even bother to look up. "Surname?" she asks Elton. "John," he tells her. "Initial?" she asks. "E," Elton says. Then she asks him, "Do you have any means of identification?" "My God!" we all said. "Are you joking? Don't you realise who this is?" "I'm sorry," the girl says. "To issue a prepaid ticket I have to have identification." All that Elton's carrying in this white suit is the diary that he carries everywhere with him, and some cash. There's no way we can get the girl to accept that he's E. John without a formal ID. The only way he can get the ticket is to pay out all the cash he has on him.'

Among all the teenage heroes Elton's fame allowed him to meet, none meant more to him than John Lennon. They had been introduced by Tony King, the ex-DJM song plugger who went on to become an executive at Apple in its final days. Friendship did not immediately blossom, for Lennon was by then in exile in New York, and in their spasmodic encounters Elton was too consumed by adulatory shyness to establish much of a rapport. 'I nursed the friendship along for quite a time,' Tony King says. 'I knew that once they did get to know each other, they'd be friends for life.'

Distant though Elton now was from Dick James, the Beatles and their vast folklore remained an insistent subtext to his life. Tony King's secretary at Apple was a girl named Margo Stevens, a Beatles fan who had found her way inside after a vigil of years on the front doorstep. Margo got to know Elton well on his many visits to King's office. When Apple folded as a record company late in 1974, it was easy for King to get her a job with Big Pig Music, the publishing division of Rocket.

Across the Atlantic, John Lennon had been going through troubled times. His marriage to Yoko Ono – that power supposedly greater than the Beatles – seemed to have broken down. In addition, he was fighting attempts by US Immigration, backed up by the CIA, to deport him as an undesirable alien.

In 1973, Lennon had left Yoko and their New York apartment, and gone to Los Angeles for the year on the loose he would subsequently call his 'lost weekend'. It was during these months of rediscovered bachelorhood that he and Elton properly became friends. A sequence in Lennon's posthumous movie autobiography, *Imagine*, shows them together in some nameless velvet-curtained West Coast dive, waltzing with a manly figure in drag, who is just recognisable as their mutual friend and intermediary Tony King.

Hero-worship was not all on the younger musician's side. Lennon was amazed by Elton's stage act, especially remembering what used to be expected of him in the Beatles' performing days. 'We only had to do twenty minutes – and that still used to seem like an hour to me,' he told Elton. 'There were four of us, but you do two and a half hours on your own. How the fuck do you do it?' He would often say that the pressure on the Beatles in the Sixties seemed minuscule compared to what Elton had to endure.

Bernie Taupin, who also was in Los Angeles for much of that

time, thinks the stories of Lennon's lost weekend mostly exaggerated. 'Everyone likes to make out that in that time away from Yoko, he was terrible and unhappy and drunk all the time, getting thrown out of the Troubadour with Harry Nilsson and sticking Kotex on his head. All I know is that every time I went around with him he was perfectly normal. I remember going with him to see Bob Marley at the Roxy, and we had a great night.'

To Bernie, Lennon was always the same generous enthusiast who had given that vital early accolade to the lyrics of 'Your Song'. 'He was always very sweet, and totally encouraging. He made a point of telling me he liked the things I wrote, which always meant a huge amount to me. And always incredibly modest about the fantastic things he'd done. He'd say things like, "Er, I wrote this song called 'Across The Universe', I don't know if you've heard of it, but anyway . . ."'

Elton's next single was planned both as a homage and a boost to Lennon's caved-in self-confidence. The ultimate Seventies star plunged off on another new way by covering the ultimate Beatles Sixties song, 'Lucy in the Sky with Diamonds'. The session took place at Caribou ranch in July, with help from Lennon himself, characteristically billed as 'the Reggae guitars of Dr Winston O'Boogie'. Those who had thought no one but Lennon could ever sing the song were to be charmed by Elton's version, modern in its reggae lilt but also perfectly mirroring that 1967 'summer of love' when Reggie Dwight used to wander round London, a forlorn Tiny Tim with his plastic carrier bag.

The following month, Elton was in a New York studio doing backup vocals for Lennon's new album, *Walls and Bridges*. The result was 'Whatever Gets You Thru the Night', a scattergun rocker which Elton's simplicity and energy helped to make more accessible than any Lennon song since 'Imagine'.

In the euphoria of the session, Elton asked Lennon if he'd also do the song with him live onstage – an enormous question. Since leaving the Beatles, Lennon had refused all attempts to get him to perform, bar one charity show in 1972. As far as millions of adoring fans were concerned, he had not been seen singing with a guitar since the Beatles' farewell concert on the Apple office roof. His stage fright, always chronic, had become something like psychosis in the years of New York hermitage. In a spirit of pure banter he replied to Elton that if 'Whatever Gets You Thru the Night' made number one, they would perform it onstage together.

Elton's arrival back at Caribou studios for the second time in six months was not quite what MCA meant by 'slowing down'. For a follow-up to *Caribou*, it had been decided merely to release a compilation album, *Elton John's Greatest Hits*. But a new album for early 1975 had to be written and recorded before he began his traditional grand autumn tour of America.

The attacks on *Caribou* had chastened Bernie, perhaps even more than Elton. In atonement he planned a *tour de force* – no grab-bag of borrowed styles and characters this time, but a concept album, as none before had been, recreating his and Elton's early partnership and life together in the half-childlike, half-mythic style of C. S. Lewis or J. R. R. Tolkien. For Elton he chose the pseudonym 'Captain Fantastic', evoking caped superheroes of Fifties comic books. Bernie himself, simple country boy with head full of Wild West dreams, would be 'the Brown Dirt Cowboy'.

For the first time, the lyrics were not dashed off and fired at Elton in eight-minute bursts, but worked on all together, as if stanzas in a narrative poem like the Macaulay epics that Bernie's grandfather used to read to him in Owmby-by-Spital. One stanza was to be a portrait of Elton as Reggie Dwight, that day Bernie had first met him at the DJM studio. Another was to recall their early vicissitudes as songwriters and all-night vigils in Oxford Street coffee bars. Another was to describe the ménage at the Furlong Road flat with Linda Woodrow, when a wedding all but took place, and Brown Dirt Cowboy had been obliged to pull Captain Fantastic's head out of the gas oven.

It was an ambitious project and Bernie, for the first time in his career, found himself rewriting, recasting, agonising and rubbing things out. Elton, however, underwent no such creative agonies. He wrote the music for the entire epic while crossing to New York on the final voyage of the French luxury liner SS *France*. 'I'd tried to book the ship's music-room, but an opera singer had got it for the whole five days. The only time she wasn't there was when she scoffed her lunch for two hours. So every lunchtime I'd nip in there and grab the piano just for those two hours.'

The recording at Caribou – each stanza in the order Bernie had written it – took longer than any in the John–Taupin oeuvre to date. As Elton himself remarked in some awe, 'It's the first time we ever took a month to make an album.'

The breach was now healed with his producer, Gus Dudgeon. For Dudgeon considered that these new songs more than made up for the sloppiness of *Caribou*. 'The whole thing is perfect, it's absolutely perfect,' he told a music magazine. 'I can't fault it. I've managed to get the best sound I've ever got, and it's the loudest album I've ever cut, despite its being twenty-five and a half minutes long on one side. It's the best the band have ever played, it's the best

Elton has ever played and it's the best collection of songs. He sings
better than he's ever sung. There's not one song on there that's less
than incredible.'

The simple private Boeing airliner of last year had been refitted in a
style better suiting MCA's $8-million property. It was now *Starship 1*,
a purpose-built flying palace for rock royalty in transit. The original
space for 138 people had been converted to accommodate only forty
in a luxurious den with couches, armchairs, cocktail bar, gourmet
kitchen, hi-fi and movies on video. For the monarch himself, there
was a master suite, complete with fur-covered bed that Hugh Hefner
might have envied. The red, white and blue fuselage was embellished
with stars and (to prove how democratic monarchs can be) the legend
ELTON JOHN BAND TOUR 1974.

Thirty-three people assembled for a group photograph before
Starship 1 took to the skies. There was Elton, in turquoise and white
jumpsuit and Somerset Maugham panama, leaning on a thin ebony
cane. There was Bernie Taupin, and Kiki Dee, the warm-up act.
There were Nigel and Dee and their consorts, and Davey Johnstone,
who now went out with Kiki, and the clerkly percussionist Ray
Cooper. There were the four-man Muscle Shoals Horns, augmenting
the stage line-up. There was John Reid in a décolleté blue boilersuit,
holding a clipboard. There was Howard Rose, the American booking
agent. There was Elton's original media champion from the *LA Times*,
Robert Hilburn. There were Rocket people, roadies, sound and
lighting men, personal assistants, gofers: truly a kingly court of straggled
hair, fitted plaid shirts, flared jeans, clogs and peep-toed platforms.

The group also included one pair of newlyweds. Rocket's young
promotion man Clive Banks had recently married Moira Bellas, a
press officer with Warner Bros Records. Elton had attended their
wedding – and shown more than a passing interest in the bride's
Chrissie Walsh dress. 'It had a winter theme,' Moira remembers. 'It
was white, covered with a mass of blue appliqué icicles. When
everyone else saw it, they said, "Mm, lovely dress." When Elton saw
it, he said, "Mm, have to get one of those."'

His insistence that Clive Banks should go on the tour, and bring
Moira as well, was typical Elton generosity. 'He made you feel that,
however huge he'd become, you were a part of it,' Banks remembers.
'At that time, I'd never even flown in a plane before. Suddenly here
I am on the other side of the world, travelling round in this massive
private jet which had showers and beds in it, and cocktail bars and a
piano.'

Starship 1 drastically reduced the fatigue of constant travel between one-night stands. For the tour's opening Southern leg, Elton could base himself in New Orleans, flying out each day to his concerts in Dallas, Houston, Mobile and Tuscaloosa. The short afternoon hops were beguiled by games of backgammon and pool, and brand-new movies like *The Exorcist*. Robert Hilburn remembers that, for some reason possibly connected with high altitude, the movie's famous scenes of revolving heads and squirting green bile reduced everyone to hysterical laughter.

John Reid, working with Howard Rose, had produced the smoothest tour organisation yet. 'It was like some presidential thing,' Clive Banks remembers. 'We'd fly in to a private airstrip. There'd be a fleet of limos waiting. We'd be taken into town with a police escort, driving down the wrong lane of the freeway. The entourage would be shoved in right at the front of the audience. Fifteen or twenty minutes later, Elton would be onstage. A couple of numbers before the end, we'd get the nod to go back to the limos. Elton would come out, get into the back of his, straight out to the airstrip again, and an hour later we'd be back in New Orleans.'

There were, inevitably, some hitches. In Dallas, when *Starship 1* landed, the limo fleet was waiting at the wrong end of the airstrip and had to race down the runway, as Robert Hilburn said, 'like cowboys trying to catch up with lost cattle'. In Mobile, the stage sound monitors gave such trouble that Elton furiously kicked one over, and refused to do an encore until the tumultuous clapping, stamping and whistling changed his mind. Though the concerts were usually miracles of mass good humour, the occasional security man would be seen mishandling boys or girls in the traditional rush to the stage during 'Saturday Night's Alright for Fighting'. This always enraged Elton – and also enraged John Reid, beyond any seeming care for his personal safety. 'John used to go berserk if the security men turned on the kids,' Dee Murray remembered. 'I've seen him do some incredible things – launch himself off a lighting tower to mix it with some huge Texan bouncer built like an all-in wrestler. You couldn't fault the guy for guts.'

The staging was the most extravagant yet, with Elton's name and each of the band's spelt out in neon above them. Elton's new stage costumes also touched new heights of the asexually bizarre. One was a black lurex bodystocking from which dozens of coloured balls sprouted on tendrils of piano wire. Another – by Hollywood designer Elizabeth Courtney – was a pink and silver sequinned catsuit worn with an outsize Edwardian dowager duchess hat, trailing huge white and pink ostrich boas. Another was mingled green, yellow and scarlet plumes, with a collar of pheasant feathers two feet long. Another was

a jumpsuit and cloak of diamanté-sewn orange and gold, worn with
the jewelled skullcap of some fourteenth-century French dauphin.
There was also a multicoloured cloak that spread over half the stage
behind him, and a top hat trimmed with further snatchings from a
giant pheasant's tail. To set these off, there were spectacles framed by
feathered whorls, bonsai palm trees or thick circles of cuddly white
mink.

Robert Hilburn was amazed to see how, even as the most
fantastical apparition, Elton still drove himself unmercifully through
every second of his two-and-a-half-hour set. The Aztec winged god,
dowager duchess or French dauphin seldom lasted more than minutes
in the frantic exertion and crippling heat. Feathered bonnet, skullcap,
cloak or boa would be thrown off, leaving a spangled, half-naked
figure whose abundant body hair contrasted ever more painfully with
his monkish tonsure. 'The whole point of touring is to strive for
something better,' he told Hilburn. 'Forget about the costumes and
staging – it's the music that counts. If you don't keep improving,
you're wasting your time. I've said it before: I don't want to end up
like Chuck Berry or Little Richard – and I don't mean to degrade
those people. But I couldn't stand the thought of coming on and
playing "Crocodile Rock" ten years from now. That would be a
nightmare.

'Sure, you can get excited about your own success, but that
doesn't mean you're satisfied. I may have a number one record, but
then I'll see someone on television and think, "God, I wish I could
play like that." There's always something to strive for.'

Hilburn was used to world-weary rock superstars who toured
only as an act of supreme condescension, treating their audience with
indifference or disdain, refusing to sign autographs or pose for
pictures, finding every excuse to delay their final, ungracious appearance on stage. Compared with these dilatory oiks, Elton's punctuality,
civility – most of all, his undiminished enthusiasm – seemed marvellous. 'I can't understand people who say they don't like doing
concerts. It's the greatest thing in the world to stand on a stage and
see people in the front rows smiling, and know they came to see
you. That's why I get so upset if I play badly. There's nothing worse
than knowing thousands of people have gone away, thinking "Oh
boy, what a drag." That's what you struggle against every night.'

Even Elton's own London staff had not grasped the full magni-
tude of his American fame. 'Nowadays when someone like Michael
Jackson comes to London, you can avoid him, because there are
other things going on,' Clive Banks says. 'But when Elton was on
that tour in 1974, the whole of America knew he was there. When

he came in to each city to play, there literally was talk of nothing else. In Los Angeles especially it was impossible to get away from him. You'd go into a shop – just a grocery – and you'd hear his name, Elton, Elton, Elton . . . "Have you got your tickets?" "Is he doing an extra show?" "You're English, you must know him." It was a buzz totally all over town.'

In Los Angeles Elton had been booked for three consecutive nights at the 18,500-seat Forum arena in Inglewood. A fourth show was hastily added when all 55,500 tickets were sold within six hours of the box office opening. Elton confessed to Robert Hilburn that when people told him things like that, he still had difficulty in believing them. The fretful, pessimistic ghost of Reggie Dwight would never quite go away. 'I keep ringing them up and saying, "Are you sure we're sold out? Are you sure?"'

His opening night back in LA was the now traditional celebrity-studded night, attended by Elizabeth Taylor, Barbra Streisand, Ringo Starr, David Cassidy and Harry Nilsson. During the finale Elton lost his temper again, this time with ushers who were blocking the fans' surge to the stage. Rushing to a side mike, he shouted at the ushers to 'get the fuck out of it'.

Based in Malibu, in a beach-front house rented from Olivia Newton-John, he spent the time between concerts in his favourite LA pastime, 'looting'. As usual, he bought with equal prodigality for whomever happened to be with him. Like others of his entourage with scruples, Clive Banks grew adept at sidestepping the ludicrous generosity. 'He'd go into some store to buy an eight-track player, which were quite novel things then. There'd be three or four other people with him, and he'd buy one for each of them – "five eight-track players, please", like ordering a round of drinks or ice cream. You felt there was a bit of guilt there, like he felt he really ought not to be buying these expensive things just for him.'

It was a generosity that made no distinction between a superstar friend and a relatively junior member of his entourage. Hearing that Clive Banks's birthday fell in the LA week, Elton organised a surprise party for him at Chasen's restaurant. 'I didn't even want to go out that night,' Banks remembers. 'I was complaining because, it being Chasen's, I had to borrow a jacket and a tie to wear. I walk in, and there's this huge table with everyone round it, and Elton's at the piano, playing "Happy Birthday to You". Cheech and Chong are at the table, and Fred Astaire's sitting downstairs. I remember, Fred Astaire said "Hello" to Elton.'

He was, once again, in his almost predictable place at the top of American and British charts – this time with both an album and a single. The compilation *Elton John's Greatest Hits*, released in November, not only went to the number-one spot faster than any of its predecessors, but also stayed there longer: eleven weeks in Britain, ten in America. 'Lucy in the Sky with Diamonds' was number one in America and ten in Britain. He ate up the airwaves with new songs, with old songs back to 1970, with his fan's cover version of a song that previously had been thought to be unrepeatable.

Whatever he touched, however incidentally, seemed to grow golden wings and fly. His protégée Kiki Dee, making her first American tour in his retinue, now also had her first American Top 20 single, 'I've Got the Music in Me' – a hit that owed its hilarious energy to drastic intervention by Elton. 'Kiki had a bit of a studio complex, and couldn't seem to get the vocal together,' Gus Dudgeon, the producer, remembers. 'While she was doing it, Elton crept in through a back door, hid behind a screen, took off all his clothes and suddenly streaked across the studio, stark naked. Kiki nearly freaked, but kept on singing. That's why the vocal came out so great.'

Best of all was the fillip he had given to his backup guitarist on 'Lucy', Dr Winston O'Boogie. For, with Elton singing backup vocals, 'Whatever Gets You Thru the Night' had pushed John Lennon back into the pop mainstream. In November, it went to number one in America – Lennon's only number-one single outside the Beatles in his lifetime.

Elton had gleefully contacted Lennon and reminded him of his promise to repeat their duet onstage if it made the top spot. Whether Lennon would keep that promise was far from certain, however. The obviously perfect time would be the climactic moment of Elton's present tour, his New York concert at Madison Square Garden on Thanksgiving night, 28 November. But the curse of the Beatles remained strong. The man for whom the world had screamed its heart out, ten years before, was more frightened than the newest novice of facing an audience with a guitar. And, even if he could nerve himself to go on, he genuinely doubted whether anyone would be that interested.

His life, anyway, was still in chaos, torn between his Chinese girlfriend May Pang and pleadings with Yoko to resuscitate their marriage. Thus far, Yoko had remained impervious. 'I'd been married twice before, and divorced,' she says. 'For me, that was what happened to marriages. They ended.'

Even when Lennon agreed to rehearse with Elton, there still were doubts about whether he would really go through with it. 'They'd booked a little studio in New York to run through some numbers with the band,' David Croker remembered. 'When I got there, they were leaving – it was all over. They couldn't have been rehearsing longer than about an hour and a half.'

Meanwhile the word was out, in New York and London. There was, at least, a strong chance that Elton John's Thanksgiving concert at Madison Square Garden would include an appearance by John Lennon. With or without Lennon, it was to be a gala occasion, crowning a still more stupendous tour, attended by a large British media contingent flown to New York at Rocket Records' expense.

Among the party was Margo Stevens, secretary to Elton's friend Tony King, the girl who had spent literally years of her life waiting on Beatle doorsteps. Margo naturally had longed to see John Lennon onstage again, but could not afford the fare to New York. Hearing of this, Elton bought her a first-class air ticket and reserved a room for her at the Sherry-Netherland hotel. 'He rang me up out of the blue and said, "Is your passport in order? Can you be at Heathrow airport first thing tomorrow morning?"'

At Heathrow airport, she joined Rocket's VIP group, among them Sheila and Fred Farebrother and Alan Freeman, the veteran disc jockey, whom Elton had asked to do a walk-on at the concert. 'I went through the security check with Alan Freeman, which was a mistake,' Margo remembers. 'He was covered with chains and medallions, which set off all the anti-terrorist alarms.'

In New York, someone else was taking a strong interest in Elton's Thanksgiving concert and its attendant rumour. Yoko Ono contacted Tony King and asked him to arrange tickets for her and her current man-friend. As she admits now, she did not know with what precise objective. 'I asked for a seat where I could see the stage, but where I couldn't be seen.'

Up until the very last minute, Lennon himself seemed to be looking for a chance to duck out. Margo Stevens, who talked to him only hours before the concert, remembers him still doubting and havering. When he turned up at Madison Square Garden, it was in a plain black suit and dark glasses, as if trying to resist the notion he had ever been a rock-'n'-roll performer. Backstage he was so nervous, he went into the men's room and vomited. He even momentarily forgot the order of the strings on his guitar, and had to ask Davey Johnstone, from Elton's band, to tune it for him. Just before show-time, a messenger delivered two identical gift boxes, one for him, one for Elton. Inside each was a white gardenia and a note: 'Best of luck and all my love, Yoko.' 'Thank goodness Yoko's not here tonight,' Lennon said. 'Otherwise I know I'd never be able to go out there.'

No one was completely certain it would happen until halfway

through the concert, when Elton paused at the piano, in his huge pheasant-feathered top hat. 'Seeing as it's Thanksgiving,' he said, 'we thought we'd make tonight a little bit of a joyous occasion by inviting someone up with us on to the stage . . .'

In the wings, still hesitating, Lennon suddenly turned to Bernie Taupin. 'He said, "I'm not going on unless you go on with me",' Bernie remembers. 'So I just went forward a little way with him, then he sort of hugged me, and I said, "You're on your own."'

The moment when Lennon's black-suited figure appeared will never be forgotten by anyone who saw it. The whole Madison Square Garden audience, 18,000 people, rose to their feet as one, with a roar far and away above the routine adulation of pop. House lights were turned full on, showing him the full scale and expression of the delight at every point. 'I'd heard of applause literally making a place shake, but I'd never seen it before,' David Croker said. 'That night, though, it was true, you could feel the floorboards quivering under your feet.'

The roar went on and on, Lennon trying to hide his bewilderment by pulling faces and pretending to loll against the piano, while Elton looked on and beamed like some proud parent at prize day. Even now, Lennon did not realise that Yoko was in the audience. 'I knew he was getting a wonderful reception,' she says. 'But when he bowed, it was too quickly and too many times. And I suddenly thought, "He looks so lonely up there."'

The set was brief and, progressively, brilliant. Lennon sang 'Whatever Gets You Thru the Night' as promised, with Elton's backup vocal like a friendly instructor, keeping him on track. Elton sang 'Lucy in the Sky with Diamonds', backed by John. Lennon's confidence was so much restored that he took a dig at his estranged soul mate, Paul McCartney. 'We thought we'd do a number of an old estranged fiancé of mine, called Paul . . .' he said with a sly grin amid complicit laughter. The song was 'I Saw Her Standing There', from days when Beatles songs were as perfect in their way as primitive paintings, and Reggie Dwight used to sit in his bedroom, dreaming, as the yellow and black Parlophone label flicked round and round.

'Everybody around me was crying,' Margo Stevens remembers. 'John was hugging Elton, and Elton seemed to be crying, too. What was really incredible was how, when the audience finally let John go off, Elton managed to pick up his own performance and carry on again. When he did 'Candle in the Wind', it was the first time I'd seen everybody strike lighters and matches in the darkness. He finished with 'The Bitch Is Back', and John came on again, so did

Bernie. By that time you as a spectator were completely wrung out and drained, so God knows what it must have felt like for Elton.'

Afterwards, Yoko and her date for the evening came backstage to visit John and his date for the evening. 'We immediately started talking, each of us totally forgetting the person we were supposed to be with,' Yoko says. 'After that, John invited me to an art show. We started dating all over again.' Their marriage tested and found durable, they settled down in the Dakota Building to have a child and – so they thought – to grow old together.

As for Elton, clasped in John Lennon's hug, with 18,000 voices blessing his loyalty, respect and unselfishness, all he could stammer out was, 'This has been a very emotional night for me . . .' Thanksgiving, 1974, indeed, was to prove his career's uttermost high-water mark. And on that authentically historic night, the same could be said of him as nearly always. He had been a very, very good boy.

ELEVEN

'My God! It's all going to crumble and go to Hell!'

EARLY in 1975, Sue Ayton returned to the Dick James organisation. Elton's friend, and almost-girlfriend, of the late Sixties had left her job as Dick James's secretary to get married, three years earlier. Now divorced and seeking a job back in the music business, she happened to meet Stephen James, who by then was largely running Dick James Music on his father's behalf. Happy to regain such a valued employee, Stephen offered her the job of managing DJM's international division.

Back in her old surroundings, Sue Ayton quickly noticed the huge change in DJM's relationship with Elton. 'When I'd left in 1972, he'd still been coming in all the time, to see Dick or talk about the next album with Stephen. But now you hardly ever saw him. In all that second time I was there, I think he came in about twice.'

Little now remained of the edifice which Dick James had constructed around Reggie Dwight in 1967. His management had been relinquished to John Reid in May 1973. The publishing agreement, for Elton and Bernie Taupin together, had ended in November that same year and had not been renewed. All that was left was Elton's four-year recording agreement, due to expire in February 1975.

Though reconciled to losing Elton's management and publishing (the latter bearable, since his pre-1973 songs remained copyright of DJM), James naturally had no wish to lose the world's biggest recording star. Nor was it yet a foregone conclusion that he would. Despite their recent estrangement, Elton was unswerving in acknowledgement of his professional debt to DJM and his affection for Dick James personally. His own Rocket label, so he constantly stressed, was not a vehicle for himself, but for new young talent. It was with some hope, therefore, that Stephen James approached John Reid in 1974 and asked if the recording contract could be renewed.

Reid did not refuse outright, especially since, in addition to an increase in future royalties, DJM also offered to boost the percentage on product already released. What Stephen James describes as 'quite meaningful' discussions took place between John Reid and him towards the end of 1974. The sticking point was Reid's insistence that DJM should put money into Rocket and that a £30,000 advance be paid on future British albums, which were then to be released unconditionally. 'He was saying we had to release stuff whether we liked it or not,' Stephen James remembers. 'That was the point when I decided to back out.'

Elton's recording agreement would thus terminate with his next album, *Captain Fantastic and the Brown Dirt Cowboy*. But that did not quite sever all links with the James organisation. Over the past two years, he had fallen behind with the annual quota of albums he was contracted to deliver to DJM. After *Captain Fantastic* he still owed two more – a studio-made one and a 'floater', the contractual term for a live album or compilation of past hits. Though legally separated, artist and record company had to continue in harness for at least another year.

This uncomfortable situation was made more so by the hostility that existed between Stephen James and John Reid. To Stephen, Reid was the viper who had betrayed his father's trust, using everything James senior had taught him to steal away and alienate DJM's most priceless asset. To Reid, Stephen was a pampered boss's son, contemptibly unaware of the tooth-and-claw struggle others had to go through to attain success. Things had got so bad between them that the simplest negotiation took on the character of fight to the death. 'I remember once trying to arrange a meeting for them at the MIDEM song festival,' Sue Ayton says. 'Each of them had set a time that didn't suit the other, and I couldn't get either of them to back down.'

Captain Fantastic and the Brown Dirt Cowboy provoked the most spectacular ructions yet. The sleeve concept had been masterminded by Bernie Taupin, whose idea it was to commission Alan Aldridge, the leading Pop Art illustrator of that day. Aldridge's design matched any of his famous reinterpretations of *Alice in Wonderland* or *The Butterfly Ball*. On the front cover, Elton as metropolitan Captain Fantastic, in top hat, silver goggles, mauve pompoms and spats, bestrode an Aldridge phantasmagoria of humanoid fish and birds in pierrot ruffles and jester's caps. On the back, Bernie Taupin as rural Brown Dirt Cowboy floated in a bubble, surrounded by pensive farm animals and insects. Two smaller bubbles contained the Elton John Band; in a third, tiny one sat a figure in a pink tie looking suspiciously like John Reid.

The Aldridge design was presented to Stephen James along with a bill far exceeding DJM's budget for album artwork. Faced with such costly *faits accomplis* in the past, Stephen had always swallowed his annoyance for the long-term aim of keeping Elton happy. But now no such constraints applied. He therefore told Reid that the design was too expensive – as well as 'too introverted and indulgent' – and that DJM would not pay for it. If Elton insisted on using it, the cost would have to be met by his own organisation.

Hours of battle finally produced a compromise, symbolising what a gulf now lay between Captain Fantastic and those who had launched him. The Alan Aldridge design would be used, but would not be paid for by DJM. The copyright would belong to Rocket, who would lease it to DJM for the lifetime of the album.

'Philadelphia Freedom', released on 28 February, was inspired by Elton's latest bout of fan-worship. In his tennis jag the previous summer, he had been thrilled to meet several Wimbledon champions, past and present, including Jimmy Connors and Billie Jean King. He was now an ardent supporter of Billie Jean's World Tennis League team, the Philadelphia Freedoms, and, for a stupefying few minutes, had even been allowed to play against her on court. In return he told Bernie they must write a song dedicated to Billie Jean King, Philadelphia and the general notion of striving against odds and winning through.

Philadelphia at the time was emerging as a music city to rival New York, with orchestral-backed vocal groups like the O'Jays, the Three Degrees and Harold Melvin and the Blue Notes. To add that modish dimension to 'Philadelphia Freedom', a string arrangement was commissioned from Gene Page, the man behind the sexually charged ballads of Barry White. The B-side was the version of 'I Saw Her Standing There' recorded live with John Lennon at Madison Square Garden. Further underlining the democracy among Elton and his stage partners, both sides carried a collective credit, 'the Elton John Band'.

'Philadelphia Freedom' went to number one in America – Elton's third there in twelve months – but only to twelve in Britain. Its home sales were not helped by a dispute between Elton and BBC1's *Top of the Pops* show, still the most crucial exposure for any new single. A new ruling by the British Musicians' Union required that any song performed on television must have its orchestral track specially pre-recorded. Elton protested that Gene Page's string effects could not be reproduced by British session men and, instead, offered his own tape of Page's arrangement. When this was not acceptable to the Musicians' Union, he refused to appear on *Top of the Pops*.

The first months of 1975 brought an extended lull in Elton's touring and recording schedule. His bass player Dee Murray remembered Elton coming up to him at a party the previous Christmas and jubilantly saying, 'Guess what! We don't have to tour next year!' 'Ah, that's great, man,' Murray replied with an enthusiasm he was afterwards to regret.

Without the customary year-opening British tour there was nothing on the diary until *Captain Fantastic*'s release in May, and the subsequent new album sessions at Caribou. Nor was there to be a summer tour but, instead, one single gigantic Elton concert at Wembley Stadium, with a supporting bill including the Beach Boys. Its future thus comfortably mapped out, basking in the collective kudos of 'Philadelphia Freedom', the Elton John Band dispersed for an extended holiday.

Only Elton himself, as usual, found it chronically difficult to relax or be still. In March he turned up on BBC Radio One, in his other incarnation as EJ the DJ, playing new releases and old favourites in a seventy-five-minute programme interspersed with Goon voices and football jokes. The show's producer remembers standing outside Broadcasting House in Portland Place, waiting with some trepidation for superstar and retinue to arrive. 'This Rolls-Royce came along, and Elton got out of it on his own. I said, "Is someone bringing the records you're going to play?" "No," he said. "They're in here", and he opened the boot of the Rolls. There was a great big cardboard carton full of records inside. He just hauled it out and carried it up to the studio.'

He could also be seen in a film, performing yet another cover version of a classic rock song. The previous year he had been asked to appear in the screen version of *Tommy*, the Who's 'rock opera', directed by the explosive Ken Russell. He hummed and hawed endlessly until offered the role of the Pinball Wizard, singing unarguably the best song Pete Townshend ever wrote. His costume included a pair of monstrous Doc Marten boots on which he had to learn to walk stiltwise, attached by metal callipers. In his three days on the set, Ken Russell remembers, he was 'no problem whatever'. The omnivorous hoarder's only stipulation was that he be allowed to take the giant boots home afterwards.

In early May, he returned to America to promote an album already known to be the most successful of his career. For on advance orders alone *Captain Fantastic and the Brown Dirt Cowboy* had already sold a million copies, going gold two days after its US release and so being guaranteed instant entry at number one in every trade paper's album chart.

Serious rock critics, too, were looking forward to an Elton John album as they had not done since the teenybop market claimed him. Even from normally taciturn sources, like Gus Dudgeon, word of mouth buzzed with epithets like 'brilliant', 'perfect' and 'masterpiece'. The title could scarcely have been bettered as a piece of advance hype, with its image of Elton as caped crusader, punching aside past disappointments like *Caribou* and soaring to new heights. The critics, in any case, realised that, even at his most frothily insubstantial, Elton spoke for the half-completed decade like no one else across the whole pop spectrum from hard rock to easy listening. *Captain Fantastic* thus was the most eagerly awaited new album since *Sgt. Pepper's Lonely Hearts Club Band*.

It certainly was like no Elton album ever before, a suite of songs as sequential and vividly personal as his previous ones had been fragmented and oblique. Bernie Taupin had written the story of their early friendship and beginnings as songwriters, in episodes as clear as the allusive magpie poet could contrive. Elton sang the saga that was half his autobiography with a new passion, involvement, sarcasm, bitterness, and occasional triumph when some old score or other was finally paid off.

As with *Sgt. Pepper*, the most sophisticated sounds of contemporary pop were mixed with everyday language, to constantly arresting and charming effect. Captain Fantastic, in the opening track, was easily recognisable as the anything-but-fantastic Reggie Dwight, in fur coat and spectacles, circa 1967: 'hardly a hero . . . Someone his mother might know . . .'. 'Tower of Babel' evoked the inhospitable London that town and country mouse used to tramp round together in their cheap little fun furs. 'Bitter Fingers' remembered their frustration as the Tin Pan Alley Twins, trying to turn out 'a hit and run' at Dick James's behest for Tom Jones or the Eurovision Song Contest. 'Writing' was about the process of composition itself, and the equality of the partnership trying 'to instigate the structure of another line or two'. 'Tell Me When the Whistle Blows' was an echo of vaulted Kings Cross station on Friday nights, when Brown Dirt Cowboy would catch his 5.15 pm train back up to Lincolnshire. 'Curtains' was a lament for 'Scarecrow', the first of their songs that Elton ever put on demo in DJM's four-track studio, afterwards letting Bernie take the acetate home to show his Uncle Henry and Aunt Tati in Putney.

Here and there, memory probed deeper than their life of 'corn-flakes and classics' and 'waking up to washing up'. 'We All Fall in Love Sometimes' was a discreet acknowledgement of the brotherhood that had sustained them in their tiny bunk bedsitter out in Pinner and past every stop along the Metropolitan Line. In deeper confessional vein, 'Someone Saved My Life Tonight' was Elton's thank-you note, partly to Bernie for pulling his head from the gas oven, and partly to Long John Baldry for bullying him out of marrying Linda Woodrow. 'You almost had your hooks in me, didn't you dear?' he sang with more than a shadow of a jeer at the long-departed Linda.

Packaged with each album was a giveaway miscellany also put together by Bernie: one book of printed lyrics and another of Elton memorabilia – old snapshots, extracts from his diary, Bernie's original handwritten words and extracts from *Jackie* magazine's Elton John strip cartoon.

The design caused something like marketing mayhem. In America, MCA's president, Mike Maitland, jibbed at the profit-erosion represented by two elaborate giveaway books, of which, on advance orders alone, a million copies must be manufactured. A further small but vital detail was that Alan Aldridge's cover had neglected to include the customary list of tracks. In American stores, prospective customers would rip open the wrapper to read the tracks on the disc itself, scattering the giveaway booklets heedlessly on the floor.

In Britain, DJM manufactured the sleeve without protest – not having had to pay for it – but then caused further upset by pricing it as if it were a double not a single LP. 'It's their decision, not mine,' Elton told *Melody Maker*, evidently seething with annoyance. 'There's only one album left to do in the DJM contract,' he added. 'After that I'm free.'

Captain Fantastic was played to the international press at two lavish receptions, one at Media Sound Studios in New York, the other, decidedly more memorable, at the Universal Pictures complex in Los Angeles.

'I flew over for the LA launch,' Stephen James remembers. 'There were about sixty of us, MCA executives, press and radio people, in this private cinema on the Universal lot. They'd laid on an audiovisual thing, with a slide show to watch as you listened to each side of the album. And while we were listening to the first side, it was obvious that something had gone wrong with the sound.

'When the first side ended, the house lights went up. John Reid got out of his seat and stormed down to the engineer who was in charge of the hi-fi monitors. John screamed at this guy, something like "The sound's a fucking shambles!" The guy turned to John and said, "Sorry, it's the best I can do." John kept screaming at him, really violent, "The whole fucking album's being ruined, and it's your fault!" This engineer was pretty laid back, considering he's about six foot two and John's only about five eight. He says, "I'm doing the best I can", and John says, "It ain't fuckin' good enough", and he swung at this guy and hit him straight in the mouth.

'The guy tried to walk away, but John kept hitting him; then everyone rushed forward and got hold of John, and this engineer finally could walk away, blood streaming from his mouth. It took about half an hour to calm things down.

'The whole episode really scared me. I thought, "The next time I'm in a meeting with John and I say no to him, is he going to do that to me?"'

Dee Murray was spending his time off on a scuba-diving holiday in the West Indies. One day, a phone call for him came through from London. The sun-worshipping bass player picked up the receiver, not supposing that he had a care in the world.

'It was Elton,' Murray remembered. 'I could tell right off that he was embarrassed about something. He said, "I've decided to change the band. I think you, Nigel and I have gone as far as we can together."' Nigel Olsson had already received a similar call, summarily firing him.

The decision came as a total shock to both, especially after so many recent signs – including the personalised neon ones above their heads – that the Elton John Band was an indestructible democracy. Elton subsequently revealed that he'd been brooding about personnel changes since just after the 1974 American tour. 'When I got back home afterwards, I was depressed for about two weeks. At first I didn't know why – I thought I was just unhappy. Then I realised: I had to change the band.'

The change was only a partial one. Lead guitarist Davey Johnstone and percussionist Ray Cooper stayed in the new, expanded line-up recruited from both Britain and America. To replace Nigel Olsson on drums, Elton brought in Roger Pope, who had been a session player on his first album, *Empty Sky*. Another face from the past was Caleb Quaye, his fellow Tin Pan Alley messenger boy, afterwards DJM's studio engineer, and guitarist with Pope in the mildly famous Hookfoot. Elton's idea was to use Caleb as a second lead guitarist, counterpointing Davey Johnstone's technical wizardry with a more visceral bluesy sound. To take over from Dee Murray on bass he brought in Kenny Passarelli, a young American with Afro hair and a handsome Latin face, who had co-written a country-rock hit, 'Rocky Mountain Way'. Like Dee's firing, Passarelli's hiring was effected by a single phone call. 'I just decided he was right,' Elton remembered. 'So I rang him and said, "We've never spoken before, but would you like to be in my band?"'

The most novel part of the new blueprint was a second keyboard player to supplement Elton's own piano playing both with organ and the Moog synthesisers that now dominated recorded pop. He was, quite simply, fed up with doing all the onstage keyboard work himself. A second player would give him more freedom to move round the stage, sing away from his piano, even feature on alternative instruments, like lead guitar. But finding a keyboard player to play in the shadow of Elton John wasn't easy. Three major names he approached all turned him down flat. Finally Howard Rose, his American agent, came up with James Newton Howard, an American synthesiser wizard, currently to be heard on a Top 10 single by Melissa Manchester.

There was little time for Elton and his new musicians to mesh in with one another. Their first public appearance was to be on 21 June, at the giant Wembley Stadium concert with Elton headlining over the Beach Boys. For this, his single major British appearance of 1975, he planned a *tour de force*. *Captain Fantastic and the Brown Dirt Cowboy* was to be played in its entirety before the 72,000-strong Wembley audience.

A crash course of rehearsals took place in Amsterdam throughout the week before the concert. Fit and bouncy from his Arizona tennis ranch, Elton took the new line-up through thirty-five numbers, with the added unfamiliarity of a three-member backup vocal group. That the city sweltered in an early summer heatwave was no brake to his frenetic energy. Between rehearsals, instead of relaxing with cold beer as they would have liked, the band found themselves being organised by Elton into running races beside the canals.

Melody Maker's choice of interviewer to talk to him in Amsterdam was a portent of the change soon to engulf music journalism. Instead of the bonhomious Chris Charlesworth or Alan Hollinghurst, the job went to Caroline Coon, a countercultural celebrity, mainly known for her work with the drug charity Release. Tall and beautiful, with immaculate liberal credentials, she appealed strongly to Elton, and for most of that week was granted the freedom of his inner circle, and almost total confidence.

Coon describes him at the Amsterdam Hilton, sprawling on his bed in a tracksuit, enthusing about the new band, with no word of regret over the dumping of Nigel and Dee. 'I've always wanted to be part of a good driving rock-'n'-roll band. The old band never used to drive – we just used to rattle on. Whenever we played anything live, it was always twice the tempo of the recording, and that was always a bit off-putting to me. I want to chug rather than race.'

He is full of respectful praise for his new colleagues, especially the 'inspiration' of James Newton Howard, and Roger Pope and Caleb, both 'amazing musicians'. 'With Kenny and James, it's worked out that I'm literally the worst musician in the band. I've got to work to keep up with them, which is going to make me play harder and better.'

Caroline Coon deftly catches Elton's own attitude to his success, that mixture of disbelief, bemusement, excitement, pessimism, even occasional irritation that nothing on earth seems able to make it stop. 'In America I've got "Philadelphia Freedom" going up the charts again. I wish the bloody thing would piss off. And "Pinball Wizard" is being played to death. I can see why people get sick and tired of it. I know that in America for the next three or four years I could get a gold on my name alone. As Pete Townshend said, I could shit bricks and people would go out and buy them . . . On the other hand, you can't force people to buy garbage. I just have to keep being very, very self-critical.'

'Someone Saved My Life Tonight' – now out as a single – had unleashed intense music press speculation as to who saved Elton's life, on which night and from what. To Caroline Coon he gives a brief version of the Linda Woodrow story and his eleventh-hour rescue by Long John Baldry. Why hasn't he settled down with any woman since Linda, Coon boldly inquires. 'I haven't settled down with anyone,' Elton replies. 'And the reason is because I haven't met anyone who I want to settle down with. And touring on the road is fun for me. I've seen so many musicians' marriages going through difficulties on the road. You can't take your old lady with you all the time because it's a bore and you want a little bit of freedom – that's a rock-'n'-roll musician's outlook on life. So I don't want to get settled down for a while yet.'

Coon – whose questions are becoming subtly more and more pointed – asks if he likes women enough to want that kind of relationship at any time.

'Oh yeah, of course. I find it easier to get to know ladies in America, though. English ladies put up so many fronts. American ladies are very bold, and that breaks the ice for me. I can never say boo to a goose to anyone. I'm very shy. I need someone to help me out.'

Caroline Coon clearly suspects an entirely different dimension, though her point of inquiry is 'We All Fall in Love Sometimes', the song about Elton's early times with Bernie Taupin. Did he, she asks, 'find it difficult to reveal the extent of his love for Bernie?'

'Oh, not at all. He loved me. We hit rock bottom together so many times, and at that point in my life he was the only person I could really call a friend. We found a spark together, and a way of writing that's still with us.'

The interview, spread over four pages in *Melody Maker*'s pre-Wembley extravaganza, was the most self-revealing Elton had ever given. If the final revelation was still a year off, ample hints were there for anyone who cared to look.

To Caroline Coon's seductive questioning, he responds almost like a patient under psychotherapy, talking freely about his childhood inferiority complex, his feeling of being unloved by his father, and sense of rejection when Stanley Dwight had four children by another wife. 'I'm very self-destructive,' he says at one point. 'I get terribly, stubbornly depressed. It's my desperate craving for affection coming out. I'll get in a mood and I'll sit at home for two days in bed, getting more and more depressed, wondering if it's all worth it.

'My manager can't help me when I'm depressed because, since he's my manager, I fight him. But Muff Winwood or Tony King will ring up and say "Run out of Pledge, have we?" Because, you see, I Hoover and dust. I used to love ironing, too. It soothed me. I'm one of those people who go around emptying ashtrays, washing them and putting them back. And so, as soon as I get depressed, one of my friends has only got to phone and send me up a bit about something like that, and I'll come out of it.

'I don't know why I get depressed. I never can figure it out. I can be very happy and then all of a sudden I'm on a come-down . . . I consider myself slightly insane, in a funny way.'

The Elton John Wembley festival on 21 June was one of very few Seventies rock events that could be called wholly pleasant. The fate that seldom smiles on British open-air gatherings decreed a day of balmy, unbroken sun. With the good weather went an equally miraculous good mood in both spectators and organisers, banishing the usual incipient violence of one and paranoia of the other. Seventy-two thousand people packed round the Art Déco oval, shirtless, topless and happy, made Wembley Stadium look more like a crowded Blackpool beach on some prewar bank holiday.

Even without its two headline stars, the programme of music – selected by Elton – would have been a generous one. First onstage, in mid-morning, were Rocket's group Stackridge, followed by the black funk band Rufus, the country-rock singer Joe Walsh, and a little-known California band, the Eagles. Some time in mid-afternoon, the Beach Boys would make their second-on-the-bill appearance. Elton and his new, augmented band would not appear until sunset, playing the whole of *Captain Fantastic* as a two-and-a-half-hour climax.

He was at Wembley for most of the day, nevertheless, watching from a VIP box with his numerous rock-star, showbiz and sporting guests. Snapshots by Terry O'Neill show him here with Candice Bergen; there with Jimmy Connors, brandishing a tennis racket; here with Ringo Starr, pretending to balance a pineapple on his head; there in a group shot, wearing bathrobe and socks, surrounded by Paul and Linda McCartney, Billie Jean King, Harry Nilsson and Martina Navratilova.

Outside, meanwhile, the huge, impacted mass of bare skin and blue denim seethed with rising pleasure and excitement. In early afternoon, the Eagles came onstage to demonstrate the sweetly cynical laid-back country rock that Elton had already predicted would make them the cult band of the late Seventies. By the end of their set, the Wembley crowd was not only delighted, but very nearly satisfied. Four hours before the main attraction was due to appear, his third on the bill had all but stolen the show.

That coup was left, however, to the second on the bill. At around six o'clock, the Beach Boys massed onstage: Carl and Dennis Wilson, Mike Love, Bruce Johnston and supernumerary musicians, all in Bermuda shorts, like so many bearded lifeguards. The absence of their founding genius Brian Wilson, after years of rumoured mental trouble, had aroused fears that the ultimate happiness band might no longer sound the same. But they sounded as coolly carefree as ever, pouring out all their Sixties surf hits in brilliant sunshine, to the utter joy of that congested urban beach.

By the time the Beach Boys had played their final encore, the best of the perfect day was over. A lengthy pause then ensued, as the sun sank behind the stadium rim and the stage was elaborately reset, not just with amps and drum-kits, but also with fairy lights, music stands and potted plants. This sudden atmosphere of pretentiousness and fuss produced a restless stirring in the audience. When Elton and the new band finally took their places amid the foliage, under a neon sign reading FANTASTIC, hundreds of people were trickling out of the stadium.

It was a moment when all Elton's accumulated stagecraft seemed to desert him. Following the Beach Boys need not have been disastrous if he had given his usual performance, crazily costumed and spring-heeled, countering their greatest hits with equally great hits of his own. Instead, he had opted to play the whole of *Captain Fantastic*, sombrely dressed – for him – and scarcely even rising from the piano. After 'Surfin' USA', 'Little Deuce Coupe', 'Fun Fun Fun' and 'Good Vibrations', the last thing his listeners felt disposed to hear were long, introspective tracks whose autobiographical nuances were mostly lost in the deepening dark. The recital proceeded in a spirit best described as dogged, with cheers in real volume only for his latest single, 'Someone Saved My Life Tonight'. But that night, nobody could.

The music critics were merciless, totally forgetting that the bands who'd stolen Elton's show had been sponsored by him in the first place. *Melody Maker*'s headline put it all too vividly: BEACH BOYS' CUP RUNNETH OVER. ELTON LEFT TO PICK UP THE EMPTIES.

His career was starting to wane in Britain, though none would realise it for a long time yet. Enormous ships, holed below the water-line, can still steam bravely ahead for miles as if nothing has happened.

Signs of malaise had been manifest even before Elton's Wembley Stadium flop. His last two American number-one singles, 'Lucy in the Sky with Diamonds' and 'Philadelphia Freedom', had risen no higher than 10 and 12 respectively in the UK charts. 'Someone Saved My Life Tonight', now number four in America, did not even make the British Top 20. Indeed, for all the sweated triumphs of conquering his native land, there was one final accolade that Britain obstinately withheld. In all these phenomenal five years, Elton John had never had a UK number-one single.

In America – by familiar contrast – the great ship appeared to steam on as unstoppably as ever. Elton was by far and away America's most listened-to recording artist, not only on his monster new album or on his nose-to-tail hit singles, but on everything else he had recorded back to *Empty Sky* in 1969. In album sales he had surpassed the Beatles a dozen times over; added to the backlog of gold and platinum was now his *Greatest Hits* album which, a year after release, had sold 5 million copies, grossing $8 million. By mid-1975 in America, it was pretty well impossible to turn on any radio anywhere across the continent without hearing classics like 'Daniel', 'Crocodile Rock', 'Your Song', 'Honky Cat' and 'Bennie and the Jets'; cult favourites like 'Burn Down the Mission', 'Levon', 'Tiny Dancer' and 'Take Me to the Pilot'; cover versions like 'Pinball Wizard', 'I Saw Her Standing There', 'Get Back' and 'My Baby Left Me'; revived rarities like 'Honey Roll', 'Razor Face' and 'Mona Lisa and Mad Hatters'. The writer Greg Shaw conducted an experiment, spinning his radio dial for six hours and finding an Elton track, on average, once every two minutes. Many stations sold themselves to their listeners on his name alone, calling themselves 'your number-one Elton John station', 'the station that plays more Elton John than anyone' or 'your official Elton John spot on the dial'.

'If you ever die,' John Lennon once told him sardonically, 'I'm gonna throw my radio out of the window.'

He was now back in the land that appreciated him most, making an album with the new band at Caribou. The customarily brief sessions were interrupted by a trip to Denver, where the Rolling Stones' current tour happened to be passing through. After playing a guest number with the Stones, Elton was aggrieved to read in *Rolling Stone* magazine that his matey walk-on style had not gone down well with the supersnobs of rock. 'Mick Jagger asked me to sit in on "Honky Tonk Woman", which I did, and then left the stage to watch the show,' he explained later. 'Then this roadie tells me Billy Preston wants me back to join them, so I go. Then I read how Keith is pissed that I wouldn't split the stage. I'm fed up with all the damned fucking lies.'

On 25 August came the fifth anniversary of his first triumphal American appearance at the Los Angeles Troubadour club. To mark the occasion, Elton returned to the Troubadour for a three-night charity appearance whose few hundred tickets were so desperately over-subscribed, they had to be allotted by prize draw. It was not quite an altruistic gesture, since his original contract with the Troubadour's canny owner, Doug Weston, had contained a clause binding him to a return date exactly five years hence. The opening night was a Hollywood gala occasion, with tickets at $250 each, attended by celebrities like Tony Curtis, Mae West and Cher. The six performances raised $150,000 for the Jules Stein Eye Institute at UCLA.

Covering the event for the *Los Angeles Times* was Robert Hilburn, whose original ecstatic review had touched off Elton's American landslide. To Hilburn, the excitement of that début night in 1970 was scarcely recaptured now. 'There'd been so much excitement at the thought of seeing Elton back at the Troubadour, and fighting for tickets, that when he finally walked onstage, it was almost an anticlimax. He had that big band, which sounded deafening in a small place; people were pressed tight up against the stage; the whole effect, with all those celebrities and VIPs, was overpowering. But not so magical any more.'

With the Troubadour dates went a souvenir book entitled *Five Years of Fun*, with pictures of Elton at great performing moments and backstage with all his celebrity friends. Here he was with Elizabeth

Taylor; with Steve McQueen; with *Hawaii Five-O* star Jack Lord. Here he was letting Richard Chamberlain and Tatum O'Neal try on pairs of his glasses. Here he was being simultaneously photographed by Terry O'Neill, Annie Leibovitz and Tim Hine. Here he was sitting on a male acrobat's shoulders with a female acrobat seated on his shoulders. No one would have guessed that at the time he was suffering from what he subsequently termed 'a mini-nervous breakdown'.

His absence in America for almost all that remained of 1975 was interpreted by some British papers as pique following the Wembley flop. The reasoning was somewhat more pragmatic. Difficulties had arisen with the US Internal Revenue Service over Elton's tax liabilities on an American income conservatively estimated at $7 million per year. On record royalties alone, DJM USA had recently received an assessment of $620,000, for which his overseas employment company, Sackville, was asked to provide indemnity. Part of a labyrinthine tax strategy worked out by John Reid and his accountants was that Elton should spend the next few months resident in Los Angeles.

For so short a time, a rented mansion would have sufficed but, instead, Elton decided he would buy one. After viewing several superstar properties, he found what he thought he wanted in the remoter reaches of Benedict Canyon, Beverly Hills. This was a $1million Moorish-style folly, built by the silent-screen star John Gilbert and later owned by David O. Selznick and his wife Jennifer Jones. In the courtyard was a fountain and a gazebo where another former occupant, Greta Garbo, was said to have spent much time.

Few who visited Elton there could see the charm of the place, with its gloomy wood panelling and musty ghosts of old Hollywood ruin and loneliness. 'There was a darkness about that house,' an ex-Rocket employee remembers. 'You felt like you wouldn't care to be alone there at night.' Elton, destined to be much alone there at night, might have been a conduit for every melancholy spirit that lingered there.

The Selznick house never felt much like a home. To begin with, John Reid was there only intermittently. Elton and Reid had by now almost ended the domestic phase of their relationship. Close and interdependent as they remained, each had his own separate life and lifestyle. The imbalance grew with Elton anchored to Los Angeles but Reid still able to fly off to London and around Europe with the frenetic energy that almost equalled his charge's.

Living in an LA canyon house had never felt quite comfortable since the Manson murders of 1969. As a further uneasy dimension,

Elton's property backed on to that of Alice Cooper, a shrine to every spaced-out weirdo who'd ever bitten off a chicken's head or tattooed himself with a blunt breadknife. One night, in what seemed entirely appropriate fashion, Alice's house burst into flames. Elton was disturbed by a succession of longhairs ringing his bell to ask if they could park in his drive and watch the conflagration.

As a precaution against importuning fans, if nothing worse, his own address was kept a closely guarded secret and his telephone number changed every two weeks. His security, even so, proved easily penetrable. One night, he awoke to find a strange girl sitting on his bed. 'I'm a bit blind without my glasses . . . I said "Who are you?" and she said, "Oh, don't you know me?" She'd gotten in without a key, and was just sitting there. Christ, it could have been someone with a fucking gun.'

Not that John Reid's absences left him short of company or diversion. Bernie Taupin was in Los Angeles, as were various members of the band, looking forward to the short American tour scheduled for October. There was his agent, Howard Rose; his PR man, Dick Grant; his personal co-ordinator, Connie Papas. There were his musician friends, flying in from New York or London, and his movie-star friends, venturing out from their Moorish or Spanish follies in the Hollywood Hills. Every night at Chasen's or Le Restaurant, he was the centre of a group seldom numbering less than a dozen.

No other city provides new friends as lavishly as Los Angeles, and on his previous visits Elton had acquired an entourage as large and competitive as Elvis Presley's Memphis Mafia or Mick Jagger's mini-Versailles. Feeling lonely, even abandoned, there, cut off from all his normal, commonsensical English roots, exacerbated that monarchical rock star compulsion to have people constantly on hand, running his errands, laughing at his jokes, participating in his puns, reassuring him by word and gesture at every second that he was totally and utterly wonderful. There are people all over the world who derive a handsome livelihood from doing this. But in Los Angeles it is practically a vocation.

The acquisition of an entourage always has one important side effect. This is to alienate, and usually drive out, genuine friends, unwilling to join in the prevailing sycophancy. One such in Elton's case was Sharon Lawrence, from Rocket's LA office. She quit at the end of 1974, feeling that the original, hard-working and motivated Rocket US team had been infiltrated by people of more doubtful value. 'I used to call them the *nouveau riche*. They were the ones who'd say they wanted a Porsche and half an hour later, Elton would have bought them one. I could see a lot of trouble coming, tax trouble coming. The end for me was when I found out some people were doing drugs in the office. I said, "I want nothing more to do with this."'

Having been a close friend of Jimi Hendrix, Sharon knew only too well how a fragile soul could be destroyed by parasitic hangers-on, tempting him into alcoholism and drugs. But she had always believed Elton's character too robust to run such a risk. She remembered him as the clean-living rock star, up playing tennis before breakfast, immune to temptation by the softest drug, horrified to see any of his idols on that fatal downward path. Many was the time she had seen him in a corner with someone he admired, fervently begging them, 'Don't do this to yourself.'

Since Elton's return to Los Angeles, Sharon Lawrence had purposely kept away from him. 'I wasn't working for Rocket any more, and I didn't want to be drawn back into that circle of dependence that Elton creates. I knew that if I sat down with him, we'd end up agonising about his life back to the age of two. He'd have me involved up to the neck in every one of his troubles and anxieties in the same way as always.

'Mutual friends who had seen him kept telling me about the awful things he was doing to himself. People who weren't of the entourage, who genuinely liked and respected Elton, were appalled at what was going down. "Can't you talk to him?" they kept saying to me. "Even if it's only a phone call or letter? He always used to listen to you."'

Finally, Elton himself telephoned. 'It was three in the morning,' Sharon remembers, 'which in itself was an abnormal thing for Elton. He said, "Reid's out of town. Please come over. I want to play you the new album, and I really need to talk to someone."'

Next day, putting aside other engagements, Sharon drove to the Alhambra folly in Benedict Canyon. 'As soon as I walked into that house, I thought, "My God! This is no place for anyone to be." There was an enormous formal drawing-room, full of inglenooks, that you couldn't imagine anyone sitting in. The only daylight seemed to be at the back, as you got nearer the garden. If you were feeling in any way down or depressed, that house would sure finish you off.'

The sight of Elton filled her with horror. 'I remembered this person who was mildly temperamental, who could be a bit neurotic and difficult, but who was basically happy and organised. Now he looked ghastly, he was incredibly strung up, anxious and panicky. In the few months since I'd seen him, he seemed to have become a complete wreck.'

He played her the new album, to be released in October as *Rock of the Westies*. 'He seemed most panicked about that,' Sharon remembers. 'He put it on at full volume and sat there staring at me, waiting for me to say it was brilliant. I didn't think so, but I said it was because he seemed to need that so desperately. While I was still at the house, John Reid came back. I realised that Elton had been in a real snit because John had gone away, and had got me over there to prove he could get along without him. It was like, "There you are – other people care about me, too."'

Various factors were to blame for Elton's condition. The rotor-ride had stopped again, flinging him to earth with a still more sickening thud. After months of giddy motion, when audiences provided every stimulus he needed, the concertless days stretched ahead with terrible tedium. There was nothing to do but put on expensive clothes, go to superb restaurants, eat fabulous food, drink marvellous wine, be courted and flattered and sit among all his myriad, well-dusted possessions. Exhaustion and anticlimax combined to produce the mood where buoyant Elton vanished and glum, pessimistic Reggie Dwight returned. These were the black plunges that took him, as well as everyone round him, totally by surprise; when all his gold and platinum discs seemed to crumple to ash; when the same thought came as years ago, in the background of Bluesology or making cut-price LPs for Woolworth's: I'm still not getting anywhere.

At such a vulnerable moment, he should have been in Virginia Water, with its support system of family and real friends. Instead, he was in Los Angeles where 'life in the fast lane', as the Eagles' song had it, frequently meant driving at 100 mph, blindfolded, with both hands off the wheel.

'There always was that strange dichotomy in Elton,' Sharon Lawrence says. 'Part of him adored and treasured his success, but another part seemed to want to do its utmost to destroy it. I've seen it with other big stars who start to take risks, knowing they have everything to lose. It's like they're consciously saying, "If people love me, then how much do they love me? How far can I go and still get away with it?" Elton and John Reid were alike in that respect. There was something in both of them that liked walking on the very edge.'

Whatever the circumstances, Elton John was still the best value any press interviewer could get. While living in LA, he did one of *Playboy* magazine's famous interviews, submitting to the same earnest question-and-answer format as had such international figures as Albert Schweitzer, Martin Luther King, Malcolm X and Marshall McLuhan. Articulate and spontaneous as ever, he revealed more than

Playboy had ever expected to learn about the pains and anxieties of being the world's number-one rock star.

The interview, *Playboy* reported, took place beneath 'a Bedouin-style canopy' overlooking Greta Garbo's gazebo. Elton, on one of his periodic slimming benders, arrived fresh from several sets of tennis. Paradoxically, at this time of mental stress he was physically fitter than he had been for months.

Topics covered a wide spectrum, from Elton's annual income (he did not seriously quibble at $7 million) to Art Nouveau and the 'boringness' of most people he met in the rock business. There was an early, highly prophetic exchange about American tabloid papers, like the *National Star* and *National Enquirer*, which had taken to printing the bizarrest rumour and speculation about show-business celebrities in the guise of genuine news. 'When Evel Knievel jumped that canyon, I was supposedly sitting by his side, singing the National Anthem. And I'm in my house, going "Oh yeah?" . . . When I read something in the *National Star* which is absolute rubbish, I say, "Well, how dare they print that?" Then I'll turn to the next page and read about someone else, and go "Hm – did they really do that?" I mean, I'm the first person to get sucked in.'

He was even prepared to talk about that old poisoner of happiness, his disappearing hair. '[It's] a real drag, because it didn't happen to the rest of my family. It must be because I was a silly cunt, and dyed my hair a lot. So, since I've discovered I don't want to be bald, I might have a hair transplant. It's just a matter of going down there with the courage to say, "I want some more hair please."'

Playboy asked in all innocence if he suffered from fear of failure or rejection. 'Sure. I think how, suddenly overnight, my records could stop selling. In this business, nothing's for certain. I'm constantly saying, "This is ridiculous. It can't go on for ever." But really I'm quite ready for the time when record sales level off or decrease, and I know that around the corner the next "biggest something" is lurking.

'I like the struggle to stay at the top. It's what keeps me going. I don't begrudge anyone else his success. You have to pay attention to what others are doing, keep listening to what's happening in order to grow. For example, Stevie Wonder can eat me for breakfast as far as musicianship goes, but that doesn't make me angry or jealous or uptight. I'd give anything to have his talent, but that doesn't make me paranoid.'

Playboy, too, hovered around a question that could not yet be asked outright. Instead, it was wrapped in a comment about David Bowie's and Mick Jagger's increasing androgyny, and Led Zeppelin's recent appearance at an LA party in drag. Did Elton 'get off on the bisexuality scene'?

'I really don't know what to say about it,' Elton replied, smoothly turning the topic to who, of either gender, could enter a room and make him gasp. 'Jagger, Sinatra, Elvis, probably. Also people like Noël Coward, Edith Piaf and Katharine Hepburn.'

To a question about drugs, his reply was equally non-committal. 'I've got a completely split personality. One minute I'm up, then I just change like the wind. I'd like to take LSD to find out what it's like but . . . it's like going into the unknown with a paranoid attitude. One half of me would love to do it, but the other half owns up to the fact that it might be a bit of a disaster.'

A routine question about childhood prompted the interview's most extraordinary passage. Elton's answer was to unlock the store of loneliness and pain which had been Reggie Dwight's second nature, but which seemed to have been long buried beneath outsize glasses and silver lamé jumpsuits. He described the solitary life he had mainly led as a small boy, his 'introverted nature' and the 'terrible inferiority complex' his physical appearance had given him. In particular, he launched into a furious diatribe against his father, opening up unsuspected scar tissue all the way back to his very birth. He told *Playboy* that Stanley Dwight had been away on an RAF posting when he was born and had not returned home for 'about two years afterwards'. On to the Garbo vista were suddenly imposed snapshots from an unhappy little house in Potter Street, Pinner, and an irascible RAF officer making his son's life a hell of petty rules, discomfort and tension. 'My father was so stupid with me, it was ridiculous. I couldn't eat celery without making a noise . . . it was just pure hate.'

Playboy readers, expecting the lowdown on a swinger, instead saw that lonely boy in his bedroom, pouring into gramophone records all the love he said his father had rejected. 'I grew up with inanimate objects as my friends, and I still believe they have feelings. That's why I keep hold of all my possessions. I'll look at them and remember when they gave me a bit of happiness – which is more than human beings have given me.'

Bitterest of all was he about his parents' divorce, and the way he alleged Stanley had treated his mother. 'She had to bear all the costs. She more or less gave up everything and had to admit to adultery, even though he was doing the same thing behind her back. He was such a sneak. Then he went away and four months later got married to this woman and had four kids in four years. My pride was really snipped, 'cause he was supposed to hate kids. I guess I was just a mistake in the first place.'

It was not in Elton's nature to manufacture calumnies, against Stanley or anyone else. Much of what he said was doubtless what he himself had been told, for instance about Stanley's supposed reluctance to see him even on finally returning from that mythical two-year foreign posting ('No, I'll wait till morning'). The mystery was why he should have so suddenly erupted against a father with whom he had appeared on good terms since the divorce and who, whatever their personality differences, had often been good to him. One can only attribute it to the stressed mental state that had so worried Sharon Lawrence, and long hours of brooding alone in his gloomy canyon house.

That particular part of the *Playboy* interview was widely reported by British newspapers. It caused total astonishment to Stanley Dwight, whose relationship with Elton had never given the smallest hint of such smouldering resentment. Though steadfastly unwilling to discuss the matter with reporters, he did unbend to a *Daily Mail* writer, Sally Brompton, who tracked him to his house in Cheshire. To her Stanley protested that he had not missed Reggie's birth, and had kept a home RAF posting until his son was fifteen months old. He had not met his second wife until after finally parting from Sheila, nor had he forced Sheila to pay the costs of the divorce. He had never 'hated' children, nor regarded his firstborn as 'a mistake'. His solicitor was even prompting him to sue *Playboy*, or even Elton personally, but Stanley would not. 'I don't want to do anything that would alienate Reggie. I just don't understand why he's started saying all these awful things.'

He recalled their apparently amiable last meeting, when Elton had played football in the garden with his four young half brothers and later slipped the two-thousand-pound cheque for a Peugeot 504 into his 'Aunt Edna's' pocket. Since then Stanley had detected a sea-change in his attitude, but was at a loss to understand why. He no longer telephoned on Christmas Day, sent birthday cards or replied to the boys' letters. Stanley had tried to ring him once on his ex-directory number, but had been unable to get through.

'He doesn't seem very happy to me,' Stanley told the *Daily Mail*. 'Last time we saw him I asked him who his friends were, and he said Elvis Presley and Billie Jean King. But when he was a child, they were his idols. How can someone you've only just met be described as a friend? There are friends and friends. And I think Reggie has to buy his friendships.'

Perhaps the most hurtful blow to Stanley was Elton's assertion that his father thoroughly disapproved of his music, but that he did 'accept the odd Cortina'. The Ford Cortina was perhaps the naffest car of that era; Stanley – who said he'd in fact tried to refuse his son's £2,000 cheque to buy a Peugeot – therefore sounded both grasping and philistine.

The next Elton John album took its name from that autumn's short US and Canadian tour whose thirteen venues all happened to lie west of the Rocky Mountains. Elton being unable to resist any wordplay – and his entourage unable to resist hailing any Elton wordplay as comic genius – West of the Rockies became *Rock of the Westies*.

Recorded at Caribou the previous July, it was earmarked as the studio album Elton had to deliver to Dick James Music in final settlement of his contract. Elton, however, liked the finished album too much to use it merely as kiss-off to DJM. 'I heard he wanted to get out of giving it to us,' Stephen James remembers. 'I even had to threaten to sue him if he didn't honour the agreement we had.'

Elton's enthusiasm for *Rock of the Westies* is difficult to fathom. After the inventiveness and soul-baring of *Captain Fantastic*, it was a relapse into mainstream pop at its most predictable, even cynical. The meaningless pun introduced a meaningless miscellany in which one obvious chart hit – the Hawaiian-flavoured 'Island Girl' – was placed like a single bright red maraschino cherry among listless tinned grapefruit. The remaining titles have long since been consigned to the John–Taupin slush pile: 'Dan Dare (Pilot of the Future)'; 'Street Kids'; 'Hard Luck Story'; 'Billy Bones and the White Bird'; 'I Feel Like a Bullet (in the Gun of Robert Ford)'. If you care, Robert Ford was the assassin of the Western outlaw hero Jesse James. It says much for Bernie Taupin's own far from bucolic state in this era that he should have fallen back on the five-year-old style of *Tumbleweed Connection*.

Yet the huge ship steamed on regardless. Like *Captain Fantastic*, *Rock of the Westies* went gold on advance orders of a million plus, entering the American album charts at number one. 'Island Girl' went to number one in the singles chart, remaining there for three weeks. Back in Britain, meanwhile, the album made only number five; the single only number 14. Again, that barely perceptible wrench below the water-line.

For Elton, the Rock of the Westies tour was punishing in a way none had ever been before. Exhilarated as he was to have created a new band that worked, the thought of sitting down and playing filled him with increasing weariness and dread. 'We were having a great time – but something inside me was so revolted by the thought of constant touring that I just wanted to say, "I've had enough".

Apparently my memory went as well. I used to go to rehearsals and then, for no reason, I'd just blow up, walk out and come back three hours later. I can't remember things I said or things I did. I think, "My God! Did I really do that?"'

The tour was to end with an event symbolising the special relationship between Elton and Los Angeles. At the end of November, he was to play two consecutive nights at the LA Dodgers' baseball stadium, to a total audience of 100,000. That week was to be designated Elton John Week in Los Angeles and to include the ceremonial laying of his name among the stars on the sidewalk outside Graumann's Chinese Theater.

While millions envied the star, one or two worried about the person, shut away in his gloomy Alhambra in Benedict Canyon. Chief among them was Sharon Lawrence to whom he had made that uncharacteristic 3 am call. Determined as she was not to be drawn back into Elton's 'circle of dependence', Sharon could not subdue an alarm and foreboding that felt horribly familiar. 'I'd spent all that earlier time around Jimi Hendrix. I knew that when a person's in a vulnerable state, anything they say can be a signal that should make you feel nervous.'

Even some of Elton's fellow rock stars now felt worried about the course he was taking, though few had the will or words to try to talk him out of it. One who did was a person to whom Elton himself had been a staunch friend in a similar period of drift. 'I know John Lennon tried to help him,' Sharon Lawrence says. 'He took Elton aside, and used just the same words Elton once had to him: "Look – I always admired you. Don't do this to yourself."'

It seemed that nothing anyone said could help. The robustly sensible character Lennon and Sharon Lawrence remembered was being drawn inexorably out of the sun, into a shadowy, murky netherworld. 'I had one other totally chaotic phone call from him,' Sharon remembers. 'He could hardly talk. "I'll bet you never thought you'd get a call like this from me," he said.' Not long afterwards, she heard from Elton's housekeeper that he had tried to commit suicide by swallowing a bottle of sleeping-pills.

His two Dodger Stadium concerts, and the ancillary celebrations of Elton John Week, were marked by the biggest display so far of Rocket Records' fun and largesse. A specially chartered Boeing 707 flew the entire London office staff out to LA for a week, together with Elton's and John Reid's parents and VIP friends like Bryan Forbes and Nanette Newman, the footballer Rodney Marsh and chat-show host Russell Harty, accompanied by a London Weekend Television film crew. For the journey over, each guest received a

Rocket monogrammed flight bag of inflight goodies including an Instamatic camera and a *Beano* comic.

Rocket's staff now included Linda Mallarkey and Marie Thacker, the two diehard fans who had waited so many hours for Elton at airports and cricket matches. Linda ran his British fan club while Marie was a general office junior. They had originally planned to follow the tour under their own steam, blueing every penny of their savings. When John Reid found out, he paid for their plane tickets and hotels and, in not uncharacteristic fashion, sent a car to bring them to the concert at Oakland Coliseum. Afterwards, they were put into Elton's limousine and allowed to accompany him back to LA on one of the two Boeing 707s he had on standby that week.

The London party was put up on unlimited tab at the Westwood Holiday Inn. An elaborate programme of amusements included trips to Disneyland and a party on *Madman*, the 65-foot boat that had been Elton's last birthday present to John Reid. For the ceremonial laying of Elton's name on the sidewalk outside Graumann's, Hollywood Boulevard had to be closed – the first time in over 1,500 such ceremonies that such a thing had been known. There was also a party to launch Neil Sedaka's new album, when Elton appeared dressed as the Lone Ranger, with a black mask fixed over his glasses.

Few of the assembled liggers noticed what an air of strain underlay their £50,000 junket. Nor did they notice that, for most of Elton John Week, Elton himself was a strangely fleeting presence. His usual music press interviewers like Steve Clark and Charles Shaar Murray were surprised to be curtly denied their usual access. Few even among his favourite celebrity guests were invited to visit him up at his Garbo mansion. Among those who did manage to cross the threshold was Margo Stevens, the Rocket secretary. Margo's eyes – sharpened in her former years of vigil outside Beatles' houses – were quick to spot something seriously amiss. 'Elton looked terribly pale and drawn,' she remembers. 'We were told that he'd been very ill.'

Whatever the illness, it could not be allowed to show in the figure, dressed in a sparkly lurex version of an LA Dodgers baseball suit, that played to its first steeply tiered 50,000 faces in the evening sunshine of 26 November. Bryan Forbes, standing in the wings, noticed a phenomenon unchanged since early switchback tours in ramshackle station wagons. By the end of Elton's two-hour performance, his finger-ends were streaked in blood.

It should have been his zenith, down there in Dodger Stadium's roaring bowl. But to Sharon Lawrence the sound of the rotor-ride seemed frightening. 'It suddenly came to me: "My God, all this is going to crumble and go to Hell!"'

TWELVE

'Christ! I wish I had someone to share all this with'

FINANCIALLY, the most sensible course for Elton at the end of 1975 would have been to become permanently resident in America. As a high-earning Briton living temporarily abroad, he was caught between two tax systems. The huge dollar sums he had grossed in America were still the subject of protracted wrangling with the Internal Revenue Service. Something like $3 million in concert earnings, back to 1973, had been frozen pending the outcome of negotiations over his US residential status. To this unreachable reserve had been added the proceeds of his last tour, including $1.1 million for his two Dodger Stadium concerts. If and when Elton moved the money to Britain, he risked being taxed on it a second time at the Wilson Labour government's top rate of almost 90 per cent, so losing the whole amount and a great deal more besides.

Several major British pop stars had already fled into tax exile, following the early lead of the Rolling Stones. Tom Jones lived permanently in Hollywood, in a Tudor-style hacienda to whose poolside he had nostalgically exported the red telephone kiosk from the street where he grew up in Tonypandy, Wales. Elton's old friend Rod Stewart was now also in California, living with Peter Sellers's ex-wife Britt Ekland, his every purchase minutely computed by her on a pocket calculator.

Had Elton himself opted to settle in America in 1976, a very different story would remain to be told. With his immaculate social record, US Immigration would readily have granted him H-1 status as a person likely to improve the nation's cultural fabric. Spared the coming musical cataclysm in Britain, he would doubtless have become an American entertainment institution midway between Frank Sinatra and the Grateful Dead. Whatever else he might have lost, he would have gained the complete privacy that being colossally rich in so large a country allows. Very likely, the only 'revelation' to come would have been a tour of his house by some voyeuristic TV programme like *Lifestyles Of The Rich And Famous*.

But to a tax exile even after the shortest time, Britain begins to look alluring; a tiny green island in the Atlantic, to which phone calls peal quaintly, as in the hallway of a quiet country hotel. One can easily forget all about British income tax, British weather, British envy and the unspeakable elements of the British press.

To symbolise his homecoming there was the now traditional Elton John Christmas show at the Hammersmith Odeon, with dry-ice clouds pumped over the front-row spectators like a vaporous form of champagne toast. Soon afterwards, *Melody Maker*'s lead story announced his first British tour in more than two years, with venues ranging from Earls Court arena to Bailey's night club, Watford. The days of Garbo reclusiveness in Hollywood seemed over. Reg, clearly, was doing everything possible to get back in touch with his roots.

The clearest sign of patriotic intent to grit his teeth and pay British income tax was purchase of an English stately home. Hercules, his Virginia Water bungalow, now could barely contain the myriad possessions stuffed into it and, in addition, had to be protected from marauding fans by an electronic security fence. Elton had long since tired of Hercules and, in early 1976, put it up for sale at £125,000, a sum thought reasonable for exotic fixtures like gold taps in the bathroom. When no buyer could be found, he was forced to drop the price to £80,000.

In May 1975, he had reportedly been about to pay £800,000 for Wargrave Manor, former home of property magnate Nigel Broackes, a Thames-side Georgian mansion on a 78-acre estate that included a farm, assorted tenantry and a herd of Friesian cattle. At the last moment, however, the deal fell through, and Elton went off to Beverly Hills, leaving the search to be carried on by his mother.

To help her, Sheila enlisted Margo Stevens, the deeply sane as well as quite crazy girl who had joined Rocket after years as the most tenacious Beatle fan ever known. Though strictly speaking just an assistant at Big Pig, Rocket's music-publishing division, Margo had a warm personal relationship with Elton and his parents. It was therefore no surprise to her to be rung up by Sheila and asked to go out househunting for Elton.

Together they found Woodside in the Berkshire village of Old Windsor. A redbrick Queen Anne-type house of no outstanding architectural beauty, it stood on a 37-acre estate and was provided with every amenity a rock-star millionaire could demand: private cinema, interior lift, stabling, staff cottage and swimming pool. From the rolling, three-lake garden, it was possible to see Windsor Castle and the flagstaff which denotes whether or not the Queen is in residence. The price – a mere bagatelle after Wargrave Manor – was just under £400,000.

Elton himself was by now in Barbados, holidaying at a rented mansion in the exclusive St James enclave with a predominantly male group including John Reid, Bernie Taupin, Gus Dudgeon and the photographer David Nutter. The portfolio produced by Nutter shows him heavily engaged in water sports, skiing and para-gliding as ferociously as he played piano onstage. His spirits buoyant again, he chafed at the formality of his black butlers and maids, and kept urging them unsuccessfully to 'loosen up' and 'join in the fun'. 'There was one girl in particular who'd never even smile,' Gus Dudgeon remembers. 'One day when we were eating, Elton said, "I'm really going to get through to her." So, when a big bowl of custard was brought in, he plunged his head straight into it. Then he let out an awful scream. He'd thought the custard was cold, but it was boiling hot.'

Back in England, the purchase of Woodside settled, Sheila asked Margo Stevens to leave her job at Rocket and become Elton's live-in housekeeper. Though inexperienced in domestic work beyond a little children's nannying, Margo agreed to give it a try. Elton rang her from Barbados to say how delighted he was that she'd taken the job.

In the spring of 1976 came still more conclusive proof that, far from intending to migrate overseas, Elton was as committed as he possibly could be to Britain and the British way of life. He was elected chairman of Watford Football Club.

It was an ambition that Elton had cherished, though scarcely dared articulate, from the day Vic Lewis had arranged for him to join the Watford board. As expected, his public support had benefited the club enormously, though still not enough to improve its abysmal standing in the Football League. The 1974–5 season had seen it drop out of the Third Division and into the Fourth. The 1975–6 season, just ending as Elton's chairmanship began, found Watford at eighth place in that ignominious bottom echelon, with no visible prospect of ever hauling itself out again.

For Vic Lewis, the association with Elton and Watford was to end even more sourly than his years as Elton's booking agent. On delivering Elton to the club as a director and obvious vast potential asset, Lewis, too, had been given a seat on the board. The following season, Elton announced he wanted John Reid to become a Watford director also. By then his wishes could not be ignored and, to create the requisite vacancy, Vic Lewis was asked to resign. The man whom

Elton had to thank for batting at Lord's – as well as persuading him to go on the road with a band – calls this episode 'the worst blow I ever received'.

Elton's acceptance of the chairmanship seemed the answer to all Watford's prayers. The club was in deep financial trouble, compounded of its disastrous match record and benign, old-fashioned management. In the season just past it had made a trading loss of £80,000. Despite Elton's benefit concert, and various loans from other directors, its bank overdraft stood at £100,000. Among the new chairman's first official duties was to preside at a series of crisis financial meetings. The club's bank manager had called in the directors and warned that the deficit could not be allowed to run on.

Elton, however, quickly dispelled any idea of himself as Watford's golden goose. 'This won't be just a happy little bandwagon, with me picking up the bills,' he said. As with Rocket Records, the last thing he intended to do was splash out millions regardless. The idea was to make Watford financially stable and self-sufficient by exploiting its own neglected or unrealised natural assets. He was equally anxious to reassure those who might think his involvement merely a rock superstar's passing whim. He pledged '100 per cent effort' in working with the board to solve Watford's budget crisis and restore it to respectable standing in the League. If necessary, he said, he would cut back on touring in order to have more time for the club.

Everything was to be played fair and square, businesslike and dignified, without undue reliance on his own huge capacity to attract crowds. 'If Elton John being chairman puts 2,000 on the gate, I shall be happy. But I don't believe in gimmicks, and I'm not doing anything drastic until I settle in. I'm in the hot seat now.'

The first new player signed under his tenure certainly felt no hint of multimillionaire munificence. In May 1976, Watford paid Leyton Orient £3,000 for their striker Tommy Walley – a sum more akin to transfer fees 20 years earlier when Elton's cousin, Roy Dwight, was a professional. But with Watford's bank manager on the warpath, even that small outlay required justification. 'It's ridiculous that a club of Watford's potential should be in this position,' Elton said. 'We feel that Tommy's experience will give us the character we require.'

He was by now touring Britain again, in conscious parallel with the supersonic airliner that had lately made its inaugural flight. 'Louder than Concorde', proclaimed the tour T-shirts, '. . . but not quite as pretty'. The witticism came from an exalted source. After one of Elton's private royal command performances, Princess Margaret had told him, 'This tour of yours sounds as if it'll be louder than Concorde.'

The tour continued a habit, still rare among rock stars, of performing in aid of charity and good causes. As well as taking on the Watford chairmanship, Elton had become involved with the Sports Aid Foundation, a government-backed body set up to provide financial support for British athletes in every field. One of his two concerts at Earls Court arena was a benefit for the Sports Aid Foundation, raising £40,000. From the stage, he spoke passionately about the need to encourage young sportsmen and women, and said that other musicians, too, should be rallied to the cause: 'No one knows what sport means to people in this business.' Afterwards, he received an award from Labour's Sports Minister, Denis Howell. Rock music and government had never consorted so openly before.

He was still the same old Reg, although to discover this one had to penetrate many layers of superstar protection. Even so old and close a friend as Sue Ayton, from Dick James's office, found herself brusquely fended off by those who now arranged Elton's social programme and screened all those seeking audience with him. Sue, however, persisted in wanting to see him and, when he played Earls Court, managed to get backstage on a pass given her by the sound engineer, Clive Franks. 'I got a lot of very black looks, like "Who does this girl think she is?"' she remembers now. 'Then, finally, I caught sight of Elton. He was standing at the end of this long concourse, with minders all round him.

'As soon as he saw me, it was all right. He came hurrying over, got me a drink, was as sweet as ever. "Do ring Sheila," he said. "She'd love to hear from you. I'll give you her number." Then, because Elton had been nice to me, suddenly everyone else was being very nice to me, asking if I was all right, showing me to my seat. I'd have loved to keep in touch with him and see his mother again, because we'd all been such friends before. But now there was all this other stuff one had to go through, I decided I just couldn't be bothered.'

The 'Louder Than Concorde' tour more than wiped away his Wembley Stadium flop ten months before. Besieged box offices from Taunton to Dundee told the same story. As a crowd puller, a surreal clothes horse, stage acrobat and marathon man, Elton John was still without peer.

On record, however, the position was less clearcut. In Britain, he had not had a Top 10 single since 'Lucy in the Sky with Diamonds' just got in, a year earlier. He was used to chart rebuffs in his native land and, up to now, had always been able to turn away from them to his constantly escalating American success. But early in 1976, his US chart ratings also began to slip.

The tireless record buyer had always been keenly aware of the competition he faced, on both sides of the Atlantic. Now he was aware of a fundamental change in the trend that had carried him to the top. After five years of chart dominance by solo singers, the fashion once again was for bands. In Britain, the chief agents were the Bay City Rollers, a gruesomely underpowered Scottish Beach Boy parody who, none the less, created enough hysteria among teenyboppers for the term 'Rollermania' to be coined. By mid-1976, almost all the names with whom Elton competed for chart access were bands. In Britain there was Queen, a group first of all remarkable for barefaced nerve in choosing such a name, their singer Freddie Mercury a camp white satin waif with the vocal range of a choirboy who had sold his soul to Satan before matins. There was 10 cc, a confederation of session wizards whose songs were an anti-American comic strip: 'Rubber Bullets', 'Wall Street Shuffle', 'I'm Mandy, Fly Me.' There was the leering country band Dr Hook, the warm-cocoa-bland Hot Chocolate, the Sixties rip-off band Darts. There was Roxy Music, Supertramp, Thin Lizzy, Sad Café and Bebop Deluxe. In America, there was the new age of country rock, combining old-fashioned pedal-steel and bottleneck blues guitar with modern lyrics about trans-American life, freeways, truckstops, diners and motels. There were Poco, Little Feat, Lynyrd Skynyrd, the Allman Brothers, the Doobie Brothers and the Eagles. There were the jazz-oriented Weather Report and the sex-oriented Steely Dan, named after a dildo in William Burroughs's *The Naked Lunch.*

With the change to bands went a change in content, away from solo plaintiveness, pensiveness and *faux naïveté*, towards the grown-up, the jaded and cynical. In fairness, the lyrics Bernie Taupin had fed to Elton had often been quite as mordant and strange as the Eagles' 'Hotel California' or Steely Dan's 'Haitian Divorce'. But the abiding Elton images were of whimsy and nostalgia. His world-conquering hits suddenly seemed like just another set of the W. D. and H. O. Wills cigarette cards that everyone was now throwing away.

He had left the avant-garde, and was moving, slowly but inexorably, to the middle of the road. The audiences that flocked to his shows were no longer kids on the cutting edge, but people with a past, looking for excuses to remember it. The fact was brought home in an American poll to find the country's three most popular musical acts. One was Elton. Another was the anodyne country singer John Denver. The third was the orchestra leader Lawrence Welk. 'Lawrence Welk!' Elton repeated incredulously. 'It's like being compared with Mantovani!'

As usual, he fretted endlessly over the problem, and how to solve it. He concluded that he had released too many singles that were slow ballads, and would do better in the charts with more hard-edged rockers, like 'Crocodile Rock' and 'Saturday Night's Alright for Fighting'. The approach of his twenty-ninth birthday – panic time in every young man's life – sharpened his desire not to be consigned to some easy-listening geriatric home.

He had chosen two tracks to make a second single from *Rock of the Westies*. One was the cumbersomely named Western love song 'I Feel Like a Bullet (in the Gun of Robert Ford)'. The other was 'Grow Some Funk of Your Own', a rocker with the same kind of hammering chorus as 'Saturday Night'. Elton, even so, suddenly grew keen on putting out 'Robert Ford' as the A-side. It proved a disastrous decision: the song was laboured as well as obscure, and many US radio stations, notably WABC in New York, rejected it outright. WABC's programme director later recalled the pressure that Elton exerted to try to push the single on to his playlist. 'An enormous cake arrived at my office, about half the size of my desk surface. On top of it was a decoration in the shape of a gun, and the message, "Give Robert Ford a shot". But we still didn't play the single. A week later, another cake arrived, this time as big as my desktop. With it was another message: "Disregard previous cake. Grow Some Funk is the A-side."'

The change of plan brought only minor comfort. 'Grow Some Funk of Your Own' – merely frenetic where 'Saturday Night' had been compulsive – rose no higher than number 14 in America. In Britain, it did not even make the Top 50.

Hits still happened, but they were hits of yesterday rather than tomorrow. In April, DJM put out a live album compilation named *Here And There*, the non-studio 'floater' to which they were entitled before finally letting Elton go. Side A featured a long-ago Elton performance at London's Royal Festival Hall; side B was a selection from his Thanksgiving 1974 concert at Madison Square Garden. Second-hand and blurred concert oldies like 'Border Song', 'Take Me to the Pilot' and 'Bennie and the Jets' still proved golden enough to take him to number four in the US and six in Britain. That same month, he had his first British Top 10 single since 'Lucy in the Sky with Diamonds'. But it was with his two-year-old version of 'Pinball Wizard', from the Who's five-year-old rock opera, *Tommy*.

Even when hits became harder to find for Elton himself, they

kept on happening for the performers he had encouraged and
promoted. Late in 1975, Neil Sedaka had a second US number-one
single on Rocket with 'Bad Blood', an exuberant rock-'n'-roll
number, featuring Elton on backup vocals. Despite his turbulent
private life, the session man proved as reliable as always. 'I was
nervous that he wouldn't show,' Neil Sedaka remembers. 'Then,
right at the end of the session, a limo drew up, and Elton walked in.
In seven takes he'd got the whole background vocal down.'

'Bad Blood' became Sedaka's biggest-ever US and Canadian hit,
selling 2 million copies. Rocket's promotion was as efficient as it
could be. 'I'd been downhearted because my last single, "That's
Where the Music Takes Me", hadn't been getting airplay on a certain
chain of radio stations,' Neil Sedaka remembers. 'When "Bad Blood"
came out, I called John Reid and said I was nervous these same
stations would pass on it. John called me back and told me it had
been accepted by the chain, and was already on twenty out of the
thirty stations. Within four weeks, it was number one.'

Still more remarkable was the renaissance that Rocket Records
gave Cliff Richard, a performer who, in almost twenty years of
consistent British chart success, had never achieved more than the
faintest pinprick in the American market. Early in 1976, Richard's
manager, Peter Gormley, sent John Reid tapes of two new songs,
'Miss You Nights', and 'Devil Woman'. Reid's instant response was
to sign the Peter Pan of British pop on Rocket US, with a vow to
get him the American hit he had been looking for since 'Move It' in
1958.

For Elton, a devout Cliff fan all that time, breaking him in the
US became a matter of personal honour. Sharon Lawrence was lured
back to Rocket to organise a publicity tour and introduce Richard
to the right media people. It helped that the songs were excellent, in
particular 'Devil Woman', a number far sexier than its vehemently
Christian vocalist had permitted himself before. In the summer of
1976, 'Devil Woman' went to number eight in America, staying in
the Top 40 for twelve weeks and earning a gold disc for sales of one
million plus.

Elton's own biggest single to date was to come in the form of a
dividend for unselfish work on another's behalf. He was now
contractually free of DJM, and at liberty to sign with any of the other
British record companies that clamoured for him. Instead, he had
decided to do what he had previously said he would not, and record
on his own Rocket label. A distribution deal for Britain was signed
with EMI, the company of which both John Reid and Rocket's
managing director David Croker were alumni.

Elton's debut on the Rocket label caused consternation within the company. He announced he wanted it to be a duet with Kiki Dee, the singer he had laboured so long to reinspire and establish. The song was 'Don't Go Breaking My Heart', a love duet in the Motown style of Marvin Gaye and Tammi Terrell. Reinforcing a suspicion that he was winding people up as he loved to do, it did not bear the usual John–Taupin byline, but was credited to 'Ann Orson and Carte Blanche'.

Various people came to David Croker, Rocket's managing director, and said that such a debut for Elton on the label would be disastrous. 'I didn't really know either way,' Croker remembered. 'I just thought it was a rather up-market form of pop. And duets just weren't fashionable.'

In July 1976, 'Don't Go Breaking My Heart' became Elton's first ever British number-one single – a triumph he was not to know again for fourteen years. The breezy pledge of undying love to Kiki even prompted some speculation that they might be more than friends. That was how generally safe his secret still remained.

When Margo Stevens became Elton's housekeeper at Woodside, she received one crucial piece of advice from her Rocket colleagues. 'Everyone said the same thing. "If he gets in a mood, leave him alone. Don't try to talk to him or reason him out of it. He gets that way sometimes, and there's nothing anyone can do about it. He'll come out of it on his own if you leave him, and be quite all right." It struck me at the time it was the way grown-ups might talk about a difficult child.'

Elton's move to his new house, early in 1976, was accompanied by one other major change. John Reid did not go to Old Windsor with him. Their domestic relationship had ended, by mutual consent, apparently without recrimination or pain on either side. There was no question but that Reid should continue as Elton's manager nor that, by the curious role reversal their life together had evolved, Elton should be somehow responsible for Reid. Close as they still were, and would always be, they now had different lives, different friends and different addresses. With the considerable wealth he had amassed, and barely spent, since 1971, Reid had bought a new house of his own in London. It was one of the elegant white houses in Montpelier Square that he had coveted as a humble assistant at Austin Reed's menswear store.

Elton was elated by his move to Woodside, seeing it as a real home whereas Hercules had ended up merely a base camp and storehouse. 'I'm basically a home-loving person,' he told Paul Gambaccini in a radio interview. 'I'm tired of wandering round the world. It's time to put down some real roots. I've been having a really good time, walking through the fields, looking at the cows. It may sound corny, but there you go.'

Extensive as the house was, every newly decorated room was at once crowded with Elton's possessions, the crimson buttonback sofas, the Art Nouveau lamps, the pot plants, the jukeboxes, the Rembrandts, the neon signs, the outsized Doc Marten boots from *Tommy*, the rail after rail of clothes. The first room to be finished was his record library, an infinity of vertical spines, dimly lit and vaguely sinister, like some data centre at MI5 or the Pentagon.

The domestic layout comprised six self-contained suites, one Elton's own, another kept for John Reid, the rest allotted to aides and friends who came to stay. There was also an office used by Elton's mother Sheila, his day-time châtelaine. When no guests happened to be there, he occupied the main house alone. Margo Stevens's quarters were a self-contained flat in a lodge building called the Orangery. Another outlying cottage was given to Elton's chauffeur, Bob Halley, and his wife, Pearl.

As housekeeper, Margo's duties were not onerous. She had to cook Elton's breakfast, look after his dogs, Bruce and Brian, and his cockatoo, Ollie, an excitable bird whose flappings sometimes set off the house burglar alarms. The rest was housework, taking care to observe the ritual pristine cleanliness and immutably fixed place of everything Elton owned. 'There was a big Casa Pupo rug on the floor in the front hall. I remember Sheila telling me that he liked all its tassels to point in the same direction.'

Elton's habits, when alone, were exceedingly simple. Off the road, he seldom bothered to dress up, spending whole days in nothing more elaborate than a tracksuit and sneakers. The meals that Margo had to prepare for him would be beans on toast, bacon sandwiches, a slice of bread coated with the beef dripping that was permanently kept in the larder. Another proletarian passion was HP sauce, cases of which had to be shipped to him wherever he happened to be on tour. He drank endless cups of tea, had a ragingly sweet tooth and, like a good boy, would eat anything put in front of him, with the single exception of eggs. 'He hated the yolks or the whites. I can't remember now which it was.'

Margo was surprised by how little lavish entertaining went on at Woodside. 'I can only remember one party. Cliff Richard was there, so were Dave Clark and Cathy McGowan. Another time, Freddie Mercury, of Queen, came to dinner. I didn't have to cook for that:

it was all catered by Friends, the restaurant John Reid started. And Princess Margaret came to tea, with her two children. When Elton sat down to play for them afterwards, he completely forgot the words of "Candle in the Wind".'

Despite all the people serving and protecting him, he often seemed a lonely figure to Margo, cast adrift in the cluttered, spotless rooms of his Queen Anne labyrinth. 'The house would be full of people; then, suddenly, there'd be no one there but Elton. A lot of nights, he didn't seem to have anywhere to go or anyone to be with. He'd say to me, "Do you feel like coming over and watching TV for a while?" One time in the kitchen, we had a food fight. We did it just like you see in films – emptying jars of coffee over each other's heads, squirting Fairy liquid, pushing cake into each other's faces. It was something I'd wanted to do all my life. Elton said he had, too.'

At other times he would appear totally self-sufficient, as the boy in Metroland had been, poring over the record albums that now needed an entire library to house them. 'And he'd get spasms of building bonfires and burning things,' Margo Stevens remembers. 'I can see him now, trooping out into the garden in a woolly hat, boots and this bright green Teddy-boy drape jacket.'

The combustibility of his emotions was not revealed to Margo until the night of the party attended by Cliff Richard and Cathy McGowan. 'After everyone had gone, Elton and I were in the kitchen with Bob and Pearl Halley. Something or other was said about the party that upset Elton. He picked up this heavy glass ashtray and flung it across the kitchen. It hit the rail of the café curtains along the window, and smashed. Elton stormed out of the room and up to his suite.'

The procedure for such moments had been firmly impressed on Margo, as on everyone else present. 'They all said, "Leave him alone, he has these Little Moments, he'll get over it." But I thought that was stupid. If someone's upset, you ought at least to try to find out what's wrong.

'So I went upstairs and knocked on the door of Elton's suite. He opened it, still furious, but obviously wanting someone to pour out his heart to. "What the fuck do they all expect me to be?" he said. "What do they want from me?" I just went and hugged him, until he'd calmed down. "I bet they're all talking about me down there," he said. "Let's go and listen." So the two of us crept down the back stairs and listened, and everyone *was* talking about him.

'I think that all his life, whenever he got angry or upset or hurt, people had just backed off and left him alone. I don't think anyone had gone up to him, hugged him and said, "What is it? Do you want to talk?"'

The 1976 American tour likewise was billed as 'Louder Than Concorde' – ironically since, having spent untold fortunes on a supersonic transatlantic plane, Britain now learned that America was refusing to admit Concorde into its airspace.

No hint of any such rejection now greeted that other British export who, in performance terms, had long ago exceeded Mach 3. His live album *Here And There* had reached number four in April; 'Don't Go Breaking My Heart', with Kiki Dee, had been a number-one single in August. His concerts sold out fast enough to raise smoke from the Ticketron computers. Mainstream FM radio still provided a basic Elton John diet, varied by odd, aberrant bites of Linda Ronstadt, Jim Stafford, George McCrae and the Hues Corporation. Despite all misgivings, his American fame was still there intact, huge, inexplicable and comfortingly ridiculous. The *Melody Maker* journalist Chris Charlesworth arrived to cover the tour with an Elton John sticker on his inflight satchel. As he waited to claim his baggage in transit, a young man came up and asked for his autograph.

For all that, the tour was a weary and bleary affair, its atmosphere progressively like those hangovers which set in before the binge is quite over. It had been the most colossal six-year binge. Corks had not yet ceased to pop, nor streamers to fly. But the bubbly now had an acrid taste. Elton was terminally bored with going on the road. In Britain that spring he had tried to regain enthusiasm by leaving the superstar tour circuit of great halls in regional capitals, playing instead to smaller crowds in out-of-the-way places he had not seen since Bluesology days. David Nutter's photographs show him travelling almost as a tourist, inconspicuous in parka and tracksuit, visiting Scottish castles, sitting among grubby ashtrays in roadside pubs, queuing at village shops for mundane English ice cream, huddled in the rain next to amusing road signs, eating fish and chips from newspaper and posing on Blackpool promenade in front of the Tower.

America permitted no such relaxation. Here it was just like last year, the year before and the year before that, the same giddy rotor-ride through heart-sinkingly familiar terrain. The same hotel suites of soulless Versailles luxury. The same private Boeing, *Starship 1*, with its cocktail bar and fur-covered kingsize bed. The same police motorcyclists, outriding the same air-conditioned stretch limousines. The same hustle through backstage areas of breeze blocks and chicken wire. The same dressing rooms, filled with flowers and well-wishing celebrities. The same walk out on to huge indoor or massive outdoor stages, to discover the same infinities of faces, adoring voices and upstretched arms.

Besides, there was now a greater preoccupation than music on Elton's mind. Earning a fortune in America seemed small by comparison with his chairmanship of Watford Football Club and his responsibility to help save the club from financial disaster. He even interrupted the tour to fly back and preside at the Watford board's annual general meeting.

His stage wardrobe reflected this new state of mind. His American fans, to their disappointment, beheld no feathered space cowboy, no beplumed Edwardian dowager, no glittery Venetian doge. Most nights, he performed in plain tracksuit and sneakers, the same outfit that the Watford first team would be wearing across the time zones in practice sessions at Vicarage Road. To these were added a miscellany hastily scooped up from his sartorial back catalogue: the matador jacket, seen on several previous tours, with big bars down its lapels; baseball caps, striped T-shirts, ski overalls, a fluffy duck suit, a straw boater, his old Uncle Sam top hat. To complete the ragbag ensemble, a dangling outsize carrot or strawberry. More than once, going out to greet the adoring continent, Elton looked a downright mess.

Different, too, was his view of the audience whose welcome had once been able to lift him from the blackest misery and self-doubt. Now, instead of 'smiling faces', he saw only a prison wall whose seething bricks happened to be human. Instead of renewing love, he felt pressure, even danger. Into his fathomlessly pessimistic mind popped a thought which, in 1976, still seemed laughable. Suppose that, in some nameless fan, adoration should metamorphose into hate? Suppose that, on some or other tropic stadium night, somebody should take a shot at him?

One fact weighed heavily, above all. In six months would come his thirtieth birthday, the formal end of youth. Unequipped as he was for an idol, he had at least always possessed that one fundamental qualification. He could pass, just about, as a balding young pop star. What was the world to make, though, of a balding, ageing pop star?

The exhaustions of touring, which youth had always thoughtlessly shrugged off, now began to take visible toll. One of David Nutter's photographs shows Elton aboard *Starship 1*, not drinking, playing piano, opening presents or looning as usual, but stretched on a sofa, dead to the world. Another picture shows him slumped in a chair, in striped lapels, striped socks and sparkly shoes, an outsize banana attached to his chest. His face looks worn away with fatigue. The eyes, through the joke glasses, are glazed and uncomprehending.

For Bernie Taupin, even more than Elton, *ennui* was growing intolerable. He had been on virtually every American tour since 1970, watching from the wings, night after night, week after week. Elton always insisted on having him there, to emphasise that the music was 50 per cent his and give him his rightful share of the applause. All these years, touring had seemed like the most wonderful free ride from luxury jet to hotel suite, from room service to party. But Bernie, too, was starting to feel the years.

He insisted that he was happy just to be around, listening to Elton sing his words and seeing their effect on audiences. He was an eternal VIP in his security badge giving 'Access to all backstage areas'; a star with no role but to socialise in dressing rooms, pick his way over the ramps protecting electric cables, and watch for the signal to take his place in the limo before Elton's finale began. His was an odd blend of fame and obscurity, a back-room boy without whom the front-of-curtain man could not function; Boswell to Elton's piano-pounding Johnson. So reticent had he been about personal publicity that few of the millions who knew his lyrics by heart had any clear idea of what he looked like, or even how to pronounce his surname. At twenty-six, he was just as famous and just as obscure as he had been at twenty-two. His collected lyrics had just been published as an opulent book, with cover by Alan Aldridge and each song interpreted by a leading pop illustrator. Bernie's title for it echoed his caustic view of himself: *The One Who Writes the Words for Elton John.*

His private life was now very different from that early country idyll at Piglet-in-the-Wilds. His American wife, Maxine, had left him after barely four years of marriage. To compound the injury, Maxine started an affair with Elton's bass player Kenny Passarelli, who had formerly been Bernie's closest crony on the road.

He himself was now dating various people, including the singer Lynsey de Paul, and living mostly in his Los Angeles house. 'The place was virtually empty,' he remembers. 'All that was there were a couple of beds and some hi-fi equipment. Just like the rock-star houses I remembered seeing when Elton and I first came to America.'

The shy Lincolnshire poet was scarcely visible in David Nutter's picture of Bernie backstage, wearing a Stetson and sunglasses and swigging beer from a bottle. He had put on weight, thanks to heavy drinking, and, like many musician friends, had acquired a cocaine habit. With the ritual self-effacement went an ego, he himself admits, that rivalled any to be found on the public rock stage. These were the high days of contractual riders, special clauses under which rock superstars compelled promoters to provide Byzantine dressing-room amenities, from Can-Can girls and vintage brandy to Smarties with all the red ones taken out. Bernie's personal rider on tour with Elton was that he must always be provided with Coors beer. Budweiser would not do, nor Miller, nor Schlitz, nor Michelob, nor any of the other myriad American brews with their barely distinguishable tastes. If Coors were not available for Bernie where the tour happened to be, special supplies had to be airlifted in.

Kenny Passarelli continued to play in the band, which was unchanged but for the absence through illness of percussionist Ray Cooper. To show how Elton valued Cooper, a life-size dummy of him stood onstage until he was well enough to fly from Britain for the tour's final dates. Kiki Dee also appeared in the New York shows, to sing the hit duet with Elton that some still took to signal more than friendship.

It was, to outward appearance, the usual triumphal trans-American journey, magnetising the usual throng of backstage celebrities: Shirley MacLaine, Don Covay, The Jacksons, Queen, Frankie Valli from the Four Seasons, Leonard Nimoy, from TV's *Star Trek*. In Atlanta, Elton met Mayor Maynard Jackson. In Philadelphia, he met Mayor Frank Rizzo. The readers of *Playboy* magazine had voted him world's number-one vocalist and keyboard player, and Bernie and him world's number-one songwriters. To receive the awards, they were invited to Hugh Hefner's Playboy mansion in Chicago, that fabled pleasure grotto where the Rolling Stones, a few years before, had caroused in whirlpools with compliant Bunnies, but where Elton and Bernie now just played pinball with Hefner and his new centrefold love, Barbi Benton. In David Nutter's photographs, the occasion has an oddly tired and passé feel, Elton and Bernie in their flared, waisted suits with shirt collars open over butterfly lapels; even Hefner hippyish now, in a horrid little denim safari suit. Seventies fashion is already dead though, alas, it will never, ever quite lie down.

There was only one great American idol that Elton had not yet met, and on this tour he finally got to meet Elvis Presley. But by now little resemblance could be seen to the marvellous young punk who had revolutionised the posture, intonation and wet dreams of postwar British youth. In 1976, just a year before his death from narcotics abuse, 'the King' was a walking mummy, encrusted with Seventies tomb-ornaments, obese, incontinent and almost blind. 'We went to see him do a show,' Bernie Taupin remembers, 'but it was absolutely pitiful. He was so drugged, he could hardly sing – he just stood there, handing out scarves. Then we were taken backstage to see him. There was this dressing room, full of Memphis Mafia, with Elvis in the middle of them on a stool, wrapped in towels. He looked awful, he was sweating, with the dye from his hair running down his face. And all these guys in suits around him in a kind of huddle. I don't think he even knew who we were. As we walked away afterwards, Elton said, "He's not long for this world." ' The awful spectacle of a great star, falling apart among servants and minders, shocked both of them to the core.

In New York in August, Elton broke the box-office record for a rock act at Madison Square Garden, playing seven consecutive nights to a total of 137,900 people. The last night's finale included Kiki Dee, Alice Cooper, Billie Jean King and the burly drag queen Divine. Its climax was Elton's appearance dressed as the Statue of Liberty, authentic in every detail but the white-framed glasses and stuck-out chin. That selfsame aureoled maiden, with torch aloft, had beckoned Reg Dwight from *New Musical Express* in the summer of 1967, when Liberty Records advertised for new talent.

At the start of the tour, MCA had announced to the US media that Elton would not be giving any press or TV interviews this time. The tireless provider of good copy was weary of doing that, too. Exceptions were made only for the two most serious music papers in Britain and America respectively, *Melody Maker* and *Rolling Stone*. Much as the obligation might bore him, when Elton gave an interview, he still could not help but give a good one. In this case, each of the lucky recipients was to find itself sitting on a world scoop.

To *Melody Maker*'s Chris Charlesworth, inflight on *Starship 1*, Elton revealed that the present tour would be his last for the foreseeable future. 'I've done it for six years, and I'm fed up with it,' he said. 'Not fed up with playing so much as with having no base and constantly roaming around. I don't want the pressure of having to tour for another two years or so.'

The idea had been fermenting in Elton's mind for many months. What had clearly brought it to a head was his meeting with Elvis Presley in Washington. He had suddenly seen with awful clarity how he himself might end like Elvis. 'I mean . . . I used to like walking round New York, but I can't do it any more. I can't go out of the hotel without someone causing a fuss, and, no matter how hard I try, I can't disguise myself. I can't live my life in a shell, like Elvis Presley or whoever. I have to do something positive, and getting associated with a soccer club is my way of doing it. I'm still dealing with people, but in a much more human situation. It won't be quite so insane as the music business.'

He stressed this wasn't permanent retirement, just a lay-off to give him leisure at his new house and time to devote to Rocket and Watford. His stage band was not to be broken up, but put on ice until he needed them again. 'I want to carry on being involved in music and sport together,' he told Chris Charlesworth. 'I want to be chairman of Watford, even if they are in a precarious position. I have wild ambitions for them because their ground can hold thousands, unlike most Fourth Division clubs. I dream about standing there in the directors' box on the night they win promotion. All the time, that's my one dream.'

Rolling Stone won its access despite having recently upset Elton with its story about Mick Jagger and him. The magazine had championed him since his earliest days and, in much lively, honest coverage, had only rarely given offence. Elton's 1973 *Rolling Stone* interview was considered one of the best with its rollicking tales of bedsitter life in Tin Pan Alley and Islington. To sustain another cover story, however, something more than recycled family and musical history would be needed. This, true to form, Elton provided in spades.

The last unrevealed detail about himself, though widely known and generally suspected, had never been officially confirmed. Everything about Elton John's public persona and private lifestyle suggested that he was homosexual. In fact, he was bisexual, capable of relationships both with women and men; prone to that capricious weather vane of the psyche that, without warning, can blow to totally opposite compass points. Most males, if they would admit it, pass through a bisexual phase at some time in their lives, but only for a tiny minority does the irresolution become permanent. As a rule, the immature homosexual phase moves on of its own accord to a mature and conclusive heterosexual one. The condition, where we can study it – in E. M. Forster's *Maurice*, or the modern, courageous writings of Colin Spencer – commonly shows male bisexuals ending up happily married, with children. For those tormented or perplexed by their condition, there was that ray of hope.

The secret that Elton had kept so sedulously through the early Seventies seemed of dwindling importance in 1976. Such had been glitter rock's blurring of gender that to be – or seem to be – bisexual was almost a requirement for chart-success. This was the time when David Bowie filled stadia across the world with his androgynous posturing; when the Rolling Stones wore Victorian sailor suits with full make-up; when Gary Glitter moved ever closer to the stage techniques of Danny La Rue; when Freddie Mercury flaunted a sateen ballet dancer's bottom in front of a band named Queen; when even so ravening a heterosexual as Rod Stewart found profit in coming onstage decked out in frills and turquoise satin tights like the fairy from atop some whorehouse Christmas tree.

Seventies fashion seemed to have swept away all former notions of macho masculinity. The least chic figures, from businessmen to trade union leaders, now wore their hair straggly-long, their sideburns to the extremities of their cheeks, their clothes in the flared, waisted and scalloped style which hinted, however vaguely, at the Regency fop. The dourest northern England industrial town now had at least one pub that put on lunch-time drag shows to huge, appreciative stag audiences, and at least one hairdresser's window displaying the word 'Unisex'. The very construction workers now wore floral patterns with prissy shades of pale green and plum, sported small gold rings in their ears and used tall canisters of hair lacquer to tint their ashen pompadours.

How Elton's secret had not leaked out into the British press — even then notoriously more sensationalist than the American — must count as a minor miracle of news management, and self-management. Certainly, it was known to every national journalist who covered pop, like David Wigg of the *Daily Express*. Again we find a parallel with the Beatles, whose human and fallible aspects were resolutely ignored by Fleet Street for the first three years of their career. The stories that sold papers were about cuddly mop-tops, and so these were provided whatever evidence might crop up to the contrary. Similarly with Elton now, the story that sold papers was of Mr Nice Guy: the rock star like no other in his clean-living ways, who put off his wild outfits to reveal a paragon, quiet, virtuous and devoted to his mother — 'The Cliff Richard of rock'.

Elton himself, honest to the core, did not enjoy lying even by omission. More than once in the past year, he had teetered on the edge of confessing all, prompted by interviewers like Caroline Coon or *Playboy* magazine. What had chiefly restrained him was his new role as chairman of Watford, and the very different standards that applied in the world of football. Here his mother had been powerfully influential, urging him to cut down the camp when he attended Watford functions in his official capacity, and to do nothing that might harm the image of the club.

John Reid was particularly anxious that Elton should not come clean, even though their personal relationship had now ended. His reasons were hard-headed business ones. David Bowie had admitted to being homosexual in 1972; otherwise, through all the primping, pouting, drag-queenly world of glitter rock, there was not one performer who owned himself other than 100 per cent normal in the Victorian sense. Besides, Bowie had come out at a time when pop musicians received almost no coverage in the mainstream British and American press. Elton, by contrast, was a world figure, with connections to high society, even to royalty, and a reputation for having a positive influence on the morals of the young. However permissive and tolerant the climate might seem, no one could predict the effect of such news on his record sales and concert drawing power.

All this had been impressed on Elton many times, but – as Reid was well aware – one never knew what he might do on the spur of the moment. Accordingly, Rocket's press officer, Caroline Boucher, had orders to eavesdrop on his interviews, and to intervene whenever revelation seemed to be trembling on the horizon. Harder-nosed Fleet Street men, like *The Sun*'s Bob Hart and the *Mail*'s Mike Housego were by now vying with each other to nail the story. 'I came into the room just in time to stop Hart getting it,' Caroline Boucher remembers. *The Sun* being then still a paper that required genuine quotes to prop up its stories, Bob Hart remained in hot pursuit.

Caroline Boucher, alas, was not on hand when Elton met *Rolling Stone*'s interviewer, Cliff Jahr. By now, at the end of his tour, the quiet Dr Jekyll who had discussed football and normality with Chris Charlesworth had turned into a hyper and mischievous Mr Hyde. Earlier, he had appeared on WNEW radio, goosey on Dom Pérignon, and intemperately attacked the *New York Times* for its review of him at Madison Square Garden. 'If you're listening, asshole,' he said to the *Times*' pop critic, John Rockwell, 'come down here, and I'll destroy you. I'll rip you to pieces on the air . . . I bet he's about four foot one. I bet he's got bogeys up his nose. I bet his feet smell.'

In New York – where homosexuality was now a familiar part of everyday life and gay pride a strong social movement – far more pressure existed to come out. David Bowie seemed to be pointing the finger, saying in a recent *Playboy* interview that Elton was 'the Liberace, the token queen of rock . . . I consider myself responsible for a whole new school of pretensions – they know who they are. Don't you Elton?' Elton seemed to be relaxing his usual discretion, talking campily on WNEW radio, using a drag queen in his stage show, even letting Divine take him to Crisco Disco, a leading gay night spot (named after the frying oil that was a popular sexual lubricant).

The interview destined to break the mould took place in the hotel suite, normally used by Elizabeth Taylor, where Elton had spent two weeks virtually a prisoner between concerts. To make it more homey, it had been stuffed with ornaments from his LA house: potted trees, Teddy bears, piles of records and two pinball machines, respectively lighting up the names Captain Fantastic and Goodbye Yellow Brick Road. Cliff Jahr was initially somewhat dismayed by the tired, shy figure who sat opposite him, seldom meeting his eyes. Only later did he realise how consummately Elton had played to the tape recorder.

After some initial stonewalling about what David Bowie might have meant, and a fracas that had occurred at the door of Crisco Disco, Jahr came right to the point. What happened when Elton came home at night? Did he have 'love and affection'?

'Not really. I go home and fall in love with my vinyl,' Elton replied. 'I suppose I have a certain amount of love and affection as far as "affection" goes. From friends and stuff. My sexual life? Um. I haven't really met anyone I'd want to have any big scenes with. It's strange that I haven't. I know everyone should have a certain amount of sex, and I do, but that's it, and I desperately want to have an affair. I crave to be loved. That's the part of my life I want to have come together in the next two or three years, and it's partly why I'm quitting the road. My life in the last six years has been a Disney film, and now I want to have a person in my life.

'I don't know what I want to be exactly. I'm just going through a stage where any sign of affection would be welcome on a sexual level. I'd rather fall in love with a woman eventually because I think a woman probably lasts much longer than a man. But I really don't know. I've never talked like this before. Ha ha. But I'm not going to turn off the tape. I haven't met anyone I would like to settle down with – of either sex.'

No press officer having rushed in with a stop-watch, Jahr was free to ask on the record, 'You're bisexual?'

'There's nothing wrong with going to bed with someone of your own sex,' Elton said. 'I think everyone's bisexual to a certain degree. I don't think it's just me. I think you're bisexual. I think everyone is.'

He'd never said so in print before?

'Probably not. It's going to be terrible with my football club. It's so hetero, it's unbelievable. But I mean, who cares? I just think people should be very free with sex – they should draw the line at goats.'

Had his first experience been with a man or woman?

'Um, when I was twenty-one, with a woman. The famous one.'

And how soon after that the first man?

'Um. The famous woman frightened me off sex for so long that I don't remember really. I think it was probably a good year or two.'

Had he and Bernie Taupin been lovers?

'No, absolutely not. Everybody thinks we were, but if we had been, I don't think we would have lasted so long. We're more like brothers than anything else. The press probably thought John Reid and I were an affair, but there's never been a serious person the whole time.'

Was he afraid that, on reading these disclosures, *Rolling Stone* readers would go 'Wow!'

'Well, I don't think so. There shouldn't be too much reaction . . . Nobody's had the balls to ask me about it before. I would have said something all along if someone had asked me, but I'm not going to come out and say something just to be − I don't want to shove it all over the front pages like some people I could mention. To be on the front of newspapers with my tongue down somebody's throat. That's really appalling.

'I'd like to have children, but I don't know if the time is right. I just want to settle down and sort of be lazy for a while. There are a couple of people back in England. I do have a crush on someone, but I can't say who it is − someone I met two or three times, who is American . . . I go for older women. Listen, Shirley MacLaine would do me fine . . .'

Only now was there an interruption. John Reid entered from the next room, where he had been playing pinball. But even this did not inhibit Elton, who − Jahr afterwards wrote − seemed relieved to have the whole thing out in the open at last.

'As soon as anyone tries to find out about me or to get to know me, I turn off,' he continued. 'I'm afraid of getting hurt. I was hurt so much as a kid. I'm afraid of plunging into something that's going to fuck me up. It's reached a point in my life where I get to my house and my animals and think, "Who am I going to . . .?" I'm certainly not going to bed with my horse. Ha ha. And I think, "Christ, I wish I had someone to share all this with."'

ELTON'S FRANK TALK: THE LONELY LIFE OF A SUPERSTAR was *Rolling Stone*'s principal cover line on 7 November, 1976. With it went a picture of Elton, lounging cheerfully enough in his big white specs and a sweater decorated with striped-shirted footballers. Inside was a more suitably sombre portrait, in straw boater, with heart-shaped spectacles. 'My life in the last six years has been a

Disney film,' ran the subheading. 'Now I have to have a person in my life.'

The treatment could not have been more tasteful and sympathetic and *Rolling Stone*'s liberal young readership, for the most part, responded in kind. Next issue, half the magazine's correspondence column was given to readers' letters on the subject, aptly headed 'Dear Johns'. 'This is undoubtedly the best interview with Elton John I've ever read,' wrote Kathryn Cwikla, of Wethersfield, Connecticut. 'It is very sensitive and in parts touching.' 'He has opened my mind completely,' wrote C. Deley of Lima, Ohio. 'I'm never going to judge anyone by what they are physically, but instead by what an individual is inside . . .' A few were negative. 'My disgust is matched only by my disappointment, which are both overshadowed by pity,' wrote Lisa Crane of Provo, Utah. 'I pity him for his sexual illusions and perversions . . .' 'Elton John, leading proponent of fungus rock, is no more artistic than articulate,' wrote Bryan Johnson of Saginaw, Michigan. 'Life is real, Elton and what will you do with yours? You're a commercial success, and that's about it.'

In Britain, the story broke in the mildest possible way. The mass-circulation dailies, *Mirror*, *Mail* and *Express*, reported Elton's confession on inside pages, merely as pick-ups of the *Rolling Stone* interview, in tones of no surprise and with no attempt to mount a wolf-pack-style follow-up. *The Sun*, amazingly, did not think it worth mentioning at all. The big fear was the Sunday tabloids, especially the *News of the World* with its voyeuristic relish for stories of sex and rock 'n' roll. But even in the 'News of the Screws', treatment was downbeat. ELTON: MY LOVE LIFE ISN'T SO STRANGE said a headline in lower-case white reversed on black. The *News of the World*'s reporter had caught Elton as he arrived with the Watford team to play an away match in Rochdale, Lancashire. Elton – 'wearing a check suit with orange trimmings, and pink-framed spectacles' – was as forthcoming as always.

'I don't see why people should be so surprised,' he was quoted as saying. 'The only reason I hadn't spoken about it before was that no one asked me. It's not important, nor is it a big thing in my life. I don't see why it should affect the fan worship I've got. It hasn't hurt David Bowie, and I don't see why it should hurt me.'

Even the *News of the World* was content merely to repeat the relevant parts of the (uncredited) *Rolling Stone* interview, and Elton's denial that he'd ever had an affair with Bernie Taupin. Beside the headline was a picture of Bernie with the caption: 'Elton denied gossip about him'.

All in all there was not a fraction of the harassment and persecution that would attend a far less legitimate story about Elton eleven years later. Apart from a call to his father (who had heard the news with blank bewilderment) Elton's family was left in peace. Not until some time afterwards did his mother give her response. 'I was upset at first,' Sheila admitted. 'But I think it was a brave thing for him to do. I would still like to think he can find happiness with a male or female – I don't care.'

Elton's great fear, as he admitted to Cliff Jahr, was the response of Watford, his fellow directors and, even more, the team he was trying to inspire to League promotion. All at Watford, too, diplomatically expressed total astonishment, from the club secretary, Ron Rollitt, to Keith Mercer, the twenty-year-old forward who had joined Elton in practice kick-arounds with Rod Stewart. The consensus, among fellow directors and in the changing-room, was that it should make no difference. Elton was by now more than just Watford's only possible path to salvation. He was also liked and respected. The revelations about a private life he had kept far from Vicarage Road changed nothing.

The wider world of football, however, was to show no such forbearance. Nor did it recognise any fine distinction of terms. Throughout the Football League, Watford now found itself stigmatised as the club led by a 'poof'. Under football-crowd logic, that made Watford players, too, by association, 'poofs'. The team had to endure being so called, both by spectators and by their opponents on the field of play. Elton's own appearance in the Rochdale directors' box was to begin an era calling on every possible reserve of chin-jutting doggedness. Shouts of 'poof' and 'queer' from rival supporters would prove the least among such public ordeals. At one later match he attended, the crowd spent twenty minutes chanting 'Elton John's a homosexual' to the tune of 'Glory, Glory, Hallelujah'.

An unfortunate postscript was supplied by the cover of Elton's new album, *Blue Moves*. For this he had chosen a painting from his own, now impressive, collection, 'The Guardian Readers' by Patrick Procktor. Hawk eyes in Fleet Street noted that in Procktor's delicate group, every figure was that of a young man.

As part of the album's promotion, fifty copies were to have been given away as prizes for a readers' competition in *The Sun*. This was cancelled because, as the paper disingenuously explained, the album cover 'didn't have a woman on it'.

Blue Moves was Elton's first album for Rocket and as such was intended to be a blockbuster. He insisted it must be a double album, the first since *Goodbye Yellow Brick Road* in 1973. His new distributor,

EMI, acceded to his wishes, even though double albums were far trickier things to sell in the price-sensitive record market of 1976.

Blue Moves turned out to be anything but the bright herald of a new era. Bernie Taupin's new lyrics had a downbeat, pessimistic tone, the consequence of his breakup with Maxine and his general feeling of uncertainty and drift. 'Between Seventeen and Twenty', for instance, mourned the absurdly young age at which he had married, believing that everything would be House at Pooh Corner-perfect. Nor did other titles, like 'Cage the Songbird', 'Somebody's Final Song', 'If There's a God in Heaven (What's He Waiting for?)' and 'Sorry Seems to Be the Hardest Word', point to a happy or optimistic viewpoint. To lighten the tone, there were two instrumentals: one by Elton's guitarist Caleb Quaye; the other entitled 'Theme From a Non-Existent TV Series'.

Gloomy or not, *Blue Moves* almost joined the great range of Elton album peaks, climbing to number three in both Britain and America. It was in fact not the start of an era, but the end of one. The days of looking down from those twin summits – fearing the moment when he might slip to number two – were gone for ever.

Choosing 'Sorry Seems to Be the Hardest Word' as the first single from the album could hardly have been more appropriate. Unhappy love lament though it was, it came across more as a polite note from that usually well-behaved Metroland boy to anyone whose sensibilities he might recently have offended. 'It's a sad sad situation' he sang in a moment of unintended truth, the superstar suddenly as forlorn and vulnerable as Reggie Dwight had ever been. He seemed to be asking for mercy and, in general, receiving it.

THIRTEEN

'There's a lot more to me than being on the road'

I N July 1976, the British pop tycoon Richard Branson threw a lavish garden party at the country house he used as a studio for his record organisation, Virgin. Among the guests was Caroline Coon, the liberal activist turned music writer, accompanied by a blond youth who seemed ill at ease among all the Seventies rock aristocrats. By day, the youth was an electrician at Barclay's brewery, a job involving so little work, he had to be paid extra for being bored. By night, he played drums in a new band, the Sex Pistols.

Six months later, the Sex Pistols were the terrorists of British pop. A group stupendously lacking all natural ability, they had come together in a Chelsea boutique called Sex, owned by the designer Vivienne Westwood. Their manager was Westwood's boyfriend, Malcolm McLaren, a shock-headed elf who combined aspirations to be a rock-'n'-roll Svengali in the Larry Parnes mould with vague theories about music as a tool of radical politics. The Sex Pistols, for McLaren, reincarnated the primeval state of rock 'n' roll, twenty years earlier. They were as musically inept as the Fifties establishment had considered Elvis Presley. Their performances unleashed the same chaos and destruction that Bill Haley's Comets had wrought in clubs, theatres and cinemas. Their discordant voices fell on Seventies' ears as terribly as had Little Richard's first 'awopbopaloobopalopbamboom'.

In his quartet of talentless Cockney youths McLaren brilliantly focused the Seventies' twin propensities, for pastiche and mindless violence. Their lead singer was named Johnny Rotten, antithesis of all smiling idols at the mike, a shambling teenage heap with shabby clothes, filthy, spiky hair and green teeth, who sang in a demented whinge, in the intervals swearing at his audience, spitting at them, throwing bottles or lashing out with his fists. The bass player was named Sid Vicious, a genuine psychopath who would publicly cut bits off himself with knives or broken glass.

As exponents of 'punk rock' – a term hijacked by McLaren from the era of Lou Reed and the Velvet Underground – the Sex Pistols blazed a trail that made the Rolling Stones' Sixties outrages seem tame by comparison. They preached 'anarchy in the UK', encouraged brawling and bloodshed at their gigs, insulted the Queen, spat vodka at press photographers, destroyed toilets at the office of their record company and vomited in the public concourse at Heathrow airport. They inspired a new dance, 'pogoing', and a new form of audience appreciation, 'gobbing'. Their apotheosis was a family talk show on Thames Television when Johnny Rotten, the self-proclaimed 'Antichrist', repeatedly shouted four-letter words at his boggling middle-aged interviewer.

Even Malcolm McLaren, however, did not realise how perfect were his creation to be heroes in 1977. For the first time in twenty years, a generation was coming to teenagerdom in a world where it was not so very wonderful to be young. The former perquisites of youth – garish clothes, extravagant hair, wild music and feckless hedonism – now belonged to all age groups under the woozy make-believe Seventies sun. In both America and Britain, youth shared the same realities as everyone else: spiralling inflation, fear of terrorist bombs, decaying infrastructure and inner-city slums. In Britain in this year, one in every two school-leavers could expect to go straight into the unemployment line. Yet the music they heard was still glittery flimflam, played by complacent, ageing longhairs on acoustic guitars or fiddly mandolins.

Johnny Rotten's spit of Luddite rage was the signal for instantaneous general revolt. Like Steven Spielberg gremlins, punk rock bands started popping out everywhere, with similarly uninviting names – the Damned, the Clash – similar lack of melodic talent and similar huge juvenile audiences. The unifying factor was furious contempt for Seventies rock culture in all its forms, the huge arenas, the four-hour delays, the million-pound light shows and house-size amps, the permed yellow hair, the frilly shirts, the dobros and mandolins, the harmony, the clarity, the dexterity, the vanity, the snobbery, the hype. So punk-rock bands sang off key and struggled to find three-finger chords in claustrophobic clubs on gimcrack stages within spitting distance – literally – of the audience. It was not music so much as a kind of mass satire, taunting the rock status quo with cacophonous parodies of itself, mocking its supposedly ageless gods as preposterous dinosaurs.

With the music that negated music came fashion negating fashion – a look drawn from horror movies and the wardrobe of the sadomasochist, including cactus-spiked green hair, rubber trousers incapacitatingly tied together at the knee, shirts and coats deliberately rent into shreds and large safety pins worn as ornaments by being driven through nose or cheek. From here on, the way to show oneself past youth, or at the nadir of style, was to wear anything structured, anything waisted or − God forbid! − anything flared.

Re-enacting the 'British Invasion' of ten years before (in every particular but charm) punk rock spread to New York, then Los Angeles, then all points in between, turning an entire industry on its head and consigning millions who had believed themselves trendy to premature middle age. The flower children's young brothers and sisters, who had seized power in 1972, and replaced Bob Dylan with Gary Glitter, now themselves fell victim to an even more comprehensive revenge.

A prescient few in the rock establishment did not join the general chorus of horror and disgust. Among them was a 'dinosaur' who could be presumed at the very top of the punks' extermination list. Elton had always said, 'It's a sign of people getting old when they start grousing about the new groups.' In his thirty-first year, he was not about to slip into that habit.

He had always been remarkably free from musical prejudice, able to stand back and see how even tinselly nine-days wonders like the Osmonds or Bay City Rollers perfectly satisfied their particular audiences. To Elton, punk rock was like turning back the clock to mid-Fifties skiffle days, when anyone could pick up a guitar and have a bash. He was also fascinated by the implications for the record industry, as the major companies were forced to recognise the huge following of punk music, and back-street labels, run by boys with safety pins through their faces, suddenly became a force in the marketplace.

He could congratulate himself on perfect timing, having got out of the rock-idol business just a split second before it dissolved into bloody revolution. The sensible and realistic side of him knew, and was reconciled to the fact, that his incredible reign over mass musical taste was over. 'He was no way giving up,' David Croker, Rocket's then general manager, remembered. 'He was going to carry on putting out records and being himself, no matter which way the business went. But he wouldn't be King of the World any more.'

At Rocket, as at all record companies of the old order, life went on, shaken but still resolute, rather like that of tsarist aristocrats after the Bolsheviks had captured the streets. Elton was amply fulfilling his promise to use retirement for the development and production of Rocket's smaller in-house talents. He worked on a second album for

Kiki Dee, and helped bring on two new bands, China and Blue, whose names, six months before, had seemed the very height of fashion.

He was further involved in the colourful and diversifying activities of John Reid Enterprises. For, now that there was no longer an Elton John road show to steer around the world, Reid was busily extending his entrepreneurial empire. As well as his first and paramount client, he now managed Queen, with the competitively flamboyant Freddy Mercury. Under Reid's tutelage, Queen had had a massive single hit with 'Bohemian Rhapsody', a six-minute operetta for which many people – Elton included – had predicted failure. What chiefly sold the single was a video film, made specially for television, showing Mercury and his band in a narcissistic kaleidoscope. The age of pop video started here.

Reid's enterprises, however, now extended far beyond the world of pop. In 1976, he had acquired an interest in the Edinburgh Playhouse theatre – hence its choice as venue for Elton's supposed farewell UK performance that September. Pursuing his long-time interest in food and cookery, Reid also opened a restaurant called Friends in London's Covent Garden. Elton put money into Friends, and – gossip writers were promised – might even occasionally turn up there, playing piano for the customers.

Something else was on John Reid's back burner, coming slowly but inexorably to the boil. This was the matter of Elton's contracts with the Dick James Organisation, which, although now expired, still regulated his publishing income up to 1973 and his recording income up to 1975. Reid had first queried these agreements in 1971, when he took over Elton's management on DJM's behalf. He had been probing around the matter ever since, constrained from open challenge by the need to keep Dick James co-operative while the contracts remained in force. Now that all had ended, the gloves could finally come off.

In 1976, he poached another key executive from DJM, persuading the lawyer Geoffrey Ellis to come across to John Reid Enterprises. Ellis was soon involved in Reid's efforts to prove that Elton's DJM contracts had not been fair and that, in the years since 1967, he and Bernie Taupin had received less than their due share of publishing royalties.

The matter was already being pursued by Reid's accountants, Shears and Co., who, in mid-1976, conducted an audit of DJM's books with regard to royalties due to Elton and Bernie Taupin up to December 1975. Geoffrey Ellis could provide further information relating to their publishing royalties from overseas. In 1975, DJM had made changes in the network of sub-publishers who collected royalties on their behalf throughout Europe. Barry Lyons of Shears accordingly wrote to DJM, asking for details of their foreign sub-publishers and licensees, and relevant contracts and agreements. DJM replied that the new arrangements were for internal convenience only, and that the contracts were based on 'normal commercial practice'. Since Elton and Bernie had 'a privileged form of agreement' with DJM's This Record Co., which guaranteed them a fixed percentage of its income, their royalty earnings would not be affected.

In October 1977, Shears finally obtained details of the new European sub-publishing arrangements. They were passed to an accountant named Alan Feigenbaum, whose reading of them suggested that, on the contrary, Elton and Bernie's income was adversely affected, possibly by as much as 50 per cent. Geoffrey Ellis reported these findings to John Reid, who instructed Feigenbaum to compute the full total of the presumed losses.

Geoffrey Ellis was too distinguished and discreet a figure ever to bear the brunt of Reid's temper. But he was, several times, a fascinated spectator. Life with Brian Epstein had been placid by comparison.

'There was one occasion when John had been in Los Angeles, and was expected back in the office that day. We were very much involved in negotiations about income tax and on the day of his return, I had to go to a meeting with a leading tax counsel. A phone call was put through to me at the chambers. It was John, asking me to come back to the office. "When?" I said. "This is an extremely important meeting." "As soon as you can," he said. "I've fired all the staff."

'When I got back to South Audley Street, it was like the aftermath of an explosion. There was an eerie silence . . . every desk deserted. John had come back from Los Angeles in a temper, and told everyone to go. "There were too many hangers-on," he said. "You and I can run this place just between the two of us." I walked through the building, and found a couple of girls huddled together in the telephone-room.

'"All right, John," I said. "But we do need secretaries. And we do need people to answer the telephone." Within a few days, everyone had trickled back and was working normally again.'

Explosive as Reid was, he still managed to inspire loyalty, even affection, among the Rocket staff. 'He could be quite sweet as well, though he did his best not to show it,' Margo Stevens remembers. 'There was one time when he'd been in Paris, and came back, steaming through the office the way he always did – like the

Road-Runner. Some of us were sitting on the floor, putting together stuff to mail out. As John came past, he threw something at me. It was a bottle of perfume.'

In almost schizophrenic contrast with the fear that Reid inspired at Rocket were the magnificent perks its employees received, like being flown to Los Angeles by chartered jet for a week. Christmas was a time of Dickensian largesse as Elton made his arrival with the traditional cornucopia from Cartier. 'He went around the whole office, handing out Cartier watches and pens,' Geoffrey Ellis remembers. 'Everyone got something – not just me but my secretary as well. And every single one had a personal card attached.'

He was equally generous at Watford, throwing parties for individual players who did well in matches, sending piles of new albums in an attempt to improve the team's generally abysmal pop musical taste. He took pains to get to know everyone at the club, not only the team and the office and ground staff but also their wives and children. One of his great pleasures was to be the summer garden party he organised for Watford employees and their families at Woodside, with sports events and games and everything else that Reggie Dwight used to miss in summers long ago, shut indoors at his eternal piano practice.

There was more to Elton's chairmanship of Watford, however, than simply being Mr Nice Guy. He had decided early on that the club's existing manager, Mike Keen, was not the person to lift it from the doldrums. After a further lacklustre season, when Watford managed to rise by only one place in Division Four, from eighth to seventh, Keen was ousted from the managership in favour of Elton's personal nominee.

He had long had his talent spotter's eye on Graham Taylor, the young player-manager who had spectacularly revived the fortunes of another moribund Fourth Division club, Lincoln City. In June 1977, he phoned Taylor and offered him the Watford job. Taylor, who had recently turned down an offer to manage First Division West Bromwich Albion, saw little to tempt him initially. 'I thought it was the last thing I wanted,' he says now. 'To go back into the Fourth Division, managing some southern club, with an outrageous pop star messing around as chairman.

'What impressed me was Elton's reaction when I rang him to say no. I expected him to try to hustle me with big talk about money and potential. But he didn't argue, didn't try to change my mind. Just wished me all the best at Lincoln, and said he hoped he might see me one day. By the time I rang off, I wanted to meet him.'

Several other candidates for the Watford job were mooted,

including the former England team captain Bobby Robson. Elton, meanwhile, waited for Graham Taylor's return from summer holiday, then approached him again. This time Taylor agreed, won over by the simplicity of Elton's dream for Watford. 'He said he wanted to take them to the top, and into Europe. I said, "Do you have an idea what that will cost?" and he said no. I told him, "Well, you ought to say a million to start with." '

Taylor's diagnosis of Watford's problem was brutally frank. He told the board and the players that their club was sloppy and rundown, and that, regardless of Elton's money, any success could only be attained by single-minded dedication and hard work. On this, and every other point, Elton and he found themselves in total sympathy. Both agreed, above all, that, rather than spending money on flash new players, Watford's primary need was to build up its support within the local community. A programme of improvements began at Vicarage Road with the emphasis on facilities to encourage parents to bring their children to matches.

Graham Taylor also took a firm line with Elton himself, whose chief pleasure as chairman had been to fraternise with the players, kicking around with them at practice or posing for zany photographs in the changing room. All that must stop, Taylor decreed. Football at Watford from here on was to be a totally serious business.

By only a few weeks into the 1977–8 season, Taylor seemed to be justifying his £125,000 contract. Two of Watford's home games drew more than 11,000 spectators each, a respectable tally for any Second Division side. They looked set fair to end up as Fourth Division champions and win their longed-for promotion back into the Third.

Pictures of Elton with Graham Taylor in the Watford directors' box showed him wearing an outsize tweed eight-piece cap like some gangster extra from Bonnie and Clyde. Out of the performing limelight, he had finally nerved himself to the last possible remedy for his vanishing hair. In September, the *Daily Express* reported that he had flown to Paris to consult plastic surgeon John Reed about a transplant operation – similar to that recently performed on Frank Sinatra – whereby hairs with healthy follicles were removed from abundant growth at the back of the neck and sewn in individual plugs over the denuded crown. Mr Reed had delivered his predictable opinion that such an operation would 'take'.

The cloth cap, and a large collection like it, concealed a crop of freshly grafted hair plugs and resultant, uncomfortable scar tissue. Elton had been told he must wait six months to see if the transplant operation had been a success; in the meantime, he should expose his scalp to the air as much as possible. He paid as much attention to that as to earlier advice that drenchings of gold, silver, scarlet or green dye could not possibly do his cursed hair follicles anything but harm.

Elton's housekeeper Margo Stevens was dusting the banisters at Woodside one day when she overheard a conversation between his mother and his chauffeur's wife. 'Well, she won't like it,' Sheila said, 'but there it is . . . she's got to go.'

Shortly afterwards, Margo was given notice. The official reason was that the house was about to be reinsured, and the insurance company objected to a single girl living alone in the Orangery. But, via her old boss, Elton's great friend Tony King, Margo heard a different story. She was thought to have become too officious in her duties, for instance locking up Elton's private suite in his absence and keeping the key jealously to herself. It was even alleged that she'd stolen some money and jewellery.

Both charges Margo indignantly denies. 'The only reason I locked his suite was because there were builders in the house at the time, and you didn't know who might walk in there and pinch something. As for stealing money, the only thing I can imagine they meant was one time when Elton had lost his piano ring, and I had to go through all his clothes searching for it. As I looked, I kept finding wads of dollars in pockets, and jewellery still pinned to lapels. I took the whole lot down to Sheila, who had an office in the house, and handed it all over to her.'

Many people knew Margo as the besotted Beatle fan who, in former years, would climb into Paul McCartney's house and walk through the rooms, looking but never stealing so much as a piece of lavatory paper. Among those who testified to her utter trustworthiness was Charlie Watts, the Rolling Stones' drummer, for whom she had often babysat.

None the less, the slur remained. Not only was Margo asked to leave Woodside; she also heard that her old job at Rocket was no longer open to her. Instead, she received compensation of £500.

'I still don't really know what happened,' she says today. 'All I can think is that Sheila got it into her head that I had some designs on Elton. I remember one day when he came into the house, and we were both standing there. He came straight up to me and said, "I've just bought some new furniture. You're going to love it." Maybe Sheila was a bit put out by that.

'Elton himself was away when they got rid of me. Just before he left, I remember, he came into the kitchen where I was working, and gave me some money. So perhaps he knew what was going to happen. I've no idea whether he did or not.'

That reduced Elton's domestic staff to just the chauffeur, Bob Halley, and his wife, Pearl. Subsequently, Bob and Pearl's marriage broke up, and Bob served Elton alone, sometimes waiting in his Rolls for seven hours at a stretch outside Friends in Covent Garden or the Rainbow on Sunset Strip.

To the fifty or so other Elton John employees, in early 1977, a stern edict went out. Elton had cut himself loose from all normal pressures, performing, writing, recording or giving interviews. He would stay at home in Old Windsor, being quiet and private. Underlining the point, only three people in the whole organisation had the Woodside telephone number: his mother, John Reid and Reid's secretary. A telex machine at the house handled all other communication. Anyone wishing to reach Elton must speak to the office, which would then − or not as the case might be − telex Elton at home. The flaw in this perfect plan was that Elton found telexes exciting; every fifteen minutes or so, he would go to the machine to see if anything new had come through on it, and feel disappointed if nothing had.

There were other signs that, much as he might ostensibly crave quiet and seclusion, Elton could never succeed in maintaining a totally low profile. In this period, *The Times*'s Personal Column contained two items, enigmatic even by its time-honoured standard. One said:

Pauline from Sheffield would like to announce it is a year since she last had a man.

The other said:

Lord Choc Ice would like to announce it is 10 years since he travelled on a bus.

Pauline from Sheffield was, of course, Pauline Matthews, aka Kiki Dee, whose sex life had always been of brotherly concern to her sponsor and producer. And even those who had not travelled with him on his last bus journey − with Uni Records into Los Angeles − had no trouble in guessing the identity of Lord Choc Ice. John Reid happened to be travelling abroad when the ads appeared but, on seeing them in his airmail *Times*, instantly knew whose little joke they were.

★

Less than a year previously, Lord Choc Ice had had the top-selling single in Britain and America. Now he seemed unable to gain the slightest toehold in either chart. His two 1977 singles were each trampled to invisibility by the punk rock horde. 'Crazy Water', released only in Britain that February, stalled at number 27. 'Bite Your Lip (Get Up and Dance!)', four months later, reached the same low-water mark on both sides of the Atlantic, stiffing at 28.

His only 1977 album was a second volume of past hits, compiled by DJM from the later material under their copyright, with the surprise addition of 'Don't Go Breaking My Heart' and 'Sorry Seems to Be the Hardest Word'. Fearing another substandard compilation, Elton instructed Rocket to lease the track to DJM. From here on, his only contact with his old mentors would be via accountants and lawyers.

The rise of *Elton John's Greatest Hits Volume II* to number six in Britain and 21 in America only seemed to confirm what a back number he now was. While punk mobs howled and looted, the aristos in their tattered flares huddled for comfort around 'Philadelphia Freedom', 'Island Girl' and 'Bennie and the Jets'.

For eleven months Elton steadfastly kept up his retreat, breaking it only at one, irresistible command. In May 1977, he was part of the Royal Windsor Big Top Show, a circus and variety spectacular given for the Queen as part of her Silver Jubilee celebrations. His confession of bisexuality had made no difference to his acceptability as a royal entertainer nor to his involvement in prestigious charity work. That same month, the *Daily Telegraph*'s Court Circular reported that Princess Alexandra and the Honourable Angus Ogilvy had 'attended a gala performance by Elton John in aid of the Queen's Silver Jubilee Appeal at the Rainbow Theatre, Finsbury Park. Lady Mary Fitzalan-Howard was also in attendance.'

The Rainbow concert, though successful, had an embarrassing sequel. Introducing one number, Elton could not resist a mischievous ad lib to amuse the rock-business cognoscenti: 'This one's for Charlie – he's doing well tonight.' It was evidently explained to Princess Alexandra that, in certain circles, 'Charlie' referred to something other than her cousin, the Prince of Wales. On meeting Elton at the backstage party later, Her Royal Highness decided to get to the bottom of the matter. 'How do you play for two and a half hours at a stretch?' she asked him. 'Do you take some sort of drug? Do you take cocaine?'

An astonished Elton told reporters what the Princess had said, then was obliged to apologise for repeating royal remarks made privately. 'I very much hope I have not embarrassed the Princess. I thought it was very amusing, and that's why I repeated it. Of course I do not take cocaine . . . it [the in-concert reference to "Charlie"] was only meant as a light-hearted comment.'

That November brought another unbreakable commitment. Earlier in the year, he had become one of the sponsors of Goaldiggers, a charity set up to provide football pitches and equipment for deprived children. The climax of a Goaldiggers fund-raising drive was to be a gala concert at Wembley Arena, jointly organised with the Variety Club of Great Britain. Elton, who had already made a special promo record for Goaldiggers, agreed to be top of the bill.

He appeared alone at the piano, still in the cloth cap that covered his hair transplant – as multifarious types of headgear would for ever after. Though given a huge welcome by 8,000 embattled Seventies children, his thirty-minute solo spot seemed subdued, even melancholic. David Croker, for one, could see he wasn't enjoying himself. 'He hadn't played a huge venue like this for over a year, and he thought it was going to feel great to be doing it again. But, you could see, it still felt like shit.'

He seemed to revive and become the old manic, acrobatic Elton when Davey Johnstone, Ray Cooper and Rocket's band China joined him onstage for a thunderous version of Marvin Gaye's 'I Heard It Through the Grapevine'. Then, rippling the intro to 'Don't Let the Sun Go Down on Me', he came out with an announcement even his closest followers had not known he meant to make:

'I haven't been touring for a long while. It's been a painful decision for me, whether to carry on touring or not. But I've made the decision – and this is going to be the last show. There's a lot more to me than being on the road.' To anguished gasps and cries of 'No', he replied, 'Thank you very much. I really enjoyed tonight. But it's the last one.'

'If this was a wake, it will not be forgotten by any of the 8,000 present,' wrote the *Daily Telegraph*'s John Coldstream. 'It was a glorious way to go, but the concert stage will be a less colourful place even if Watford FC is the richer.'

III

HERCULES

FOURTEEN

Mr Cheveux

NINETEEN seventy-eight was rock music's Year Zero. The old order had been wiped from existence as totally as the era of music hall, silent movies, harpoon whaling or steam trains. The new order, Eighties children two years premature, controlled everything.

Punk rock in its impurest form was a fairly short-lived British phenomenon. From that generalised shrieking and jeering, the eternal 2 per cent of true talent soon emerged as, thankfully, it always has and always will. A few months were sufficient to separate the talentless opportunists from bands of manifest ability and originality: the Police, the Jam, the Boomtown Rats. Out of the 'gobbing' rabble, names like Elvis Costello, Paul Weller and Sting began to be recognised as songwriters and showmen to rival any gone before. The spirit of aggressive egalitarianism quickly produced punk-influenced reggae, from bands that mixed black and white personnel as democratically as did the dole queues of the outside world. The most notable, indeed, called themselves UB40, after the harsh government form issued to all applying for unemployment benefit. One needs no better example of how welded to real life rock had become, and how redundant now seemed the tinsel age of *Captain Fantastic* and *Goodbye Yellow Brick Road*.

Nowhere was the revolution more visible than in Britain's weekly music press. The *New Musical Express*, *Sounds* and, finally, even the illustrious *Melody Maker* dropped their conventional newspaper format, substituting the garish asymmetry of post-punk publications like *Blitz* and *The Face*. The once straightforward, literate feature articles were replaced by tracts of teenage free association, sprayed on to the page with the same wild predictability as the graffiti now infesting walls, buildings and underpasses. There was no point any longer in being an articulate rock musician since no articulate rock writers were there to take note of the fact.

Meanwhile, the megastars who had been eclipsed were exiles in their own land, holed up on their country estates, seldom daring to venture forth with their horribly outmoded flared silhouettes. For many, the blow was compounded by serious drug and alcohol problems, produced by long years of heedless excess. From their common predicament, one might have expected to see evolve a spirit of mutual sympathy and support. But rock stars – all except one – had never been very good at keeping in touch.

Eric Clapton, the nonpareil of British rock guitarists, was one major star whom the late Seventies found in a rough patch, both professionally and personally. He had never been a particular friend of Elton's, but Elton possessed the knack of keeping even peripheral friendships in good repair. 'Suddenly, out of the blue, you'd get a Fortnum and Mason hamper at Christmas, with a label on it, "Love from Elton",' Clapton remembers. 'Or you'd get a note, or a message with a hotel operator, or you'd hear he'd dedicated a tune to you onstage. Some little thing was always turning up to make you feel good.'

Whatever complex new twists Elton's life might be taking, the indestructible good boy in him seldom forgot a friend's birthday. 'It was my fiftieth,' Bryan Forbes remembers. 'We were having a big party in the garden at Wentworth. Elton wasn't in the country at the time, but I knew I'd be bound to hear from him in some way or another.

'But my birthday arrived – and no word from Elton. As we were having our party on the lawn, I suddenly heard something that sounded like a Welsh miners' brass band coming up the drive. It *was* a Welsh miners' brass band! Wherever Elton was, he'd got in touch with them, booked them and bussed them all the way up from the Rhondda Valley to Surrey. They played to us for the rest of the afternoon.'

One Watford match Saturday, during drinks in the club boardroom, Elton spotted a familiar face. It was George Hill, landlord of the pub where Reggie Dwight had got his first break as a solo performer, for £1 10s a night back in prehistoric 1962. George was still running the Northwood Hills Hotel, and, after the game, invited Elton over to see his wife, Ann, and look round the old place again. Elton stayed a couple of hours, reminiscing about those days when fifteen-year-old Reggie would sing mournful Jim Reeves songs in a ginger tweed sports jacket, undeterred by showers of ash-trays and empty crisp packets.

The Hills' son Andrew, just a toddler back then, was now about to leave school and begin an engineering course at Loughborough College. Andy Hill, too, was a Watford fanatic, and frequently ran into Elton during or after matches at Vicarage Road. One day in the spring of 1977, the superstar came up with a proposal that left the eighteen-year-old school-leaver speechless. 'You oughtn't to go straight from A-levels to college,' Elton told him. 'You should take some time off first, to have fun and broaden your outlook. Be my personal assistant for a year, and see the world.'

So Andy Hill, with experience of nothing but pub and school life in deepest Metroland, went straight to the number-one spot in Elton John's entourage, at a salary of £100 per week. His first duty was to be Elton's sole travelling companion on a six-week trip, taking in Washington, Los Angeles and Maui. 'Elton turned up for the Concorde flight trip in white shorts,' Andy Hill remembers. 'And each of his socks was a different colour, and each of his shoes was a different pattern.'

After a family gathering at Elton's LA house, master and personal assistant flew on to Maui for two weeks' intensive tennis coaching. Andy Hill soon discovered his fiercely competitive nature. 'I said I could beat him at squash, so we played; he was determined to beat me, and he did. It was the same with tennis. When Elton played anything, even if it was only pinball, he played to win.'

At tennis school on the loveliest Hawaiian island, Andy saw Elton at his most carefree and relaxed. 'He wasn't recognised. No one bothered him. He could go round just like an ordinary person. So he, in turn, was very open and friendly to everyone. I remember, one day some people came round collecting for "Save the Whale". Elton knew this guy who ran one of the local bars, and he said "Why don't we do a gig for Save the Whale?" So one night he just went and played the piano on his own in this bar. By the time he'd finished, of course, the word was out, and there were hundreds of people in the street, waiting for him.

'I discovered his sense of humour, as well, when we were leaving, and went to say goodbye to the tennis pro who'd been coaching him for the two weeks. When we arrived at this bloke's bungalow, he wasn't there. Elton said, "Why don't we take every bit of furniture out of his bedroom?" So we took out everything – his bed, the tables, chairs, lamps – and arranged them in exactly the same position in the garden.'

Another duty for the awestruck 18-year-old was to accompany Elton to his Paris hair-transplant clinic. The initial operation, performed by France's leading trichological surgeon Dr Pierre Pouteaux, followed a new and allegedly superior method called 'square grafting'. Sections of hair-bearing scalp were taken from the back of the neck, then cut into tiny squares and punched over the barren crown as in a checkerboard design. The advantage was that, if the grafts took, growth would be faster and the covering denser than from patches transplanted at random. The disadvantage was that several further uncomfortable operations were necessary until all the white cranial squares had been filled in.

Elton's first transplant experience bore his familiar imprint of mingled farce and pain. Emerging from the clinic, head bound in lint and gauze, he was ushered by Andy Hill to a waiting limousine. As he went to get in, he struck his vulnerable cranium an almighty blow on the rim of the car door. 'He thought he might have knocked some of the hair-plugs loose,' Andy remembers. 'So we had to go back into the clinic and have them checked out. I thought it was funny at the time. But I can see now he must have been in agony.'

It was in this second retirement period that Elton adopted the habit of travelling under elaborately comic aliases. An early alter ego – in tribute to his French trichological experiences – was Mr Cheveux. 'A lot of the time, people still knew who he was,' Andy Hill says. 'But sometimes they didn't. Once we were on a flight where first class had been overbooked, and, seeing this Mr Hill and Mr Cheveux, the airline just put us on the list to be downgraded to economy. Elton nearly went barmy! Luckily, at the last minute they realised who he was, and managed to find us a couple of seats in first.'

In the political swirls and eddies that surrounded Elton, Andy seemed to bear a charmed life. John Reid, for some reason, had no objection to his employment. Apart from one wobbly moment at Wembley, when Elton's hats failed to arrive backstage, he never found himself on the receiving end of a Reid explosion. 'Being so young, I didn't realise what a powerful figure John was. I wasn't in awe of him, which he seemed to like. I could sometimes even be a bit cheeky to him.' The only edge of animosity came from Elton's chauffeur, Bob Halley, who clearly had himself hoped to be promoted from mere driving to Andy's privileged place at the sovereign's right hand.

Though officially termed 'personal assistant', Andy Hill's administrative duties were of the lightest. Virtually all arrangements on

Elton's behalf were made through John Reid's office at 40 South Audley Street, where he was nominally based. As weeks passed in unstrenuous, peripatetic luxury, in Los Angeles, Hawaii and Seattle, Andy realised what was the true and exclusive nature of his job. It was simply to go with Elton everywhere, and keep him company, day and night.

Like others before him, he was amazed to see how much of the superstar's life was unglamorous, funless and solitary. 'Everyone else in the organisation had a circle of friends that they could call on at the end of the day. Elton had good friends, but they didn't make any kind of structure around him. I couldn't believe how this incredible figure, who was the envy of millions, used to go back to an empty house most nights, and just be there on his own.'

At Woodside the main social events were squash or tennis tournaments, with Elton in obsessive combat against Andy Hill, Bryan Ferry or the more athletic members of Rod Stewart's new stage band. 'He was seeing quite a lot of Rod, and Rod's manager, Billy Gaff, who was a big friend of John Reid. Elton and Rod had this incredible love-hate relationship. They were terrific friends, but couldn't be together without continually trying to put each other down and score off each other. Like, Rod would buy some really horrible, cheap plonk, then stick expensive labels on it and say to Elton, "Hey I've got some incredible wine here: you ought to try it."'

They continued to call each other the camp nicknames dating from the Long John Baldry era. To Rod, Elton was Sharon; to Elton, Rod was Phyllis. When Rod was on tour with his album *Blondes Have More Fun*, Elton had a big banner hung outside Olympia: 'Blondes may have more fun, but brunettes have lots more money. Happy Xmas, love, Sharon.' It was taken down rather hastily by Rod's roadies.

Apart from Concorde trips abroad, Andy's chief duty was to accompany Elton to Watford matches, home and away. Throughout that season, 1977–8, they did not miss a single one, travelling by helicopter if the venue was too far in the chilly north for Bob Halley to pilot the long-distance Daimler.

In this sphere, at least, Elton's spirits were soaring. The inspirational management of his protégé Graham Taylor had transformed the sleepy, sloppy Watford team into an enthusiastic, highly motivated unit that was now scything through its Fourth Division opponents. By the end of Taylor's first full season, Watford's goal tally had earned them 71 League points, a club record. They finished

as Division Four champions, winning promotion to Division Three
with a 2–0 away win over Bournemouth. The result, said a rhapsodic
Elton, was 'better than having a record at number one'.

The ground and its terraces also had been transformed with new
fencing, bright new paint and a staff outfitted in blazers of canary
yellow. The run-down adjoining greyhound track had been closed,
without protest or regret. New amenities were constantly being
added, underlining Elton's wish for a 'family club', free of the male
macho mayhem that usually cursed English football. The most telling
innovation was a 500-seat family enclosure in front of the directors'
box, where parents with children had their own catering and toilet
facilities and personalised seats. Child members received a gift at
every match and, on their birthdays, a card signed by all the team.
Every player had written into his contract an obligation to meet and
talk to young supporters. There was a Christmas party each year, and
before the home match nearest Easter, Elton would personally
distribute up to 750 chocolate eggs.

Especially at away matches in northerly towns like Rochdale and
Scunthorpe, the opposing supporters were still apt to chant disagreeable things about Elton and his sexuality to improvised tunes of pop
songs or hymns. But Watford's fans now had an answering chant to
characterise themselves in their ever more consistent triumph: 'Elton
John's Taylor-made Army!'

With Watford on its feet and running, signs of the chairman's
personal munificence began to appear. Two record transfer fees were
paid to buy in outside players, Ray Train for £50,000, then Steve
Sims for £170,000. What was his club's aim for 1979? the *Daily
Express* asked Elton. 'Third Division champions, and promotion
again,' he replied. 'There's no point in just consolidating. You've got
to be positive in football.'

One revealing photograph from this era shows Elton in his floppy
tweed cap, grinning proudly amid Watford's victors, towel-wrapped
and steamy from the after-match communal bath. Another photograph shows him actually in the bath with them. 'You could always
tell how much he himself would have loved to be a footballer,' Andy
Hill remembers. 'There was one testimonial match where, in fact, he
did turn out to play for Watford. I think it was probably the proudest
moment of his life.'

From his inside vantage point Andy Hill saw how there were
two Eltons in constant, unpredictable alternation: one brash and
buoyant, the other shy and self-conscious; one hectically happy, the
other bleakly morose; one decent, considerate and civilised, the other
prone to explosive moods and Georgie-Porgy tantrums. 'I saw him

in the dressing room at Wembley, the night he announced his retirement, throwing flower arrangements around, shouting, "I'm not bloody well going on!" It was just to get attention, because he thought no one cared about him and the pressure he was under, having to go out in front of all those people and perform. Most of the time, he really needed people. If there was a big match on TV, he'd ring me and say, "Do you want to come to the house and watch it with me? And can you pick up some smoked salmon from Harrods on the way?" Another time, I'd go to the house and Bob Halley would say, "Elton doesn't want to see anyone at all for two days." '

Even the fabled Elton generosity, that splashed out Cartier watches, jewels, even cars on the most casual acquaintances, coexisted with an innate shrewdness. 'I've seen him bet £100 on the toss of a coin,' Andy Hill says. 'He could be the easiest touch in the world sometimes, and at other times watch the pennies just like anyone who didn't have his kind of money. I remember, while we were rehearsing with Davey Johnstone's band, China, at Shepperton studios, everybody got hungry and Elton gave me £20 to go out and fetch some hamburgers. When I got back, the first thing he said to me was "How much were they?" and, when I told him, "Where's the change?" '

His constant saving grace was a sense of humour that could usually pull him back from Elton number two's black abyss with a healing draught of Elton number one's rational and self-mocking laughter. Nor was the tireless practical joker lacking in humour when, as sometimes happened, the joke was turned back on him. 'While we were in Los Angeles, he got a message saying there was a fancy-dress party at the Rocket office,' Andy Hill remembers. 'Elton got really dolled up for it, in a woman's frock, a huge wig and roller skates. But it was all a big leg-pull. When he arrived there, in this incredible get-up, on skates, everyone there was in suits, holding the annual general meeting.'

Elton's interest in Andy Hill was entirely circumspect. Taking him on as personal assistant had been no more than a kind of long-belated thank you to George Hill for that first chance at the Northwood Hills Hotel. As well as being good-looking, Andy was a thoroughly presentable, intelligent and articulate boy, whose Metro-land innocence brought out all Elton's latent elder-brotherliness. 'His attitude to me was always very free. It was always "Enjoy yourself, do what you like." But once, he did give me a talking-to. Once, while we were in LA, I was with some people on a boat at Malibu. We'd been drinking, and we dived off the boat to get to shore and see some actor who was supposed to have draught Guinness in his garden. When Elton found out, he was furious. "Don't you realise how dangerous that was?" he said to me. "You're never ever to do it again!"'

None the less, Andy Hill was privy to the seamy side of rock superstar life, which now went on behind closed doors as if in hiding from the punk thought police. At parties, cocaine was still provided as copiously as sherbet powder, arranged into neat ploughman's lines with golden razor blades and sniffed up through spills of tightly rolled brand new £10 notes. Whatever the horrors of the Top 20 and this week's *NME*, 'Charlie' was still doing just fine.

Andy also had to deal with the succession of temporary companions who had passed through Elton's life since he parted, domestically, from John Reid. These companions, usually of the American blond surfer type, were each taken up with an enthusiasm that seldom convinced Elton's nucleus of true, loving friends, like Nanette Newman. 'With Elton, there were never half-measures,' she says now. 'Whenever he started a relationship, it was always the one; the love of his life.'

The liaisons rarely lasted longer than a day or two. 'They usually weren't very bright,' Andy Hill remembers. 'Elton would get bored, and embarrassed by the whole thing, and want to get rid of them as quickly as possible. There was one named HG who stayed around some time. Elton told me to buy him a car, so I took him to a Ford showroom. But this guy wasn't interested in Fords; he wanted a Ferrari. I told Elton, and Elton said, "OK. Get him a Ferrari."'

For all that Elton's sexual nature was now public knowledge, he remained utterly discreet. When the growing horde of tabloid paparazzi sighted him, it would invariably be with John Reid, in the conventional mode of star and guard-dog manager. Separate as their lives were, they still saw each other constantly, even took the occasional holiday together. July 1977 found them in the south of France, revisiting the St Tropez waterfront where Elton had played the Papagayo club with Bluesology – and, one night, almost electrocuted himself. There was a John Reid-style contretemps after a local club refused to admit them. Reid tried to climb over the back wall and fell off, breaking his right foot in three places.

When Watford held a formal dinner or reception, the club chairman would arrive escorted by a female employee of Rocket Records or John Reid Enterprises. This was not entirely diplomatic artifice. Elton was still strongly, if spasmodically, attracted to women. Digress as he might, he always carried a clear mental picture of his ideal type. She would be American, some years older than himself, experienced and understanding enough to untie all the knots, accept all the conundrums and so, finally, bring him into line. His mother cherished much the same hopeful vision, as was revealed in a rare interview with *People* magazine. 'Deep, deep down, I know he would love to get married and have a family,' Sheila said. 'The sort of woman he'd marry would understand [the bisexuality] anyway.'

For a while, it seemed that he might be about to start a relationship with Melanie Green, the pretty seventeen-year-old daughter of a well-known London investment banker. They met in 1976, at a charity dinner attended by Prince Charles; thereafter Melanie became a noticeable fixture backstage and at post-concert parties. When Andy Hill arrived in 1977, she would still occasionally fly over to see Elton from Switzerland, where she was at finishing school.

'There's no doubt in my mind that Elton was born to be straight,' Andy Hill says. 'If he hadn't gone into the music business and met all those other people, he'd be living in Pinner now, happily married, surrounded by kids.'

Ceasing to perform was not the only great change in Elton's life during this era of massive general upheaval and uproar. He was also without the collaborator representing 50 per cent, if not more, of his artistic self. Bernie Taupin and he had ceased to write songs together.

Their last album, *Blue Moves*, though commercially successful, had been anything but the euphoric short-distance gallop to which both were accustomed. Bernie, in particular, had felt under intolerable pressure. 'By that point, we seemed to have achieved everything there was to achieve. Elton had filled every major stadium in the world. We'd written strings of number ones – eventually, things that went straight into the charts at number one. You couldn't fart without hearing Elton John. At that point, it felt like there was no way we could go any further. There was only one way to go from here.

'*Blue Moves*, Elton always says, was the doom-and-gloom album, and that's pretty much how I felt at the time. My marriage had broken up; I had a lot of negative thoughts about everything. For instance, 'Someone's Last Song' is about committing suicide. For the first time, when we began work, I found myself thinking, "I don't know if I've got it in me. I don't know if I want to do this any more."'

There was little resemblance now to the shy farm boy who had come down from Lincolnshire with his pockets full of wistful poems. Bestubbled and overweight, he looked more like one of the Mafia

hoods who populated his new homeland. His drinking had reached
the problem stage, though Bernie himself did not yet realise it. 'I
used to wake up in the morning in my house on North Doheny
Drive – the rock star's empty house – and the first thing I'd do
would be to reach over to the refrigerator by my bed. I'd take out a
beer, empty half of it away, then fill it up with vodka. I'd drink that
every morning before I got up. When I went anywhere in a limo,
I'd take a gallon jug full of vodka and orange juice. People were
starting to say, "Hey, you've got a problem", but I wouldn't believe
them. I said, "No, I'm just having a good time."

'I was doing drugs, too – though the funny thing was, I never
smoked dope. It was basically cocaine, and dabbling in smack a
couple of times. But not through a needle; always ingesting it. I went
through my period of hallucinations, too – magic mushrooms, acid,
stuff like that.'

In the post-*Blue Moves* period, two things happened to Bernie.
He began a relationship with a high-powered Californian woman
named Loree Rodkin. And he visited a doctor for treatment for a
routine ailment. After examining him, the doctor told him his liver
was in terrible shape and that if he didn't do something soon, the
consequences might be disastrous.

'I'd started this new relationship, which seemed promising, so I
took it on myself to go away and dry out. I went to Acapulco and
lived on my own for three months. I had this big house at a place
called Horseshoe Bay, and I stayed there, just getting the sun, and
thinking about other forms of writing that I might do. Loree came
back and forth, but basically I was alone there. I kept a diary and as I
wrote it, gradually, I could feel my mind unfogging and clearing, and
it was beautiful. In the evening, I could look over the bay and see
the stars and the night lights, and I began to realise the world wasn't
such a bad place after all.'

There was never any kind of falling out between Elton and
Bernie, nor even formal acknowledgement that they had ceased
collaborating. It simply happened that when the album-making
feeling next came over Elton, as it did in late 1977, Bernie was 5,000
miles away, with little on his mind but the daily struggle against
wanting a drink.

Coincidentally, Elton had also parted from Gus Dudgeon, the
producer who had supervised all fourteen of his albums since the
breakthrough one in 1970. The reasons, Dudgeon says, were mani-
fold. 'I remember, at the time of *Blue Moves*, I rang up America to
see how Kiki was doing with "I Got the Music in Me". My wife
said, "You never even asked how Elton was doing." I said, "Oh I

know he's all right." And I suddenly realised, the challenge there used to be in producing Elton had gone. We just assumed we were a team with a magic touch.'

As producer, Dudgeon had always enjoyed a unique measure of independence in Elton's highly political circle. 'I was only contracted album by album, which meant I worked directly for Elton. At the same time, because I had other projects, like Joan Armatrading, I was apart from all the political stuff. When Elton wanted to record, he called me, and we recorded. I didn't have to belong to all the Yes men, telling him that everything he said was wonderful and marvellous.'

Dudgeon's chief discontent was in his capacity as a director of Rocket. 'The problem was that, with Elton and John Reid travelling all over the world, and Bernie Taupin away in America, you could hardly ever get all the directors in one place for a meeting. I was getting fed up because I didn't think we were signing the people we had a chance to. I'd wanted to sign Dave Edmunds, but wasn't allowed to. "Oh no," they said. "He'll never have another hit." Another person I wanted to sign was Barry Humphries [aka Dame Edna Everage]. "No," they said. "He's an actor." "But he's in this great show, Housewife, Superstar. He's going to be enormous," I said, but they still wouldn't listen.

'There was going to be this one board meeting when I had a lot of complaints to bring up. Neil Sedaka was very unhappy with the label, and thinking of signing somewhere else, but no one was even trying to keep him. And I was very dissatisfied with the way the accounts were being kept. I said, "Things have really got to be a lot better, or I'm quitting." I realised that no one was saying, "Don't go, Gus" – and I was out.'

It was cavalier treatment for the man who had masterminded Elton's career on records and had very often produced hits from shit. Subsequently he sold out his Rocket shares to John Reid, and continued his highly successful career with other artists, among them Elkie Brooks and Chris Rea.

Elton was on fire with enthusiasm for a project requiring neither Gus Dudgeon nor Bernie Taupin. His first studio sessions in more than a year were to be produced by Thom Bell, creator of the Philadelphia sound, lightweight orchestral soul music which had dominated the mid-Seventies charts. As well as producing, Bell was to supply the songs and arrangements in the pattern of his earlier huge successes with Harold Melvin, the O'Jays and the Three Degrees. The album was made at Bell's Sigma Sound Studios in Philadelphia and the Kay Smith Studio in Seattle. Andy Hill, who sat in on the Seattle sessions, remembers them as 'outstanding'. But when Thom Bell delivered the finished album, Elton decided it was overproduced and the orchestration were 'too sweet'. The whole project was then peremptorily shelved.

From easy-listening soul music, he switched abruptly to the idea of meeting the new, dark forces of rock music head on. In March 1978, he released a one-off single called 'Ego', a stockpile Bernie Taupin song, recorded at the Mill Studios, Cookham, Berkshire, with production jointly credited to Clive Franks and Elton himself.

With it came images of a new-look Elton, hopefully more in accord with the stark, grainy tastes of punk. Gone was the familiar bespectacled face, with its air of intense anxiety or its manic gap-toothed grin. Instead, a dramatic, chiselled countenance, minus glasses and so artfully lit and retouched as to be barely recognisable, scowled forth from under beetling brows. After years of spectacle-wearing, he had taken to contact lenses, enduring the fiddles with eyelids, tiny containers and distilled water for the sake of a hopefully vast improvement in his personal attractiveness. Gone with the specs was the floppy tweed cap, revealing a manifest miracle. Where there had formerly been weak strands of thinning blond there was now dark hair, not thick but apparently firm and all-enveloping.

Elton was determined that 'Ego' should be launched with every proper modish marketing device. With the single came a video film showing the new unspectacled Elton, seated in an ornate room, receiving a large crowd of reverent courtiers. He explained it was meant to satirise 'the type of people you can meet in this business, with over-inflated ideas and big talk. The type of people I loathe.' But to many, the ego in question seemed to be Elton's own as he motioned people to this or that side of the room like some latter-day, wigless Sun King. Forty thousand pounds was spent on the video, as against the £4,000 that Queen's 'Bohemian Rhapsody' one had cost only two years before. Elton may be said to have single-handedly started the trend of pop videos with budgets as big as feature films.

There was instant massive media interest, though little of it in the new single. All that any Fleet Street news editor wanted to know was the exact nature and consistency of the dark substance under Elton's tweed cap. The fact that he resolutely kept his cap on for the video's West End cinema première and through all pre-release interviews added to the feverish speculation. During his talk with disc jockey Kenny Everett on London's Capital Radio, a listener phoned in to say she'd donate £10 to charity if Elton would remove the cap. This Elton briefly did, giving Everett and his studio staff as much newsworthiness as if they had witnessed some landing by Martians. 'There was hair, filmy hair, but hair all over as far as I could see,' Kenny Everett later testified to the *Daily Mail*. Studio engineer Keith Muirhead got into the story for having missed the revelation. 'It happened so quickly and I was so busy, I didn't even see it.'

Alas, the record was a resounding flop which did not even approach the Top 20 in either America or Britain. To compound the snub, Elton's costly video promo film was refused by BBC TV's *Top of the Pops*, whose policy was to feature only songs that had made the British Top 30.

Previous failures had been greeted by Elton – in public at least – with resigned good sportsmanship. But, when 'Ego' stiffed at 34, his response was to launch a bitter attack on the 'inaccuracy' of the chart which the British Market Research Bureau supplied to the BBC. Complaining that alternative charts, notably the *NME*'s, showed 'Ego' in the lower 20s and even rising, he threatened to withdraw Rocket's advertising from papers carrying the BMRB's lists. Rocket's managing director David Croker and promotion manager Arthur Sherriff were bitterly blamed for the video's non-appearance on *Top of the Pops*. 'John Reid rang me up and screamed abuse at me,' Croker remembered. 'Told me I was fired on the spot.' ROCKETS FLY AS ELTON'S EGO FLOPS said Nigel Dempster's *Daily Mail* diary, reporting that Arthur Sherriff had been dismissed by John Reid through the company lawyer, and was now having to sign on the dole.

On Elton's next album, Bernie Taupin's place as lyricist was taken by Gary Osborne, an ebullient blond character who had been the monarch's attentive friend since the time of his Wembley Stadium Beach Boys show. Osborne had written the lyrics to Kiki Dee's 'Amoureuse' though he was slightly better known as a writer of TV jingles for a bank, a building society, a brand of toothpaste and the health drink Lucozade.

Elton's decision to team with Gary Osborne was not based on any serious idea that he'd found a rival to Bernie Taupin. Whereas Bernie was always different, and could often be brilliant, Osborne at his best was only very adequate. It was his personality that appealed to Elton: whatever they might produce, at least they could do it with ease and the necessary quota of laughs. 'Gary was such a character, with his flowing blond hair, his big coats and his great long fingers,' Andy Hill remembers. 'Elton had always wanted more hair, and longer fingers. I think he just wished he was Gary Osborne.'

On the allusively named *A Single Man*, released in October 1978, all but one of the tracks bore a Gary Osborne lyric; bread and butter where Bernie Taupin would have provided sherry trifle. The exception was an instrumental written by Elton alone, deriving from his love of the sombre and funereal. During the album sessions, a seventeen-year-old Rocket messenger named Guy Burchett was killed in a motorcycle crash. Elton had known and liked the boy and, on the day of the accident, sat down and produced 'Song for Guy', a lachrymose piano piece with no vocal beyond a vague accompanying murmur. Two songs, 'Georgia' and 'Big Dipper', had backup vocals by the Watford team, bussed in to the Mill Studio as if to an away match.

Though nominally the chief product of his own organisation, Rocket, Elton now began what would be an extended pass-the-parcel progress around the major companies that handled manufacture and distribution for independent labels. With *A Single Man*, Rocket severed its British distribution deal with EMI, who, naturally, had come in for some of the blame for the 'Ego' flop. A new contract was signed with the Dutch-based Phonogram company, previously Philips. Elton was thus back, indirectly, with the people who had first signed him up in Bluesology.

The advance single was 'Part-Time Love', a Gary Osborne pensée set to a tune that, as usual, had sprung in a few seconds from Elton's meandering fingertips. If banal by *Captain Fantastic* standards, it was at least catchy, unpretentious, and endowed with enough of Elton's old charm to break his two-year chart jinx. Within a week or two, it had made the British Top 30, finally entitling Elton to appear on *Top of the Pops* amid the punk riffraff in his floppy hat, his face oddly rigid and embalmed-looking, like some tight-lipped housewife out shopping in a neighbourhood gone to the dogs.

In late November, when 'Part-Time Love' was still clambering towards its eventual 15th place in the British charts, a second Elton single was suddenly lobbed out after it. The approach of Christmas had brought the customary crop of Christmas records, hoping to cash in on seasonal sentiment. 'Song for Guy', his piano requiem for the young Rocket messenger boy, seemed an ideal contender.

The funereal piece was scarcely in the shops when it took on an unpleasant real-life dimension. Elton collapsed at home, complaining of acute chest pains and unable to get his breath. The doctor who was called suspected a heart attack, and had him rushed by ambulance to the special coronary unit at the London Clinic. The trouble was subsequently diagnosed as 'exhaustion', brought on by the rigours of promoting his new album and playing five-a-side football in a charity match for Goaldiggers. David Croker, who had known Elton for years, made a more informed diagnosis. 'It was an anxiety attack.'

The medical emergency, however, proved more effective than any amount of expensive promotion and hype. News that Elton John was in hospital after a suspected heart emergency prompted an immediate, rather ghoulish clamour for his new single with its well-publicised theme of mourning and death. 'Song for Guy' shot to number four in Britain. It would probably have reached number one but for a pre-Christmas manufacturing decision by Elton's new British distributor, Phonogram. 'They'd got two big hits – "Song For Guy" and "YMCA" by Village People,' David Croker remembered. 'They decided to give the final big retail push to Village People.'

The London Clinic's advice to Elton to cut down on anxiety and take things easier fell on unresponsive ears. Less than a month after his 'funny heart thing', as he continued to call it, Rocket Records announced that his retirement was over. He would begin playing live concerts again early in 1979.

The change of heart came suddenly that December, when Elton accepted an invitation to perform at the British music industry's annual equivalent to the Oscar ceremony. The huge welcome he received – plus seeing *A Single Man* now at number eight in Britain and 15 in America – convinced him there truly was life after punk rock.

At the outset, all was meant to be modest, low-profile and small scale. The mad, manic Elton of the mid-Seventies, he announced, had been laid to rest for ever. There would be no more huge stadium shows; no more stages crowded with people; no more Hollywood stairways, flashing neon or pouring dry ice. He would play only intimate venues, to small audiences, not even using the band he had kept in cold storage for almost two years. There would be just him on piano and Ray Cooper on percussion. And no more gallivanting round the world. England, his England was the only place to be. The Northwood Hills saloon-bar entertainer would come back into his own.

But over lunch with the British rock promoter Harvey Gold-smith, everything suddenly changed yet again. 'Elton said he didn't want to do another European tour, because it was too boring,' Goldsmith remembers. 'He said he'd do a couple in Paris, but he wanted to play somewhere "interesting". I said, "Like where?" He said, "Russia." I said, "OK".'

The attitude of Russia to rock throughout its first twenty-five years had been a steadfast and stony-faced 'Nyet'. Born as it had been at the height of the Fifties Cold War, it figured almost top of the Kremlin's list of contemptible capitalist vices. From the Elvis Presley era onward, *Pravda*, the official newspaper, and Tass, the official news agency, had regularly fulminated against the 'decadent' and 'primitive' music, and its power to turn young people's thoughts away from healthy pursuits, like building dams, driving combine harvesters and manufacturing safety pins.

In this, as much else, *Pravda* and Tass were wilfully blind. Russian youth was as besotted by rock music as youth everywhere, even though forced to hear it illicitly via overseas radio services and hugely expensive black market records. So great had the interest become, there had even been a few tentative concert appearances in Moscow by anodyne European acts, like Cliff Richard and Boney M. But in the eyes of the regime, the music simply did not exist.

'I decided the only way to go was strictly by the book,' Harvey Goldsmith says. 'So I went through all the proper official channels at the Foreign Office. They said they'd pass on the request to the Russian Ministry of Culture, but they had no idea what the response would be.'

Goldsmith's approach came at a fortunate moment. Russia in the Brezhnev era had been gradually unbending to Western culture and consumerism. The men in the Kremlin realised the passion of young Russians for rock music, and saw the wisdom of providing it under official auspices, rather than seeing it grow as an underground movement. An additional factor was that the 1980 Olympic Games were due to be held in Moscow, prompting a major push in national PR and a determined thaw in the country's traditional image of frozen joylessness. Rock music was thus to be officially recognised and, for the right kind of Western rock star, every door would be opened.

There had long been in existence an Anglo-Soviet cultural treaty, under which Russian ballet troupes or balalaika players could perform in Britain, and Britain would send over corresponding amounts of opera, Shakespeare plays and readings from Charles Dickens. In January 1979, an official of the Soviet Ministry of Culture, Vladimir Kokonin, flew to London to renew this treaty for the next two years. During his visit, he attended one of Elton's new-style intimate shows in Oxford, flanked by Foreign Office minders and Soviet Embassy staff. 'There was a lunch at Lancaster House, which I went to,' Harvey Goldsmith says. 'At the end, this Russian got up and said the treaty would be renewed, there'd be more opera, Dickens and Shakespeare, "and we shall provide music for the masses." Everyone turned round and started toasting me, and I suddenly realised we were in.'

It was arranged that Elton should go in late May, when the Russian winter had finally ended, giving a total of eight concerts in Leningrad and Moscow. To complete the cultural tie, there would be an unprecedented live hook-up with BBC Radio One, and the tape of the broadcast would be released by the Soviet record label Melodiya. Five days before departure, Harvey Goldsmith was approached by the comedy scriptwriters Dick Clement and Ian La Frenais with a plan to make a film documentary of the trip. The deal agreed, extra visas had to be provided for a film crew. 'Normally, visas took ages to come through, but these appeared like lightning,' Goldsmith remembers. 'That was how much the Russians wanted us.'

The fee was a purely nominal one of £4,000. But in addition the Russians offered flights and first-class hotel accommodation for twelve people. Elton, once again, made it a family trip, inviting his mother and stepfather. The party would also include John Reid, Ray Cooper, Clive Franks, Harvey Goldsmith and Geoffrey Ellis, Reid's legal adviser, somewhat bemused to be taking his first-ever Rocket 'freebie'.

Thus, Elton's intended small-scale and semi-private return from retirement materialised in an eleven-country tour, beginning in Stockholm, Sweden, moving on to Paris and the Theatre Royal, Drury Lane in London and then – at yet another superstar whim – Tel Aviv, Israel. The new-style show featured Elton alone at the piano for its first hour, then augmented by Ray Cooper's percussion for a further hour and a half.

The sell-out success of this trans-European comeback was matched by that of the football team he had unwillingly left behind. Again, under Graham Taylor, Watford contrived a leap forward in the dying moments of the season, winning promotion from Division Three to Division Two in their very last match. Subsequently they reached the semi-final of the Football League Cup, losing 3–1 on aggregate to Roy Dwight's old team, Nottingham Forest. Elton was ecstatic and, on leaving for Russia, presented Taylor with the gold disc he had just received for sales of *A Single Man*.

On Sunday 20 May he arrived at Moscow airport, suitably attired in worker's cloth cap, satin anorak and pantaloons tucked, Cossack-style, into patent leather boots. With him and his twelve-person entourage also came Ian La Frenais, a film crew and a large contingent of British and American reporters, poised to record every utterance of what the *Daily Mail* had already dubbed 'the bizarre Czar of rock'. Appropriately, the press group included Robert Hilburn, whose review in the *Los Angeles Times*, nine years before, had given Elton the key to another, seemingly impenetrable continent.

Expecting frozen wastes, he found an 88-degree-Fahrenheit heatwave, which forced him to doff his cap as immigration officials scrutinised his passport and stared at his Cossack outfit. Quotable quips came nineteen to the dozen. 'I don't know if they've heard of Watford in Russia, but they soon will. Mind you, this could be the last time you see me. If they don't like you in Moscow, you end up down a salt mine.'

From the airport, Elton and his entourage were driven to Moscow railway station, to board the midnight Red Arrow express for the eight-and-a-half-hour journey to Leningrad. A special deluxe carriage had been provided to shield the superstar from normal Soviet railway experiences, such as dirt, acrid tobacco smoke, sleeping compartments shared by men and women, and washroom taps emitting nothing but liquid rust.

Elton's four Leningrad concerts were to be at the 3,800-seat Bolshoi Concert Hall, close to the square containing the tsars' Winter Palace and the Hermitage. All four had sold out as soon as they were announced, and eight-rouble ($8 or £4.50) tickets were now changing hands on the black market for almost twenty times their face value. One boy to whom Robert Hilburn talked had travelled from Kiev, 1,000 miles away, but still had been unable to get in to any of the concerts.

As promoter and liaison man, Harvey Goldsmith's chief concern was that Goskoncert, the government booking agency, still did not fully appreciate the kind of show Elton did, or the effect it might have on young members of its audience. 'I tried to put it all up front. "Look, the kids may get into the aisles and dance. And if there's any problem with the material he's going to do, tell me now." But none of it seemed to be a problem.'

In fact, most tickets had gone to the privileged élite whose lives had little to do with the familiar Soviet images of shabbiness, shortage and queuing. Ninety per cent of the first night's audience were Party officials, their wives and families, filling the front rows, with the lucky few genuine Elton fans crammed in far to the rear. British journalist Paul Donovan sat between a twenty-one-year-old girl, the height of fashion in her scalloped early Seventies jacket, and two nervous boys in the blue jeans that were Communist Russia's most prized contraband. Before the performance there was a lengthy broadcast address, including biographical sketches of Elton and Ray Cooper. Out in the street, meanwhile, thousands of teenagers who had been unable to get tickets were held back by massed police, militiamen and bobble-hatted sailors from the Baltic Fleet.

Taking the stage in another variant of his cloth-capped worker-cum-Cossack outfit, contact lenses once again replacing glasses, Elton said, 'Dobriy vecher' (good evening) then sat at a solitary Steinway grand piano to play old hits now as well known in Russia as anywhere else: 'Your Song', 'Daniel', 'Don't Let the Sun Go Down on Me' and 'Rocket Man' (translated in the programme as 'Cosmonaut').

It was anything but easy work. As the Leninesque leprechaun toiled at his keyboard, the front rows of Party officials, deserving bureaucrats and hand-picked members of obedient 'youth leagues' all watched in stolid silence, occasionally turning round, puzzled by the stubborn cheering and clapping from the real rock fans at the back. Not even the heartbroken sincerity of 'Candle in the Wind' could dispel the atmosphere of some village Women's Institute talk, going subtly but disastrously wrong. Robert Hilburn felt an eerie déjà vu of that other uneasy overture at the Troubadour. 'When Elton kicked away the piano bench à Jerry Lee Lewis and fell to his knees during "Bennie and the Jets",' Hilburn wrote, 'it was easy to imagine he was really praying for help.'

He persevered, however, in the best tradition of Reggie Dwight, projecting over the rigid official heads to the far-away but persistent signs of life. And, in the second hour, aided by Ray Cooper's percussive pyrotechnics, everything suddenly ignited. The genuine fans broke out of their rearward ghetto, surging down the aisles, clapping, whistling, dancing, making peace V-signs, flinging carnations and tulips on to the stage. The dozens of ushers, guards, invigilators and name-takers made no move to intervene. In a society founded on iron crowd control, it was an incredible moment.

The finale was a home run through all his old bourgeois rabble-rousers, 'Saturday Night's Alright for Fighting', 'Pinball Wizard', 'Crocodile [or, as it might be, Krokodil] Rock' and, as an audacious farewell touch, the Beatles' borscht Beach Boy parody, 'Back in the USSR'. 'I never meant to do that song,' Elton admitted later. 'It just popped into my head. I didn't know the chords, or any of the words except the title. So I just kept singing that over and over again.'

Unprecedented scenes continued for half an hour after Elton and Ray Cooper had left the tulip-strewn stage, with teenagers refusing to disperse, standing firm against officialdom with chants of 'Elton, Elton'. Outside, hundreds more broke through the police barriers to press around the exits, buttonholing those who emerged with cries of 'What was he like?' and entreaties to buy their official programmes.

In his third-floor dressing-room, Elton could hear the same kind of desperately adoring cries that had once fallen on deaf Romanoff ears. 'These kids are really incredible,' he said, genuinely moved. 'They're starved of music. I hope I'm just the first of many who come here to play for them.' At the time, he had no idea that the 2,000 filling the tram-lined street were those who had not been able to watch him perform.

The American and British press, next morning, were as jubilant as if Russia had given up communism overnight. ELTON JOHN, SUPER-CZAR, ROCKS THEM BACK IN THE USSR, said the London *Daily Mail*. ELTON JOHN STUNS SOVIET ROCK FANS, said the *Daily Telegraph*. ROCK STAR RISES OVER RUSSIA, said the *Los Angeles Times*. LENINGRAD'S YOUNG PEOPLE MOB ELTON JOHN, said the *New York Times*.

Even the Russian press was indulgent, after its own peculiar fashion. *Pravda*'s story about Elton seized on his many public references to his unhappy boyhood, clearly deducing rock to be a by-product of decaying family values in the West. A piece in Russia's nearest approach to a teenage magazine noted, with Tolstoyan innocence, that Elton's style was marked by its 'gay originality . . . While some people like this style, others find it excessively naughty.'

None the less, there were some attempts at censorship. At the three remaining Leningrad concerts, the fans were checked from rushing down to the stage front. Elton was asked not to finish with 'Back in the USSR' – though he did so, anyway. But he agreed to a request that he shouldn't kick his piano stool over, nor offend Russian sensibilities by attacking the Steinway grand quite so hard.

He was, for the most part, the model of politeness and diplomacy, taking a keen interest in all things Russian, laughing off the dreary 'international' cuisine and snail's-pace restaurant service, standing still for endless pictures with his arm round his mum's shoulders or sportingly getting down in the traditional Cossack pose of crouch-and-kick. The only slight wobble occurred on the third day, after a night of much Russian champagne mixed with tinned mandarin juice, and high jinks with the film crew, which climaxed in Elton's throwing a full glass of vodka into Harvey Goldsmith's face.

The next morning, he was to make a specially arranged tour of the Winter Palace and Hermitage museums, which would also serve as a sequence in the film by Dick Clement and Ian La Frenais. He had been eager to see the museums' imperial treasures and collection of French Impressionist paintings but, when the time came, was unable to haul himself out of bed. He arrived at the Hermitage two hours late, still deeply hung over, and, after only two minutes, walked off in a sudden tantrum, leaving his film crew with no footage and his Russian guides staring in mystification and pique. ELTON SNUBS RUSSIANS IN WINTER PALACE REVOLT, the *Daily Mail* duly reported.

His four Moscow concerts were in the Rossiya Concert Hall, overlooking the onion domes of St Basil's Cathedral and the cobbled expanse of Red Square, where soldiers mount goose-stepping guard on Lenin's tomb around the clock. Once again, the bulk of the tickets had gone to Party officials and favourites, leaving only a few hundred to be fought for by hungry young rock fans. Many occupants of the front rows arrived in the chauffeur-driven Chaika limousines available only to senior Politbureau members. The running order was the same as in Leningrad, including 'Back in the USSR', but with one curious addition. Halfway through his first solo hour, Elton suddenly switched from Steinway grand to Yamaha electric piano and struck up 'He'll Have to Go', the same mournful Jim Reeves ballad with which fifteen-year-old Reggie Dwight had begun his uphill residency at the Northwood Hills Hotel.

As at his Leningrad first night, the beginning was muted and the end spectacular, with hundreds of young Russians forgetting Party decorum and rushing down the aisles to the stage front. Presents were continually handed up to Elton aides: a cuddly toy, flowers, books and numerous handwritten notes. At one point, a string of pearls landed on the stage. Elton returned for three encores, even though his throat had been giving him trouble. 'It started to go dodgy at the sound check,' he said afterwards. 'But somehow I shouted and screamed and gargled my way through.'

The second night's concert was beamed live to BBC Radio One, available throughout the United Kingdom and in many European countries as well. No rock star before had reached so many people at once, over so many cultural and political divides.

Between concerts, he, Sheila and Derf, pursued by their constant semicircle of snapping photographers, strolled round the red-walled Kremlin precincts and attended a performance of *Swan Lake* in the sumptuous Bolshoi Theatre. Elton was also shown the extensive building preparations for the following year's Olympic Games, an event which excited him so much that he offered to write a theme song to accompany the official Games logo of a cuddly little cartoon Russian bear. Another afternoon, he went to a football match between Moscow Dynamo and the Red Army, was presented with a football autographed by the Red Army team, and promised to try to organise some friendly matches between them and Watford.

At one of his press conferences, a Russian journalist asked in halting English whether he was against apartheid in sport. 'Yes,' he replied. 'I object to apartheid, whether it's because of colour, class or sexual preference.' In Russia at that time, as everyone present knew, the punishment for homosexuality was five years' imprisonment.

A *Daily Telegraph* leading article struck the only sceptical note, accusing Russia of using Elton's concerts to placate its young in the time-honoured dictatorial tradition of 'bread and circuses'. What had happened in Moscow and Leningrad, the *Telegraph* said, was that rock music had been detached from Western democracy and been remoulded as part of a new, subtler communism. But even the *Telegraph* leader writer had only benign feelings towards the performer whose music had proved so international and ideologically malleable.

For everyone on the Russian side, the enterprise had been a phenomenal success. Normally po-faced and cautious diplomats at Britain's Moscow embassy were openly calling it the biggest step forward in East–West understanding since Nikita Khrushchev had visited Hollywood. The ultimate sign of Soviet capitulation occurred after the third concert, when Tass filled its office display windows with publicity material and posters of Elton.

He arrived back at Heathrow airport on 31 May, 'knackered' but exhilarated, still wearing his big cap and Watford scarf. Pinned to his anorak was a badge reading 'Lend us a quid', stressing how unmercenary had been the purpose of the trip. With him came Harvey Goldsmith, carrying the blue bag in which the Russians had paid out £4,000 in notes so ancient, they had to be taken to the Bank of England and exchanged for new ones.

Sipping restorative Lucozade, Elton told his airport press conference the tour had been 'one of the most memorable and happy I've ever been on. We took along the Ludo, the Monopoly and the backgammon, thinking we'd be locked up in our hotel all night. But the country isn't dark, grey, grim or drab – it's beautiful, and the people are very warm. Leningrad is a marvellous city, and the hospitality was tremendous.'

So was he now a convert to communism and totalitarianism? 'I'm against bigotry and prejudice and persecution,' he replied. 'But if that stopped me playing my music, I wouldn't play it here, because of the National Front or the campaign against homosexuality. You don't go in with guns blazing, saying, "I want this and that." You've got to approach things gently. I'd be very presumptuous to consider myself an ambassador of any sort, but I'm glad to do my bit.'

Ignoring press pleas to take off his cap, he was then ushered to his Rolls-Royce and driven off to satisfy pent-up cravings for an Indian curry and a cup of tea brewed in a pot, not a samovar.

He kept his promise and wrote a song for the 1980 Moscow Olympic Games. But by that time, the cuddly little cartoon bear had sent tanks to invade Afghanistan, and the Games were subject to an international boycott. At the Foreign Office's 'suggestion', Elton's song never found its way to his new friends in Moscow.

The spent force and yesterday's man was back in his old niche as the world's most talked-about rock star. As in 1971, when his professional demise also was confidently predicted, Elton had contrived to reinvent himself.

The autumn of 1979 found him on top form again, both as performer and communicator, taking time off from a new American tour (headlined 'Back in the USSA') to hold court in a $1,000-per-day suite at the New York Waldorf Towers. An extravagant centre spread in the *Daily Mirror* shows him in décolleté silk pyjamas, posing in exaggeratedly camp style, cheeks drawn in and lips puckered, one hand archly patting the back of his head. An adjacent mirror reflects the new hair transplant, dark, patchy and vague, like sandbars seen through the shallow waters of Scapa Flow.

The new non-glitter, contact-lens look is accompanied by a new honesty and plain-spokenness about himself. He is now completely open about his bisexuality, and will talk about it to any interviewer, freely and without embarrassment. 'I realise it's not everyone's cup of tea, and I try not to dwell on it too much,' he tells the *Mirror*'s Alasdair Buchan. 'But I had to get it off my chest. That's the way I am, and it's no good hiding it.'

The camp pose, however, is pure parody, showing not what he is but what he isn't. His point is that not all men with homosexual tendencies conform to the mincing stereotype of current gay comedians like Larry Grayson and John Inman. 'A lot of them are just very confused, frightened people. I know it was far easier for me to come out than for many others. They go through a hell of a lot of pain, and I would support anyone who was totally frank, because it's never easy. I've had a lot of letters from people who think they're gay, but live in small communities where it would be very hard to say so. I rarely write back to anyone, but I wrote back to every one of those people and said, "If you ever get down in the dumps, write again."'

He also speaks for the first time about his mother's feelings on the subject. 'From the beginning, she always said, "Listen. Don't ever

be deceitful to me. Tell me, even if you think I won't like it." I
never thought I'd go to bed with someone of my own sex. When I
did, she was the first person I phoned and told. I said "You told me
never to be deceitful, so this is what happened."'

So tasteful and sympathetic was his treatment by the British
tabloids that Sheila herself gave two lengthy interviews, confiding to
the *Daily Express* WHY I WORRY ABOUT MY YOUNG ELTON, and
telling the *Daily Mail* about THE JEKYLL AND HYDE THAT IS MY
SON ELTON.

Tactfully prompted by the *Express*'s David Wigg, she admitted
that Elton's telephone call had been a shock, but said she had long
ago come to terms with what he was. 'A lot of people didn't admire
him for saying it. Some used to shout odd names after him. But he
was strong enough to come out of the closet when there's thousands
more that won't. Half the people who look at him and say, "Oh,
he's a queen" are the same way, if they'd be honest with themselves.
But I don't think he'd ever have been if it wasn't for show business.
Show business did it, definitely.

'Loneliness – that's what I worry about for him more than
anything else. I think he's desperate. He's got all the possessions you
could wish for, but that doesn't make him happy. He hasn't anyone
to share it with, and that's what he needs. He says he'd like to have
a family. Unfortunately, his lifestyle doesn't allow him to meet
anybody. And he won't allow himself. It's as if he holds back all the
time. I feel that he's got everything – but nothing.'

Also back at full strength was the studio workaholic, keen as ever to
release twice as much product as the market could stand. That April,
three tracks from the abandoned Thom Bell album project had been
resurrected, remixed and issued as a new-style twelve-inch single.
Though none was a hit in Britain, the Beatle-echoey 'Mama Can't
Buy You Love' reached number nine in America, firing up Elton's
enthusiasm for a still bigger comeback in the land that had originally
made him.

Straight after touring Europe, Israel and Russia, he was off making
another album, commuting between Musicland studios in Munich
and Rusk Sound Studios in Hollywood. His style flew in yet another
direction, flavoured now by the disco sound that had been in vogue
since John Travolta's movie *Saturday Night Fever*. For the new album,
Victim of Love, he teamed with songwriter-producer Pete Bellotte,
the man behind new disco stars like the erotic Donna Summer. In
his keenness to fit the new mould, Elton left all the songwriting on
Victim of Love to Bellotte and other lyricists, bizarrely miscellaneous.

There was even a version of the Chuck Berry classic 'Johnny B. Goode'.

The words might have served as an admonition to Elton's manager. For in this period, as the superstar regained the ascendant in every possible constructive and positive way, John Reid was at his most unruly and controversial.

In 1978, Reid had astounded his and Elton's joint circle by becoming engaged to Sarah Forbes, Bryan and Nanette's eighteen-year-old daughter. The eleven-year difference in their ages might have mattered less had Reid not known Sarah as a little girl in the Wentworth days, and had she not known him in his apparently permanent domestic relationship with Elton. The engagement caused particular discomfort to Elton, for whom Sarah was still the little girl who had presented him with a Rolls-Royce-embroidered cushion. Reid was apparently quite serious, even phoning Nina Myskow, who had just joined *The Sun* from *Jackie* magazine, to give her the story exclusively. To general relief, however, the engagement was called off after a few weeks. Sarah Forbes went on to marry the actor John Standing – also some years her senior – and has remained on friendly terms with Reid.

In October 1979, Elton's disco album, *Victim Of Love*, was released, quickly stiffing at number 35 in America and 41 in Britain. Its namesake single did no better, making only 31 in America but not even registering in Britain's charts. John Reid's enraged response was another mass sacking of Rocket Records staff, including the managing director David Croker, whom he had sacked a year previously for the 'Ego' flop but afterwards reinstated.

'The pathetic sight of a small group of colourfully dressed people locked out on a Mayfair pavement is the latest evidence of pop millionaire John Reid's increasing eccentricity,' Nigel Dempster's *Daily Mail* diary reported. 'Passers-by in South Audley Street were treated to the vision of Rocket staff being unceremoniously bundled out on to the pavement . . . A victim of last year's screaming match, former promotions manager Arthur Sherriff, tells me, "These sackings are an annual event at the very least."'

Like Elton, Reid was a walking weather-house rotation of Jekyll and Hyde. The public shrieker and punch-thrower also hankered for respectability and social standing and, for a time, even contemplated entering politics. In 1979, he got involved with the Conservative Party, just as it was preparing to fight its first general election under Margaret Thatcher's leadership. He cultivated the acquaintanceship of several Tory MPs and let it be known that, if offered a Parliamentary seat, he would willingly stand. The party responded to these overtures, seeing in him the kind of thrustful young self-made man it needed for its new meritocratic image. Reid underwent serious grooming and self-grooming as a prospective candidate, absorbing policy, attending cocktail parties, even speaking at one or two dinners to test his oratorical gifts.

Three weeks before the election, he was asked to stand for the far northern seat of Orkney and Shetland, but refused, deciding that, after all, pop managership and politics did not mix. Certainly, the career of a bright young Thatcherite MP would hardly have been compatible with stories like this, from the 1 October issue of *The Sun*:

ELTON'S MANAGER IS ARRESTED AFTER 'HITTING DOORMAN'

Superstar Elton John's manager has been arrested for allegedly attacking a hotel doorman with a walking stick.

Police said that John Reid, 30, lost his temper over a car parked outside the posh Fairmont Hotel in San Francisco's Nob Hill. The doorman, John Figuero, asked Reid to shut the car door because it was blocking other traffic.

Mr Charles Sandovic, the police spokesman, said yesterday: 'Reid is said to have become very abusive, and attacked the doorman with the black, silver-tipped cane he was carrying.

'He allegedly struck Figuero several times on the back and has been charged with battery.'

Figuero had to have medical treatment to his back and is considering suing Reid.

Because Reid is a Londoner and his only identification was his British passport, he was charged at the city's central jail, but bailed in his own recognisance.

FIFTEEN

The Sun Also Rises

LONG before the Seventies had limped to an end, they were generally agreed to have been an unmitigated disaster. The whole decade seemed little but a long hangover from the Sixties, in which the carried-on ideals of 'love' and 'peace' had looked increasingly fatuous and futile. Though public pressure had finally ended the Vietnam war, other nasty little wars raged unchecked, and largely forgotten, in Nicaragua, Cambodia, Northern Ireland, the Lebanon. Notions of human brotherhood had barely alleviated the problem of world famine, or the plight of untold political prisoners under innumerable repressive regimes. Across Europe, terrorist murder was an almost daily fact of life, very often committed by young men whose long hair, blue denim and 'Have a nice day' patches were identical with those of the fraternal multitudes at Sixties rock festivals.

America's election of a wholly liberal, wholly moral president, Jimmy Carter, had brought about only chronic financial instability and a ghastly dip in national pride, epitomised by the taking hostage of an entire embassy in Teheran. In Britain, under successive Labour governments, the welfare state was running amok, with millions apparently preferring unemployment benefit to work, inflation out of control and trade union tyranny rampant. In Britain, 1979 was the so-called Winter of Discontent, when strikes paralysed public transport, schools and hospitals, and rubbish sacks festered in mountains on the streets. Different indeed from the winter of 1969, with its golden, regretful afterglow. In 1979, no one could get out of the old decade fast enough.

The decade ahead glowed with compensatory allure. After those ten long years of dragged-out whimsy and illusion, the Eighties approached Britain in a heady aura of cool realism. Science and technology, fifteen years at the nadir of chic, suddenly made a remarkable comeback. The fashionable rage was 'high tech', a gaunt modernity of design in furniture and decor, sweeping away pine floors, Victorian dressers, Art Deco ducks and Portobello Road bric-a-brac. Personal computers appeared in thousands of homes, no longer a vaguely sinister appendage to government, but a miraculously labour-saving, 'user-friendly' domestic pet. Cars lost their Seventies flimsiness and hollowness, growing chunky and soft-bumpered, full of user-friendly dials, lights, even voices, to assist and reassure their drivers. Movies like *Star Wars*, *Buck Rogers* and *Battlestar Galactica* made science fiction more popular than it had been since the mid-Fifties. New pop stars, like Gary Numan, all seemed to be rocket men, singing in the flat, jerky automaton voices from studios apparently located somewhere in inner space.

That long-delayed miracle, 'the Future', seemed ready to dawn at long last. One could hardly wait to kick away the Seventies' useless husk, and cross into the Eighties' vista of chaste black rooms, house-trained robots, bright chromium and cosy red indicator lights.

By coincidence, at this pivotal point between epochs, America and Britain each acquired a new leader. In both cases, the national choice was one which, a very few years before, would have seemed inconceivable. America's was a former actor in Hollywood B-pictures, already so aged and bewildered that he was unable to frame the simplest utterance without help from teleprompters and cue cards. Britain's was a nondescript Tory woman whose shrill voice rose and fell curiously out of synch' with her words, like an imperfectly dubbed foreign film.

Outwardly dissimilar as Ronald Reagan and Margaret Thatcher might seem, there was – as they would soon reveal – a profound kinship between them. For both were creations of publicity and marketing campaigns, so stupendously resourced as to make even the hype machine of rock music seem moderate by comparison. And both, lacking any self-consciousness or shame, were perfect mouthpieces for their respective parties' promise to the electorate. An end to the woozy liberalism and *laissez-faire* chaos of government in the Sixties and Seventies. A new atmosphere of purpose, efficiency and hard work. A new spirit of enterprise, self-help, national pride and feeling good about oneself.

Like the Sixties and Seventies, the Eighties had to run a couple of years before revealing their true character. In 1982, Margaret Thatcher sent a naval force to recapture one of Britain's last colonial territories, the Falkland Islands, from an Argentinian invasion force. A few months later, Ronald Reagan dispatched troops to crush an alleged communist coup on the West Indian island of Grenada. What will engross future historians may not be the cause or necessity of these operations so much as the way each was successfully used to sell leader to nation by their respective marketing organisations. To America, in the invasion of Grenada's undefended beaches, Reagan had magically wiped away the agony of Vietnam. To Britain, for mowing down the Argentinian boy-conscripts, Margaret Thatcher became Winston Churchill born again. Thus was the seal set on the two most astonishingly successful Western leaders of modern times.

Mrs Thatcher's transformation was accomplished with the help of one wholly unlooked-for ally. For fifty years, Britain's only significant mass circulation tabloid newspaper had been the left-wing *Daily Mirror*. In 1969, the Australian press tycoon Rupert Murdoch had bought the *Mirror*'s ailing broadsheet stablemate *The Sun*, turning it into a tabloid identical in every respect save that on its third page every day, flouting all Fleet Street convention, there appeared a bare-breasted young woman. For all the resultant controversy among moralists and feminists, *The Sun* had remained a conventional product, vying with its competitors first and foremost in the retailing of news. But with the Falklands war, its hour – as well as Margaret Thatcher's – had come.

Though Argentina had always been the most anglophile of Latin American countries, *The Sun* instantly characterised its people with primitive racism as 'Argies'. It declared itself 'the Paper Behind Our Boys', following the government line in tones of hysterical chauvinism not heard in Britain since August 1914. Broadcasters who questioned the conduct of the war were denounced in *Sun* editorials as 'traitors'. The quintessential moment occurred when pictures came back of Argentina's archaic cruiser *General Belgrano* being blown apart by British missiles. *The Sun*'s headline, displaying all the humane sensibility of a football thug putting the boot in, was GOTCHA!

So for Britain, once again, the Future failed to arrive. Overnight, the 1980s leapt back to the 1880s, our dreadnoughts masters of the seas again, our jolly tars triumphant and the dagoes licked. Instead of that high-tech vista came a landscape testifying to our regained glory as a great war-making power. In the microchip age, the great buzzwords turned out to be 'traditional', 'original' and 'classic'. Pubs transformed themselves into semblances of Boer War gin palaces or Dickensian coffee rooms. Fortunes were made in the mass-production of bogus nineteenth-century goods, from 'Victorian villager' soap-on-a-rope to 'Victorian country house' chutney and mustard foot-soak. Such things had existed, of course, in the Sixties and Seventies, but were always recognised as pastiche. In the Eighties, they began to be believed. Mrs Thatcher herself spoke of restoring

'Victorian values' and in this, at least, spoke the truth. For the values that returned were the Victorian ones which the previous two decades, for all their faults, had seemed to diminish: class snobbery, social cruelty, racism and blind prejudice.

All this was faithfully reflected in *The Sun*. Even before GOTCHA! the paper had adopted a formula uniquely blending the nationalistic and moral fervour of the new age with the reality of its tastes and appetites. News, in the form of daily political and social happenings, had little place in *The Sun*. Its world was the fantasy one of show business, television soap opera, royal tittle-tattle and its own daily bingo game and mammarily remarkable but airheaded 'Page Three girls'. The all-time classic *Sun* story illustrates the paper's huge distance from any traditional purposes of journalism. In 1986, the ex-girl-friend of a TV comedian named Freddie Starr gave it an anecdote, already three years old. Feeling hungry one night in 1983, Starr had picked up her pet hamster, jokily put it between two pieces of bread and pretended to bite into it. By any sane news value, the tired little tale barely rated mention at the foot of some show-biz gossip column. In *The Sun* it made front-page splash in three-inch headlines, FREDDIE STARR ATE MY HAMSTER!

Even by the dubious standard of Fleet Street, the paper's ethics and practices were unique. People whom it wished to feature in its 'stories', whether famous or obscure, were pursued and harassed with utter ruthlessness, into their homes, into hospital, even on to the very mortuary slab. On two infamous occasions, both connected with the Falklands war, 'interviews' were fabricated with people who had refused to speak to the paper. Its editorials – written in kindergarten English, for an imagined attention span of about eight seconds – combined slavish pro-Thatcherism with rabid xenophobia. Not only its prejudices but also its language echoed that of the construction site. To *The Sun*, French people were 'Frogs', Germans 'Krauts', Japanese 'Nips', and homosexuals 'poofs'.

The result was a commercial triumph, selling over 4 million copies and claiming to reach 13 million readers daily, to the near-eclipse of the essentially decent and ethical *Daily Mirror*. The *Mirror*'s response was to ape *The Sun* – a lead quickly followed by its other daily rival, the *Star*, and the *Sunday People* and *News of the World*. Britain's press in the Eighties could therefore sink to its all-time low with all-powerful justification: 'It's what people want.'

The change of tone where Elton was concerned happened as the decades revolved. In November 1979, he was talking about his bisexuality to a *Daily Express* whose editorial tone was as sympathetically restrained as some social worker or therapist. In August 1980, the same paper's William Hickey diary carried this ominously unpleasant item:

> The only woman in Elton John's life has left him.
> His mother.
> After nursing her gay little lad through the rigours of stardom for the past 10 years, Mrs Sheila Farebrother has decided to make a go of it on her own.
> She has bought a house in Brighton, miles away from her son's Windsor mansion. And no longer will she be popping in every day to make sure her superstar son's smalls are laundered.
> Of course, Elton is 33, and it's high time he and his mum went their separate ways.
> But the two have relied on each other for so long that it comes as a surprise.
> Indeed, whenever there was a handbag fight between Elton and his diminutive manager John Reid, Sheila used to come into the offices to sort it out . . .
> There's only one problem now that Sheila is moving on. Who will water Elton's newly-transplanted thatch?

At the beginning, ironically, few seemed likelier to prosper in Mrs Thatcher's Golden Age. Almost the first image we have of Elton in the Eighties is his black-windowed Rolls turning into the gateway of the Houses of Parliament. The occasion was a party to launch the *Guinness Book of Hits of the Seventies*, compiled by Elton's chief media mouthpiece Paul Gambaccini, and attended also by lesser hit-makers such as Freddie Mercury and Gary Glitter. Elton upstaged all, arriving – with Kiki Dee – in a schoolboy's cap and striped blazer, to set off £400,000-worth of jewellery including a diamond-encrusted watch. During the reception in a panelled Commons committee-room, he was seen chatting with Norman St John Stevas, then Leader of the House. 'I'm trying to make him into a Tory,' St John Stevas quipped.

A small kerfuffle subsequently broke out when it was alleged that, on a conducted tour of the Commons Chamber after the party, Elton had been allowed to sit in the Speaker's Chair. A Conservative MP, John Carlisle, wrote to Norman St John Stevas, complaining it was 'a gross breach of respect'. But the Cartier-encrusted schoolboy remained uncensured.

His apparently secure place in the national pantheon seemed confirmed by his inclusion in a 1980 BBC-TV series *Best of British*, singling out those who had most enhanced Britain's international prestige in recent years. Again the interviewer was Paul Gambaccini, whose on-camera arrival at Woodside gives a vivid picture of the state in which Elton now lived. We see Gambaccini's car turn off the Old Windsor road into a tree-lined precinct, guarded by police, slalomed by traffic cones and punctuated by signboards warning 'Trespassers Will Be Prosecuted' and 'Guard Dogs On Patrol'. A quarter of a mile on, we reach the iron main gate, its electronic entryphone to be buzzed by 'Authorised Callers Only'. Thence down the long drive, past its signpost 'Elton Road', bumping over sleeping policemen with the caution of an armoured convoy in Belfast. Here, finally, is the chunky Queen Anne house and its occupant, as well-guarded and sequestered as ever Elvis was at Graceland.

We see Elton at his piano, surrounded by the same vermilion leather buttonback sofas he had at Hercules. Both his face and waistline have noticeably filled out again. His transplanted hair is apparently so abundant that a loose strand can even be made to fall carelessly down over his forehead. He wears a plain white sweater with the sleeves pushed up, and almost no jewellery. He could be any young businessman showing off the rewards of the Thatcher enterprise culture.

His view of the decade just past is characteristically forthright. 'Great from a career point of view but from a personal point of view, terrible. A lot of the time, I was a complete mess. Around 1975, especially, I started acting like a real spoiled brat. There are parts of it I can't even remember.'

He describes the effort he has made – in his own estimation, at least – to come down to earth and join the human race again. 'I'd go away on my own, following the England football team; I'd check into a hotel, then ring my mother and say, "Well! I made it!" She'd say, "So? A grown man feels proud because he's unpacked his own suitcase?"' With due apology, he yet again mentions what a beneficent stabilising influence Watford has been. 'There, people don't treat me as anything special. I can just be myself. It's wonderful.'

The programme also fascinatingly demonstrates Elton's ability to produce a pop melody almost instantaneously from any words handed to him. In this case, the words are some of the most resounding ever written in English, John Donne's famous 'No man is an island . . .' The scrap of paper from Paul Gambaccini is briefly studied. The pudgy fingers reach and press. In five or six seconds, the voice has found the hook. A new track is nearly ready for the guys in the band:

No man is an Island
Entire of it self
Every man is a peece of the Continent
A part of the maine . . .

Any man's death diminishes me
Because I am involved in Mankinde.
And therefore, never send to know for whom the bell tolls.
It tolls for thee.

The *Daily Telegraph*'s TV critic, Sylvia Clayton, wasn't impressed. 'The cadences he produced, rather like a syncopated hymn, put me in mind of Oscar Wilde's Canon Chasuble, who had a sermon adaptable for any occasion.' She felt it was wrong to present so interesting and articulate a personality in the Japanese or Irish mode of 'living national treasure'.

Professionally, he was back from the wilderness. Pop had passed through its punk holocaust and was moving forward again, which, as ever, meant circling back and back. For up-and-coming bands, the *sine qua non*, once more, was skill, together with an eclecticism pop had never seen before. New line-ups featured saxes, trumpets, even trombones, experimenting with idioms traditionally excluded from the genre, Latin American, even jazz and bebop. Stage clothes made the same total about-face, from punkdom's tatters and knee-manacles to a revival of the mid-Sixties Mod style, embellished by floppy haircuts, frills, cloaks and enough similar poetic flourishes to label a new movement, the New Romantics. Most of its musicians had been small boys in the early Seventies, and enjoyed the glitter and froth of music then, much as earlier small boys had enjoyed comic books and Saturday morning cinema. The new chart sensation Adam Ant performed in bizarre period clothes amid extravagant settings, all much like those which had first established Elton John. The New Romantic band Spandau Ballet unashamedly acknowledged him as their chief inspiration. An international genre of singer-songwriters, like Billy Joel and Barry Manilow, produced hits as prolifically as he had done in the mid-Seventies, accompanying themselves on piano in the same high, passionate register. It was even revealed that Simon Le Bon, lead vocalist of Duran Duran, had grown up in the same Middlesex suburb as Elton, and even attended the same school. Pinner was a pop powerhouse at last.

Elton's 1980 album, *21 at 33*, took its title from the supposition that his thirty-third birthday coincided with his twenty-first LP. It was, in fact, counting compilations, only his eighteenth, but what did that matter except to mathematical pedants? *21 at 33* proved a commercial success, which restored Elton to the musical foreground in America and Britain, as well as restoring an irreplaceable element to his psyche. For Bernie Taupin and he were back writing songs together, as of old.

Bernie, too, felt he had survived the previous decade, and all its extravagant gifts to him, only by the skin of his teeth. 'The last thing I want to do is glorify the way I was,' he says. 'I hate that press cliché of calling you a survivor just because you've got through binges of drink and drugs, and making a hero out of someone like Jim Morrison, who kills himself with sheer excess. There's nothing heroic in being a fall-down drunk. It's pathetic – and I was pathetic.'

Drying out in Acapulco, in the post-*Blue Moves* period, had dealt with only part of Bernie's problem. Despite the fortune he had earned in song royalties since 1970, his finances were in a chaotic mess. 'For years, I'd spent money without thinking, and borrowed it without thinking. I hadn't cared about anything but getting wasted and having a good time. And suddenly came the day I realised it wasn't a bottomless coffer. The reserves were running dry.'

In 1978, he acquired a new manager, Michael Lippman, who set about the long process of putting his business affairs in order. At the same time, his affair with the celebrated Loree Rodkin came to a painful – though, alas, not final – conclusion. Ten years later, Rodkin would still be pointing to Bernie's scalp, among others, on her belt in an interview with *Vanity Fair* magazine.

Not long after splitting up with Loree Rodkin, he went to a friend's birthday party at the Beverly Hilton hotel. 'I was still feeling pretty sad about life, and hadn't wanted to go to this thing, but I was persuaded to. Standing at the bar there was the most stunning girl I'd ever seen. It sounds silly, but as soon as I looked at her, I thought, "That's the woman for me."'

He discovered her name was Toni Russo, and that her sister was Renée Russo, the top American fashion model of that time. For all his incurably romantic ardour, that seemed as far as Bernie was destined to get. 'I tried to set up a date with her, but she didn't want to know about me. I sent her flowers, but it was still no good. Then she started working as manageress at Lou Adler's club, and, when I walked in one night, there she was behind the bar. So I started talking to her again, and from there we just evolved into a relationship.'

Marrying Toni Russo, in 1979, was Bernie's final salvation from the Seventies. 'She was the one who put everything back together for me. I don't think anyone in my life, apart from my parents, has done more for me, physically and mentally. I'd always dreamed of writing other things, outside the things I did with Elton. I'd talked about it so much, but Toni was the one who really played hardball with me, and said, "Well, don't talk about it all the time. Do it."

'The really phenomenal thing she did was to pull everything together on the financial front. The people I'd had looking after my affairs were very lax, mainly because I couldn't be bothered, and there was no one sitting on top of them, saying, "What's going on?" Toni was the one who got my new manager, Michael Lippman, to go in and find out what was there, and put together a whole new crew to invest it properly.'

The gulf between Elton and him closed as wordlessly as it had opened. In the summer of 1979, while Elton was recording at Superbear Studios in Nice, he asked Bernie and Toni over to stay at the house he had rented in nearby Grasse. As part of the pleasant reunion, Bernie wrote three songs for *21 at 33*, including a memoir of his Acapulco exile called 'Two Rooms at the End of the World'.

The way was not yet open to their old total collaboration. Gary Osborne was still around, contributing three tracks, including the album's hit single, 'Little Jeannie'. In addition – to prove he could keep up with the times – Elton had tried writing with two lyricists of the new generation. One was Rocket Records' expensive new artiste, Judie Tzuke. The other was Tom Robinson, a performer admirable in many respects, not least his sane, plain-spoken declaration that one should be 'glad to be gay'.

Again, the album was co-produced by Elton with his former engineer Clive Franks. Bringing Bernie over was part of a conscious wish to reassemble as many as possible of the team who had made so many hits so easily in carefree days at Château d'Hierouville. The band he put together included his stalwart lead guitarist Davey Johnstone, and even his original bass player and drummer, Dee Murray and Nigel Olsson. In true Seventies longhair style, neither bore any grudge for their unceremonious sacking, five years before. 'I got a call when I was in Los Angeles,' Dee remembered. 'It was the office, the way it always used to be. "Elton's recording, would you like to do some sessions?" I said, "Yeah, great." We seemed to pick up just where we'd left off.'

21 at 33 was Elton's best received album since *Blue Moves*, reaching number twelve in Britain and thirteen in America. The real astonishment was 'Little Jeannie', Gary Osborne's routine ballad, which reached only thirty-three in Britain, but flew to number three on the American singles charts.

Having a US hit album and single meant more to Elton now than it had ever done. His confession of bisexuality, while seeming to cause little backlash at the time, had done long-term damage to his popularity in God-fearing and straitlaced Middle America. To be permitted back to the top of *Billboard*'s and *Cash Box*'s charts seemed to indicate that the whole thing had finally blown over, on both sides of the Atlantic. 'Talking about it affected my popularity far more in the States than in Britain,' Elton himself acknowledged, adding what was to prove the unhappiest false prophecy of his career. 'There are far more maniacally religious people, who care about that sort of thing, in America. The British public, on the other hand, like you to be more upfront. They don't make such issues into big deals.'

His total rehabilitation in America was confirmed by that autumn's sell-out tour, backed by the *21 at 33* studio band, including Dee Murray and Nigel Olsson, and featuring an array of new stage outfits in his most extravagant Seventies styles. One was a sequinned cowboy outfit, another a floppy-capped chauffeur's uniform with two piano keyboards down its front like crisscrossed black-and-white bandoliers. His new publicity picture showed him in a New York policeman's wired cap and uniform tunic, embellished by a double lion's-head brooch at the throat. His face also appeared on an issue of novelty $1 bills, a distinction granted only to select VIPs like President Reagan, Frank Sinatra and the late Elvis Presley.

The climax of the 1980 tour was a free concert in New York's Central Park, with Elton performing to his largest-ever audience, an estimated 400,000. It was a glorious Fall afternoon, as much symbolising the reclamation of the park itself from muggers and fear by cyclists, joggers and skateboarders. The high point was Elton's appearance in a Daisy Duck costume, shaking his yellow beak, stomping webbed feet and wagging the tail that Nature had already started, back in those illicit rock-'n'-roll sessions on the school Steinway.

Among the songs from eighteen albums was a cover version specially relevant to Central Park, with its red-gold trees and skinny-tailed grey squirrels. Striking up John Lennon's 'Imagine', and looking away to the dark cupolas of the Dakota Building, Elton simply said, 'This one's by a friend of mine.'

In 1980, Elton's close-knit executive team lost a key member. David Croker resigned his managing directorship of Rocket Records to join the Hansa production company, handling rival attractions like Japan and Boney M. He subsequently embarked on a totally new career, one for which life with John Reid – being regularly screamed at, fired and rehired – might seem not unsuitable preparation. After years of taking heat in a metaphorical kitchen, David Croker became executive chef with a London catering company.

His successor at Rocket was a go-ahead young man named John Hall, who had arrived as promotions manager a year earlier, having previously owned his own label, Ebony. Hall's task was to reinvigorate an organisation from which all the Seventies champagne fizz seemed to have vanished. The original roster with its outmoded names – Longdancer, Stackridge, China – was moribund. Neil Sedaka, the great hitmaker for Rocket USA, had been allowed to drift away to another label. Apart from Elton and Kiki Dee, no Rocket act had come near a chart hit for years. The company which its co-founder had committed to 'working its b****cks off' seemed flat, dispirited and unready to face the challenge of a brand new decade.

The main hope was Judie Tzuke, a David Croker signing, who combined songwriting abilities with a bruised and melancholy aura much like Kiki Dee's. Her second single for Rocket, 'Stay With Me Till Dawn', was indeed a torch song virtually identical to 'Amoureuse', and an almost exactly similar medium British hit. Elton's label seemed to make a speciality of girl singers prone to extravagant pillow-talk.

During the next couple of years, under John Hall, Rocket enjoyed more hits than ever in its history. The successful artistes were a strangely assorted bunch, reflecting the chaos and caprice of charts in those post-punk days. After Judie Tzuke, a band called the Lambrettas, signed by Hall himself, had a British number seven single with the old Coasters song, 'Poison Ivy'. The surprise number six hit to end them all was an ageing country-and-westerner named Fred Wedlock, singing a lament for all beer-bellies stuffed into blue jeans, called 'The Oldest Swinger in Town'.

Elton was delighted with these several successes, on top of his own resurgence in the British and US charts. One night at the Plaza Athenée Hotel in Paris, he impulsively offered John Hall a substantial share in Rocket. 'He said, "Got a pen, Beryl?" to John Reid, and wrote it out there and then inside a matchbook that I was to get something like 40 per cent of the company,' Hall remembers. 'I could see John sweating while it was going on, and feel pairs of eyes boring into this matchbook, like some slowed-up scene in a Clint

Eastwood movie. Elton made me take it, so I just handed it to John and said, "If you want to give me this, fair enough." And he didn't.'

The operation that John Hall ran through the dawning Eighties was very different from what had begun, back in that seemingly boundless early Seventies sunshine. The days of 'looning' and 'ligging', of special trains to Moreton-in-Marsh, of lavish buffets torn apart and champagne bars drunk dry, of office outings to LA by charter jet and block bookings at the Beverly Hilton, of Cartier watches distributed by the carton and £50 notes pinned to Christmas cards, were gone for good. In the less than immortal words of Mrs Thatcher herself, there was to be 'no more free lunch'.

The rude awakening for Rocket came in 1979, when John Reid suddenly dismissed the company's accountants, Shears and Company. The ostensible reason was disappointing performance in a matter that obsessed the fiscally avid Scot. He remained convinced that, for all the millions Elton had earned in the Seventies, millions more might have been improperly withheld from him.

For almost six years, he had been engaged in guerrilla warfare with Elton's old mentors, Dick James Music, who held copyright on his songs up to 1973 and his record output up to 1975. The claim – backed up by diverse expert legal and commercial opinions – was that DJM's network of foreign sub-publishing arrangements took too big a slice of the royalties Elton and Bernie earned from the playing of their songs worldwide.

On Reid's instructions, Shears and Co. had conducted an audit of DJM's books and examined its sub-publishing contracts, but with markedly little result. In October 1977, DJM had written to Geoffrey Ellis at Rocket, offering £6,687 in final settlement of the alleged shortfall in Elton's and Bernie's overseas royalties up to December, 1975 – a sum clearly nowhere near that which John Reid had in mind. Shears then began a further audit at DJM for the period 1976–78. This was still in progress when Reid lost patience, dismissed Shears and appointed the firm of Arthur Andersen and Company to look after Rocket, John Reid Enterprises and Elton.

Andersen's advice was a complete restructuring both of Rocket's corporate finances and Elton's personal ones. 'The message was that the silly times were over,' John Hall says now. 'People had to grow up and realise more money was going out than was coming in. Elton had to realise it, too, for the very first time in his career.'

Rocket henceforward was run on a tight rein, belied by the 'Help yourself' smile still on the face of its Thomas Tank-engine logo. And Elton, too, while not actually forced to economise, was fencouraged to think twice before buying Ferraris for acquaintances or going round Cartier with his Safeway supermarket trolley. 'I don't spend as much money as I used to,' he admitted on his 1980 American tour. 'It used to be Rembrandts at Christmas for friends, which was a bit stupid.' (He had, in fact, given Rembrandt's etching 'The Adoration of the Shepherds' as a thirtieth-birthday present to that noted aesthete Rod Stewart.)

The other factor crucial to Rocket's health at the turn of the decade was negotiating a new recording deal for Elton in America. John Hall flew over with John Reid for this purpose, returning with a Reid story fit to join the classics of the genre.

Elton's $5-million deal with MCA, negotiated by Reid in 1974, was at that time the biggest and best ever made for a recording star. But now, at the end of its five-year span, the terms no longer seemed munificent. The putting of armlocks on to rich record companies, so ably pioneered by Reid, had become standard practice for managers throughout the music industry. Advances of $1 million per album, which once only Elton could command, were routinely paid out, to stop established stars from defecting or snap up potential money-spinners. In capital-investment terms, he rated as only a middle-sized fish in the pool.

The explosive additional factor in the affair, as always, was John Reid's personal hubris. Merely securing his client a right and proper increment was not enough for Reid. Nothing would do but that he make Elton an American deal as phenomenal for 1980 as the MCA deal had been for 1974.

'John went in to see the board of MCA,' John Hall remembers. 'They were pretty paranoid about losing Elton. Even though he wasn't hot at that time, he still accounted for an incredible amount of their turnover. They would probably have taken him on as a loss leader, just for the sake of his back catalogue.

'So John presents them with this phenomenal deal he's already boasted all around LA that he's going to do for Elton – I think it was $25 million for five albums. And having told the whole world he'd get it, he had to get it. The MCA people said, "Well, we're prepared to consider this, but for that sort of money, we'd need the rights for the whole world . . ." At that, John threw one of his massive tantrums and walked out of the room.

'I was at the meeting, but I'd already left. I heard later that John had come storming out of the boardroom into the main office, where all these secretaries were sitting, and the walls were covered with gold and platinum discs, mostly earned by Elton. John shouted

something like "I made this fuckin' company, they can stick their
fuckin' records" and got hold of one of the gold discs to tear it off
the wall. But it was screwed on tight. He's standing there, with all
the secretaries looking on, wrenching at this thing and cursing, but it
just won't budge.'

Reid now found himself in serious difficulty. Having told the
MCA board they were 'assholes', he had no possible channel for
reopening negotiations. Nor could he take his deal to any of the
other international companies capable of paying a $25 million
advance. EMI and RCA had already featured in Elton deals ending
less than happily for both sides. To go to PolyGram, Rocket's
European distributor, would mean giving worldwide rights in Elton
to a single company, with resultant loss of power both to artist and
manager.

The one company willing and eager to do a deal on Elton in
America only was a brand-new and largely untried label, Geffen
Records. Its owner, David Geffen, had run the hugely successful
Asylum label in the early Seventies, rising to still greater eminence
after Asylum's merger with Warner and Elektra to form WEA.
Setting up on his own, he had quickly wooed several major artists
from other labels, compensating for the lack of enormous advances
by a promise of imaginative and sympathetic handling. His great
coup had come with the news that John Lennon was out of domestic
retirement in New York, and recording tracks for a new album,
Double Fantasy. After reviewing multimillion dollar offers from every
major record company, Lennon – and Yoko – plumped for Geffen.

John Reid knew Geffen well, moving as they did in the same
social circle. Geffen had already approached him about signing Elton,
but – with the MCA superdeal supposedly imminent – had been
scathingly rebuffed. No deal with MCA, or any other giant, having
materialised, Reid's only option was to eat humble pie with David
Geffen. 'I was involved in it,' John Hall remembers. 'We had to call
Geffen and say, "Oh, gee, David – John's really sorry he hasn't got
back to you before now, but he hasn't been feeling very well . . ."'

A deal was made with Geffen, saving Reid's face at the eleventh
hour, though at some little cost. Instead of the much-trumpeted
$25 million advance, Geffen paid essentially what MCA had under
the 1974 deal, $1 million per album. The plus side, supposedly, was
that Elton would be handled with a flair and sensitivity MCA could
never match. 'What John had been going for was simply money,'
John Hall says. 'And that, really was the right approach. With an
artist of Elton's size, sensitive handling isn't the first priority. What you
need first of all is massive cash investment to market him properly.'

To Elton, money was of less importance than sharing a label with his greatest idol and – now – great friend. 'Lennon and I are both on Geffen now,' he told people proudly on that summer 1980 tour. 'So we may do an album together one day. I'd love that.'

In Lennon's long hermitage at the Dakota Building, indeed, Elton had been one of the few welcome regular visitors. He was godfather to Sean, the son Yoko had borne after three traumatic miscarriages. The baby, with his Lennon face and Japanese eyes, in many ways became a surrogate for the child Elton himself still longed to have.

Liking and admiring Lennon did not blind Elton to his many foibles and inconsistencies. The man who had engraved 'Imagine no possessions' on the mind of a generation now owned a vast property empire, including a farm and a prize herd of Holstein cattle. Yoko was an acquirer who put even Elton into the shade. 'I couldn't believe it,' he said after visiting the biggest of their three apartments at the Dakota. 'Yoko has a refrigerated room just for keeping her fur coats. She's got rooms full of those clothes racks like you see at Marks and Spencer. She makes me look ridiculous. I buy things in threes or fours, but she buys them in fifties. The funny thing is, you never see her wearing them. She's always got up in some tatty old blouse.'

For Lennon's fortieth birthday that October, Elton sent him a card, poking gentle fun at the words of his best-known song:

> *Imagine six apartments.*
> *It isn't hard to do.*
> *One is full of fur coats,*
> *The other's full of shoes.*

On the night of 8 December, Lennon returned home after an evening at New York's Hit Factory recording studio. As he and Yoko got out of their car and walked under the Dakota's Gothic arch, a young man, for whom Lennon had earlier autographed an album, stepped forward and fired five shots from a .38 handgun at point-blank range into his back. He managed to stagger into the Dakota vestibule, but died before an ambulance could get him to Roosevelt Hospital.

Other murders of modern times may have aroused similar world-wide grief and shock. But for no one else was universal grief more deeply personal. It would have astonished Lennon himself, who was convinced that the Beatles meant little to people any more, and, a few days before his death, had asked a British disc jockey if there might be 'any interest' in his appearing onstage again, as at Madison Square Garden in 1974.

The grief was greatest among the dozens of musicians, both British and American, who counted Lennon among their earliest inspiration. In a special memorial issue, *Rolling Stone* sought professional tributes from Ray Charles, Chuck Berry, Mick Jagger and a host of others. But, surprisingly, not from that once-upon-a-time Beatle fanatic in Pinner, who would prove Lennon's only rival in the command of mass personal friendship.

For Yoko, the shock included a reaction common among bereaved partners. In the days immediately after John's death, some of his characteristics seemed to transfer to her. Her eyesight, formerly excellent, suddenly became as bad as his. She also found herself developing his craving for chocolate.

Despite the vast outpouring of sympathy, very few people could find anything practical to do for her. One exception was an outsize chocolate cake, delivered to the Dakota Building with a card saying 'Love from Elton'.

In 1981, Elton's appearance changed yet again. The Cossack urchin look, of eight-piece caps and pantaloons tucked into boots, abruptly vanished. So did the contact lenses, the hollow face and bushy eyebrows. So did any further chance to monitor progress, or lack of it, in the hair-plugs checkered over his scalp. From here on, apart from a few involuntary unveilings, the transplant would remain covered, like the Lord's wicket awaiting the end of rain.

The new Elton was a figure much attuned to the Eighties spirit of new Victorianism. It wore striped blazers, wing-poke collars with bow ties or cravats and over its bombarded cranium a straw boater tilted in the rakish style of Maurice Chevalier. Its torso – chunky once again – assumed a little parallel sideways twist, creating a silhouette that ultimately would be as recognisable as Chevalier's or Chaplin's. The eyes, that had so urgently wanted to meet others head on, hid away again behind dark glasses. In the right earlobe, a plain gold ring continued to make its small but unabashed self-declaration.

For most of 1981, Britain's press had little time to spare for Elton, or any rock star. Fleet Street was plunged into an obsession with royalty that even the Victorians might have considered excessive. The thirty-two-year-old Prince of Wales had announced his imminent marriage to Lady Diana Spencer, nineteen-year-old daughter of Earl Spencer. The royal choice, unprecedently, was a stunner, tall, buxom and blonde, with the legs of a fashion model. This 'fairy tale' romance roused the tabloids to outpourings of gush not seen in print since Nannie Crawford blew the whistle on Princess Lillibet.

The advent of Princess Diana was but one sign of greatly increased trendiness in the House of Windsor. Both the Queen's younger sons, Prince Edward and Prince Andrew, were now young men, of character very different from the circumspect Prince Charles. Andrew, in particular, was emerging as a hero of the new 'hooray Henry' class with his fondness for squirting soda siphons, and an indiscreet love life that led the tabloids to dub him 'Randy Andy'.

There remained, even so, only one rock performer with the equivalent of a royal 'By appointment' warrant. For Prince Andrew's twenty-first birthday party at Windsor Castle, Elton was invited to provide the cabaret. Six hundred guests, including Mrs Thatcher and her husband, watched him perform against a backdrop of castle walls, on which laser beams projected the word CONGRATULATIONS. The thank-you letter afterwards sent to Rocket Records was signed 'Diana Spencer'.

Otherwise, the year found him in another professional trough, following a pattern that Rocket's young boss, John Hall, was quick to identify. 'It was always the same with Elton. He'd do one or two bad albums, and everyone would think that was the finish – he'd finally played himself out. Then he'd suddenly pull another great one out of nowhere.'

His album for 1981 was *The Fox*, a further *mélange* of collaborations with Gary Osborne, Bernie Taupin and Tom Robinson, co-produced by Chris Thomas, who had previously worked with the Sex Pistols, Paul McCartney and the Pretenders. It did respectably in Britain, reaching number twelve, but, as his first US release on Geffen, made only a disappointing twenty-one. Around it came a meteor shower of unsuccessful singles: 'Nobody Wins' and 'Just Like Belgium' from *The Fox*, plus DJM's opportunistic release of his three live tracks with John Lennon onstage at Madison Square Garden.

John Hall is almost unique among ex-Rocket employees in remembering his time there as happy and his treatment as generous and appreciative. 'I never got any of the fabled presents. I tried to distance myself from all that – even bought my own Cartier watch. But Elton was always great to me, and to my family. He adored my two kids, and they adored him. I remember when I took them to the Central Park gig, Elton had just landed by helicopter, and was in the middle of this huge entourage. But when he saw my kids, he came straight over, sat down and started talking to them.'

The sovereign's inner circle had lately taken on a new complexity. Bob Halley, his former chauffeur, was now the principal person in his life, a twenty-four-hour-a-day 'personal assistant'. As Rocket

Records' head, John Hall had to deal with the ticklish emotional triangle formed by Elton, Halley and John Reid. 'Bob was the closest person to Elton on a day-to-day basis. But John and Elton still had something incredibly strong between them. They might have screaming rows and throw things at one another, or deliberately not call one another for weeks on end. But you knew there was something between them that no other relationship either of them might have could ever affect.'

Hall, despite himself, was drawn into what an earlier member, Sharon Lawrence, had called 'Elton's circle of dependence'. 'He seemed to have all these celebrity friends, and be hanging out with top musicians, like Rod, and Freddie Mercury. But I'd still find myself sitting up with him into the small hours. He could be incredibly funny, because he'd got this total recall of stories and the way people talked. And the more he drank, the sharper he got. He could drink brandy all night, and be totally fresh when everyone else was dropping dead.

'He loved to play cards as well, though he hated to lose, and never paid you what he owed you. He'd just go on doubling the stakes until he started winning by the law of averages. I think it was Gary Osborne who told him one night he'd got to pay up. "All right, what do you want?" Elton said. "I want that," Gary said, pointing to one of his cars. So Elton just gave him the car.'

Hall saw the total meticulousness that Elton could bring to bear, even in the staging of his characteristic little jokes. In March 1981, at a Christie's auction, he paid £14,000 for the original scripts of BBC Radio's *Goon Show*, to which he had been addicted since boyhood. Six thousand pages of script, with notes by Spike Milligan and Peter Sellers, were added to the dustless treasure house at Old Windsor. The Rocket spokeswoman who gave out Elton's press statement was instructed to speak in the accent of his favourite *Goon Show* character, Bluebottle: 'I have boughted dem because I loved dem.'

'The thing you had to recognise about Elton was that he was totally unpredictable,' John Hall says. 'I've had private planes waiting at Heathrow to take him to international conferences, with PolyGram executives waiting. At the last minute, there's a phone call: it's Bob Halley. "He's not coming. He doesn't feel well."

'A lot of the time, it was sheer stress – not just what other people put on him but also what he put on himself. He'd be on one of his awful diets, not eating anything at all. Or not drinking anything except water. Or he'd be in a depression because he thought he'd overeaten, or about his hair. Nobody really knew what he went through with those transplants. I've seen his head raw and bleeding.

'But the one area where you could totally rely on him was live performance. I've seen him blow out network TV shows – just turn round and say, "I'm not going to do it." But in all those hundreds of live gigs all over the world, he's never, if he could help it, let anyone down. Ever.'

In 1978, a letter had been forwarded to Elton via Graham Taylor at Watford football club. It was from his stepmother, Edna, telling him that his father's health was bad, and growing worse.

After the pillorying in *Playboy* magazine, Stanley Dwight had moved his family from Cheshire to Ruthin, North Wales. But it was no simple matter to turn off that sudden, unwelcome spotlight. Journalists from all over the world still ferreted out his ex-directory telephone number or turned up on his doorstep, inviting him to tell his side of the story. Whenever Elton made headlines, as with his declaration of bisexuality or his heart scare, the pressure on Stanley redoubled.

On many occasions, Edna Dwight now says, he was offered substantial cash inducements to give an interview as Elton's maligned father. But, despite continually straitened financial circumstances, he resolutely refused to speak to anyone. Nor, even in the most private conversations with his wife, did he ever utter a word of criticism or reproach against Elton.

Even in Ruthin's quiet, hilly streets, Stanley was pointed out as Elton John's father and whispered about as the parade-ground martinet who reputedly had all but stifled a colossal talent. It was locally assumed that Elton had bought the Dwights' modest home for them and that he was paying for his four young half-brothers to attend private school (in fact, they had all won scholarships).

In 1978, Stanley suffered a heart attack. After a spell in hospital under observation, he was allowed to return to work at Unilever, but was never again to be his old vigorous, resourceful self. Edna remains convinced his deteriorating health was mainly caused by the strain of unending press harassment, his distress over Elton's public condemnation of him and the subsequent wall of silence between them. Ironically, it was not long afterwards that Elton was rushed to the London Clinic with his own heart scare. Stanley, Edna says, sent him a bunch of flowers and a get-well card without mentioning his own illness.

Hence Edna's letter to Elton care of Graham Taylor, which she says she sent without Stanley's knowledge. Elton at the time was away in Europe but sent Stanley some flowers and a telegram, wishing him well and promising to visit him on his return. But, according to Edna, no visit followed.

In 1981, Stanley suffered a haemorrhage that robbed him of sight in one eye, and over the next year his health went rapidly further downhill. He was admitted to hospital suffering from ischaemic heart disease and angina, and kept in intensive care until his condition could be stabilised. Two months later, he was hospitalised again with osteoarthritis in his neck and other joints. By September 1982, his heart condition was so serious that he was sent to Sefton General Hospital in Liverpool and told that his only hope was a quadruple bypass operation. A month later, he was back in hospital for a temporal artertis biopsy which meant that, in addition to extensive heart medication, he would spend the rest of his life on steroids.

That October, his son Geoffrey managed to see Elton backstage after an appearance with Freddie Mercury in Manchester. To Geoffrey's surprise, Elton already knew about their father's impending heart surgery and promised to telephone him. The call came through a month later, just as Stanley came in from work after driving through a blizzard. Edna remembers him sitting on the stairs still in his overcoat, talking to his son with tears in his eyes.

The ice melted instantly, she says, with both chatting away about music and football as if the glacial recent years had never been. Elton offered to pay for his father to have the heart-bypass operation as a private patient, but Stanley insisted he was quite happy with his treatment under the NHS. Elton then spoke to Edna herself, repeating his offer and making her promise to let him know directly Stanley went into hospital. Edna says he told her: 'I've been doing some thinking. I've got a dad and four brothers I haven't seen much of for a long time, and it's about time I got to know them better. After all, blood is thicker than water.' As an earnest indication of this, he mentioned that Watford would be playing away to Liverpool in a few weeks time. Did Stanley think he would be well enough to attend the match with him? Stanley replied that he would.

The appointment was duly confirmed, in December 1982, and Stanley kept it even though blizzards were still raging and his health was now extremely bad. As he and Edna crossed on the Mersey ferry to Liverpool, they saw Elton's private helicopter coming in to land at Speke Airport. 'The memory of Stan's face as he gazed up at it will be with me always,' Edna says.

Elton, she remembers, showed tender solicitude for his father, who was grey-faced and unsteady, taking Stanley's arm to help him up the steps to the Anfield ground. They watched the match from the directors' box and, although Watford lost, Stanley still witnessed the spectacle of the Liverpool crowd swaying in unison and chanting 'Elton! Elton!' Afterwards, he watched his son sign autographs and –

says Edna – was profoundly moved when Elton borrowed his pen
but forgot to return it and took it away in his pocket.

Later in the directors' lounge, Stanley showed him pictures of his
four half brothers and Elton asked for one to keep. He also said that,
after the operation, he'd like to come and stay for the weekend with
Stanley and Edna in Ruthin. His father's reply, according to Edna,
was 'You're welcome any time. You're one of the family,
remember.'

Stanley underwent his eight-and-a-half-hour quadruple bypass
operation in January 1983. Elton, by then in Australia, sent a huge
basket of carnations and a message: 'Tell Dad I have been thinking
of him all day. I think he is very brave. I am very proud of him and
love him very much.' But father and son were never to meet again.

Dick and Stephen James had long been braced to the idea that John
Reid might sooner or later bring some kind of legal action against
them. Virtually from the day Elton left DJM in 1975, Reid had been
on their tail, questioning the terms of agreements they had allowed
him to study at leisure as their employee. Stephen James had many
times regretted what he considered his father's early indulgence of
Reid, and his own failure to throw the importunate Scot neck and
crop into the street.

The primary claim from Reid repeated that painful syndrome
that Dick James had already experienced as publisher of John Lennon
and Paul McCartney. Under the agreement Elton and Bernie Taupin
had signed in 1967, all their songs up to 1973 remained the copyright
of Dick James Music. Reid's assertion was that, however much
'standard practice', it had been unfair to allow two inexperienced
teenagers thus to sign away their work. Likewise, the recording
agreements Elton had signed with DJM, in 1968 and 1970, had not
given him a nearly big enough share of the £200 million his records
had earned worldwide. He, not DJM, should own the master
recordings of all those gold-mine albums and singles. In addition, he
should be paid the difference between his past record income and
what he would have received under a 'fair' contract.

The second prong of Reid's attack centred on changes DJM had
made to the network of foreign sub-publishers through whom
overseas royalties were collected. According to DJM, the changes
had been purely for administrative convenience. Reid, however,
remained convinced that these new DJM foreign satellites were
deducting a greater, and unjustified, proportion of Elton and Bernie's
overseas publishing income.

The Jameses, on their side, pointed to the large capital sum they had sunk into launching Elton, an investment which, for three years, seemed unlikely to be recouped. In their view, they had been generous over his contractual obligations. At the end of the recording agreement he, by their reckoning, still owed them a further studio album, but had nevertheless brought out *Blue Moves* on Rocket. 'We could have sued him to get *Blue Moves*, which turned out to be a big hit,' Stephen James says. 'But my father didn't want to get into a legal fight with Elton. All we finally got to settle the contract was two tracks licensed to us by Rocket for our second *Elton John's Greatest Hits* album.'

Dick James, by this time, was one of the most distinguished figures in the British entertainment industry. He had been chairman of the Music Publishers Association, and vice chairman of the Performing Right Society. His company had three times earned the Queen's Award for industry for its export record, and James himself had received an Ivor Novello Award for services to entertainment. A mild heart attack in 1973 had forced him to stop smoking but otherwise he had scarcely slackened pace, still actively running the publishing side of DJM while Stephen ran the recording.

In manner and appearance, he remained as amiable and cuddly as ever. In 1980, he gave two long interviews to the present writer about his years with the Beatles and the acrimonious end of that publishing arrangement. 'But then we found Elton John,' he said, still evidently regarding it as a second instalment of stupendous luck. Ever ready to oblige a Fifties nostalgic, he even warbled a few lines of his own most unforgettable hit as a professional singer:

> *Feared by the bad,*
> *Loved by the good,*
> *Robin Hood!*
> *Robin Hood!*
> *Robin Hood!*

Reid's discharge of arrows at Dick James was sporadic – ceasing, for instance, when he needed DJM's co-operation at the time of Elton's tax difficulties in America. By 1980, the question of the song copyrights had receded against that of the alleged shortfall in Elton's royalties via DJM's reconstructed overseas subsidiaries. However, lengthy auditing of DJM's books by Rocket's accountants, Shears and Co., had found no discrepancy anywhere near the scale Reid had hoped for. For the years 1976–9, the figure Shears finally came up with was £12,178 pounds – mere small change, not worth a single day's court costs.

The galvanising factor was Reid's 1980 change of accountants to Arthur Andersen. A partner at Andersen's, Julian Lee, reactivated the question of the song copyrights in John Reid's mind. The opinion of a QC, Gerald Butler, was sought, both on that matter and the question of Elton's overseas royalties. The QC's opinion was that Elton's publishing agreements with DJM were 'valid and not open to attack', and he did not advise suing for the recovery of the song copyrights. The only feasible claim was for loss of royalties, and this would depend on expert testimony as to whether DJM's new overseas sub-publishing arrangements were 'commercially reasonable'.

Julian Lee's advice to Reid was to 'push harder'. To Reid, however, the stumbling-block was Elton, who remained fond of Dick James and would only sue if the sums were large enough, and he became 'sufficiently aggrieved'. Arthur Andersen then began a fresh audit of the DJM group's books.

In 1981, Dick James's heart trouble recurred and, like Stanley Dwight, he underwent quadruple bypass surgery to forestall what might have proved a serious heart attack. His doctor's orders were that from now on he should take things much more easily. He therefore stepped down as managing director of DJM, handing the whole company over to Stephen while remaining its chairman. His plan henceforward was to come into the office only for an hour or so each day and to enjoy retirement with his wife at their penthouse in St John's Wood and their luxurious flat in Cannes.

Wounding as the various skirmishes with John Reid had been, they did not seriously undermine James's equanimity, nor unsettle his conviction that all his dealings with and on behalf of Elton had been utterly straight and above board. It was just the 'John and Paul Syndrome' all over again; an artist once grateful and thankful, now carpingly discontent. However microscopically the original agreements with Elton might be examined, there was one thing of which Dick James was righteously and securely certain. They had followed faithfully the standard practice throughout the industry.

In 1982, however, standard practice throughout the industry was turned on its head. The singer Gilbert O'Sullivan began legal action against his former manager and publisher Gordon Mills, on grounds precisely the same as John Reid's dispute with Dick James Music. O'Sullivan had joined Mills's company, MAM, on terms remarkably like Elton's at DJM, receiving a £10 per-week retainer as a combination in-house songwriter and odd-job boy. His string of huge Seventies hits, like 'Nothing Rhymed', 'Clair' and 'Alone Again (Naturally)', had grossed £14.5 million pounds for MAM, of which O'Sullivan claimed to have received barely half a million.

The O'Sullivan case was heard in the High Court during May 1982. It resulted in total victory for the singer-songwriter against the manager and publisher who claimed to have invented him. The judge, Mr Justice Mars-Jones, ruled that the agreements between Gordon Mills and O'Sullivan took unfair advantage of O'Sullivan's youth and innocence, and therefore could be said to constitute a 'restraint of trade'. Mills was ordered to relinquish all Gilbert O'Sullivan copyrights, deliver up all master recordings of his songs and pay him massive back royalties, with interest.

When Dick James read the verdict in the Gilbert O'Sullivan case, he knew it could not be long before a similar lawsuit was launched against him by John Reid. In an effort to head it off, he phoned Reid and asked him to lunch, intending to make a conciliatory proposal. 'We agreed we'd offer to sell back the masters of Elton's records to him,' Stephen James says. 'If that went well, we'd also discuss selling back the song copyrights. John agreed to meet us for lunch, but at the last minute he rang up and cancelled.'

Three weeks later, DJM received formal notice of court action from Reid's solicitors. The full claim, when it arrived, corresponded almost word for word with Gilbert O'Sullivan's against Gordon Mills.

If Lord Choc Ice was in another temporary trough, the chairman of Watford Football Club was starting the biggest roll of his career. Under Graham Taylor's management, the 1981–2 season had been Watford's best yet, with bigger and bigger crowds cheering the emergence of gifted young players like John Barnes, Kenny Jackett and Nigel Callaghan. The rising tide of success reached its first climax when the club's youth team won the FA Youth Cup. Then, on 4 May, 1982, in front of 20,000 home fans, Watford beat Swansea City 2–0, so winning promotion to Division One for the first time in its ninety-year history.

The extent of Elton's support was revealed in the 1982 accounts, which showed he had so far provided a total of £1.2 million in interest-free loans. Currently he was suffering less frustration from dud singles than from Watford's local planning authority, which had mysteriously opposed the building of a new grandstand to accommodate the greatly increased numbers at Vicarage Road. He was also spearheading a somewhat implausible plan to turn Watford, the town, into a tourist attraction. The club had affiliated itself with a hotel chain, which now offered weekend package tours, including a VIP seat at a Watford home game, for less than £20 per head.

The euphoria of Watford's Division One debut, that autumn,

might have been expected to flavour Elton's first British concert tour for five years. He was determined to do it, despite a year as slow on record as Watford's young strikers had been quick to the opposing goalmouth. His 1982 album, *Jump Up!*, had been a disappointment, reaching number thirteen in Britain and seventeen in America. Recorded at George Martin's AIR studios in Montserrat, it was a further uneasy mix of words by Bernie Taupin and Gary Osborne, with a stray track oddly provided by the *Evita* lyricist Tim Rice. Its only successful single was 'Blue Eyes', a Gary Osborne love song at near-standstill tempo, which made number eight in Britain and twelve in America. When Elton sang 'Baby's got blue eyes', then and ever afterwards, it seemed like nothing so much as a longing for fatherhood.

Most disappointing was what befell 'Empty Garden', an elegy for John Lennon which Bernie Taupin had written in a haze of grief the day after his great friend's death. At a time when cheap and tawdry 'tributes' to Lennon were still coining fortunes, this right and tasteful one – as angrily sad as 'Candle in the Wind' – reached only thirteen in America and fifty-one in Britain. Another hopefully topical track, 'Princess', issued in Britain only as a single, did not even get into the Top 50.

The pre-tour photograph showed Elton in a uniform of mitre-shaped cap, gold-epauletted hussar tunic, sash, frogged breeches and tasselled topboots, looking rather like one of the Argentinian generalissimos who had launched the Falklands invasion. THE GAY HUSSAR! chortled a *Daily Mirror* picture spread, whose caption of barely a hundred words managed to make two further nudge-nudge references to homosexuality.

It was to be an Elton tour in traditional style, winding up at his old London Yuletide home, the Hammersmith Odeon. The act was fundamentally the same as had packed them in by the million through the Seventies. New songs first, then album evergreens and, finally, the ceremonial kicking away of the piano stool for his time-honoured stand-up rock-'n'-roll finale.

Again his stage band mixed new blood with old stalwarts Davey Johnstone, Dee Murray and Nigel Olsson. Unluckily, British winter took its toll and just before the Hammersmith first night, Olsson succumbed to influenza. Elton was not told of his absence until minutes before going onstage. As a result, the gold-laced general faced his cheering fans in the very worst possible mood.

His ill-humour mounted throughout the show, reaching a crescendo when he kicked away his piano stool for the rock-'n'-roll sequence. As a rule, Hammersmith Odeon had a conventional parapet stage, with a deep pit below, into which objects hurled from the stage could tumble harmlessly. For this week, however, unknown to Elton, a fabric slope had been built from the stage edge almost to the front row of the audience. The piano stool – whacked away with extra, peevish force – skidded over this ramp and hit a spectator on the shoulder.

The piano stool's victim, twenty-four-year-old Seana Connolly, suffered bruising on her cheek and the top of her right arm. 'She was one of those real die-hard Elton fans,' John Hall remembers. 'She'd got every album and loved him since she was ten. So I said, "Look, we're very sorry, it was an accident, please come back and meet Elton after the show." I took her to the dressing room, and Elton apologised to her, and gave her a bottle of champagne and a leather jacket. "To show you how really sorry I am," he said, "I'd like to buy you a dress as well."

'So the next day, someone from the office took this girl out, and she bought the world's most expensive dress. That night, we were having a big end-of-tour party at Xenon, and I'd also invited her along to that. We sent the limo for her and, of course, she turned up in the dress Elton had bought her. And it's one of those with a cutaway at the top of the arm, to highlight the bruise she got from the piano stool. After all the trouble we'd gone to to keep the thing quiet, there she is parading round Xenon, showing her bruise off to everyone.'

Those two Hammersmith concerts brought a flurry of tabloid headlines which made rock's good boy sound more like some latter day Johnny Rotten. Some reports claimed that, after the flying piano stool incident, he had snapped at Seana Connolly, 'If you're so bloody hurt, call an RSPCA man.' *The Sun* alleged that a group of stage-door fans had seen him afterwards, still in his banana republic generalissimo's outfit, banging his head 'at least six times' on the bonnet of his Rolls-Royce. 'It was like watching a child throwing a temper tantrum because he can't get his own way,' one of the purported witnesses said. 'He yelled at someone, "Right, you're fired! I don't want to see you again!" [and] was then whisked away in another car.'

Nor had his mood much mellowed twenty-four hours later, when he arrived at the lavish end-of-tour party at Xenon. According to the ever-watchful *Daily Mail*, he did not show up until 1 am, and then 'brushed aside the good wishes of friends like David Essex, Pamela Stephenson, Billy Connolly and Lulu . . . Elton refused to mix with guests, and sat in a corner, surrounded by aides. After fifteen minutes, he left, saying, "I've had enough of this."'

SIXTEEN

'Good on yer, poofter'

THE 'party-destroyer', who could wipe out festivity with almost
ectoplasmic emanations of black rage, might just as bafflingly
switch back to being the life and soul of the party.

In April 1983, he accepted an invitation to what should have
been only effortless, unadulterated luxury. It came from Cartier, the
French jewellery house of whose products he was among the world's
foremost bulk buyers. Cartier were launching a new range of 22-
carat gold sunglasses and, to celebrate, flew a party of VIPs from all
over Europe to a party at the luxury Tunisian resort of Monastir.
Elton and John Reid were asked to join the British contingent, along
with the Queen's cousin Lady Elizabeth Shakerley, the Countess of
Lichfield, actor Christopher Cazenove, singers Hazel O'Connor and
Lynsey de Paul, and assorted Fleet Street gossip columnists.

Unfortunately, none of the gold timepieces at Cartier had registered the fact that April is typhoon season in Monastir. Arriving after
an uncomfortable four-hour flight, the VIPs found gale-force winds
and driving rain. The beach marquee in which the glamorous sunglasses were to be launched had already partly collapsed and blown
into the sea. At the resort's luxury Hannibal Palace Hotel, as much
chaos reigned as if its namesake's war elephants had lately passed
through. Some of the celebrities found that no rooms had been booked
for them, and had to be decanted into a neighbouring, inferior
establishment. Cries of agony from practised liggers arose on discov-
ering that room service and phone calls were not included in Cartier's
hospitality. A grand gala 'welcome' dinner, cooked to be served at
9.30 pm, did not start reaching the tables until almost midnight.

Among those present was the *Daily Express*'s William Hickey
diarist, Christopher Wilson. 'By about 1 am, when this pretty awful
dinner had been served, everyone was pretty pissed off,' Wilson
remembers. 'The only chance of rescuing the whole ghastly occasion

was that Elton John might play something. No one was quite sure if he would, because he looked just as pissed off as everyone else. But in the end, he did go up to the piano and start to play.

'I've never seen anyone turn a room full of people around so totally. In about twenty minutes, he had everyone clapping, singing, standing on tables. It was an incredible performance, that seemed to come from absolutely nowhere. And once he got going, there was no stopping him. As a finale, he led all these quite starchy jet-set types, in their evening dress and jewellery, in a Pied Piper line out of the hotel and down to the beach, where the remains of this marquee were still standing. He grabbed Hazel O'Connor and danced with her among the ruins, then he dropped his trousers and wiggled his bare arse. Which, everyone felt, summed the whole thing up perfectly.'

Any royal gala by now put Elton John automatically at the top of the A-list. Early in 1983, the Queen visited America, welcomed thither by President and Mrs Reagan with all the taste and restraint of their Hollywood background. The climax was a dinner in Tinseltown itself, organised and hosted by the First Lady and attended by movie greats such as James Stewart, Bette Davis, Fred Astaire and Gene Kelly. Elton was chosen to sit at Nancy Reagan's own top table, along with the Queen, Prince Philip and a miscellany of British stars like Michael Caine, Julie Andrews and Jane Seymour.

It was an occasion with all the hallmarks of Reagan taste, taking place on a movie sound-stage normally used for filming TV series like *M.A.S.H.* The cabaret – introduced by Johnny Carson's straight man – featured Dionne Warwick, and a duet between Frank Sinatra and Perry Como. The evening's longueurs made Elton once again forget politeness and protocol. To *The Sun*'s Los Angeles correspondent he said the royal dinner had been 'so boring, I almost fell asleep'. He thought it 'a shame' that, fenced around by Britishers like himself, the Queen had had no chance to meet the real stars of Hollywood. About the cabaret he was equally scornful, saying that Sinatra and Como had been under-rehearsed and Dionne Warwick, too, was 'boring'. ELTON RAPS QUEEN'S HOLLYWOOD PARTY, *The Sun* said with a wink to its four million initiates.

Most of 1983 was spent jetting around the world in search of the perfect party, or in retreat from it. Two months after baring his bottom at the Tunisian hurricane, he was standing on the Great Wall of China. Though China would soon succumb to rock music, as Russia had done, Elton was not this time to be the catalyst. He was there only as chairman of Watford, watching the club play two exhibition matches in Beijing and a third in Shanghai.

In China, Elton John the rock star was still virtually unknown. He could walk around as he pleased, conspicuous to Chinese eyes only as a foreigner. 'This is one of the few places in the world I can go without being recognised,' he said. 'It's a terrific feeling not to have people staring at you. I haven't known it for thirteen years.'

He visited tourist spots, as incognito as a man could be dressed in an Edwardian boater, a wing-poke collar and three-piece checked suit, and surrounded by footballers and photographers. At the tomb of Mao Tse Tung he respectfully removed his hat, giving the assembled press a collective world scoop. 'Elton John doffed his hat in memory of Chairman Mao . . . and revealed a costly failure,' the *Daily Mail* reported. 'Six hair transplants, for which he paid £1,800, have left him with only some fine wisps to cover his baldness.' There was a picture of an undeniably bald-looking Elton, boater pressed to chest, with Chairman Mao, above, seeming to look tactfully in the other direction.

Watford won all three of their friendly matches against Chinese teams, the third against the national side in Bejing's Workers' Stadium, watched by a crowd of 70,000 plus an estimated 400 million on television. Afterwards, there was a banquet in the club's honour on the Great Wall of the People. Elton confessed to being 'covered with goosepimples the whole time'.

Standing on the Great Wall, surrounded by 2,000 years of history, he sucked an ice lolly and gave thanks to Watford yet again for helping him not to be a rock ego monster. 'I was carried away with my own importance,' he told his circle of busily scribbling scribes. 'I've used my status wrongly in the past. But this club has done so much for me, because nobody there will put up with all that. In my business, it was luxury jets, the best hotels and shows in front of 20,000 people. Then I'd walk into Watford, and the washing-up lady would toddle across and say, 'I don't like your new record.' I needed that. They may have sniggered behind my back, but they've tolerated me until I've had time to mature.'

Especial thanks went to the club's manager Graham Taylor for keeping him on the rails with a bluntness none of his rock entourage would have dared. 'Three years ago, I was very unhappy, and drinking a lot of brandy. The team were playing Luton on Boxing Day, and I turned up in a coat that had cost £300 but looked like a dressing gown. The next morning, Graham called me round to his house. He put a bottle of brandy on the table and said, "Here you

are. Are you going to drink that? What the hell's wrong with you?"
He brought me to my senses.'

There was an impromptu concert at the team's hotel, and a visit
to an antiques export store, where Elton spent £50,000 on Chinese
souvenirs including a set of stone lions weighing six tons each. The
Watford players received their first sight of his Safeway trolley
shopping method. 'He just went in and said, "I'll have that, that and
that",' one of them reported incredulously.

His frequent, well-publicised absences from home brought an
inevitable consequence. Despite its electronic gates, roaming guard
dogs and labyrinthine defences, Woodside was burgled in March
1983. The thief or thieves got into Elton's private suite, making off
with a diamond and sapphire ring worth £50,000, a £6,000 Cartier
watch and £100 in cash. Since none of the house's internal alarms
had been triggered, and there was no sign of forced entry, the police
suspected an inside job. 'But that just cannot be,' a spokesman for
Elton said. 'All the people around at the time were trusted colleagues
and friends.' In a separate but equally unsettling incident, one of the
guard dogs went missing and was later found dead in a stream at
Egham, a few miles away.

Two months after returning from China, he was off again, flying
to South Africa to make a guest appearance with Rod Stewart at the
Sun City leisure complex in Bophuthatswana. Though later to join
the anti-apartheid boycott of Sun City, Elton at this time thought its
Superbowl stadium was 'wonderful', and made tentative plans for a
£700,000 concert season there the following October.

His stage appearance with Rod Stewart reactivated the carping,
camping friendship that had existed since the early Seventies. Plans
were announced for them to make a world tour together, and also
co-star in a film as modern counterparts of Bing Crosby and Bob
Hope in the old 'Road' pictures. The tour's opening was set for
Sydney, Australia, early in 1984. But that autumn, appearing on
Channel 4's American football programme, Elton suddenly
announced that it was all off. Nor was any more heard of the film,
with its putative female star Liza Minnelli.

In September, he flew to West Germany to see Watford play
their first-ever UEFA Cup match. Despite losing to FC Kaisersläu-
tern, they were 'not bad', the Sunday Telegraph said, 'for a club who
six years ago were restricted to lunge and bash matches in the Fourth
Division against teams like Rochdale'. Their famous young striker
John Barnes had been picked for Bobby Robson's England squad,
and the million-pound sale of Luther Blisset to AC Milan had bought
another potential star, eighteen-year-old Walsall defender Lee Sin-

nott. Elton watched every moment of practice and match, and signed autographs tirelessly.

On 17 November, he was due to fly to Los Angeles to give a benefit performance for the American Cancer Society at the Beverly Hilton. His Steinway grand was already set up onstage when word came that he'd gone down with glandular fever, and was too ill to leave Old Windsor.

George Martin's AIR Studios were the means by which history's most successful record producer finally made some personal profit. As a label head for EMI, Martin masterminded the Beatles' multibillion-pound recording career for a salary that, at its highest, only just cleared £3,000 per year. Though far from mercenary, he frequently had cause to chafe against EMI's institutional meanness. At the end of 1963, a year in which Beatles hits had stuffed the British charts, George Martin received a memo telling him he did not qualify for the staff's Christmas bonus.

The result was AIR – Associated Independent Recording – founded by Martin and three partners in 1965, happily anticipating a new era of independent record production companies. A few years later, seeking further capital, Martin considered selling out to Dick James, but withdrew when James's offer proved less than favourable. So small is the British record world, and so abiding the fall-out from the Beatles.

By the early Eighties, AIR was the brand-leader among British independent production companies. To its studios in London, it had added a second complex on the West Indies island of Montserrat, where artists could work with total concentration in congenial surroundings. AIR-Montserrat became the place to record for every-one from Paul McCartney and Eric Clapton to Phil Collins and the Police.

Elton had first gone there in 1982, to make his rather static and unenergised *Jump Up!* album. He returned the following summer to record *Too Low for Zero*, a production equally nothing like its implied nadir of despair. Dismissing Gary Osborne and all his other part-time and would-be collaborators, he went into the studio with a full set of Bernie Taupin lyrics for the first time since *Blue Moves* in 1976. 'I told Elton, "We've got to collaborate totally, or it's never going to be any good",' Bernie says. 'To me, our songs had always worked in total, with a feeling of continuity between them. I didn't want to keep on doing odd or obscure tracks on albums of other people's work. We had to try to get back to that complete closeness and understanding we had when we started out.'

Bernie himself was back on form, steadied by his new marriage, and writing with a simplicity and subtlety that made all former competitors redundant. *Too Low for Zero* contained two classic Elton tracks that carried him triumphantly back to the singles charts in both Britain and America. 'I Guess That's Why They Call It the Blues' was a love letter from Bernie to his new wife, Toni, borrowed by Elton's voice with the usual purging of all lascivious intent. When he sang of 'rolling like thunder under the covers', he could as well have meant a game of sardines after lights out in a school dormitory. 'I'm Still Standing' was the Brown Dirt Cowboy's overt tribute to a surrogate brother who, like himself, seemed to have weathered the Seventies intact, and to be bound now for sunny and mellow uplands. A third single from the album did less well, but deserves mention for its eerily prophetic title: 'Kiss The Bride'.

On returning from Montserrat, Elton had to go into AIR's London studios to finish off some vocal overdubs. Working as tape-operator on these final sessions was a girl named Renate Blauel.

Tape op' or second engineer in a recording studio is a subordinate job, generally combined with fetching coffee and phoning for taxis. This tape op' was slightly unusual, in being female and German, in her late twenties, with dark curly hair and the kind of dimply, pointed face usually associated with frilly-sleeved serving wenches in Bavarian bierkellers.

Even so, the people around Elton had little cause to notice Renate at the beginning. 'She was very nice,' John Hall remembers. 'Quiet. Unassuming. Usually wearing jeans and a sweater or T-shirt. To my mind, she always looked a bit masculine. But none of us took any real trouble to talk to her or get to know her. She was just a nice girl, who was a very unimportant part of what was going on. Then we noticed that whenever Elton came in, he'd say something to her. She'd laugh. They've suddenly got this little relationship going. And when the album comes out, there's a dedication: "Special thanks to Renate Blauel".

'It was a time when Elton was coming back with Top 30 singles, and being asked to do *Top of the Pops* again. The rule there was still that you had to pre-record a special version of your backing instrumental and vocal tracks. Elton would say, "No, fuck it! I'm not going to do it." I'd say, "You've got to do it, or you can't be on *Top of the Pops*." He'd say, "All right, I'll do the backing tracks at AIR – and can you get that Renate girl there as well? I'm not going to do it unless she's there."

'Then it comes time for the next album, *Breaking Hearts*, which he's going to do in Montserrat again. We've booked the studio, the band, everything's lined up. Then Elton suddenly says, "I'm not going." Total consternation! "I'm not going," he says, "unless Renate goes out there, too." So the whole million-dollar production comes to a standstill unless we can get this tape op' to Montserrat for him.'

The *Breaking Hearts* sessions flowed into Christmas 1983. Elton's journalist friend Nina Myskow – now TV critic of the *Sunday People* – also happened to be staying on the island. 'I'd no idea Elton would be there,' she remembers. 'Not till I arrived at Antigua airport and met John Reid also on his way out. He was in the duty-free shop, serving behind the counter.'

No sign of a romance was yet visible, even to Nina Myskow's practised eye. 'Renate was just one of the boys, in her usual jeans and T-shirt. Elton didn't seem to be taking any special notice of her. One night, I remember, she wore a dress – the first time I'd ever seen her in one. The change was extraordinary. She looked really sweet and terribly pretty.'

After seeing in the New Year on Montserrat, Elton was due to fly to Sydney to begin a tour of Australia and New Zealand. Again, the mystifying ultimatum was given. Renate Blauel had to be taken along.

Three weeks later, the tour party were at the Sebel Town House hotel, Elton's usual Sydney hideaway. His bass player Dee Murray and some others were having a late-night drink in the bar. Elton and Renate had gone out to dinner by themselves.

'I looked up and there they were in the doorway, holding hands,' Dee remembered. 'Elton said, "Guess what, man. I'm engaged."'

Why he did it should have been no mystery to anyone who had ever seen him with Bryan Forbes's little girls, or presenting Easter eggs to Watford junior members, or talking to John Hall's kids in Central Park, or with Sean Lennon, or a small Chinese boy who presented him with a painting near the Great Wall. Every friend and employee to whose children he was a doting godfather or uncle knew how desperately he wanted a family of his own.

The analogy of poor serving girl swept off her feet by millionaire Prince Charming was not wholly apt. Renate came from a respectable, even well-to-do West German background. Her father was a Munich publisher, Joachim Blauel. She had emigrated to London at twenty-two, partly as an act of rebellion against her parents, and drifted into the music business after various jobs including a spell with Lufthansa, the German airline. That dimpled, rather impersonal face might well be imagined above a trim Lufthansa blue jacket, scanning the aisle before take-off to ensure no tray tables were down and all seats were in the fully upright position.

In the male-dominated world of recordings studios, she had done remarkably well. Even today, only one in a hundred second engineers is likely to be a woman. Her superiors at AIR thought highly of her. 'She was more than good, she was very good,' remembers Bill Price, the engineer she assisted on *Too Low For Zero*. 'She was totally capable and reliable, and she had that peculiar Teutonic thoroughness.'

Outside work, her life was so low-profile as to be almost invisible. She lived alone in a £34-per-week flat in a Victorian house in Kilburn, north London. She had no boyfriend that her AIR colleagues ever saw. Her invariable dress of jeans and T-shirt suggested rather limited interest in men. She unbent to her fellow engineers only in revealing she could play piano a little, and had ambitions one day to produce records in her own right.

In one sense, she was the perfect person for Elton to woo. Much as he craved affection, he had always recoiled and withdrawn from anyone who came too precipitately close. The gulf in status between Renate and him gave him absolute control over the relationship. He could advance by whatever cautiously infinitesimal steps he chose.

It was further significant that they should have met in a recording studio, the one place in the world, other than onstage, where Elton felt completely at home. Almost their entire courtship was conducted over a control desk, in their common element of dead air, teacups, echo chambers, red lights and reverbs. He would make a joke. She would press a switch and smile. And suddenly the weather-vane swung from its wavery south-west back to strong due north.

One night in Montserrat they disappeared to have dinner together at an open-air restaurant called the Chicken Shack, where fried chicken was served in paper wrappings like English fish and chips. Renate afterwards said that this was the first occasion on which Elton proposed to her.

The affair proceeded with as much propriety as if they were teenage virgins. In Sydney, even after their engagement, they continued to occupy separate rooms. Elton was constantly attentive and chivalrous. He would make jokes. She would smile. He seemed as delighted and excited as a person could be.

'Rock on! Here comes the bridegroom,' said the *Daily Mail*, in one of the kinder British press comments on the affair. 'The pop world was rocked last night by news that millionaire superstar Elton John is to marry next week ... Last night, the 36-year-old singer and composer who has admitted to being bisexual, and once said he wanted to marry "but I don't care if it's a boy or a girl", was said to be over the moon with joy.'

His family and closest associates had already heard the news from Elton on the phone from Sydney. Clive Franks, his recording engineer, Graham Taylor, his football-club manager, Kiki Dee, his long-time token girlfriend, each listened to the bashful voice across the world in utter astonishment. The least surprised was Bernie Taupin, who had of course witnessed an almost exactly similar frantic courtship of Linda Woodrow, fifteen years earlier. 'It was unexpected, but it wasn't in the least out of character,' Bernie says now. 'I always knew that if Elton suddenly got a bee in his bonnet about wanting a family, it was likely to happen pretty suddenly.'

The great fascination within Elton's circle was how John Reid would react. Especially fascinated were those who remembered Elton's discomfiture, a few years earlier, when Reid had announced his own deeply unsuitable engagement to Bryan Forbes's daughter Sarah. 'John's attitude over the whole thing was quite weird,' an ex-Rocket employee says. 'He obviously didn't think much of Renate, and he was likely to be against anyone who threatened his power over Elton. But he seemed to regard the whole thing as terribly funny.'

The death of Soviet premier Yuri Andropov was relegated to out-of-the-way pages as Britain's tabloids fought for exclusive insights into the woman who had brought about this amazing transformation. *The Sun*'s first picture of 'vivacious brunette Renate Blauel', unfortunately, showed a girl who was not Renate laughing by Elton's side. Sunday's *News of the World* printed two pictures of the correct 'leggy brunette Renate Blauel', plus a good proportion of the few remarks she was ever destined to make on the record. She admitted she had 'heard all kinds of stories about Elton, that he's supposed to be bisexual. But that doesn't worry me at all ... He's wonderful, the nicest guy I've ever met. He makes me laugh and he's very considerate. I'm feeling just fabulous. This is the greatest day of my life.'

The *Mail on Sunday* tracked down the Indian restaurant where Elton had proposed, and quizzed its assistant manager, Mr Debu Benerjee, for his observations of the climactic moment. 'It was very romantic,' Mr Benerjee recalled. 'I could see they were in love. We put them at a corner table and had some nice sitar music wafting softly over them. Perhaps that is what did it.

'They ordered tandoori chicken, beef curry, kebab and pilau rice and poppadums. They seemed totally preoccupied with each other.

Mr Elton John didn't even notice another diner who came up to the table to ask for his autograph. The lady with him was very beautiful, and dressed in a beige-coloured dress. I couldn't hear the conversation, but it was obvious they were discussing something very serious. He kept reaching over and touching her hand. Then, when the meal was over, they sat back and smiled at each other a lot over coffee.'

Back in London, equally frantic newshounds were turning over the details of Renate's career as an AIR Studios tape operator and her modest, solitary home life in Kilburn. The *News of the World* quoted an unnamed female friend whom Renate had rung from Australia with the news. 'I thought it was a joke, and I said to her, "Put Elton on the line." I asked him if it was true, and he said, "Yes" . . . [She's] obviously very keen to marry Elton. She told me, "I really do love him very much."' Before announcing the engagement, Elton had phoned Renate's father, Joachim, in Munich, and had asked for her hand 'in a nice old-fashioned way'.

At her new home near Brighton, Sheila Farebrother appeared as enthusiastic as a mother could be who had never laid eyes on her prospective daughter-in-law. From what Elton had told her, Sheila felt 'instinctively' that Renate was the right choice. 'She's thirty, not some slip of a girl, which was what I first feared. She seems the kind of girl who'll keep Elton in his place.' His eighty-four-year-old grandmother, Ivy, added, 'I'm thrilled. I had to take a tablet to calm myself down.' But there had been no call to his father, Stanley Dwight, now retired and living in Ruthin, north Wales. 'I don't hear from him any more,' Stanley told the *News of the World* bleakly. 'We live in two different worlds.'

The first anti-gay catcall came from the *Daily Express*, whose William Hickey diary on 13 February was headed 'Elton John and the boys he leaves behind':

As close friends around the globe reel from the shock of self-confessed bisexual Elton John's wedding announcement, what about the lads? Probably none is more startled than his personal assistant and live-in companion of more than eight years, Bob Halley.

. . . Halley, who started life with Elton as his chauffeur, has faithfully followed him almost everywhere, to the collapse of his own marriage in the 1970s, when he split from his wife, Pearl.

He and his boss even wear His and His earrings, one each of a pair of diamond solitaires. And he was in Montserrat when Elton met Renate at Christmas while recording there.

Elton, Halley and a blond Australian friend called Gary lived a few miles from the recording studio in a villa, to which the pop star retired early from a New Year's Eve party.

. . . Halley, in his early thirties, is also in Sydney, at the Sebel Town House hotel, where John and Renate have adjoining suites. The poor chap was apparently still mute with shock yesterday, refusing all telephone calls to his own room.

The *People* even succeeded in tracking down the only previous Elton John fiancée. Twice married since, with four children, the former Linda Woodrow now lived with an American serviceman in the village of Hilton, near Cambridge. She had not seen or heard from Elton since he and Bernie had fled from their Islington flat in 1969. She was aware of Elton's many satirical references to her in interviews – as well as in 'Someone Saved My Life Tonight' – and, after hearing for the umpteenth time that she was to blame for putting him off heterosexuality, had resolved to sue for libel. 'I went to a solicitor in Huntingdon, who said he'd take the case. I paid this guy £1,500, but then nothing ever came of it.'

ELTON JILTED ME, screamed the *People*'s front page, above a picture of Linda in her Cambridgeshire garden: 'He was lousy lover says star's old flame.' There followed a reprise of their nine-month romance and its sudden end, thickly planted with signposts to Elton's bisexuality. Linda recalled that, although 'not openly gay', he had 'worn a lot of jewellery and perfume' and had been a 'Mother's boy', constantly phoning home. 'I'm not a bitter woman,' she was quoted as saying. 'I really hope he makes a success of marriage . . . If Renate is expecting romance, though, she's picked the wrong guy. He was lousy in bed.'

The marriage was to be on 14 February, St Valentine's Day. The couple wanted a traditional white wedding, and had chosen St Mark's, an Anglican church in the aptly named Sydney suburb of Darling Point. Normally, under New South Wales law, applicants for a marriage-licence were subject to a thirty-day wait. Elton was granted a special waiver after explaining that concert commitments would not allow him to get married in Australia any later this tour.

In the preceding twenty-four hours, Elton stayed in his hotel suite while Renate shopped for clothes, displaying what would be a consummate skill in avoiding paparazzi. Unloosed on Sydney's expensive boutiques with a blank cheque from her husband-to-be, a second latent skill began to reveal itself. 'The jeans and T-shirts we'd always seen Renate in suddenly just went,' Dee Murray remembered.

'Suddenly, each time you saw her, it was in another nifty little designer number.' Elton emerged only once, furiously pushing through a crowd of reporters, one of whom asked whether he'd bought Renate a ring yet. 'No – and I don't intend to,' he shouted over his shoulder.

A hundred wedding guests were specially flown in from Britain and America, among them Olivia Newton-John, Michael and Mary Parkinson and Barry Humphries. Renate's parents did not attend, and even Sheila and Derf Farebrother decided they would rather share the occasion via a special TV hook-up. To the *Daily Mail*, Sheila revealed that her wedding present to Elton would be a pram. 'He's sensible and likes home life, and most of all he loves children,' she said. 'And I don't think he'll waste any time in making sure he gets some.'

Tradition and old-world charm held sway throughout. Just before the wedding it was suggested to Elton that, following recent superstar precedent, Renate should be asked to sign a 'pre-nuptial agreement', defining her claim on his fortune in the event of a divorce. But, despite all that he had to safeguard, Elton thought a pre-nuptial agreement would be callous and unromantic, and refused to consider the idea.

Two thousand people stood outside St Mark's to see him arrive, seventeen minutes early, in a white tailcoat, a striped shirt with bow tie and his trademark boater. Renate wore a high-necked gown of white silk and Swiss lace and Elton's wedding gift, a heart-shaped gold pendant set with sixty-three diamonds. Bernie Taupin and John Reid were joint best men, and Toni Taupin was one of three pink-clad female attendants. The newlyweds posed at the church door to the strains of 'Kiss the Bride', from *Too Low For Zero*, played through the open window of an adjacent house. In their most-reproduced wedding picture, bride inclines her face to kiss her marginally shorter, boatered bridegroom, somewhat like the famous Buckingham Palace balcony shot of Prince Charles and Princess Diana.

Afterwards, there was a £50,000 reception in an apricot-coloured assembly-room at the Sebel Town House. The guests ate lobster, king prawns, oysters, scallops, smoked salmon, mud crabs, trout, lamb, venison, loin of beef, stuffed quail glazed with honey, pork, turkey and lemon chicken, washed down with Roederer's Cristal champagne, 1959 Puligny Montrachet, 1976 Château Latour and schnapps. Music was provided by a seven-piece string orchestra. Below the obligatory Commonwealth member's portraits of the Queen and Prince Philip stood two giant ice-blocks spelling ER – not for Elizabeth Regina but for Elton and Renate.

The bridegroom made a warm and funny speech, admitting that, left to him alone, the wedding might never have come off. Having asked Renate to marry him at breakneck speed, he had immediately started worrying about how they could possibly find a church and clergy, and order a cake in time. 'It isn't that unpleasant – like going to the dentist,' Renate had reminded him. He could even laugh at the comment from one Australian onlooker as he and his bride had emerged from St Mark's. 'Good on you sport, you old poof! You finally made it!' this well-wisher had shouted. 'It just goes to show how wrong you all were,' Elton had shouted back.

Next morning's British papers all carried the same post-nuptial picture of Elton and – in the *Daily Mirror*'s gracious phrase – his 'Prussian possum'. The prize, however, went to *The Sun*. Picking up the remark of the church-door barracker as repeated by Elton, altering it to make it more offensive, and leaving off quote marks – so that quote imperceptibly became editorial comment – *The Sun*'s headline to Elton's wedding was GOOD ON YER, POOFTER.

The day after it appeared, John Reid spotted *The Sun*'s Sydney correspondent, Nick Ferrari, in the lobby of the Sebel Town House. What happened next Ferrari told in a second dispatch which, for all that he had not written the offending headline, was still somewhat overweening in its tone of innocent astonishment:

ELTON'S TOUGH MINDER BEATS UP SUN MAN

I was savagely beaten up yesterday in an astonishing attack by Elton John's tough-guy manager, John Reid.

He thumped me in the face and dragged me through a crowded hotel lobby after exploding with rage over yesterday's *Sun* headline on Elton's wedding. Furious Reid claimed the headline . . . was '★★★★ing disgraceful'.

Short, stocky Reid, who had been drinking with friends in the bar of the luxurious Sebel Town House hotel, Sydney, suddenly lurched across the lobby towards me.

CRASH! He hauled me from my seat and ripped my shirt.

BANG! He dragged me through the lobby before stunned guests.

WALLOP! Reid hit me in the face and slammed my head against a lift door before staff dragged him away.

I made no attempt to fight back. I just tried to restrain him and talk quietly.

All I said was that I had reported what Elton said in an amusing speech at his wedding reception . . .

The tabloids kept up the pursuit to New Zealand, where Elton and Renate were to honeymoon between his three sold-out concerts. 'I can definitely predict we'll be starting a family,' Elton announced on arrival at Christchurch. In Auckland, there was a different kind of disturbance outside their hotel. Anti-apartheid groups staged an angry protest over Elton's recent appearance with Rod Stewart in South Africa.

The newlyweds' return to Heathrow airport, a month later, showed how rapidly Renate was settling down to her new life. With them off the plane came thirty suitcases, half gold-monogrammed 'EHJ', the other half 'RB'. Their similar garb, of rather medical-looking overalls, gave spice to a rumour sent ahead from the Antipodes. Was Renate already pregnant? 'No way,' Elton replied, also scotching a claim that his honeymoon had been marred by an attack of chickenpox.

Larger Australian purchases were shipped home separately. They included a Sydney tram to which Elton had taken a fancy and bought for $10,000, paying a further $22,000 for its journey from one side of the world to the other. Since it would not pass through Wood-side's front gates, the only method of delivery seemed to be to fly it in dangling from a pair of Chinook helicopters. This plan had to be abandoned because of the nearness of Heathrow airport, and Elton's mental visions of some headline like JUMBO JET COLLIDES WITH TRAM. In the end, the main road outside was closed, and the tram heaved through a gap in the security perimeter. A ten-foot concrete runway was specially built to display it among the flowerbeds and topiary work.

Elton was as explicit as always about the kind of marriage he hoped this would be. 'We're not going to be the type of couple who go out to discos – I'm tired of them anyway – and dinner parties. We just want to spend some time together. We want to have a home life. I simply want to be a family man – and I'm not getting any younger.'

To all such *gemütlich* ideas, Renate signified agreement with her dimply smile. Even so, she made it clear she would not be content with the merely decorative role of rockbiz wife. 'Just because I'm getting married to a famous superstar, it doesn't mean I'm going to give up my job as a recording engineer,' she announced at their wedding reception. To underline the point, Elton's new album, *Breaking Hearts*, bore the credit line 'Engineered by Renate', the verb in this case seeming to imply much more than mere operation of switches and winding-back of tape.

Despite all he had said, domestic life with Elton was not something Renate was ever to experience in any abundance. In early April 1984, he brought her to her new home. Less than a week later, he departed on a European tour. Renate did not accompany him.

Two further absentees were conspicuous in the band he took with him. Nigel Olsson and Dee Murray, his original drummer and bass player, dropped in the mid-1970s and reinstated in the early 1980s, now found themselves dropped again, in Dee's case without warning or explanation. 'The *Breaking Hearts* tour went well, and ended very happily. Elton presented a Cartier watch to everyone who'd been with him on the road. I went off on vacation – same as I had in '74 – expecting a call from the office when I got back about where to meet up with the band again. But – same as in '74 – the call never came.'

His diplomatic triumphs in Russia and China, understandably, had rather gone to Elton's head. He saw himself now less as rock star than roving ambassador, with a gift of communication no diplomat had ever possessed to bridge the chasms between West and East. His spring 1984 European tour included three appearances in Poland, where the Gdansk shipyard workers' Solidarity trade union still waged its pioneering struggle against Russian-prescribed totalitarian rule. On Elton's arrival, with two private aircraft, it was announced he would also be visiting Solidarity's embattled leader, Lech Walesa. They met in Walesa's Gdansk flat, to sip tea from glasses under a portrait of the Pope. Walesa – who bore an eerie likeness to the DJ Paul Gambaccini – tried on Elton's cowboy hat, accepted two cassettes of his music and, later, was guest of honour at the Gdansk concert. 'Visits from people like you are a great help to me,' Walesa told him, adding, perhaps too modestly for a Nobel Peace Prize winner, 'It shows that I have not been forgotten.'

In Munich, joined by Renate, Elton paid what would be his one and only visit to his new German parents-in-law. Joachim and Gisela Blauel entertained him to dinner at their bungalow in the respectable suburb of Gauting. According to Elton later, 'Everything went well, just great. They are lovely people.' *The Sun*'s most faithful tabloid imitator, the *Daily Star*, published a picture of him with Renate after the meeting. Above was a headline transforming the Blauels' quoted opinion of him into yet another anti-homosexual jeer. HE'S A NICE BOY!

There was another, larger distraction from simple conjugal bliss. From midway through Watford's second season in Division One, the possibility had been growing that, for the first time in history, the FA Cup might be within their grasp. On top of Graham Taylor's inspired management, they had received a magical 'draw', matching them against easily trounced opponents like Second Division Charlton and Brighton, and relegation-doomed Birmingham. Their luck held when, reaching the barely conceivable heights of the semi-final, they found themselves facing only Third Division Plymouth. That 1–0 victory guaranteed what, even a year before, would have been unthinkable. Watford were through to the FA Cup Final, playing the Merseyside stars Everton.

Flying back from Berlin for the big occasion, at Wembley Stadium on 19 May, Elton found himself elevated to still greater heights of ambassadorial conciliation. Football in the 1980s had been increasingly plagued by violence, both among spectators and on the field. Merseyside supporters in particular enjoyed a Europe-wide reputation akin to that of Attila's Huns. To lessen the chance of crowd mayhem at Watford's Cup Final, Elton agreed to make a special pre-match appearance, driving round the Wembley pitch before kick-off with Everton's chairman, Philip Carter, in an open-top vintage car.

That day at Wembley expunged two stains from the Dwight escutcheon. Not only his own concert flop here in 1975, but also his cousin Roy's broken leg in 1959, were more than redeemed as Elton sat with Renate in the royal box, just a few places from the Duchess of Kent, who was to present the trophy. Hatless and dressed in a comparatively sober checked suit, he still had to face what the *Sunday Times* called 'good-natured mockery' from the Everton crowd. He was clearly overcome with emotion and during the traditional singing of 'Abide With Me', was seen to brush tears from his eyes. All that spoiled the dignity and spontaneity of the occasion was an outsize plug for his latest single, an electronic scoreboard lit up with the words 'Sad Songs (Say So Much)'.

Alas, Watford's dreams were to end with the drive up the stadium's triumphal avenue. Two weeks earlier, their captain Wilf Rostron, had been sent off in a match against Luton, and so was barred from appearing at Wembley. Against a giant side like Everton, Graham Taylor's only strategy could be to score first, and carry the game on sheer audacity. Though several openings for Watford occurred, the only goal in the first half came from Everton. Next to Elton, Renate was seen to smile in delight, then grow abruptly serious again as her husband explained it was not their side who had scored. A further blow came after half-time when the referee allowed a suspect goal by Everton striker Andy Gray. Try as they might, Watford could do no better than hold the score at 2–0.

On the credit side, thanks chiefly to Elton, it was a Cup Final of unusual good humour, from which the game's general morale received a desperately needed boost. Not one single player was booked for a foul, nor one flurry of kicks and punches noticed on the terraces. Some Watford and Everton fans were even seen sharing cans of lager.

After the final whistle, Elton ran out on to the turf to commiserate with Taylor and his team, especially goalkeeper Kenny Sherwood, the victim of that second, questionable goal. Win or lose, it had been a stupendous day for the club he had almost single-handedly reinvented. Later, there was a grand welcome home parade through Watford, followed by a lavish party for 230 guests at John Reid's house. The chairman switched roles again, getting up with Kiki Dee to sing their old hit 'Don't Go Breaking My Heart'. Shortly afterwards, Graham Taylor signed a further six-year managerial contract. As Elton, at his most sportsmanlike and philosophical, kept saying, there was always another year.

However lofty and dignified a personage he became, there was no escaping a perennial note of Reggie Dwight. Back on tour, his aides were now exercised by a tricky problem. So rapid was the progress from one capital to the next, no hotel had time to wash and dry the superstar's underwear. In Prague, with a backlog of twelve days' Elton undies, the American embassy had to be begged for a loan of its spin-dryer. No such high-level help could be found in Paris, where pairs of Calvin Klein briefs were spotted hanging over the balcony of Elton's suite at the Ritz. There was evident need for Sheila to be still there, doing Reg's washing and, in her own special way, 'whitening it up a bit'.

For Dick James, the music industry's luckiest man, things could hardly have turned out more unfortunately. After his quadruple bypass heart surgery, his doctor had warned him to cut right down on work and stress. A few months later, here he was, plunged into feverish preparation to fight a lawsuit which, if successful, would deal him and his organisation a crippling financial blow.

The writ which had taken John Reid nine years to unloose was, when finally received, a formidable document, covering every aspect of Elton's former involvement with Dick James Music. It challenged the publishing agreement he and Bernie Taupin had signed in 1967, and the recording deals he had signed in 1967 and 1970. It disputed the overseas sub-publishing arrangements by which Elton and Bernie's 'mechanical' royalties were collected. It even attacked the short-lived management agreement between Elton and Dick James,

claiming that as manager, obligated to get his client the best possible
deal, James should never have allowed the publishing and recording
agreements to stand.

The remedies sought were the same as in Gilbert O'Sullivan's
trail-blazingly successful action against Gordon Mills and MAM, two
years earlier. Elton and Bernie should receive back copyright in the
144 songs published during their six-year contract with DJM, including their greatest hits, 'Your Song', 'Daniel', 'Candle in the Wind'
and 'Goodbye Yellow Brick Road'. Elton, not DJM, should own
the masters of his huge cache of Seventies hit singles and perennially
in-demand albums, including *Elton John*, *Honky Château* and *Captain
Fantastic*. DJM also should give up the thirty-six unpublished songs
and twenty-four unreleased tracks it held in its vaults. In addition,
Elton and Bernie should be paid as damages the difference between
what they had received under their DJM agreements and what it was
alleged they ought to have received, plus compound interest for the
intervening years.

English lawsuits, unlike American ones, are not valued in
advance. But estimates were that a victory on all fronts, and a
judgment like that awarded Gilbert O'Sullivan, could cost DJM as
much as £30 million. Small wonder that, against all medical advice,
Dick James devoted every possible moment to preparing and worrying about his company's defence.

In the time-consuming and costly pre-trial months of meeting
lawyers, giving statements and ferreting out papers, DJM acquired an
unexpected ally. This was their former executive Geoffrey Ellis,
whom John Reid had wooed away in 1976. No longer with John
Reid Enterprises, Ellis felt strongly enough about Dick James's
integrity to assist DJM in the case on an advisory basis. Ever correct,
he stipulated he could reveal nothing he had learned during his years
with Reid. Great reliance also was placed on Sidney Goldwater, the
company accountant and Dick James's old and close friend, who had
been instrumental in drawing up the foreign sub-publishing arrangements at the centre of the dispute.

Confident as James was that all in his organisation could bear the
minutest legal scrutiny, he was far from his old, calmly ebullient self.
It wounded him enormously that Elton's lawsuit named him personally, along with his companies DJM and This Record Co. 'He felt
they'd always had this special relationship, almost like father and son,'
Stephen James remembers. 'He couldn't understand why Elton had
turned on him.' He was convinced that, if Elton and he could sit
down and talk together as of old, everything could be sorted out
without recourse to litigation. But Elton, as ever, was an elusive

pimpernel, jetting all over the world in apparent contradiction of his desire for a home life with Renate. August 1984 found him dangling from a helicopter in the south of France for a video to accompany his new single, 'Passengers'. By autumn, he was back on another American tour, so strenuous that he collapsed onstage with a 'virus infection', this time in Charlotte, North Carolina. Next he was reported in New York, in an incident revealing how much changed was the wide-eyed fan of yore. Emerging from a Madison Avenue store, he encountered Doris Day, the freckled *chanteuse* whose films, like *Calamity Jane*, he used to soak up on Technicolor afternoons in Metroland. 'Hello,' she said. 'I'm a fan.' But Elton walked past, not even recognising her.

That winter, Dick James finally succeeded in contacting Elton and arranging to meet him privately and discuss the lawsuit. 'We arranged to see him in a hotel, one afternoon at two o'clock,' Stephen James says. 'We got there at 1.30 and had a sandwich in the coffee shop. At about 1.45, we were paged and told there was a phone call for us. It was John Reid. He said he and his solicitor had talked Elton out of coming to see us.

'I still bitterly resent the fact that my father was never allowed to talk to Elton personally before going into court. I'm convinced that if they'd sat down on their own, they could have sorted it all out. Because we were willing to sell him back the master recordings, and discuss selling back the song copyrights. And I don't think Elton wanted to go through with it, and what it did to my father.'

After several delays, the case opened in the Chancery Division of the High Court, before Mr Justice Nicholls, on 4 June, 1985. Elton, Bernie and Elton's two companies, William A. Bong Ltd and Happenstance Ltd, were represented by Mark Littman QC and three junior counsel. Dick James and his organisation were represented by George Newman QC and two juniors. DJM contested the suit on all counts, and Dick James denied personal responsibility for the disputed contracts. Into court with both sides came a huge volume of paperwork, drawn from forty separate files. The plaintiffs' statement of claim alone ran to 100 pages, and the bundle of pleadings to more than 400. The giving of oral evidence took thirty days and the full hearing something like fifty. For much of that time, Elton's straw boater lay on a table in court, giving the dry, dusty, pedantic proceedings its rakish Edwardian signature.

Mark Littman's opening address quickly set the tone of the proceedings. He portrayed Dick James as an unscrupulous predator who had taken advantage of Elton and Bernie's extreme youth and inexperience to bind them to 'onerous' and 'one-sided' contracts and, in addition to having a stranglehold on their work, had systematically siphoned their royalty earnings off into a network of overseas 'shell' companies. In other words, a picture conforming to every stereotype and caricature of the cigar-chewing, swindling pop mogul. 'The whole suit was obviously aimed personally at my father,' Stephen James says. 'Elton himself never seemed comfortable about that. During the whole time in court, I never once saw him look at my father – not even when my father was in the witness box. At the end of each day, Elton was hustled off through a far door, so there was no chance of them meeting outside.'

A few days into the case, a meeting was set up with John Reid to see if, even at this late stage, some agreement might be hammered out. 'I went by myself to meet him at their solicitors, Frere Cholmeley,' Stephen James says. 'My father at that stage said he couldn't bear to be in the same room as John Reid. The offer from John was basically that, if we gave up the song copyrights and record masters, he'd give us a million dollars to go away. I said, "Why are you talking about dollars? We should be thinking in pounds. And, anyway, you left a nought off there." John told me to eff off, and I left.'

The James side suffered an early blow, both strategically and to morale. Sidney Goldwater, Dick James's accountant and a crucial witness on the sub-publishing question, was found to be suffering from cancer and so could not be expected to appear in court. The cancer proved inoperable and, only a few weeks after its diagnosis, Goldwater was dead. This sudden loss of his old friend caused Dick James further unhappiness and anxiety.

Elton's side had been diligent in tracing figures from his earliest past who could present James in an unfavourable light. Among the first to be contacted was Ray Williams, who had discovered Elton, via *New Musical Express* back in 1967, had first teamed him with Bernie Taupin, but had ended up with zilch per cent of the eventual goldmine. Though not called as a witness, Williams added background to the picture of Dick James as ruthless mogul, recalling how James had arbitrarily terminated his contract as personal manager in 1970, and how, in his short tenure, he had never been allowed to see any of Elton's agreements with DJM.

The case against the publishing contract was a reprise of days long ago in Tin Pan Alley and Frome Court, Pinner. Sheila Farebrother told how she had backed her son in his desire to become a musician, allowing him to drop out of school before A levels; scraping up £25 to buy him an old car when he began at Mills Music; even helping him draft his fateful reply to Ray Williams's *NME* advertisement. She said she had signed the first publishing agreement on his behalf as a minor, having no real idea what it meant. 'It was just like the others he came home with and said, "Sign this, Mum", and I would sign it. I didn't carefully consider it. I don't even understand them now.'

Another figure from the distant past was Muff Winwood, the A & R man for Island Records who had befriended Elton and Bernie during their Pinner exile in 1969. Winwood recalled how frustrated Elton had been over the failure of his early singles, and how he had wanted to quit DJM for Island and let Winwood and Lionel Conway take over his management from Dick James. He described how Island's owner, Chris Blackwell, had offered him a £10,000 advance and, in looking over his DJM contracts, had opined there were 'holes' in them. The question had then been dropped, thanks chiefly to James's agreement that Elton and Bernie could write what they chose and that Elton should be allowed to make his first album, *Empty Sky*.

John Reid made an impressive witness. In his calm, quiet, orderly Scots voice, he told how he had become 'suspicious' about the overseas royalty earnings just after leaving DJM's employ to become Elton's independent manager in 1972. He recalled, at that early stage, consulting Paul McCartney's brother-in-law John Eastman, and Eastman's view that there was 'a strong case' against Dick James for not accounting properly and levying a 50 per cent retention rate on American mechanical royalties. Reid's pursuit of the matter via two firms of accountants over eight years earned the only compliment to come from Mr Justice Nicholls, who, in the eventual judgment, described him as 'a young man both astute and tenacious'.

Evidence from a solicitor named Charles Levison, whose firm Harbottle and Lewis had drawn up John Reid's management contract with Elton, gave some insight into Reid's own earnings in commission since 1972. He himself agreed that, under his entitlement to 10 per cent of Elton's record income, he had received £579,136 between 1973 and 1976, and a further £676,733 up to December 1982. It was the only faint allusion to the fact that a massive payout for Elton also would mean a proportionate payout for Reid.

Bernie Taupin had flown in for the hearing from Los Angeles, a dapper, urbane, suntanned figure, very different from the shy country boy frequently referred to in evidence. He described how many of the songs in the £30 million jackpot had been written by him in that tiny shared bedsitter at 30a Frome Court, then carried, postman-like, along the tiny hall to Elton at the living-room piano. On the complex business matters under dispute, however, Bernie could shed little light. Ever bookish and vague, he had taken in virtually nothing of the papers he'd signed with Elton down the years; of meetings with lawyers and accountants, employment companies and tax shelters. 'It got a bit monotonous,' he remembers now. 'To question after question, I could only give the same reply. "I'm sorry, I just don't remember." '

Elton himself, soberly dark-suited, his exiguous new hair scraped back into a ponytail, took the stand at the start of the second week. Throughout his evidence, he was treated with noticeable deference by Mr Justice Nicholls, who, at several points, seemed worried that the proceedings might be overtiring him.

He recalled the day in 1967 when Bernie and he had been summoned to Dick James's office over the illicit use of DJM's studio, not knowing that their demos had already found favour with James. Sitting outside the great man's room had been 'very frightening', Elton said: 'a bit like waiting for your O-level results'. James's offer to sign them both as writers had been 'unbelievable, like a dream come true'. The subsequent agreements, publishing, recording and management, had seemed 'heaven-sent'. 'I was very young. It was a very exciting period. I didn't think of going to a solicitor. I just trusted Mr James. I was very naïve and wet behind the ears. Anything anyone told me to sign, I signed. Everything was done on trust.'

To him, in those days, James's terms had often seemed munificent. Receiving a £50 advance and £15 a week to write songs was 'the big time' for two boys who had previously been paid nothing. Likewise, being allowed to make the *Elton John* album as an unknown, at a cost of £7,000 to £8,000, had come 'like manna from Heaven'. The resultant hike in his record royalty rate from 20 to 60 per cent – i.e. 2 per cent of retail sale price to 6 per cent – at the time had seemed like 'a shot in the arm'.

His assertion that 'vast sums' of his royalties had been 'whittled away' brought a sharp counterattack from DJM's counsel, George Newman QC. Balance sheets were passed to Elton, showing that up to December 1982, he had received £13.4 million from record sales. In publishing royalties he had received a further £1.16 million and Bernie Taupin just over £1 million. Over the same period, This Record Co. had made profits of £7 million and DJM Records £1.5 million. Would Elton care to comment on these figures? 'I can't comment on them,' he replied. 'I'm not a chartered accountant. My lawyers told me there had been mishandling of money, and I just told them to get on with it [the lawsuit]. I was led to believe that vast sums were involved.'

Never in question was the perseverance of the James Organisation in launching Elton's career nor that, in the most adverse judgement, DJM would be entitled to a reasonable return on palpable long-term faith and investment. The same balance sheets showed that, if it had taken three years to establish Elton John as an international star, it had taken five to see any profit back from him. In 1972, the year of *Honky Château*, 'Daniel' and 'Crocodile Rock', he still represented a deficit of £197,000. Only in 1973, the year of *Goodbye Yellow Brick Road* and the Hollywood Bowl concert, had he shot to a £236,000 profit.

The disputed recording agreement also showed how what had once been faith in an unknown artist looked like rank exploitation with the hindsight of that artist's global success. In 1967, when Philips refused to release an album by Elton, DJM had set up its own DJM record label, handling all aspects of production bar actual manufacture. DJM Records then paid its production company, This Record Co., a 10 per cent royalty, on which Elton's royalty was calculated. This 10 per cent UK rate had never been increased even though the going rate – for performers far smaller than Elton – quickly rose to around 16 per cent.

The two-tier system of This Record Co., the production company, and DJM, the record label, had at the time seemed flattering to Elton, a way of ensuring total artistic control over his records. However, his contract entitled him only to a share of profits from This Record Co. The DJM label also generated profits from manufacture, distribution and sales, of which he was entitled to not a penny. It was alleged that this side of the arrangement had never been explained to him, and that even John Reid had been ignorant of it until Geoffrey Ellis suggested broadening the audit from publishing to recording.

Even more serious allegations were made about the DJM foreign subsidiaries which, after 1975, had collected Elton and Bernie's song royalties in Australia, Japan, France, Scandinavia, the Netherlands and Italy. Elton and Bernie were by now on a 60–40 publishing split with DJM, but that was not as straightforward as it sounded. First, an administrator, responsible for collection in each territory, deducted a 15 per cent charge. Thirty-five per cent then remained in the overseas subsidiary while 50 per cent came home to be split 40–60 between DJM and the writers. According to their counsel, it was not just that DJM failed to explain the system and the full impact of its deductions to Elton and Bernie. There had been a deliberate cover-up of 'the critical factors which showed the diversion to be wrongful'.

Stephen James spent four days in the box, an ordeal for which there can be no adequate preparation. 'I'd been coached a bit by our lawyers in what to say, but it wasn't of much help. Up there, you're totally on your own. You're not even supposed to look at your own counsel. They can ask you anything they like, and you never know where it's coming from next.' He was cross-examined by junior counsel, often on matters of detailed accountancy that lay outside his knowledge. To him, as head of This Record Co., the crucial question was put. Why had Elton's UK royalty rate been permanently pegged at a beginner's 6 per cent of retail? Stephen replied that it had been more than compensated for by the higher than average rate that DJM had obtained for him throughout the rest of the world, especially with MCA in America. To have raised his UK royalty to the going rate, and lowered his American rate commensurately would have reduced his income by something like £2 million.

Dick James himself was in the box for five days. Despite recent traumas, he gave a relaxed performance in the face of hard and hostile questioning by Mark Littman QC. He recalled how, having 'a minute or two to spare', he had interviewed Elton and Bernie, divined their talent and signed it up for a £100 advance, which was, for those days, 'on the right side of generous'. The original 50–50 publishing split had been standard practice then and, indeed, still was today. Elton's royalty rate from This Record Co. might seem small in modern terms, but it had been generous at the time – Elton himself had freely admitted thinking so. DJM had done him proud, given that the chances of ever breaking him had been so remote for so many years.

Only once did James become ruffled. This was when Mark Littman suggested that DJM's Swiss subsidiary had merely been a front for him personally to siphon Elton and Bernie's royalties into a Swiss bank account. 'My father was terribly upset, and terribly annoyed,' Stephen James says. 'He thought it was a disgraceful suggestion.'

In July, Britain's legal system went into its summer recess and the case had to be adjourned for two months. The Jameses were cautiously optimistic, sensing that the judge inclined to their version of the evidence. Dick James felt he had acquitted himself well in the witness box, and began to think this aberrant stretch of bad luck might finally be nearing an end.

It had taken twenty-five years, but social conscience was taking root in pop music at last. Late in 1984, BBC television showed a horrifying report on the famine in Ethiopia, and the impotence of government and relief agencies in combating it. Among many shocked and outraged by the pictures was Bob Geldof, Irish lead singer with the Boomtown Rats. Mobilising his many friends in the music business, Geldof organised the making of a special ensemble single to raise funds for Ethiopian famine relief. 'Do They Know It's Christmas?', featuring performers like Boy George, Spandau Ballet and Big Country under the collective name Band Aid, was a massive British hit in December; the first 'Christmas record' ever truly deserving the name. There quickly followed an American counterpart, 'Feed the World', with a still more impressive artist roster, from Michael Jackson and Cyndi Lauper to Bruce Springsteen and Bob Dylan. What had been the most selfish and self-centred of all media suddenly transformed itself into the most community-minded and caring.

The past year in Britain had been one of extreme ugliness, as a misconceived and badly led miners' strike tested Margaret Thatcher's avowed intent to smash trade union power. TV images from home also became horrific, with a new-style paramilitary police force sealing off whole counties, and ferocious baton charges against those whom Mrs Thatcher repellently termed 'the enemy within'. Among the miners' few public supporters were young left-wing pop musicians like Paul Weller, Jimmy Somerville and Billy Bragg. There was a rebirth of the mid-Sixties 'protest song'. Even pop's latest teenybop sensation, the two-man group Wham!, gave a concert to raise money for wives and families hit by the strike.

In May 1985, football thuggery wrought its worst mayhem yet. A mindless riot by British supporters at the Heysel stadium in Brussels caused thirty-nine deaths from crushing and led English clubs to be banned from all matches in Europe for the next five years. The chairman of Watford was specially depressed to think how all his cleaning-up and peacemaking initiatives had been set back.

The brightest spot of the year – indeed, of the Eighties so far – came on 13 July. From Bob Geldof's Band Aid record had grown the concept of Live Aid, a giant concert for the Ethiopian famine, televised simultaneously from Wembley Stadium in London and JFK Stadium in Philadelphia, and featuring almost every major American and British pop name in a marathon eight-hour bill: Bob Dylan, the Rolling Stones, David Bowie, Tina Turner, Phil Collins, Sting, U2, Madonna, Queen, Paul Young, Geldof himself with the Boomtown Rats, and scores of others.

Such an occasion could not possibly leave out the performer who had pioneered these sensibilities fifteen years in advance of everyone else. Elton was allotted an unprecedented thirty-minute spot at the end of the day's marathon from Wembley, playing bespangled

antiques like 'Rocket Man' and 'Bennie and the Jets' in a striped
lamé frock coat and Queen Mary toque, backed by an augmented
band and a vocal quartet including Kiki Dee.

In his role as Big Daddy to the new glitter rockers, he also
introduced George Michael of Wham!, whose potential as a writer
and solo performer he had spotted well ahead of the crowd. Michael
then sang 'Don't Let the Sun Go Down on Me', a dual tribute to
Elton's influence and his special way of bestowing public compli-
ments. It was all a far cry from the High Courts of Justice, from
writs, depositions, statements of claim, dusty robes, grey wigs, pink
ribbon and green sealing-wax.

To build up strength for the second part of the case, Dick James
went away with his wife to their flat in Cannes. After only three or
four days there, they went to bed one night, leaving the doors to
their balcony open. At about 1 am, Mrs James awoke to find a
burglar standing over her. The burglar hit James in the face, then
jumped over the balcony, which was six storeys high. It afterwards
transpired he was a thief famous up and down the Riviera, a trained
acrobat, able to perform near-impossible climbs and leaps from
balcony to balcony.

'That was the last straw for my father,' Stephen James says. 'He
was so distressed by the whole thing, he couldn't sleep without
sedation for about three weeks afterwards. And he said he never
wanted to go back to that flat. He felt his luck had became so bad
that it could never turn back again.'

Proceedings in the High Court resumed on 1 October. In his
closing speech for the defendants, George Newman QC submitted
that there was 'not a scintilla of evidence' that Dick James had used
'undue influence' to make Elton and Bernie sign away their song
copyrights. 'There is no evidence of browbeating, persuasion or use
of muscle in any way. The fact that they might have been in awe of
Dick James and his position is neither here nor there. You might be
in awe of your bank manager. Elton John simply has never had a
complaint about his career and about what was done for him in the
way of exploitation and promotion. In fact, he is very fond of Dick
James, and is grateful to him in many ways. He has amassed a
considerable fortune because of what Dick James has done for him.'

Winding up for the plaintiffs, Mark Littman QC denied that
Elton and Bernie had brought the case merely at the suggestion of
lawyers. 'As long as these agreements remain in respect of this very
large body of master recordings and songs – a third of them unissued
– it is very reasonable to bring such a claim.' Though their confidence

in Dick James had naturally been 'shaken' over the alleged siphoning of royalties abroad, they were 'more concerned with the future than with the past'.

On 29 November, Mr Justice Nicholls delivered his verdict in a four-hour judgment. Essentially, he found against DJM on almost all counts, but at the same time awarded Elton and Bernie only a fraction of what they had claimed. Clearing Dick James of all personal blame or liability, he was nevertheless to use words that wounded James to the quick.

The crux of the judgment was that, in dealings with their two protégés, especially as minors, DJM's prime duty had been that of a 'fiduciary', or trustee. The onus on Dick James throughout had been to secure Elton and Bernie the fairest possible terms rather than to do smart business on his own company's account. It was a piece of brand-new law, with obvious far-reaching consequences for the whole British music industry.

On this principle, the 1967 publishing agreement, assigning Elton and Bernie's entire songwriting output for the next six years to DJM, had been 'an unfair transaction'. Though James had not consciously sought to take advantage of them, and had acted in good faith and according to standard music-business procedure, this did not fully answer the claim of undue influence. 'One can obtain an unfair advantage by the exercise of a dominant influence without intending to be unfair.' In the same way, while similarly acknowledging Dick James's good faith, the 1968 recording agreement, with its fixed low royalty rate, had also been unfair. The amended agreement of 1970, increasing the royalty rate, had not been unfair, given that at the time Elton still had to make a hit record. But it had been 'not generous'.

The judge's harshest words were directed at the internal structure of Dick James Music and its adverse impact on Elton and Bernie's income as writers and Elton's as a recording artist. The way in which DJM's own record label paid its production company a systematically low royalty, as the basis of Elton's UK record royalty, 'could not stand scrutiny' as a discharge of fiduciary duty. Nor could the fact that the record company earned profits of which Elton received nothing. Under his contract, he should have received a share in all proceeds from the licensing and exploitation of his records.

Most damning was Mr Justice Nicholls about DJM's overseas subsidiaries, and the two separate bites taken out of Elton and Bernie's foreign royalties before they reached London. In the judge's view, it was not right for subsidiaries with neither offices nor staff to deduct 35 per cent on top of the 15 per cent already taken by the outside administrator. He refused to accept Stephen James's assertion that even subsidiaries without offices incurred expenses from such things as promotion, advertising and business travel.

Dick James, as 'an able businessman' had realised what John Reid would say about such a system, and so it had been kept dark in successive royalty statements and in all correspondence and discussion about sub-publishing. Elton's side had not known the full story until after the start of the present action. All this had been 'unconscionable' behaviour on DJM's part.

Three factors, however, militated against the setting aside of the publishing and recording agreements, despite their breaches of fiduciary duty. The first was DJM's undoubted success in marketing Elton and Bernie's work, which, even on unfair terms, had given them undreamed-of fame and wealth. The second was that throughout Elton's time with DJM, he had had a good relationship with Dick James, and felt he had 'no particular axe to grind'. The third was that so many years had been allowed to elapse between the signing of the agreements and the decision to bring a lawsuit. 'The balance of justice', therefore, was against rescinding either. The song copyrights and record masters would remain with DJM.

Damages were granted on two counts. First, on Elton's UK record royalty, where the judge ruled he should have received 12 per cent, not 5.4 per cent of the retail sale price, and that DJM must make good the difference, with interest. Second, on foreign sub-publishing, where 35 per cent had been improperly withheld from the calculation of his and Bernie's overseas royalties. These were now to be recomputed as 60 per cent, not of 50 but 85 per cent. In addition, the retention rate of DJM-USA was retroactively lowered from 50 to 25 per cent.

Dick James was absolved of all personal responsibility or liability on every count. There was no order as to which side should pay the costs of the action – by then estimated at between £1 million and £1.5 million.

In interviews with the trade paper *Music Week*, both sides claimed victory. John Reid said that, although Elton had not won back his song copyrights, 'a moral victory' had been won on the UK royalty rate and sub-publishing. Dick James's riposte was that DJM had 'lost a battle but won the war'. Each expressed regret that the action had ever been brought and said it need not have dragged on so long, enriching lawyers along the way, if the other had been prepared to see reason. Dick James added a heartfelt lament on behalf of all music publishers now likely to be hit by the John and Paul, or Elton and Bernie, syndrome. 'It seems rather incongruous that you can go back with a contract after seventeen years and expect to renegotiate. We never heard in the past that Cole Porter, Jerome Kern or George Gershwin disputed the contracts they'd made with their publishers.'

No one denied that the lawsuit had redrawn the ground rules for British music publishers and their writers. To Elton, personally, however, only marginal benefits had accrued. Copyright in his greatest hits still remained in other hands. The hoped-for fortune in damages had nowhere near materialised. Initial estimates of the royalty repayment went as high as £5 million. But, according to Stephen James, it ended up as 'a six-figure sum – less than a million', not enough to justify lodging an appeal.

But if Dick James Music was relatively undiminished, James himself had been devastated. He could not get over the fact that Elton, his surrogate son, had turned on him, nor that, even though cleared of personal blame, his cherished business integrity had come under repeated attack in court. The word 'unconscionable', in particular, returned again and again to haunt him – proof, above all, that his fabulous luck had turned bad and would never turn good again.

His heart trouble, amazingly, had not recurred during the protracted strain of the lawsuit, the death of his friend Sidney Goldwater or the incident with the burglar at his flat. But, as heart specialists know, there can often be more danger to a serious cardiac condition when pressure ceases and adrenalin is suddenly shut off. Barely three months later, on 1st February, 1986, James suffered a massive heart attack at his St John's Wood home and died before he could be taken to hospital.

Stephen James has no doubt where the blame lies. 'I'm sure that if it hadn't been for the strain of the court case and the impugning of his reputation, which hurt him so much, he would never have had the attack, and might still be alive today. I still feel so furious that something so unimportant by comparison with my father's life should have caused that. It hadn't been the way I'd expected him to go.'

Elton was shocked and distressed by his old mentor's death, and patently troubled by thoughts that the lawsuit might have played a part in bringing it about. His lawyers were ordered to reach a settlement as rapidly as possible with DJM over the royalty repayments. Since Dick James had been absolved of personal liability in the case, Elton also agreed to meet his legal costs, paying them into an estate eventually valued at £6.8 million.

However, there was one touch that the punctilious good boy of old might have managed a little better. 'After my father died, I got a message that Elton was very upset, and wanted to send his condolences,' Stephen James remembers. 'It was phoned through to me by someone at John Reid's office.'

SEVENTEEN

Gotcha!

THE first reports, around 1982, were merely of another bizarre American invention. New York, that unique repository of dirt and germs, had created a brand-new disease. It was a virus which attacked antibodies in the bloodstream, destroying the body's immune system and causing death from the torrent of infection which then rushed in. Weirdly, it was thought to occur in only four social groups, haemophiliacs, Haitian immigrants, intravenous drug users and male homosexuals, among whom it was communicated by sexual and oral contact. Its cumbersome name, Acquired Immune Deficiency Syndrome was shortened to a computer-style acronym, AIDS.

In a short time, the haemophiliacs, junkies and Haitians had been cast off like so much ballast from a rising balloon. AIDS was reported primarily as a disease of homosexual males, endemic among New York's huge gay population, especially at Lower East Side pick-up joints and 'bath houses', where up to twenty casual promiscuous encounters per person per night might take place. A spate of deaths followed among figures prominent in the art and fashion world and in Hollywood, some of them men never dreamed to be other than totally hetero. This was a new and ghastly version of 'coming out'.

The first British AIDS cases made even worse impact on a society which prided itself on having virtually eliminated sexually-transmitted disease. That the figures were still infinitesimal, especially compared with those of cancer or heart disease, brought little comfort from the medical authorities. The lethal virus had been found to act with horrible leisureliness, taking up to eight years to incubate in a body which for all that time might think itself quite healthy. From the few dozen at present, future cases were projected in the thousands, even the millions. Late twentieth-century Europe was suddenly looking at another medieval Black Death.

The growing incidence of victims among heterosexuals – and those whose sexuality was irrelevant, like newborn babies and nuns – continued to make little general impression. To the public at large, AIDS was a disease of homosexual men, one which seemed to confirm everything ever alleged about their promiscuity and predatoriness. In the rising panic, all final traces of Seventies liberal tolerance disappeared. A brush fire of homophobia swept through Britain, fanned by the Victorian voices that were once again in the ascendant. Several prominent Christians, in and out of the pulpit, went so far as to suggest that AIDS was more than a medical catastrophe. It was nothing less than God's will; a Heaven-sent scourge on all those guilty of 'unnatural' acts, whom a too-tolerant society by now almost recognised as legitimate human beings.

So the young men wasted away. The modern Pecksniffs told them it was their own fault for being so disgusting. And tabloid newspapers began to scent circulation in what *The Sun*'s headline writers with their usual humanity had already termed 'the Gay Plague'.

There was never any doubt that Elton genuinely loved Renate. Months after their wedding, he was still talking about it in wonderment to his long-time friend Nina Myskow. 'He told me that when he turned round in that church and saw Renate coming down the aisle towards him, he thought she was the most beautiful thing he'd ever seen in his life. And there were tears in his eyes when he said it.'

The myths that have grown up around Renate can be quickly disposed of. She was no mere gold-digger, taking advantage of a momentary mad whim on Elton's part to plug into his millions. Nor was she, as would also be alleged, a lesbian, conniving in a mutually convenient show marriage. She loved Elton back, with a wholehearted simplicity that very nearly overcame the handicaps of their relationship. There was probably no one in his life who ever got closer to him, or was finally rejected with such anguish.

Renate's rather wooden exterior proved to have been deeply misleading. 'She was a really intelligent, lively girl,' Nina Myskow says. 'She had a great sense of humour, and she was one of the most thoughtful people you could ever meet. Even as this big-time pop star's wife, she had a quality that was totally modest and unassertive. And she knew just the way to get along with Elton. When they were together, they were good together.'

Those who had seen the romance grow in half-smiles over a

studio control desk wondered if it could ever have a sexual side. It did and, to begin with at least, it was totally successful. Two people equally shy and uncertain can often bring about miracles together. 'I know they had a physical relationship,' Nina Myskow says. 'Elton used to talk a lot about having children. Though, being him, in the next breath he'd say, "Ah, you've only got to sit next to a crying baby on a plane to be put off them for life."'

On one level, being married suited him perfectly. He called Renate 'the wife' as naturally as if they had settled in a mock-Tudor semi in Pinner, Northwood or Dollis Hill. He would write letters and cards to 'Wifey' signing them 'Hubby'. It amused him to picture them as Darby and Joan, with mugs of Bournevita cocoa, in tartan pompom slippers, seated on either side of a Magicoal fire.

No other rock star's wife was ever treated with such old-world chivalry. 'Whenever they were together, Elton paid attention to Renate all the time,' Nanette Newman remembers. 'He'd always be leaning over to kiss her or squeeze her hand. He always seemed worried that she might feel neglected or left out.'

It was wonderful to him to have someone in his life whom he could spoil, publicly and legitimately. His lavishness with Renate passed all previous bounds. He showered gifts on her, jewellery, flowers, clothes and still more clothes for her stupendously expanded wardrobe. Her great weakness, like his own, was chocolate. At Easter, Harrods would be ordered to send its most prodigious chocolate egg for 'the wife'.

Thoughtful and sensitive on that same level, he realised the problems Renate faced in integrating into his environment. In particular, he wanted her to feel at home at his Old Windsor mansion. When they returned there after their wedding in Australia, he told her to do anything she wanted that would make the house nicer for her.

The difficulty was that every room was packed with fifteen years' worth of Elton's bulk-bought treasures, the mazes of Bugatti furniture, the labyrinths of Asprey's silver, the phalanxes of Lalique glass, the forests of many-hued Tiffany lamps, the seraglios of Art Nouveau dancing girls and nymphs, all in their places like exhibits in a museum. From the model of Pharoah Tutankhamun's throne across the vista of mock-Renaissance sideboard, brass palm trees and Majorelle marquetry card tables to the Victorian clubman's chair with attached jockey-weighing scales, nothing that met Renate's eye could be called lived-in or homey. 'She was totally bemused by the place,' an ex-Rocket employee remembers. 'She didn't know where she was supposed to sit or not to sit. She hardly liked to turn round unless something got knocked over or broken.'

Renate's influence was confined to the kitchen, which she began to have completely rebuilt, and the master bedroom suite, where she and Elton shared a carved wooden bed modelled on that of Empress Josephine. So worried was Elton by her lack of territorial demands that he insisted she should have one of the five remaining suites as her private domain, decorated and furnished just as she wanted it.

One of the few journalists permitted into Woodside after Renate's arrival was David Wigg of the *Daily Express*. The perennially 'safe' Wigg duly reported on a wild man of pop, calmed and mellowed by a good woman's love. 'I had everything but I had nothing,' Elton told him. 'I needed the challenge of changing my life, making it more fulfilling and sharing. I could see myself ending up as an eccentric, living alone and being incredibly fussy, rather like Quentin Crisp, except that I dust and he doesn't. I didn't want that.'

His verdict on marriage so far? 'Fabulous. I'm so happy, and very much in love. Being married has made me so much calmer. I'm less argumentative now, and more reasonable. I don't get my own way any more, but it's so nice to come home and actually share things.' Even so, he admitted that he could be a terrible person to live with. 'I'm so set in my ways. I've got certain methods of doing everything. Like, I can't speak at breakfast. I've got to have total silence. When you share a house with someone else, that can be a problem, but so far it hasn't been. The wife's got her own suite of rooms that she can go to if she wants to, but otherwise we share most things in the house. She's taking over, and making it more of a home than it was before. She just adds little things to the place, like flowers, and the way she puts things together make it more homely. It's a woman's touch, and I like that.'

He returned constantly to the theme of having children, always stressing the plural. 'I was an only child, and I didn't enjoy that much. Ideally, I'd like to have two, but you never know. Please God that we can have one. We've been trying for children, but it hasn't happened yet. If we find we can't have them, we'll consider adoption. There are so many kids who don't have a home. I think adoption is wonderful.'

So why, if he was so calm and happy with Renate, did he plunge right back into his old frenetic and frequently miserable way of life? Why, longing for children so much, did he embark on the one course that guaranteed he would never have any? Why, with happiness within his grasp, did he almost immediately fling it away?

It seems clear that Elton had hoped marriage to Renate would cancel out his homosexual side and that, within a very short time, he realised that had not happened. Plenty of marriages have worked in such circumstances, and Renate evidently possessed sufficient understanding and patience to give this one a more than healthy chance, on any terms Elton chose. But he himself was too conventional for any kind of open relationship à la V. Sackville-West and Harold Nicolson. 'It wasn't enough for Elton that the marriage should work,' Nina Myskow says. 'It had to be seen to work. So being apart, with the excuse he had to go off on tour, was better than being together in any way that could cause comment or criticism.'

Renate was not left completely alone. A live-in couple ran the house, and there were frequent callers, from Elton's business organisation and family. His grandmother had by now been installed in the Orangery, and Sheila often drove up from Sussex to see her, sometimes bringing along Ivy's other daughter, Win. No evidence exists of especially warm relations between Renate and her British in-laws.

The curious feature of her months at Woodside is how little she used its magnificent facilities. Private cinema, swimming pool, squash court and games room had no allure to her, and she seldom even went out into the 38 acres of perfectly manicured grounds. Apart from one or two visits to health farms, she preferred not to leave the house. Much of her time – even in the most brilliant summer weather – was spent lying on an expensive sunbed Elton had bought her. She became fascinated by computers, and would spend all day, and all night as well, up in her private suite tapping the keys of a PC. Almost the only pastime she and Elton shared outside a recording studio was watching video films, which he would bring home from his trips in huge quantity. With a meticulousness he warmly approved, Renate set herself to cataloguing the videos in a set of expensive leather-bound ledgers.

Even from a distance, Elton remained hugely protective of her. He was specially concerned to shield her from the politics that always raged inside his court, and told her that when she wanted something, she must always come straight to him, rather than speaking to Bob Halley or John Reid. The woman who, a year ago, had possessed only jeans and a few T-shirts now had need of a personal assistant to catalogue her clothes. 'John didn't think she ought to have one,' Nina Myskow remembers. 'So she had to go to Elton about that. He got very annoyed that she shouldn't immediately have been given what she asked for.'

He relied on John Reid to be supportive of her in his absence, and bristled extremely if ever Reid proved dilatory in the job. 'John was supposed to be coming over to dinner one night while Elton was away,' Nina Myskow remembers. 'At about five-thirty, the phone goes. Typical John – he's cancelling. Then Elton rings up from the States and asks "How are things going for the dinner party tonight?" "John's not coming," Renate says. "Oh, isn't he!" Elton says. "Just you wait and see!" Half an hour later, the phone rings again. It's John. He is coming after all.'

A curious sense of the relationship leaked into Elton's album, *Ice on Fire*, released in 1985 while the court battle with DJM was just drawing to an end. That the marriage had already hit trouble was obvious to close friends like Nina Myskow. 'I remember being at the house for dinner one awful night. Renate was away at a health farm, and Elton wouldn't get up. I just saw these trays being brought out of his room, covered with Mars-bar wrappers and sandwich crusts.'

Ice on Fire marked the return to the fold of his best-ever record producer, Gus Dudgeon. Seven years after being peremptorily dropped, Dudgeon got a phone call from Elton out of the blue. 'He said, "There never was a team like you and me. You've got to produce my next one." I said, "All right, but I've got to hear the songs first." He said, "Christ! It can't still be like that!" I said, "That's the way it always was."'

The album included a duet between Elton and George Michael whose title, 'Wrap Her Up', was all too apt a summary of Renate's situation. Still more unconsciously evocative was 'Nikita', in which Elton sang to a lonely Russian girl 'in your little corner of the world', but as bleakly as if he meant a German girl at home in Old Windsor, painstakingly listing video films in a leather-bound book.

The accompanying video was directed by Ken Russell, British cinema's white-haired *enfant terrible*, who had cast Elton in his screen version of *Tommy*. Underlining the new hetero image, Russell made Nikita a blonde East German guard on the Berlin Wall and Elton her wooer from a capitalist Rolls-Royce. A dream sequence followed in which Elton was seen with Nikita at a Watford game, strapped to the gigantic Doc Marten boots Ken Russell had originally made him wear as the Pinball Wizard.

'Nikita' was his biggest single for years, reaching number three in Britain and seven in America and more than answering the long-time demand of an enormous public for 'another song like Daniel'. For what not even Ken Russell realised at the time was that Nikita is actually a man's name.

★

Above: New-look Elton with Watford players fresh from the bath.
(Rex Features)

Below left: Elton with Kiki Dee when the road was starting to get tougher.
(Rex Features)

Below right: Elton pays court to tennis champ Billie-Jean King.
(Terry O'Neill, Camera Press)

Opposite page, below left: Elton as the Pinball Wizard in Tommy. (Rex Features)

Opposite page, bottom left: Wedding day, 1984. (Camera Press)

Main photograph: Back to Seventies lunacy in the Eighties. (Rex Features)

Left: With 'Phyllis', aka Rod Stewart, at a football match. (John Evans, Camera Press)

Right: The superstar in middle age: everybody's Uncle Reg. (Rex Feaures/ The Sun)

Left and below: Wardrobe treasures destined to be sold at Sotheby's. (Sotheby's)

Above left: A towering musical talent. (Camera Press)

Above right: Elton and John Reid, 'the keeper of the gate' who lost it.
(Richard Young, Rex Features)

Below: With Gianni Versace, soon to be 'blown away in his Versace flip-flops.'
(Theodore Wood, Camera Press)

Elton at his 50th birthday party with Sheila and Derf. (Richard Young, Rex Features)

Above: Elton introduces David Furnish to his old friend Princess Margaret.
(Ian McIlgorm, Camera Press)

Below: Elton and Furnish together at a London film premiere.
(William Conran, Camera Press)

September 6, 1997: 'Now the stars spell out your name.' (Camera Press)

By early 1986, British gossip columns had begun to describe Elton's marriage as 'shaky'. There was constant hammering on about his 'gay past', and scarcely veiled speculation that Renate might be hiding something similar. The solitary former boyfriend to be dredged up from her Kilburn bedsitter days reported that on their nights together, she slept in the bed while he occupied the sofa. 'Renate didn't want a passionate relationship,' complained this conveniently anonymous voice. 'She only wanted to live like brother and sister.'

Elton's former lifestyle was more specifically and damagingly under the spotlight. In 1985, police had charged a man with stealing the £6,000 gold and diamond Cartier watch which had gone missing from his bedroom at Woodside two years earlier. It had been recovered in a dawn raid on the West Croydon home of twenty-one-year-old Cornelius Culwick, who had at first tried to hide it in his pyjama trousers. Asked where he got the watch, Culwick had allegedly replied, 'I'll give you a clue – the Pinball Wizard. Now work it out.'

Culwick denied stealing the watch, claiming it had been a gift from a bisexual friend named Tommy Williams, who had been given it by Elton himself. The case went for trial at the Old Bailey, and Elton was obliged to appear as a prosecution witness. He said that on the night the watch disappeared, he had come home with Tommy Williams and 'two other men', and had changed into a bathrobe, taking off the watch and a sapphire ring. 'At about 1 am, my friends came to my suite, and we then went to the video room until about 4 am. I fell asleep on the sofa until about 9 am.'

The theft charge was amended to one of 'dishonest handling', and the case dragged on over several months, Culwick alleging along the way that he'd had 'a gay fling' with Elton. He was eventually acquitted and also given back the watch, since Elton had not attempted to reclaim it. 'EX-LOVER' CAN KEEP ELTON'S WATCH was the *Daily Express* headline.

Elton met the ceaseless media probing and digging with his usual total unpredictability. February 1986 found him celebrating his second wedding anniversary on a French TV programme called *The Truth Game*, in which celebrities were invited to bare their innermost souls to phone-in questioners.

An early caller asked with Gallic forthrightness if his marriage to Renate wasn't just camouflage for his homosexuality. He replied with all his old winning frankness and good humour. 'I'm not trying to hide my homosexuality at all. It was just that I met someone whom I liked a lot and wanted to marry. It happened at a moment when I was tired of my old style of living. But I don't regret anything I did, nor my style of life before. I have nothing to hide. I regret nothing.'

Another caller said he remembered once seeing Elton on a beach in St Tropez 'surrounded by beautiful boys'. 'Before, he saw me with a beautiful boy,' Elton replied. 'Now I'm with a beautiful woman . . .'

He was just as forthcoming on *The Tube*, a new British TV rock show, hosted by Bob Geldof's girl-friend, Paula Yates. Though guests on *The Tube* were expected to speak only in ten-second sound bites, Elton gave them an extended confessional. 'When I announced I was gay in 1976, it really hurt me a lot. In America, a lot of radio stations stopped playing my records. I even thought about committing suicide. If I hadn't had Watford, I might have become a very big casualty. But I had to learn to take defeat well. If you take your seat at a football ground and 20,000 people are singing, "Elton John's a homosexual", you learn fairly quickly.'

Nor was he afraid to stand up and be counted in the growing horror of the AIDS epidemic. Three years on, only minimal government resources had been allotted to fight the disease, and sufferers were still cast out of society like lepers. Pop music, in its new humanitarian mood, offered one of the earliest pleas for compassion and charity. On the Band Aid principle, a special fund-raising single, 'That's What Friends Are For', was recorded by Dionne Warwick, backed by three 'friends', Gladys Knight, Stevie Wonder and Elton.

His charity performances continued, though less noticeable now in the general mania of rock stars for doing good works. He gave an open-air concert in St James's Park to raise funds to help young drug addicts, and became a stalwart of the Prince's Trust, Prince Charles's youth charity, appearing in its giant Wembley gala with Tina Turner and Phil Collins. Once, Elton had been the only pop figure within miles of royalty. Now you could barely see him in the throngs of them, bowing stiffly to the Prince of Wales or whispering discreet designer-stubbly jokes into Princess Diana's scrumptious little ear.

Yet where was Mrs John? people continued to ask. He seemed to bring her out only on the most formal public occasions, in his capacity as Watford chairman or when receiving some ceremonial accolade from the music industry. In February 1986, he collected a belated BPI award for his 1979 Russian tour, handed over with an unconvincing warm smile by the Conservative Party chairman, Norman Tebbit. Infuriated by both occasion and presenter, Elton was believed to have smashed the statuette to pieces. In April, Renate appeared again as he received two Ivor Novello Awards, one for 'outstanding' services to music, the other for 'Nikita' as the 'year's best song'.

A media invitation he could hardly refuse, affording maximum prestige with zero controversy, was appearing on BBC Radio's *Desert Island Discs*. The plodding old radio fantasy, in which a famous 'castaway' chooses his or her eight favourite records, has become a mark of recognition only just short of the Queen's honours list. To obtain Elton, the strict rule was waived that castaways, even if royal, must make their selection from a studio at Broadcasting House. The interviewer, Michael Parkinson, travelled specially down to Old Windsor.

Elton's *Desert Island Discs* remains among the best ever broadcast. As well as choosing music from Thelonius Monk through Elgar's 'Nimrod' to Nina Simone's 'I Put a Spell on You', he was at his most winningly lucid, modest and funny. In the biographical inter-ludes, he deftly summed up his career and performing rationale, talked of Watford and John Lennon and, with no trace of mawkish-ness, remembered cuddling a boy with incurable cancer on a Barba-dos beach. *Desert Island Discs* has an enormous audience. This focusing of Elton at his best in the public mind could not have come at a more timely moment.

Michael Parkinson was a reliable old friend. The one indirect mention of Renate occurred when Elton chose 'Abide With Me' to remind him of Watford's Cup Final. 'Apart from getting married,' he said, 'that was the happiest day of my life.'

The tabloids had been quick to spot his seeming fascination with George Michael of Wham!. That June, Wham! gave a giant concert at Wembley Stadium, in brilliant summer weather recalling another spectacular, long ago, starring the Beach Boys. Elton was among the backstage guests, holding court to young acolytes like Simon Le Bon of Duran Duran and Holly Johnson of Frankie Goes to Hollywood. With him he brought a 60-foot mobile trailer stuffed with food and liquor, an expanse of synthetic lawn and a portable swimming pool. He joined Wham! onstage, playing piano in a Ronald McDonald orange wig, red nose and clown suit while George Michael sang 'Candle in the Wind'. In the finale Elton came back again, wearing a fluorescent pink tracksuit and a matching Marie-Antoinette wig.

In July, Britain was convulsed by its second royal wedding of the decade. Prince Andrew, aka Randy Andy, took unto himself Sarah Ferguson, daughter of Prince Philip's polo manager, a jovial redhead whom the tabloid press instantly dubbed 'Fergie'. Even this regal occasion brought Elton and Renate's marriage back into the spotlight.

Like Randy Andy, Fergie was an avid Elton fan. She also became a personal friend, unhampered by the constraints of royalty. Her favourite Elton track was 'Song for Guy', so he recorded a special new piano-only track for her as a wedding gift. She in return was to join his long line of sympathetic female listeners.

Elton and Renate were among the highly unconventional wedding guests invited to join the Queen, the Queen Mother, the Prince and Princess of Wales, the Princess Royal and Princess Margaret at Westminster Abbey. Elton in addition attended Prince Andrew's stag party at the Guards Polo Club, which Fergie and Princess Diana attempted to gatecrash, disguised as policewomen.

On his wedding morning, the Queen gave her boisterous second son the more dignified title of Duke of York. During the Abbey service, many eyes wandered to a morning-suited figure whose doffed grey top hat revealed wispy zigzags of transplanted hair. Renate sat close, in a couture outfit of suit, pillbox hat and veil, cosily gripping his arm. It was said in the gossip columns that their marriage had got its second wind, and that their new friends 'the Yorks' had been instrumental in providing it.

Renate was with Elton when he travelled to New York in early September for a four-night appearance at Madison Square Garden. An American Elton fanatic named Wayne Newton, surreptitiously backstage at the Garden, observed the rather curious way in which husband and wife arrived. 'I heard this voice singing, and then Elton walked past me, totally alone. About ten minutes later, there was the slam of a car door, and Renate came in with Bob Halley, Elton's bodyguard and another man. She came only for the first and third nights. She'd stay in the dressing room until after the show started, then be ushered up to the wings. And she'd leave well before the end of the show.'

The four Madison Square Garden nights were the first sign that something might be going wrong with Elton's voice. 'I heard that before the first night, he hadn't been able to speak at all,' Wayne Newton says. 'He'd made a joke of it by arriving backstage dressed as Harpo Marx, and running through honking a motor horn. Another night, I was there before the show at around 6 pm when no one was onstage but Elton and his piano tuner. He played for about five minutes, and then his voice completely cut out. They were four great shows that week, but in every one there'd be moments when his voice just went. On the last night, the audience were virtually singing the words because he couldn't. I heard he was due to go to Australia, then coming back to the States in January. I couldn't see how he was going to make it.'

On 17 October, he was back in London to do BBC TV's Terry Wogan show, hosted in the great Irishman's absence by Esther Rantzen. He made his appearance in a huge yellow Tina Turner wig and a silver lamé teagown, topped by enormous silver angel wings. 'I'm forty next year,' he explained in a voice noticeably lower and huskier than usual. 'I'm having a great time onstage, and I feel just in the mood to put on all this kind of stuff just once more. People expect me to make a fool of myself, and I always do.'

For his Australian tour, he had gone back to his old Seventies designer Bill Mackie, and ordered a wardrobe as preposterous and obliteratingly heavy as anything seen by the glitter age. As well as the Tina Turner gown, there was a Mephistopheles costume with a four-foot-high scarlet ruff, a bespangled Ali Baba turban and bloomers, and a Mozart suit, worn with cascading white wig and beauty spot. Before Elton on the coffee table was a Mohican wig in fluorescent pink, trimmed with a Fergie-style black velvet bow.

He took the opportunity to stress again that he and Renate were truly happy, and all the gossips were wrong. 'When we were in America there were all these headlines that our marriage was on the rocks, and we were having private conversations with the Duke and Duchess of York. I mean, can you imagine it? "She threw a sausage at me, Your Highness . . ." The press over here are unbelievable.'

As if in confirmation of marital harmony, his new album, *Leather Jackets*, included a track written by Renate under the pseudonym Lady Choc Ice. There was also a credit line: 'Special thanks to Lady Choc Ice for being a continued source of inspiration.'

However, when he left for Australia in November, Renate did not accompany him. And within a week or so, rumours of a rift between them had broken out again. Q magazine published an interview with Elton, insisting that they were still happy and his marriage had not been 'a cover-up'. This was enough for the *Daily Star* to headline its pick-up story ELTON SLAMS GOSSIP ABOUT RENATE and for *The Sun* to tag its even shorter précis ELTON IN GAY 'COVER-UP' ROW.

Renewed tabloid interest in his family life was swelled by the unluckiest of coincidences. On 5 November, his half-brother Geoffrey Dwight – one of the four sons from his father's second marriage – was sentenced to a term of youth custody by a court in Mold, north Wales. It was said that twenty-year-old Geoffrey and an older accomplice had broken into a lonely farmhouse and robbed the young couple there after tying them up and terrorising them with pickaxe handles. Both accused pleaded guilty, explaining in mitigation that they had thought the house belonged to a local drugs dealer.

Since Elton had last seen him, Geoffrey had evidently gone downhill, giving up university to become a timber salesman, then falling in with the worst possible company. Despite the long silence between Elton and his father and half-brothers, a message was sent, asking him to attend court as a character witness for Geoffrey. But he was on tour on the other side of the world.

With his Seventies wardrobe, the Australian tour saw a stage format harking back to even earlier. The first half of each show was all-out rock, with Elton leading his thirteen-piece band as Mohican, Mephistopheles or Tina Turner taking tea at the Ritz. The second half featured him in his Mozart suit, white wig and beauty spot, playing antique album-tracks like 'The King Must Die' and 'Madman Across the Water', accompanied by the Melbourne Symphony Orchestra. There were to be twenty-seven separate shows, ending with a climactic Christmas season at the enormous Sydney Entertainment Centre. The Sydney concerts were to be filmed by American ABC television and also recorded for a double live album to be released in 1987.

By the end of the first week in Australia, Elton's voice had started breaking down again. Gus Dudgeon, arriving to supervise the live album, was shocked by its sudden deterioration. 'He did two concerts in Perth that went fine, then on the third night, he was sitting in his dressing room beforehand, and suddenly found he couldn't speak at all. The concert had to be cancelled, and Elton was told by a doctor not to speak at all for four days. He had to go around with a little blackboard, writing down everything he wanted to say.'

The tour had been specially timed to allow Elton to follow the winter Test cricket series between England and Australia. He became the England touring team's unofficial mascot, supporting them at all their matches, joining their group pictures in baggy T-shirt, pads and cap. It was worth the whole trip to see them win back the Ashes from Australia after a tense final day's play in Melbourne. At the celebration party that night, he presided over a hired mobile disco as voluntary DJ.

Even his well-known hero worship of great sportsmen was now turned round to provide winks and nudges in the British tabloids. He had long been friendly with England's captain Ian Botham, a figure fully as controversial as any rock star. Euphoric after the Melbourne Test he gave an interview to a *Sun* journalist, chiefly for the purpose of answering back Botham's numerous attackers in the media. 'It's not just Ian's cricket I adore – it's his love of life, his generosity, his complete openness. I've only ever met one other person like him, and that was John Lennon.' *The Sun*'s double-page spread was headlined WHY I LOVE BEEFY BOTHAM, BY ELTON.

The approach of Christmas was celebrated with his usual expansiveness. All eighty-eight of his temporary colleagues in the Melbourne Symphony Orchestra received £500 Cartier watches. Ian Botham, recovering from an onfield injury, inspired a typical Elton jape. A Cartier bag was delivered to Botham, containing a cricketer's genital-protecting box. The *Daily Star*'s subsequent gossip paragraph should by rights have drawn the earliest libel writ. '. . . As for Elton, it is a box upon whose contents he will never be permitted to gaze. Still, it is the thought that counts.'

He was by now at Sydney Entertainment Centre, playing nightly to 12,000 people, with 101 musicians round him on the special set built for ABC's end-of-week telerecording. Gus Dudgeon stood by to mix the sound for ABC and also record tracks for the projected double live album, though increasingly alarmed by the worsening throat problem. 'After about a number and a half, it would start. It was just as if he'd got a faulty mike that kept cutting out, then coming on again. You'd see him singing with all his might, but there'd be no sound coming out. By the end of the first half of the show, it would seem to be all right. Then after the interval, when he came back as Mozart, it would start going again.'

After a third night of problems in Sydney, Elton was persuaded to forget about theatre doctors and honey-and-lemon remedies and consult a serious throat specialist. 'We were all in the bar at the Sebel Town House when he came back,' Gus Dudgeon remembers. 'He said, "They think it might be throat cancer." It was a terrible moment. Elton just stood there in the crowded bar and burst into tears. John Reid shut down the place there and then. He went round turfing everyone out, saying, "I'm sorry, the bar's closed", like a little Scots bouncer. What I remember was how totally supportive of Elton everyone was, from the band right down through the road crew. People might gripe about him and say, "He's a right little asshole" but as soon as he was in trouble, everyone was behind him all the way.'

Pending further examination and tests, the specialist's advice was to cease performing immediately. Elton, however, said he would finish the week's concerts in Sydney, do the ABC telerecording and make the live album.

By the end, no one close to him knew how he was managing to carry on. 'He was having these awful coughing fits right there onstage,' Gus Dudgeon says. 'Coughing up green stuff, red stuff, God knows what. When it got really bad, the lighting man had to turn the spotlights off him, so that the audience wouldn't see. By the end of each show, he'd be literally knee-deep in used Kleenexes.'

On the very last night, his resolution almost broke. He announced he wasn't going on – but then thought of the 12,000 audience, ABC's film and the live album. Strangely enough, that show, in his idiotic lamé teagowns and wigs, with the terror of cancer hanging over him, was the most brilliant of the whole tour. When Gus Dudgeon later came to choose album tracks from several nights'-worth of performance, almost all the best proved to be from the last night.

His duty done, Elton's only thought was to get back to England as fast as possible and seek a second opinion from a Harley Street specialist. He was warned, however, that going from Australian heat into London's December cold might make the trouble even worse. Instead, he flew to Canberra, to see John Tonkin, Australia's leading ear, nose and throat surgeon. Tonkin's examination revealed the presence of several tiny lesions, or nodules, clustered around Elton's vocal cords. If they proved malignant, he could expect to have his larynx removed and – at the most hopeful – be unable ever to sing or speak properly again.

He faced the prospect with all his deepest reserves of dogged Dwight courage. His chief concern was that, after the operation, he should be told immediately if it was cancer, and the full extent of the danger he would then face. He telephoned his mother in England, cheerily telling her he was fine and not to worry, and that he'd phone her again after his surgery, as soon as he was allowed to talk. He spent the last hours before going into hospital with conspicuous *sang-froid*, watching a one-day cricket match in Perth between England and the West Indies. 'I'm not in the least bit worried,' he said. 'It's a relief to have found a doctor who can help.' Only to a few close friends did he break down in tears and confess, 'I'm scared. I'm so scared.'

The operation was performed by John Tonkin at a private Sydney clinic on 6 January, 1987. The nodules proved to be benign, and easily and permanently cauterised by surgical laser-beam. On regaining consciousness, Elton was told he would make a full recovery and that, after a period of strict convalescence, his singing voice would not be affected.

He was inundated by get-well messages and telegrams, including one from Fergie, Duchess of York. It was reported in one paper that both Fergie and the Princess of Wales had written to Elton, begging him to have the operation. His Australian publicist, Patti Mostyn, dismissed the claim as 'ridiculous'.

He was no sooner discharged from hospital than rumours about his marriage erupted afresh in the British tabloids. A man facing an operation for suspected cancer would be expected to have his wife constantly at his bedside. But Renate, throughout the whole crisis, had remained 8,000 miles away, in Los Angeles.

'Superstar Elton John's marriage is on the rocks because of his bisexual lifestyle,' said the *Sunday People*, with the tabloids' usual blithe lack of any named source, on 11 January. 'Friends say he is now determined to get a divorce after spending just three days with his wife Renate in the past four months. Self-confessed bisexual Elton has been married nearly three years, but has always bluntly refused to give up his male friends.

'. . . A friend in Australia said last night, "Renate realised from the start what Elton was about, but she never realised he would completely shut her out. The crunch came when Elton demanded she come to Australia to be with him during his surgery. He only wanted her because the press thought it strange that she was in America while he was ailing. He exploded when she refused to come and is now more than ever determined to get a divorce . . . Renate, 31, has reportedly gone to great lengths to save her marriage, but over recent months Elton has shut her out of his life. He has admitted privately that he married her because he wanted children, but the couple haven't had any success. The friend added: "Elton realised he can't go on living a lie."'

It was unlucky that, just as the tabloids began quarrying into Elton's private life yet again, his name should be dragged into a particularly sordid Australian sex trial. A former policeman named David Moore, convicted at Brisbane Supreme Court for seducing teenage boys, was said to have boasted that Elton had once been a friend of his. According to the prosecution, Moore had used Elton's name merely to impress his victims, and there was no evidence they had ever met. None the less, a juicy footnote was provided to every insubstantiated press claim that 'flings' with men were what had fatally undermined Elton's marriage.

Next from *The Sun* was a 'world picture exclusive', showing Elton, in the aftermath of his throat surgery, aboard a boat cruising in Sydney Harbour. Seated beside him, as if in corroboration of everything ever alleged, insinuated or suspected, was – a man! 'Troubled rock star Elton John found a shoulder to cry on yesterday, as his best pal flew in to cheer him up,' *The Sun* reported with its

usual meticulous choice of words. 'The friend in need is hunky
bachelor Peter Ikin, who helped organise Elton's wedding to his
now-estranged wife, Renate . . . And Elton needs a friend more than
ever at the moment, as he reels from his MARRIAGE breakdown, his
THROAT operation and being named in a sordid SEX case . . . Peter,
a record company boss, took the lonely rock star for a three-hour
boat trip around Sydney Harbour yesterday . . . David Brown, who
shares a Sydney home with Peter, said "Whenever Elton is in town,
he always spends time with Peter."'

The *News of the World*, on 18 January, claimed to have reached
the heart of the matter: GAY ELTON WED TO PLEASE HIS MUM. The
story that followed was a little masterpiece of the stilted police-court
language which tabloid newspapers invent on their victims' behalf.
'Elton John sat down with his mother and frankly confessed the bad
news. "I'm gay," he said. But then came the good news. "I'll still try
to make you a grandma," he pledged.

'Now, as part of that amazing pact with his mum, the superstar
will beg his estranged wife, Renate: "Let's stay married and try for
the baby I crave." . . . For Elton is trapped between two women.
WIFE Renate refuses to start a family unless Elton drops his self-
confessed bisexual lifestyle. MUM Sheila Farebrother accepts her son
has had male lovers, but is desperate for a grandchild . . .'

Renate, in Los Angeles, had succeeded in totally eluding the
scores of journalists pursuing her. 'She has shunned the reflected
limelight in a way that would be worthy of Greta Garbo,' *Today*
admitted with a touch of grudging admiration. 'She is said to be
working but on what is a mystery, even to her publicist, Sarah
McMullen. All she will say is that Renate plans to fly to Sydney on
January 22.'

Her father Joachim, in Munich, reportedly corroborated this
intention. Elton was said to be spending £200,000 on chartering Sir
Justin Hickey's luxury yacht *Lady Patricia* – 'a floating Paradise with
mirrored master suite, bedroom ceiling included' – to take her on a
cruising second honeymoon.

Instead, Renate flew back to Britain and, with an unpredictability
worthy of her spouse, gave an exclusive interview to the *Daily Express*.
Far from contemplating divorce, she said, Elton and she were planning
a second marriage ceremony. 'I really don't know where these awful
rumours started,' she told the *Express*'s Roger Taverner in the kitchen
at Woodside. 'The truth is, we are as close as we ever were, and this is
very close. The reason we are apart at the moment is that I must get
on with my own career. Elton knows that and wants it that way.'

She revealed she had become a record producer in her own right, and was working on a single with her friend Sylvia Griffin, former lead singer with a band called Kissing the Pink and now another client of John Reid. Ms Griffin, a wide-awake blonde, was pictured with her at the studio control desk. Roger Taverner was even allowed to hear the demo they had made, a song called 'Lonely Heart', co-written by Elton and Gary Osborne.

Why had Renate not been at his bedside during the cancer scare in Australia? 'We talked about it for a long time before he went to the hospital for the tests. I had been told by the doctors that it was not serious. Elton said there was no need for me to be there. We agreed we would speak on the phone every day, which we do.'

In Australia, meanwhile, Elton joined Lionel Ritchie onstage, playing piano only, since still forbidden either to sing or speak. One TV news report followed him through his hotel lobby, in a black satin suit and zebra-skin Nehru cap, clutching the child's scribbling board that was his only means of communication. 'Thanks for everything' he wrote on it to his audience, before giving a forced little smile and a thumbs-up sign and slipping through a half-opened door. His poorest and most ill-dressed fans were already starting to feel fortunate by comparison.

We can see, therefore, that what *The Sun* was shortly to unloose on Elton did not happen in isolation. For five or six years already, he had been the target of anti-gay smears and sneers in Britain's tabloid press, a public whipping-boy for the growing phobia about AIDS. The unwritten law that rock stars never sue allowed things to be written about him that in any other context would instantly have drawn libel writs. The *Express*, the *Star*, the *People* and *News of the World* had all, at one time or another, had their knives into Elton. It was just that, under its then editor, Kelvin McKenzie, *The Sun* went furthest and sank lowest.

Early in 1987, the paper had received a tip-off from one of its network of paid spies and informers. The tip-off led to a nineteen-year-old male prostitute, or rent boy, named Stephen Hardy, who told a story calculated to make any *Sun* man salivate. He claimed to have attended gay parties at the home of Rod Stewart's manager, Billy Gaff, in Finchampstead, Berkshire, and to have been involved in drug-taking and homosexual orgies there with Elton John.

No one can object to a tabloid publishing an exposé, however nasty, if sufficient informed sources have been found to corroborate it. Behind the screaming headlines of old-fashioned scandal sheets could always be found the most meticulous delving and triple-checking. To *The Sun*, however, the word of Stephen Hardy was basis enough for another great coup in the tradition of GOTCHA! and FREDDIE STARR ATE MY HAMSTER. Hardy was paid £2,000 for his revelations, with further regular sweeteners of £250.

ELTON IN VICE BOYS SCANDAL was *The Sun*'s four-deck front page splash on 25 February. There followed the 'confession' of Stephen Hardy under the alias Graham X. He claimed to have been the pimp who had recruited teenage rent boys for parties at Billy Gaff's house, specifically as sexual partners for Gaff and Elton. Over a period of months, he said he had supplied 'at least ten youngsters, who were each paid a minimum of £100 each, plus all the cocaine they could stand'. According to Graham X, aided by *The Sun*'s distinctive typography, Elton 'LOVED his boys to be tattooed skinheads or punks with spiky hair, SNORTED cocaine throughout the orgies, which lasted up to four days, and BEGGED the teenagers to indulge in his bondage fantasies. The sordid rent-boy sessions began just eighteen months after Elton's highly publicised Valentine's Day marriage to German bride Renate Blauel.'

The story was presented not as an exultant soft-porn feast, but as a solemn moral duty, with Graham X, in the bosom of *The Sun*, now reformed and penitent. 'I am ashamed of what I did . . . I am speaking out to show how widespread this sort of thing is and to warn other gullible young kids to steer clear of people like these.'

Inside, hammering home the moral message, was a double-page spread, ELTON'S LUST FOR BONDAGE, in which Graham X 'confessed' to his own sexual encounters with Elton at Billy Gaff's house. He said that on the first occasion, Elton had been lying on a bed in a pair of skimpy leather shorts, 'looking like Cleopatra and twirling a sex aid between his fingers'. He claimed he had been shown bondage accessories, and that Elton had fantasised about tying him to a tree in the woods before making love to him. On a later occasion, he said, he had witnessed a foursome between Elton, Billy Gaff and two rent boys, which had ended with them swapping partners.

Ironically, it was none of this spun-out sleaze, but the spurious attempts to give it social uplift, which would prove *The Sun*'s undoing. In a foot-of-page 'box' story, Graham X told how he had repented his rent-boy life after falling in love with a girl, but had carried out one final pimping mission to pay for their engagement ring. So 'he took two youngsters to Gaff's home on 30 April last year. It was the last time he saw Elton.'

It was the only specific date mentioned in the whole story, and in *The Sun*'s own office there was someone who recognised it as deeply unsafe. Nina Myskow had returned to the paper a few months earlier after a stint as TV critic for the *Sunday People*. Knowing she was a long-time friend of Elton, *The Sun*'s legal adviser showed her the Graham X copy a couple of weeks before publication. Nina still kept up with Elton intermittently and was sure she remembered that on 30 April, 1986, he and his assistant Bob Halley had both been out of Britain. 'I said, "If you're going to go with this stuff, for God's sake make sure you check and double check that date."' Her advice fell on deaf ears.

In fact, on 30 April, 1986 – as many more of his friends, like Bryan Forbes, remembered – Elton had been in New York, staying at the Carlyle Hotel. He had had lunch with his old confidant Tony King, then gone to see his costume designer, Bill Mackie. Any number of people could confirm that he had remained in New York one further night, flying home, with Bob Halley, by Concorde early on 1 May.

That one slip, if nothing else, made *The Sun* vulnerable to a massive libel suit. Even so, there were those around Elton who urged him in the strongest terms not to sue. Mick Jagger, in particular, phoned to warn against it, citing his own experience with the *News of the World* twenty years earlier. That, too, had arisen from the grossest of factual errors. Jagger had been accused of boasting about his drug consumption in an interview with two *News of the World* reporters who did not realise they were actually talking to another Rolling Stone, Brian Jones. Jagger had issued a libel writ, only to be followed and spied on by the paper until finally set up for the Redlands drug bust that led to his and Keith Richard's imprisonment. If Elton tried to fight *The Sun*, even on this seemingly winnable count, what campaign of still dirtier tricks could be expected before the case finally came to court? In Jagger's view, the best course was to follow rock-star precedent since 1967, and just take it until it stopped.

Elton disagreed. On the day of *The Sun*'s first Graham X stories, a writ for libel arrived from his solicitors, Frere Cholmeley. So full of confident glee was the paper at this stage that its second front-page Elton John 'world exclusive', next morning, bore an additional come-on tag: 'The story they're all suing over'.

In this instalment, ELTON'S KINKY KICKS, Graham X claimed that Elton would snort cocaine through rolled-up $100 bills 'to set himself up for orgies with rent boys', and that he insisted his youthful partners also be 'drugged with vast amounts of coke before they were brought to his bed'. A second inside spread, ELTON'S DRUG CAPERS, alleged, through Graham X, that Elton would take as many as three lines of cocaine in an hour, sometimes dividing it up with an American Express Gold credit card, and throwing the $100 bills away after he'd used them. Here, too, the nineteen-year-old uneducated rent boy expanded into psychological analysis. 'It was as though he needed the drug as a crutch because he believed in some strange way that the boys wouldn't talk to him if he wasn't stoned on drugs.'

A bold-type side bar announced, on a note of palpable triumph, that Elton was suing over the first day's story and that his lawyers had unsuccessfully sought a High Court injunction to halt the series. Continuing the public service motif, it was said that Scotland Yard had begun an investigation into the whole matter, and were preparing to interrogate Graham X. 'Tomorrow . . .' a streamer at the bottom promised, 'Elton's Pink Tutu Party'.

The Sun's chief rival, the *Daily Mirror*, had by now also thrown its hat into the ring. The *Mirror* still retained some shreds of its old decency, and had not gone quite as far as other tabloids in the recent spate of gay-bashing. It would, besides, do anything in its power to wound, insult or embarrass *The Sun*. So, on 26 February, as ELTON'S KINKY KICKS hit the streets, the *Mirror* came trumpeting to his defence. A page-five story set out the evidence that Elton could not possibly have attended a homosexual orgy in Berkshire on 30 April, 1986, because at the time he was 5,000 miles away in New York.

A detailed examination of the star's diary – which only Elton's own office could have made possible – reconstructed almost his entire day's itinerary. There were confirmed sightings of him all around Manhattan, from the *New York Daily News*, his clothes designer, Bill Mackie, even a restaurant that had turned him away for refusing to remove his hat. There was also a statement from Billy Gaff, who not only denied that Elton had ever been at his house but could prove that at the time of the alleged orgy, he, too, had been out of Britain. That day, Gaff said, in one of the saga's more delectable touches, he had been flying home from the Philippines 'after meetings with the vice president to discuss a new national anthem'.

The *Mirror* was not about to let *The Sun* off the hook. Next morning, it produced a second story, THE BIG LIE, offering documentary proof that Elton had not returned from New York to Britain until 1 May, 1986. The *Mirror* had found his and Bob Halley's names on the passenger list for Concorde's 9.30 am flight, and obtained a copy of the invoice from the limousine company that took them to JFK Airport. On the Concorde manifest, Elton's name bore a special notation, 'famous singer', in case he should not be recognised. The airport limo had been driven by a man named Walt.

The Sun, meanwhile, had adopted the time-honoured voice of editorial courage, and was 'standing by' its story. Instead of the promised revelations about a 'pink tutu party', its third Graham X instalment was the rent boy's retort that 'Elton can say what he likes, but deep in his heart he knows I'm telling 100 per cent the truth [*sic*]. I know why he is saying he has never met me or been to bed with boys I supplied for him and Billy Gaff. He wants to protect his image as the Royal favourite, loved by millions of fans. I'm sorry to have to tell his wife, but he did have sex with the teenagers I brought to Gaff's home . . .' The front-page headline – that familiar *Sun* device of turning quote into editorial comment – was YOU'RE A LIAR, ELTON!

The slip-up over the date was certainly unfortunate. But *The Sun* had infinite faith in its own power as a newsprint bludgeon. It believed that if it kept hitting Elton, he would eventually cave in, the way people always did. The chance of eventually winding up in court would be of little account against the damage suffered meantime, not just by the victim himself but also by his family, business associates and friends.

Elton was aware of all the risks. He knew what a drawn-out battle with a ruthless tabloid might do to his mother and stepfather, and the many other respectable, inoffensive members of his family. He knew what it might do to the football club in whose junior enclosure he had often appeared, presenting children with Easter eggs. He knew what it might do to his social life and cherished royal connections. Above all, he knew what it might do to his already strained and vulnerable marriage. His biggest fear, Nina Myskow remembers, was that Renate would be hurt.

None the less, the dogged Dwight chin was firmly stuck out. ELTON'S KINKY CAPERS brought a second libel writ. YOU'RE A LIAR, ELTON brought a third. Estimates of the damages he would be seeking rose from £5 million to £20 million. His solicitor, Frank Presland, said that as long as the Graham X series continued, the writs would keep on coming.

Elton himself, still in Australia, put on a light-hearted front. Acting as MC at a record-awards ceremony, he was defiantly full of his usual camp one-liners. A female guest admired a brooch he was wearing. 'You get one of those when you sleep with a queen,' Elton told her. To a male guest he said he'd always thought 'bondage' was a surfers' beach in Sydney. His hair had become platinum blond, cut in a star shape high above the ears. 'Blondes have more fun,' he explained.

The only press interview he would give was to John Blake, who had written the *Daily Mirror's* BIG LIE story. This time there was no joking. 'I have travelled the world and seen a lot of things, but I have never even heard of any orgies with underage boys. And I swear I have never, ever seen anything like the things that were described. The outfits I was supposed to have worn, and all of the rest of it, were just plain ridiculous.

'No matter what happens, I will go into court, swear on the Bible and tell the truth about everything. I'm going to nail the paper that wrote all those lies. I'm doing it to clear my name, not for the money. But £50 million would not be enough to compensate for all the harm they have done me . . . I don't care what comes out in court about my life. They can throw every single thing at me, and I'll still nail them.'

He said he would be returning to Britain to face up to *The Sun*, and celebrate his fortieth birthday on 25 March. 'And it's also about time I saw the wife again . . . We've had to put up with an awful lot of nonsense during our time apart. But the fact is, our marriage is fine. I love her, she loves me, and we are happy . . . It was arranged before Christmas that we would have to spend these months apart . . . Renate has been in the studio with a girl singer, and she's been working very hard. If you are in the Air Force, you are often away from your wife for six or seven months at a time. And, really, it's pretty much the same for me.'

One had to know about Elton's father, and the relationship of a foreign-posted RAF officer in the Fifties with a lonely, obsessive, insecure small boy, to relish the full poignancy of that.

EIGHTEEN

Reg Strikes Back

E LTON'S fortieth birthday party was held at Lockwood House, a ten-bedroomed Georgian mansion which John Reid had lately acquired, near Rickmansworth, Hertfordshire. NATO-style security surrounded a bash as munificent as any thrown by Rocket in the spendthrift Seventies. Guards with Doberman pinscher dogs checked passes before allowing access to the lit-up house and the five marquees in its grounds. The 350 guests included rock superstars George Harrison, Ringo Starr, Eric Clapton, Phil Collins, Bob Geldof, and Lionel Ritchie, designer Zandra Rhodes, actor Sir John Mills, actresses Hazel O'Connor and Britt Ekland, film directors Ken Russell and Michael Winner, impresarios Richard Branson and Mickie Most, local MP Tristan Garel-Jones and the entire Watford football team. Just before midnight, the Duke and Duchess of York arrived, racing up the drive in a chauffeur-driven Jaguar, followed by a car full of armed Special Branch men. 'The Yorks' at least, seemed unworried by what *The Sun* said.

The party was also expected to be a grand public reunion for Elton and Renate. He arrived alone, however, and before long it became painfully obvious that Renate would not be joining him. Friends who asked after her were told that she'd gone down with flu.

Elton seemed in good spirits none the less, cutting his sarcophagus-sized birthday cake and pulling pink ribbons from the £80,000 Ferrari Testarossa sports car that was John Reid's present. A chorus of 'Happy birthday to you' from an ad hoc supergroup including two ex-Beatles showed how solidly behind him were all his music business friends. In his speech he apologised for Renate's absence, showing off an antique diamond and ruby watch which he said she had given him. His only allusion to other current troubles was to sing a few bars of 'My Way'.

Afterwards there was a firework display which awoke patients in nearby Mount Vernon Hospital and brought two fire engines racing to the scene. Police received over a hundred calls from disturbed local residents, some of whom believed the nearby air base at Northwood to be under attack.

Renate's non-appearance on such a night could lead to only one conclusion. It was confirmed next day by a press announcement from John Reid's office. Elton and Renate had decided to 'continue living apart', though there were no plans at present for a divorce and they remained on 'very good personal terms'. In particular it was emphasised that the separation had nothing to do with *The Sun*'s rent-boy claims, which had come after their decision to part and which both found 'deeply distressing and intrusive'.

Fleet Street's wolf pack were not long in providing background details. Renate had already left Woodside and was to move into a £300,000 flat, bought and decorated for her by Elton, in Adam and Eve Mews, Kensington. Lawyers were said to be at work on a divorce settlement after Renate had turned down Elton's original offer of £2 million.

All the stories mentioned Renate's friendship with Sylvia Griffin, clearly implying a lesbian relationship. Though neither could be found, it was safe to assume, in kindergarten tabloidese, that Elton's fugitive wife was being 'comforted' by her 'close pal'. The *News of the World* claimed the marriage had latterly become a *ménage à trois*, with Elton lavishing expensive gifts on Sylvia, even allowing her to accompany Renate and him on holiday. '. . . A close friend of Sylvia believes that Renate turned more and more to her as the strain of marriage to bisexual Elton took its toll . . . Now she and Renate are believed to be planning a get-away-from-it-all break together, probably in California . . .' A second *News of the World* 'exclusive', ELTON WEEPS ON FERGIE'S SHOULDER, said he had spent much of his fortieth birthday party pouring out his marital troubles to a sympathetic Duchess of York.

The Sun's coverage managed to combine voyeuristic relish at the split with sycophantic slavering over Fergie's presence at the party, and further stabs at Elton on the rent-boy question. The front-page splash, ELTON ENDS SHAM MARRIAGE, made it all seem the inevitable result of Graham X's revelations, and promised a further 'dossier' linking Elton with teenage boys 'back to the 1970s'. The centre spread, A MARRIAGE BUILT ON LIES, listed all Elton and Renate's previous press quotes about their marriage, each with the word LIE beside it. The implication was that his word about rent-boys could

not be believed either. On the same page, schizophrenically, was
ROYAL RAVER! FERGIE'S NIGHT OF STAR MAGIC. (Completing the
flavour of that day's edition, one could turn to a story about Japanese
imports to Britain, headed HOW THE NIPS DO US DOWN.)

Outwardly, *The Sun* appeared as brassily confident as ever. But
behind the death-dealing three-inch heads and white-on-black thun-
derbolts, things were starting to go awry. In particular, twinges of
scepticism were tardily being felt about that 'world exclusive's' one
and only source. It was finally borne in on *The Sun* that a hard-up
rent boy might not be the most reliable or truthful person.

To stop rival papers getting to Stephen Hardy, a task force of *Sun*
heavies had smuggled him, his girlfriend and their baby out of
Britain, keeping them for a month at secret addresses in Paris, Malaga
and Gibraltar. All this effort and expense was wasted, however, when
the *Daily Star* found a gay picture magazine named *Vulcan* for which
Hardy had posed three years earlier. EXPOSED! THE WORM THAT
TURNED ON ELTON, chortled the *Star*. The two unedifying pictures
of a scrawny nude boy were accompanied by character notes that
caused further wincing over at *The Sun*'s Wapping offices. 'When he
walked through the door, we knew he was trouble,' said a man who
had been at the *Vulcan* photo session. 'He is capable of doing anything
for money.'

The obvious urgent need, if Graham X could not be trusted, was
to find other rent boys able to tell the same tale. In earlier times,
such work would have been entrusted to hard-digging reporters. *The
Sun*, however, chose as its investigator a young Scot named John
Boyce, a former rent boy who professed nine criminal convictions
for fraud and one for attempted murder. Boyce was offered £1,750
for every signed affidavit he could deliver from a rent boy claiming
to have slept with Elton. Of this, the rent boy would receive £500
while Boyce pocketed the remainder. He later described his work
method in a television interview: 'We used to bring people to hotel
rooms and they would tell us that they had an affair with Elton John
and, you know . . . I mean it was all pure crap.'

Besides which, the game plan against Elton, mysteriously, wasn't
working. *The Sun* was hitting him with everything it had, but he still
wasn't turning tail and running. Every new 'world exclusive' that
was expected to produce a hasty climb-down instead produced a
further libel writ. The more people urged him to give in and cut his
losses, the more resolute Elton became. He would repeat what he
had said on the phone to Mick Jagger's advice that it wasn't worth
it. 'They can say I'm a fat old sod, they can say I'm an untalented

bastard, they can call me a poof, but they mustn't lie about me because I'm going to fight. And I'm determined to be a winner.'

On 13 April, *The Sun* struck again with ELTON PROBE: HEAVY MOB MOVE IN. The story was that gay men who had agreed to co-operate in the 'Elton John investigation' were now suffering 'vicious attacks and threats of violence'. One 'gay couple' had had their house broken into, their furniture smashed and dog excrement smeared on the walls, and a message for the *Sun* informant had been left behind: 'It will be his kneecaps, not the furniture next time'. A second 'witness' was said to have been warned via a phone call to his elderly mother to 'keep his nose out of other people's business or we'll cut it off for him'. A third had been menaced by 'heavies' in a pub and 'several more' had received threatening phone-calls.

'There is no evidence to suggest that Elton is aware of these attacks,' *The Sun* continued magnanimously. 'But it is known that certain violent elements of the pop-gay community [*sic*] are incensed by our revelations.' Readers were left to draw their own conclusions from a picture of Elton in gangster-looking dark glasses, over a subhead SINGING TO BEAT A KILLER which only close inspection revealed to be unconnected with the criminal underworld. 'Elton sings at Wednesday's AIDS fund-raising concert in London,' the caption noted. 'Friends say he would be horrified to think people were threatening gays in revenge for *The Sun*'s revelations about his escapades with rent boys.'

With libel writs out, both sides were under legal obligation not to comment further on the case. *The Sun*, however, showed no sign of honouring the *sub judice* rule. And pressure was growing on Elton to make some kind of public statement about the torrent of accu-sations against him.

Television was clearly the only medium that could hope to equal *The Sun*'s massive daily circulation. It was, besides, the medium in which Elton had always most excelled. He therefore turned to his old friend Michael Parkinson who, though no longer a prime-time chatshow host, was still among Britain's best-liked TV interviewers. It was agreed that he should appear on Parkinson's Yorkshire Tele-vision show *One to One*. The programme was recorded before a studio audience on 14 April for network transmission on 2 May.

The Sun, meanwhile, was still straining every muscle and resource to trawl up further filth on Elton. At one point, a tip-off came that he was to meet his mother for lunch at an out-of-town restaurant. *The Sun* sent so many spies to eavesdrop that there was no room in the restaurant for their quarry, who had to be put into an overflow establishment down the road. In any case, the target proved to be only Sheila Farebrother and someone from John Reid's office. Elton himself was not even in the country at the time.

In mid-April, the operation seemed to strike paydirt. A person was found who claimed to be an ex-lover of Elton's, but who this time offered evidence in the form of three Polaroid photographs. In a hush-hush operation that would have done credit to John le Carré, *The Sun* bought the Polaroids for £10,000.

Before publishing them, as a cat might toy with a mouse, it made sure that Elton himself received copies. His lawyers at the time had been seeking a High Court injunction to prevent any further 'revelations' from appearing. To *The Sun*'s added triumph, this was now abandoned.

ELTON PORN PHOTO SHAME hit the streets on Thursday 16 April. With the splash headline went a fuzzy nude shot of Elton in sunglasses, cropped at the waistline. Inside was a somewhat clearer head and shoulders shot of him in a striped football shirt, his arm round the shoulders of a boy cuddling what seemed to be a pillow. The third Polaroid allegedly showed him 'having sex with a young man'. This, *The Sun* said, was 'too disgusting to be printed in a family newspaper'.

The treasure trove was not quite what it had first appeared. As Elton's physique and, even more, his hairline showed, the Polaroids had been taken years earlier, possibly as long ago as 1976. In those far-off liberal times, several famous gay men had posed as full frontal nudes, most famously the painter David Hockney. In the unpublished sex-shot, the other participant was someone clearly old enough to be acceptable under the law as a 'consenting adult'. As to the boy Elton was shown cuddling, *The Sun*'s own caption readily admitted: 'There is no suggestion of any sexual liaison between them'.

The Polaroids, however embarrassing, were merely evidence of the bisexuality which Elton had freely admitted eleven years before. They had no connection with Graham X or rent boys and, in particular, none with the patently untrue claim that Elton had attended a cocaine and rent-boy orgy at Billy Gaff's house on 30 April, 1986.

In this issue a new informant, 'Malcolm M', described as a '19-year-old artist', claimed he had been involved in 'a sordid five-day gay sex and cocaine orgy' with Elton and another man at Woodside during 'the early Eighties'. In *The Sun*'s familiar typographical style, Malcolm M claimed that Elton 'PLIED him with massive amounts of cocaine, cannabis and champagne, PERSUADED him to perform horrible gay perversions, COMMITTED other degrading sex acts on him, FLEW in another gay lover to take part in a three-in-a-bed homosexual session, and INVITED the teenager to fly to Paris to continue the orgy.' The 'five-day bash', with a Californian surfer named as Vance, was said to have happened at a time when Elton was filming at Shepperton studios. 'I had to control my laughter,' Malcolm M was quoted as saying. 'Elton John was the biggest pop star going and all he wanted to do was to be degraded. He looked pathetic, stretched out there on the green carpet.'

The ELTON'S FIVE-DAY ORGY centre spread featured a new departure – a *Sun* editorial, denouncing Elton and praising the paper's own courage and steadfast championing of truth and light:

Elton John is a pop star of great talent.

His gifts have earned him riches and the adulation of millions.

But he is not entitled to live above the law.

In February, *The Sun* published a series on his lifestyle. It was not a pretty story.

Threatened

It involved drug-taking and illegal homosexual exploits with young boys.

Elton's reply was volcanic. It was LIES he said, and he threatened to sue *The Sun* for £20 million.

Other newspapers, less concerned with the truth than with their dreadful circulation figures, tried to take advantage by supporting his campaign against us. The singer assembled a battery of lawyers to muzzle us. Then we received fresh evidence in the shape of pornographic pictures showing Elton involved in sex with a young man.

The lawyers dropped their action as eagerly as a patron saint denounces sin.

The Sun has no hard feelings towards Elton John. We wish him no ill. Certainly, we shall never pursue him maliciously.

But he must stop telling LIES about *The Sun*.

In return, we shall stop telling the TRUTH about him.

Next day, 16 April, came I RAN COKE FOR ELTON. A twenty-seven-year-old 'showbiz executive', codename John D, claimed to have taken Elton supplies of cocaine, for which he was sometimes so eager that he 'tore at the packet with his teeth'. John D was said to have worked as an office boy at Rocket Records, and there to have witnessed 'much drug-abuse and homosexual activity' between Elton and various young men. Like Graham X and Malcolm M, John D was now a reformed character, speaking to his tabloid father confessor only for the greater public good. 'I very much regret getting involved with drugs and the Elton John scene. I'm lucky to be alive.'

Overleaf on page six could be found an example of *Sun* cartoon humour. A crudely drawn fat figure in straw boater and large spectacles was shown vanishing into a cupboard labelled 'Closet'. 'I'm not coming out again 'til this lot's all over,' the caption read.

With public interest in the affair at its height, Yorkshire TV had hastily brought forward transmission of Elton's interview with Michael Parkinson from 2 May to 18 April. *The Sun* knew in advance much of what he would say and, that morning, spoke in another editorial:

> *The Sun* urges its 12 million readers to sit down tonight and watch Elton John's performance on the Michael Parkinson show.
>
> Not since Vivien Leigh in *Gone With the Wind* has there been such an extraordinary piece of acting.
>
> For Mr John is lying through his back teeth. HE knows it, his MANAGEMENT knows it and his FRIENDS know it.
>
> Sickening
>
> But in a desperate attempt to bamboozle fans and family alike, he claims our sex and drug allegations are all lies.
>
> His public denials are as sickening as his private perversions.
>
> If you believe Elton, you'll believe in fairies.

Onscreen that night, Michael Parkinson faced a haggard and dejected-looking figure. Since last seen in public, Elton had acquired a thick growth of beard. He was, for him, drably dressed, in a shapeless flying suit and red Watford FC baseball cap. None would have recognised the silver-clad Rocket Man who used to trip forth on four-inch platforms in Parkinson shows of the happy Seventies.

It was the gentlest possible interrogation by a plainly sympathetic old friend, but Elton still put up an impressive performance. He repeated that *The Sun*'s allegations were 'all lies', and he intended to prove so in court, no matter what the toll on him and his family. He revealed that Sheila, 'at the end of her tether' with scandal and press harassment, had decided to emigrate to Spain. He himself was being followed and spied on and, during a recent trip to America, had actually found an electronic bug in his hotel suite. There had even been attempts to persuade Renate's doctor to reveal confidential medical details about him. 'They probably want to examine my sperm,' Elton said. 'You would have thought they had buckets of the stuff.' The studio audience, and viewers at home, loved it.

He said he would be going to Los Angeles for a few months, but denied he intended to settle there permanently. He also denied recent press reports that he intended to sell Watford. 'The reason I would never sell . . . is because they are people who would fight and die for me.'

The real revelation, however, was that he had spent the past week with Renate, who would be awaiting him afterwards back in Old Windsor. 'We're really good friends,' Elton said. 'The marriage isn't over *per se*. We've just separated for a little while . . . We're known as the Odd Couple, apparently. That's fair enough. But we still get on very well with each other. I still love her. She still loves me.'

I STILL LOVE MY RENATE! was *The Sun*'s headline, under a white-on-black flash STRANGE BUT TRUE.

Lady Choc Ice had, indeed, come back, as an announcement from John Reid's office confirmed soon afterwards. She had kept in constant touch with Elton in their month apart, making it clear she did not believe a word of *The Sun*'s stories. 'The lady's dignity throughout the whole thing taught me a hell of a lot,' Elton admitted. 'Her faith in me never wavered for a minute. So something good came out of it.'

Renate was resolutely by his side once more at Watford that May as he watched the closing games of the 1986–87 football season. He was determined that *The Sun*'s campaign should not drive him into hiding and, in particular, not spoil his life's chief pleasure and pride.

Watford's attitude to his troubles gave Elton much heart. *The Sun*'s soccer-thug taunts found few echoes on the Vicarage Road terraces. Scores of letters came in from ordinary supporters whose young sons and daughters used the family enclosure. Their message was nearly always the same. What Elton did in his private life was his business so long as he continued to behave with dignity as chairman of Watford.

Nor did all this ghastly personal publicity seem to have any adverse effect on Watford's performance or morale. The Vicarage Road ground now boasted a new £2.2 million west grandstand – largely paid for by Elton – and attendance and receipts were at an all-time high. In 1986, Watford had made a second bid for Wembley glory, reaching the quarter-final of the FA Cup before losing to mighty Liverpool. This year, they had won right through to the semi-final, going down at last 4–1 to Tottenham Hotspur.

A double blow to Watford and Elton personally came in May, when Graham Taylor resigned his managership to join Second Division Aston Villa. His explanation was that, after ten triumphant years with Elton at Watford, it was time to move on to a fresh challenge. Elton was magnanimous over the loss of a partner as important to him, in many ways, as Bernie Taupin had once been. Though three years of Taylor's Watford contract remained, no compensation was sought from Aston Villa. So Graham Taylor left Vicarage Road and embarked on the route which, three years later, would lead him to managership of England.

Elton maintained his deliberately high profile with Watford, welcoming Taylor's replacement, Dave Bassett, and announcing that he would accompany the team on their second tour of China that August. At the welcome party for Bassett, he joked that he'd thought of standing in the imminent general election, but 'after all the recent publicity, my chances might not have been too great'. Some tabloid photographers shouted to him and Dave Bassett, a good-looking young Cockney, to move closer together. 'Now come on, don't start that,' Elton snapped.

Interspersed with scandal and smear were Elton stories that could still raise the old familiar smile. In August he took another step from his Pinner origins by acquiring a coat of arms. Two years had been spent by an artist at the College of Heralds on focusing all things associated with Elton John into a heraldic device. A shield with a black-and-white piano keyboard top was surmounted by a figure of Pan playing blue pipes (for Bluesology) with a golden football caught under one hoof. The shield's lower part was 'gules and or', ie Watford's colours of red and gold. The motto beneath was a pun in Spanish, *El Tono es bueno*: The Music, or Elton, is good.

In Beijing with the Watford touring team, he announced that his vocal chords had totally recovered from their recent surgery. 'At one point, about two months after the operation, I was very frightened because I couldn't get any falsettos. I think my voice is lower in pitch, but I've got my falsettos back.' He said he would be giving his voice 'at least a year and a bit off' and meanwhile planned to write music, for stage or screen. He had already been asked to score a film about Peter Wright, the former MI5 man whose book *Spycatcher* was currently embarrassing the Thatcher government.

His only record releases for 1987 were the *Live in Australia* album and, as a single, the stage version of 'Your Song' he had managed to perform in his Mozart wig and beauty spot before his voice totally collapsed. Having pulled off another brilliant technical production for him, Gus Dudgeon was astonished to be dispensed with yet again. 'I remember, I went to Renate's birthday party, and Elton was really friendly,' Dudgeon says. ' "You and I are a team," he told me. "We'll always work together." As I was leaving, I saw John Reid give me a peculiar look. I said to my wife, "I've been dropped." And sure enough, I had.'

Elton seemed overjoyed to be with Renate again, showering her with expensive presents and splurging on exotic fitments for the home that was going to work this time. John Reid's managerial acquisitions now included Princess Margaret's son Viscount Linley, who had emerged as a fashionable Chelsea furniture designer. The viscount was commissioned to build a new marital bed for Elton and Renate to replace their Empress Josephine replica. Delivered in October, the Linley bed was a sumptuous affair, with towered and battlemented half-screens and E and R initials entwined on its headboard. With it came an equally regal bill for £75,000.

They seemed a united and even carefree couple early that month, when Elton received a special award from the American Society of Composers, Authors and Publishers for twenty years' achievement in music. Renate was pictured kissing him over his Golden Note statuette, both of them looking as bemusedly happy as on their wedding day.

In private, however, Elton's battle with *The Sun* was taking a heavy toll. After publication of the Polaroid pictures, and the allegations of Malcolm M and John D, his lawyers had issued two more libel writs. Two had also been issued against the *Daily Star*, for repeating the alleged defamation. With the pile of writs already against *The Sun*, that brought the grand total to twelve.

Since February, he had received hundreds of letters from friends and fans alike, sympathising with his ordeal and expressing revulsion at what *The Sun* was doing. The punctilious good boy wrote back to everyone personally, often sending flowers along with his note. He was continually amazed to discover how much he was loved, and what little difference smearing headlines made to that.

None the less, some of the mud was sticking. Just before *The Sun*'s onslaught, Elton had made a series of television commercials for Cadbury's chunky chocolate bars. Britain's chocolate companies were almost all founded by Quakers, and the possible effect of ELTON'S KINKY KICKS on chunky bar family sales had the Cadbury's men quaking in their boots. The TV ads were cancelled forthwith.

Though other papers dared not join *The Sun*'s frontal attack, there was constant sniggering and swiping from the sidelines. One gossip columnist managed to inject homophobia even into a report that Elton and John Reid had visited the White House, and had tea with President Reagan. 'I wonder who was mother?' the writer concluded archly. Another vicious little paragraph noted that Elton was looking for a new house in Los Angeles, and commended the one formerly owned by Rock Hudson. It was just a few months since Hudson's death, ravaged by AIDS.

Cruellest of all was a *News of the World* story that, but for the rent-boy allegations, Elton would have received a knighthood in the Queen's Birthday Honours. He himself was said to have confided to 'friends' that the scandal had 'destroyed his close friendship with the Royal Family'. Prince Andrew, Fergie and the other pop-loving 'young Royals' had allegedly been banned from mixing socially with him ever again. 'The Yorks' had defied this ban by attending his fortieth birthday party and in so doing, had 'infuriated' the Queen and Prince Philip. But 'kind-hearted Fergie did accept a phone call from the tormented singer last week. He called her at a villa in Barbados, where she was on holiday, and cried down the line about his troubles while she tried to reassure him . . . The Duchess told him she did not believe [the] allegations . . . But she admitted that she could not see him in the near future, and had no plans to do so . . . A member of the Royal Household said: "It's quite inconceivable that any member of the family could recognise Elton John after this . . . I can't think that the Queen could give him any honour now, though he was certainly in line for one."'

There were those around Elton who seriously doubted whether he could survive all this punishment. Especially fearful were those who remembered two suicide attempts, at moments of far less extremity. As an unnamed 'friend' gloomily put it in one interview: '*The Sun* might just as well have sent him a rope and told him to get on with it.'

Much of the time, he was resolutely upbeat. He knew that at the end of the road, as things stood, was a massive court case that would inflict incalculable further damage on himself and his family. He would be obliged to go into the witness-box and allow his private life to be dissected for days on end by some ruthless, supercilious QC. Whatever the personal and financial cost – and whatever the pragmatic legal advice – he was determined not only to survive but come out a winner.

On other days, his resolve would collapse, and engulfing despair come flooding in. 'I hardly went out, because I couldn't stop crying,' he later admitted. 'One minute I'd be fine, the next – "waaaa". I'd

get up, have breakfast, then go back to bed. Eat ice lollies and watch
TV all day.' In his depression, he was eating 'six times what I should
have' and drinking more heavily than ever in his life. 'I started
drinking vodka martinis. You're supposed to sip them . . . but I used
to just woosh them back. I would need three or four before I went
out in the evening. Then I'd go on to red wine.'

Bernie Taupin recognised the danger signs, having been through
his own bout of runaway drinking ten years before. After a party for
John Reid's father, at which Elton was scarcely coherent, Bernie told
him what no one else would dare. 'I've never seen you so embarrassing as you were last night. If I'd had a tape recorder with me, you'd
never drink again.'

At the nadir, he locked himself in his suite and remained there
for almost a week, refusing all entreaties to open the door. Alarm
grew that he might be about to do something desperate. The situation
was saved by Renate, who ran outside, got a ladder, climbed up to
his window and tapped on it. Elton was instantly shaken out of his
black mood. 'He thought it was wonderful that someone cared
enough about him to do that,' Nina Myskow remembers. '"And
she's scared of heights," he kept saying. He couldn't get over it.'

On Remembrance Sunday, 1987, IRA terrorists bombed a
church parade at Enniskillen, Northern Ireland. Among those fatally
injured was a young nurse named Marie Wilson. Her father, Gordon
Wilson, later gave a moving TV interview in which he described
holding her hand in the rubble and talking to her as she lay dying.

Seeing and hearing Gordon Wilson was what brought Elton
conclusively round from his glooms, forebodings and despair. 'That
man was so forgiving, so gracious . . . I thought, "Christ, this is what
courage is about. Elton, just shut up, will you. Shut up immediately
and get back to work."'

Meanwhile, within *The Sun*'s compound at Wapping, all was far
from well. The paper had believed its gamble on the rent-boy story
would be justified by huge rises in circulation. But its marketing
people reported a strange phenomenon. On days when it ran an
Elton John exposé, circulation actually fell. On *pièce de résistance* issues
like ELTON PORN PHOTO SHAME the fall could be as much as 200,000
copies. When no Elton John story occupied the front page, sales
returned to normal once more.

The fact was that *Sun* readers did not like seeing Elton on the
rack. Seventeen years of being publicly decent, sane and positive – as
well as adding immeasurably to life's fun – paid off for him now in

spectacular dividends. Even those whom the 'revelation' had titillated at first, soon wearied of their grinding overkill. *The Sun* had lost what credibility it ever had as a moral crusader, and merely seemed to be pursuing a vendetta.

The paper's proprietor Rupert Murdoch had always hitherto allowed it a free rein. But even Murdoch was becoming concerned that the exposés could do him more harm than good. His media empire in America and Australia included many TV stations that could well suffer retaliatory withdrawal of Elton concert films and videos. As a rule, libel actions against his newspapers represented the merest small change to Murdoch. But he seems to have had a premonition, long before any of his staff, that this one would cost him dear.

In July 1987, the stakes in the game were raised dramatically. The novelist Jeffrey Archer had sued the *Daily Star* for a story alleging he was involved with a London call-girl. A drawn-out and spectacular High Court trial found against the *Star* and, by bizarre custom, left the amount of Archer's damages to be set by the jury. They awarded him half a million pounds, the largest libel damages in British legal history. Those at Wapping who had felt uneasy twinges about the Elton John affair began feeling them with redoubled force.

Yet the 'investigators' were still allowed to go about their business. And on 28 September, as surely as one of its own much-derided 'Japs', the paper took a long curved knife and publicly disembowelled itself.

Its reporter in the Thames Valley, covering Old Windsor, filed a story that two Rottweiler guard dogs on Elton's estate had had their 'voice boxes sliced through' to prevent them barking. With the story – a revealing insight into *The Sun*'s editorial procedures – came a note from the reporter saying he was 'not 100 per cent sure' it was true.

MYSTERY OF ELTON'S SILENT DOGS led the next day's paper none the less, under a thin guise of concern for dumb animals. RSPCA officials were said to be 'furious' at the 'evil and outrageous operation' on the Rottweilers. The only quoted source was 'one of Elton's staff', who claimed to have seen the dogs in the Woodside grounds, being walked by a guard on a long lead. 'They looked frightening,' the source had allegedly said, 'but all they could do was snarl and whimper. Afterwards, one of Elton's men said they couldn't make any noise because they'd had their voice boxes cut. Nobody in the grounds would know the dogs were there until it was too late. They're like silent assassins.'

With the spread went a large picture of an open-mouthed Rottweiler, and a reminder that 'the most savage breed in the world . . . will not release their jaws when locked on a victim.' The clear insinuation was that the dogs had been mutilated to make their attacks on trespassers even more terrifying.

The story was nonsense, as *The Sun* found out within hours of running it. One of its photographers, dispatched to Old Windsor to get pictures of the 'silent assassins', reported back that he could find only two Alsatians, both with barks in working order. As a spokesman for Elton confirmed soon afterwards, those were the only dogs he owned. His solicitors, meanwhile, had issued his seventeenth libel writ.

Its entrails all over its desert boots, *The Sun* still kept on slugging. October 15 brought a new front-page splash: YARD BID TO GRAB SUN FILE ON ELTON. Scotland Yard detectives were said to have demanded access to the paper's 'dossier' on 'Elton's sordid sex-life', believing it of 'substantial value' in long-term investigations into the corruption of young boys. The dossier, 'gathered during months of inquiry into London's sordid vice trade', was said to contain testimony from 'dozens of rent boys . . . along with pals and former associates of Elton'.

Next day came news of one legal action, at least, in which *The Sun* could claim unequivocal victory. A judge at the Old Bailey had refused the police a court order to seize the dossier. Its contents, whatever they might be, enjoyed full legal privilege, having been collected in defence of a libel action.

The unkindest cut of all for *The Sun* was that its original rent-boy informant, Stephen Hardy, had now fallen into the hands of its arch-rival, the *Daily Mirror*. On 6 November, the *Mirror* administered the *coup de grâce*, an interview with Hardy under the heading MY SEX LIES OVER ELTON. 'It's all a pack of lies,' Hardy was quoted as saying of *The Sun*'s original 'world exclusive'. 'I made it all up. I only did it for the money, and *The Sun* was easy to con. I've never even met Elton John . . . I've never been to one of his concerts or bought one of his records. In fact, I hate his music.'

The process of wholesale divestment had begun, though it would not be noticeable for some little time yet.

In November 1987, the Rocket record company finally reached the end of the line. Its once proud roster had run down to a few obscure names like Anya and Splash, and, apart from Elton, it had not registered a hit for several years. Its two last supporting acts were told their contracts would not be renewed and that from here on,

Rocket would exist only as a vehicle for Elton John product. Just what he had always said he didn't want, back in those idealistic Seventies days of smiley tank-engine logos, give-away tote bags and office trips to Los Angeles.

Less than a week later, an even bigger dream seemed to have reached its end. Elton announced he was resigning as chairman of Watford and selling his 95 per cent stake in the club for £2 million.

His reason was that he could not go on being Watford's sole financial support. 'I love the club passionately, but I'm no longer touring, so there's no cash flow coming in. It would be difficult to provide cash for Watford, and the club has reached a stage where it needs financial security. I could continue as chairman, but I don't want to destroy what's been achieved, by an act of folly on my part. As much as it hurts me to step down, I know I leave the club having done a lot for it. Now I cannot go on. I don't want to burn myself out.'

The prospective buyer was press and publishing tycoon Robert Maxwell, who had lately diversified his interests with the purchase of two other First Division clubs, Derby County and Oxford United. Elton was initially doubtful about Maxwell, but was won over by the fact that his company, BPCC, had its headquarters in the Watford area and, as large local employers, would have an interest in maintaining a 'family' club. Since Maxwell was already chairman of Derby and his son Kevin of Oxford, BPCC's chief executive John Holloran was appointed to take over at Vicarage Road. Elton would receive the title of Life President and retain a seat on the board.

However, the Football Association opposed the sale under its regulation 60, which prohibited the control of more than one club by any individual or family. A High Court injunction was successfully sought, preventing the transfer of Elton's shares to BPCC. For a time, pop star and press tycoon formed a weird alliance, the latter implausibly sporting an Elton-style baseball cap. The FA agreed to drop its ban if Maxwell would balance his takeover of Watford by selling his interests in Oxford United. But in late December, Elton called the whole deal off. For the present anyway, that part of his life was too precious to throw out.

For Christmas cards that year he commissioned a series of cartoons designed to show how happy Renate and he still were, despite everything. On one card, Renate sat on a couch, wrapping presents and asking, 'What are you wearing for Christmas, Elton?' Behind her stood Elton, dressed as a laden and lit-up Christmas tree.

The Watford sale saga rumbled on into 1988. In January, the

strip-club king Paul Raymond offered to match Robert Maxwell's
£2 million offer for Elton's shares. To add to the turmoil, Dave
Bassett had resigned after only half a season as manager, and the
club's poor showing that year had doomed it to Division Two in
1988–9. Elton had found a successor to Bassett in Steve Harrison,
Watford's former full back and coach. But Harrison would not sign
unless given assurances that the club had a stable future. Elton pledged
to spend half a million pounds, if necessary, to restore Watford to
Division One, and promised he had no intention of making it the
adjunct to Raymond's Revuebar. 'I'm not going anywhere,' he said.
'I will not be selling my soul to the devil.'

On 16 January, *The Sun* mustered a last full front-page assault,
ELTON JOHN QUIZZED BY VICE POLICE. Elton was said to have been
questioned 'for THREE HOURS' by the head of Scotland Yard's Vice
Squad, Chief Superintendent Bill Carnie, and two other senior
detectives at his solicitor's office in Lincoln's Inn. But, by previous
standards, the reporting was almost eerily circumspect. 'At 9.06 pm,
the Vice Squad men left, but Mr Carnie would only say: "There is
no statement." Elton . . . was escorted to the waiting car by his
lawyers. The star shook their hands, then smiled briefly for a *Sun*
photographer, saying "Thank you, gentlemen." ' The only result of
this meeting – if, indeed, it took place in the way *The Sun* claimed –
was to eliminate him from any police inquiries on any subject
whatever.

Elton's public restraint towards *Sun* representatives was not emu-
lated by his manager. A few weeks later, in a West End night club,
John Reid spotted Elton being buttonholed by a *Sun* reporter named
Rick Sky. What happened next was retailed next morning in the
paper's usual gobsmacked typography: 'Reid shouted abuse as he
GRABBED our man and SHOOK him. Then he BASHED Rick's head
against a pillar five times and PUSHED him out of the club while
punching him on the chest. Rick was taken to hospital with blood
streaming on to his shirt . . . [he] suffered a deep cut on the back
of his head, and doctors put three stitches in the wound.' A
photograph showed the superstar, in tasselled smoking cap, being
ushered from the scene by his manager with checked jacket rumpled
and tie askew.

Reid was charged with assault, and subsequently appeared in the
dock at Bow Street Magistrates' Court. He was fined £150 after
telling magistrate William Robbins, 'I'm very sorry. I'd had a few
drinks.' ELTON THUG FINED, *The Sun* noted with righteous satisfaction. Elton was furious over the incident, and stormed at Reid to
remember that such outbursts always rebounded directly on to him.

'It's always "Elton Aide Beats Up *Sun* Man". And they do like to get the letters AID next to my name.'

But *The Sun* had not finished, either with Reid or the letters AID. Next week came a story dredged up from the fortieth birthday party that 'bully-boy pop supremo John Reid' had given for Elton at his Hertfordshire house, more than a year earlier. It was alleged that the noise of the fireworks had frightened a neighbour's pregnant mare into premature labour and the foal had been born dead. The mare's owner had intended taking Reid to court, but at the last minute he had sent her £2,753 in compensation. ELTON AIDE'S WILD PARTY KILLED MY HORSE, apart from its satisfactory arrangement of capitals, had a resonance akin to FREDDIE STARR ATE MY HAMSTER.

In March, Elton returned to AIR Studios in London to make his first album since the throat surgery, and so discover whether or not he still had a singing voice. To lend moral support, producer Chris Thomas had assembled a squad of star helpers, including Pete Townshend on acoustic guitar and Carl Wilson and Bruce Johnston of the Beach Boys to do backing vocals. Another track featured vocals by Elton's two original band musicians, the perennially forgiving Dee Murray and Nigel Olsson. The sessions took longer than expected, owing to the accidental wiping of several half-completed songs; immediately afterwards Elton flew to Los Angeles to celebrate his forty-first birthday. There was no sign of Renate.

In early April he had been scheduled to join Ian Botham on the latter's sponsored walk in aid of leukaemia research. The plan was to follow Hannibal's invasion route across the Alps to Italy, leading a symbolic elephant. The event was cancelled, however, and instead Elton flew to Hawaii, where George Michael was on tour. Checking in to a £1,000-per-night suite at the Honolulu Hilton, he spent a week sunbathing with George Michael and cheering him on from the front row of his concert audience. There still was no sign of Renate.

Almost exactly twenty years earlier, he had bolted from his first fiancée, summoning his stepfather's van to take away his records, cushions and books. And now – albeit on an infinitely more opulent and elaborate level – history was to repeat itself.

A press release from Sotheby's, the international auction house, announced that Elton was to dispose of his entire collection of antiques and art. The reason given was that he planned to sell Woodside and to move to a smaller house further into the country where Renate and he could live a more secluded life. The auction, at Sotheby's New Bond Street salesrooms, later that summer, was expected to realise as much as £3 million.

Coming so soon after his attempt to sell Watford, the announcement aroused speculation that Elton might be running short of cash. However, a recent survey in *The Sunday Times Magazine* had rated him Britain's 95th richest person, with an estimated fortune of £42 million. The same survey had rated John Reid 176th, with an estimated £12 million.

Elton's story was that, at 41, he had suddenly lost his lifelong mania for collecting, and his reliance on inanimate objects as the sole dependable source of happiness. He had woken up one day at Woodside and realised the full enormity of his two-decade shopping spree. 'It was like Harrods' warehouse. There was stuff sitting unopened in crates, which was preposterous. Literally everything was covered. Every wall, every surface. It was suffocating me.'

He still talked resolutely about 'us' and 'our home' and making the fresh start that selling everything would allow. But by this stage, few who knew him believed in that quieter new place in the country where married life would finally begin. 'Clearing out the house was a typical Elton way of going about things,' Nina Myskow says. 'What he was really clearing out was Renate.'

During Renate's final days at Woodside, in March or April of 1988, she invited Nina there for the weekend. Elton was still away, in Los Angeles or Hawaii. The Sotheby people were soon to arrive with their rescuing vans, like Derf Farebrother, twenty years earlier, to strip the place bare.

Renate by now spent almost all her time in the one part of the house she could call her own. This was a screened-off alcove at one end of the private suite Elton had insisted she should have. It contained her computer, her clothes and some furniture in her own modest, tentative taste. 'It was a bit like a bedsitter,' Nina Myskow remembers. 'Very feminine. Flowered covers and pot-pourri. Almost Biba feathers kind of style.'

Nina herself slept at the top of the house in the Bugatti Suite, named for its collection of quasi-Egyptian spiked and tasselled furnishings by Carlo Bugatti. Nearby were rooms of Elton's stage costumes and of artworks never unpacked from their delivery crates.

She spent a curious couple of days, sitting with Renate in her screened-off little bedsit, or downstairs in the sumptuous newly rebuilt kitchen. 'The fridge alone was like a room in its own right. You could walk in and find anything you wanted. All the facilities were magnificent. But all the time one felt slightly illicit. As if having been invited by Elton's wife wasn't really sufficient excuse to be there.'

Lying around, as always, was a large selection of the newest hardback books. Nina picked up Kitty Kelley's biography of Frank Sinatra and was leafing through it when a piece of paper slipped from between the pages. 'It was a note from Renate to Elton. I tried to put it back without reading it, but couldn't help seeing a few words. It said she really loved him, but didn't want to stand in his way or be a problem to him. And she didn't want anything from him.'

Already this year, the treasure troves of two other noted materialists had come under the auctioneer's hammer, attracting huge publicity and fetching bonanza prices. In Los Angeles, Liberace's furs, jewellery and mink-lined, chandelier-hung limousines had gone for $2 million. Then in New York, Andy Warhol's collection of art and kitsch had made an unbelievable $25 million. Warhol and Liberace had followed convention, at least, in being dead before their estates were sold off. It was something new for a superstar publicly to dispose of his own valuables, as if he were about to take a vow of poverty and become a wandering friar.

This new phenomenon, the 'celebrity sale', had made even dignified auction houses see the value in pop-style hype and razzmatazz. Both Sotheby's and their arch rival Christie's had courted Elton for his business as avidly as any record company of yore. Sotheby's won the day in a presentation combining talk-'em-up pre-sale showmanship with reverent good taste. The firm's senior director Marcus Linell, accompanied by its 'Head of Collectibles' and its jewellery and fine art experts, then paid an exploratory visit to Woodside. Having seen the hoard – which by that time had overflowed even into the squash court – they came away marvelling that anyone could actually live there.

Elton's overriding stipulation was that everything must go. Not only the art treasures and costly antiques, the 150 Art Nouveau lamps and 200 Art Déco nymphs, the jukeboxes and pinball machines, but all his other possessions, down to the most private and personal. The clothes he had worn onstage since 1970, his jewellery, his shoes, his collected spectacles, his massed gold discs, even his luggage, were put out to be assessed, graded and priced. Every expensive toy, and every cheap one, that had ever caught his looter's eye, every relentlessly hoarded and obsessively dusted ornament, conversation piece, souvenir, knick-knack and keepsake was dismissed without a backward glance. He was disposing not simply of assets but of his whole past. Taking him at his word, Sotheby's even removed the soap dish from

Bob Halley's bathroom. Three days were needed to transport the hoard in a fleet of pantechnicons from Old Windsor to Old Bond Street.

Sotheby's success with Elton had much to do with its chairman, the former Tory arts minister Lord Gowrie. They had met ten years earlier, when Gowrie was a dealer in contemporary art, and sold Elton an important portrait by Francis Bacon. This 'great masterpiece' he persuaded Elton to hold back from the sale, along with a handful of other paintings. Nor, finally, were the superstar's fourteen cars included, nor his prodigious record library, nor his Goon Show scripts, nor his £75,000 marital bed.

Characteristically, the grand sell-off was no sooner announced than Elton started buying once more, abetted by his new friends in aprons of green baize. In July, Sotheby's held a sale of works by Russian avant-garde painters who, until recently, had been unable to exhibit even in their own country. Elton paid £44,000 for two works by the husband-and-wife team Igor and Svetlana Kopystianski.

The Elton John sale was scheduled for four days early in September. Meanwhile, lavish picture spreads of the merchandise to be auctioned appeared in every major newspaper and magazine, with Elton posing in their midst like an opulent Albert Steptoe. Selected items were taken on tour to New York, Los Angeles, Tokyo and Sydney. The Victoria and Albert Museum mounted a special summer exhibition of 500 lots, including pictures by Magritte and L. S. Lowry, Bugatti furniture, Art Nouveau figures, jewellery, spectacles and stage costumes. It was another notable 'first' for glam rock sequins and glasses spelling 'Elton' to be given the same historical weight as cabinets of royal armour and Iron Age axe-heads.

The catalogue ran to four volumes, contained in a white slip case and costing £40. Volume 1, 'Stage Costume and Memorabilia', showed Elton perched on the edge of a pinball machine, flanked by his hussar and aquamarine feather outfits and wearing the stole of artificial bananas from his Bob Mackie pirate suit. Volume 2, 'Jewellery', showed him in close-up under his boater brim, displaying a large diamond and sapphire ring, a diamond and sapphire double wrist band and an onyx and diamond brooch with a tassel as long as a fly switch. Volume 3, 'Art Nouveau and Art Déco', showed him holding the spike of a Bugatti chair, surrounded by mottled glass and ethereal figurines. Volume 4, 'Diverse Collections', showed him with a gold palm tree, Warhol's 'Marilyn', Magritte's blue fish swathed in pearls, a replica of Tutankhamun's state throne, a jewelled papier-mâché cabinet, an umbrella stand and a stool on two legs clothed in checked trousers and white shoes.

Everything received the same scrupulous description and provenance. Thus: '1163. Rembrandt Harmensz Van Rijn. Self-portrait . . . Etching, a very good impression of the second state . . .' Thus: '1851. A Smoky Plastic Musical Guitar, modern, revolving on a spigot and playing "Love Me Tender".' Thus: '782. A Salon Suite with Decorative Aubusson Tapestry Coverings, designed by Raoul Dufy, *circa* 1925–30.' Thus: '1853. A Cutey-Doll Radio, modern, wearing a see-through negligée, with dual controls, her body containing the works.' Thus: '119. A Presentation Platinum Disc for the Album *Rock of the Westies*.' Thus: '88. Pinball Wizard movie prop boots from the film *Tommy*, the fibre-glass giant Doc Marten lace-up boots with platform supports above and metal callipers and leather supports for attaching to the legs.' Thus: '215. A Camisole belonging to Judy Garland in *Meet Me In St Louis*.' Thus: '281. Multi-coloured Jockey Cap, by Interstellar Propellors, with twin-bladed propellor mounted on the crown.' Thus: '76. A pair of 'sun-blind' novelty spectacles, the yellow frames stamped 'Roma' with unfolding semi-circular fabric sun-blinds.'

Thus the original lounge suite he had brought for Hercules ('of slightly concave outline, upholstered in red leather'); his monogrammed Louis Vuitton cases and cabin trunks ('each with traditional tan leather and brass-bound exterior'); his long-ago blue Levi suit 'applied with commercially produced embroidered patches'); his John Lennon lithographs ('inscribed "To Elton/Let's hope it's a good one/Love Yoko and Sean"'); and his souvenir programme 'signed in black ball pen by Elvis Presley'.

The lots jammed Sotheby's storerooms, spilling into corridors and even Lord Gowrie's own office. They included a selection of footwear, like '144. A pair of monogrammed high platform boots, the silver-leather zippered boots lettered E and J in scarlet with leather stacked heels and silver and scarlet platform soles.' His lordship's Sloaney secretary, too young to remember glam rock, asked Elton if he'd really worn such things on stage. 'They were for day wear, darling,' he said. 'I used to run for taxis in those.'

The great Woodside turn-out also made a cover for Elton's new album, which showed his stage costumes on their manikins, massed like a small army beyond a foreground heap of feathers, glasses, boaters, bananas and Minnie Mouse ears. Its title, too, reflected his disinvention of two decades as well as his continuing firm resolve against *The Sun*. Recognising a self cast off in 1968, but never really lost, the album was called *Reg Strikes Back*.

Any other rock star passing through such ordeals would have shown his anger and anguish in his music. But Elton, as always, was singing Bernie Taupin's words, and Bernie's horizons were quite clear. *Reg Strikes Back* was no furious thunderbolt but a cheery miscellany on topics far from home, whose references to Elton's current state were only of the most accidental kind. Elton had found solace in recording it, especially since it showed his voice to be not only unimpaired but even improved. One particular track, 'Since God Invented Girls', yet another homage to Brian Wilson and the Beach Boys, found him making notes as high and harmonies as complex as Wilson ever had. Only the straining eye could see any emotional subtext in titles like 'Poor Cow' and 'I Don't Wanna Go on with You Like That', and lines like 'This overload is edging me further out to sea / I need to put some distance between overkill and me.'

It was clear by now that *The Sun*'s onslaught had had no adverse effect on Elton's career in Britain or America. In January 1988, as the world was crashing round his ears, he had had a surprise single hit with his live Australian concert version of 'Candle in the Wind', which made number five in Britain and six in America. *The Sun*'s so-called corrupter of youth was hard to reconcile with his video image, Mozart-wigged and husky-voiced, impassionedly singing of Marilyn Monroe as 'something more than sexual'.

Reg Strikes Back further proved that his public had not deserted him, reaching seventeen in the UK and eighteen in America, while its best single, 'I Don't Wanna Go On with You Like That', was an American number two. Any idea that he had lost his royal friends was also quashed when, in June, he appeared in a gala concert for the Prince of Wales's Prince's Trust with Eric Clapton, Rick Astley, Joe Cocker and Leonard Cohen.

Feeling 'like a man who's taken a cleansing shower' after the Woodside purge, he plunged into a variety of new projects, none of them leading to a smaller, quieter house in the country. He agreed to appear in Ken Russell's film version of *The Rainbow* by D. H. Lawrence, playing the cameo role of Uncle Henry. He got involved in a compact-disc version of Dylan Thomas's *Under Milk Wood*, writing new music for Polly Garter's song, to be sung by Bonnie Tyler. He dropped out of *The Rainbow* – just before he was due to appear on camera – but was then mooted to play Liberace in an American TV movie.

The 2,000 lots on preview in five rooms at Sotheby's brought him his first reviews in salesroom columns rather than musical ones. 'His collection . . . is the opposite of a connoisseur's choice,' said the *Daily Telegraph*. 'It is two decades of impulse-buying, done with a splendid sense of humour, but its interest in excellence is incidental.

It is not a "collection" in any disciplined sense; it is an assemblage, a magpie's nest piled high with glamour and glitz. What there is, as art, starts with Art Nouveau glass, chosen to be big, colourful, ritzy and flamboyant. The 20th-century furniture is more impressive and better-chosen. The jewellery . . . oddly mixes the tastes of a conservative duchess and a mid-Thirties flapper.'

In the Warhol sale, even insignificant trinkets had commanded huge prices thanks to the great artist's personal imprimatur. To give the Elton sale a 'Warhol factor', each lot came with a special label warranting it to be of the Elton John Collection and stamped with a logo of straw hat and spectacles.

The four-day sale, when it came, was conducted more like a rock concert, with police and crash barriers in New Bond Street, and Elton fans packed among the dealers and collectors. Six hundred people, in six separate rooms, competed for the treasures, with telephone bids coming in from others all over the world. Even Elton's mother had a representative there to snap up some keepsakes of her boy's past. He himself did not attend the sale, being on tour again in America.

From the first day's business, on 6 September, it was obvious that prices were going wild. The Magritte gouache, 'Hommage à Alphonse Allais', went to a Brussels buyer for £70,200, twice the anticipated price. Three Lowrys, 'The Beach at Penarth', 'Moreton-in-Marsh' (Elton's souvenir of Rocket Records' inauguration) and 'A Yacht at Lytham' went respectively for £46,200, £41,800 and £17,600, again roughly double the estimates. An Allen Jones 'kneeling nude' glass table, expected to make up to £7,000 went to a Japanese buyer for £20,900. Furnishings and glass were equally astonishing. The Dufy Aubusson suite made £90,200, again doubling Sotheby's prediction, as did a Morris and Co. carpet, designed for Merton Abbey in 1900, which fetched £71,500. A Daum vase with applied red glass tulips went for £56,100. Two Tiffany lamps went for £37,400 and £36,300. The jewellery fetched £400,000, its prize piece a diamond and onyx Cartier watch, which went to a Japanese department store for £25,300, twelve times the catalogue estimate.

Of the £14.8 million made in four days, more than £1 million came from Elton's personal effects, showing what frantic desire now existed to invest in pop music memorabilia. A collector from Nashville paid £44,000 for eleven of his stage costumes. His Dodger Stadium suit, thought to be worth £1,800, went for £6,200 and his 'Eiffel Tower boater' for £4,000, ten times the estimate. His 1939 Wurlitzer jukebox fetched £17,600, his light-up 'Elton' glasses

£9,900, his mink-framed Dior ones £950 and his signed picture of Elvis Presley £2,500, five times as much as expected. The giant Pinball Wizard boots, expected to make under £2,000, went for £11,000 to a director of the Doc Marten company. The propellor baseball cap, expected to fetch £40, went for £800. A straw boater, which could be bought new in Oxford Street for £20, went for £825, and a painted mirror, $5 on any Venice Beach stall, for £285. A white-haired woman unsuccessfully bid £3,600 for the silver E and J platform boots, which went to America for £4,950. A cushion like the *Madman Across the Water* album-sleeve went to Gus Dudgeon, the album's producer, for £2,950. Even the ELTON JOHN SALE banners hanging outside were added as extra lots, and fetched £550.

No break-up ever happened with more sad cordiality. All through the final months, Elton kept in daily touch with Renate on the mobile phone he now carried everywhere. The smallest upset or piece of news still made him instinctively turn to her. One day she found a message on the answering machine from Elton in a hotel room somewhere in America. He said he'd awoken to find a small earthquake going on, but it had stopped now and he was going back to sleep again.

The end was officially confirmed on 18 November. Elton and Renate were to divorce 'by mutual consent . . . and with no fault attaching to either party'. He was especially emphatic on that point, remembering his own parents' divorce and the way his mother had been named as the guilty party.

A bleakly formal statement from Renate was issued via John Reid's office: 'Both of us have been and will be so busy with our own work commitments that we are seeing too little of each other. And for that reason it seems unavoidable that we are growing apart. We are, however, parting on the most amicable terms and genuinely intend to remain best friends. Moreover we are both confident that all personal matters will be resolved without any animosity. I am obviously saddened to see our marriage end, and I wish Elton all the happiness in the world and I know that he wishes me the same.'

The orgy of tabloid headlines was generally sympathetic in tone. With each one went the wedding-day picture of boatered, wing-poke bridegroom and bewildered bride, as unreal now as figures under glass in a shake-up snowstorm. *Today*'s full colour extravaganza used an all-too-inviting simile: ELTON'S MARRIAGE FLICKERED AND WENT OUT LIKE A CANDLE IN THE WIND.

The Sun called them BRIDE 'N' DOOM, surrounding the words with a broken heart-shape. Two inside pages explained WHY THE

ODD COUPLE WERE DESTINED TO GET DIVORCED, helped by one picture of Elton giving a kiss to Phil Collins, another of him with his arm round George Michael and a third of him dressed as a panto-mime dame. Significantly, however, there was no mention of cocaine, orgies or escapades with rent boys.

The only interview Elton gave was to his old friend Nina Myskow, for the *Mail on Sunday*. 'I gave it my best shot,' he said. 'And it's certainly not Renate's fault. She's done nothing wrong. That's what makes it so hard. I feel this terrible guilt because she was so supportive when things were going badly for me. She was absolutely wonderful.'

He admitted to Nina that at the time of the worst *Sun* stories, he'd thought of seeking psychiatric help. 'Lots of my friends say it's wonderful to be able to unburden yourself. But I think I should overcome my own problems.'

Though Renate had made no pre-nuptial agreement, there was speculation that her divorce settlement might be as high as £10 million. Her only visible acquisition, however, was a seventeenth-century cottage in Godalming, Surrey. 'She chose it just because she liked its name,' Nina Myskow says. 'It was called Cobblers.'

Ever unpredictable, having refused interviews to all network TV shows, Elton suddenly agreed to talk to Thames, London's local channel, in the garden at Woodside. The inevitable questions about Renate were fielded with deft grace. 'I'd rather not say anything about the marriage situation. It's only fair to my wife, who's been so dignified throughout this whole thing.' That evidently meant most of all to him.

Elton apart, there had been signs all through 1988 that the tide was turning against *The Sun*. Its persecution of the dying TV star Russell Harty, another 'self-confessed' homosexual, aroused widespread pro-test and brought a memorable denunciation by Alan Bennett from the pulpit at Harty's memorial service. More flak flew when, in reporting the horrific Ealing Vicarage rape case, it ignored all conven-tions of decency and identified the victim. Then in October, it went too far with the royal family, ending a long-standing convention that the Queen never answers back. To obtain a first sight of Fergie's new baby daughter, *The Sun* hijacked a royal family group photograph destined to be the Queen's next Christmas card. The Queen brought proceedings for breach of copyright and Scotland Yard's Serious Crime Squad began an investigation into how the picture had been misappropriated. *The Sun* was forced to pay £100,000 to four Palace-nominated charities and publish a grovelling front-page apology.

To add to all this, its bully-boy muscle had been resisted in unprecedented fashion. The 'poofter' pop star had not turned tail and run. Its Elton John exposé must be defended in court, using a chief witness who had already confessed, in the columns of its greatest rival, that he'd told 'a pack of lies'.

In the libel action over Graham X's allegations against Elton, *The Sun* knew it stood no chance whatever. What it still could do was make that trial a personal nightmare for Elton, bringing forward its other witnesses to smear him and reporting everything under the protection of full legal privilege. If the paper was going down, it would have the consolation of taking Elton with it.

At this point, Elton's lawyers pulled off a coup that can only be called dazzling. They arranged that the first libel case into court was the subject of Elton's seventeenth and last writ – the instantly disprovable allegation that he owned Rottweiler dogs whose barks had been silenced. *The Sun* was thus faced with an action in which muck-raking would be useless, one which it had to lose and which would, moreover, unleash hysterical laughter up and down Fleet Street. The case of the voiceless Rottweilers was set to begin in the High Court on 12 December, before Mr Justice Michael Davies. But lawyers from Wapping were already talking to lawyers from Lincoln's Inn.

Later that week, Nina Myskow was invited to dinner with Elton and John Reid at Reid's house. 'When I got there, Elton took me outside into the drive,' Nina remembers. 'He said, "I've won. *The Sun* are going to pay me a million pounds." Then he burst into tears.'

On 12 December, the morning that the Rottweiler libel action was due to open in the High Court, *The Sun*'s splash headline was two words: SORRY ELTON. As a rule, in British papers apologies are minuscule paragraphs in legalese, buried at the foot of inside pages. Never before had one appeared this way as a lead story in house-style prose, every word of it approved in advance by the plaintiff's lawyers:

> *The Sun* last night agreed to pay megastar Elton John £1 million libel damages.
>
> The settlement followed allegations published in *The Sun* last year about his private life.
>
> A delighted Elton said last night: 'This is the best Christmas present I could wish for.
>
> 'Life is too short to bear grudges and I don't bear *The Sun* any malice.'

Later a *Sun* spokesman apologised to Elton for running the stories which they acknowledge to be completely untrue.

The spokesman said: 'We are delighted that Elton and *The Sun* have become friends again and are very sorry that we were lied to by a teenager living in a world of fantasy.'

Elton said: 'Now I welcome the fact that my name has been cleared.'

The settlement included *The Sun* paying damages concerning an article about Elton's alleged cruelty to dogs.

The spokesman said: 'We accept that he loves his pets and we are very sorry we suggested otherwise.'

The Sun is paying Elton's legal costs.

Inside was a centre spread in which Elton repaid the compliment by giving *The Sun* an exclusive interview. The Rottweiler of Fleet Street was transformed to fawning puppy dog as it proudly told how its late quarry was 'fighting fit and ready for action', having lost twenty-eight pounds in less than two months. 'He has completely changed his lifestyle by cutting out BOOZE and his DIET of stodgy food and going on a rigid training EXERCISE . . .' The interview itself was presented in a manner verging on the schizophrenic. 'Things hadn't gone well for me in 1987, and I was feeling desperately depressed . . .' Elton was quoted as saying. 'I needed to get fit and healthy again after the worst year of my life . . .' A second instalment retailed his views on current pop hits, under the strapline WHEN STARS MAKE FRIENDS, THEY MAKE FRIENDS WITH THE SUN. Having failed to pierce his jugular, the paper now seemed intent on licking Elton to death.

The damages doubled Jeffrey Archer's record jury award a year earlier, and *The Sun* was estimated to be liable for about as much again in costs. Elton had in addition received what few thought he ever could, 'an apology to match the smear'.

But not everybody was thrilled. The judge who had been due to sit in the Rottweiler case, Mr Justice Michael Davies, complained the court had been 'manipulated' by *The Sun*'s 'pre-emptive strike' in announcing the settlement before it had been formally put before him. 'Reading it, one would think that Elton John and the newspaper had formed a mutual admiration society,' the judge commented acidly. Recording 'extreme disapproval and distaste', he pointed out that courts of law were a forum for trials and disputes. They were not 'a supine adjunct to a publicity machine for pop stars and newspapers'.

The Elton John case dealt *The Sun* a blow that would change it, and all tabloids, for ever. As well as costing the paper dear in both cash and circulation, it had a galvanising effect on other show business celebrities who had previously accepted their fate as supine soft targets. Like Mexican villagers in *The Magnificent Seven*, they realised that if you turned and fought, the ogre was not invincible. A wholly unanticipated factor, the moral sensibility of its buyers, also now had to enter into *The Sun*'s thinking. A year afterwards, it suffered a further damaging loss in circulation – including a boycott on Mersey-side – after claiming that victims in the Hillsborough soccer stadium tragedy had had their pockets picked as they lay dying. As a result, it began seriously to clean up its act, even appointing an ombudsman to deal with reader complaints.

What was never fully appreciated was how much Elton had *The Sun* over a barrel. In the original apology headline dictated by his lawyers, SORRY ELTON was followed by an exclamation mark. Between editions, for aesthetic reasons, the editor decided to drop the exclamation mark. But before even this could be done, it had to be cleared with Elton's lawyers.

NINETEEN

'I just want to smell a few roses'

O N 28 August, 1989, Elton appeared in a special bank holiday one-to-one edition of *Wogan*. It was the British television public's first chance to see him since his victory over *The Sun*, and the total change he had announced in every department of his life. Goodwill still waxed strong, if the studio audience was anything to go by. Congratulatory applause, whistles and whoops greeted him as he walked out on to the gimcrack chat-show set.

This born-again, new-look, low-key Elton wore modest rimless glasses, an unadorned dark blue Gianni Versace suit and lavender turtleneck shirt. Over the platinum blond hair strands curved a purple bead-trimmed Nehru cap. He might have been the leader of some Rajneeshi-style religious sect who had just purchased an entire American state for his disciples. Lounging on the couch next to Terry Wogan, his coat sleeves slipped up his forearms and one silk sock-top disclosed a band of white shin. Almost all the two stone, euphorically sweated off in late 1988, seemed to have found its way back again.

He was as good-humoured and fluent as ever in responding to Wogan's clueless blarney, which included an observation that his 'old bones' must by now be feeling the strain of performing and going on tour. He contrived to keep smiling even through a photo and film montage containing scenes of his wedding to Renate and blow-ups of the worst rent-boy stories from *The Sun*.

'In all these years, you've never had a British number-one single,' Wogan reminded him at one point. 'Does that rankle at all?'

The lavender Nehru twitched his glasses up his nose, in the mannerism all interviewers had noted, right back to Cyril Gee at Mills Music in 1965.

'No, not really,' he answered – and, ever the record trivia hound, could instantly list all those bizarre or unlikely names who had achieved what he, somehow, never could. 'Laurel and Hardy had one, Richard Harris, even Arthur Mullard's had a British number one. It would have been nice, but it doesn't bother me. I don't suppose I ever will have one now.'

The Sun's million-pound pay-out had been poured into a life that seemed totally dismantled. Not only had wife and possessions gone from Woodside but the mansion itself had now been gutted, pending total renovation and refurnishing. Its owner spoke vaguely of a new 'traditional' look, replacing the Art Deco labyrinth with chaste vistas of Laura Ashley print, quiet furnishings and open fires. Meanwhile, for the foreseeable future, the only residents were his ninety-year-old grandmother, Ivy, whom he'd installed in the Orangery, and his servants and security staff.

Throughout that spring, summer and autumn, Elton was back onstage – 'the only place where I feel safe' – pushing himself to constant new extremes of self-flagellating celebration. While playing Bercy stadium, near Paris, he collapsed from heat exhaustion and had to be revived with damp towels and water before continuing. Two nights later, he spent a reported £200,000 on a party to celebrate his forty-second birthday, bringing over 200 guests including Tina Turner, Ringo Starr and Viscount Linley, all of whom were put up at exclusive hotels and ferried by fleets of limousines to the château hired for the occasion. Food and drink were served by footmen in powdered wigs and, after cutting his cake, a nine-foot-high replica of the Eiffel Tower, Elton sat down at the piano and belted out number after number. 'He was more like a man celebrating his twenty-first birthday than his forty-second,' one guest commented. 'The Romans couldn't have done it better. There was champagne by the bucketful, and a snap of fingers brought a host of flunkeys to your table.'

In August, he was reported to have spent £6,000 on wines at a single dinner for himself and a fourteen-strong party at a restaurant in Dallas, Texas. In September, he cancelled his two concerts in Tampa, Florida, after going down with influenza. In October, he was said to have 'keeled over with exhaustion, which called off his final US show, in Worcester, Massachusetts, and caused speculation that he might be suffering from the 'yuppie virus', myalgic encephalitis. That same week, an 'ailing' and 'burned-out Elton' checked into a £560-per-night suite at the Ritz Hotel, Paris, under orders to take a month's complete rest before going on to tour the Far East, Australia and New Zealand. In November, he was due to top the bill at a music festival in Antwerp, Belgium, and also receive a Diamond Career Award for services to music. This performance, too, was cancelled when Elton's people notified the festival organisers that he was 'not yet fully fit'.

There were intermittent rumours that, after his trials with the British press, he intended to live permanently overseas. The *Daily Star* claimed he had already paid £4.5 million for an enormous estate in Palm Beach, Florida. An aerial photograph was provided, showing the high tower from which Elton would allegedly gaze at the Atlantic like a muezzin in a minaret. The story brought an instant denial from his lawyers – a force now held in awe throughout Fleet Street. This time there was no writ, only a complaint of inaccuracy to the Press Council. But the *Star* was still rattled enough to print a fulsome retraction within days. None could doubt that Elton's battle with *The Sun* had fundamentally changed the way in which tabloid newspapers went about their business.

He admitted that, in the darkest days of *The Sun*'s onslaught, he had often been tempted to take permanent refuge abroad. 'But I couldn't just run away. I had to stay and take it until I'd totally cleared my name. Anyway, Britain's my home. It always has been and it always will be.'

His mother and stepfather now lived, safe from tabloid harassment, on the Spanish island of Minorca. But his remaining close family, on Sheila's side, were still in Britain, around the mock-Tudor fringes of Metroland. The millionaire gypsy kept in touch as conscientiously as his whirlwind schedule would allow. His Aunt Win and his younger cousin Paul – now married with a baby daughter – both lived on the same modest street in Ruislip, Middlesex. Every so often, Paul would get a phone call from his mother to come along quickly as Elton had looked in for a few minutes en route across the world. He was devoted to his grandmother, who, even though living in his mansion grounds, made no distinction between him and her other grandchildren and great-grandchildren. It meant much to him that, when the Duke and Duchess of York attended one of his huge parties, Fergie made a special point of talking to his 'Nan'.

Fractured and frenzied as Elton's existence might seem, it maintained its perennial fixed points of normality and sanity. He still played tennis like a podgy whirling dervish, in early mornings after the heaviest carousing. He was as much a football fan as ever, timing his latest world circumnavigation to end in time for the 1990 Cup Final. But his days as Watford FC's saviour and bottomless piggy bank were definitely over. In December 1989, he tried for the second time to sell his 92 per cent stake in the club, this time to a London-based leisure company, Wrighton Enterprises. As with the abortive Robert Maxwell deal, the sale was to bring him £2 million, removing the club's drain on his finances while leaving him its figurehead life president. But a month later, it was announced that the negotiations had 'failed to come to fruition'.

The social connections that meant so much to him proved to have been unharmed by *The Sun*'s muck-raking. He remained on the guest list for parties at Windsor Castle when, it was said, the Queen relied on him as a jiving partner to Bill Haley's 'Rock Around the Clock'. At a luncheon he gave at Woodside before its shutdown for refurbishment, the Queen Mother was among his guests. 'I sat next to her,' Bernie Taupin remembers. 'We talked about gardening – and summer pudding. While we were out in the garden, we could see the tower of Windsor Castle, where the flag was flying. "Oh," the Queen Mother said. "My daughter's at home."'

Despite these social triumphs, the company Elton relished most was still that of musicians, especially his fellow time-travellers through the Sixties and Seventies: Eric Clapton, Ringo Starr, George Harrison, Freddie Mercury. His favourite pastime was still hanging out into the small hours, behind a myriad of bottles and glasses, reminiscing about the vast lengths of road that stretched behind. Despite his wealth and freewill, he remained the music industry's biggest workaholic, never really happy unless head-clamped between cans in some airless underground booth. He was still a tireless accumulator of records, tapes and compact discs, an omnivorous hoarder of record trivia, an astrological porer over Top 20, 40 and 100 charts, a forensic dissecter of any new sound that might be turned to his own purposes. For all his global fame, he remained at heart a session man, always willing to sing or play backup anonymously for others, just as in the long-ago days of Marble Arch and Pickettywitch. In 1987, he played piano and electric piano on George Harrison's album *Cloud Nine*. In 1988, he co-produced the title track of Olivia Newton-John's album, *The Rumour*, as well as contributing piano tracks and vocals. In 1989, he duetted with Aretha Franklin on her single, 'Through the Storm'. In 1990, he played piano on new albums by Jon Bon Jovi and his undiminished idol, Bob Dylan.

Advancing into middle age, he was still utterly without musical prejudice, able to find something to praise as well as much to damn in every new era of commercial pop. Madonna he damned, in typically waspish style, for not singing live at her concerts. But, just as he once had liked the Osmonds, he now liked the milk-fed puppets of Stock, Aitken and Waterman's Hit Factory studio. Rick Astley, in particular, he said, had 'a terrific voice'. He liked the peroxide Goss twins, natural heirs to the Bay City Rollers. He believed George Michael to be a virtuoso ranking with any of his own time. There was no one with whom he wouldn't share a stage, and none who did not jump at the chance to share one with him.

He continued unique among his species as a mixture of egomaniacal arrogance, infantile petulance, punctilious chivalry, sensitivity, generosity and the fine-tuned thoughtfulness of that good boy at Pinner County Grammar School. In 1989, the comedienne Marti Caine was found to be suffering from cancer. Returning one day to her theatre dressing-room, she found it full of white flowers sent by Elton. That same year his old journalistic friend Nina Myskow – now herself a considerable celebrity – was 'turned over' by the *News of the World* in a miniature version of what Elton had gone through with *The Sun*. He immediately sent her an enormous bouquet and a sympathetic cheer-up note. In 1990, burglars ransacked the house of his young cousin Paul, making off with the TV set, the stereo and other valuables. When Elton heard of it, he paid for every lost item to be replaced.

For someone who had ended so many eras and made so many fresh starts, his life possessed a remarkable degree of continuity. His close friends and associates in 1990 were fundamentally the same as in 1970. There was Tony King, his long-time confidant and accomplice in outrage, now living in New York and working for Mick Jagger. There was Steve Brown, Elton and Bernie's original saviour and mentor at Dick James Music, now reclaimed from agriculture and back in his old crucial role as co-ordinator of albums and tours. There was Bob Halley, who had survived fourteen years with Elton, first as chauffeur, then as live-in companion and finally as selfless twenty-four-hours-a-day personal factotum.

Continuity, above all, was represented by John Reid, his manager for almost twenty years and still seemingly impregnable so, despite regular rumours of terminal rifts between them. The relationship between them in some ways resembled that of Elvis Presley and Colonel Parker, in others that of Richard Burton and Elizabeth Taylor. They were like old marrieds, endlessly divorced and reconciled, unable to live with one another or survive longer than a few months apart. They still could have rows rivalling the big scene in *Who's Afraid of Virginia Woolf?* and thereafter refuse to communicate except through their respective courtiers. Then one would throw a stupendous party for the other, or present him with some breathtaking new toy, and harmony would be restored. In 1990, *Music Week* published one of the very few pictures ever seen of Reid and Elton together. Superstar's puggy face looks down on manager's foxy one with that old paradoxical elder brother smile. Little seems to have changed since the days at the Water Garden, when streetwise John first taught innocent Reggie to eat poussin instead of Instant Whip.

The peculiar, unstable, indestructible chemistry between them was best observed by John Hall, the young head of Rocket Records to whom Elton once almost signed away something like 40 per cent of the company. Hall did well enough without, going on to found the Filmtrax organisation and, eventually, to sell it for $95 million.

John Hall dissents from the view that Reid was the worst thing ever to happen to Elton. 'There's a strength about him that Elton always needed. He's the one who fights battles for Elton. He'll go out into the playground and bash big boys up. He doesn't care. And he'll protect Elton until the last drop of blood is spilt. You can say he's only looking after his own interests, but there's always been much more to it than that. What's between them is a love, a mutual need; you simply couldn't have one without the other. Elton is the prize and John Reid is the keeper of the gate.'

He retained his oldest associate of all, his original surrogate brother, country mouse to his town mouse, Brown Dirt Cowboy to his Captain Fantastic, Piglet to his Winnie-the-Pooh. Twenty-two years on, when stubby fingers stretched on piano keys, there was still only one person who could fill in the empty bubble overhead.

Bernie Taupin, now aged thirty-nine, lived permanently in Los Angeles. He, too, had gone through the Eighties couture mill, no longer dressing in Take Six flares and Navajo amulets, but in luminous grey Versace suits, cream silk blouses and string ties clasped by pieces of designer silverware. His dark hair remained intact, flattened back with gel and slung in a modish ponytail. He was a figure of mature sophistication who these days, grandly, preferred to be known as plain 'Taupin'. Yet, tanned by California life, his face still had the shy yet faintly dangerous good looks of some uppish young Indian brave.

Despite his blissful childhood in Lincolnshire, Bernie felt little nostalgia for England. His faint East Midland burr was now larded with Americanisms – 'Sir', for instance, when calling a waiter. He had lately brought his parents over to live in LA, severing the last link with Market Rasen and Owmby-by-Spital. Having so long absorbed America through every pore, he had decided to exchange his resident-alien status for full US citizenship.

His place in pop music remained unique. Twenty years had produced no other megastar musician with a lyric-writing partner who received equal credit. The great Elton John evergreen hits, 'Your Song', 'Goodbye Yellow Brick Road', 'Daniel', 'Crocodile

Rock', 'Candle in the Wind', all were universally acknowledged to be as much Bernie's as Elton's. The supreme accolade for him had been to attend a Frank Sinatra concert, and hear Sinatra perform 'Your Song' alongside the best of Cole Porter, Ira Gershwin and Sammy Cahn. And at the intermission, a Sinatra bodyguard tapped him on the shoulder and croaked, 'Frank wants to see ya.'

Bernie's career in the Eighties had considerably diversified. He had released two albums as a vocalist in his own right, and made his first essay as a director of pop videos. He also had formed an extramural partnership with the British musician Martin Page. Together they had written two number one US singles, 'We Built This City' for Jefferson Starship, and 'These Dreams' for the female rock band Heart. The possibility that Bernie Taupin might be on the open market had produced a flood of offers, some from young bands like Level 42 and Curiosity Killed the Cat. Though much flattered, Bernie politely declined, preferring to save himself for the voice and the psyche he knew best.

He lived quietly with his second wife Toni in the house on North Doheny Drive which he had bought in 1972. His main interest was his library, divided between English literary first editions and rare volumes about the American West. The former hard-drinking lie-abed had become a fitness fanatic, rising early to work out for several hours each day, taking alcohol only moderately, in the form of good-quality wines. Even more than in the Seventies, personal publicity was abhorrent to him. He received an unwelcome dollop of it in 1988 when his former girlfriend Loree Rodkin gave disparaging details about their time together in an interview with *Vanity Fair*. The next issue carried a dignified riposte from Bernie, calling Rodkin a 'primal diva', interested only in her social career and dental bridgework. There may have been the makings of a new lyric here.

He had long wanted to write narrative prose, rather than irresistible half-line hooks, and, encouraged by Toni, finally squared himself to the task. The result was an autobiography called *A Cradle of Haloes*, recreating his Lincolnshire childhood and adolescence after the style of Laurie Lee's *Cider with Rosie*. With his own odd mixture of star ego and sensitive consideration, he gave Owmby-by-Spital another name, fearing that crowds of reverential pop fans might descend on the place and give annoyance to his parents' former neighbours. *A Cradle of Haloes* was not critically praised. But Bernie continued undaunted, working on a book of poems, provisionally called *The Devil at High Noon*, and a movie screenplay about an offbeat Western desperado named Sam Bass.

In late 1988, he was in London, doing publicity for *A Cradle of Haloes* before joining Elton at sessions for a new album in Denmark. He appeared on Radio Two's Gloria Hunniford programme, answering questions about their exploits together with the gravitas of an Auden-in-exile. At the same time, he made no attempt to conceal how instantaneous and painless their collaboration had been, nor how many sources they had blithely plundered over the years.

'Like "Rocket Man",' Gloria Hunniford ventured. 'Didn't the idea for that one come from David Bowie?'

'Oh no,' Bernie replied. 'We didn't steal that one from Bowie. We stole it from another bloke, called Tom Rapp.'

He might have added that he was about to join Elton in Denmark to produce the most derivative song collection of their entire career. The idea came from Elton, remembering black vocal groups like the Drifters, with whom he had toured as a humble keyboard player twenty-five years earlier. He would make his twenty-sixth album a homage to the Drifters, the Impressions, the Miracles, with their smiles in unison, their shape-drawing dance routines, their easygoing French-fried world of 'Saturday Night at the Movies' and 'Under the Boardwalk'. At the same time, there would be an edge of modern pastiche, like the Billy Joel album which contained 'Uptown Girl'.

Elton named this 1989 album *Sleeping with the Past*, despite the probability of much unfriendly sniggering. With pre-emptive chutzpah, he joked to Terry Wogan that he had half thought of issuing it with an illustrated catalogue. Any sexual charge, however, was instantly defused by the cover, which showed just his face, asleep in its granny specs, as innocent as the Ovaltine moon over Metroland.

The first track issued as a single was 'Healing Hands', a rousing neo-spiritual about love as a redemptive power, 'a light where the darkness ends'. With it went a high-fashion black-and-white video, featuring Elton in wide-brimmed Zorro hat and gale-blown cloak, intercut with yearning faces clasped between hands that might have modelled for Velasquez. It was, by the highest Taupin–John standards, a very good song. Against 1989's chainsaw drill of hip-hop, it seemed as old-fashionedly ingenious and well made as a Cecil B. de Mille movie or a Terence Rattigan play. Its tone of heartfelt thanks for a good woman's love was unhappily ironic; not long afterwards, Bernie Taupin and Toni were to separate.

Elton played 'Healing Hands' as a finale to his Wogan appearance, seated in Nehru cap before a digital piano, with a back-projected light show which the BBC must have been hoarding since his *Sounds for Saturday* concert in 1971. Though *Sleeping with the Past* made both the British and US album Top 20, the old jinx remained. 'Healing

Hands' failed to become a hit single. So did its follow-up, 'Sacrifice'. The impression – as so many times down the years – was of a career gently but inexorably in decline.

The Seventies may have seemed a formless, aimless jumble at the time. But here, on the threshold to the Nineties, they were starting to look better and better. It was like some magic-mushroom-induced dream to remember a time when Britain was governed by the liberal Left rather than the repressive Right; when the rich did not grow constantly richer at the expense of the poor; when social snobbery seemed extinct; when public utilities were not in the hands of private speculators; when tabloid newspapers published news; and when the destiny of youth was to have fun, not to sleep rough on the streets and be liable for the poll tax.

As 1990 dawned, however, there were signs that the garish greed and philistinism of the Thatcher decade might have run their course. Hype now governed everything, and the Nineties received heavy advanced hype as a new era of social reconciliation and 'caring'. Since no one could have 'cared' less than Mrs Thatcher, any small step in that direction by her successors was bound to be highly conspicuous. Those in government now at least acknowledged the problems – for instance, that of endemic homelessness, most shamingly in the nation's capital. Blind eyes ceased to be turned on the cardboard cities around Waterloo and the Strand.

One area where compassion definitely had increased was with regard to AIDS sufferers. The disease was now known to be the scourge not only of junkies and gays but of every sexually active man and woman throughout the world. Through the medium of infected blood, it had been transmitted to celibate haemophiliacs, nuns, children, even unborn babies. The few thousand who suffered its terminal disintegration represented but a fraction of this ghastly spread. Hundreds of thousands, possibly millions, unknowingly carried the HIV virus as a ticking time bomb inside them. No one who had slept with anyone over the past decade could feel entirely easy, now or for half a dozen years to come.

Thanks to his freely admitted bisexual past, Elton clearly was in a high risk category. He owned up to being terrified of AIDS, characteristically, during a 1988 interview for *Woman's Own* magazine. 'Sure, the AIDS problem worries me – it should worry everyone,' he said. 'People ask me if I've ever had an AIDS test. Well, I have. I have blood tests all the time.'

That fear was bound to increase as AIDS plied its knife ever wider through the once carefree, careless world of show business, media and the arts. In four or five years, it had cut down the Hollywood star Rock Hudson, the clothes designers Willie Smith and Perry Ellis, the photographer Robert Mapplethorpe, the actor Ian Charleson, not to mention innumerable celebrity lovers, ex-lovers and friends of friends. Among its saddest victims was Liberace, Elton's great exemplar in piano showmanship and sartorial excess. He was personally grieved, and John Reid still more so, by the death of David Bell, an influential figure in British television and an *éminence grise* to both throughout their careers.

Most public figures at personal risk from AIDS maintained a careful silence on the subject. Elton, however, was among the most visible supporters both of research into finding a cure and of the charities set up to shelter and counsel AIDS victims. It was in large part his doing that rock music's new conscience now embraced the problem, drawing millions into awareness of it via multi-star fund-raising concerts and charity records like his pioneering one with Dionne Warwick and Stevie Wonder. Even now, no one could rival Elton for the grand gesture. In June 1990, he re-released his year-old 'Sacrifice', announcing that all its British royalties would be donated to four AIDS charities: London Lighthouse, Body Positive, Jefferies Research Wing Trust and the Terence Higgins Trust.

That same month, he appeared at a huge charity concert in the grounds of Knebworth Hall, Hertfordshire. The good cause was Music Therapy, a system of using music to teach handicapped children which Elton had already supported for more than a decade. At Knebworth, he contrived to make his old show-stopping impact, even against the massed talents of Eric Clapton, Phil Collins, Cliff Richard, Paul McCartney and Pink Floyd. He later complained that the bill had featured too many 'dinosaurs' like himself, and not enough new young talent.

Not the least factor in changing public attitudes to AIDS had been the courage shown by many of its sufferers. Among the most notable in America was a teenage boy named Ryan White, one of the blameless multitude accidentally infected via blood transfusion. The subsequent story of his parents' ostracism by neighbours and Ryan's own persecution at school, until the family was obliged to flee from its home in Indianapolis, represented the very worst anti-AIDS ignorance and prejudice. Though already terminally ill, Ryan thereafter became an indefatigable campaigner for the rights and dignity of other AIDS sufferers. His bravery won him a nationwide audience and earned a personal commendation from former president Ronald Reagan.

Elton, in America at the time, was deeply moved by the Ryan

White story. Like several other celebrities, he travelled to see the dying boy and pay public tribute to his spirit and fortitude. But this was no big-star flying visit. He remained with Ryan until the end, and even then still stayed around, comforting the White family, taking responsibilities off their shoulders, attending the funeral and helping carry the coffin. It was as if a miraculous elder brother had descended out of the blue, just a few days too late.

Willing as British pop fans now were to help AIDS sufferers, and warmly as they esteemed Elton John, what befell his 'charity single' still defies explanation. On its first release, a year previously, 'Sacrifice' had seemed no more than a pleasant period piece, unfashionably slow, heart-searching and tuneful. Reissued in June 1990 – a double A-side with the equally unsuccessful 'Healing Hands' – it suddenly took fire. After twenty-two years' trying, long after having given up hope, Elton suddenly received his heart's desire. He had a British number-one single.

'Sacrifice'/'Healing Hands' stayed at the top for five weeks, finally selling more than 600,000 copies. Adding the proceeds from a follow-up single, 'Club at the End of the Street', Elton was able to present a cheque for £328,000 to his four nominated AIDS organisations. Back on the Terry Wogan show that summer, he announced that in future all royalties from his British singles would be donated to charity.

By the end of 1990, further remarkable things had happened. His *Sleeping with the Past*, a respectable British number six a year earlier, also now leapt back, on the strength of its hit single, to become his first British number-one album since 1977. A few weeks later, he was back in that top spot a second time, with a new compilation album, *The Very Best of Elton John*. Two number-one albums and- a smash number-one single made him PolyGram Records' only million-seller in 1990 and, ultimately, Britain's highest-grossing artist on record during the whole year. He had not been so big since Captain Fantastic soared up in silver-winged boots, accompanied by the faithful Brown Dirt Cowboy.

For all those Captain Fantastic years, there was now a heavy price to be paid. In April 1990, John Reid was reported to have entered a detoxification clinic at the Cedars Sinai Medical Center, Los Angeles. A 'source close to Reid' was quoted as saying, 'John has always been a big party man. He likes to go over the top in every way [but] even he now accepts that his dabbling with drugs and drink has gone too far.' Not long afterwards, Elton himself was said to be undergoing treatment at a clinic specialising in 'eating disorders'.

In the autumn of 1990, he returned to *The Sun*'s front page in a story claiming he had joined Alcoholics Anonymous. Despite the paper's obsequious care in calling him 'brave Elton', and praising him editorially for his courage in trying to kick a destructive habit, it was widely speculated that more thunderbolt writs might be hurled towards Wapping. However, none was. And an AA member subsequently reported seeing Elton regularly at two London group sessions, one in Hinde Street, Marylebone, the other in Earls Court. He was said to be throwing himself into the spirit of the thing, testifying frankly about his addiction and joining with enthusiasm in the frequent, mutually supportive group hugs.

From people who met him or talked to him during late 1990, the reports were uniformly good. With Woodside still under renovation, he had moved into a large rented house in London's Holland Park. He had finally done a deal over Watford, selling out to a London property and hire-car magnate named Jack Petchey, while retaining the title of life president. His two British number-one albums seemed to have temporarily sated even his addiction to work, and he had announced he would take the whole of 1991 off. To his oldest friends and associates – Steve Brown, Bernie Taupin, Clive Banks – he seemed at last to have put all his troubles and traumas behind him. Brown, indeed, told an interviewer that, in twenty years, he had never seen Elton happier, more positive about the future or personally at ease.

All such reports seemed confirmed in December 1990, when he agreed to appear on Jonathan Ross's Channel 4 talk show. This unveiled yet another brand-new Elton, lighter by two stone, wearing a wide-brimmed fedora and triumphantly loose-hanging green Versace suit. The Ross show went out 'live', and in the dressing room beforehand there was a brief Little Moment, with Elton threatening to walk out because his spot was a few minutes delayed. But once before the cameras, he was his usual candid and lucid self, willing – even anxious – to talk about this further absolutely fresh beginning to his life. He had lost the weight, he said, by giving up sugar and white flour, and by a regimen of abstinence that was for keeps. 'I used to get depressed; I'd overeat and overdrink, and it used to get ridiculous. Because I always wanted too much. Whenever I had a hit record or met someone, I was never happy with just that. I always wanted more. I never gave myself time to stop and smell the roses. Well, now I can stop and I'm going to. I just want to smell a few roses.'

He said the great change had been brought about by the ten days he'd spent with the dying AIDS victim, Ryan White, and his family.

'God, what those people went through. And they had such dignity. Such grace. For all they'd suffered, they bore no grudge towards anyone. They never complained. And I was someone who'd go into a hotel suite and complain because I didn't like it. And I've had such blessings in my life. After that, I'm never, ever going to complain again . . .'

Dignity and grace had always shown themselves to be part of Elton's character, far outweighing the selfish, petulant side. And, without wishing to add to the weight of therapy he was ultimately to undergo, one can legitimately deduce that he must have inherited those qualities from somewhere.

On 15 December 1991, his father, Stanley Dwight, died at home in Hoylake, Cheshire, aged only 66. They had not met since watching the Watford–Liverpool match together at Anfield eight years previously. Elton's promise to come and spend a weekend with his father had not been fulfilled, although, his stepmother Edna says, he referred to it several times in phone calls after Stanley's heart-bypass operation and even named a specific date. Edna says she even began to ready the spare room for his arrival. Then, without explanation, the phone-calls stopped again.

Stanley's final years were increasingly painful and difficult. His quadruple bypass proved only partially successful and he had to take early retirement from his job at Unilever. In 1985 alone, he was hospitalised five different times. In addition to his heart problem, he developed a duodenal ulcer, continued to be racked by osteoarthritis and was eventually confined to a wheelchair. That had been his main reason for moving house again, from hilly north Wales back to the flat Cheshire Wirral. Despite often being in great pain, Edna says, he managed to remain cheerful and positive.

In Hoylake, despite his obvious extreme illness, he was still badgered ceaselessly by journalists to dish the dirt on Elton. Stanley remained adamant in refusing to give any press interviews. Nor would he hear a word against Elton, even when the tabloids were ablaze with rent-boy allegations. Edna recalls his uncharacteristic anger towards her when she suggested there might be some truth in *The Sun*'s story. 'Stan told me I was never to say such a thing ever again. I said "But how can you be so sure it isn't true?" "Because he's my son," Stan said.'

By early 1991, Stanley's health had deteriorated so far that Edna felt she must make contact with Elton, which she did via John Reid. Elton telephoned her from France and, she says, agreed to a meeting with her to discuss Stanley's condition. Shortly afterwards, they heard that Elton had given an interview on Sky Television in which he repeated that he'd been afraid of his father when he was a child.

The Dwights' small bungalow in Hoylake was immediately besieged by journalists seeking to amplify the quote. One of them, a female reporter from the *Sunday People*, who seemed more sympathetic and understanding than the rest, talked her way inside and obtained a brief, non-committal interview with Stanley. The paper's headline the next Sunday was DYING DAD'S LOVE FOR ELTON. HE SENDS HEARTBREAK MESSAGE TO STAR THROUGH THE PEOPLE. On the same day, the *Sunday Mirror*, which had not spoken to Stanley, carried the headline ANGER OF ELTON'S DYING DAD. STAR HAS SNUBBED US FOR YEARS. By Edna Dwight's account, Elton then telephoned her to say he was 'annoyed' by the tabloid headlines and that there was no question now of their meeting. 'He said "I'm not going to get involved in a slanging-match" and put the phone down.'

After Stanley's death, his son Geoffrey made contact with Elton and told him the date and time of the funeral. According to Geoffrey, Elton replied that it would be 'hypocritical' of him to attend and he'd made his peace with his father. But he added: 'I'll be at home at Windsor all next week if you should need anything.'

'We never wanted anything from him,' Edna Dwight says. 'Stan certainly never did – only a little of his time.'

INTERLUDE

Tea and Sympathy

THE street is one of the least grand to be found in London's white and leafy Holland Park district. On the corner is a down-to-earth pub with a blackboard menu of bar-food and a beer-garden behind a latticework fence. Opposite runs a terrace of plain-fronted two-storey villas, built in the early 19th-century as servants' quarters for mansions in the neighbouring squares. Though prettified and gleaming, they are still very far from millionaire residences. Only one, half-way along, stands out from its neighbours. Grafted on to its narrow façade is a mock-Georgian pedimented doorway that seems to belong to some much larger and grander establishment. It is also the only house in the row with an illuminated security buzzer, and a pale green Rolls-Royce parked outside.

The buzzer's soft electric chord sets off a frantic barking behind the outsize front door. At the same moment, an unmistakable bodyguard figure walks rapidly across the road from the pub's beer-garden.

The barking proves to come from no Rottweiler or Alsatian but from a rangy grey-and-white mutt with good-natured eyes and a silly, bearded face, frisking and worrying around the striped trousers of a black American major domo. 'Thomas thinks everyone comes here to see him,' the major domo explains, leading the way down a narrow, dusky hall. To the left is a polished sideboard, bearing many silver-framed photographs of the same multi-hatted celebrity, hobnobbing with royalty, sports personalities and movie stars. To the right is a small sunken drawing room with primrose-coloured walls and chintzy armchairs. And here, at long last, stands Elton John.

For more than two years, I have been his unauthorised biographer, resigned to his management's firm refusal of all access to him. Now, in 1991, my book is now on sale in the UK, replete with the anecdotes of friends, business colleagues, even close family; packed with musical, historical and sartorial detail, but, alas, containing not one first-hand quote from its subject. Two afternoons ago, while I was drowsing on my office couch in post-publication tristesse, the telephone rang. I picked it up, expecting to hear my wife. 'Hi,' a familiar light, rapid voice said. 'This is Elton. I'm reading the book. It seems pretty accurate so far. Maybe you'd like to come round for a cup of tea.'

It is the strangest experience, after one has chronicled someone's whole life at second hand, finally to meet him face to face. It is like shaking hands with a character from a novel. The physical details I have tenaciously highlighted and emphasised over 500 pages dwindle to the minor key of real life. In person he is taller than I expected; paler and much thinner. He is wearing a blue baseball cap, a creased T-shirt, striped buccaneer pants and purple pointed shoes, intricately crosslaced. One trait, at least, is as the novelist recorded. As he talks, a jumpy forefinger constantly points up to twitch his glasses straight on his nose.

What follows is not an interview. In an interview, one asks questions, hoping to tease or startle the information out. Here it is understood that I know every twist and cranny of Elton's life during its first forty-three years. We begin *in medias res*, where my narrative ended in late 1990. There are next to no questions. He talks for two hours as if dictating a supplementary chapter; at times, as if to his psychiatrist.

'I just wanted to explain why I couldn't co-operate while you were writing the book. It was nothing against you personally. It was just that two years ago when you asked me, I was so totally fucked up I couldn't have done anything like that. But I'm okay now. I've found someone I really love. I'm so in love, it's wonderful. I'm quite comfortable about being gay. I've finally resolved every one of the problems that I had. I'm really happy and optimistic, for the first time ever.'

Even to his biographer, all this is pure revelation. For two years ago, when Elton went into semi-retirement, he seemed to have no more problems left to overcome. As he says now, 'There was still one thing I hadn't sorted out. That was me.'

'I was cocaine-addicted. I was an alcoholic. I had a sexual addiction. I was bulimic for six years. It was all through being paranoid about my weight but not able to stop eating. So in the end I'd gorge myself, then deliberately make myself sick. For breakfast I'd have an enormous fry-up, followed by 20 pots of Sainsbury's cockles and then a tub of Häagen-Dazs vanilla ice cream, so that I'd throw it all up again. I never stood still. I was always rushing, always thinking about the next thing. If I was eating a curry, I couldn't wait to throw it up so that I could have the next one.'

Drugs, drink and his stupendous fame had turned him into a monster of ego and megalomania rivalling any in the rock pantheon. The difference with Elton was that a normal, sensible part of him could always stand back and watch it happening. 'I could be unbelievably horrible and stupid. On tours, I'd get on a plane, then get off it, maybe six or eight times. I'd walk out of a hotel suite because I didn't like the colour of the bedspread. I remember looking out of my room at the Inn on the Park one day and saying, 'It's too windy. Can someone please do something about it?'

His famous tantrums used to astonish him as much as any of their victims. 'What you call "Elton's Little Moments" in the book is spot-on. I never knew where they came from. At one time, I even started having seizures.' (This bears out an American source who told me that, in the late Seventies, she became worried that Elton might be suffering from epilepsy.)

He himself now puts much of the blame on his unhappy, repressed childhood in the Art Déco tedium of Pinner. 'My father never showed me any affection, and that made me keep everything in. I was always held up by my family as the paragon of what a child should be, which, I think, never left me. I wish I'd had the courage to really express my feelings – like not going onstage and performing when I felt I couldn't face it. But I always made myself do it. I was too afraid of letting people down.'

Without prompting, he describes his second suicide attempt, at the very zenith of his fame, in November 1975. It was 'Elton John Week' in Los Angeles. His footprints had joined those of the movie immortals on Hollywood Boulevard. He was playing sold-out nightly concerts at Dodger Stadium and living in David Selznick's old mansion in the Hollywood Hills. One day, when his proud relations were gathered around his swimming pool, Elton swallowed sixty Valium tablets. 'I jumped into the pool in front of my mother and my seventy-five-year-old grandmother, screaming "I'm going to die!" I always remember that, as they pulled me out, I heard my gran say "I suppose we've all got to go home now."'

His excesses gradually estranged him from his mother, that once tireless ally and champion. 'My mum had always supported me and never reproached me, even when I went on record and said I was bisexual. But by the mid-eighties, even she'd had enough. She and my stepfather left England and went to live in Minorca.'

The first straw at which he clutched was having to leave his Old
Windsor house during the post-marital gutting and refurbishment
that would eventually take almost three years. Lodged in Elton's
mind was the awful memory of having met Elvis Presley in 1977,
only weeks before Presley's death, in a similar, suffocating mansion.
'He looked terrible – all bloated, with hair-dye trickling down his
forehead. He had dozens of people round him, supposedly looking
after him, but he already seemed like a corpse. I knew that if I
didn't do something now, I could end up in exactly the same way.'

The solution was to rent this small house in Holland Park and
make one last, desperate stab at a 'normal' existence. 'My whole life,
I'd never lived on my own. First I lived at home with my mum,
then I lived with John [Reid], then I was on tour with people
constantly around me. In the morning I'd get up, wash, get ready for
the day and from then on there were dozens of people to do
everything for me. I decided I was going to live alone here, and do
everything for myself – make my own phone-calls, pack my own
bags to go away. For weeks I stayed in my bedroom, too scared to
go out, just doing *The Times* crossword puzzle. In the end, I could
do the whole thing in about ten minutes.'

Much of the time his only companion was Thomas, the lanky
grey and white mongrel now sprawling untidily on the carpet. 'I
decided I'd have a dog, so I went to find one at Battersea Dogs'
Home. All the dogs in the cages were barking like mad – only one
was just lying there, looking as miserable as I felt. I said "that's the
one for me."'

He had already met Hugh, the young American he then described
as 'the love of my life'. In almost twenty years of covert relationships,
on and off the road, nothing remotely like it had ever struck him
before. 'I had a sexual addiction as bad as any of the others. For the
first time, I knew someone I wanted to be totally monogamous with.
Before, I only took hostages.'

The blight on their love affair was Elton's cocaine addiction, and
the drug's deadly illusion of sharpening, not destroying, the user's
faculties. 'After I'd had a line of coke I could set the whole world to
rights. I'd say to people "You want to do this and that . . ." It never
occurred to me that I was the one who needed help most of all.
Finally, it was Hugh who said to me, "You've got to get straight.
Love has to be a two-way relationship. At the moment it's a three-
way relationship – you, me and coke."'

Hugh also had a drug problem and begged Elton to accompany
him into 'detox'. For initial therapy, each had to make a list of what
he considered the other's worst faults. 'Hugh's list started "Elton does

drugs, he's alcoholic, he's bulimic, he has terrible fits of rage . . ." My list began "Hugh never puts his CDs away tidily . . ." '

When Hugh began detoxification in earnest, Elton's first thought was that their relationship was over. 'I went to see him in hospital, and it was awful. I came back to this house and wrecked the whole place, tore up all his photographs. Then I realised it was him I loved, there was no one else. If we were going to have a future, I had to get myself properly back on the rails.'

The problem was finding a rehabilitation programme that could help someone so comprehensively self-abused. All the big-star clinics turned Elton away, saying he had too many addictions for them to handle. The only 'detox' centre that would take him was at the Parkside Lutheran Hospital in Chicago. Inmates had to endure a spartan regime, living two to a room in army-style beds and doing their own laundry. 'I had to take all these little packets of detergent in my luggage. On the journey there, the one thing that terrified me was that I wouldn't be able to work the washing-machine. When I saw the place, I almost checked out. But then I thought, "Elton, there's nowhere else to go." '

Part of his therapy at Parkside was to write a letter to cocaine, bidding it a formal and conclusive farewell. He fetches the letter, on neatly handwritten yellow sheets, and reads it aloud. It is Elton John's *De Profundis*, a beautifully composed elegy, as if the wicked white powder were some beautiful, heedless woman. 'I have sent cars – even planes – to pick you up . . .' One wonders afresh why someone so literate and articulate has always been afraid to write lyrics for his own songs. When he read the cocaine letter to Bernie Taupin, it made Bernie cry.

During the treatment in Chicago, Elton and his mother became reconciled. 'She'd write to me. I'd cry when I read her letters. She's told me she'd cry when she read mine. Now that I'm okay, she's come back to live in England again. The funny thing is, while she was in Minorca her health got bad. Since she got home, she's been perfectly well. It must have been all psychological, because of worrying about me.'

He also began attending AA meetings in Los Angeles and at two centres in London. 'It was wonderful, the way they just accepted me. They didn't care who I was. For the first time in twenty years I could feel totally anonymous. The incredible thing about AA is that, whatever your addiction has made you do, there's never any blame, only sympathy and love. At one meeting, we all had to confess to something in our pasts that we were really ashamed of. I confessed that I'd only got married to please my mother. Then a young woman got up and confessed to something so tragic and traumatic that I thought I ought to do better with my confession, so I told them about something really really bad that I'd once done.'

Though never conventionally religious, he now makes frequent reference to the 'Higher Power' which AA encourages its members to invoke in their battle against self. The group's emphasis on human contact, hand-holding and hugging, has been no less revelatory to someone who always found difficulty with giving and receiving affection. 'After one meeting, this boy came up to me very shyly and said "Do you mind if I speak to you?" He wanted to confess to me that he was gay. After that, he slipped – what we call going back on the booze. We didn't see him for a while and when he next came to a group, he'd been sleeping rough, and looked it. I hugged him, and sat and held his hand through the whole meeting.'

The former Nero-gorging bulimic now follows a healthy regime of three meals per day with no snacking in between, no sugar or white flour. His major domo and a maid enter with a silver tray of tea, smoked salmon sandwiches sprinkled with cress, and a dark chocolate cake under a glass dome. The new self-help Elton pours my tea, adds milk to it and cuts me a slice of the 'chocky cake' he himself is forbidden. He tips forward his baseball cap, giving a brief glimpse of the crown where hair-transplant surgeons have worked as long and intricately as embroiderers on the Bayeux Tapestry. All in vain, it would appear. There are just a few dark strands floating in parallel, like seaweed on an ebb tide.

Now apparently settled and monogamous, he divides his time between his London house and Hugh in America. 'We do ordinary things together that I've never done in my whole life. We go to Paris like ordinary tourists, and go up the Eiffel Tower. I'd never been up the Eiffel Tower before. We go to Hawaii and swim in the ocean. I'd been to Hawaii about nine times on tours, but never thought of going in the ocean.' When travelling alone, he asks a fellow AA group member to accompany him. Under AA rules, only two people are needed to constitute an official meeting.

He speaks fondly of Renate, whom he certainly married for love if also to please his mother. It remains miraculous to him that Renate was not after his millions, but genuinely wanted the relationship to work on any terms Elton chose. He still appreciates her dignity and restraint, during their drawn-out public separation, and a loyalty to him which never wavered. 'When *The Sun* came out with their rent-boy stories, Renate was ready to go into court and speak for me. And we'd already decided to split up by that time.'

Around him today there are few signs of the impulse-buying

sprees that once crammed Woodside, his country house, to the roof. On the walls hang one or two paintings of quietly manifest quality. In a raised recess stands an electric piano and a multi-coloured jukebox of compact discs. His one remaining addiction is buying clothes. 'I still do it at incredible speed. It's all a hangover from childhood, when my mum would bring me up to London to look at a coat she wanted to buy. "I don't know," she'd always say. "We'd better come back next week and have another look . . ." '

He acknowledges that, while his fame has brought huge problems, it also brought moments undreamed by a boy named Reg from suburban Middlesex. 'Like playing for Prince Andrew's 21st birthday party at Windsor Castle. When I arrived, there was no one there but the dance band and Princess Diana. We danced the Charleston alone on the floor for twenty minutes. Then Princess Anne came up to me and said "Would you like to dance?" What am I going to say? "No – fuck off"? We went into this disco where the music was so quiet, you could hardly hear it. As we're bobbing up and down, the Queen comes up with an equerry and says "Do you mind if we join you?" Just at that moment, the music segues into Bill Haley's *Rock Around The Clock*. So I'm dancing to *Rock Around The Clock* with the Queen of England.'

After almost three years, Woodside is nearly ready for him to move back. In place of the former Art Nouveau, Lalique and Bugatti warehouse there is now a mature country squire's residence, all quiet colours, understated prints and open fireplaces. In the grounds is a new ornamental lake containing three million gallons of water. Thomas, the mongrel, will be introduced to Elton's other pet dogs, two German shepherds and two Irish wolfhounds. One corner of the garden is kept as a cemetery for his dogs down the years. 'There are all these little headstones with names like Bruce and Brian. Anyone looking at them might think they were old boyfriends I'd bumped off.'

He is as interested as ever in the contemporary music scene, as acerbic as ever in his comments about it. He detests rap and the posturing and laziness of young bands who think the only key to success is making a trendy video. 'The way to get on isn't any different from when I started in the early Seventies. You've got to go out there and grab the audience; travel America coast to coast as number two on the bill; build up your following in Europe. Nothing beats working your ass off.'

Since the triple surprise success of 1990 – his first UK number one single and two number one albums – his name has stayed up there among pop's young lions and lionesses. A boxed four-CD set, *To Be Continued* . . . , includes rarities like his first recorded vocal,

'Come Back, Baby', with Bluesology. Also in 1991 came *Two Rooms*, an album breaking the convention that Elton John/Bernie Taupin songs are seldom, if ever, covered by other artists. Assorted British and American superstar friends paid tribute to the partnership with original and oddball cover-versions – Eric Clapton, for instance, doing 'Border Song', and Kate Bush an eccentric squeezebox version of 'Rocket Man'.

Now, the only remaining problem for Elton is 'what next?' For years, people have been saying that he and Bernie should develop their colossally successful partnership by writing a stage musical. 'The trouble is, I'm not really that keen on musicals. To be honest, I've no idea what I'll be doing over the next few years. It could just as well be something charitable.'

His parting words are about my biography: 'Thanks for all the dedication.' Before I leave, he writes my name and phone number carefully in his neat little self-help Filofax. 'I'm off to the States in a few days. But I'll let you know what I think of the book when I finish it. I'll call you and maybe we can go to dinner . . .'

Since then, nothing.

POSTSCRIPT

'It's crazy – but it keeps me sane'

'**Y**ou make some sort of major confessional statement roughly every five or six years,' I remarked to Elton when we met. Sure enough, in the wake of Bryan Forbes's documentary and the *Playboy* and *Rolling Stone* interviews of the Seventies, the gargantuan car-boot sale of the Eighties and the born-again declarations that punctuated the early Nineties, here he is bang on schedule, coming clean yet again.

Even for Elton, his passion for soul-searching intensified by years of therapy, it is an extraordinary exercise. In 1995, David Furnish, the 30-year-old Canadian who succeeded Hugh Williams as his partner, has been given unlimited licence to shoot video footage on and around that year's Elton John World Tour. The resulting documentary, entitled *Tantrums and Tiaras*, is premiered on ITV on 7 July, 1996.

From its pre-title sequence alone, we realise we are to discover new meaning in the phrase 'warts and all'. Here is Elton, clad in a leopardskin overcoat, arriving for a video-shoot to discover that the outfit he wishes to wear has been inadvertently left somewhere else. Here is the same Elton who vowed 'I'm never, ever going to complain again', unloosing a ferocious fusillade of fucks that will make the film transmittable only in the late evening 'post-watershed' hours. Here is the loyal, sensible – though, it will prove, not eternal – Steve Brown, like some bearded Biblical martyr, vainly trying to defuse the explosive Little Moment.

As ever, the other Elton is only a heartbeat away. Or perhaps one should say, the other Eltons. Here he is greeting John Reid in his old camp Kenneth Williams voice, with no hint of impending terminal estrangement: ''Ello, Mister Reid! Bona to see you . . . She looks worth a few bob, doesn't she? The fabulous Beryl!' Here he is like a schoolboy in his stout-legged shorts, wrestling on a sofa with his one-time driver, now personal assistant, Bob Halley. Here he is returning to Woodside on his birthday and being presented with a Kerry Blue puppy by a domestic staff whose maternal cooing may be part of the job specification. Here he is, like a child transfigured, beaming and kissing the puppy's head as he names it Graham. Here he is, trotting through an interior once crowded with jukeboxes, pinball machines and Art Nouveau nymphs but since its £5 million refurbishment presenting as many vistas of aggressive good taste as a bound volume of *House & Garden*. 'I always love coming home,' he confides. 'There's a lot of love in this house. It used to be a rampant party house. I did a lot of drugs here . . .'

A recurrent sequence shows Elton alone with Furnish in their bedroom, wearing only a white bathrobe and responding to questions in the confidential murmur of pillow talk. In the first, he opens a letter and reads out what seems to be a fan's query, ' "Would you call yourself a mummy's boy?" Yeah, I am. I think I've always been a mummy's boy.' For amplification, here is his mother, Sheila, now aged seventy, still a chic, good-looking woman in her turquoise trouser-suit, still impressively level-headed and perceptive. The spectre of Elton's father is evoked yet again, with unspoken memories of footballs that could not be kicked and celery that could not be crunched. 'I don't think he ever really liked you,' Sheila says. 'If ever he could have a little dig at you, in things like table manners . . . You were frightened of him, weren't you?'

Sheila's composure breaks down as she recalls number two of the three nadirs of her son's life, which came in 1975 amid the multiple ironies of 'Elton John Week' in Los Angeles and culminated with the suicide attempt in his pool. 'It was a terrible time . . . I couldn't get near you, could I?' She describes watching him onstage, a ghastly spectre with torn and bleeding fingertips, and being convinced he was going to die. A Russell Harty documentary filmed her weeping in the wings and assumed that her tears were of joy.

We see the bearded Halley, an Elton functionary for twenty-one years whose most prized attribute must be his belligerent *lèse-majesté*. 'I'd be dead without Bob,' Elton declares, while an expressive upward roll of Halley's eyes suggests this is no mere hyperbole. We are given a peep into the journal where Elton lists the performance of every record he releases. With its meticulous tabulation and colour coding in highlighter pens, it would do credit to any honours graduate from accountancy school. Back to the boudoir, the soft lights and the white bathrobe. 'I'm good at giving love, but not receiving it,' Elton admits. 'I've always wanted a close, loving relationship . . . but then that part of me that I've created always wants to push it away.'

'Is there enough balance in your life?' David asks. 'What is balance for you?' 'Spending enough time with you probably,' Elton replies. When the probing becomes too deep, he demurs with a little 'Ssh!'

Here he is paying a visit to his nonogenarian grandmother, Ivy, before leaving for Paris and the Oscars ceremony in Hollywood. His beloved 'Nan' has lived for years in the Orangery, Woodside's former gatehouse, in a comfortably furnished apartment, provided with every care. On her sitting-room table stands a lavish bouquet of flowers, something she receives from her grandson each week without fail wherever he happens to be. 'Did you see me on *Top of the Pops?*' Elton asks. 'Yes, you were enjoying yourself,' Ivy says. 'Did you get my card from Japan?' 'Yes . . . it's very kind of you to think [of me]' 'Aw, you silly old sausage,' Elton chides her. 'Love you . . .'

Now here he is before the Oscars ceremony, catching a fretful nap in his Winnebago trailer, not so much more comfortable than the gawpers herded behind police barriers out on the street. Here he is, brandishing the statuette just presented to him by Sylvester Stallone and revealing that Ivy had died a few days earlier. 'She was the one who sat me down at the piano when I was three and made me play, so I'm accepting this in her honour.'

Here is Elton, the pivotal figure in the fight against AIDS, through the foundation he has endowed and his tireless proselytising and appearances at fund-raisers. Here is someone apparently at ease with his own sexual orientation at long last. 'I came out in America,' he tells a rapt audience of kindred spirits. 'I must have slept with a good half of you . . . I was diagnosed HIV negative. I was a lucky, lucky person. It's my job to repay that debt.'

Here is Elton, taking a few days' unaccustomed holiday with David in the South of France and not doing very well at it. Here he is, showing us the necessities without which he never travels – the massed bottles of vitamins, the freezer compartment full of Marks & Spencer's muffins ('nice and healthy') the bottles of HP brown sauce. Thence to his travelling wardrobe, a multi-dimensional closet as big as many a Riviera boutique with its rail upon rail of suits, jackets and shirts (as distinct from silk shirts, which are in a separate section), its shelf upon shelf of piled-up woollens, its rank upon rank of flawlessly shiny shoes. Pairs of glasses and sunglasses fill an entire chest of drawers. 'I like to have a choice,' he explains, pulling open each colour-coded drawer. 'Pink, blue, burgundy . . . purple, silver, gold and black . . . brown, green and red . . .' On a shelf lie two tiaras, pukka affairs, encrusted with gems, such as might decorate the iron-grey curls of Elizabeth Regina herself as she addresses a Lord Mayor's banquet or opens parliament. Why two tiaras? David's voice asks bemusedly. 'Because when you're away, you never know who you're going to meet. It is crazy, but it keeps me sane.'

Here is Elton sweltering on his terrace above Cap Ferrat, with David now transformed from dispassionate Boswell to faintly petulant spouse. Couldn't he have taken these few days off without his driver, his valet and his tennis coach? Might he consider doing some things that David would like to do? Like water ski-ing? 'No.' Going for a drive? 'No.' Lying beside the pool? 'No.' Taking a walk around the *cap* in the cool of the evening? 'Not really.'

We see Elton on the hotel tennis court, serving with all the concentration of a Wimbledon finalist. Then we see Elton suddenly cast away his racket and leave the court. We catch up with him in the lift, his eyes wild, his face strangely pouchy and elongated, as if the camera has become a distorting mirror. It is clearly a Little Moment of thermo-nuclear proportions. Back in the suite, he is so angry that he can barely speak. He picks up the telephone and orders the pilot of his private jet to airlift him back to Britain the following afternoon. 'I've had it with this place,' he mumbles. 'I'm never coming to the South of France again.'

Not until three days later (still at Cap Ferrat) does he feel equal to speaking on camera about the cause of the explosion. While he was playing tennis, a female passer-by had shouted 'Yoo-hoo' at him.

Here is Elton in Russia, Japan or Latin America, the perennial stocky, auburn-fringed figure in his checkerboard tail-suit, pounding out 'Crocodile Rock', 'Pinball Wizard' or 'I'm Still Standing' with no sense that he's fed up to the back teeth with them all. Here are the two great survivors from his various bands: lead guitarist Davey Johnstone, a stunning blond Seventies period piece, and percussionist Ray Cooper, like a crop-headed mad scientist among his skyscraper-high hats. Here is Elton in mid-performance in Santiago, Chile, suddenly finding himself unable to get his breath, staggering into the wings and sitting there with the bewildered blankness of a stroke victim. Here he is rallying and going back out to finish the show. 'They're waiting . . . You can't let them down . . . Be a good boy.'

The most bizarre sequence shows Elton in his white bathrobe watching a video of David discussing him with his therapist, the star shrink Beechy Colclough. 'I think he buys people,' says Colclough, a pixie-like man with an Ulster accent and a Jason King moustache. 'I think a lot of people just feed off him . . . He's only happy when he's playing. The thing is, he never believes the audience reaction. He hates himself . . . He's a totally addictive, compulsive person. If it hadn't been the alcohol, it would have been the drugs. If it hadn't been the drugs, it would have been the food. If it hadn't been the food, it would have been the relationships. If it hadn't been the relationships, it would have been the shopping. Only he's got all five.'

Elton is visibly shaken by what he has heard. 'Listening to you and Beechy was like [seeing] a couple of vultures picking over a carcass,' he tells David. 'You were talking about me like I was some kind of fuckin' soap powder, and I find that irritating, I find it offensive . . . A lot of it, of course, was extremely accurate, like the bit about my being compulsive and my low self-esteem . . .' What has most nettled him, it seems, were the comments about people feeding off him and the concern that he's working himself into the ground. 'Why are people always telling me to slow down, what's it to them? Because I'm responsible for other people's livelihoods apart from my own. And I like working. I've told you that before. I like working for a living.

'Everybody wants me to do what they want to do, but the actual thing is . . .' His face sets in that familiar pugnacious expression, when the groove above his top lip seems sculpted from granite. 'I'm always gonna do what I wanna do. And if people don't like that, you know, they can do what they want . . .'

Apart from his family, the warmest words in the film are reserved for his ex-wife, Renate. To Elton she is still 'one of the best people I've ever met', and he looks forward to the day when they can be real friends again. His good fortune in Renate's dignity and loyalty will be further underlined when his friend Mick Jagger – or 'Missis Jagger', as Elton calls him – ends his twenty-year relationship with Jerry Hall. As a spur to the financial arrangements, Jerry faxes Jagger's lawyer a summary of the book she intends to write unless paid enough to suppress the literary imperative.

In May 1998 came an announcement that the British pop industry little thought it would ever hear. To insiders in the business, it was as if Marks had decided to part from Spencer, Procter from Gamble or Laurel from Hardy. John Reid and the newly dubbed Sir Elton John were to go their separate ways.

The news caused as much mystification as surprise. Sir Elton's association with Reid was one of pop's few genuine institutions, the longest-ever unbroken relationship between a UK artist and a manager. However ill-starred at the beginning, it had survived all the pressures – and more – that habitually destroy such partnerships. With twenty-seven years behind them, the 'Odd Couple' of pop had triumphantly passed the silver wedding mark and looked to be going for gold.

Despite the periodic rows and bust-ups, their regard for one another seemed as deep as ever. All the extraordinary turns that Sir Elton's life had taken in the Nineties had apparently not diminished his reliance on the dour character whom he loved to satirise as 'the fabulous Beryl'. Where Sir Elton's interests were concerned, John Reid still showed the same pit-bull ferocity and protectiveness, even if no longer to the extent of hitting journalists or getting put into gaol. At Sir Elton's fiftieth birthday party the previous year, he had been guest of honour. A somewhat mellower person nowadays, he had even let the world in – just a little – on his emotions towards his pre-eminent client. Sir Elton, he revealed, had largely prompted his own decision to beat alcohol addiction in the early Nineties, and throughout his cure had been there for him with support and advice.

According to both sides, the split was by amicable mutual consent. Sir Elton, a spokesperson said, 'wanted to take more control over his own life.' Reid's equally ambiguous personal statement said, 'We felt that the time had come for us each to pursue our separate interests.'

The people closest to each party, however, had seen this moment coming for a long time, and knew that it would be anything but amicable. It could be said to have been on the cards since David Furnish became Sir Elton's official partner. As Princess Diana said, in a not wholly dissimilar context, 'There's only room for two in a marriage. There's not room for three.' The extra emotional dimension in Sir Elton's and Reid's relationship was what had created its cohesion as well as its occasional explosive instability. Furnish's growing influence on Sir Elton's life and career decisions could not but place extreme stress on that. 'David was like the new wife,' a friend says, 'and John was like the ex-wife who had never quite let go.'

The first overt sign of real trouble had come two months earlier, when a thirty-four-year-old trainee solicitor named Benjamin Prell scavenged through rubbish sacks left outside the West London offices of John Reid Enterprises and also managed to hack into the firm's computer. His haul included a mass of information relating to Sir Elton's private finances: bank and credit-card statements, receipts, invoices and confidential correspondence with his accountants. In a deal brokered by publicist Max Clifford, Prell sold the material to the *Mirror* newspaper, which began publishing it in daily instalments until restrained by a High Court injunction.

There was correspondence relating to a private concert Sir Elton had given for the Sultan of Brunei, the world's richest man, and his sharp exchange with Richard Branson over Princess Diana's funeral music. Most piquantly, there was a letter from his accountants, Price Waterhouse, expressing concern at the scale of his current spending and warning that at this rate 'available headroom', i.e. supplies of ready cash, could run out within eight weeks. The accountants urged him to rustle up some emergency millions by staging another big one-off show such as he'd given for the Sultan of Brunei, arranging a new song-publishing deal or selling off some of his art treasures. Sir Elton, understandably, was appalled to have his most personal business made public, and blamed Reid's organisation for not keeping it secure.

Another danger sign might perhaps have been read in his camp greetings to Reid ('She looks worth a bob or two, doesn't she?') in the *Tantrums and Tiaras* film. From the beginning of their association, Reid had pursued luxury and good taste with the same dedication that Sir Elton had. He now lived with the graciousness befitting a man whose personal worth was estimated at around £20 million. Like Sir Elton, he had three luxurious homes, in London, America and the South of France. A few years earlier, in an echo of Sir Elton's great Sotheby's turn-out, he had put his own art collection up for auction, including works that once belonged to Rudolf Nureyev and Jacqueline Onassis.

According to friends, Sir Elton had grown increasingly restive at these signs of what Reid earned from him. A telling moment occurred when Reid moved into a new house in Hamilton Terrace, north London's smartest boulevard, and invited Sir Elton to dinner. Sir Elton looked around the opulent interior, then wordlessly held up two fingers, crooked to resemble stumps. The message was clear: all this came off me.

Breaking away from Reid was nowhere near as traumatic as it would have been a few years earlier, when almost all of Sir Elton's human support system was based at John Reid Enterprises. The once crucial Steve Brown had left the company long since; Robert Key, another trusted associate of latter days, was now director of the Elton John Aids Foundation. The role of such people, in any case, had become gradually marginalised since the appearance of David Furnish. A new company was created, Elton John Management Ltd. To run it, Sir Elton headhunted Colin Bell, head of London Records, the label that had developed the girl group All Saints. Bell had formerly managed Tom Robinson, and had worked with Sir Elton on an unsuccessful bid to bring a gay radio station to London. Crucial to the new set-up was Frank Presland, the solicitor who had steered him to victory in his battle with *The Sun*.

Reid put on a brave face about the split, telling friends like Bryan

Forbes how 'liberated' he felt. He remained a powerful figure in the entertainment world thanks to a roster of undefecting star clients that included Lord Lloyd-Webber. He was himself now in a stable relationship (with a doctor) that by rights should have lessened the emotional impact of losing Sir Elton. Even so, it seemed to many around him that the centre had gone out of his world. 'John had been difficult in lots of ways, but he was the best manager Elton could have had,' a friend says. 'He'd have walked over red-hot coals for him.'

That all-consuming dedication brought uncomfortable repercussions for Reid in a legal battle with another disaffected client. In 1995, he had begun to represent Michael Flatley, the Irish star of stage spectaculars like *Riverdance* and *Lord of the Dance*. The relationship did not prosper, and in 1998 Reid brought a £10 million lawsuit against Flatley for breach of contract and loss of earnings. Flatley counter-sued for negligence. In that October's High Court action, he complained that Reid had never given proper attention to developing his career, having always been too much preoccupied with Elton John's business. He also complained of Reid's 'bullying, threatening, rude and abusive behaviour' which, he claimed, had made him physically sick on the very night that *Lord of the Dance* was due to open at Wembley Arena.

Flatley settled out of court, paying Reid a 'substantial' sum and withdrawing the allegations against him, but Reid was badly bruised by the experience. He attended the hearings each day, and had to sit and listen to withering criticisms of himself by, among others, the concert promoter Harvey Goldsmith.

In January 1999, the façade of an 'amiable divorce' between Reid and his once paramount client was blown away. Sir Elton began legal proceedings to recover £20 million in earnings which he claimed had 'gone astray' during his latter years under Reid's management. Writs were issued by three Elton John companies against the former managing director of John Reid Enterprises, Andrew Haydon, and the accountants Price Waterhouse Cooper.

Four months later came suggestions that Britain's second wealthiest rock star – his estimated £150 million fortune topped only by Sir Paul McCartney – might indeed be running out of financial 'headroom'. Sir Elton was said to be in talks with City bankers HSBC to raise a lump sum payment of £25 million against his publishing back-catalogue. The deal looked like a repeat of one pioneered two years earlier by David Bowie, who had earned £33 million upfront by selling rights to his future composing royalties in the form of a Wall Street bond. It was firmly denied, however, that

Sir Elton sought the £25 million to pay off pressing debts including a £7 million overdraft at a single British bank. According to his solicitor, Frank Presland, the money would be used partly to regain control of his song-copyrights back to the late Sixties.

New-found domestic happiness notwithstanding, his workload continued to be awesome. Within the space of two years, there had been another world tour, this one sponsored by Citibank, and another Disney musical collaboration with Sir Tim Rice, this one an ambitious stage version of *Aida*. Reworking Verdi's Egyptian epic brought on a songwriting jag comparable with any in the mid-Seventies, with Sir Elton completing nineteen numbers in as many days – 'a million dollars a day,' as he quipped. Ahead of the show (which had rather more teething troubles than *The Lion King*) came an album, featuring his usual crew of up-to-the-minute mates including the Spice Girls, Janet Jackson, Lenny Kravitz, Tina Turner and Sting. In addition, there had been the usual tireless appearances as a guest performer onstage, on TV talk shows and in comedy skits, good-humouredly sending up his own incendiary Little Moments. He also changed managers again, dropping Colin Bell in favour of the lawyer Frank Presland.

In July, he finally went on the record to deny the reports of his imminent insolvency – and deliver his first public broadside against John Reid. 'As far as I am concerned [he's] a liar and a cheat. The treachery and betrayal of a man I counted on as a friend and confidant and have caused me eighteen months of heartbreak. It's bad enough to lose £20 million to a man you trusted, but the money really is of secondary importance. It's the act of betrayal which really hurts.

'It is ludicrous and untrue to say I am in financial difficulty. I am not skint . . . nothing could be further from the truth.'

Reid responded simply that he had read Sir Elton's comments 'with great sadness . . . I have no intention of becoming involved in a public dispute of this kind. When Elton and I ended our business relationship last year, we both wish each other well. I have nothing further to add.'

On 3 July, Sir Elton had been en route by air for Dublin to perform at the wedding of Spice Girl Victoria Adams to Manchester United footballer David Beckham. Feeling ill during the flight, he apologetically cancelled the wedding gig and returned to France for a check-up, which pronounced him quite fit. A few days later, while playing tennis at his villa, he began suffering faintness and dizzy spells. After initial diagnoses of heatstroke and a viral infection, French doctors discovered an irregularity in his heartbeat. He was rushed to

London and there on 10 July underwent a ninety-minute operation to fit him with a heart-pacemaker.

According to friends, the faithful Bob Halley stayed by his side almost until he was wheeled into the operating theatre. After the pacemaker had been fitted, Halley was the first to reassure him: 'Don't worry, dear – we'll get you a nice one from Cartier as soon as possible.'

Discography
by Mark Lewisohn

The following discography charts Elton John's entire career, spanning UK (and principal overseas) record releases from his first session with Bluesology in 1965 to the present day.

Unless otherwise indicated, this discography excludes greatest hits and other compilations, reissues and repackages, cassettes and promotional-use-only discs, and record-company marketing devices such as coloured and shaped vinyl and picture discs, except where such items contain previously unreleased material. Concert and documentary video/laserdisk releases and TV programmes are also excluded, as are interview discs, both official and quasi-legal. Multi-format versions of singles are only mentioned where they carry additional songs over the basic release; extended, remixed or otherwise reworked versions of songs which appear on the basic single are not detailed.

First-time issued live albums and singles tracks *are* included, although the song titles may appear at first glance to be repetitious of those on previous works.

The artist credit on all singles and albums is Elton John, unless otherwise stated.

All compositions are by Elton John and Bernie Taupin, unless denoted by one of the following symbols:

[1] composed by Elton John only
[2] composed by Elton John and Bernie Taupin with one or more other writers
[3] composed by Elton John and Gary Osborne
[4] composed by Elton John and Gary Osborne with one or more other writers
[5] composed by Elton John and Tim Rice
[6] composed by Elton John with one or more other writers but not Taupin, Osborne or Rice
[7] composed by neither Elton John nor Bernie Taupin
[8] composed by Reg Dwight only (pre name-change to Elton John)
[9] composed by Reg Dwight with three other writers
§ composed by Bernie Taupin with one or more other writers but not Elton John

'Don't Go Breaking My Heart' and 'Hard Luck Story' were written by Elton John–Bernie Taupin under the pseudonyms Ann Orson–Carte Blanche. 'Cartier Commercial' was written by John–Taupin under the pseudonyms Dinah Card–Carte Blanche. 'Choc Ice Goes Mental' and 'Earn While You Learn' were written by Elton John only, under the pseudonym Lord Choc Ice.

In the USA, 'Sartorial Eloquence' was called 'Don't Ya Wanna Play This Game No More?' and 'Screw You' was retitled 'Young Man's Blues'.

SINGLES

July 1965	'Come Back, Baby'[8]/'Times Getting Tougher Than Tough'[7] (*Bluesology*)
February 1966	'Mr Frantic'[8]/'Everyday (I Have The Blues)'[7] (*Bluesology*)
October 1967	'Since I Found You Baby'[7]/'Just A Little Bit'[7] (*Stu Brown & Bluesology*)
March 1968	'I've Been Loving You'/'Here's To The Next Time'[1]
January 1969	'Lady Samantha'/'All Across The Havens'
February 1969	'The Dick Barton Theme (The Devil's Gallop)'[7]/ 'Breakdown Blues'[9] (*The Bread And Beer Band*)
May 1969	'It's Me That You Need'/'Just Like Strange Rain'
March 1970	'Border Song'/'Bad Side Of The Moon'
June 1970	'Rock And Roll Madonna'/'Grey Seal'
January 1971	'Your Song'/'Into The Old Man's Shoes'
April 1971	'Friends'/'Honey Roll'
April 1972	'Rocket Man (I Think It's Going To Be A Long, Long Time)'/'Holiday Inn', 'Goodbye'
August 1972	'Honky Cat'/'It's Me That You Need', 'Lady Samantha'
October 1972	'Crocodile Rock'/'Elderberry Wine'
January 1973	'Daniel'/'Skyline Pigeon'
June 1973	'Saturday Night's Alright For Fighting'/'Jack Rabbit', 'Whenever You're Ready (We'll Go Steady Again)'
September 1973	'Goodbye Yellow Brick Road'/'Screw You'
November 1973	'Step Into Christmas'/'Ho! Ho! Ho! (Who'd Be A Turkey At Christmas?)'
February 1974	'Candle In The Wind'/'Bennie And The Jets'
May 1974	'Don't Let The Sun Go Down On Me'/'Sick City'
August 1974	'The Bitch Is Back'/'Cold Highway'
November 1974	'Lucy In The Sky With Diamonds'[7]/'One Day At A Time'[7]

February 1975	'Philadelphia Freedom'/'I Saw Her Standing There'[7] (*A-side The Elton John Band; B-side The Elton John Band featuring John Lennon & The Muscle Shoals Horns*)
June 1975	'Someone Saved My Life Tonight'/'House Of Cards'
September 1975	'Island Girl'/'Sugar On The Floor'[7]
January 1976	'Grow Some Funk Of Your Own'[2]/'I Feel Like A Bullet (In The Gun Of Robert Ford)'
March 1976	'Pinball Wizard'[7]/'Harmony'
June 1976	'Don't Go Breaking My Heart'/'Snow Queen'[2] (*duets with Kiki Dee*)
September 1976	'Bennie And The Jets'/'Rock And Roll Madonna'
October 1976	'Sorry Seems To Be The Hardest Word'/'Shoulder Holster'
February 1977	'Crazy Water'/'Chameleon'
June 1977	'Bite Your Lip (Get Up And Dance!)'/'Chicago'[7] (*double-A-side. 'Chicago' performed by Kiki Dee only*)
March 1978	'Ego'/'Flintstone Boy'[1]
October 1978	'Part-Time Love'[3]/'I Cry At Night'
December 1978	'Song For Guy'[1]/'Lovesick'
April 1979	'Are You Ready For Love (Part 1)'[7]/'Are You Ready For Love (Part 2)'[7] (*Other format also includes* 'Three Way Love Affair'[7], 'Mama Can't Buy You Love'[7])
September 1979	'Victim Of Love'[7]/'Strangers'[3]
November 1979	'Johnny B Goode'[7]/'Thunder In The Night'[7]
May 1980	'Little Jeannie'[3]/'Conquer The Sun'[3]
August 1980	'Sartorial Eloquence'[6]/'White Man Danger'[3], 'Cartier Commercial'
November 1980	'Dear God'[3]/'Tactics'[1] (*Other format also includes* 'Steal Away Child'[3], 'Love So Cold')
March 1981	'I Saw Her Standing There'[7]/'Whatever Gets You Thru The Night'[7], 'Lucy In The Sky With Diamonds'[7] (*The Elton John Band featuring John Lennon & The Muscle Shoals Horns*)
May 1981	'Nobody Wins'[7]/'Fools In Fashion'
July 1981	'Just Like Belgium'/'Can't Get Over Getting Over Losing You'[3]
March 1982	'Blue Eyes'[3]/'Hey Papa Legba'
May 1982	'Empty Garden (Hey Hey Johnny)'/'Take Me Down To The Ocean'[3]
September 1982	'Princess'[3]/'The Retreat'
November 1982	'All Quiet On The Western Front'/'Where Have All The Good Times Gone?'
April 1983	'I Guess That's Why They Call It The Blues'[2], 'Choc Ice Goes Mental'[1] (*B-side artist credit: Lord Choc Ice, pseudonym for Elton John*)

July 1983	'I'm Still Standing'/'Earn While You Learn'[1] (*B-side artist credit: Lord Choc Ice, pseudonym for Elton John*)
October 1983	'Kiss The Bride'/'Dreamboat'[4] (*Other format also includes* 'Ego'/'Song For Guy'[1])
November 1983	'Cold As Christmas'/'Crystal' (*Other formats also include* 'Don't Go Breaking My Heart'/'Snow Queen'[2] (*duets with Kiki Dee*), 'J'Veux d'la Tendresse'[7])
May 1984	'Sad Songs (Say So Much)'/'A Simple Man'[3]
August 1984	'Passengers'[2]/'Lonely Boy'[3] (*Other format also includes* 'Blue Eyes'[3])
October 1984	'Who Wears These Shoes?'/'Tortured' (*Other format also includes* 'I Heard It Through The Grapevine'[7] *live*)
February 1985	'Breaking Hearts (Ain't What It Used To Be)'/'In Neon'
June 1985	'Act Of War (Part 1)'/'Act Of War (Part 2)' (*duet with Millie Jackson*)
October 1985	'Nikita'/'The Man Who Never Died'[1] (*Other formats also include* 'Sorry Seems To Be The Hardest Word' *live*, 'I'm Still Standing' *live*)
November 1985	'Wrap Her Up'[2]/'Restless' *live* (*A-side duet with George Michael*)
February 1986	'Cry To Heaven'/'Candy By The Pound' (*Other format also includes* 'Rock And Roll Medley' *live*: 'Whole Lotta Shakin' Going On'[7]/'I Saw Her Standing There'[7]/'Twist And Shout'[7])
September 1986	'Heartache All Over The World'/'Highlander'[1]
November 1986	'Slow Rivers'/'Billy And The Kids' (*Other format also includes* 'Lord Of The Flies') (*A-side duet with Cliff Richard*)
July 1987	'Your Song' *live*/'Don't Let The Sun Go Down On Me' *live* (*Other format also includes* 'I Need You To Turn To' *live*, 'The Greatest Discovery' *live*)
January 1988	'Candle In The Wind' *live*/'Sorry Seems To Be The Hardest Word' *live* (*Other formats also include* 'Your Song' *live*, 'Don't Let The Sun Go Down On Me' *live*)
May 1988	'I Don't Wanna Go On With You Like That'/'Rope Around A Fool' (*Other format also includes an Elton John interview*)
August 1988	'Town Of Plenty'/'Whipping Boy' (*Other format also includes* 'My Baby's A Saint', 'I Guess That's Why They Call It The Blues'[2])
November 1988	'A Word In Spanish'/'Heavy Traffic'[2] (*Other format also includes Live medley:* 'Song For Guy'[1]/'Blue Eyes'[3]/'I Guess That's Why They Call It The Blues'[2] ; 'Daniel' *live*)

August 1989	'Healing Hands'/'Dancing In The End Zone'[2] (*Other formats also include* 'Sad Songs (Say So Much)' *live*)
October 1989	'Sacrifice'/'Love Is A Cannibal'[2] (*Other format also includes* 'Durban Deep')
June 1990	'Sacrifice'/'Healing Hands' (*Other formats also include* 'Durban Deep')
August 1990	'Club At The End Of The Street'/'Whispers'[7] (*Other formats also include* 'I Don't Wanna Go On With You Like That' *live*)
October 1990	'You Gotta Love Someone'/'Medicine Man'
November 1990	'Easier To Walk Away'/'I Swear I Heard The Night Talkin'' (*Other formats also include* 'Made For Me', 'Cold As Christmas', 'Step Into Christmas')
February 1991	'Don't Let The Sun Go Down On Me'/'Song For Guy'[1] (*Other formats also include* 'Sorry Seems To Be The Hardest Word')
May 1992	'The One'/'Suit Of Wolves' (*Other formats also include* 'Fat Boys And Ugly Girls', 'Your Song', 'Don't Let The Sun Go Down On Me', 'Sacrifice')
July 1992	'Runaway Train'[2] (*Elton John & Eric Clapton*)/'Understanding Women' (*Other formats also include* 'Made For Me', 'Through The Storm'[7] (*duet with Aretha Franklin*), 'Don't Let The Sun Go Down On Me' (*duet with George Michael*), 'Slow Rivers' (*duet with Cliff Richard*))
October 1992	'The Last Song'/'The Man Who Never Died'[1] (*Other formats also include* 'Song For Guy'[1], 'Are You Ready For Love',[7] 'Three Way Love Affair'[7], 'Mama Can't Buy You Love'[7])
May 1993	'Simple Life'/'The Last Song' (*Other format also includes* 'The North')
November 1993	'True Love'[7] (*duet with Kiki Dee*)/'The Show Must Go On'[7] *live* (*Other formats also include* 'Runaway Train'[2] (*Elton John & Eric Clapton*), 'Wrap Her Up'[2] (*duet with George Michael*), 'That's What Friends Are For'[7] (*Dionne Warwick & Friends*), 'Act Of War' (*duet with Millie Jackson*))
February 1994	'Don't Go Breaking My Heart' (*duet with RuPaul*)/'Donner Pour Donner'§ (*duet with France Gall*) (*Other format also includes* 'A Woman's Needs' (*duet with Tammy Wynette*))
June 1994	'Can You Feel The Love Tonight'[5]/'Can You Feel The Love Tonight'[5] *instrumental* (*Other format also includes* 'Hakuna Matata'[5] (*not performed by Elton John*), 'Under The Stars'[7] *instrumental*)
September 1994	'Circle Of Life'[5]/'Circle Of Life'[5] *soundtrack version*

(*Other formats also include* 'Circle Of Life'[5] *cast version*, 'I Just Can't Wait To Be King'[5] *cast version*, 'This Land'[7] *instrumental*)

February 1995   'Believe'/'The One' *live* (*Other formats also include* 'Sorry Seems To Be The Hardest Word' *live*, 'Believe' *live*, 'The Last Song' *live*)

May 1995   'Made In England'/'Whatever Gets You Thru The Night'[7] (*with John Lennon*), 'Lucy In The Sky With Diamonds'[7] (*with John Lennon*), 'I Saw Her Standing There'[7] (*with John Lennon*) (*Other formats also include* 'Can You Feel The Love Tonight'[6], 'Your Song' *live*, 'Don't Let The Sun Go Down On Me' *live*, 'Daniel' *live*)

January 1996   'Please'/'Latitude' (*Other formats also include* 'Made In England', 'Honky Cat' *live*, 'Take Me To The Pilot' *live*, 'The Bitch Is Back' *live*)

December 1996   'Live Like Horses' (*Elton John & Luciano Pavarotti*) *live*/ 'Live Like Horses' (*Elton John & Luciano Pavarotti*) (*Other formats also include* 'I Guess That's Why They Call It The Blues'[2] *live*, 'Live Like Horses' *solo version*, 'Step Into Christmas', 'Blessed')

September 1997   'Candle In The Wind 1997'/'Something About The Way You Look Tonight' (*Other format also includes* 'You Can Make History (Young Again)')

February 1998   'Recover Your Soul'/'No Valentines' (*Other formats also include* 'Big Man In A Little Suit', 'I Know Why I'm In Love')

June 1998   'If The River Can Bend'/'Bennie And The Jets' (*Other formats also include* 'Saturday Night's Alright For Fighting', 'Don't Let The Sun Go Down On Me' *live*, 'I Guess That's Why They Call It The Blues' *live*, 'Sorry Seems To Be The Hardest Word' *live*)

February 1999   'Written In The Stars'[5] (with LeAnn Rimes)/'My Strongest Suit'[5] (*performed by The Spice Girls only*), 'Not Me'[5] (*performed by Boyz II Men only*), 'A Step Too Far'[5] (with Heather Headley and Sherie Scott), 'Your Song' *live* (*Other format also includes* 'Recover Your Soul' *live*)

ALBUMS

June 1969   *Empty Sky*

A: 'Empty Sky', 'Val-Hala', 'Western Ford Gateway', 'Hymn 2000'
B: 'Lady, What's Tomorrow?', 'Sails', 'The Scaffold', 'Skyline Pigeon', medley: 'Gulliver'/'Hay Chewed'[1]

April 1970   *Elton John*
A: 'Your Song', 'I Need You To Turn To', 'Take Me To The Pilot',
   'No Shoe Strings On Louise', 'First Episode At Hienton'
B: 'Sixty Years On', 'Border Song', 'The Greatest Discovery', 'The
   Cage', 'The King Must Die'

October 1970   *Tumbleweed Connection*
A: 'Ballad Of A Well-Known Gun', 'Come Down In Time', 'Country
   Comfort', 'Son Of Your Father', 'My Father's Gun'
B: 'Where To Now, St Peter?', 'Love Song'[7], 'Amoreena', 'Talking Old
   Soldiers', 'Burn Down The Mission'

April 1971   *17-11-70*
A: 'Take Me To The Pilot', 'Honky Tonk Women'[7], 'Sixty Years On',
   'Can I Put You On?'
B: 'Bad Side Of The Moon', medley: 'Burn Down The Mission'/'My
   Baby Left Me'[7]/'Get Back'[7]

May 1971   *Friends* (**Original Soundtrack Recording**)
A: 'Friends', 'Honey Roll', *'Variations On "Friends" Theme (The First
   Kiss)'*[7], 'Seasons', *'Variations On Michelle's Song (A Day In The
   Country)'*[7], 'Can I Put You On?'
B: 'Michelle's Song', *'I Meant To Do My Work Today'*[7], *'Four Moods'*[7],
   'Seasons (Reprise)'   (*Italicised titles not performed by Elton John*)

November 1971   *Madman Across The Water*
A: 'Tiny Dancer', 'Levon', 'Razor Face', 'Madman Across The Water'
B: 'Indian Sunset', 'Holiday Inn', 'Rotten Peaches', 'All The Nasties',
   'Goodbye'

May 1972   *Honky Château*
A: 'Honky Cat', 'Mellow', 'I Think I'm Going To Kill Myself', 'Susie
   (Dramas)', 'Rocket Man (I Think It's Going To Be A Long, Long
   Time)'
B: 'Salvation', 'Slave', 'Amy', 'Mona Lisas And Mad Hatters', 'Hercules'

January 1973   *Don't Shoot Me, I'm Only The Piano Player*
A: 'Daniel', 'Teacher, I Need You', 'Elderberry Wine', 'Blues For My
   Baby And Me', 'Midnight Creeper'
B: 'Have Mercy On The Criminal', 'I'm Going To Be A Teenage Idol',
   'Texan Love Song', 'Crocodile Rock', 'High-Flying Bird'

October 1973   *Goodbye Yellow Brick Road*
A: medley: 'Funeral For A Friend'/'Love Lies Bleeding', 'Candle In The
   Wind', 'Bennie And The Jets'

B: 'Goodbye Yellow Brick Road', 'This Song Has No Title', 'Grey Seal',
    'Jamaica Jerk-Off', 'I've Seen That Movie Too'
C: 'Sweet Painted Lady', 'The Ballad Of Danny Bailey (1909–34)', 'Dirty
    Little Girl', 'All The Girls Love Alice'
D: 'Your Sister Can't Twist (But She Can Rock 'n' Roll)', 'Saturday
    Night's Alright For Fighting', 'Roy Rogers', 'Social Disease',
    'Harmony'

June 1974   *Caribou*
A: 'The Bitch Is Back', 'Pinky', 'Grimsby', 'Dixie Lily', 'Solar Prestige à
    Gammon', 'You're So Static'
B: 'I've Seen The Saucers', 'Stinker', 'Don't Let The Sun Go Down On
    Me', 'Ticking'

May 1975   *Captain Fantastic And The Brown Dirt Cowboy*
A: 'Captain Fantastic And The Brown Dirt Cowboy', 'Tower Of Babel',
    'Bitter Fingers', 'Tell Me When The Whistle Blows', 'Someone Saved
    My Life Tonight'
B: '(Gotta Get A) Meal Ticket', 'Better Off Dead', 'Writing', 'We All
    Fall In Love Sometimes', 'Curtains'

October 1975   *Rock Of The Westies*
A: medley: 'Yell Help'²/'Wednesday Night'²/'Ugly'², 'Dan Dare (Pilot
    Of The Future)', 'Island Girl', 'Grow Some Funk Of Your Own'²,
    'I Feel Like A Bullet (In The Gun Of Robert Ford)'
B: 'Street Kids', 'Hard Luck Story', 'Feed Me', 'Billy Bones And The
    White Bird'

April 1976   *Here And There*
A: 'Skyline Pigeon', 'Border Song', 'Honky Cat', 'Love Song'⁷,
    'Crocodile Rock'
B: medley: 'Funeral For A Friend'/'Love Lies Bleeding', 'Rocket Man (I
    Think It's Going To Be A Long, Long Time)', 'Bennie And The Jets',
    'Take Me To The Pilot'

October 1976   *Blue Moves*
A: 'Your Starter For . . .'⁷, 'Tonight', 'One Horse Town'², 'Chameleon'
B: 'Boogie Pilgrim'², 'Cage The Songbird'², 'Crazy Water', 'Shoulder
    Holster'
C: 'Sorry Seems To Be The Hardest Word', 'Out Of The Blue',
    'Between Seventeen And Twenty'², 'The Wide-Eyed And Laughing'²,
    'Someone's Final Song'
D: 'Where's The Shoorah?', 'If There's A God In Heaven (What's He
    Waiting For?)'², 'Idol', 'Theme From A Non-Existent TV Series',
    'Bite Your Lip (Get Up And Dance!)'

October 1978 *A Single Man*

A: 'Shine On Through'[3], 'Return To Paradise'[3], 'I Don't Care'[3], 'Big Dipper'[3], 'It Ain't Gonna Be Easy'[3]

B: 'Part-Time Love'[3], 'Georgia'[3], 'Shooting Star'[3], 'Madness'[3], 'Reverie'[1], 'Song For Guy'[1]

October 1979 *Victim Of Love*

A: 'Johnny B Goode'[7], 'Warm Love In A Cold World'[7], 'Born Bad'[7]

B: 'Thunder In The Night'[7], 'Spotlight'[7], 'Street Boogie'[7], 'Victim Of Love'[7]

May 1980 *21 At 33*

A: 'Chasing The Crown', 'Little Jeannie'[3], 'Sartorial Eloquence'[6], 'Two Rooms At The End Of The World'

B: 'White Lady White Powder', 'Dear God'[3], 'Never Gonna Fall In Love Again'[6], 'Take Me Back'[3], 'Give Me The Love'[6]

May 1981 *The Fox*

A: 'Breaking Down The Barriers'[3], 'Heart In The Right Place'[3], 'Just Like Belgium', 'Nobody Wins'[7], 'Fascist Faces'

B: medley: 'Carla'[1]/'Etude'[1]/'Fanfare'[6]/'Chloe'[3], 'Heels Of The Wind', 'Elton's Song'[6], 'The Fox'

April 1982 *Jump Up!*

A: 'Dear John'[3], 'Spiteful Child', 'Ball & Chain'[3], 'Legal Boys'[5], 'I Am Your Robot', 'Blue Eyes'[3]

B: 'Empty Garden (Hey Hey Johnny)', 'Princess'[3], 'Where Have All The Good Times Gone?', 'All Quiet On The Western Front'

June 1983 *Too Low For Zero*

A: 'Cold As Christmas', 'I'm Still Standing', 'Too Low For Zero', 'Religion', 'I Guess That's Why They Call It The Blues'[2]

B: 'Crystal', 'Kiss The Bride', 'Whipping Boy', 'My Baby's A Saint', 'One More Arrow'

June 1984 *Breaking Hearts*

A: 'Restless', 'Slow Down Georgie (She's Poison)', 'Who Wears These Shoes?', 'Breaking Hearts (Ain't What It Used To Be)', 'Li'l 'frigerator'

B: 'Passengers'[2], 'In Neon', 'Burning Buildings', 'Did He Shoot Her?', 'Sad Songs (Say So Much)'

November 1985 *Ice On Fire*

A: 'This Town', 'Cry To Heaven', 'Soul Glove', 'Nikita', 'Too Young'

B: 'Wrap Her Up'[2], 'Satellite', 'Tell Me What The Papers Say', 'Candy By The Pound', 'Shoot Down The Moon' (CD and cassette versions also include 'Act Of War')

November 1986   *Leather Jackets*
A: 'Leather Jackets', 'Hoop Of Fire', 'Don't Trust That Woman'[6], 'Go It
   Alone', 'Gypsy Heart'
B: 'Slow Rivers', 'Heartache All Over The World', 'Angeline'[2], 'Memory
   Of Love'[3], 'Paris', 'I Fall Apart'

September 1987   *Live In Australia*
A: 'Sixty Years On', 'I Need You To Turn To', 'The Greatest
   Discovery', 'Tonight'
B: 'Sorry Seems To Be The Hardest Word', 'The King Must Die', 'Take
   Me To The Pilot', 'Tiny Dancer'
C: 'Have Mercy On The Criminal', 'Madman Across The Water',
   'Candle In The Wind'
D: 'Burn Down The Mission', 'Your Song', 'Don't Let The Sun Go
   Down On Me'

July 1988   *Reg Strikes Back*
A: 'Town Of Plenty', 'A Word In Spanish', 'Mona Lisas And Mad
   Hatters (Part Two)', 'I Don't Wanna Go On With You Like That',
   'Japanese Hands'
B: 'Goodbye Marlon Brando', 'The Camera Never Lies', 'Heavy
   Traffic'[2], 'Poor Cow', 'Since God Invented Girls'

September 1989   *Sleeping With The Past*
A: 'Durban Deep', 'Healing Hands', 'Whispers', 'Club At The End Of
   The Street', 'Sleeping With The Past'
B: 'Stones Throw From Hurtin'', 'Sacrifice', 'I Never Knew Her Name',
   'Amazes Me', 'Blue Avenue'

June 1992   *The One*
'Simple Life', 'The One', 'Sweat It Out', 'Runaway Train'[2], 'Whitewash
County', 'The North', 'When A Woman Doesn't Want You', 'Emily',
'On Dark Street', 'Understanding Women', 'The Last Song'

November 1993   *Duets*
'Teardrops'[7] (with kd lang), 'When I Think About Love (I Think About
You)'[7] (with PM Dawn), 'The Power' (with Little Richard), 'Shakey
Ground'[7] (with Don Henley), 'True Love'[7] (with Kiki Dee), 'If You Were
Me'[7] (with Chris Rea), 'A Woman's Needs' (with Tammy Wynette), 'Old
Friend'[7] (with Nik Kershaw), 'Go On And On'[7] (with Gladys Knight),
'Don't Go Breaking My Heart' (with RuPaul), 'Ain't Nothing Like The
Real Thing'[7] (with Marcella Detroit), 'I'm Your Puppet'[7] (with Paul
Young), 'Love Letters'[7] (with Bonnie Raitt), 'Born To Lose'[7] (with
Leonard Cohen), 'Don't Let The Sun Go Down On Me' *live* (with
George Michael), 'Duets For One'[6] (Elton John with himself)

October 1994   *The Lion King* **(Original Soundtrack Recording)**
'*Circle Of Life*'[5], '*I Just Can't Wait To Be King*'[5], '*Be Prepared*'[5], '*Hakuna Matata*'[5], '*Can You Feel The Love Tonight*'[5], '*This Land*'[7], '*. . . To Die For*'[7], '*Under The Stars*'[7], '*King Of Pride Rock*'[7], 'Circle Of Life'[5], 'I Just Can't Wait To Be King'[5], 'Can You Feel The Love Tonight'[5]

(Italicised titles not performed by Elton John)

March 1995   *Made In England*
'Believe', 'Made In England', 'House', 'Cold', 'Pain', 'Belfast', 'Latitude', 'Please', 'Man', 'Lies', 'Blessed'

September 1997   *The Big Picture*
'Long Way From Happiness', 'Live Like Horses' *solo version*, 'The End Will Come', 'If The River Can Bend', 'Love's Got A Lot To Answer For', 'Something About The Way You Look Tonight', 'The Big Picture', 'Recover Your Soul', 'January', 'I Can't Steer My Heart Clear Of You', 'Wicked Dreams'

March 1999   *Aida*
'*Another Pyramid*'[5], 'Written In The Stars'[5] (with LeAnn Rimes), '*Easy As Life*'[5], '*My Strongest Suit*'[5], 'I Know The Truth'[5] (with Janet Jackson), '*Not Me*'[5], '*Amneris' Letter*'[5], 'A Step Too Far'[5] (with Heather Headley and Sherie Scott), '*Like Father Like Son*'[5], '*Elaborate Lives*'[5], '*How I Know You*'[5], 'The Messenger'[5] (with Lulu), '*The Gods Love Nubia*'[5], '*Enchantment Passing Through*'[5], '*Orchestral Finale*'[7]

(Italicised titles not performed by Elton John)

OTHER RECORDINGS

Except where stated, this list details the Elton John record releases not shown in the preceding sections of this discography; it is *not* an attempt to list his considerable body of unreleased recordings.

June 1969
This was the month in which the debut album by The Bread And Beer Band was set for release, although it was withdrawn before issue and did not exist beyond test pressings and sample covers. The band – consisting of Reg Dwight (keyboards), Bernie Calvert (bass), Caleb Quaye (guitar), Roger Pope (drums) and two Jamaican percussionists, Rolfo and Lennox – taped two songs at EMI Studios, Abbey Road, on 2 December 1968, a version of 'The Dick Barton Theme (The Devil's Gallop)' and 'Breakdown Blues', the latter jointly written by all four band members. These formed two sides of an unsuccessful single, issued by Decca in February 1969.

Undaunted by the failure, The Bread And Beer Band taped cover-

versions of ten more songs in two further Abbey Road sessions, on 19
March and 9 April 1969. These were produced by Chris Thomas who, in
the 1980s, would produce several Elton John albums. The ten songs were
compiled into an album and test-pressings were made but the project went
no further, and it remains commercially unreleased to this day. Had it
appeared, the album would have contained the following. Reg Dwight
contributed harmony vocals to two of the songs, 'The Letter' and 'Mellow
Yellow'.

A: 'Woolly Bully', 'Mellow Yellow', 'If I Were A Carpenter', 'Zorba's
    Dance', 'The Letter'
B: 'Quick Joey Small', 'Needles And Pins', 'God Knows (A Bit Of
    Freedom)', 'Billy's Bag', 'Last Night'

April 1970
A recording of Elton John singing 'From Denver To LA' appeared on the
film soundtrack album *The Games*, released only in the USA. He did not
compose the song. Backed by an unrelated film piece, it was also issued as
the A-side of a US single, his artist credit erroneously reading 'Elton
Johns'.

March 1975
The first release of Elton John's cover of The Who's 'Pinball Wizard',
included on the soundtrack album of the film *Tommy*. The recording was
released as a single in March 1976.

April 1977
'The Goaldiggers Song'/'Jimmy, Brian, Elton & Eric' was a special Rocket
Records single, recorded to raise funds for Goaldiggers, the British football
charity. It was not released commercially and only 500 copies were
pressed. The A-side features an otherwise unissued Elton John solo
composition and recording. The B-side consists of spoken messages from
Elton John, football TV pundits Jimmy Hill and Brian Moore, and
comedian Eric Morecambe, then a director of Luton Town football club.

February 1980
Numerous compilations of Elton John recordings have been issued over
the years, mostly collections of hits. One particularly interesting album was
Lady Samantha, first issued on record at this time and available on cassette
since September 1974, which brought together 14 of the more obscure
releases from Elton John's early recording career, many of which were no
longer available in their original format.

A: 'Rock And Roll Madonna', 'Whenever You're Ready (We'll Go
    Steady Again)', 'Bad Side Of The Moon', 'Jack Rabbit', 'Into The
    Old Man's Shoes', 'It's Me That You Need', 'Ho! Ho! Ho! (Who'd
    Be A Turkey At Christmas?)'

B: 'Skyline Pigeon', 'Screw You', 'Just Like Strange Rain', 'Grey Seal', 'Honey Roll', 'Lady Samantha', 'Friends'

February 1981
Elton John recorded two songs in the French language with France Gall, one of the leading female vocalists in France, and the original singer of 'J'Veux d'la Tendresse' (see below). The songs were 'Les Aveux', meaning 'Avowal', written by Elton John with Michel Berger (Gall's husband), and 'Donner Pour Donner', meaning 'Giving For Giving', written by Berger with Bernie Taupin. In that order, as A- and B-sides, the songs were issued as a February 1981 single in France by Atlantic Records.

May 1981
'J'Veux d'la Tendresse' – the original French version of 'Nobody Wins', written by Jean-Paul Dreau but meaning, literally, 'I Want Tenderness' – was recorded by Elton John in that language, and released as a single by Rocket Records in France. (The B-side, 'Fools In Fashion', was in English.) The French language recording also replaced its English counterpart on local pressings of Elton John's album *The Fox*, issued in May 1981. 'Je Veux d'la Tendresse' was not released in the UK until December 1983, as a bonus track on the 12-inch single of 'Cold As Christmas'.

July 1981
The B-side of the US-only single release 'Chloe' (from the album *The Fox*) was the song 'Tortured', not issued in the UK until October 1984.

May 1983
'Take Me Down To The Ocean', composed by Elton John–Gary Osborne and otherwise available only as the B-side of the May 1982 single 'Empty Garden (Hey Hey Johnny)', was included on the soundtrack album of the film *Summer Lovers*.

April 1987
Elton John appeared on *The Prince's Trust 10th Anniversary Birthday Party*, the album of the Wembley Arena show on 20 June 1986, singing 'I'm Still Standing'. He was also pianist in the all-star band which perform several numbers backing guest vocalists.

August 1987
Elton John appeared on *The Prince's Trust Concert 1987*, the double-album of the Wembley Arena show on 6 June 1987, singing 'Saturday Night's Alright For Fighting' and 'Your Song'. He was also pianist in the all-star band which perform several numbers backing guest vocalists.

October 1988
A BBC-radio session recording of the *Tumbleweed Connection* track 'My Father's Gun' was included on the various artists compilation album *21 Years Of Alternative Radio 1*. It was taped in August 1970.

February 1989
Between *Reg Strikes Back* and *Sleeping With The Past*, MCA Records in the USA issued a six-track album, *The Complete Thom Bell Sessions*, featuring the full set of songs Elton John recorded in Seattle and Philadelphia in autumn 1977. Three of the titles ('Mama Can't Buy You Love', 'Are You Ready For Love' and 'Three Way Love Affair') had been issued as a single in April 1979. The other three were previously unreleased: 'Nice And Slow' (composed Elton John–Bernie Taupin–Thom Bell), 'Country Love Song' (cover-version) and 'Shine On Through' (Elton John–Gary Osborne). (A re-recording of this latter song was issued on Elton John's October 1978 album *A Single Man*, but this earlier Thom Bell version had remained unissued.) The album was originally scheduled for full international release in autumn 1982 but had been withheld.

May 1989
Elton John contributed 'I'm Ready', a new exclusive cover-version recording, to the various artists concept album *Rock, Rhythm & Blues*.

August 1989
'Love Is A Cannibal', otherwise available only as the B-side of the October 1989 single 'Sacrifice', was first released on the soundtrack album of the film *Ghostbusters II*.

July 1990
'Medicine Man', otherwise available only as the B-side of the October 1990 single 'You Gotta Love Someone', was first released on the Romanian Angel Appeal charity album *Nobody's Child*.

August 1990
Elton John appeared on *Knebworth – The Album*, the double-album of the major charity concert which took place there on 30 June 1990, singing 'Sad Songs (Say So Much)' and 'Saturday Night's Alright For Fighting'.

August 1990
Some European pressings (and a withdrawn UK pressing) of the single 'Club At The End Of The Street' featured as a bonus track a previously unissued December 1988 Elton John studio performance of Lennon–McCartney's 'Give Peace A Chance'. The recording was later included as part of the boxed-set *To Be Continued* . . . (see below).

August 1990
'You Gotta Love Someone', issued as a single and as part of the boxed-set
To Be Continued . . . in October 1990, was first released on the soundtrack
album of the film *Days Of Thunder*.

October 1990
Elton John's 25th anniversary as a recording artist was marked in the USA
by the release of a four-CD boxed retrospective, *To Be Continued* . . .
There were several rarities among the 68 tracks, such as 'Come Back,
Baby', his debut composition and the debut single by Bluesology, the
original (1970) version of 'Grey Seal' and 'Donner Pour Donner', one of
his two duets with France Gall; six others were previously unreleased: a
solo demo of 'Your Song', live versions of 'I Feel Like A Bullet (In The
Gun Of Robert Ford)' and 'Carla'/'Etude', and three more new (July
1990) recordings, 'Made For Me', 'I Swear I Heard The Night Talkin''
and 'Easier To Walk Away'. See November 1991 for details of the UK
release.

January 1991
Elton John contributed 'The Measure Of A Man', a new cover-version
recording, to the soundtrack album *Music From The Film Rocky V*.

May 1991
Elton John contributed a recording of 'The Pacifier', a solo instrumental
composition, to the Pediatric AIDS Foundation charity album *For Our
Children*, issued in the USA.

October 1991
A BBC-radio session recording of the *Tumbleweed Connection* track 'Ballad
Of A Well-Known Gun' was included on the various artists compilation
album *Before The Fall – The Peel Sessions 67–77*. It was taped in April 1970.

October 1991
Elton John was interviewed, comically, by Rowan Atkinson during a
charity concert in aid of the Terrence Higgins Trust, held at the London
Palladium in June 1991; the sketch was released on the album *The Best Of
Hysteria 3!*

November 1991
The UK version of the *To Be Continued* . . . four-CD boxed-set was
slightly different to the US original (see October 1990, above), with the
final three tracks on the fourth CD being, in order, 'Easier To Walk
Away', 'Suit Of Wolves' and 'Understanding Women'. The first of these
had been the final cut on the US compilation, a song first issued in the
UK in October 1990 on a hits compilation album, *The Very Best Of Elton*

John. 'Suit Of Wolves' and 'Understanding Women', both Elton John–Bernie Taupin compositions, were recorded in July 1991.

August 1992
Elton John contributed a recording of 'Some Other World' to the soundtrack album of the animated film *Ferngully: The Last Rainforest.* He also wrote the tune, put to the lyrics of Bruce Roberts.

October 1992
'Runaway Train', recorded by Elton John and Eric Clapton and released on Elton's album *The One* in June 1992, was first released on the soundtrack album of the film *Lethal Weapon 3.*

October 1992
Elton John sang the lead vocal and played piano on 'Up The Revolution', a song with which neither he nor Bernie Taupin had any writing involvement, released on the various artists album *The Bunbury Tails* to accompany an animated TV series of the same title.

November 1992
A BBC-radio recording of Elton John performing 'Candle In The Wind' live in concert was included on the various artists compilation album *1 And Only.* It was recorded in February 1979.

December 1992
Thirty-seven scarce or previously unreleased Elton John recordings, taped 1967–75, were compiled on to the double-CD *Rare Masters.* The collection made particular emphasis on gathering together non-album tracks (principally A- and B-sides of singles) and curios from that early period, and it included five previously unreleased tracks – alternate versions of 'Madman Across The Water' and 'Slave', and Elton John's original recordings of songs that he gave away (hence they appear in the discography section 'Compositions released only by other artists', below), 'Let Me Be Your Car', 'Planes' and 'Rock Me When He's Gone'.

September 1993
A recording of Elton John and Axl Rose's duet of Queen's 'Bohemian Rhapsody', as performed in the Freddie Mercury memorial show Concert For Life in April 1992, was issued on the album *A Tribute To Freddie Mercury.*

February 1994
Elton John And The Sounds Of Blackness contributed a cover-version recording of 'Amen' to the various artists album *All Men Are Brothers: A Tribute To Curtis Mayfield.*

May 1994

Exclusive recordings of Elton John singing the Gershwins' 'But Not For Me' and The Dixie Cups' 'Chapel Of Love' appeared on the soundtrack album for the film *Four Weddings And A Funeral*.

June 1994

Elton John sang lead vocal on two tracks on the various artists album *The Glory Of Gershwin*, 'Someone To Watch Over Me' and 'Our Love Is Here To Stay', performing with the album's main artist, Larry Adler.

December 1994

A recording of 'Don't Let The Sun Go Down On Me' from Elton John's August 1990 broadcast on MTV's *Unplugged* television show was included on the various artists compilation album *The Unplugged Collection, Volume One*.

February 1995

Elton John sang lead vocal on 'I'm Your Man', released on the various artists tribute album *Tower Of Song: The Songs Of Leonard Cohen*.

May/July 1995

A dozen Elton John albums, issued 1969–76, were re-released on CD in the UK at this time, six in May 1995, the remainder two months later (in the USA, the re-releases occurred in February and March 1996). All were remastered from the original tapes and so featured much improved sound, and eight included bonus tracks drawn from each album's time period, recordings already reissued on *Rare Masters*. Additionally, the two live albums, *17–11–70* (titled *11–17–70* in the USA) and *Here And There*, were remixed and supplemented with previously unissued recordings – the former was given one, 'Amoreena', *Here And There* was completely revamped with the addition of 16, seven recorded at the Royal Festival Hall in London in May 1974 ('Take Me To The Pilot', 'Country Comfort', 'Bad Side Of The Moon', 'Burn Down The Mission', 'Candle In The Wind', 'Your Song' and 'Saturday Night's Alright For Fighting') and nine recorded at Madison Square Garden in New York City in November 1974 ('Grey Seal', 'Daniel', 'You're So Static', 'Whatever Gets You Thru The Night', 'Lucy In The Sky With Diamonds', 'I Saw Her Standing There', 'Don't Let The Sun Go Down On Me', 'Your Song' and 'The Bitch Is Back').

September 1995

In the guise of an angel, Elton John sang 'Little Island' on the album release of Goethe's *Faust*, conceived and written by Randy Newman.

November 1995

A recording of the Elton John–Bernie Taupin song 'Red', an outtake from sessions for the album *Made In England*, appeared on the charity album *Sol En Si*, issued only in France.

September 1996
The US issue of the Elton John compilation album *Love Songs* featured a different song selection to the UK version, released in November 1995. Specifically, it included two Elton John–Bernie Taupin songs that would not be released in the UK until late 1997 and early 1998: 'You Can Make History (Young Again)' and 'No Valentines'.

November 1996
Live performances of 'I Guess That's Why They Call It The Blues' and 'Live Like Horses', the latter sung as a duet with Luciano Pavarotti, were included on the album *Pavarotti And Friends For War Child*. The tracks were issued as an Elton John single in the UK in December 1996.

April 1997
A recording of Elton John performing 'Abide With Me' was included on the US various artists compilation album *Carnival! The 1997 Rainforest Foundation Concert*.

September 1997
The BBC issued a recording of the complete funeral of Diana, Princess Of Wales, including Elton John's Westminster Abbey performance of 'Candle In The Wind 1997'. The version released as a single a few days later was a studio re-recording.

November 1997
Elton John was among the many stars who contributed vocally to a new recording of Lou Reed's 1972 song 'Perfect Day', utilised by the BBC to profit its Children In Need charity. The disc rose to number one in Britain.

April 1998
Elton John sang Noël Coward's 1931 composition 'Twentieth-Century Blues' on the various artists album *Twentieth-Century Blues: The Songs Of Noël Coward*.

May 1998
A recording of Elton John performing the Christine McVie composition 'Don't Stop' was included on the various artists album *Legacy: A Tribute To Fleetwood Mac's Rumours*.

September 1998
A recording of Elton John performing the Tammy Wynette hit 'Stand By

Your Man' was included on the various artists tribute album *Tammy Wynette . . . Remembered*.

December 1998
Elton John contributed a new recording, 'Wake Up Wendy', composed by Elton John–Bernie Taupin, to the various artists project *Chef Aid: The South Park Album*.

March 1999
A six-song Elton John mini-album was released on CD in the USA for limited-period exclusive sale through the chain of Target Records stores. Titled *Live At The Ritz*, the disc featured 'Daniel', 'Don't Let The Sun Go Down On Me', 'Sorry Seems To Be The Hardest Word', 'Something About The Way You Look Tonight', 'Take Me To The Pilot' and 'The Last Song', all recorded at the Hotel Ritz in Paris in January 1998. (Two of the numbers – 'Don't Let The Sun Go Down On Me' and 'Sorry Seems To Be The Hardest Word' – were released in the UK in June 1998 as part of the single 'If The River Can Bend', along with a third not included on *Live At The Ritz*, 'I Guess That's Why They Call It The Blues'.)

THE SONGWRITING

Compositions never released by any artist, The DJM Years, 1967–73

Many of these songs were originally recorded by Reg Dwight/Elton John in rough demonstration form, acetate pressings and tapes of which have surfaced in auction and on the collectors' market. There exists an original demonstration-use-only album comprising ten of the songs, including 'Regimental Sgt Zippo' and 'Watching The Planes Go By', and three 1990s bootleg CDs containing more than 50 such recordings – see the note at the end of the Songwriting section.

All of this information has been gathered from internal-use files at Dick James Music.

All songs are Elton John (or Reg Dwight) and Bernie Taupin compositions, unless otherwise stated. The dates indicate month of copyright registration.

September 1967
'Can't You See It' (Reg Dwight solo composition)
'Scarecrow'
'A Dandelion Dies In The Wind'
'If You Could See Me Now' (Reg Dwight solo composition)
'A Little Love Goes A Long Long Way' (Reg Dwight solo composition)
'Mr Lightning Strikerman'

'Onetime, Sometime Or Never'
'Watching The Planes Go By'

October 1967
'Where It's At' (Reg Dwight–Nicky James composition)
'Countryside Love Affair' (Reg Dwight solo composition)
'I Could Never Fall In Love With Anybody Else' (Reg Dwight solo composition)
'I Get A Little Bit Lonely' (Reg Dwight solo composition)
'Who's Gonna Love You' (Reg Dwight–Kirk Duncan composition)
'Witch's House' (Reg Dwight solo composition)
'Year Of The Teddy Bear'

November 1967
'Nina'

December 1967
'I Want To See You Smile' (Elton John–Caleb Quaye composition)

January 1968
'The Angel Tree'

February 1968
'Tartan Coloured Lady'

April 1968
'And The Clock Goes Round'
'When I Was Tealby Abbey'
'Trying To Hold On To A Love That's Dying'
'Reminds Me Of You'
'I'll Stop Living When You Stop Loving Me'

May 1968
'Regimental Sgt Zippo'
'You'll Be Sorry To See Me Go' (Elton John–Caleb Quaye composition)

June 1968
'Cry Willow Cry'
'If I Asked You'
'There Is Still A Little Love'

September 1968
'Smokestack Children'
'Two Of A Kind'
'The Girl On Angel Pavement'
'Baby I Miss You'

October 1968
'Bonnie's Gone Away'
'Just An Ordinary Man'
'Going Home'
'There's Still Time For Me'

December 1968
'Digging My Grave'

February 1969
'Child'

April 1969
'Last To Arrive'

July 1969
'I'm Going Home'

August 1969
'Big Circle Of Stone' (Elton John–Bernie Taupin–Caleb Quaye composition)

October 1969
'She Sings Rock And Roll'
'In The Morning'

December 1969
'All The Way Down To Elpaso'
'Thank You Mama'

February 1970
'Rolling Western Union'

April 1970
'Scales' (Elton John solo composition; featured in the film *Friends*)

May 1972
'Tell Me What The Doctor Said'

December 1972
'Gotta Get Back To England'

In addition to the above, two other known early Elton John–Bernie Taupin compositions, 'Indian Maiden' and 'Velvet Fountain', appear not to have been registered for copyright.

Compositions released only by other artists

Most notably before his own-name career became successful, but also on a
few subsequent occasions, Elton John has authored songs which have been
released only by other artists, not by Elton himself. This is the complete list
of such compositions, in alphabetical order. All have been written with
Bernie Taupin unless otherwise stated.

'Basque'
An instrumental, written by Elton John alone, recorded by flautist James
Galway for his album *The Wind Beneath My Wings*, released in August
1991. Elton John won a Grammy Award for this composition in 1992.

'Breakdown Blues'
(composed by Caleb Quaye–Reg Dwight–Chris Jackson–Bernie Calvert)
First released as the B-side of a single by The Bread And Beer Band in
February 1969. (Reg Dwight was a member of this group, which released
just this one single.)

'Chow Down'
(composed by Elton John–Tim Rice)
First released on the album *The Lion King – Original Broadway Cast
Recording* in November 1997.

'Crime Of Passion'
(composed by Elton John–Bernie Taupin–Davey Johnstone)
First released on the album *Radio Nights* by Public Domain in August
1998.

'The Flowers Will Never Die'
First released as the A-side of a single by Ayshea in January 1976.

'Get Out (Of This Town)'
(composed by Elton John only)
First released as the B-side of a single by Mr Bloe in May 1971.

'Hey Lord You Made The Night Too Long'
(composed by Tony Macaulay–John Baldry–Reg Dwight)
This composition surfaced only as the B-side of an export issue of Long
John Baldry's UK hit 'Let The Heartaches Begin' (Pye 7N 17408), pressed
expressly for the overseas market in November 1967, the same month that
the original disc (Pye 7N 17385) entered the UK chart. (The B-side of the
domestic edition was 'Annabella (Who Flies To Me When She's Lonely)'.)

'I Can't Go On Living Without You'
First released in Europe (but not in the UK) by Lulu in March 1969 as

part of a four-track EP of songs which, with two others, were contenders for the UK's Eurovision Song Contest contribution that year. ('Boom Bang-A-Bang' was eventually selected.)
First released in the UK as the A-side of a single by Stewart A. Brown in March 1969. (Brown was a former member of Bluesology.)

'I Loved A Man'
(words by Dylan Thomas, set to music by Elton John)
First released on the album *Under Milk Wood*, sung by Bonnie Tyler, in November 1988.

'The Last Good Man In My Life'
First released as the B-side of a single by Kiki Dee in June 1973.

'Let Me Be Your Car'
First released on the album *Smiler* by Rod Stewart in September 1974. (Elton John's demo recording of this song was included on the 1992 historical CD *Rare Masters*, above.)

'Lonely Heart'
(composed by Elton John–Gary Osborne)
First released as the third track on a 12-inch single (A-side 'Love's A State Of Mind') by Sylvia Griffin in May 1988.

'Lonnie And Josie'
First released as the A-side of a single by Kiki Dee in June 1973.

'The Madness Of King Scar'
(composed by Elton John–Tim Rice)
First released on the album *The Lion King – Original Broadway Cast Recording* in November 1997.

'The Man Who Loved To Dance'
Written by Elton John–Bernie Taupin under the pseudonyms Tripe–Onions, this was first released as the B-side of a single by Kiki Dee in January 1977.

'The Morning Report'
(composed by Elton John–Tim Rice)
First released on the album *The Lion King – Original Broadway Cast Recording* in November 1997.

'Never Going To Fall In Love . . . (Again)'
(composed by Elton John–Tom Robinson)
First released as the A-side of a single by Tom Robinson With The Voice Squad in June 1979.

'Planes'
First released as the A-side of a single by Colin Blunstone in November
1976.
(Elton John's recording of this song was included on the 1992 historical
CD *Rare Masters*, above.)

'Rock Me When He's Gone'
First released on the album *It Ain't Easy* by John Baldry in July 1971.
(Elton John's demo recording of this song was included on the 1992
historical CD *Rare Masters*, above.)

'Roll On'
(composed by Elton John–Gary Osborne)
First released on the album *Did He Jump . . . Or Was He Pushed?* by Garth
Hewitt in October 1979.

'The Rumour'
First released on the album *The Rumour* by Olivia Newton-John in
October 1988.

'Season Of The Rain'
First released as the B-side of a single by Nite People in June 1970.

'71–75 New Oxford Street'
(composed by Elton John only)
First released as the A-side of a single by Mr Bloe in May 1971.

'Sing Me No Sad Songs'
First released as the A-side of an immediately withdrawn single by Guy
Darrell in October 1969. Issued again in October 1974 on a DJM Records
various artists compilation cassette.

'Smile That Smile'
(composed by Elton John–Gary Osborne)
First released as the A-side of a single by Neil Bashan in May 1979.

'Snookeroo'
First released on the album *Goodnight Vienna* by Ringo Starr in November
1974.

'Supercool'
First released on the album *Loving And Free* by Kiki Dee in December
1973.

'Sweetheart On Parade'
(composed by Elton John–Gary Osborne)

First released on the album *Home Again* by Judy Collins in November 1984.

'Taking The Sun From My Eyes'
First released as the B-side of a single by Ayshea in February 1969.

'Thank You For Your Loving'
(composed by Caleb Quaye–Elton John)
First released as the B-side of a single by Dukes Noblemen in July 1968.

'The Tide Will Turn For Rebecca'
First released on the album *This Man Alone* by Edward Woodward in April 1970.

'Turn To Me'
First released on the album *Currency* by Plastic Penny in February 1969.

'Warthog Rhapsody'
Written by Elton John–Tim Rice for *The Lion King*, but omitted from that project, this song first appeared on the November 1995 Disney album *Rhythm Of The Pride Lands (Music Inspired By The Lion King)*, performed by Nathan Lane and Ernie Sabella.

'When The First Tear Shows'
First released as the A-side of a single by Brian Keith in November 1968.

Compositions released first by other artists, then by Elton John

The following Elton John compositions, all subsequently released by him, were initially recorded and issued by other artists. All are Elton John–Bernie Taupin compositions, unless otherwise stated.

'Bad Side Of The Moon'
First released as the A-side of a single by Toe Fat in February 1970.
First released by Elton John as the B-side of the single 'Border Song' in March 1970.

'Country Comfort'
First released on the album *Orange Bicycle* by Orange Bicycle, and on the album *Gasoline Alley* by Rod Stewart, in September 1970.
First released by Elton John on the album *Tumbleweed Connection* in October 1970.

'Empty Sky'
First released as the B-side of a single by Roy Everett in May 1969.
First released by Elton John on the album *Empty Sky* in June 1969.

'Hard Luck Story'
First released as the A-side of a single by Kiki Dee in March 1974.
    First released by Elton John on the album *Rock Of The Westies* in
October 1975.

'Indian Sunset'
First released on the album *Mary* by Mary Travers in August 1971.
    First released by Elton John on the album *Madman Across The Water* in
November 1971.

'Nice And Slow'
(composed by Thom Bell–Elton John–Bernie Taupin)
First released on the album *Don't Take Love For Granted* by Lulu in July
1979.
    First released by Elton John on the US album *The Complete Thom Bell
Sessions* in February 1989, although recorded in late-1977.

'Sixty Years On'
First released as the A-side of a single by Hayden Wood in February 1970.
    First released by Elton John on the album *Elton John* in April 1970.

'Skyline Pigeon'
First released as the A-side of a single by Roger James Cooke (Roger
Cook), and as the A-side of a single by Guy Darrell, in August 1968.
    First released by Elton John on the album *Empty Sky* in June 1969.

'Son Of Your Father'
First released as the A-side of a single by Spooky Tooth featuring Mike
Harrison in September 1969.
    First released by Elton John on the album *Tumbleweed Connection* in
October 1970.

'Take Me To The Pilot'
First released as the A-side of a single by Orange Bicycle in January 1970.
    First released by Elton John on the album *Elton John* in April 1970.

Three bootleg CDs, the first two issued in 1992, the last in 1994, compiled
Elton John's own, unreleased demo recordings of many of the above
songs, together with some alternative versions of his released early tracks
and other, miscellaneous pieces.
    Dick James Demos, Vol 1 contained 'The Tide Will Turn For Rebecca',
'Sitting Doing Nothing', 'When The First Tear Shows', 'Thank You For
Your Loving', 'Get Out (Of This Town)', 'Tartan Coloured Lady', 'The
Angel Tree', 'Turn To Me', 'I Can't Go On Living Without You', '71–75
New Oxford Street', 'When I Was Tealby Abbey', 'And The Clock Goes

Round', 'Regimental Sgt Zippo', 'A Dandelion Dies In The Wind', 'You'll Be Sorry To See Me Go', 'Come Down In Time'

Dick James Demos, Vol 2 contained 'When The First Tear Shows', 'Thank You For Your Loving', 'Sitting Doing Nothing', 'Turn To Me', 'The Angel Tree', 'Sixty Years On', 'The Flowers Will Never Die', 'Sing Me No Sad Songs', 'In The Morning', 'Where It's At', 'I Get A Little Bit Lonely', 'A Dandelion Dies In The Wind', 'You'll Be Sorry To See Me Go', 'Tartan Coloured Lady', 'Hour Glass', 'Taking The Sun From My Eyes'

The Unsurpassed Dick James Demos, Vol 3 contained 'Annabella', 'Reminds Me Of You', 'I Love You And That's All That Matters', 'Last To Arrive', 'There Is Still A Little Love', 'There's Still Time For Me', 'Sarah's Coming Back', 'Lady, What's Tomorrow?', 'I Need You To Turn To', 'Son Of Your Father', 'The Tide Will Turn For Rebecca', 'Rock And Roll Madonna', 'Grey Seal', 'The Cage', 'Rock Me When He's Gone', 'Holiday Inn', 'I Get A Little Bit Lonely', 'Scarecrow', 'Velvet Fountain'

In 1993, a UK record company, Connoisseur Collection, compiled the various-artists CD *Elton John Songbook*, comprising 19 recordings of Elton John compositions from all stages of his career. Most of the recordings have been detailed in the preceding pages, a handful were straightforward cover-versions, subsequent to Elton's own rendition. The tracks were 'Hey Lord You Made The Night Too Long' (Long John Baldry), 'Breakdown Blues' (The Bread And Beer Band), 'Turn To Me' (Plastic Penny), 'Country Comfort' (Rod Stewart), 'Border Song' (Aretha Franklin), '71–75 New Oxford Street' (Mr Bloe), 'Let Me Be Your Car' (Rod Stewart), 'Don't Let The Sun Go Down On Me' (The Three Degrees), 'Planes' (Colin Blunstone), 'Candle In The Wind' (Sandy Denny), 'Your Song' (Billy Paul), 'Philadelphia Freedom' (Esther Phillips), 'Strangers' (Randy Meisner), 'Sweetheart On Parade' (Judy Collins), 'Sorry Seems To Be The Hardest Word' (Elaine Paige), 'The Rumour' (Olivia Newton-John), 'Sacrifice' (Brenda Cochrane), 'Someone Saved My Life Tonight' (Walter Jackson) and a new recording of 'Elton's Song' by co-composer Tom Robinson.

The unreleased demos of other writers' compositions

From 1968, until achieving fame, Reg Dwight/Elton John supplemented his income by recording demonstration versions of newly-written songs for Dick James Music and other music publishing companies. Almost all were written by other composers, although it is conceivable that one or two of the following may be Elton John–Bernie Taupin songs, not registered as copyright. But although this list is the fullest yet compiled, it is certainly incomplete – it is known, for example, that Elton John recorded demos of Roger Cook–Roger Greenaway compositions, and that he also recorded a

demo for British comedian-singer-songwriter Lance Percival, yet these are
not detailed here.

The last seven songs in the list, known informally and collectively as
The Warlock Sampler, and made in July 1970, were unusual in that the
songwriters' own versions had already been issued; Elton John was hired to
give them a new voice, in order to attract cover-versions. The seven were
compiled on to an album, with around 100 copies privately pressed, along
with four further songs from the same session ('You Get Brighter', 'This
Moment', 'I Don't Mind' and 'Pied Pauper') sung by Linda Peters and
featuring Elton John on piano.

The songs here are listed chronologically, in likely order of recording;
where no details are shown the composer details cannot be traced and it is
thought that said song has not been released commercially by any artist.

'I Love You And That's All That Matters', 1968.
'She's Only Anne', 1968.
'Sitting Doing Nothing', 1968.

'Best Of Both Worlds', April 1968. Written by Don Black–Mark London
and published by Dick James Music. The song was a US hit single for Lulu
in December 1967.

'Since The Poet Came', October 1968.
'Empty Hands', *circa* 1969.
'Hanging Upside Down', *circa* 1969.
'Open Your Eyes To The Sun', *circa* 1969.

'Say Hello To Mrs Jones', *circa* 1969. Written by Martin Hall and
published by Belsize Music. The song was released as a single by Jigsaw in
January 1971.

'A Slow Fade To Blue', *circa* 1969.

'Sarah's Coming Back', spring 1969. Written by Paul Raymond–Tony
Murray and published by Dick James Music. The song was never released
commercially.

'Hour Glass', autumn 1969. Written by Tony Collacott–Jack Mowbray–
Breen Leoeuf and published by Dick James Music. The song was never
released commercially.

'United We Stand', late 1969. Written by Tony Hiller–John Goodison
(the latter under the pseudonymous surname Simons) and published by
Mills Music, the song became an international hit for Brotherhood Of
Man in spring 1970. At that time, Elton John recorded the song again for
an 'anonymous cover-version' album (see below).

'Dark Side Of The Moon', mid 1970. Written by Ben Findon–Peter Shelley–Albert Hammond–Mike Hazlewood and published by Casanova Music. The song was released as a single by The Outer Limits in May 1971.

'Green Is The Colour', June 1970. Written by Nat Kipner–Mike Bradley and published by Carlin Music. The song was never released commercially.

'If You Say Goodbye', June 1970. Written by Nat Kipner–Mike Bradley and published by Carlin Music. The song was never released commercially.

'Life Is What You Make It', June 1970. Written by Bryce Bradley and published by Carlin Music. The song was never released commercially.

'Only Love', June 1970. Written by Nat Kipner–Mike Bradley and published by Carlin Music. The song was never released commercially.

'That Old Fashioned Game', June 1970. Written by Nat Kipner–Mike Bradley and published by Carlin Music. The song was never released commercially.

'Words And Music', June 1970. Written by Nat Kipner–Mike Bradley and published by Carlin Music. The song was never released commercially.

'Day Is Done', July 1970. Written by Nick Drake and published by Warlock Music. The song had been released by Nick Drake on his September 1969 album *Five Leaves Left*.

'Saturday Sun', July 1970. Written by Nick Drake and published by Warlock Music. The song had been released by Nick Drake on his September 1969 album *Five Leaves Left*.

'Time Has Told Me', July 1970. Written by Nick Drake and published by Warlock Music. The song had been released by Nick Drake on his September 1969 album *Five Leaves Left*.

'Way To Blue', July 1970. Written by Nick Drake and published by Warlock Music. The song had been released by Nick Drake on his September 1969 album *Five Leaves Left*.

'Go Out And Get It', July 1970. Written by John Martyn and published by Warlock Music. The song had been released by John and Beverley Martyn on their February 1970 album *Stormbringer!* [On the demo recording, Elton John shared the lead vocal with Linda Peters.]

'Stormbringer', July 1970. Written by John Martyn and published by Warlock Music. The song had been released by John and Beverley Martyn on their February 1970 album *Stormbringer!*

'Sweet Honesty', July 1970. Written by Beverley Martyn and published by Warlock Music. The song had been released by John and Beverley Martyn on their February 1970 album *Stormbringer!*

The anonymous cover-version recordings

Before becoming a successful performer in his own right, Elton John supplemented his income with regular contributions to anonymous 'cover-version' recordings. These discs, usually albums or EPs, typically sold at budget price through multiple retail outlets such as Woolworths, presented sound-alike versions of current hit singles in the UK. In an effort to maintain the pretence, the sleeves did not name the decidedly unfamous singers and musicians who had worked to re-create another artist's sound.

A few brave souls have summoned the resolve to search through these difficult to locate and often unlistenable-to albums to identify which recordings feature Elton John – while some bear his easily recognisable lead vocal, he also contributed backing vocals and instrumental work to other recordings less easy to identify. However, in October 1994, an enterprising UK record label, RPM, issued a CD compiling 20 such tracks, all featuring Elton's distinctive vocal. Titled *Reg Dwight's Piano Goes Pop*, the album comprised 'My Baby Loves Lovin'', 'Cottonfields', 'Lady D'Arbanville', 'Natural Sinner', 'United We Stand', 'Spirit In The Sky', 'Travellin' Band', 'I Can't Tell The Bottom From The Top', 'Good Morning Freedom', 'Young Gifted And Black', 'In The Summertime', 'Up Around The Bend', 'Snake In The Grass', 'Neanderthal Man', 'She Sold Me Magic', 'Come And Get It', 'Love Of The Common People', 'Signed, Sealed Delivered (I'm Yours)', 'It's All In The Game', 'Yellow River'. The album was temporarily withdrawn soon after release because Elton John objected to its title, claiming that the recordings featured his vocal work, not necessarily his piano playing, and then resurfaced in March 1995 as *Chartbusters Goes Pop*. (In the USA, the album carried only 16 tracks, omitting 'Young Gifted And Black', 'In The Summertime', 'Snake In The Grass' and 'Neanderthal Man'.) A UK single was issued too, showcasing the original version and new remixes of 'United We Stand', sung as a duet with Kay Garner.

The most surprising aspect of this 'anonymous' work is that Elton John continued to make such recordings as late as August 1970, when his own third album was awaiting release and at the time of his important US concert debut at the Troubadour in Los Angeles.

The list that follows reflects Elton John's known work in the anonymous cover-version field, in approximate date order. Some songs feature his lead vocal, others his backing vocal or instrumentation. The artist whose work was being mimicked is named in parentheses.

June 1969	'Snake In The Grass' (Dave Dee, Dozy, Beaky, Mick And Tich)
August 1969	'Saved By The Bell' (Robin Gibb)
October 1969	'Don't Forget To Remember' (The Bee Gees)
January 1970	'She Sold Me Magic' (Lou Christie)
February 1970	'Come And Get It' (Badfinger)
February 1970	'Let's Work Together' (Canned Heat)
March 1970	'August October' (Robin Gibb)
March 1970	'My Baby Loves Lovin'' (White Plains)
April 1970	'Bridge Over Troubled Water' (Simon And Garfunkel)
April 1970	'Good Morning Freedom' (Blue Mink)
April 1970	'United We Stand' (Brotherhood Of Man)
May 1970	'Back Home' (The England World Cup Squad)
May 1970	'I Can't Tell The Bottom From The Top' (The Hollies)
May 1970	'Spirit In The Sky' (Norman Greenbaum)
May 1970	'Travellin' Band' (Creedence Clearwater Revival)
May 1970	'Young Gifted And Black' (Bob And Marcia)
June 1970	'Cottonfields' (The Beach Boys)
June 1970	'It's All In The Game' (The Four Tops)
June 1970	'Question' (The Moody Blues)
June 1970	'Yellow River' (Christie)
July 1970	'Down The Dustpipe' (Status Quo)
July 1970	'In The Summertime' (Mungo Jerry)
July 1970	'Love Of The Common People' (Nicky Thomas)
August 1970	'Lady D'Arbanville' (Cat Stevens)
August 1970	'Natural Sinner' (Fair Weather)
August 1970	'Neanderthal Man' (Hotlegs)
August 1970	'Rainbow' (Marmalade)
August 1970	'Signed, Sealed Delivered (I'm Yours)' (Stevie Wonder)
August 1970	'Up Around The Bend' (Creedence Clearwater Revival)

The following list reflects anonymous cover-version recordings *thought* to feature an Elton John contribution, not yet proven as fact.

August 1969	'Early In The Morning' (Vanity Fare)
August 1969	'Si Tu Dois Partir' (Fairport Convention)
August 1969	'Too Busy Thinking 'Bout My Baby' (Marvin Gaye)
September 1969	'Soul Deep' (The Box Tops)
November 1969	'Sugar Sugar' (The Archies)

November 1969	'What Does It Take (To Win Your Love)' (Junior Walker And The All-Stars)
February 1970	'Love Grows (Where My Rosemary Goes)' (Edison Lighthouse)
April 1970	'Everybody Get Together' (The Dave Clark Five)
April 1970	'Knock, Knock, Who's There?' (Mary Hopkin)
June 1970	'All Right Now' (Free)
July 1970	'Goodbye Sam Hello Samantha' (Cliff Richard)
July 1970	'I Will Survive' (Arrival)
August 1970	'I'll Say Forever My Love' (Jimmy Ruffin)
August 1970	'Lola' (The Kinks)
August 1970	'The Wonder Of You' (Elvis Presley)

Elton John's guest appearances

Since he first worked in recording studios, and particularly since he achieved international fame in 1970, Elton John has appeared as a guest performer on dozens of recordings by other artists. The list that follows details all known occurrences but, owing to anonymous/unresearchable contributions, it is incomplete. (Unless otherwise stated, none of the songs named in this section was composed by Elton John.)

Aida

According to the sleeve credits, Elton John served as musical director and contributed additional keyboards to all of the tracks on *Aida*, issued in March 1999 (for further details see the main Albums section), though, in fact, this may not be the case. But, in addition to the songs on which he sings lead, Elton John also sang backing vocal on 'Like Father Like Son', performed by Lenny Kravitz. (Note. Other songs written by Elton John and Tim Rice for *Aida*, not issued on the album, include 'The Dance Of The Robe', 'Every Story Is A Love Story', 'The Judgement', 'Night Of Nights', 'Our Nation Holds Sway' and 'The Past Is Another Land'.)

Rick Astley

Elton John contributed piano to two tracks, 'Behind The Smile' and 'Wonderful You', on the February 1991 album *Free*.

Kevin Ayers

Elton John contributed piano to three tracks, 'Circular Letter', 'Guru Banana' and 'Toujours La Voyage', on the March 1975 album *Sweet Deceiver*.

Long John Baldry/John Baldry

Bluesology, with Reg Dwight on piano, backed Long John Baldry on the two recordings that formed the B-side of his November 1967 hit 'Let The

Heartaches Begin' – 'Annabella (Who Flies To Me When She's Lonely)',
issued on the UK single, and also 'Hey Lord You Made The Night Too
Long', only released overseas. (The latter song was composed by Tony
Macaulay–John Baldry–Reg Dwight, and Reg also contributed a vocal
track.)

Elton John produced all four songs on side B of John Baldry's July
1971 album *It Ain't Easy*. These were: 'Let's Burn Down The Cornfield',
'Mr Rubin', 'Rock Me When He's Gone' (an Elton John–Bernie Taupin
composition especially donated to Baldry and otherwise unissued) and
'Flying'. Elton John also contributed piano to all four songs.

Elton John produced all five songs on side A of John Baldry's May
1972 album *Everything Stops For Tea*. These were: 'Come Back Again',
'Seventh Son', 'Wild Mountain Thyme', 'Iko Iko' and 'Jubilee Cloud'. He
also contributed vocal accompaniment to four of these, the exception
being 'Seventh Son'.

The Barron Knights

Elton John contributed piano to the group's single 'An Olympic Record',
issued in October 1968. Typical of The Barron Knights' singles, the track
wove together parodies of contemporary hits, in this instance 'Lazy
Sunday', 'I Pretend', 'Delilah', 'Cinderella Rockefella', 'Dream A Little
Dream Of Me' and 'Here Comes The Judge'.

Blue

Elton John and Clive Franks co-produced all ten tracks on the band's June
1977 Rocket Records album *Another Night Time Flight*, and Elton also
contributed piano under the alias Redget Buntovan. The tracks were
A: 'Another Night Time Flight', 'Fantasy', 'Women', 'The Shepherd',
   'Strange Thing'
B: 'Bring Back The Love', 'I'm Alone', 'Tired Of Loving You', '(Gonna)
   Capture Your Heart', 'I Understand'

Elton John and Clive Franks co-produced 'Falling', the B-side of the
single 'Another Night Time Flight' taken from the above album and issued
in July 1977.

Elton John and Clive Franks co-produced 'I'm Alone', the B-side of
the single 'Women' taken from the above album and issued in November
1977.

Elton John and Clive Franks co-produced 'Change In The Weather',
the B-side of the Rocket Records single 'Stranger's Town' issued in
February 1979.

Elton John and Clive Franks co-produced 'Danger Sign' and 'Love
Sings', two songs on the Blue album *Fool's Party*, released by Rocket
Records in April 1979. Elton also played piano on the second of these.
Together with Clive Franks and Blue, Elton also jointly produced a
third song on the album, 'Victim', and, again, played piano on the
track.

Jon Bon Jovi
Elton John contributed to two tracks on the album *The Blaze Of Glory: Young Guns II*, issued in August 1990: piano on 'Billy Get Your Guns' and piano/backing vocals on 'Dyin' Ain't Much Of A Livin''.

Jackson Browne
Under the pseudonym Rockaday Johnnie, Elton John contributed piano to 'Redneck Friend', a song on Browne's January 1974 album *For Everyman*. The track was also issued as a single two months previously, in November 1973.

The Chanter Sisters
Elton John played piano on *Birds Of A Feather*, issued in October 1970. The album contained cover-versions of four Elton John–Bernie Taupin compositions – 'Take Me To The Pilot', 'Border Song', 'Bad Side Of The Moon' and 'Country Comfort' – and although the sleeve does not declare specific, track by track musician details, it is likely that he contributed to all four.

China
With Clive Franks and China, Elton John produced both sides of the Rocket Records single 'On The Slide'/'Save Your Soul', issued in September 1977. The A-side also appeared on the band's Rocket album (see below).

   With Clive Franks and China, Elton John produced all ten tracks on the band's October 1977 Records album *China*. These were:
A: 'On The Slide', 'Meet Me Halfway', 'Broken Woman', 'Hametheme', 'Savage'
B: 'Dear You', 'One Way Ticket', 'For A While', 'Shameful Disgrace', 'This Time (It's For You)'

   Elton John also received a credit for supplying backing vocals, though to which song(s) was not specified. 'Shameful Disgrace' is likely to be one, however.

Kiki Dee
Both sides of Kiki Dee's June 1973 single for Rocket Records, 'Lonnie And Josie'/'The Last Good Man In My Life' were Elton John–Bernie Taupin compositions especially donated to Dee and otherwise unissued. The former was on the album *Loving And Free* (see below), the latter only appeared on the single. Both were produced by Elton John–Clive Franks.

   Elton John and Clive Franks co-produced Kiki Dee's entire December 1973 album *Loving And Free*, issued by Rocket Records. The content was:
A: 'Loving And Free', 'If It Rains', 'Lonnie And Josie', 'Travellin' In Style', 'You Put Something Better Inside Me'
B: 'Supercool', 'Rest My Head', 'Amoureuse', 'Song For Adam', 'Sugar On The Floor'

Two of the songs, 'Lonnie And Josie' and 'Supercool', were Elton John–Bernie Taupin compositions especially donated to Dee; Elton John also contributed musically to the album, playing keyboards on 'If It Rains', 'Lonnie And Josie', 'You Put Something Better Inside Me', 'Supercool', 'Rest My Head' (backing vocals too), 'Song For Adam' and 'Sugar On The Floor'.

Elton John and Clive Franks co-produced both sides of a Rocket Records single issued by Kiki Dee in March 1974. Side A was 'Hard Luck Story', an Elton John–Bernie Taupin song written under the pseudonyms Ann Orson–Carte Blanche, given first to Dee and not issued by Elton John until October 1975. Side B was 'Everyone Should Have Their Way'.

Both sides of Kiki Dee's January 1977 single for Rocket Records, 'First Thing In The Morning'/'The Man Who Loved To Dance' were produced by Elton John–Clive Franks. The A-side was on the album *Kiki Dee* (see below) while the latter track, the B-side, was also an Elton John–Bernie Taupin composition (although the composers' credit read Tripe–Onions) especially donated to Dee and released only here.

Elton John and Clive Franks co-produced the entire March 1977 album *Kiki Dee*, issued by Rocket Records. The content was:
A: 'How Much Fun', 'Sweet Creation', 'Into Eternity', 'Standing Room Only', 'Bad Day Child', 'Chicago'
B: 'Night Hours', 'Keep Right On', 'In Return', 'Walking', 'First Thing In The Morning'

Elton John sang duet with Kiki Dee on 'Loving You Is Sweeter Than Ever', on the June 1981 album *Perfect Timing*. It was a hit single when issued in November 1981.

Elton John and Gary Osborne co-produced 'The Loser Gets To Win', issued as a single in September 1983.

Marcella Detroit

In April 1994, five months after it had appeared on Elton John's album *Duets*, his and Marcella Detroit's recording of the Marvin Gaye–Tammi Terrell song 'Ain't Nothing Like The Real Thing' was included on her album *Jewel* and also became a hit single, credited as Marcella Detroit & Elton John.

Lonnie Donegan

Elton John contributed piano to two tracks on Donegan's January 1978 album *Puttin' On The Style*: 'Diggin' My Potatoes' and 'Puttin' On The Style'.

Lesley Duncan

Elton John contributed piano to one or more unspecified tracks on Duncan's 11-song June 1971 album *Sing Children Sing*.

Bob Dylan
Elton John contributed piano to the track '2 x 2' on Dylan's September
1990 album *Under The Red Sky*.

Fairfield Parlour
Elton John contributed backing vocals to 'Just Another Day', issued as a
single in July 1970.

Family Dogg
Elton John contributed piano to the song 'A Way Of Life', issued as a
single in April 1969.

Aretha Franklin
Elton John sang duet with Franklin on 'Through The Storm', issued as a
single in April 1989 and on the album of the same name one month later.

George Harrison
Elton John contributed piano to two songs on Harrison's November 1987
album *Cloud Nine*: 'Devil's Radio' and 'Wreck Of The Hesperus', and
electric piano to the title track 'Cloud Nine'.

The Hollies
Elton John contributed piano to 'He Ain't Heavy, He's My Brother', first
released as a single in September 1969.
    Elton John contributed piano to 'I Can't Tell The Bottom From The
Top', first released as a single in April 1970.
    Elton John contributed piano to 'Perfect Lady Housewife', first
released on the November 1970 album *Confessions Of The Mind*.

Davey Johnstone
Elton John played harmonium on 'Keep Right On', a track on Johnstone's
May 1973 Rocket Records album *Smiling Face*.

Tom Jones
Elton John contributed backing vocals to 'Delilah', first released as a single
in February 1968.
    Elton John contributed backing vocals to 'Daughter Of Darkness',
issued as a single and on the album *I Who Have Nothing* in April 1970

Lenny Kravitz
See *Aida*, above.

John Lennon
Elton John contributed piano, organ and backing vocals to two songs on
Lennon's October 1974 album *Walls And Bridges*: 'Whatever Gets You

Thru The Night' and 'Surprise Surprise (Sweet Bird Of Paradox)'. The former became Lennon's first US number one single as a solo artist.

Mauro
Elton John contributed piano and vocals to 'Love Sings', the B-side of the single 'Do You Love Me', issued in June 1996. Elton John and Clive Franks co-produced the recording.

George Michael
A recording of George Michael and Elton John duetting Elton John–Bernie Taupin's 'Don't Let The Sun Go Down On Me', recorded in concert at Wembley Arena in January 1991, was issued as a single in November 1991, peaking at number one on the UK chart. (The recording was also issued on Elton John's *Duets* album in November 1993.)

Mr Bloe
Elton John played piano on the two instrumental songs that he wrote, 'Get Out (Of This Town)' and '71–75 New Oxford Street', issued as the A- and B-sides of a single in May 1971.

Eddie Murphy
Elton John is among the many stars recruited to sing 'Yeah' on the song of this title, issued on the album *Love's Alright* in February 1993.

My Dear Watson
As a session player, Elton John contributed keyboards to this Scottish band's single 'Have You Seen Your Saviour'/'White Line Road', issued by DJM in July 1970.

Olivia Newton-John
Elton John co-produced and contributed digital piano and vocals to 'The Rumour', an Elton John–Bernie Taupin composition especially donated to Olivia Newton-John; it served as the title of her album, released in October 1988, and was also issued as a single the previous month.

Hugh Nicholson
Elton John and Clive Franks co-produced 'Love's On Fire', the B-side of his February 1979 Rocket Records single 'How Beautiful'.

Nigel Olsson
Elton John played piano on 'Only One Woman', a track on the Rocket Records album *Nigel Olsson*, released in November 1974, also issued as the A-side of a single at the same time.

Elton John played piano on 'Showdown', a track on the album *Changing Tides*, released in August 1980.

Maldwyn Pope
Elton John and Clive Franks co-produced his July 1977 Rocket Records
single 'If I Wasn't There'/'A Child's Prayer'.

Radio Heart featuring Gary Numan
Elton John played piano on 'Radio Heart', issued as a single in March
1987.

Bruce Roberts
Elton John contributed keyboards and vocals to 'When The Money's
Gone' and 'Emerald' on the October 1995 album *Intimacy*.

Jennifer Rush
Elton John sang duet with Rush on 'Flames Of Paradise', a track on her
April 1987 album *Heart Over Mind*. It was a hit single when issued that
June.

Brian and Brenda Russell
Elton John contributed piano and backing vocals to Brian and Brenda
Russell's cover-version of his and Bernie Taupin's *Captain Fantastic* track
'Tell Me When The Whistle Blows', which appeared on their June 1976
Rocket Records album *Word Called Love*.

Mike Sammes Singers
Although precise details are not known, Elton John participated in
numerous 1968–70 sessions with Sammes' in-demand troupe, principally
adding vocals to other artist's recordings.

Saxon
Elton John contributed piano to two tracks on Saxon's September 1986
album *Rock The Nations*, 'Northern Lady' and 'Party 'Til You Puke'.

The Scaffold
Elton John contributed uncredited backing vocals on several Scaffold
recordings, *circa* 1968/69, including the October 1969 single 'Gin Gan
Goolie'.

Neil Sedaka
Elton John sang harmony vocal on Sedaka's single 'Bad Blood', released in
November 1974, also included on Sedaka's February 1975 UK album
Overnight Success, titled *The Hungry Years* in the USA where Sedaka was
signed to Rocket Records and 'Bad Blood' was a number-one hit single.
       Elton John sang backing vocals on 'Steppin' Out', the title track on
Sedaka's Rocket Records album issued in the USA in June 1976.

Ringo Starr
Elton John contributed piano to 'Snookeroo', an Elton John–Bernie

Taupin composition especially donated to Starr and otherwise unissued, which appeared on his November 1974 album *Goodnight Vienna*.

Rod Stewart
Elton John contributed piano and vocals to 'Let Me Be Your Car', an Elton John–Bernie Taupin composition especially donated to Stewart and otherwise unissued, which appeared on his September 1974 album *Smiler*.

Sting
Appearing under the pseudonym Nancy Treadlight, Elton John contributed piano to Sting's recording of 'Come Down In Time', one of the 16 cover-versions of Elton John–Bernie Taupin compositions featured on the various artists CD *Two Rooms*, issued in October 1991. This multimedia project, sanctioned by the writers, also encompassed a TV programme (issued on video and laserdisc) and book.

Bernie Taupin
See below

Dionne Warwick & Friends
Elton John, Stevie Wonder and Gladys Knight all assisted Warwick with backing vocals on the AIDS charity song 'That's What Friends Are For', released as a single in November 1985 and as a track on Warwick's album *Friends* in December 1985.

Wham
Elton John played piano on 'The Edge Of Heaven', issued as the lead cut on a four-track EP in June 1986 and also included on the album *The Final* the following month.

Bernie Taupin releases

Between 1971 and 1987, Bernie Taupin released three albums credited to himself, in which his poems or lyrics were set to music for the most part written by musicians other than Elton John.

Additionally, in the late 1990s, Taupin has been a founder-member of the US band Farm Dogs; the fourth and fifth albums listed below are Farm Dogs releases.

September 1971 *Taupin*
A: *Child*: 'Birth', 'The Greatest Discovery', 'Flatters (A Beginning)', 'Brothers Together', 'Rowston Manor', 'End Of A Day', 'To A Grandfather', 'Solitude', 'Conclusion'
B: 'When The Heron Wakes', 'Like Summer Tempests', 'Today's Hero', 'Sisters Of The Cross', 'Brothers Together Again', *Verses After Dark*: 'La Petite Marionette', 'Ratcatcher', 'The Visitor'

June 1980   *He Who Rides The Tiger*
A: 'Monkey On My Back (The Last Run)', 'Born On The 4th Of July',
    'Venezuela', 'Approaching Armageddon', 'Lover's Cross'
B: 'Blitz Babies', 'Valley Nights', 'Love (The Barren Desert)', 'The
    Whores Of Paris'
Note: Elton John sang on 'Love (The Barren Desert)'.

August 1987   *Tribe*
A: 'Friend Of The Flag', 'Corrugated Iron', 'Citizen Jane', 'Hold Back
    The Night', 'She Sends Shivers'
B: 'Billy Fury', 'I Still Can't Believe That You're Gone', 'Conquistador',
    'The New Lone Ranger', 'Desperation Train'
Note: Elton John sang on 'Citizen Jane' and 'Billy Fury'.

July 1996   *Last Stand In Open Country*
'Me & My Friends', 'Cinderella '67', 'Beautiful (I Don't Want To Be)',
'Shameless', 'Burn This Bed', 'Color Bar', 'Pretty Bombs', 'Barstool', 'The
Ballad Of Dennis Hopper & Harry Dean', 'Bone Of Contention', 'In
Paradise', 'Last Stand In Open Country'

February 1998   *Immigrant Sons*
'Foreign Windows', 'Distance To The Mountain', 'Daria', 'Lightning On
The Hill', 'This Face', 'Whiskey In The Bathtub', 'Bird Of Prey', 'Leaving
Buffalo', 'Workin In The Fields', 'America On Trial', 'Nothin' Gonna Kill
The Kid', 'Aimless Driving', 'Deep Dark Secret', 'Stars & Seeds'

Bernie Taupin's other compositions

In addition to his own and the Farm Dogs albums detailed above, more
than 40 songs written by Bernie Taupin with composers and musicians
other than Elton John have been released to date.

'Lover Come Back To Me', The Hudson Brothers, 1974; 'Lonely School
Year', The Hudson Brothers, 1975; 'Broken Woman', China, 1977;
'Savage', China, 1977; 'From The Inside', Alice Cooper, 1978; 'Wish I
Were Born In Beverly Hills', Alice Cooper, 1978; 'The Quiet Room',
Alice Cooper, 1978; 'Nurse Rozetta', Alice Cooper, 1978; 'Millie And
Billie', Alice Cooper, 1978; 'Serious', Alice Cooper, 1978; 'How You
Gonna See Me Now', Alice Cooper, 1978; 'For Veronica's Sake', Alice
Cooper, 1978; 'Jacknife Johnny', Alice Cooper, 1978; 'Inmates (We're All
Crazy)', Alice Cooper, 1978 *(the preceding ten tracks comprised the Alice Cooper
album* From The Inside*)*; 'No Tricks', Alice Cooper, 1978; 'If I Weren't
So Romantic I'd Shoot You', Derringer, 1978; 'Julie', Cher, 1980; 'For
The Working Girl', Melissa Manchester, 1980; 'Never Give Up On A
Dream', Rod Stewart, 1981; 'Sonny', Rod Stewart, 1981; 'Johnny And
Mary', Melissa Manchester, 1982; 'Guess I'll Always Love You', Rod

Stewart, 1982; 'Hey Ricky (You're A Low Down Heel)', Melissa Manchester, 1983; 'White Rose', Melissa Manchester, 1983; 'Satisfied', Rod Stewart, 1983; 'Into The Heartland', The Motels, 1984; 'These Dreams', Heart, 1985; 'We Built This City', Starship, 1985; 'Love Rusts', Starship, 1985; 'I Engineer', Animotion, 1986; 'When The Phone Stops Ringing', Boomerang, 1986; 'Hard Lesson To Learn', Rod Stewart, 1986; 'The Burn', Starship, 1989; 'Light In Your Heart', Martin Page, 1990; 'Deal For Life', John Waite, 1990; 'Dip Your Wings', Peter Cetera, 1992; 'The Rain', Carlene Carter, 1993; 'Monkey In My Dreams', Martin Page, 1994; 'In The House Of Stone And Light', Martin Page, 1995; 'Dance With Life (The Brilliant Light)', Bryan Ferry, 1996.

Mark Lewisohn wishes to acknowledge the assistance of Brendan Glover and Alan McCormack in helping to cast light on a few of the particularly cloudy aspects of Elton John's recording career.

Author's Note

THIS did not start out as an authorised biography of Elton John. When I first approached him via the John Reid organisation I was told that, although no obstacles would be put in my way, I could not have direct access to Elton himself because he was about to write his own book. As I later discovered, this was the time when he was battling to overcome his various addictions and communicating with almost no one. However, I was fortunate to enjoy the full co-operation of Bernie Taupin, who granted me many hours of interview in London and Miami. Towards the end of my researches, I was even able to ask direct questions of Elton via Bernie. It was only after the first hardback edition came out that Elton summoned me to his London house and virtually dictated an extra chapter about his various cures and his relationship with Hugh Williams. Subsequently, in an interview with Sky television, he said that my book had got him 'spot-on'. So 'retroactively authorised' seems a fair description.

My grateful thanks to Sue Ayton, Long John Baldry, Clive Banks, Jack Baverstock, Andrew Bendel, Don Black, Caroline Boucher, Sally Brompton, Paul Buckmaster, Eric Clapton, Ray Coleman, David Croker, Elton Dean, Gus Dudgeon, Kirk Duncan, Edna Dwight, Roy Dwight, Geoff Dyson, Mick Eaves, Janet Edrof, Geoffrey Ellis, Peter Emery, Bryan Forbes and Nanette Newman, Cyril Gee, Harvey Goldsmith, Roger Greenaway, John Gunnell, John Hall, Linda Hannon, John Harvey, Pat Higgs, Andrew Hill, George Hill, Neil Hubbard, Nicky James, Stephen James, Bill Johnson, Tony King, David Larkham, Sharon Lawrence, Joan Lewis, Vic Lewis, Kenny Lynch, Linda Mallarkey, Bob Miller, Dee Murray, Nina Myskow, Yoko Ono, Helen Piena, Caleb Quaye, Terri Quaye, Annie Reavey, Russ Regan, Tommy Roberts, Paul Robinson, Johnny Rogan, Ken Russell, Gill Saitch, Gay Search, Neil and Leba Sedaka, Margo Stevens, Rod Stewart, Robert and Daphne Taupin,

Alistair Taylor, Arnold Tendler, Penny Valentine, Helen Walters, Michael Watts, Jack Westgate Smith, Doug Weston, Ray Williams, Richard Williams, Chris Wilson, Norm Winter, Al Woodrow and Neil Woodrow.

I owe much to my two editors, Gail Rebuck – whose idea this book was – and Robyn Sisman. My agent, Michael Sissons, has been enthusiastic and supportive, as always. Chris Carne of Calancraft Computers was a saviour at moments of technical panic. In helping me on discographical matters and tracking down obscure sources, Mark Lewisohn constantly proved himself a researcher of true brilliance. Nor could I have gone the distance without Sue, my energy and inspiration on so many disgruntled summer mornings.

Index